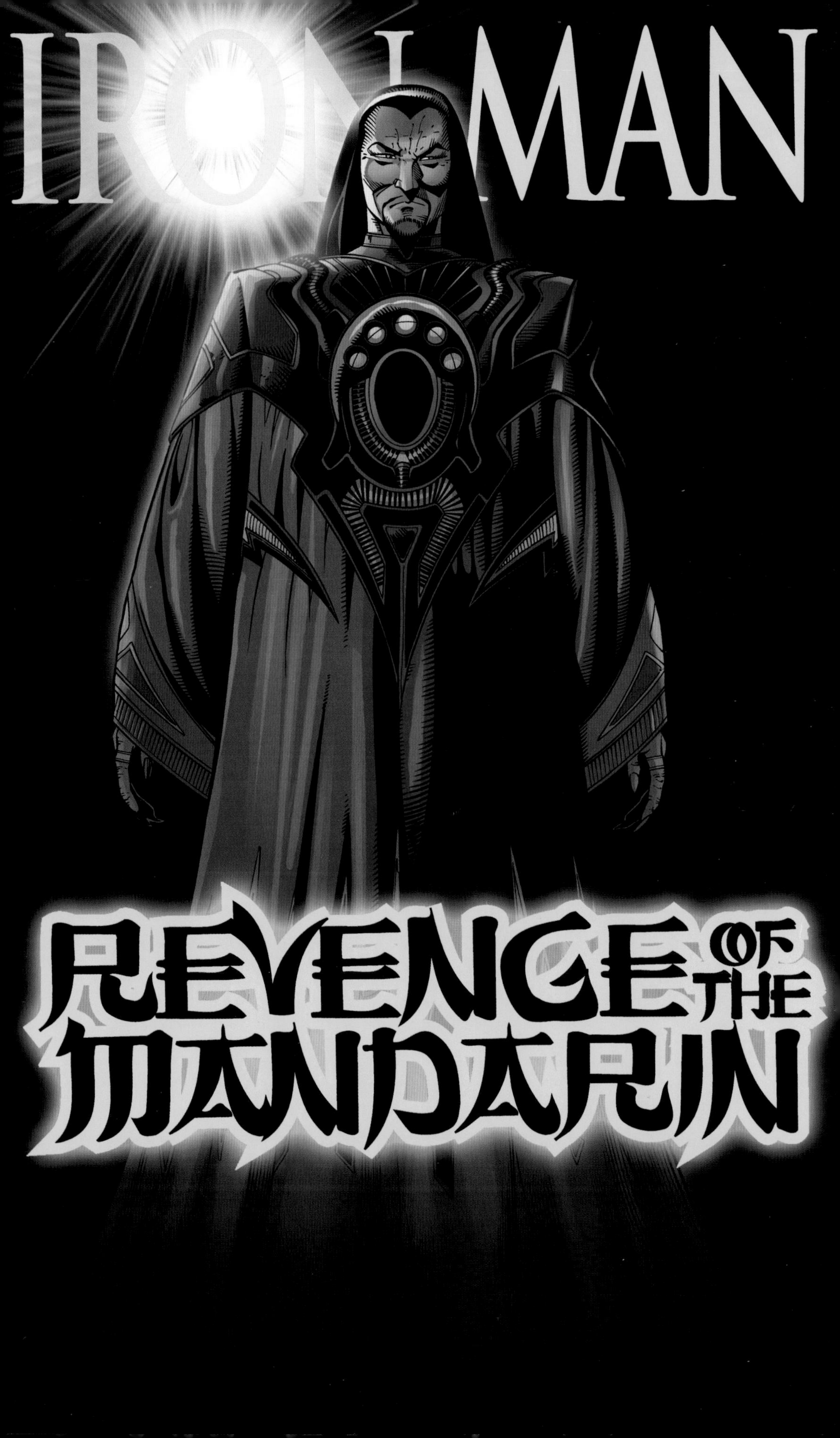
IRON MAN
REVENGE OF THE MANDARIN

IRON MAN

WRITERS
KURT BUSIEK, ROGER STERN & CHRIS CLAREMONT WITH MARK WAID

PENCILERS
SEAN CHEN, PATRICK ZIRCHER & SALVADOR LARROCA

INKERS
ERIC CANNON, SEAN PARSONS, LARY STUCKER, RANDY EMBERLIN, LARRY MAHLSTEDT & ART THIBERT WITH BUD LaROSA

COLORISTS
STEVE OLIFF, TOM SMITH & LIQUID! GRAPHICS

LETTERERS
RICHARD STARKINGS & COMICRAFT WITH DAVE LANPHEAR, WES ABBOTT & ALBERT DESCHESNE

EDITORS
BOBBIE CHASE & MATT IDELSON

COVER ARTISTS
SEAN CHEN, LARY STUCKER & LIQUID! GRAPHICS

IRON MAN: REVENGE OF THE MANDARIN. Contains material originally published in magazine form as IRON MAN #8-14, IRON MAN/CAPTAIN AMERICA ANNUAL '98 and FANTASTIC FOUR #15. First printing 2012. ISBN# 978-0-7851-6260-5. Published by MARVEL WORLDWIDE, INC., a subsidiary of MARVEL ENTERTAINMENT, LLC. OFFICE OF PUBLICATION: 135 West 50th Street, New York, NY 10020. Copyright © 1998, 1999 and 2012 Marvel Characters, Inc. All rights reserved. $39.99 per copy in the U.S. and $43.99 in Canada (GST #R127032852); Canadian Agreement #40668537. All characters featured in this issue and the distinctive names and likenesses thereof, and all related indicia are trademarks of Marvel Characters, Inc. No similarity between any of the names, characters, persons, and/or institutions in this magazine with those of any living or dead person or institution is intended, and any such similarity which may exist is purely coincidental. Printed in China. ALAN FINE, EVP - Office of the President, Marvel Worldwide, Inc. and EVP & CMO Marvel Characters B.V.; DAN BUCKLEY, Publisher & President - Print, Animation & Digital Divisions; JOE QUESADA, Chief Creative Officer; TOM BREVOORT, SVP of Publishing; DAVID BOGART, SVP of Operations & Procurement, Publishing; RUWAN JAYATILLEKE, SVP & Associate Publisher, Publishing; C.B. CEBULSKI, SVP of Creator & Content Development; DAVID GABRIEL, SVP of Publishing Sales & Circulation; MICHAEL PASCIULLO, SVP of Brand Planning & Communications; JIM O'KEEFE, VP of Operations & Logistics; DAN CARR, Executive Director of Publishing Technology; SUSAN CRESPI, Editorial Operations Manager; ALEX MORALES, Publishing Operations Manager; STAN LEE, Chairman Emeritus. For information regarding advertising in Marvel Comics or on Marvel.com, please contact John Dokes, SVP Integrated Sales and Marketing, at jdokes@marvel.com. For Marvel subscription inquiries, please call 800-217-9158. Manufactured between 4/30/2012 and 6/11/2012 by R.R. DONNELLEY ASIA PRINTING SOLUTIONS, DONGGUAN, GUANGDONG, CHINA.

10 9 8 7 6 5 4 3 2 1

COLLECTION EDITOR
NELSON RIBEIRO

ASSISTANT EDITORS
ALEX STARBUCK

EDITORS, SPECIAL PROJECTS
MARK D. BEAZLEY & JENNIFER GRÜNWALD

SENIOR EDITOR, SPECIAL PROJECTS
JEFF YOUNGQUIST

SENIOR VICE PRESIDENT OF SALES
DAVID GABRIEL

RESEARCH
KEVIN WASSER

LAYOUT
JEPH YORK

PRODUCTION
RYAN DEVALL & JERRON QUALITY COLOR

SENIOR VICE PRESIDENT OF SALES
DAVID GABRIEL

EDITOR IN CHIEF
AXEL ALONSO

CHIEF CREATIVE OFFICER
JOE QUESADA

PUBLISHER
DAN BUCKLEY

EXECUTIVE PRODUCER
ALAN FINE

SPECIAL THANKS TO JACOB ROUGEMONT

REVENGE OF THE MANDARIN

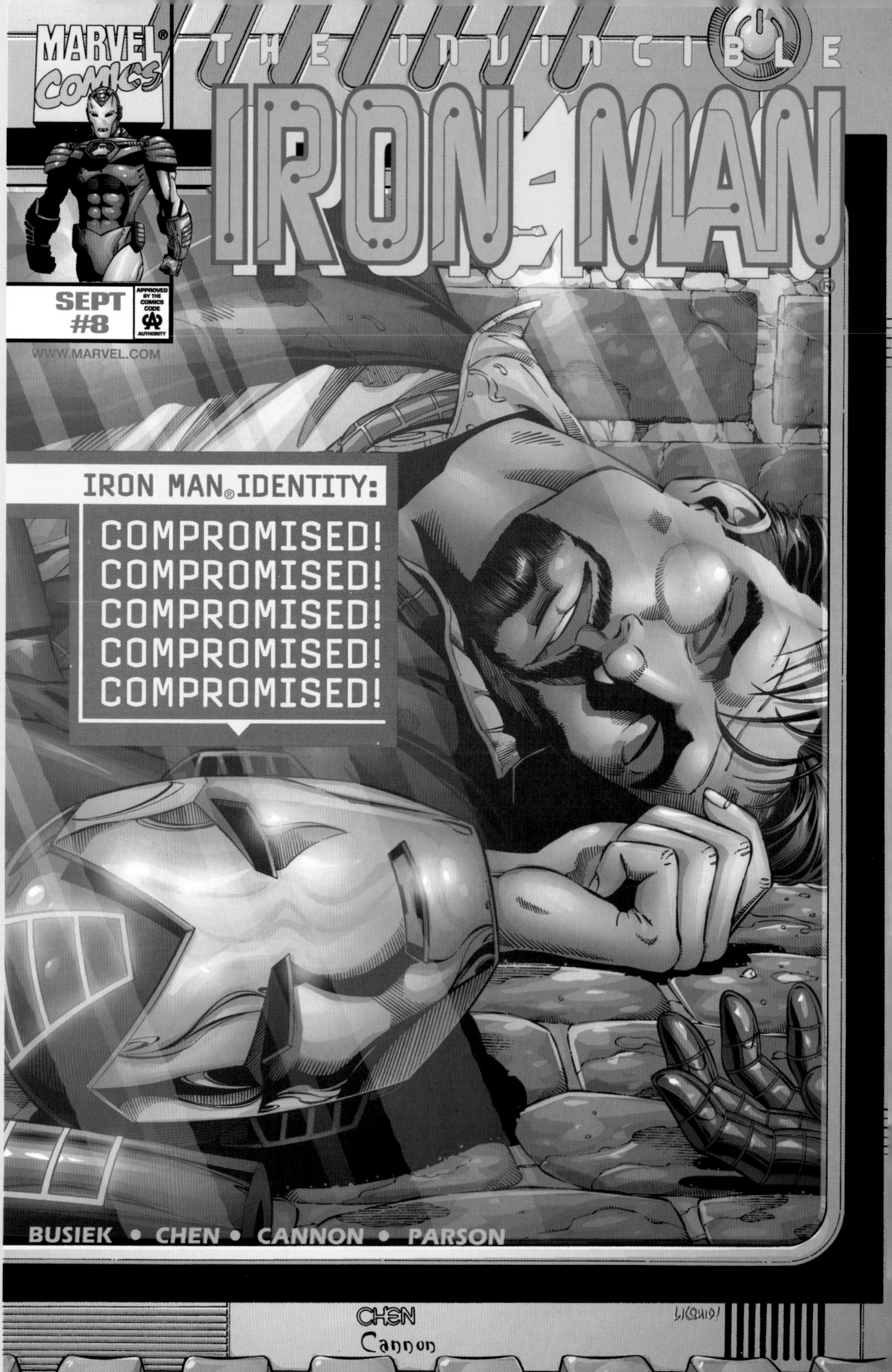
MARVEL COMICS
THE INVINCIBLE
IRON MAN
SEPT
#8
APPROVED BY THE COMICS CODE AUTHORITY
WWW.MARVEL.COM
IRON MAN® IDENTITY:
COMPROMISED!
COMPROMISED!
COMPROMISED!
COMPROMISED!
COMPROMISED!
BUSIEK • CHEN • CANNON • PARSON
CHEN
Cannon

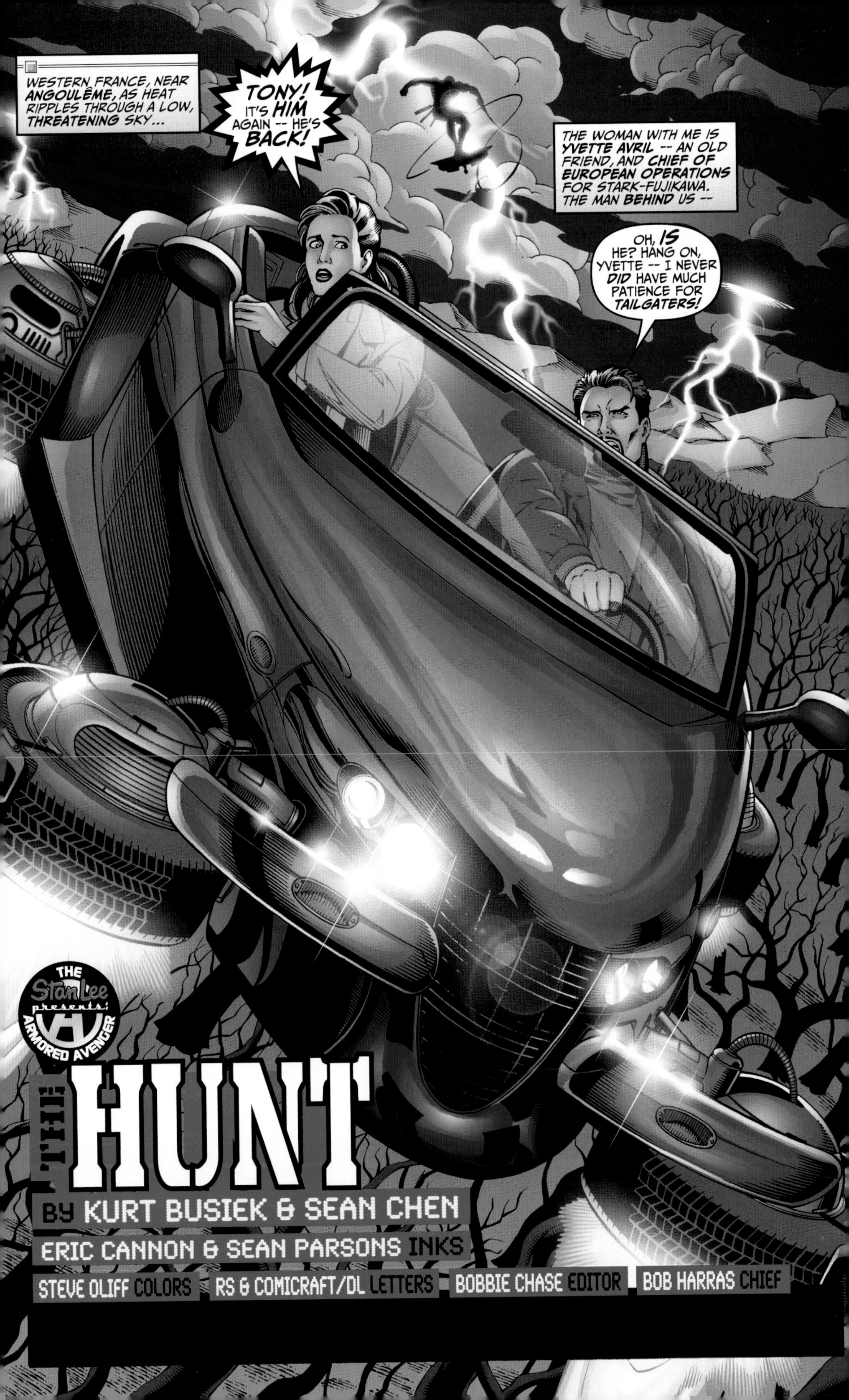
WESTERN FRANCE, NEAR ANGOULÊME, AS HEAT RIPPLES THROUGH A LOW, THREATENING SKY...
TONY! IT'S HIM AGAIN -- HE'S BACK!
THE WOMAN WITH ME IS YVETTE AVRIL -- AN OLD FRIEND, AND CHIEF OF EUROPEAN OPERATIONS FOR STARK-FUJIKAWA. THE MAN BEHIND US --
OH, IS HE? HANG ON, YVETTE -- I NEVER DID HAVE MUCH PATIENCE FOR TAILGATERS!
THE Stan Lee presents: ARMORED AVENGER
THE HUNT
BY KURT BUSIEK & SEAN CHEN
ERIC CANNON & SEAN PARSONS INKS
STEVE OLIFF COLORS
RS & COMICRAFT/DL LETTERS
BOBBIE CHASE EDITOR
BOB HARRAS CHIEF

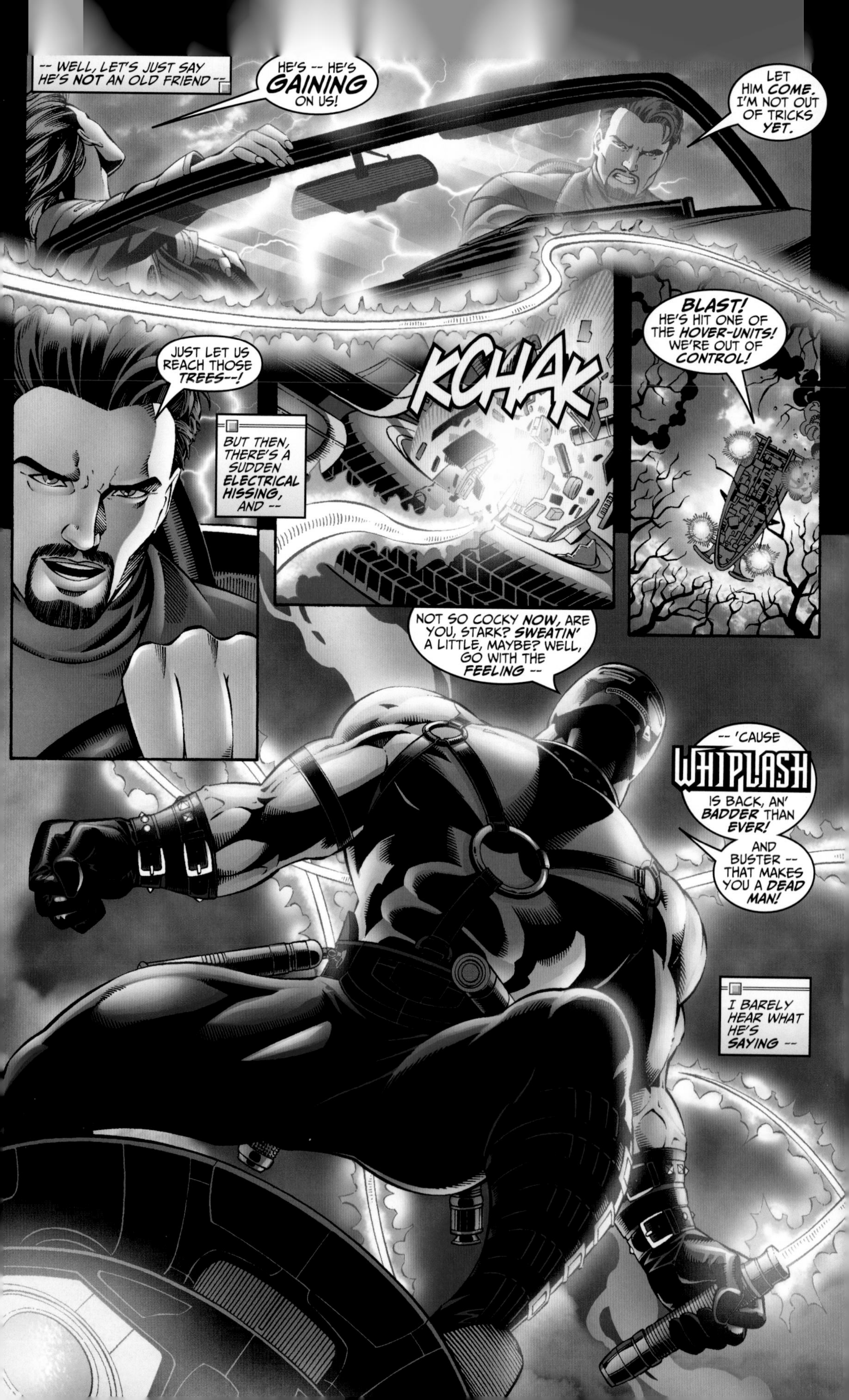
-- WELL, LET'S JUST SAY HE'S NOT AN OLD FRIEND --
HE'S -- HE'S GAINING ON US!
LET HIM COME. I'M NOT OUT OF TRICKS YET.
JUST LET US REACH THOSE TREES--!
BUT THEN, THERE'S A SUDDEN ELECTRICAL HISSING, AND --
KCHAK
BLAST! HE'S HIT ONE OF THE HOVER-UNITS! WE'RE OUT OF CONTROL!
NOT SO COCKY NOW, ARE YOU, STARK? SWEATIN' A LITTLE, MAYBE? WELL, GO WITH THE FEELING --
-- 'CAUSE WHIPLASH IS BACK, AN' BADDER THAN EVER!
AND BUSTER -- THAT MAKES YOU A DEAD MAN!
I BARELY HEAR WHAT HE'S SAYING --

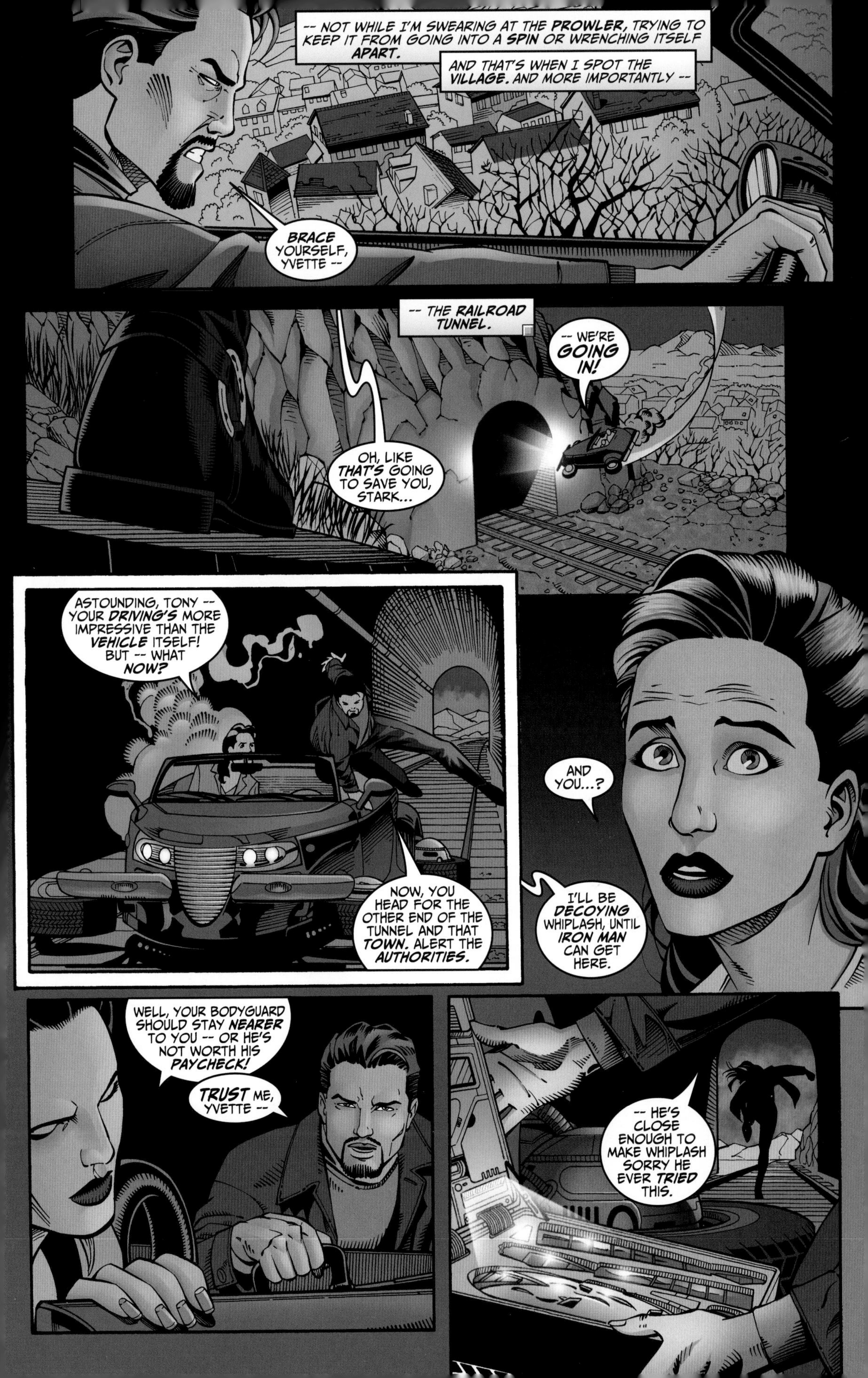
-- NOT WHILE I'M SWEARING AT THE PROWLER, TRYING TO KEEP IT FROM GOING INTO A SPIN OR WRENCHING ITSELF APART.
AND THAT'S WHEN I SPOT THE VILLAGE. AND MORE IMPORTANTLY --
BRACE YOURSELF, YVETTE --
-- THE RAILROAD TUNNEL.
-- WE'RE GOING IN!
OH, LIKE THAT'S GOING TO SAVE YOU, STARK...
ASTOUNDING, TONY -- YOUR DRIVING'S MORE IMPRESSIVE THAN THE VEHICLE ITSELF! BUT -- WHAT NOW?
NOW, YOU HEAD FOR THE OTHER END OF THE TUNNEL AND THAT TOWN. ALERT THE AUTHORITIES.
AND YOU...?
I'LL BE DECOYING WHIPLASH, UNTIL IRON MAN CAN GET HERE.
WELL, YOUR BODYGUARD SHOULD STAY NEARER TO YOU -- OR HE'S NOT WORTH HIS PAYCHECK!
TRUST ME, YVETTE --
-- HE'S CLOSE ENOUGH TO MAKE WHIPLASH SORRY HE EVER TRIED THIS.

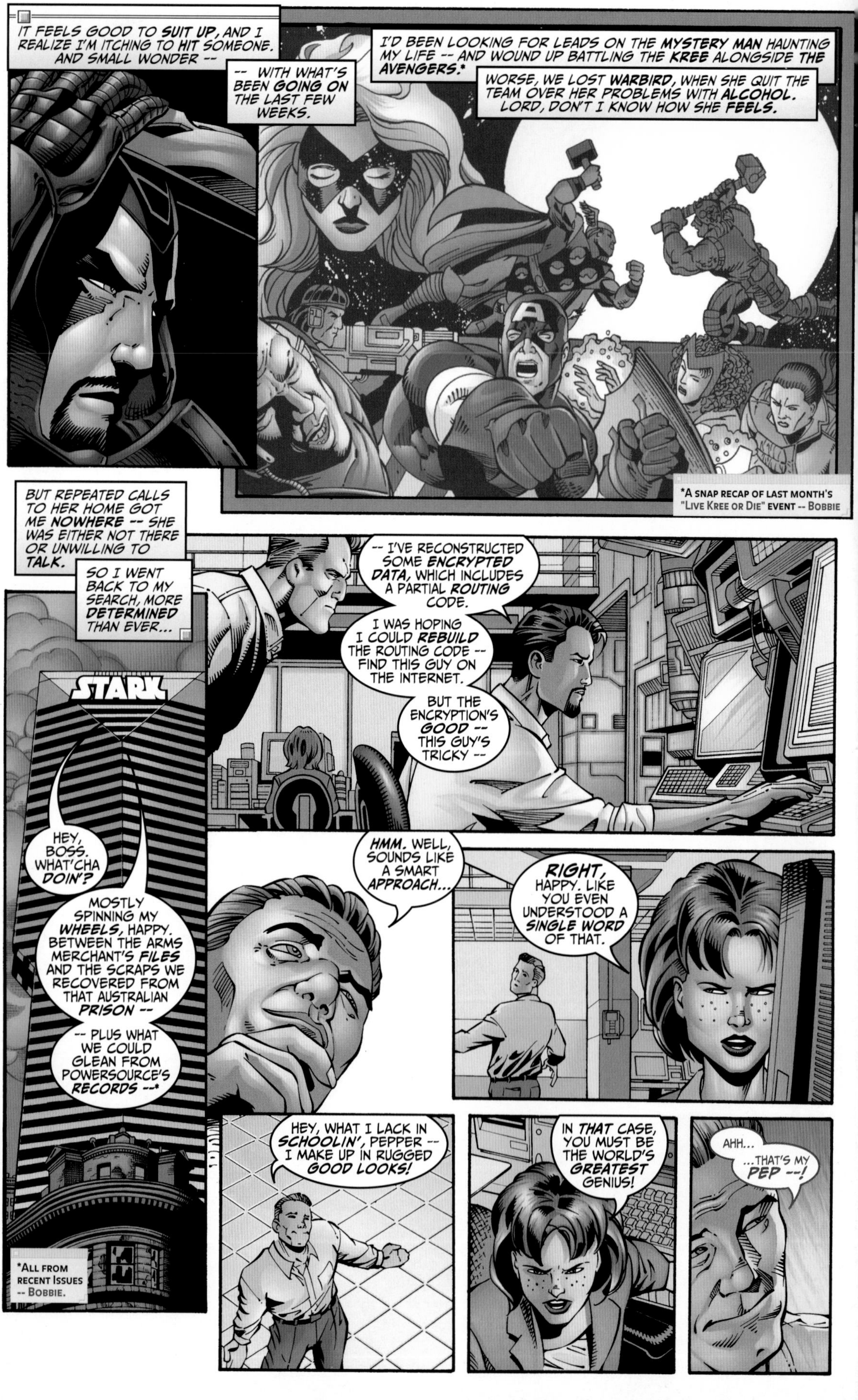
IT FEELS GOOD TO SUIT UP, AND I REALIZE I'M ITCHING TO HIT SOMEONE. AND SMALL WONDER --
-- WITH WHAT'S BEEN GOING ON THE LAST FEW WEEKS.
I'D BEEN LOOKING FOR LEADS ON THE MYSTERY MAN HAUNTING MY LIFE -- AND WOUND UP BATTLING THE KREE ALONGSIDE THE AVENGERS.*
WORSE, WE LOST WARBIRD, WHEN SHE QUIT THE TEAM OVER HER PROBLEMS WITH ALCOHOL. LORD, DON'T I KNOW HOW SHE FEELS.
*A SNAP RECAP OF LAST MONTH'S "LIVE KREE OR DIE" EVENT -- BOBBIE
BUT REPEATED CALLS TO HER HOME GOT ME NOWHERE -- SHE WAS EITHER NOT THERE OR UNWILLING TO TALK.
SO I WENT BACK TO MY SEARCH, MORE DETERMINED THAN EVER...
STARK
HEY, BOSS. WHAT'CHA DOIN'?
MOSTLY SPINNING MY WHEELS, HAPPY. BETWEEN THE ARMS MERCHANT'S FILES AND THE SCRAPS WE RECOVERED FROM THAT AUSTRALIAN PRISON --
-- PLUS WHAT WE COULD GLEAN FROM POWERSOURCE'S RECORDS --*
-- I'VE RECONSTRUCTED SOME ENCRYPTED DATA, WHICH INCLUDES A PARTIAL ROUTING CODE.
I WAS HOPING I COULD REBUILD THE ROUTING CODE -- FIND THIS GUY ON THE INTERNET.
BUT THE ENCRYPTION'S GOOD -- THIS GUY'S TRICKY --
*ALL FROM RECENT ISSUES -- BOBBIE.
HMM. WELL, SOUNDS LIKE A SMART APPROACH...
RIGHT, HAPPY. LIKE YOU EVEN UNDERSTOOD A SINGLE WORD OF THAT.
HEY, WHAT I LACK IN SCHOOLIN', PEPPER -- I MAKE UP IN RUGGED GOOD LOOKS!
IN THAT CASE, YOU MUST BE THE WORLD'S GREATEST GENIUS!
AHH...
...THAT'S MY PEP --!

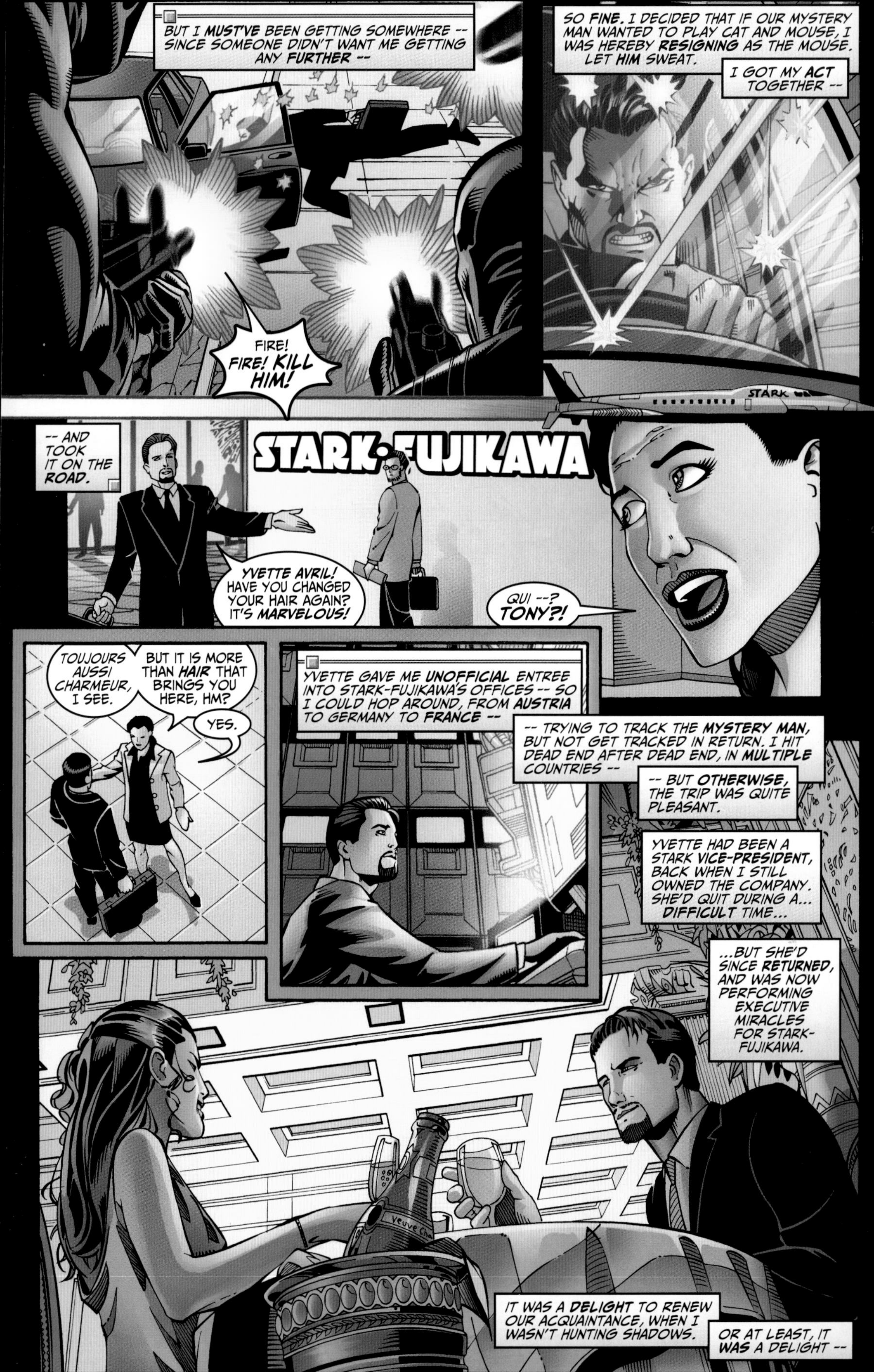
BUT I MUST'VE BEEN GETTING SOMEWHERE -- SINCE SOMEONE DIDN'T WANT ME GETTING ANY FURTHER --
FIRE! FIRE! KILL HIM!
SO FINE. I DECIDED THAT IF OUR MYSTERY MAN WANTED TO PLAY CAT AND MOUSE, I WAS HEREBY RESIGNING AS THE MOUSE. LET HIM SWEAT.
I GOT MY ACT TOGETHER --
STARK
-- AND TOOK IT ON THE ROAD.
STARK-FUJIKAWA
YVETTE AVRIL! HAVE YOU CHANGED YOUR HAIR AGAIN? IT'S MARVELOUS!
QUI --? TONY?!
TOUJOURS AUSSI CHARMEUR, I SEE.
BUT IT IS MORE THAN HAIR THAT BRINGS YOU HERE, HM?
YES.
YVETTE GAVE ME UNOFFICIAL ENTREE INTO STARK-FUJIKAWA'S OFFICES -- SO I COULD HOP AROUND, FROM AUSTRIA TO GERMANY TO FRANCE --
-- TRYING TO TRACK THE MYSTERY MAN, BUT NOT GET TRACKED IN RETURN. I HIT DEAD END AFTER DEAD END, IN MULTIPLE COUNTRIES --
-- BUT OTHERWISE, THE TRIP WAS QUITE PLEASANT.
YVETTE HAD BEEN A STARK VICE-PRESIDENT, BACK WHEN I STILL OWNED THE COMPANY. SHE'D QUIT DURING A... DIFFICULT TIME...
...BUT SHE'D SINCE RETURNED, AND WAS NOW PERFORMING EXECUTIVE MIRACLES FOR STARK-FUJIKAWA.
IT WAS A DELIGHT TO RENEW OUR ACQUAINTANCE, WHEN I WASN'T HUNTING SHADOWS.
OR AT LEAST, IT WAS A DELIGHT --

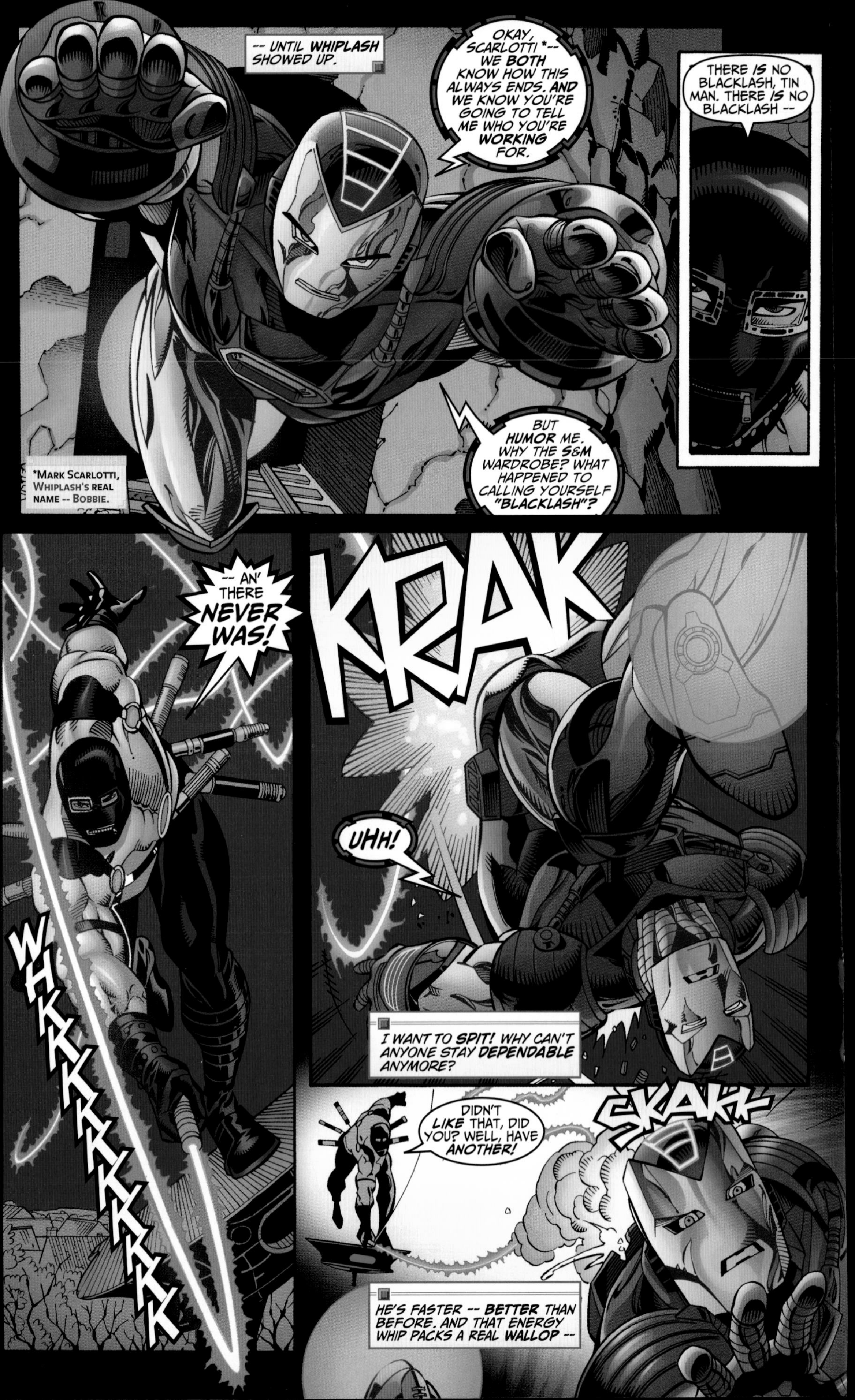
-- UNTIL WHIPLASH SHOWED UP.
OKAY, SCARLOTTI *-- WE BOTH KNOW HOW THIS ALWAYS ENDS. AND WE KNOW YOU'RE GOING TO TELL ME WHO YOU'RE WORKING FOR.
BUT HUMOR ME. WHY THE S&M WARDROBE? WHAT HAPPENED TO CALLING YOURSELF "BLACKLASH"?
*MARK SCARLOTTI, WHIPLASH'S REAL NAME -- BOBBIE.
THERE IS NO BLACKLASH, TIN MAN. THERE IS NO BLACKLASH --
-- AN' THERE NEVER WAS!
WHKKKKKKKKK
KRAK
UHH!
I WANT TO SPIT! WHY CAN'T ANYONE STAY DEPENDABLE ANYMORE?
DIDN'T LIKE THAT, DID YOU? WELL, HAVE ANOTHER!
SKAKK
HE'S FASTER -- BETTER THAN BEFORE. AND THAT ENERGY WHIP PACKS A REAL WALLOP --

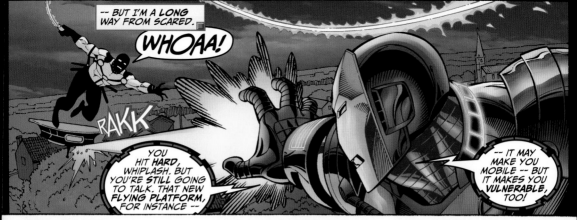

-- BUT I'M A LONG WAY FROM SCARED.

WHOAA!

RAKK

YOU HIT **HARD**, WHIPLASH. BUT YOU'RE STILL GOING TO TALK. THAT NEW FLYING PLATFORM, FOR INSTANCE --

-- IT MAY MAKE YOU MOBILE -- BUT IT MAKES YOU **VULNERABLE**, TOO!

OH, YEAH?

NICE TO KNOW --

-- THAT EVEN AVENGERS CAN BE MORONS!

KZZT

TNK

NOW -- WHERE WERE WE? OH, RIGHT --

-- I WAS KICKIN' YER BUTT!

KRAK

H-UHH!

HIS WHIPS -- MUST WORK ON A MOLECULAR LEVEL, MAKING WHATEVER THEY TOUCH **BRITTLE** -- MY ARMOR ACTUALLY **CRACKS** --

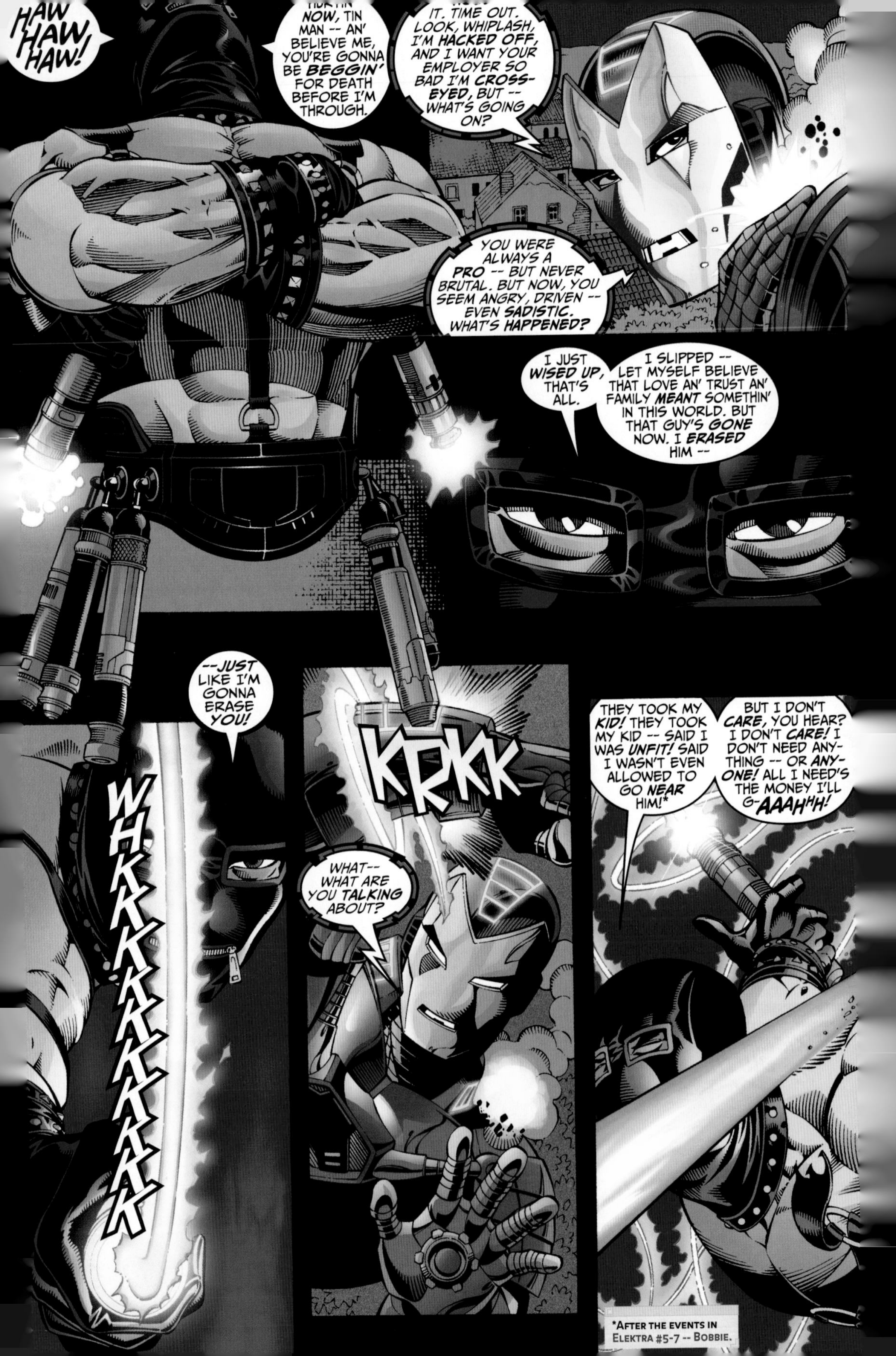

HAW HAW HAW!
NOW, TIN MAN -- AN' BELIEVE ME, YOU'RE GONNA BE BEGGIN' FOR DEATH BEFORE I'M THROUGH.
IT. TIME OUT. LOOK, WHIPLASH, I'M HACKED OFF, AND I WANT YOUR EMPLOYER SO BAD I'M CROSS-EYED, BUT -- WHAT'S GOING ON?
YOU WERE ALWAYS A PRO -- BUT NEVER BRUTAL. BUT NOW, YOU SEEM ANGRY, DRIVEN -- EVEN SADISTIC. WHAT'S HAPPENED?
I JUST WISED UP, THAT'S ALL.
I SLIPPED -- LET MYSELF BELIEVE THAT LOVE AN' TRUST AN' FAMILY MEANT SOMETHIN' IN THIS WORLD. BUT THAT GUY'S GONE NOW. I ERASED HIM --
--JUST LIKE I'M GONNA ERASE YOU!
WHKKKKKKKKKK
KRKK
WHAT-- WHAT ARE YOU TALKING ABOUT?
THEY TOOK MY KID! THEY TOOK MY KID -- SAID I WAS UNFIT! SAID I WASN'T EVEN ALLOWED TO GO NEAR HIM!*
BUT I DON'T CARE, YOU HEAR? I DON'T CARE! I DON'T NEED ANY-THING -- OR ANY-ONE! ALL I NEED'S THE MONEY I'LL G-AAAHHH!
*AFTER THE EVENTS IN ELEKTRA #5-7 -- BOBBIE.

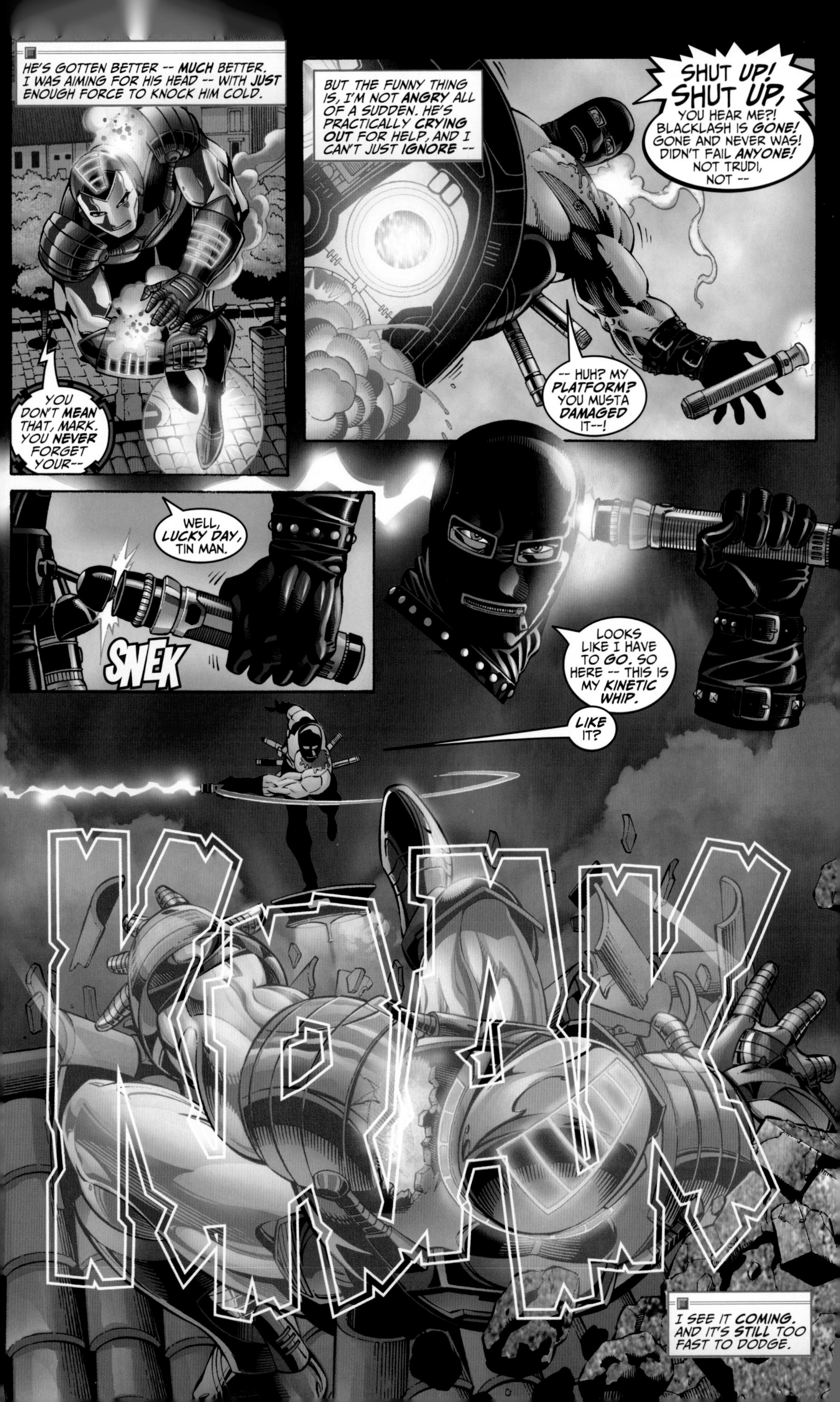

HE'S GOTTEN BETTER -- MUCH BETTER. I WAS AIMING FOR HIS HEAD -- WITH JUST ENOUGH FORCE TO KNOCK HIM COLD.
YOU DON'T MEAN THAT, MARK. YOU NEVER FORGET YOUR--
BUT THE FUNNY THING IS, I'M NOT ANGRY ALL OF A SUDDEN. HE'S PRACTICALLY CRYING OUT FOR HELP, AND I CAN'T JUST IGNORE --
SHUT UP! SHUT UP, YOU HEAR ME?! BLACKLASH IS GONE! GONE AND NEVER WAS! DIDN'T FAIL ANYONE! NOT TRUDI, NOT --
-- HUH? MY PLATFORM? YOU MUSTA DAMAGED IT--!
WELL, LUCKY DAY, TIN MAN.
SNEK
LOOKS LIKE I HAVE TO GO. SO HERE -- THIS IS MY KINETIC WHIP.
LIKE IT?
KRAKK
I SEE IT COMING. AND IT'S STILL TOO FAST TO DODGE.

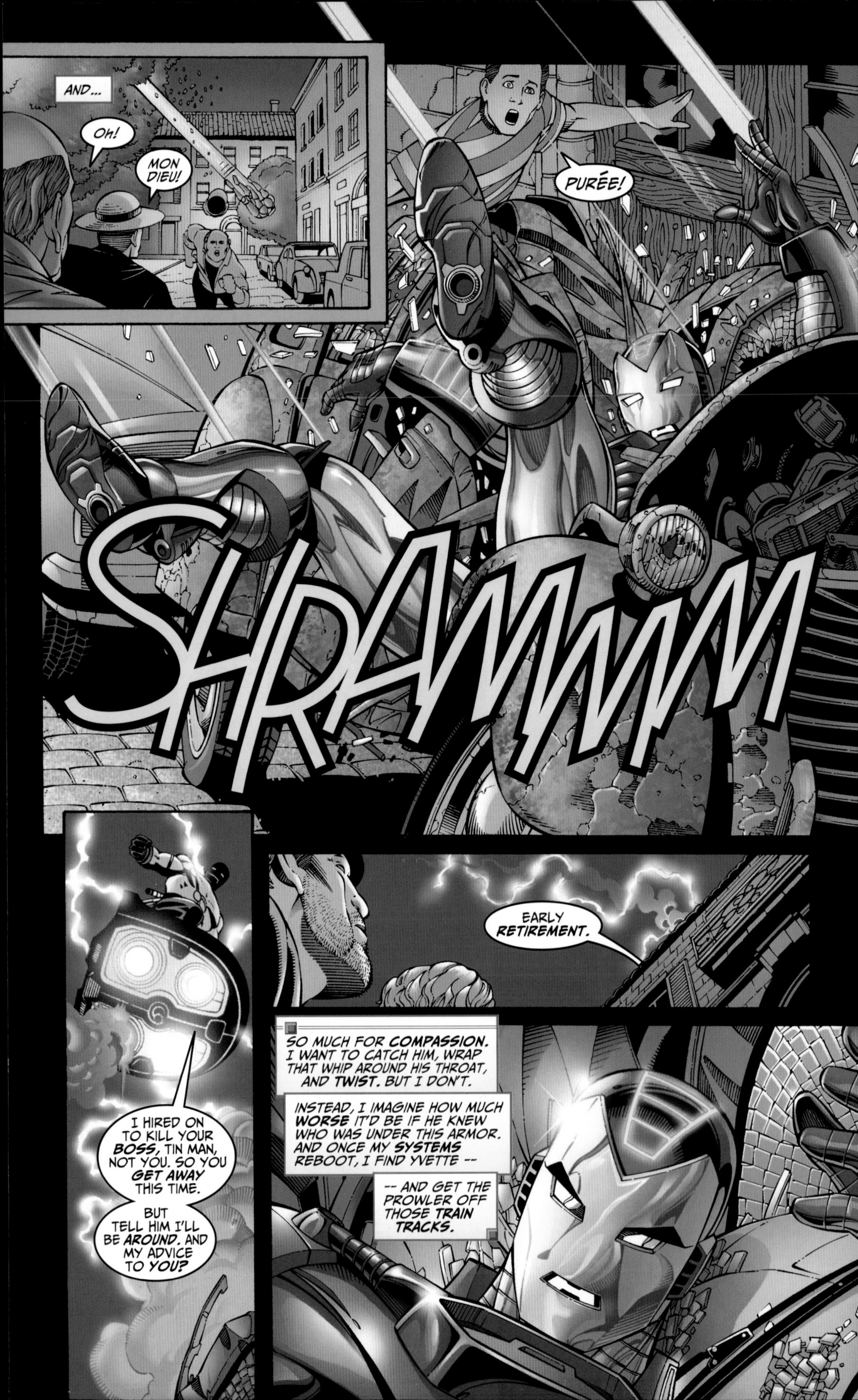
AND...
Oh!
MON DIEU!
PURÉE!
SHRAMMM
I HIRED ON TO KILL YOUR BOSS, TIN MAN, NOT YOU. SO YOU GET AWAY THIS TIME.
BUT TELL HIM I'LL BE AROUND. AND MY ADVICE TO YOU?
EARLY RETIREMENT.
SO MUCH FOR COMPASSION. I WANT TO CATCH HIM, WRAP THAT WHIP AROUND HIS THROAT, AND TWIST. BUT I DON'T.
INSTEAD, I IMAGINE HOW MUCH WORSE IT'D BE IF HE KNEW WHO WAS UNDER THIS ARMOR. AND ONCE MY SYSTEMS REBOOT, I FIND YVETTE --
-- AND GET THE PROWLER OFF THOSE TRAIN TRACKS.

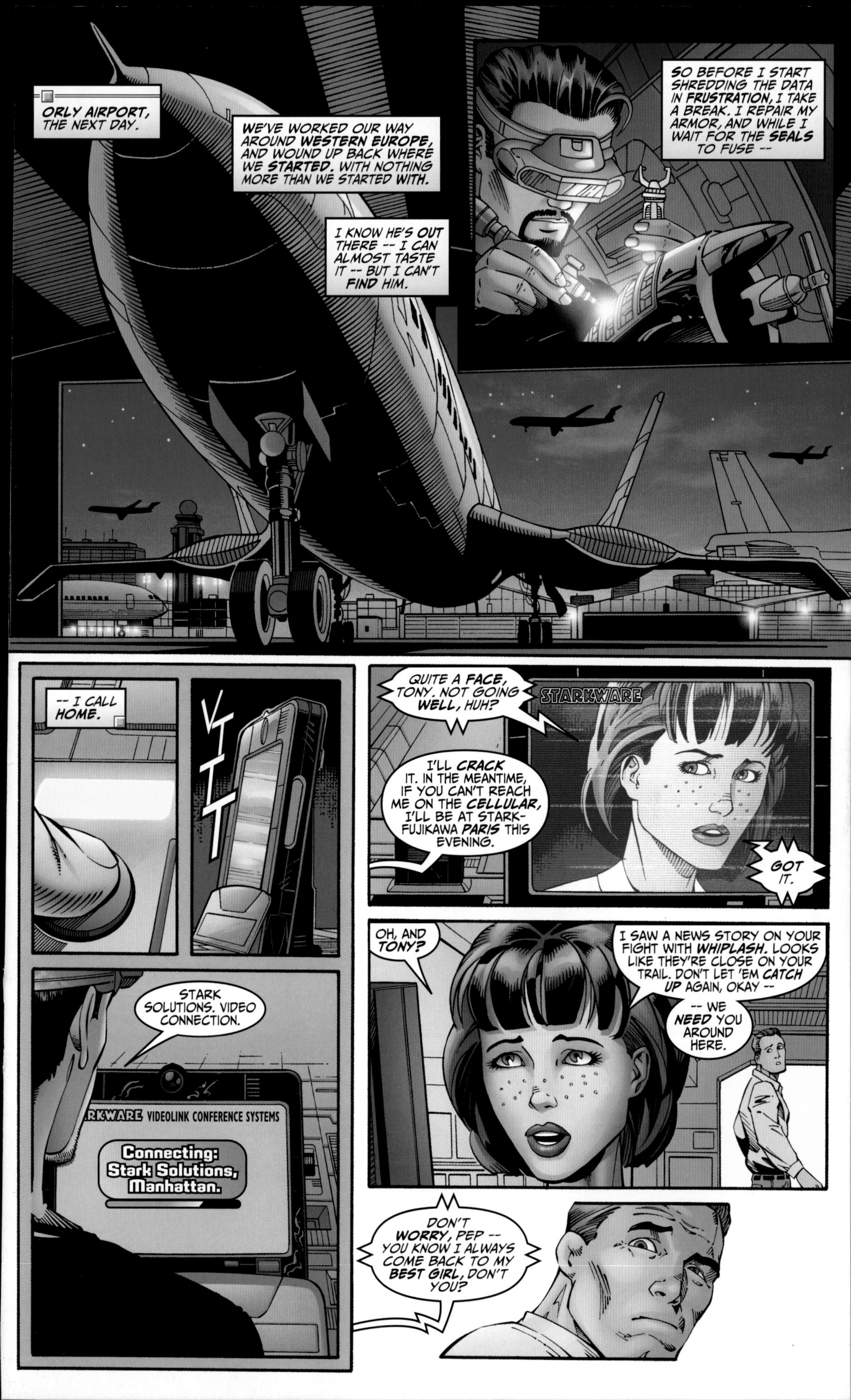
ORLY AIRPORT, THE NEXT DAY.
WE'VE WORKED OUR WAY AROUND WESTERN EUROPE, AND WOUND UP BACK WHERE WE STARTED. WITH NOTHING MORE THAN WE STARTED WITH.
I KNOW HE'S OUT THERE -- I CAN ALMOST TASTE IT -- BUT I CAN'T FIND HIM.
SO BEFORE I START SHREDDING THE DATA IN FRUSTRATION, I TAKE A BREAK. I REPAIR MY ARMOR, AND WHILE I WAIT FOR THE SEALS TO FUSE --
-- I CALL HOME.
VTTT
STARK SOLUTIONS. VIDEO CONNECTION.
STARKWARE VIDEOLINK CONFERENCE SYSTEMS
Connecting: Stark Solutions, Manhattan.
QUITE A FACE, TONY. NOT GOING WELL, HUH?
STARKWARE
I'LL CRACK IT. IN THE MEANTIME, IF YOU CAN'T REACH ME ON THE CELLULAR, I'LL BE AT STARK-FUJIKAWA PARIS THIS EVENING.
GOT IT.
OH, AND TONY?
I SAW A NEWS STORY ON YOUR FIGHT WITH WHIPLASH. LOOKS LIKE THEY'RE CLOSE ON YOUR TRAIL. DON'T LET 'EM CATCH UP AGAIN, OKAY --
-- WE NEED YOU AROUND HERE.
DON'T WORRY, PEP -- YOU KNOW I ALWAYS COME BACK TO MY BEST GIRL, DON'T YOU?

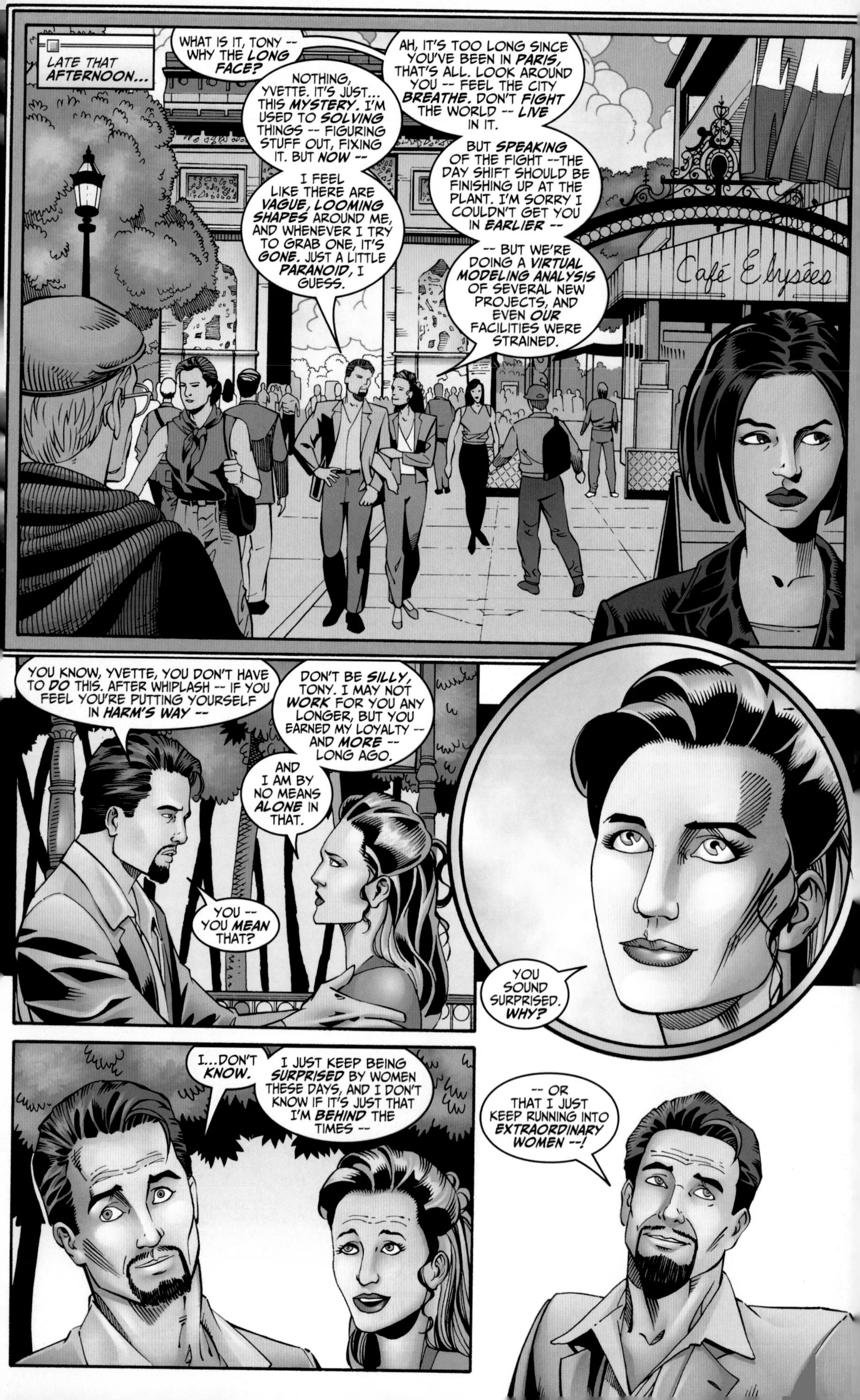

LATE THAT AFTERNOON...
WHAT IS IT, TONY -- WHY THE LONG FACE?
NOTHING, YVETTE. IT'S JUST... THIS MYSTERY. I'M USED TO SOLVING THINGS -- FIGURING STUFF OUT, FIXING IT. BUT NOW --
I FEEL LIKE THERE ARE VAGUE, LOOMING SHAPES AROUND ME, AND WHENEVER I TRY TO GRAB ONE, IT'S GONE. JUST A LITTLE PARANOID, I GUESS.
AH, IT'S TOO LONG SINCE YOU'VE BEEN IN PARIS, THAT'S ALL. LOOK AROUND YOU -- FEEL THE CITY BREATHE. DON'T FIGHT THE WORLD -- LIVE IN IT.
BUT SPEAKING OF THE FIGHT --THE DAY SHIFT SHOULD BE FINISHING UP AT THE PLANT. I'M SORRY I COULDN'T GET YOU IN EARLIER --
-- BUT WE'RE DOING A VIRTUAL MODELING ANALYSIS OF SEVERAL NEW PROJECTS, AND EVEN OUR FACILITIES WERE STRAINED.
Café Elysées
YOU KNOW, YVETTE, YOU DON'T HAVE TO DO THIS. AFTER WHIPLASH -- IF YOU FEEL YOU'RE PUTTING YOURSELF IN HARM'S WAY --
DON'T BE SILLY, TONY. I MAY NOT WORK FOR YOU ANY LONGER, BUT YOU EARNED MY LOYALTY -- AND MORE -- LONG AGO.
AND I AM BY NO MEANS ALONE IN THAT.
YOU -- YOU MEAN THAT?
YOU SOUND SURPRISED. WHY?
I...DON'T KNOW.
I JUST KEEP BEING SURPRISED BY WOMEN THESE DAYS, AND I DON'T KNOW IF IT'S JUST THAT I'M BEHIND THE TIMES --
-- OR THAT I JUST KEEP RUNNING INTO EXTRAORDINARY WOMEN --!

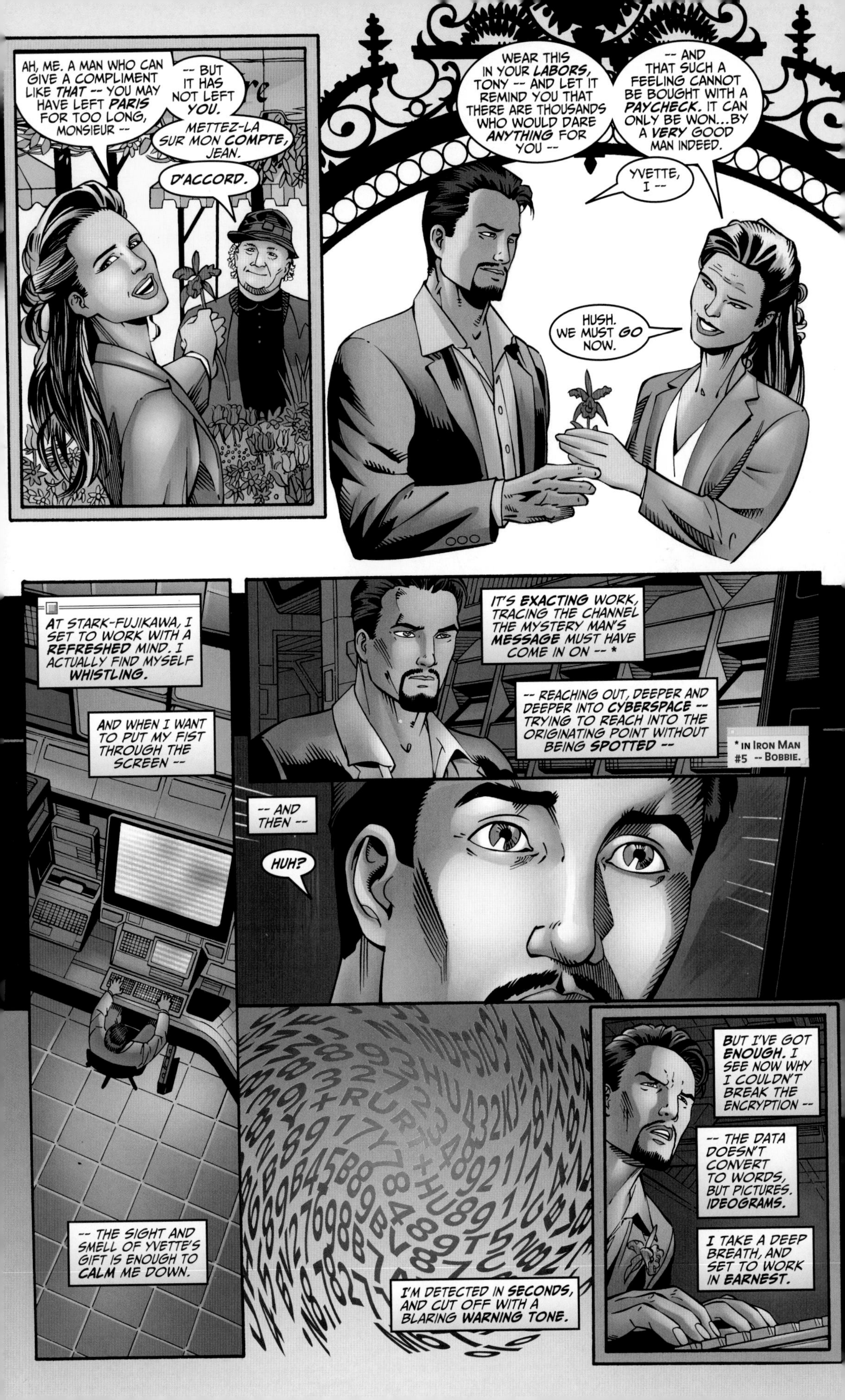

AH, ME. A MAN WHO CAN GIVE A COMPLIMENT LIKE THAT -- YOU MAY HAVE LEFT PARIS FOR TOO LONG, MONSIEUR --
-- BUT IT HAS NOT LEFT YOU.
METTEZ-LA SUR MON COMPTE, JEAN.
D'ACCORD.
WEAR THIS IN YOUR LABORS, TONY -- AND LET IT REMIND YOU THAT THERE ARE THOUSANDS WHO WOULD DARE ANYTHING FOR YOU --
-- AND THAT SUCH A FEELING CANNOT BE BOUGHT WITH A PAYCHECK. IT CAN ONLY BE WON...BY A VERY GOOD MAN INDEED.
YVETTE, I --
HUSH. WE MUST GO NOW.
AT STARK-FUJIKAWA, I SET TO WORK WITH A REFRESHED MIND. I ACTUALLY FIND MYSELF WHISTLING.
AND WHEN I WANT TO PUT MY FIST THROUGH THE SCREEN --
-- THE SIGHT AND SMELL OF YVETTE'S GIFT IS ENOUGH TO CALM ME DOWN.
IT'S EXACTING WORK, TRACING THE CHANNEL THE MYSTERY MAN'S MESSAGE MUST HAVE COME IN ON -- *
-- REACHING OUT, DEEPER AND DEEPER INTO CYBERSPACE -- TRYING TO REACH INTO THE ORIGINATING POINT WITHOUT BEING SPOTTED --
* IN IRON MAN #5 -- BOBBIE.
-- AND THEN --
HUH?
I'M DETECTED IN SECONDS, AND CUT OFF WITH A BLARING WARNING TONE.
BUT I'VE GOT ENOUGH. I SEE NOW WHY I COULDN'T BREAK THE ENCRYPTION --
-- THE DATA DOESN'T CONVERT TO WORDS, BUT PICTURES. IDEOGRAMS.
I TAKE A DEEP BREATH, AND SET TO WORK IN EARNEST.

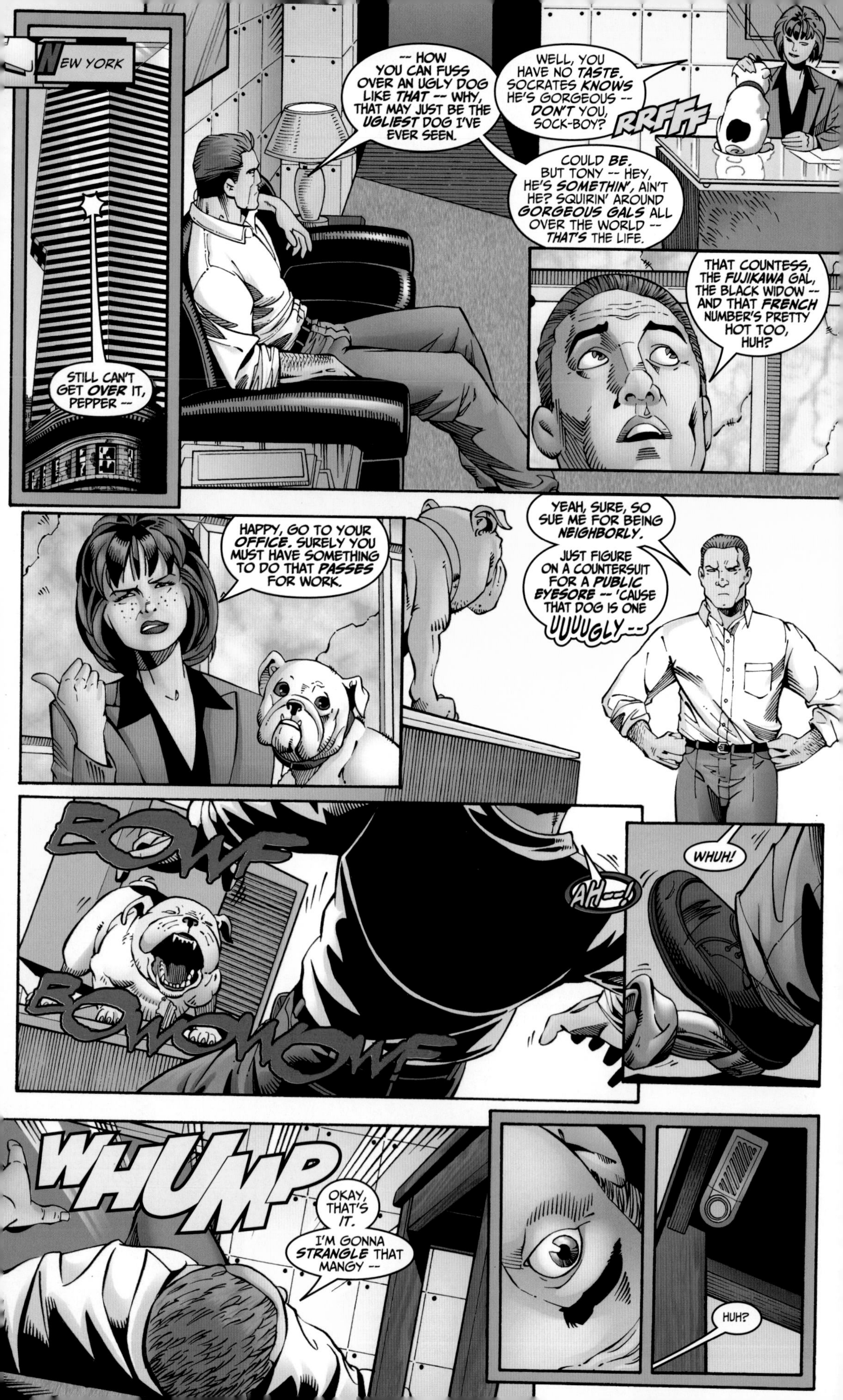
NEW YORK
STILL CAN'T GET OVER IT, PEPPER --
-- HOW YOU CAN FUSS OVER AN UGLY DOG LIKE THAT -- WHY, THAT MAY JUST BE THE UGLIEST DOG I'VE EVER SEEN.
WELL, YOU HAVE NO TASTE. SOCRATES KNOWS HE'S GORGEOUS -- DON'T YOU, SOCK-BOY?
RRFFF
COULD BE. BUT TONY -- HEY, HE'S SOMETHIN', AIN'T HE? SQUIRIN' AROUND GORGEOUS GALS ALL OVER THE WORLD -- THAT'S THE LIFE.
THAT COUNTESS, THE FUJIKAWA GAL, THE BLACK WIDOW -- AND THAT FRENCH NUMBER'S PRETTY HOT TOO, HUH?
HAPPY, GO TO YOUR OFFICE. SURELY YOU MUST HAVE SOMETHING TO DO THAT PASSES FOR WORK.
YEAH, SURE, SO SUE ME FOR BEING NEIGHBORLY.
JUST FIGURE ON A COUNTERSUIT FOR A PUBLIC EYESORE -- 'CAUSE THAT DOG IS ONE UUUUGLY --
BOWF
BOWOWOWF
AH--!
WHUH!
WHUMP
OKAY, THAT'S IT.
I'M GONNA STRANGLE THAT MANGY --
HUH?

PEPPER!

PEPPER, LOOK AT *THIS!* IT WAS UNDER THE *TABLE* THERE -- AND IT SURE AIN'T *OURS!*

I'VE SEEN *EVERY* PURCHASE ORDER FOR *EVERY* PIECE A' EQUIPMENT IN THE JOINT, AN' --

IT'S A *BUG,* HAPPY. A *LISTENING* DEVICE.

AND YOU AND I *BOTH* KNOW WHO PUT IT THERE. IT WAS THAT *DOREEN* YOU WERE SO SMITTEN WITH --

-- I *KNEW* THERE WAS SOMETHING WRONG WITH HER FROM THE START.

AW, LIKE *HECK* YOU DID. YOU WERE JUST JEALOUS, IS ALL -- EVEN THOUGH YOU DIDN'T HAVE NOTHIN' TO BE JEALOUS *ABOUT.*

IF YOU THOUGHT SHE WAS A *SPY,* YOU'D HAVE -- YOU'D HAVE --

HAPPY, WHAT?

TONY TOLD YOU WHERE HE'D *BE!* HE'S BEEN DOIN' IT *ALL ALONG!* I BUSTED THE THING NOW, BUT WHOEVER'S BEEN BUGGIN' THE *OFFICE* --

-- THEY'VE KNOWN EVERY *STEP* OF HIS TRIP!

WORSE THAN THAT, HAPPY. *MUCH* WORSE.

WE HAVE A *SECURE* LINE -- SO WE'VE TALKED TO TONY *OPENLY* ABOUT HIS OTHER IDENTITY. WHOEVER BUGGED US --

"-- THEY KNOW HE'S *IRON MAN!*"

I FINALLY *GET* IT, AND THE SCREEN RESOLVES INTO THE MAIN *IDEOGRAM.* IT'S A TRADITIONAL, PRE-REVOLUTIONARY *CHINESE CHARACTER.*

FROM THE DAYS OF *IMPERIAL CHINA.*

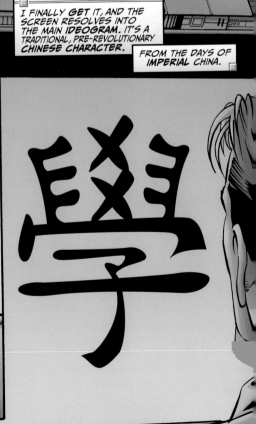

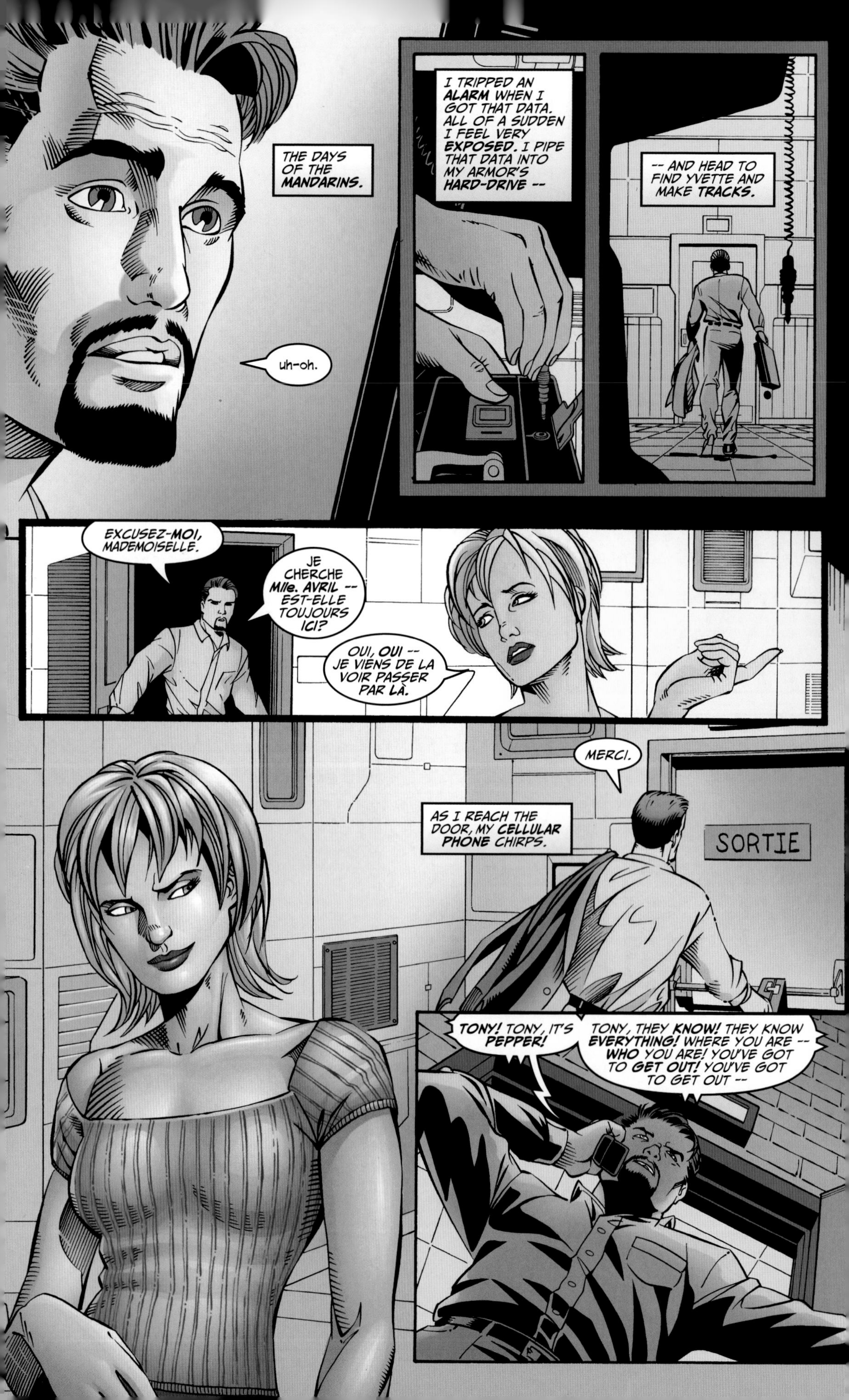
THE DAYS OF THE MANDARINS.
uh-oh.
I TRIPPED AN ALARM WHEN I GOT THAT DATA. ALL OF A SUDDEN I FEEL VERY EXPOSED. I PIPE THAT DATA INTO MY ARMOR'S HARD-DRIVE --
-- AND HEAD TO FIND YVETTE AND MAKE TRACKS.
EXCUSEZ-MOI, MADEMOISELLE.
JE CHERCHE Mlle. AVRIL -- EST-ELLE TOUJOURS ICI?
OUI, OUI -- JE VIENS DE LA VOIR PASSER PAR LÀ.
MERCI.
AS I REACH THE DOOR, MY CELLULAR PHONE CHIRPS.
SORTIE
TONY! TONY, IT'S PEPPER!
TONY, THEY KNOW! THEY KNOW EVERYTHING! WHERE YOU ARE -- WHO YOU ARE! YOU'VE GOT TO GET OUT! YOU'VE GOT TO GET OUT --

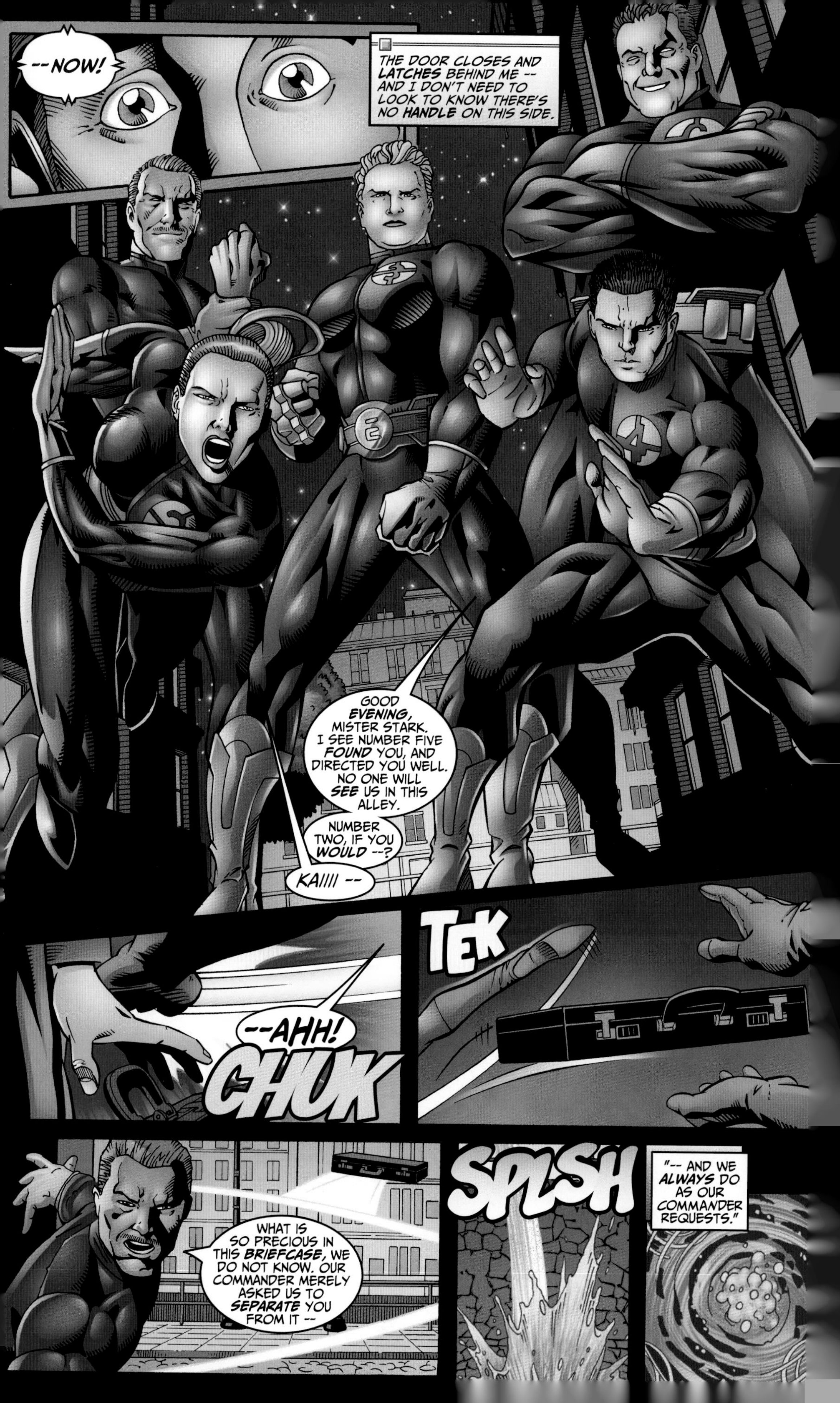

--NOW!
THE DOOR CLOSES AND LATCHES BEHIND ME -- AND I DON'T NEED TO LOOK TO KNOW THERE'S NO HANDLE ON THIS SIDE.
GOOD EVENING, MISTER STARK. I SEE NUMBER FIVE FOUND YOU, AND DIRECTED YOU WELL. NO ONE WILL SEE US IN THIS ALLEY.
NUMBER TWO, IF YOU WOULD --?
KAIIII --
--AHH!
CHUK
TEK
WHAT IS SO PRECIOUS IN THIS BRIEFCASE, WE DO NOT KNOW. OUR COMMANDER MERELY ASKED US TO SEPARATE YOU FROM IT --
SPLSH
"-- AND WE ALWAYS DO AS OUR COMMANDER REQUESTS."

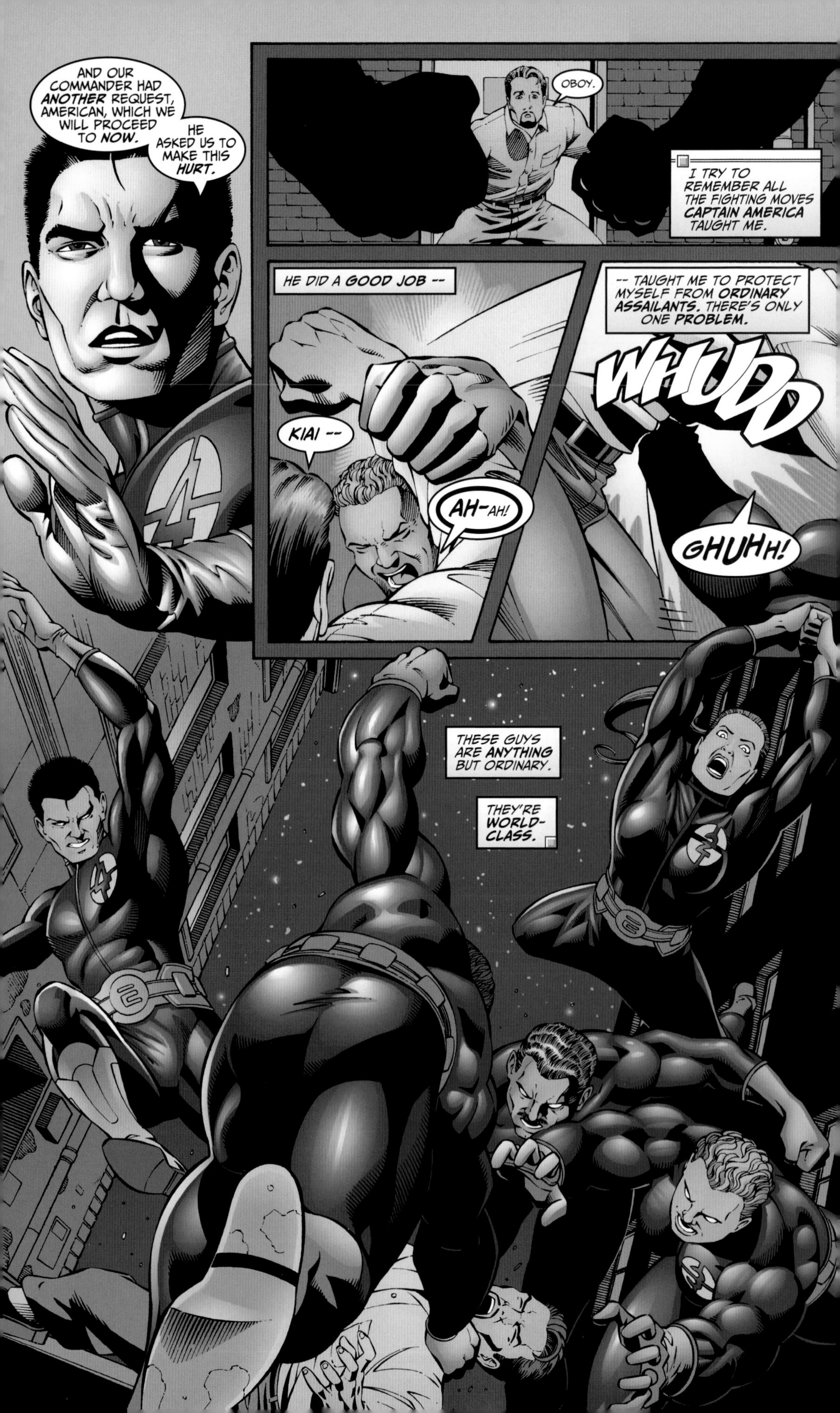
AND OUR COMMANDER HAD ANOTHER REQUEST, AMERICAN, WHICH WE WILL PROCEED TO NOW.
HE ASKED US TO MAKE THIS HURT.
OBOY.
I TRY TO REMEMBER ALL THE FIGHTING MOVES CAPTAIN AMERICA TAUGHT ME.
HE DID A GOOD JOB --
KIAI --
AH-AH!
-- TAUGHT ME TO PROTECT MYSELF FROM ORDINARY ASSAILANTS. THERE'S ONLY ONE PROBLEM.
WHUDD
GHUHH!
THESE GUYS ARE ANYTHING BUT ORDINARY.
THEY'RE WORLD-CLASS.

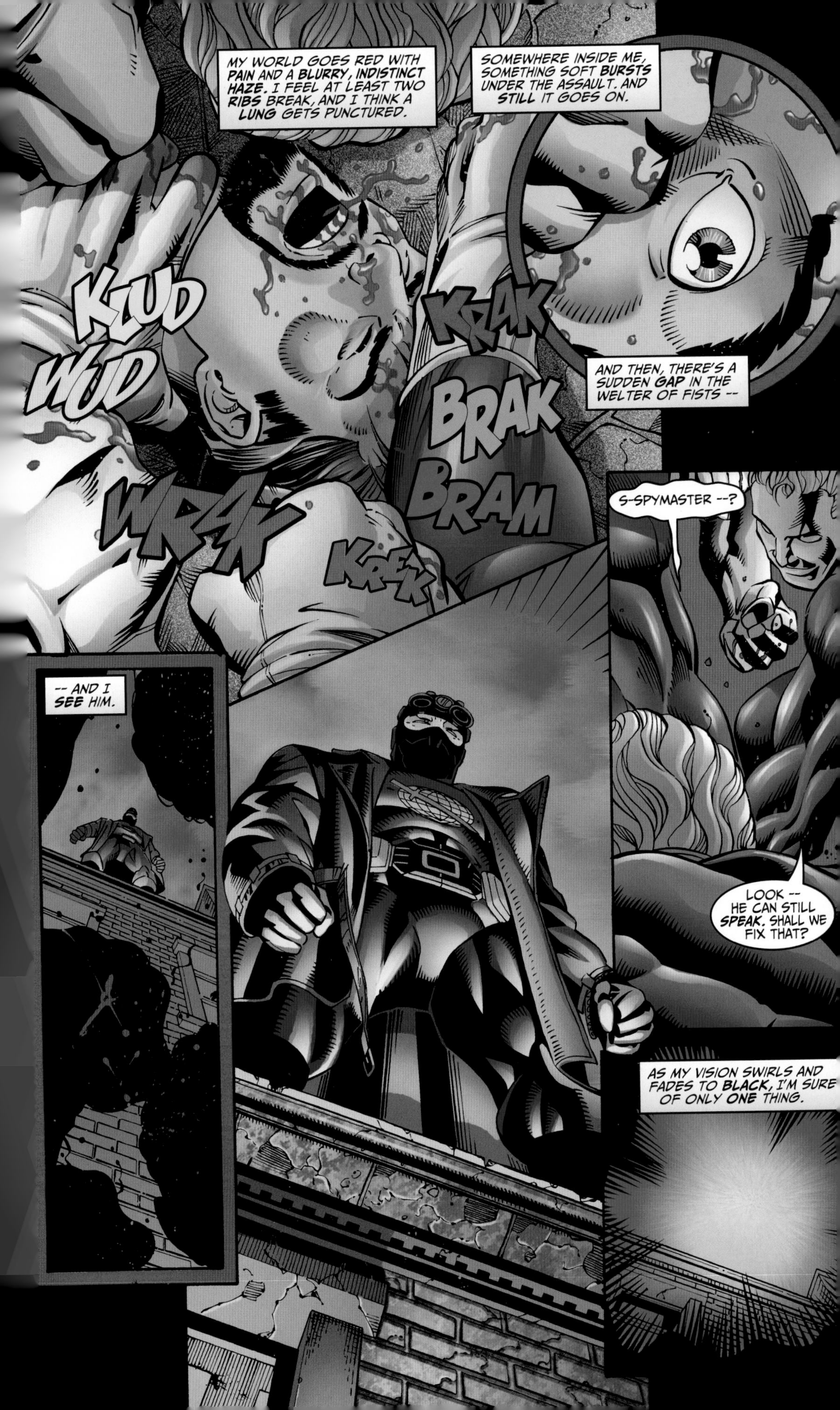
MY WORLD GOES RED WITH PAIN AND A BLURRY, INDISTINCT HAZE. I FEEL AT LEAST TWO RIBS BREAK, AND I THINK A LUNG GETS PUNCTURED.
SOMEWHERE INSIDE ME, SOMETHING SOFT BURSTS UNDER THE ASSAULT. AND STILL IT GOES ON.
KLUD
WUD
KRAK
BRAK
BRAM
WRAK
KREK
AND THEN, THERE'S A SUDDEN GAP IN THE WELTER OF FISTS --
S-SPYMASTER --?
LOOK -- HE CAN STILL SPEAK. SHALL WE FIX THAT?
-- AND I SEE HIM.
AS MY VISION SWIRLS AND FADES TO BLACK, I'M SURE OF ONLY ONE THING.

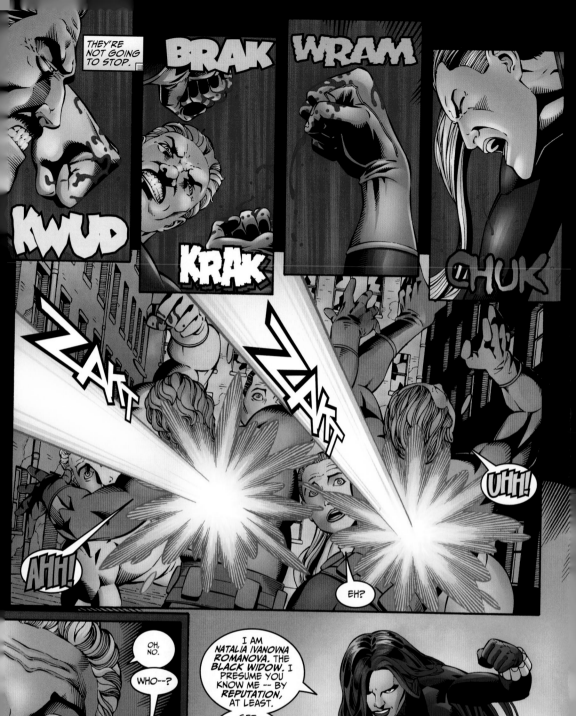

THEY'RE NOT GOING TO STOP.

BRAK

WRAM

KWUD

KRAK

CHUK

ZAKT

ZAKT

UHH!

AHH!

EH?

OH, NO.

WHO--?

I AM NATALIA IVANOVNA ROMANOVA. THE BLACK WIDOW. I PRESUME YOU KNOW ME -- BY REPUTATION, AT LEAST.

GET AWAY FROM THAT MAN. NOW.

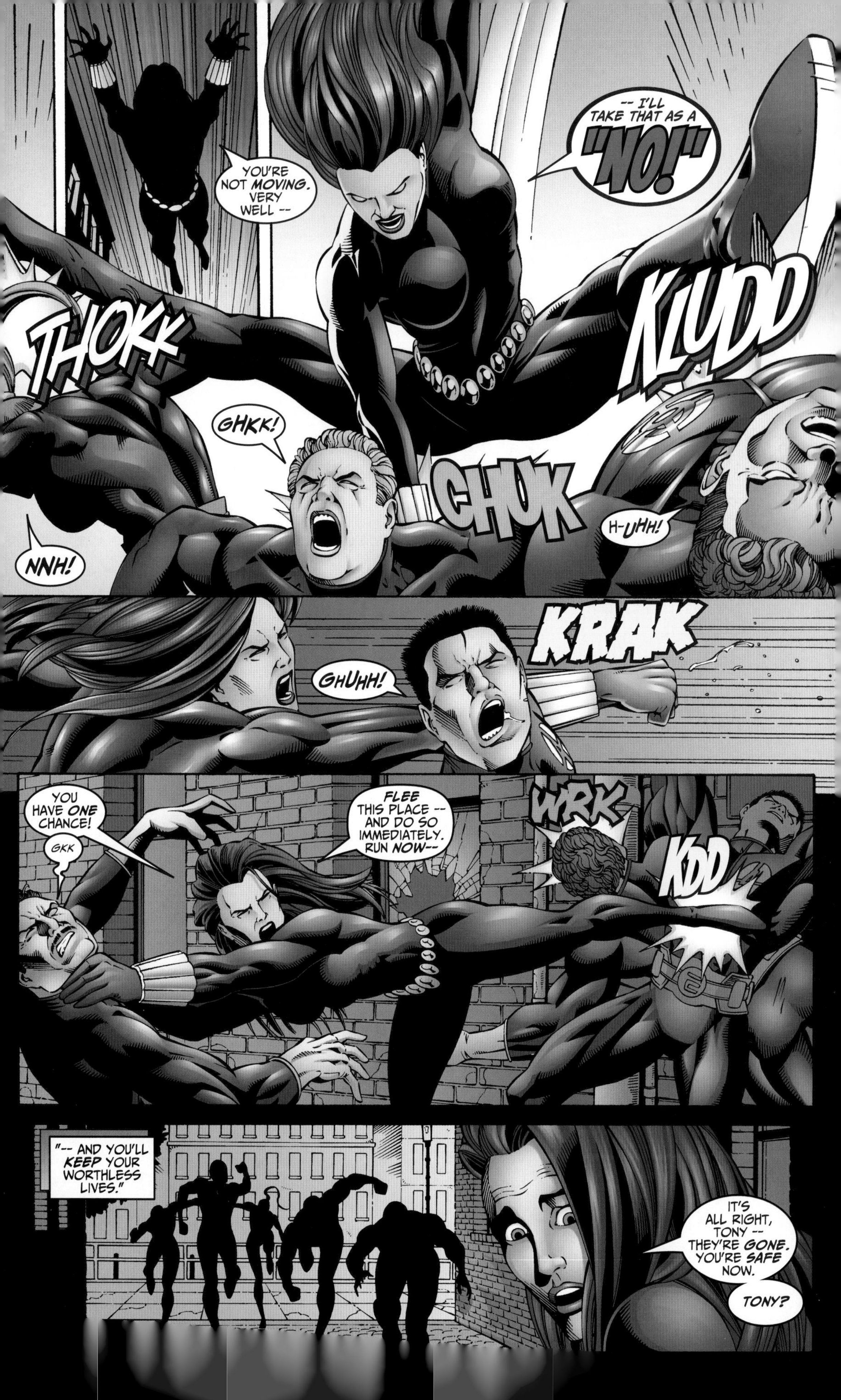
YOU'RE NOT MOVING. VERY WELL --
-- I'LL TAKE THAT AS A "NO!"
THOKK
KLUDD
GHKK!
CHUK
H-UHH!
NNH!
KRAK
GHUHH!
YOU HAVE ONE CHANCE!
GKK
FLEE THIS PLACE -- AND DO SO IMMEDIATELY. RUN NOW--
WRK
KDD
"-- AND YOU'LL KEEP YOUR WORTHLESS LIVES."
IT'S ALL RIGHT, TONY -- THEY'RE GONE. YOU'RE SAFE NOW.
TONY?

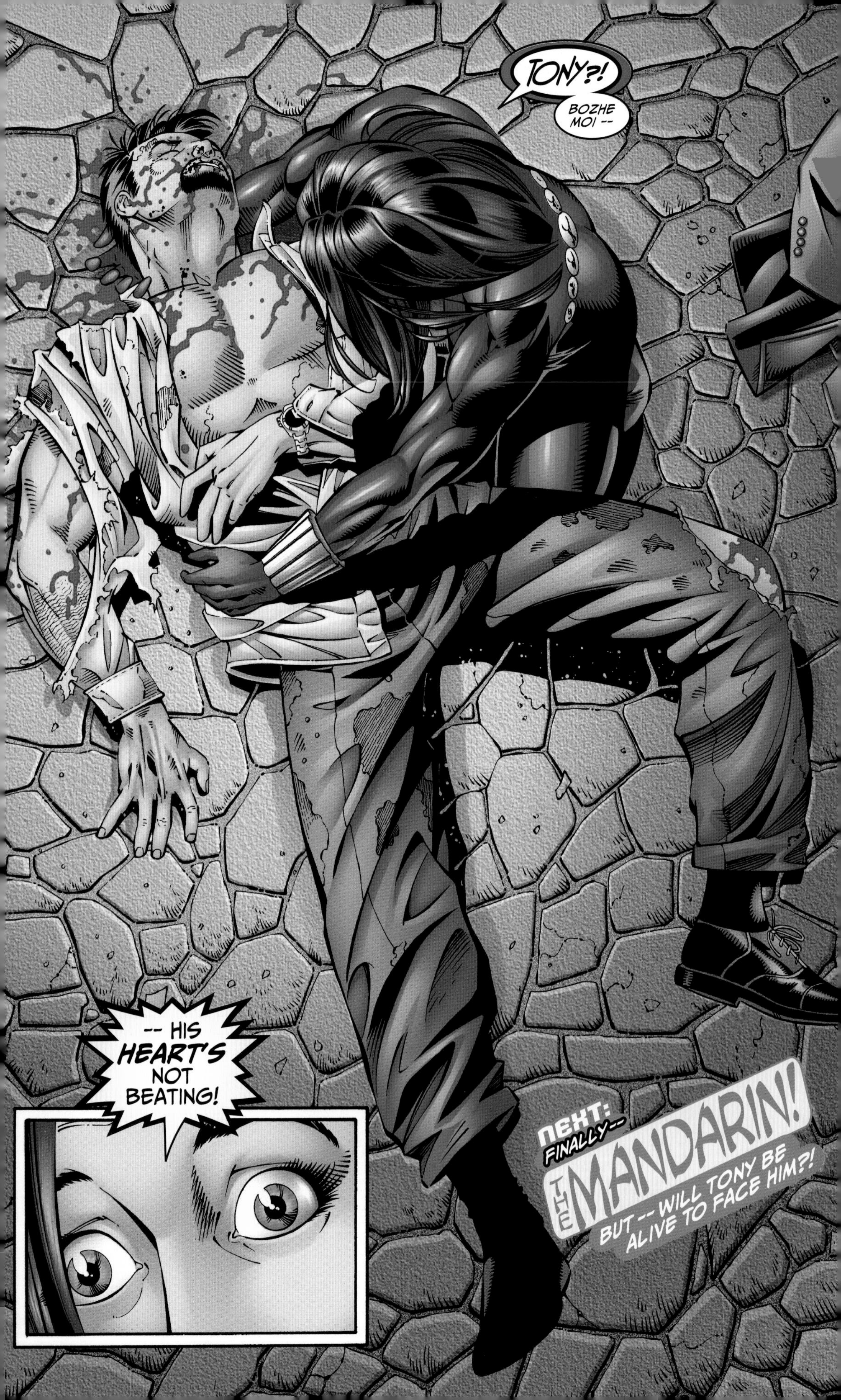
TONY?!
BOZHE MOI --
-- HIS HEART'S NOT BEATING!
NEXT: FINALLY--
THE MANDARIN!
BUT -- WILL TONY BE ALIVE TO FACE HIM?!

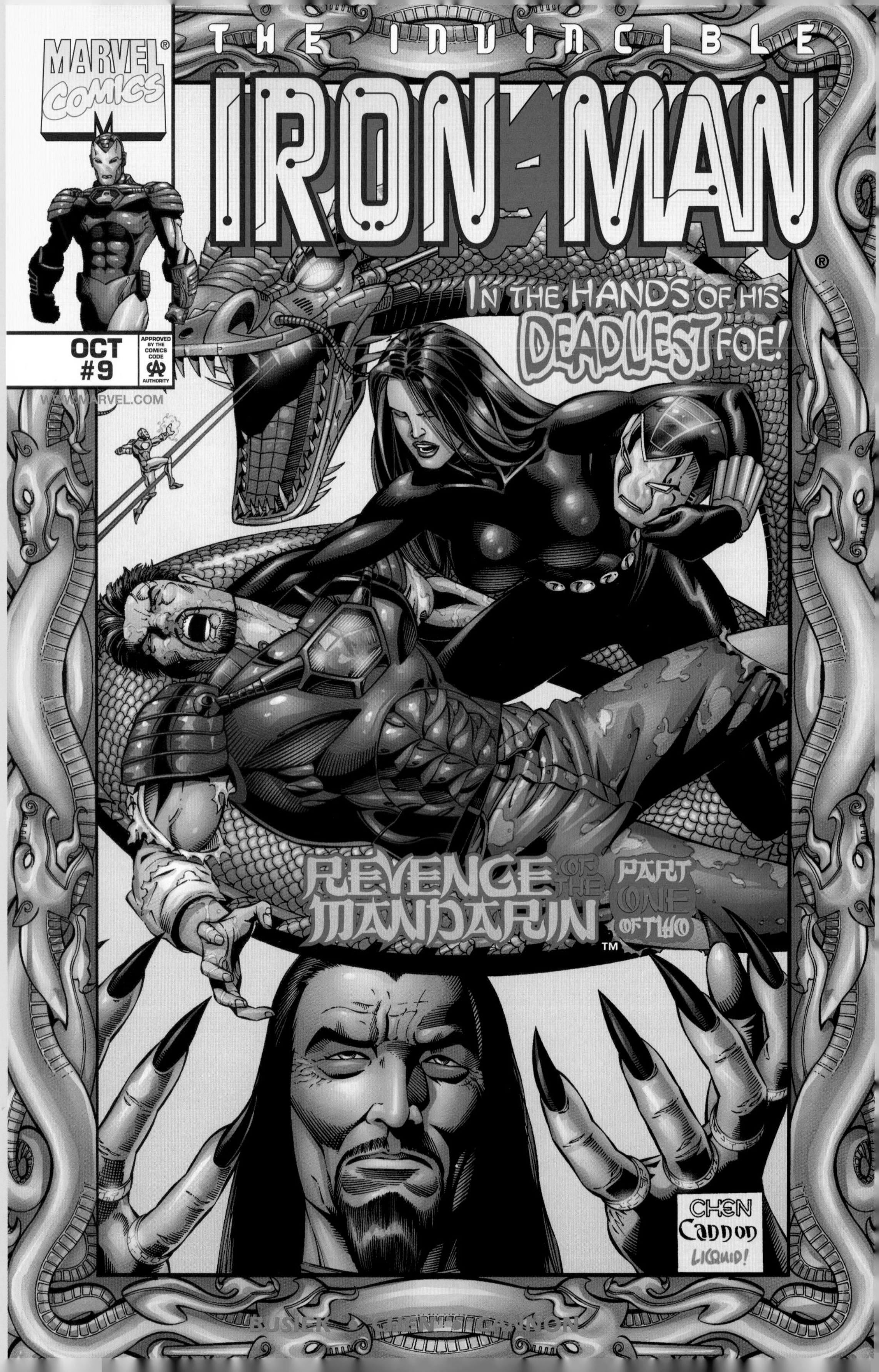
MARVEL COMICS
THE INVINCIBLE
IRON MAN
OCT
#9
APPROVED BY THE COMICS CODE AUTHORITY
WWW.MARVEL.COM
IN THE HANDS OF HIS DEADLIEST FOE!
REVENGE OF THE MANDARIN
PART ONE OF TWO
CHEN
CANNON
LIQUID!

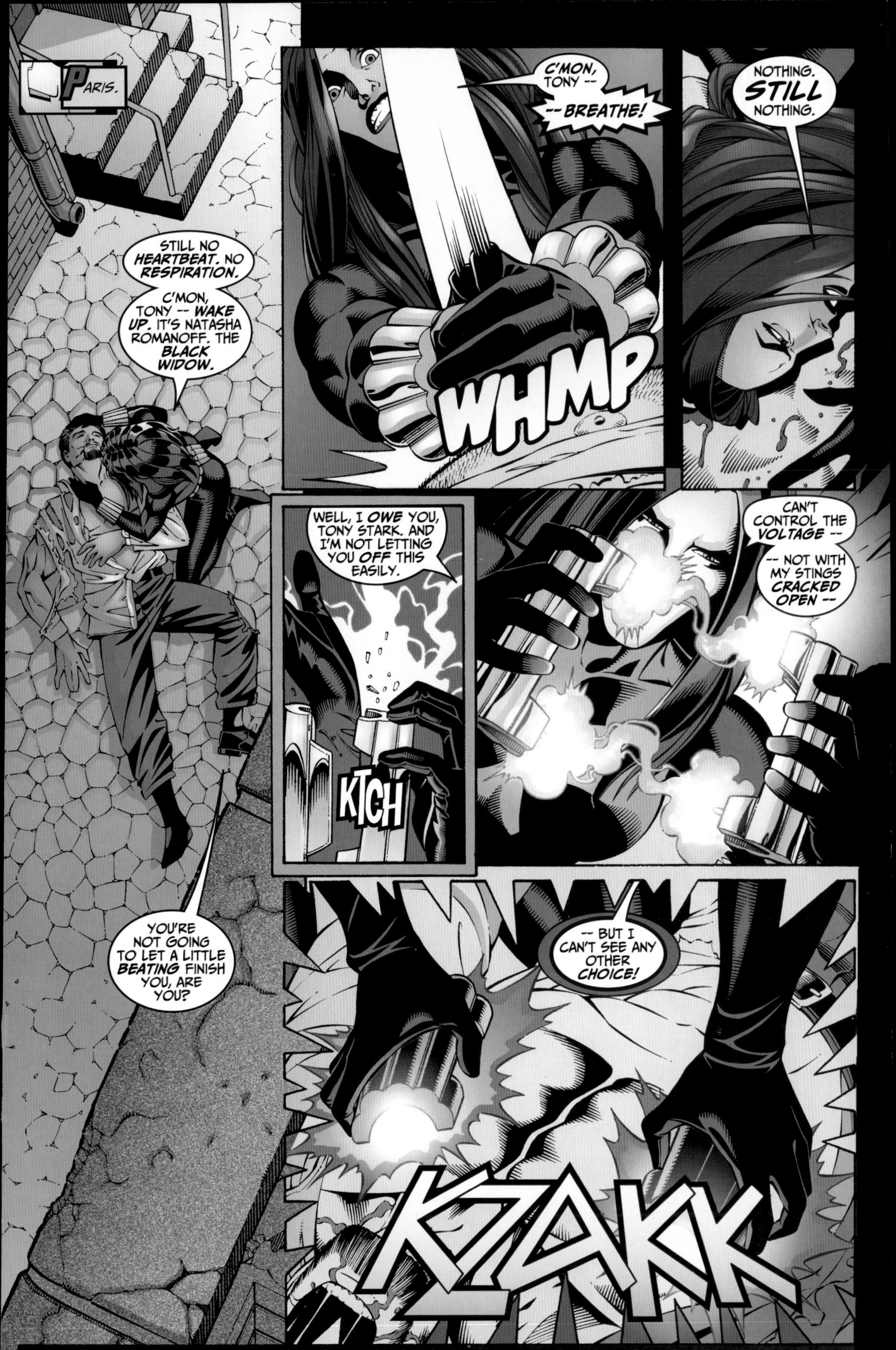

PARIS.
STILL NO HEARTBEAT. NO RESPIRATION.
C'MON, TONY -- WAKE UP. IT'S NATASHA ROMANOFF. THE BLACK WIDOW.
YOU'RE NOT GOING TO LET A LITTLE BEATING FINISH YOU, ARE YOU?
C'MON, TONY --
--BREATHE!
WHMP
NOTHING. STILL NOTHING.
WELL, I OWE YOU, TONY STARK. AND I'M NOT LETTING YOU OFF THIS EASILY.
KTCH
CAN'T CONTROL THE VOLTAGE --
-- NOT WITH MY STINGS CRACKED OPEN --
-- BUT I CAN'T SEE ANY OTHER CHOICE!
KZAKK

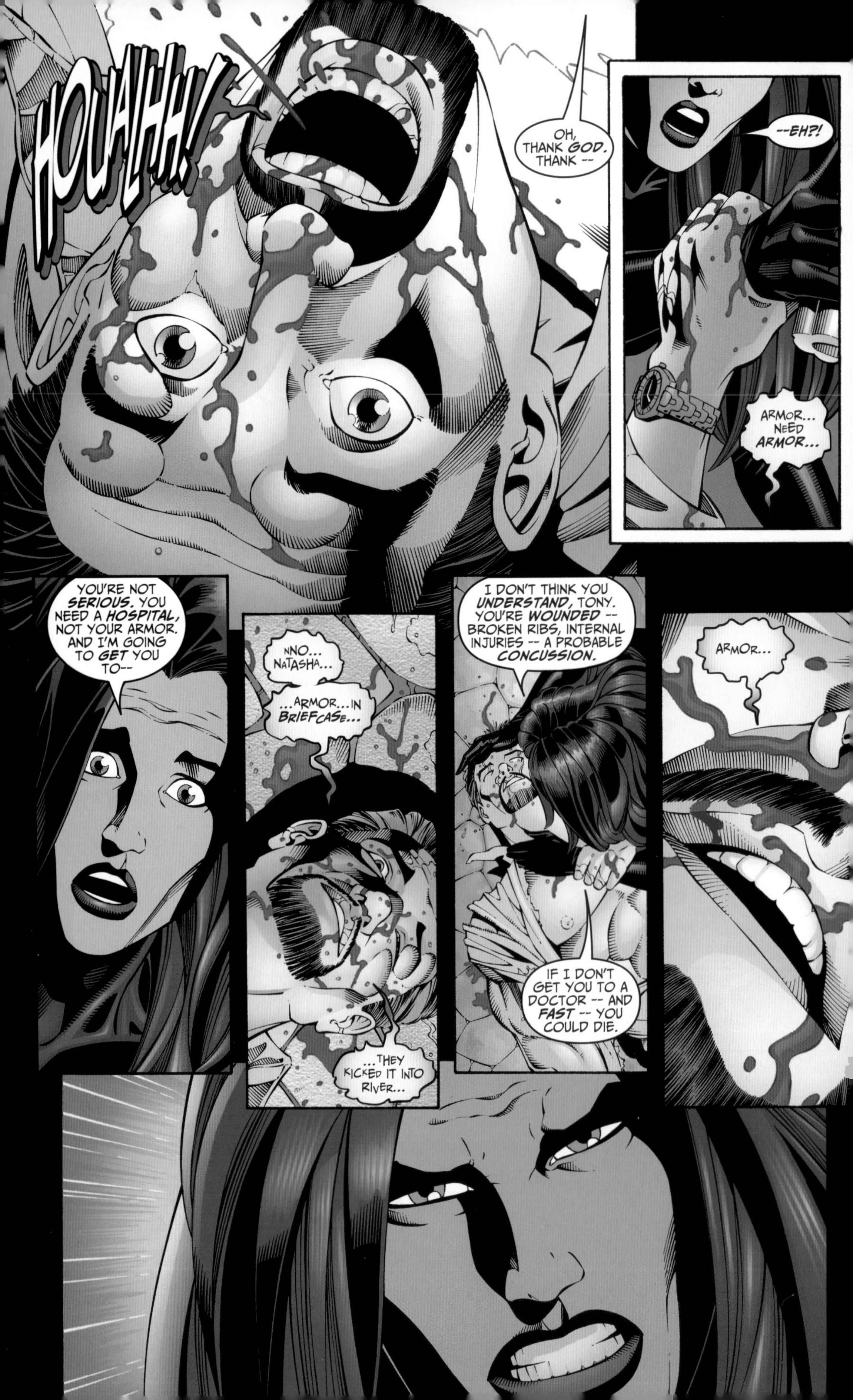
HOUAHH!
OH, THANK GOD. THANK --
--EH?!
ARMOR... NEED ARMOR...
YOU'RE NOT SERIOUS. YOU NEED A HOSPITAL, NOT YOUR ARMOR. AND I'M GOING TO GET YOU TO--
NNO... NATASHA...
...ARMOR...IN BRIEFCASE...
...THEY KICKED IT INTO RIVER...
I DON'T THINK YOU UNDERSTAND, TONY. YOU'RE WOUNDED -- BROKEN RIBS, INTERNAL INJURIES -- A PROBABLE CONCUSSION.
IF I DON'T GET YOU TO A DOCTOR -- AND FAST -- YOU COULD DIE.
ARMOR...

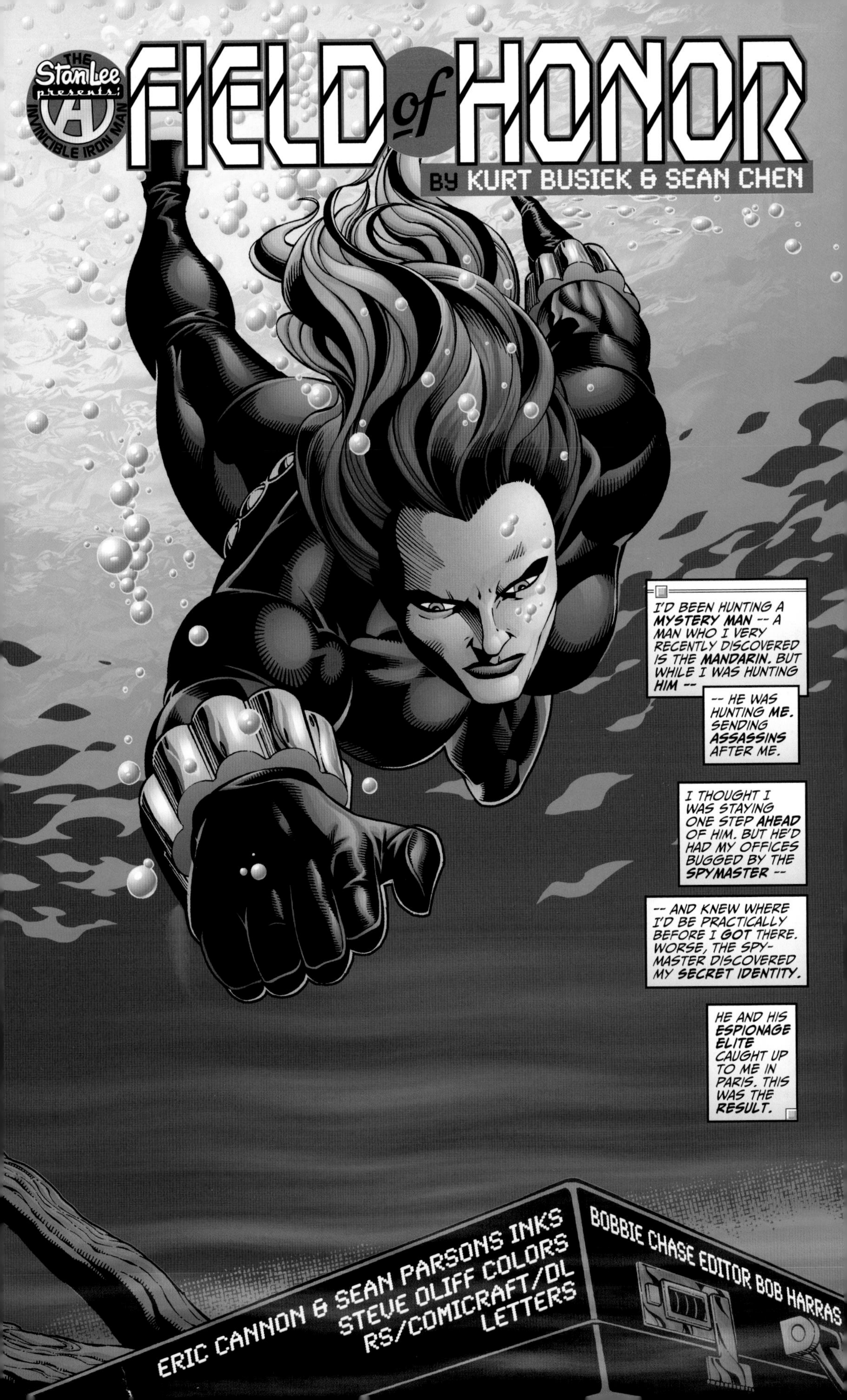
THE Stan Lee presents: INVINCIBLE IRON MAN
FIELD of HONOR
BY KURT BUSIEK & SEAN CHEN
I'D BEEN HUNTING A MYSTERY MAN -- A MAN WHO I VERY RECENTLY DISCOVERED IS THE MANDARIN. BUT WHILE I WAS HUNTING HIM --
-- HE WAS HUNTING ME. SENDING ASSASSINS AFTER ME.
I THOUGHT I WAS STAYING ONE STEP AHEAD OF HIM. BUT HE'D HAD MY OFFICES BUGGED BY THE SPYMASTER --
-- AND KNEW WHERE I'D BE PRACTICALLY BEFORE I GOT THERE. WORSE, THE SPY-MASTER DISCOVERED MY SECRET IDENTITY.
HE AND HIS ESPIONAGE ELITE CAUGHT UP TO ME IN PARIS. THIS WAS THE RESULT.
ERIC CANNON & SEAN PARSONS INKS
STEVE OLIFF COLORS
RS/COMICRAFT/DL LETTERS
BOBBIE CHASE EDITOR BOB HARRAS

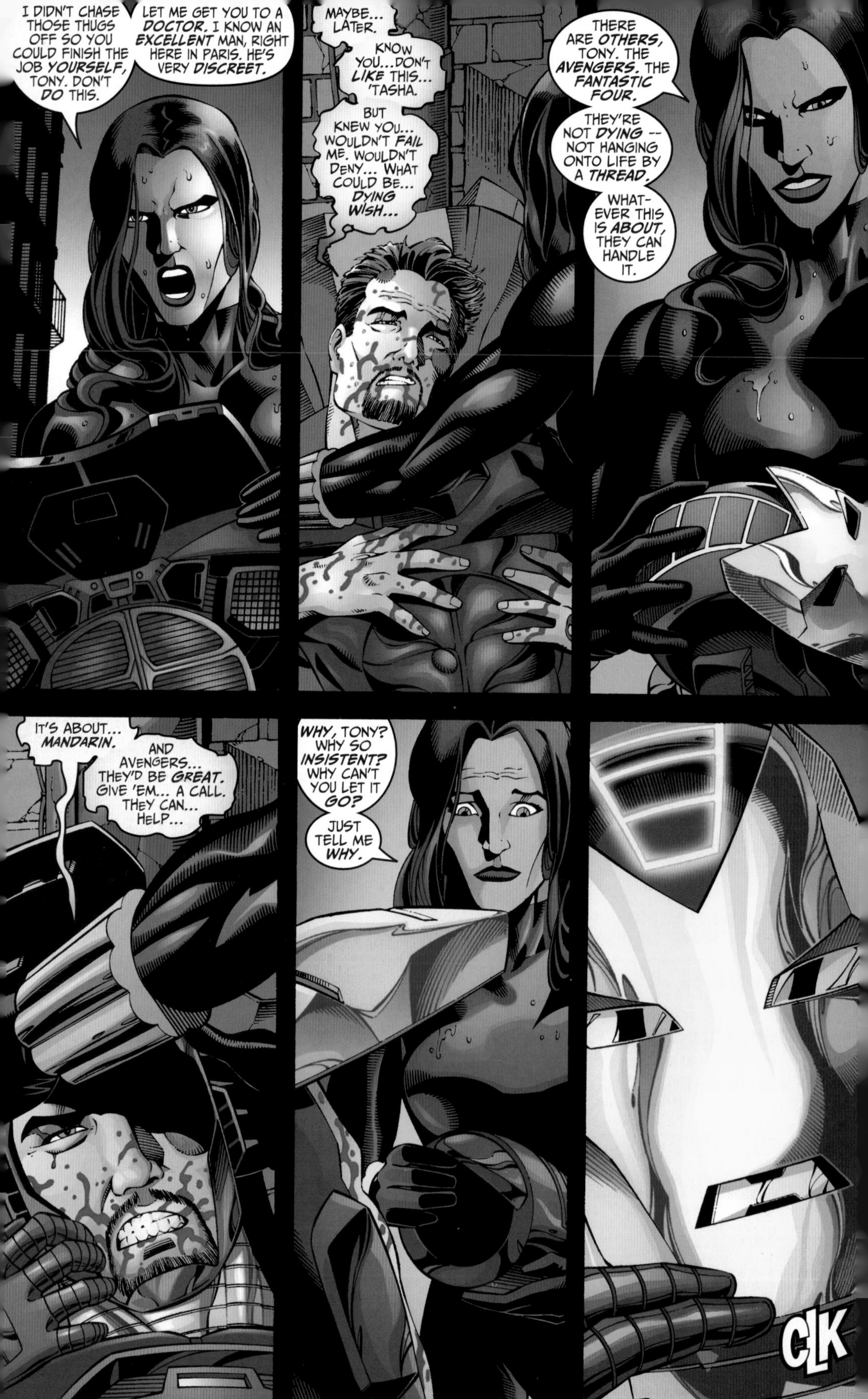
I DIDN'T CHASE THOSE THUGS OFF SO YOU COULD FINISH THE JOB YOURSELF, TONY. DON'T DO THIS.
LET ME GET YOU TO A DOCTOR. I KNOW AN EXCELLENT MAN, RIGHT HERE IN PARIS. HE'S VERY DISCREET.
MAYBE... LATER.
KNOW YOU...DON'T LIKE THIS... 'TASHA.
BUT KNEW YOU... WOULDN'T FAIL ME. WOULDN'T DENY... WHAT COULD BE... DYING WISH...
THERE ARE OTHERS, TONY. THE AVENGERS. THE FANTASTIC FOUR.
THEY'RE NOT DYING -- NOT HANGING ONTO LIFE BY A THREAD.
WHATEVER THIS IS ABOUT, THEY CAN HANDLE IT.
IT'S ABOUT... MANDARIN.
AND AVENGERS... THEY'D BE GREAT. GIVE 'EM... A CALL. THEY CAN... HELP...
WHY, TONY? WHY SO INSISTENT? WHY CAN'T YOU LET IT GO?
JUST TELL ME WHY.
CLK

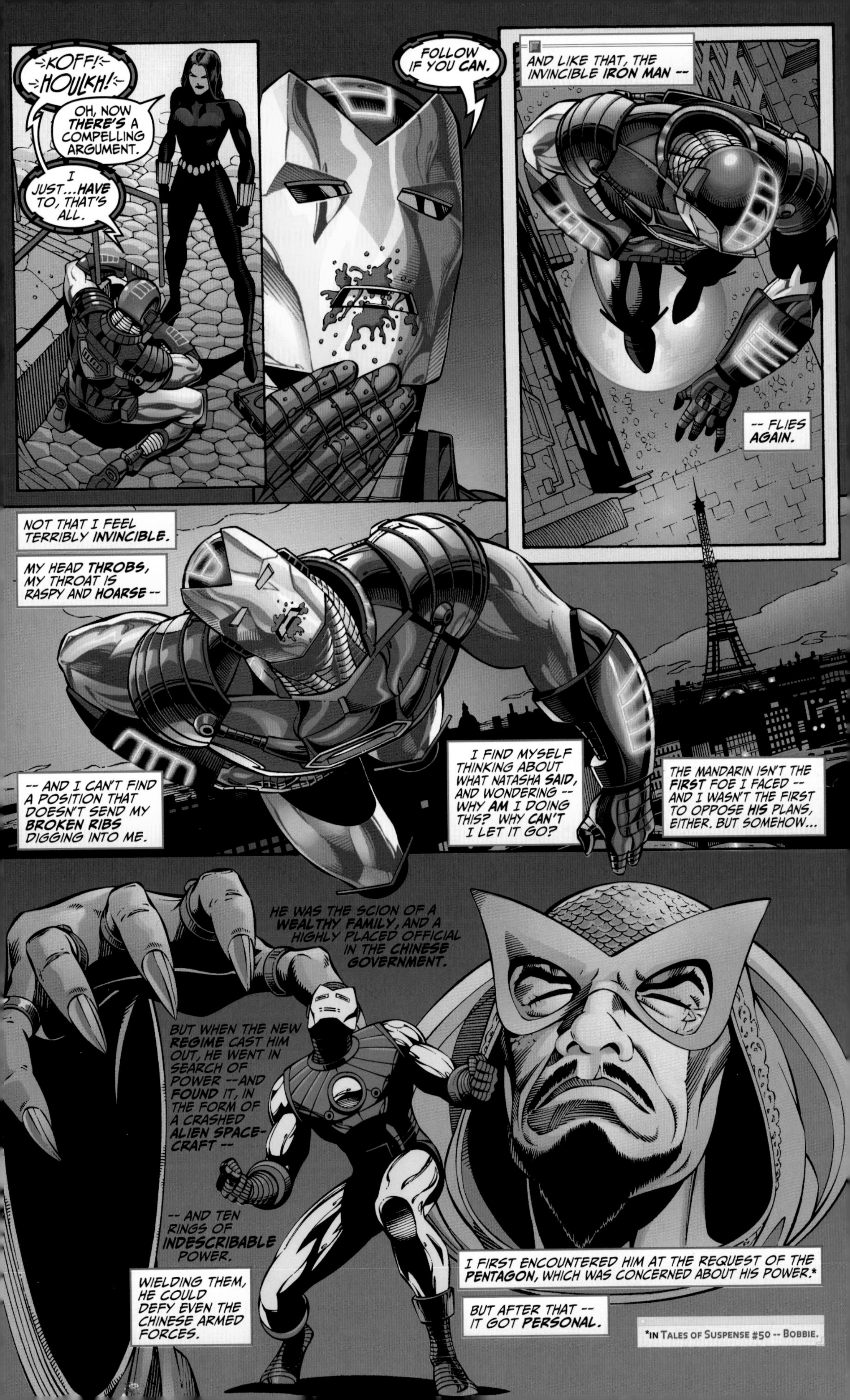

KOFF! HOULKH!
OH, NOW THERE'S A COMPELLING ARGUMENT.
I JUST... HAVE TO, THAT'S ALL.
FOLLOW IF YOU CAN.
AND LIKE THAT, THE INVINCIBLE IRON MAN --
-- FLIES AGAIN.
NOT THAT I FEEL TERRIBLY INVINCIBLE.
MY HEAD THROBS, MY THROAT IS RASPY AND HOARSE --
-- AND I CAN'T FIND A POSITION THAT DOESN'T SEND MY BROKEN RIBS DIGGING INTO ME.
I FIND MYSELF THINKING ABOUT WHAT NATASHA SAID, AND WONDERING -- WHY AM I DOING THIS? WHY CAN'T I LET IT GO?
THE MANDARIN ISN'T THE FIRST FOE I FACED -- AND I WASN'T THE FIRST TO OPPOSE HIS PLANS, EITHER. BUT SOMEHOW...
HE WAS THE SCION OF A WEALTHY FAMILY, AND A HIGHLY PLACED OFFICIAL IN THE CHINESE GOVERNMENT.
BUT WHEN THE NEW REGIME CAST HIM OUT, HE WENT IN SEARCH OF POWER -- AND FOUND IT, IN THE FORM OF A CRASHED ALIEN SPACE-CRAFT --
-- AND TEN RINGS OF INDESCRIBABLE POWER.
WIELDING THEM, HE COULD DEFY EVEN THE CHINESE ARMED FORCES.
I FIRST ENCOUNTERED HIM AT THE REQUEST OF THE PENTAGON, WHICH WAS CONCERNED ABOUT HIS POWER.*
BUT AFTER THAT -- IT GOT PERSONAL.
*IN TALES OF SUSPENSE #50 -- BOBBIE.

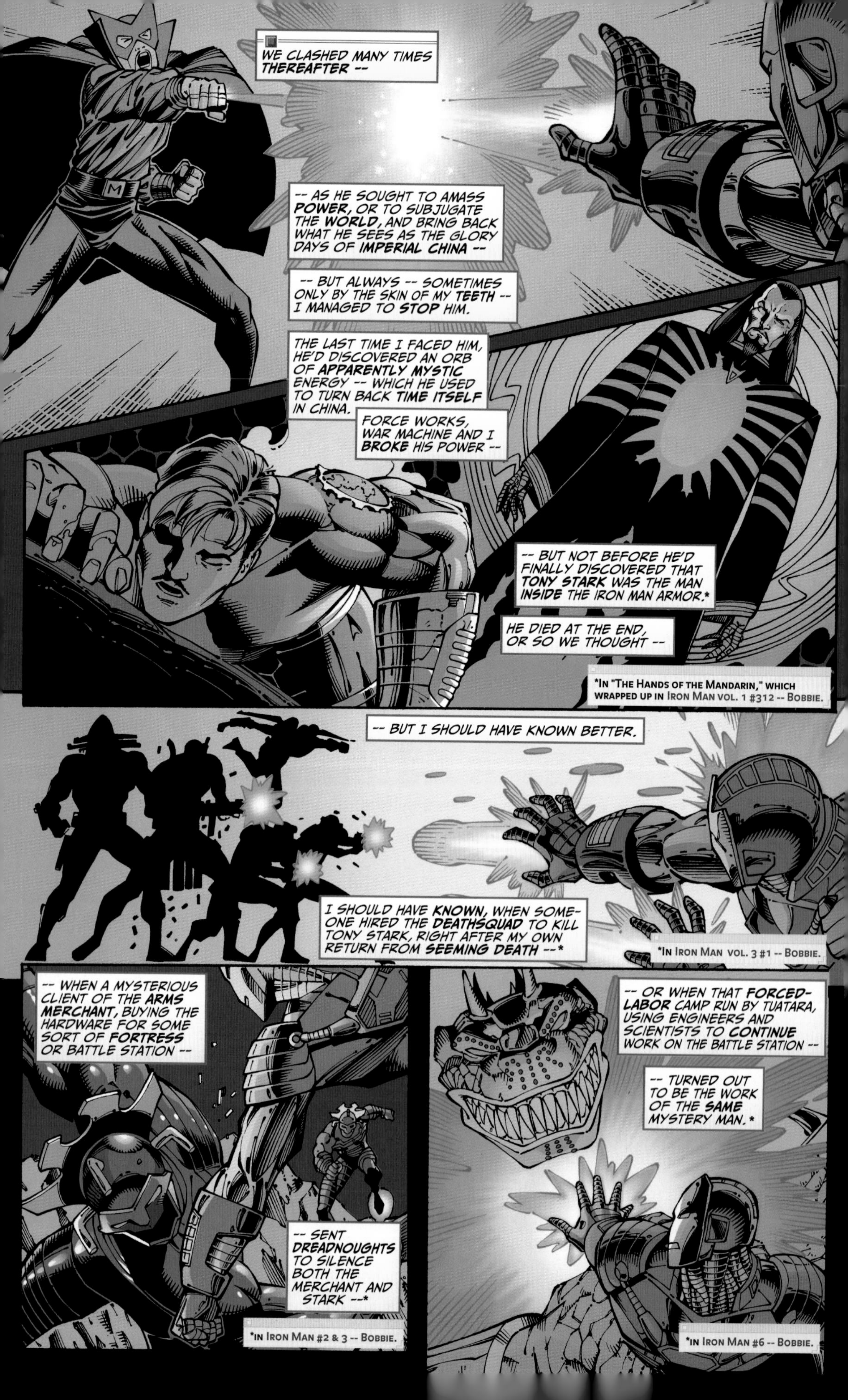

WE CLASHED MANY TIMES THEREAFTER --
-- AS HE SOUGHT TO AMASS POWER, OR TO SUBJUGATE THE WORLD, AND BRING BACK WHAT HE SEES AS THE GLORY DAYS OF IMPERIAL CHINA --
-- BUT ALWAYS -- SOMETIMES ONLY BY THE SKIN OF MY TEETH -- I MANAGED TO STOP HIM.
THE LAST TIME I FACED HIM, HE'D DISCOVERED AN ORB OF APPARENTLY MYSTIC ENERGY -- WHICH HE USED TO TURN BACK TIME ITSELF IN CHINA.
FORCE WORKS, WAR MACHINE AND I BROKE HIS POWER --
-- BUT NOT BEFORE HE'D FINALLY DISCOVERED THAT TONY STARK WAS THE MAN INSIDE THE IRON MAN ARMOR.*
HE DIED AT THE END, OR SO WE THOUGHT --
*In "The Hands of the Mandarin," which wrapped up in Iron Man vol. 1 #312 -- Bobbie.
-- BUT I SHOULD HAVE KNOWN BETTER.
I SHOULD HAVE KNOWN, WHEN SOMEONE HIRED THE DEATHSQUAD TO KILL TONY STARK, RIGHT AFTER MY OWN RETURN FROM SEEMING DEATH --*
*In Iron Man vol. 3 #1 -- Bobbie.
-- WHEN A MYSTERIOUS CLIENT OF THE ARMS MERCHANT, BUYING THE HARDWARE FOR SOME SORT OF FORTRESS OR BATTLE STATION --
-- SENT DREADNOUGHTS TO SILENCE BOTH THE MERCHANT AND STARK --*
*in Iron Man #2 & 3 -- Bobbie.
-- OR WHEN THAT FORCED-LABOR CAMP RUN BY TUATARA, USING ENGINEERS AND SCIENTISTS TO CONTINUE WORK ON THE BATTLE STATION --
-- TURNED OUT TO BE THE WORK OF THE SAME MYSTERY MAN.*
*in Iron Man #6 -- Bobbie.

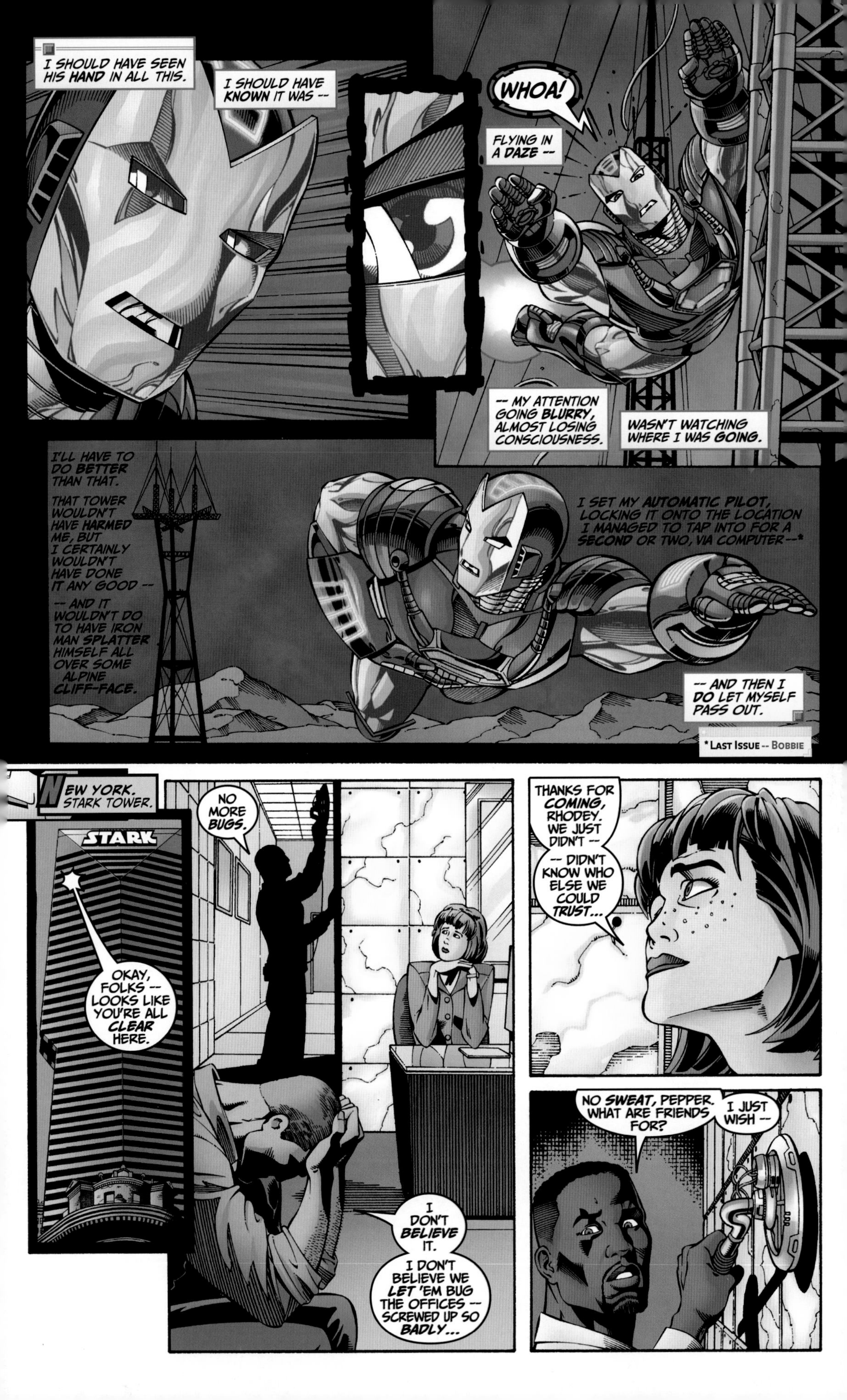

I SHOULD HAVE SEEN HIS HAND IN ALL THIS.
I SHOULD HAVE KNOWN IT WAS --
WHOA!
FLYING IN A DAZE --
-- MY ATTENTION GOING BLURRY, ALMOST LOSING CONSCIOUSNESS.
WASN'T WATCHING WHERE I WAS GOING.
I'LL HAVE TO DO BETTER THAN THAT.
THAT TOWER WOULDN'T HAVE HARMED ME, BUT I CERTAINLY WOULDN'T HAVE DONE IT ANY GOOD --
-- AND IT WOULDN'T DO TO HAVE IRON MAN SPLATTER HIMSELF ALL OVER SOME ALPINE CLIFF-FACE.
I SET MY AUTOMATIC PILOT, LOCKING IT ONTO THE LOCATION I MANAGED TO TAP INTO FOR A SECOND OR TWO, VIA COMPUTER--*
-- AND THEN I DO LET MYSELF PASS OUT.
*LAST ISSUE -- BOBBIE
NEW YORK. STARK TOWER.
STARK
OKAY, FOLKS -- LOOKS LIKE YOU'RE ALL CLEAR HERE.
NO MORE BUGS.
I DON'T BELIEVE IT.
I DON'T BELIEVE WE LET 'EM BUG THE OFFICES -- SCREWED UP SO BADLY...
THANKS FOR COMING, RHODEY. WE JUST DIDN'T --
-- DIDN'T KNOW WHO ELSE WE COULD TRUST...
NO SWEAT, PEPPER. WHAT ARE FRIENDS FOR?
I JUST WISH --

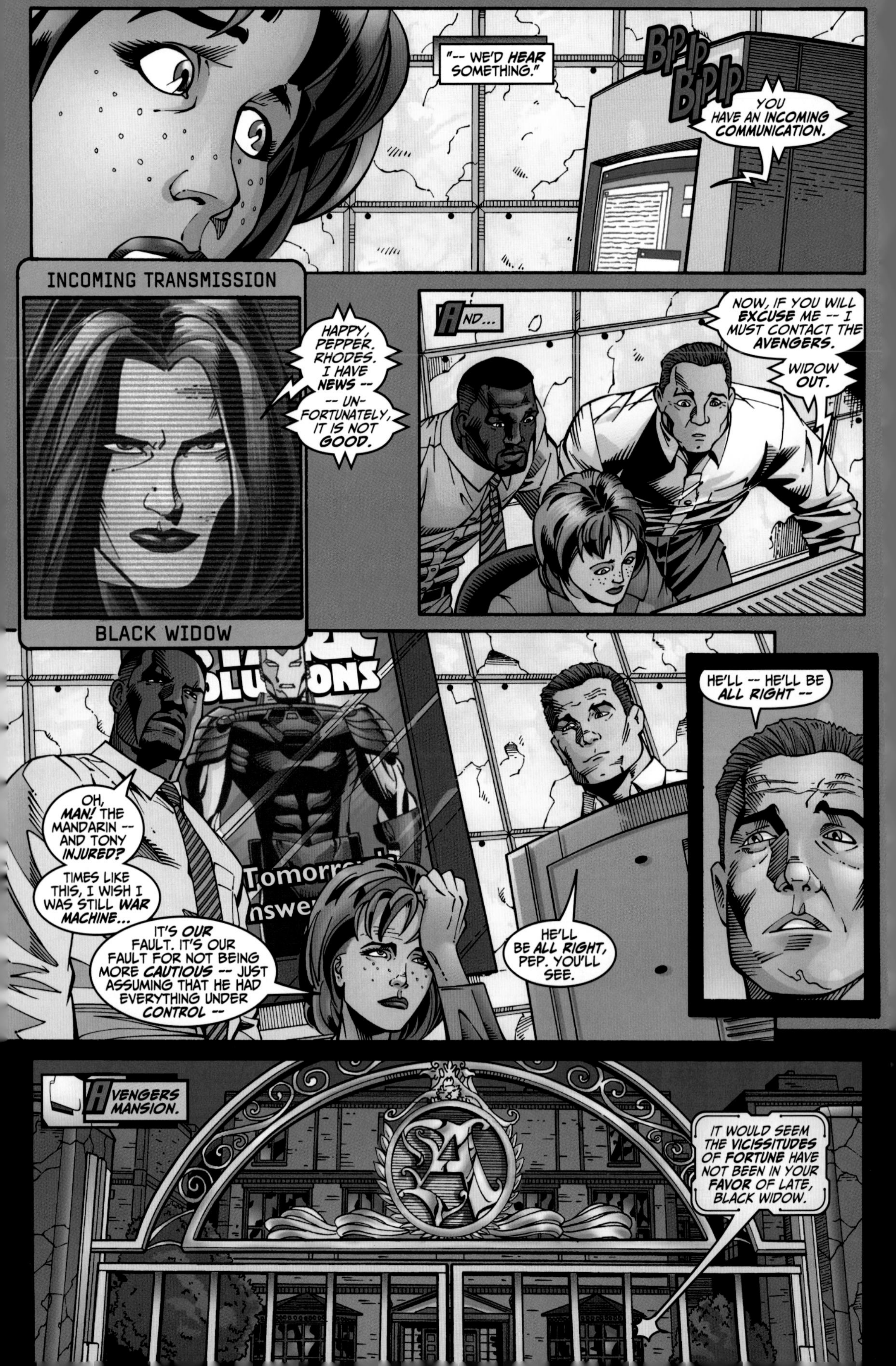

"-- WE'D HEAR SOMETHING."
BIPIP BIPIP
YOU HAVE AN INCOMING COMMUNICATION.
INCOMING TRANSMISSION
BLACK WIDOW
HAPPY, PEPPER. RHODES. I HAVE NEWS --
-- UNFORTUNATELY, IT IS NOT GOOD.
AND...
NOW, IF YOU WILL EXCUSE ME -- I MUST CONTACT THE AVENGERS.
WIDOW OUT.
OLUTIONS
OH, MAN! THE MANDARIN -- AND TONY INJURED?
TIMES LIKE THIS, I WISH I WAS STILL WAR MACHINE...
IT'S OUR FAULT. IT'S OUR FAULT FOR NOT BEING MORE CAUTIOUS -- JUST ASSUMING THAT HE HAD EVERYTHING UNDER CONTROL --
HE'LL BE ALL RIGHT, PEP. YOU'LL SEE.
HE'LL -- HE'LL BE ALL RIGHT --
AVENGERS MANSION.
IT WOULD SEEM THE VICISSITUDES OF FORTUNE HAVE NOT BEEN IN YOUR FAVOR OF LATE, BLACK WIDOW.

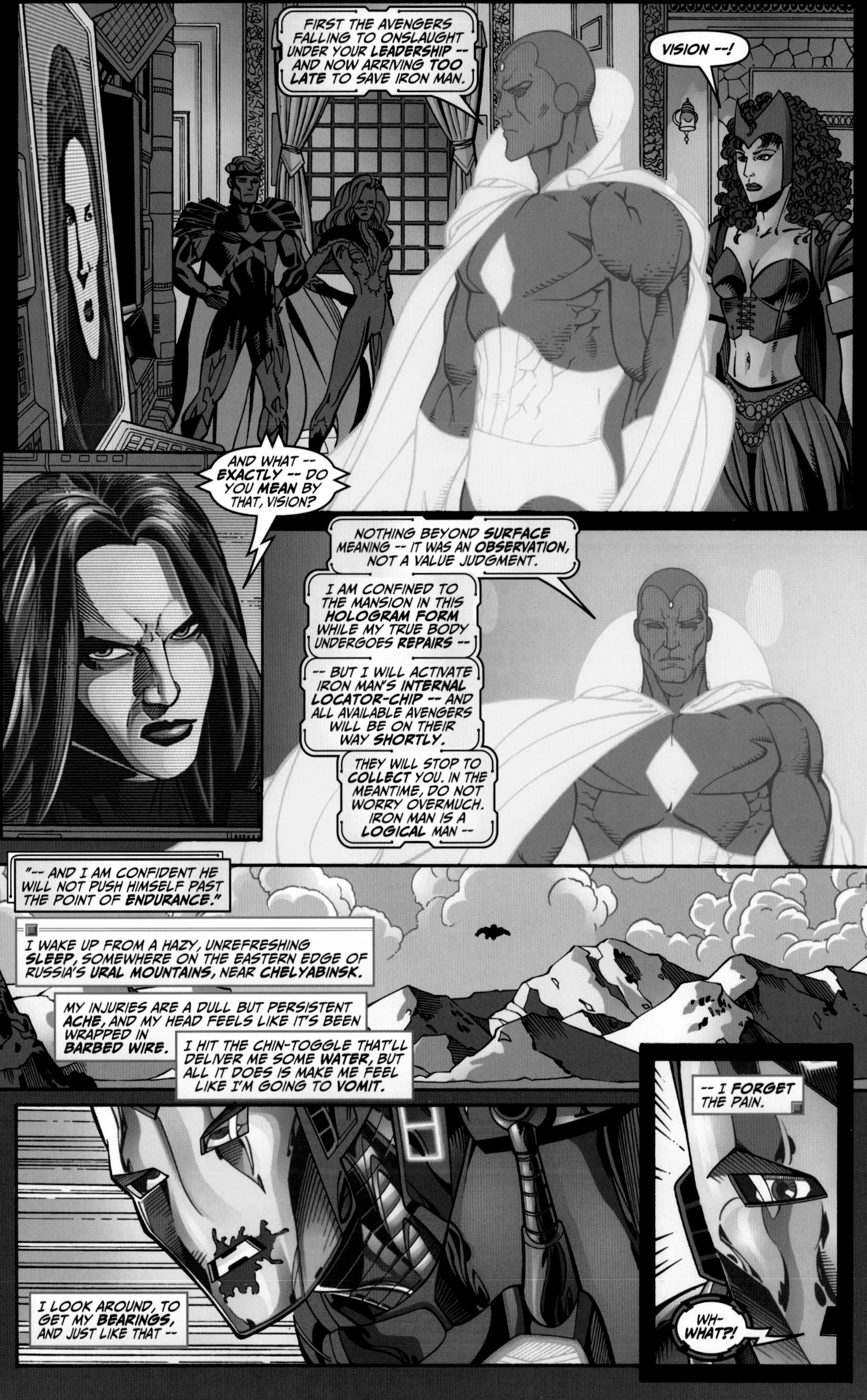
FIRST THE AVENGERS FALLING TO ONSLAUGHT UNDER YOUR LEADERSHIP -- AND NOW ARRIVING TOO LATE TO SAVE IRON MAN.
VISION --!
AND WHAT -- EXACTLY -- DO YOU MEAN BY THAT, VISION?
NOTHING BEYOND SURFACE MEANING -- IT WAS AN OBSERVATION, NOT A VALUE JUDGMENT.
I AM CONFINED TO THE MANSION IN THIS HOLOGRAM FORM WHILE MY TRUE BODY UNDERGOES REPAIRS --
-- BUT I WILL ACTIVATE IRON MAN'S INTERNAL LOCATOR-CHIP -- AND ALL AVAILABLE AVENGERS WILL BE ON THEIR WAY SHORTLY.
THEY WILL STOP TO COLLECT YOU. IN THE MEANTIME, DO NOT WORRY OVERMUCH. IRON MAN IS A LOGICAL MAN --
"-- AND I AM CONFIDENT HE WILL NOT PUSH HIMSELF PAST THE POINT OF ENDURANCE."
I WAKE UP FROM A HAZY, UNREFRESHING SLEEP, SOMEWHERE ON THE EASTERN EDGE OF RUSSIA'S URAL MOUNTAINS, NEAR CHELYABINSK.
MY INJURIES ARE A DULL BUT PERSISTENT ACHE, AND MY HEAD FEELS LIKE IT'S BEEN WRAPPED IN BARBED WIRE.
I HIT THE CHIN-TOGGLE THAT'LL DELIVER ME SOME WATER, BUT ALL IT DOES IS MAKE ME FEEL LIKE I'M GOING TO VOMIT.
I LOOK AROUND, TO GET MY BEARINGS, AND JUST LIKE THAT --
-- I FORGET THE PAIN.
WH-WHAT?!

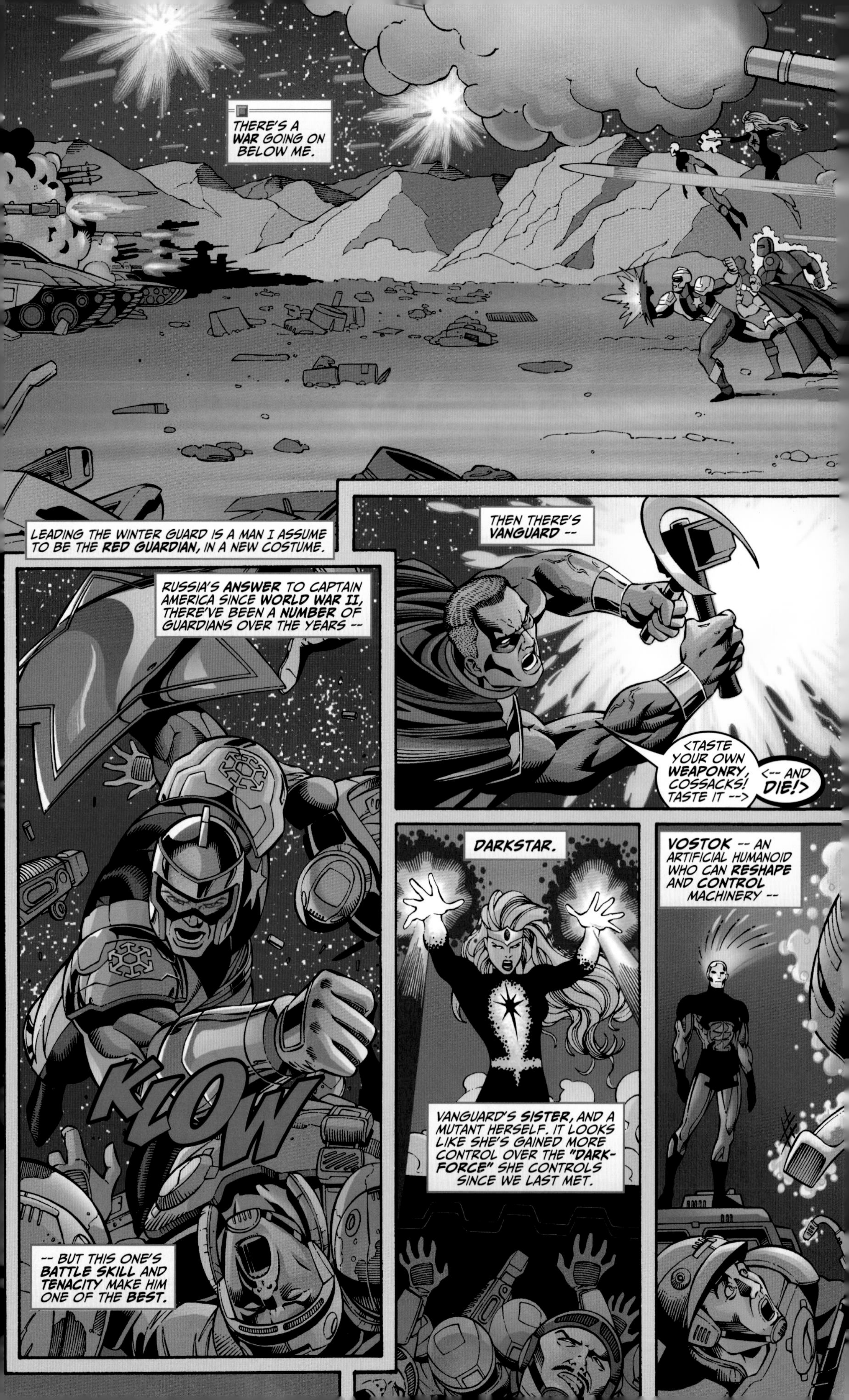
THERE'S A WAR GOING ON BELOW ME.
LEADING THE WINTER GUARD IS A MAN I ASSUME TO BE THE RED GUARDIAN, IN A NEW COSTUME.
RUSSIA'S ANSWER TO CAPTAIN AMERICA SINCE WORLD WAR II, THERE'VE BEEN A NUMBER OF GUARDIANS OVER THE YEARS --
KLOW
-- BUT THIS ONE'S BATTLE SKILL AND TENACITY MAKE HIM ONE OF THE BEST.
THEN THERE'S VANGUARD --
<TASTE YOUR OWN WEAPONRY, COSSACKS! TASTE IT -->
<-- AND DIE!>
DARKSTAR.
VANGUARD'S SISTER, AND A MUTANT HERSELF. IT LOOKS LIKE SHE'S GAINED MORE CONTROL OVER THE "DARK-FORCE" SHE CONTROLS SINCE WE LAST MET.
VOSTOK -- AN ARTIFICIAL HUMANOID WHO CAN RESHAPE AND CONTROL MACHINERY --

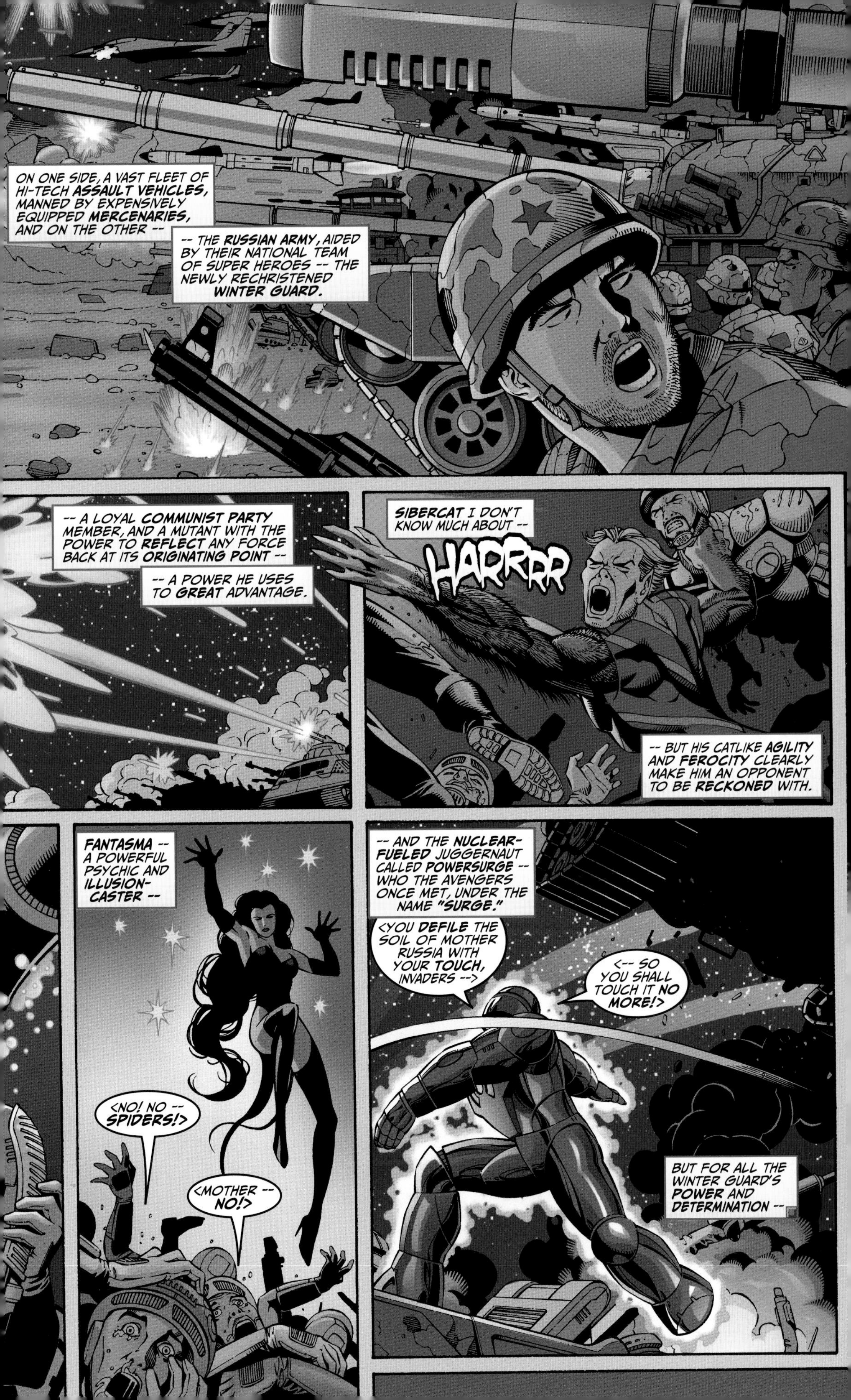
ON ONE SIDE, A VAST FLEET OF HI-TECH ASSAULT VEHICLES, MANNED BY EXPENSIVELY EQUIPPED MERCENARIES, AND ON THE OTHER --
-- THE RUSSIAN ARMY, AIDED BY THEIR NATIONAL TEAM OF SUPER HEROES -- THE NEWLY RECHRISTENED WINTER GUARD.
-- A LOYAL COMMUNIST PARTY MEMBER, AND A MUTANT WITH THE POWER TO REFLECT ANY FORCE BACK AT ITS ORIGINATING POINT --
-- A POWER HE USES TO GREAT ADVANTAGE.
SIBERCAT I DON'T KNOW MUCH ABOUT --
HARRRR
-- BUT HIS CATLIKE AGILITY AND FEROCITY CLEARLY MAKE HIM AN OPPONENT TO BE RECKONED WITH.
FANTASMA -- A POWERFUL PSYCHIC AND ILLUSION-CASTER --
<NO! NO -- SPIDERS!>
<MOTHER -- NO!>
-- AND THE NUCLEAR-FUELED JUGGERNAUT CALLED POWERSURGE -- WHO THE AVENGERS ONCE MET, UNDER THE NAME "SURGE."
<YOU DEFILE THE SOIL OF MOTHER RUSSIA WITH YOUR TOUCH, INVADERS -->
<-- SO YOU SHALL TOUCH IT NO MORE!>
BUT FOR ALL THE WINTER GUARD'S POWER AND DETERMINATION --

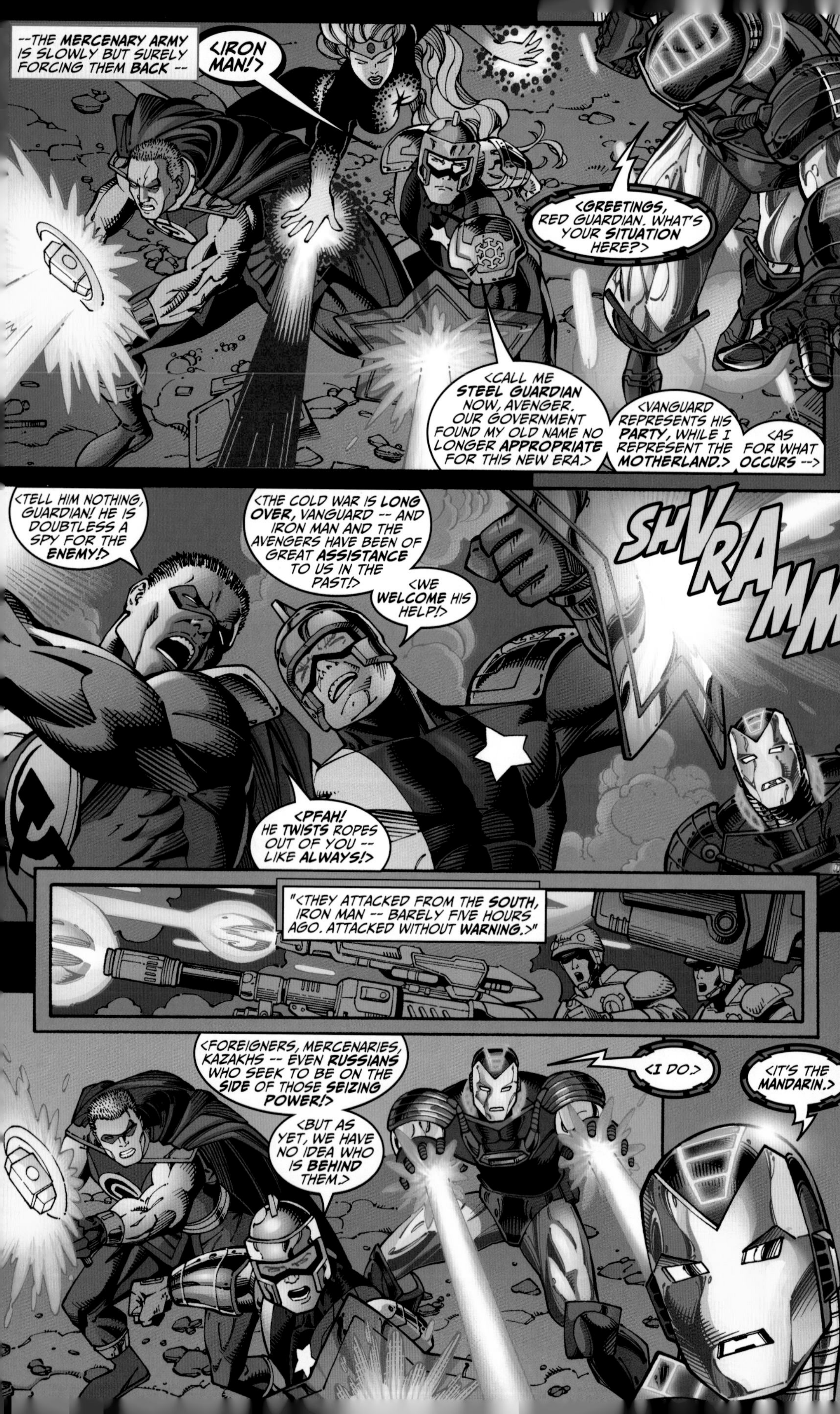
--THE MERCENARY ARMY IS SLOWLY BUT SURELY FORCING THEM BACK --
<IRON MAN!>
<GREETINGS, RED GUARDIAN. WHAT'S YOUR SITUATION HERE?>
<CALL ME STEEL GUARDIAN NOW, AVENGER. OUR GOVERNMENT FOUND MY OLD NAME NO LONGER APPROPRIATE FOR THIS NEW ERA.>
<VANGUARD REPRESENTS HIS PARTY, WHILE I REPRESENT THE MOTHERLAND.>
<AS FOR WHAT OCCURS -->
<TELL HIM NOTHING, GUARDIAN! HE IS DOUBTLESS A SPY FOR THE ENEMY!>
<THE COLD WAR IS LONG OVER, VANGUARD -- AND IRON MAN AND THE AVENGERS HAVE BEEN OF GREAT ASSISTANCE TO US IN THE PAST!>
<WE WELCOME HIS HELP!>
SHVRAMM
<PFAH! HE TWISTS ROPES OUT OF YOU -- LIKE ALWAYS!>
"<THEY ATTACKED FROM THE SOUTH, IRON MAN -- BARELY FIVE HOURS AGO. ATTACKED WITHOUT WARNING.>"
<FOREIGNERS, MERCENARIES, KAZAKHS -- EVEN RUSSIANS WHO SEEK TO BE ON THE SIDE OF THOSE SEIZING POWER!>
<BUT AS YET, WE HAVE NO IDEA WHO IS BEHIND THEM.>
<I DO.>
<IT'S THE MANDARIN.>

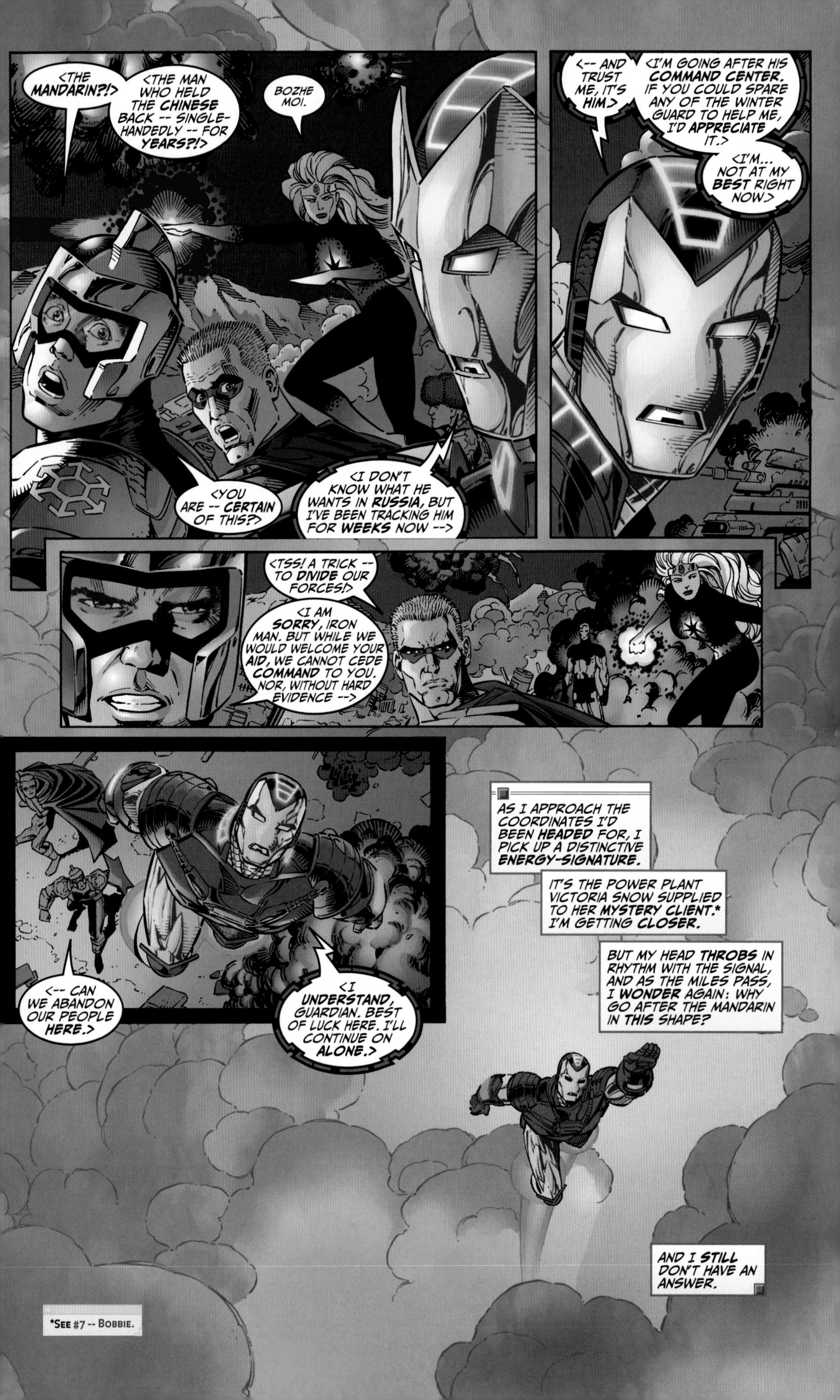
<THE MANDARIN?!>
<THE MAN WHO HELD THE CHINESE BACK -- SINGLE-HANDEDLY -- FOR YEARS?!>
BOZHE MOI.
<YOU ARE -- CERTAIN OF THIS?>
<I DON'T KNOW WHAT HE WANTS IN RUSSIA, BUT I'VE BEEN TRACKING HIM FOR WEEKS NOW -->
<-- AND TRUST ME, IT'S HIM.>
<I'M GOING AFTER HIS COMMAND CENTER. IF YOU COULD SPARE ANY OF THE WINTER GUARD TO HELP ME, I'D APPRECIATE IT.>
<I'M... NOT AT MY BEST RIGHT NOW.>
<TSS! A TRICK -- TO DIVIDE OUR FORCES!>
<I AM SORRY, IRON MAN. BUT WHILE WE WOULD WELCOME YOUR AID, WE CANNOT CEDE COMMAND TO YOU. NOR, WITHOUT HARD EVIDENCE -->
<-- CAN WE ABANDON OUR PEOPLE HERE.>
<I UNDERSTAND, GUARDIAN. BEST OF LUCK HERE. I'LL CONTINUE ON ALONE.>
AS I APPROACH THE COORDINATES I'D BEEN HEADED FOR, I PICK UP A DISTINCTIVE ENERGY-SIGNATURE.
IT'S THE POWER PLANT VICTORIA SNOW SUPPLIED TO HER MYSTERY CLIENT.* I'M GETTING CLOSER.
BUT MY HEAD THROBS IN RHYTHM WITH THE SIGNAL, AND AS THE MILES PASS, I WONDER AGAIN: WHY GO AFTER THE MANDARIN IN THIS SHAPE?
AND I STILL DON'T HAVE AN ANSWER.

*SEE #7 -- BOBBIE.

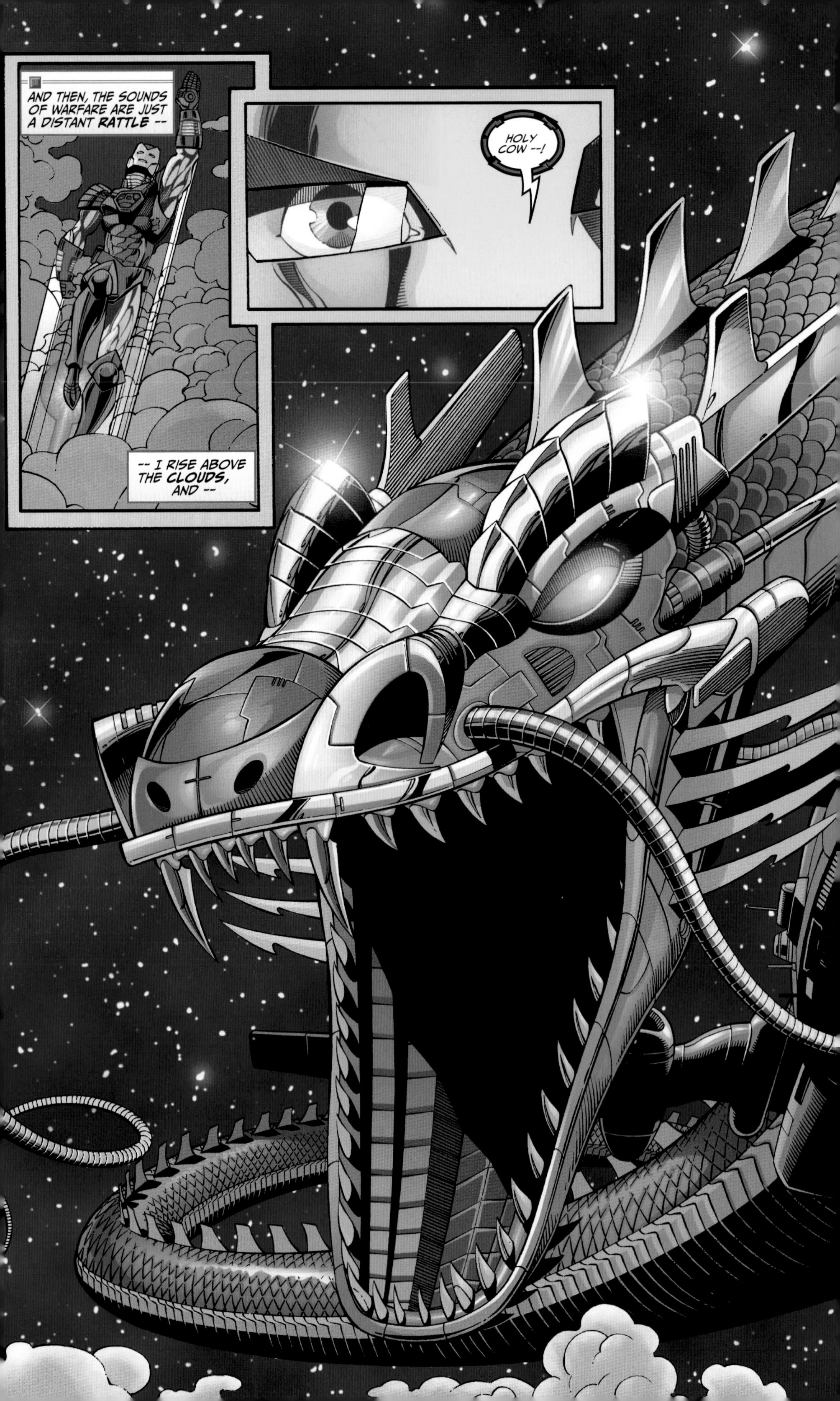
AND THEN, THE SOUNDS OF WARFARE ARE JUST A DISTANT RATTLE --
HOLY COW --!
-- I RISE ABOVE THE CLOUDS, AND --

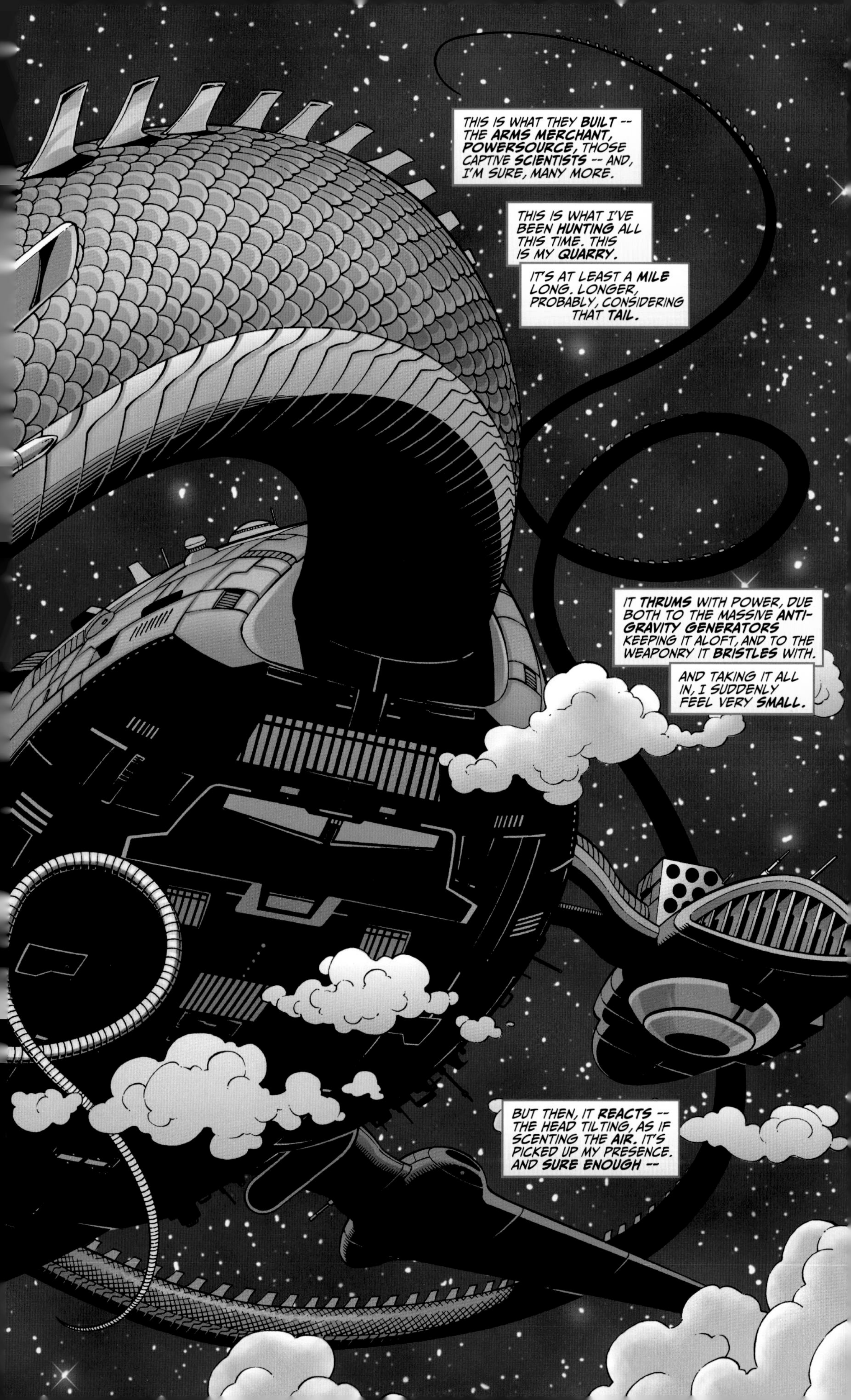
THIS IS WHAT THEY BUILT -- THE ARMS MERCHANT, POWERSOURCE, THOSE CAPTIVE SCIENTISTS -- AND, I'M SURE, MANY MORE.
THIS IS WHAT I'VE BEEN HUNTING ALL THIS TIME. THIS IS MY QUARRY.
IT'S AT LEAST A MILE LONG. LONGER, PROBABLY, CONSIDERING THAT TAIL.
IT THRUMS WITH POWER, DUE BOTH TO THE MASSIVE ANTI-GRAVITY GENERATORS KEEPING IT ALOFT, AND TO THE WEAPONRY IT BRISTLES WITH.
AND TAKING IT ALL IN, I SUDDENLY FEEL VERY SMALL.
BUT THEN, IT REACTS -- THE HEAD TILTING, AS IF SCENTING THE AIR. IT'S PICKED UP MY PRESENCE. AND SURE ENOUGH --

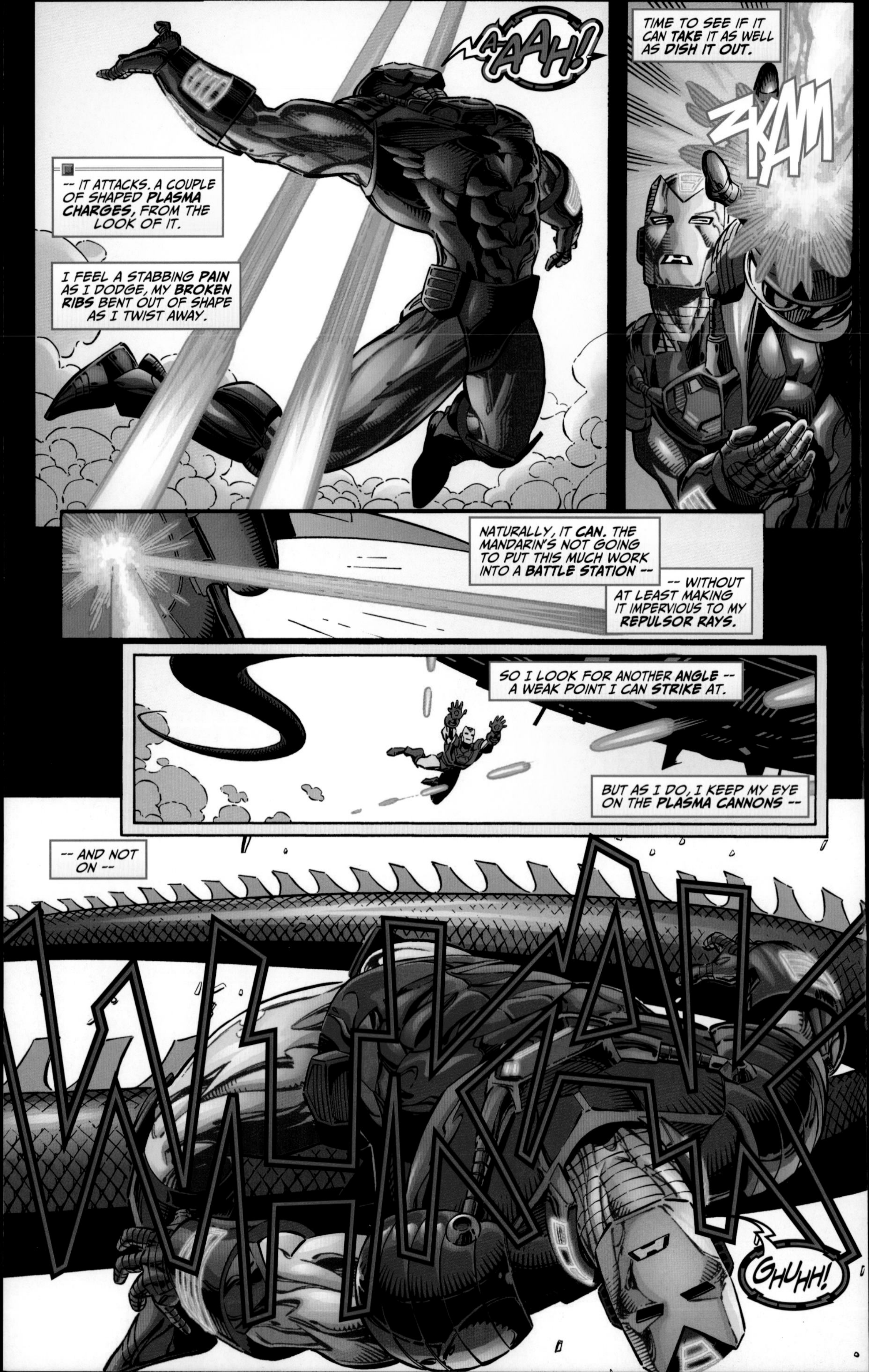
A-AAH!
-- IT ATTACKS. A COUPLE OF SHAPED PLASMA CHARGES, FROM THE LOOK OF IT.
I FEEL A STABBING PAIN AS I DODGE, MY BROKEN RIBS BENT OUT OF SHAPE AS I TWIST AWAY.
TIME TO SEE IF IT CAN TAKE IT AS WELL AS DISH IT OUT.
ZKAM
NATURALLY, IT CAN. THE MANDARIN'S NOT GOING TO PUT THIS MUCH WORK INTO A BATTLE STATION --
-- WITHOUT AT LEAST MAKING IT IMPERVIOUS TO MY REPULSOR RAYS.
SO I LOOK FOR ANOTHER ANGLE -- A WEAK POINT I CAN STRIKE AT.
BUT AS I DO, I KEEP MY EYE ON THE PLASMA CANNONS --
-- AND NOT ON --
WHAK
GHUHH!

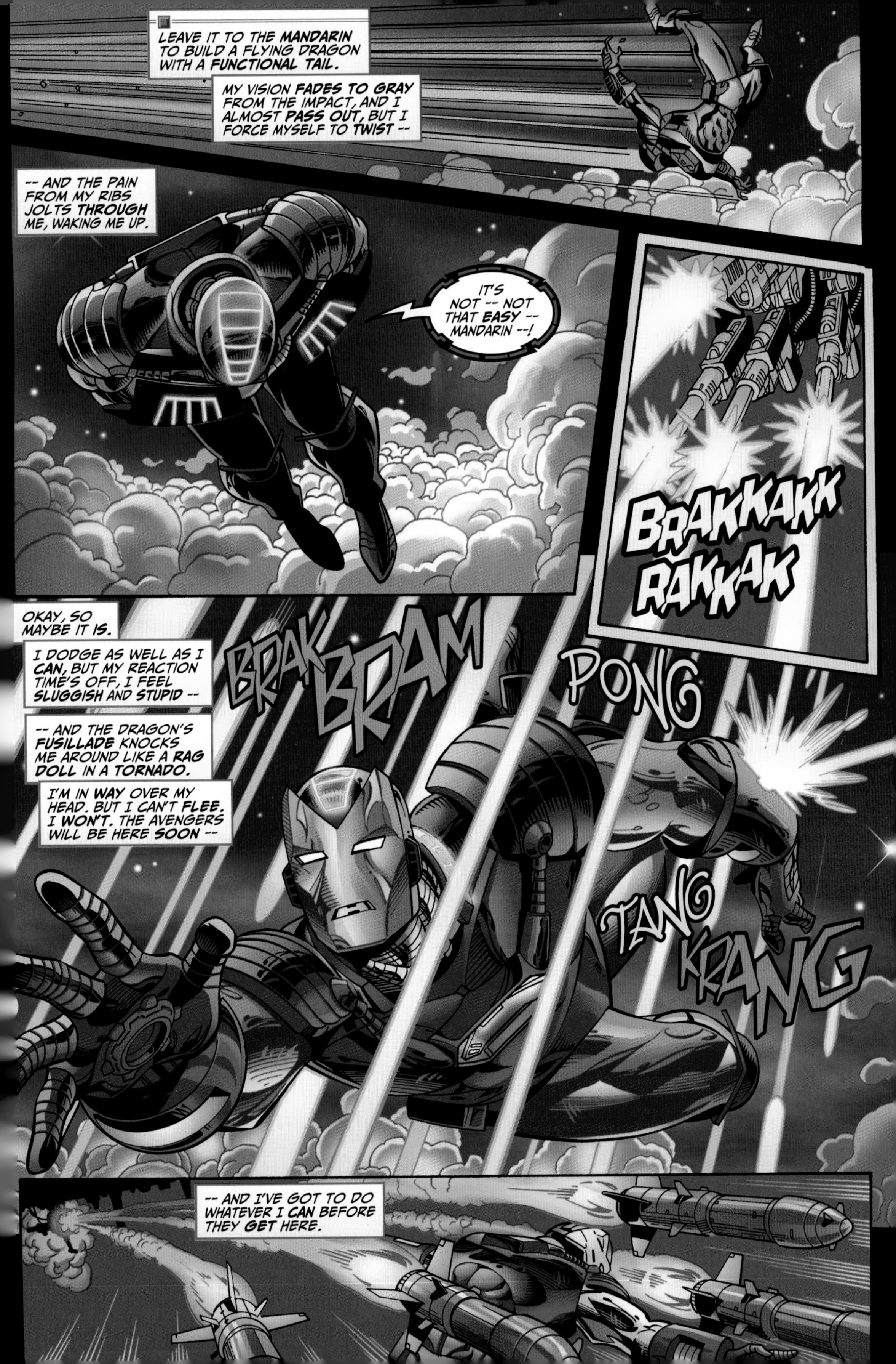
LEAVE IT TO THE MANDARIN TO BUILD A FLYING DRAGON WITH A FUNCTIONAL TAIL.
MY VISION FADES TO GRAY FROM THE IMPACT, AND I ALMOST PASS OUT, BUT I FORCE MYSELF TO TWIST --
-- AND THE PAIN FROM MY RIBS JOLTS THROUGH ME, WAKING ME UP.
IT'S NOT -- NOT THAT EASY -- MANDARIN --!
BRAKKAKK RAKKAK
OKAY, SO MAYBE IT IS.
I DODGE AS WELL AS I CAN, BUT MY REACTION TIME'S OFF, I FEEL SLUGGISH AND STUPID --
-- AND THE DRAGON'S FUSILLADE KNOCKS ME AROUND LIKE A RAG DOLL IN A TORNADO.
I'M IN WAY OVER MY HEAD. BUT I CAN'T FLEE. I WON'T. THE AVENGERS WILL BE HERE SOON --
BRAK BRAM
PONG
TANG KRANG
-- AND I'VE GOT TO DO WHATEVER I CAN BEFORE THEY GET HERE.

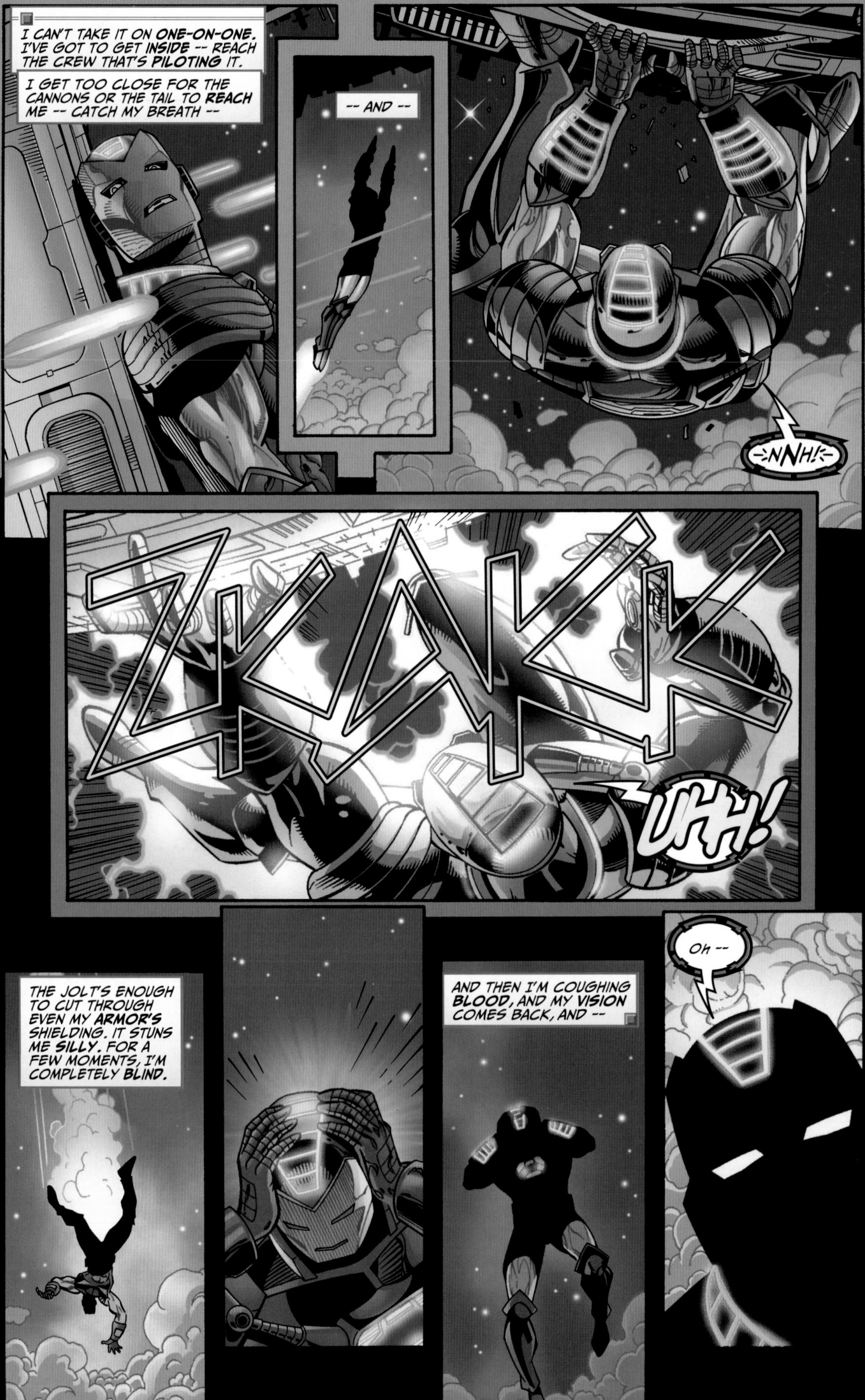
I CAN'T TAKE IT ON ONE-ON-ONE. I'VE GOT TO GET INSIDE -- REACH THE CREW THAT'S PILOTING IT.
I GET TOO CLOSE FOR THE CANNONS OR THE TAIL TO REACH ME -- CATCH MY BREATH --
-- AND --
NNH!
ZKAKK
UHH!
THE JOLT'S ENOUGH TO CUT THROUGH EVEN MY ARMOR'S SHIELDING. IT STUNS ME SILLY. FOR A FEW MOMENTS, I'M COMPLETELY BLIND.
AND THEN I'M COUGHING BLOOD, AND MY VISION COMES BACK, AND --
Oh --

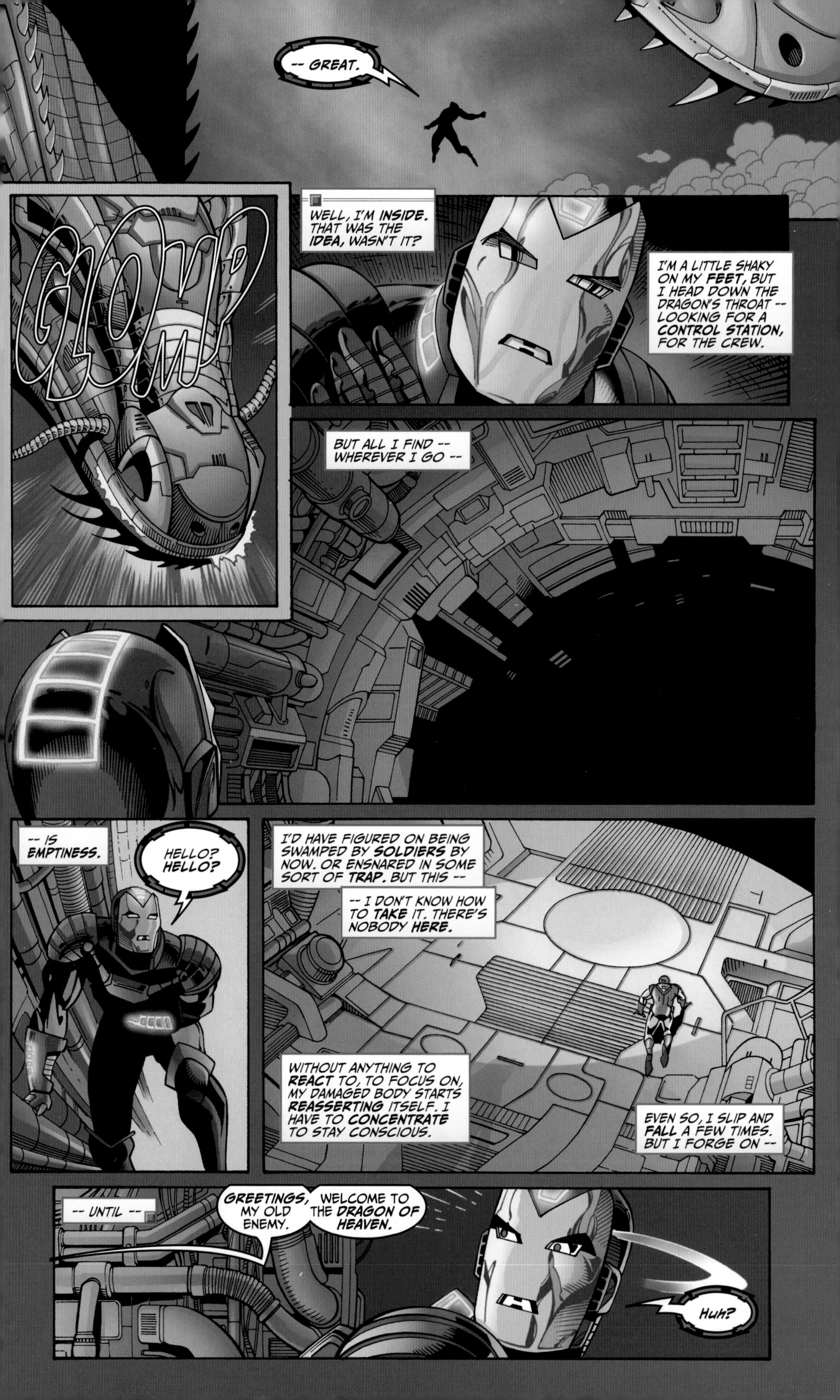
-- GREAT.
WELL, I'M INSIDE. THAT WAS THE IDEA, WASN'T IT?
I'M A LITTLE SHAKY ON MY FEET, BUT I HEAD DOWN THE DRAGON'S THROAT -- LOOKING FOR A CONTROL STATION, FOR THE CREW.
GLOMP!
BUT ALL I FIND -- WHEREVER I GO --
-- IS EMPTINESS.
HELLO? HELLO?
I'D HAVE FIGURED ON BEING SWAMPED BY SOLDIERS BY NOW. OR ENSNARED IN SOME SORT OF TRAP. BUT THIS --
-- I DON'T KNOW HOW TO TAKE IT. THERE'S NOBODY HERE.
WITHOUT ANYTHING TO REACT TO, TO FOCUS ON, MY DAMAGED BODY STARTS REASSERTING ITSELF. I HAVE TO CONCENTRATE TO STAY CONSCIOUS.
EVEN SO, I SLIP AND FALL A FEW TIMES. BUT I FORGE ON --
-- UNTIL --
GREETINGS, MY OLD ENEMY.
WELCOME TO THE DRAGON OF HEAVEN.
Huh?

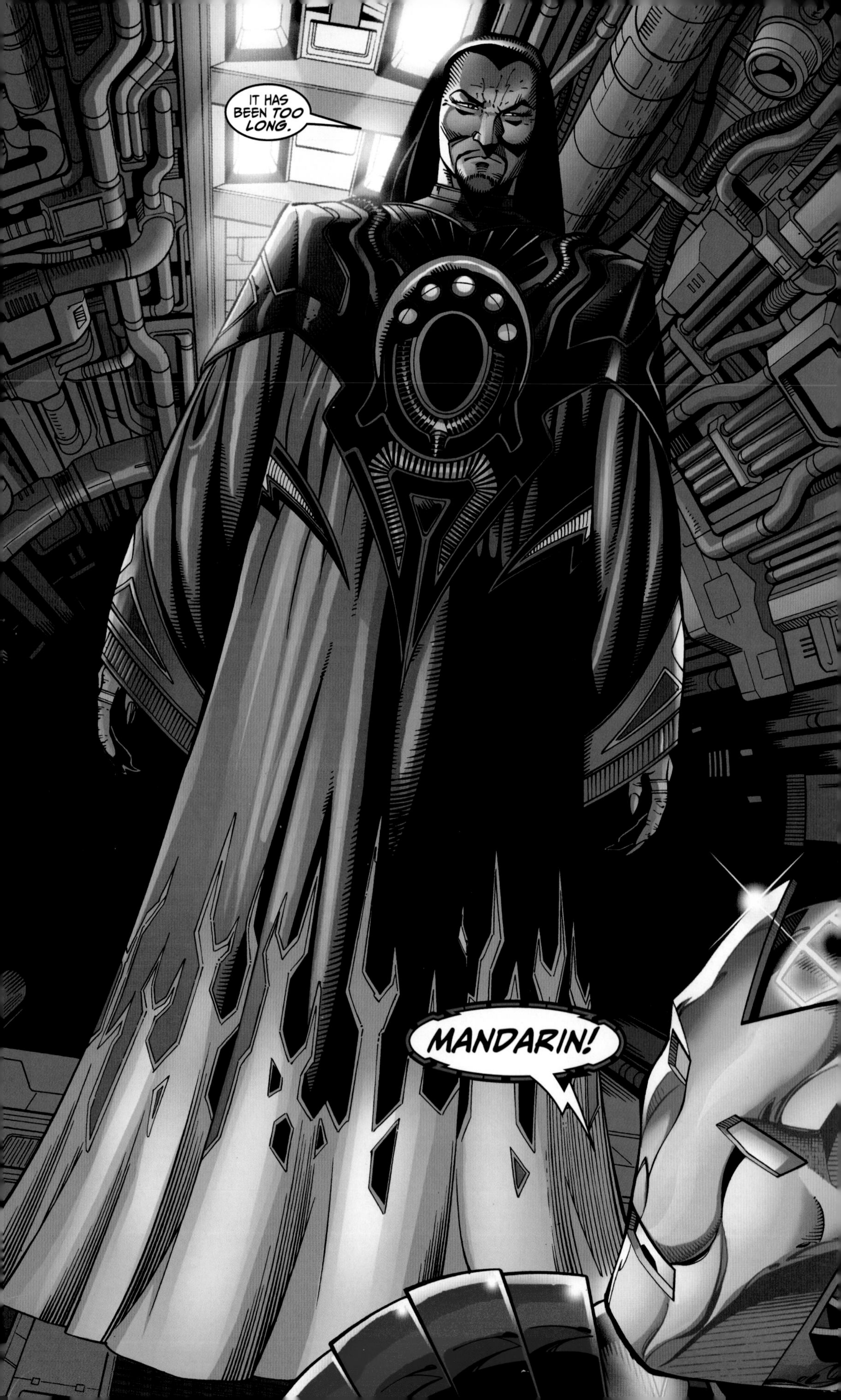
IT HAS BEEN TOO LONG.
MANDARIN!

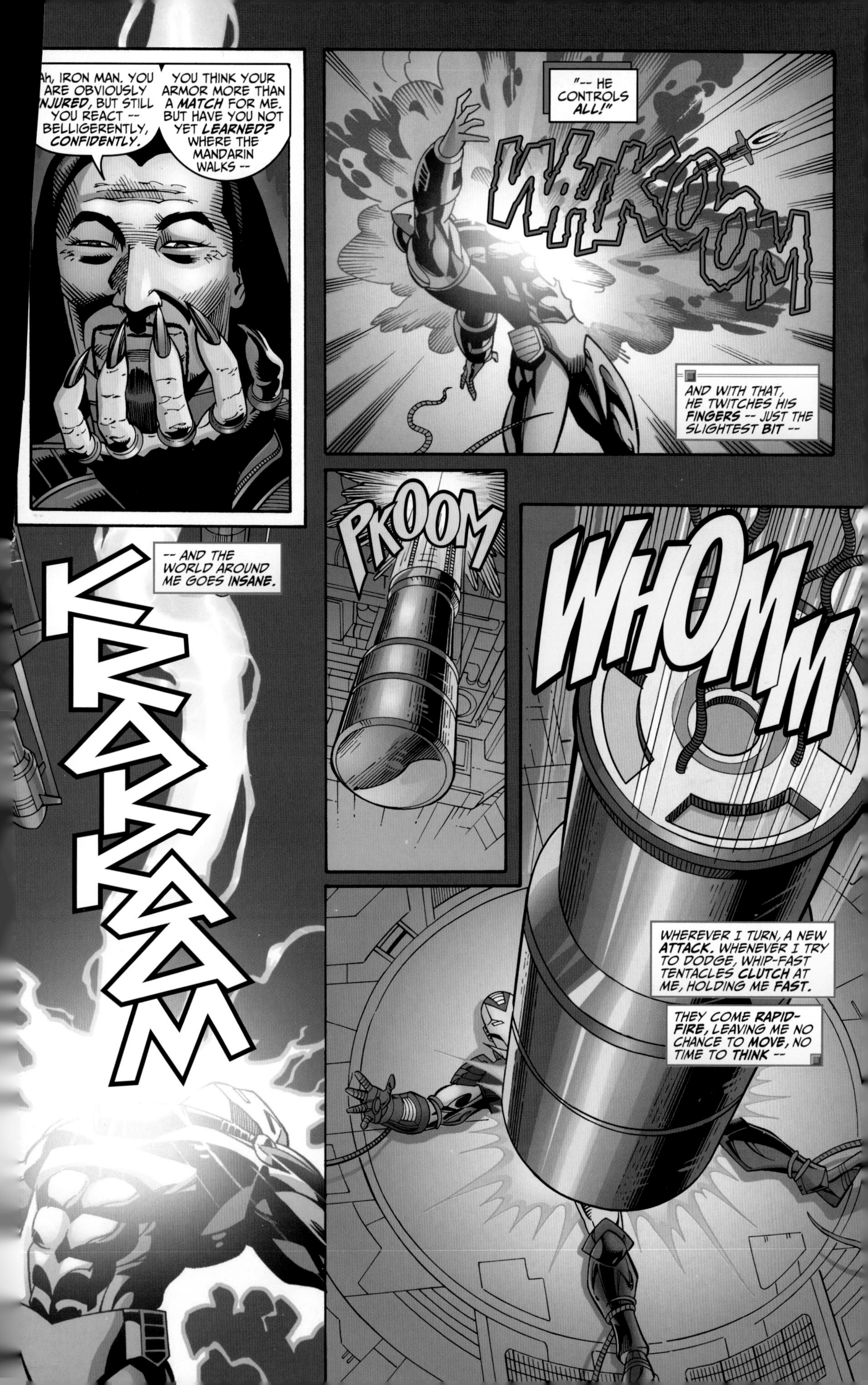

AH, IRON MAN. YOU ARE OBVIOUSLY INJURED, BUT STILL YOU REACT -- BELLIGERENTLY, CONFIDENTLY.
YOU THINK YOUR ARMOR MORE THAN A MATCH FOR ME. BUT HAVE YOU NOT YET LEARNED? WHERE THE MANDARIN WALKS --
"-- HE CONTROLS ALL!"
WHKOOM
AND WITH THAT, HE TWITCHES HIS FINGERS -- JUST THE SLIGHTEST BIT --
-- AND THE WORLD AROUND ME GOES INSANE.
KRAKAKOOM
PKOOM
WHOMM
WHEREVER I TURN, A NEW ATTACK. WHENEVER I TRY TO DODGE, WHIP-FAST TENTACLES CLUTCH AT ME, HOLDING ME FAST.
THEY COME RAPID-FIRE, LEAVING ME NO CHANCE TO MOVE, NO TIME TO THINK --

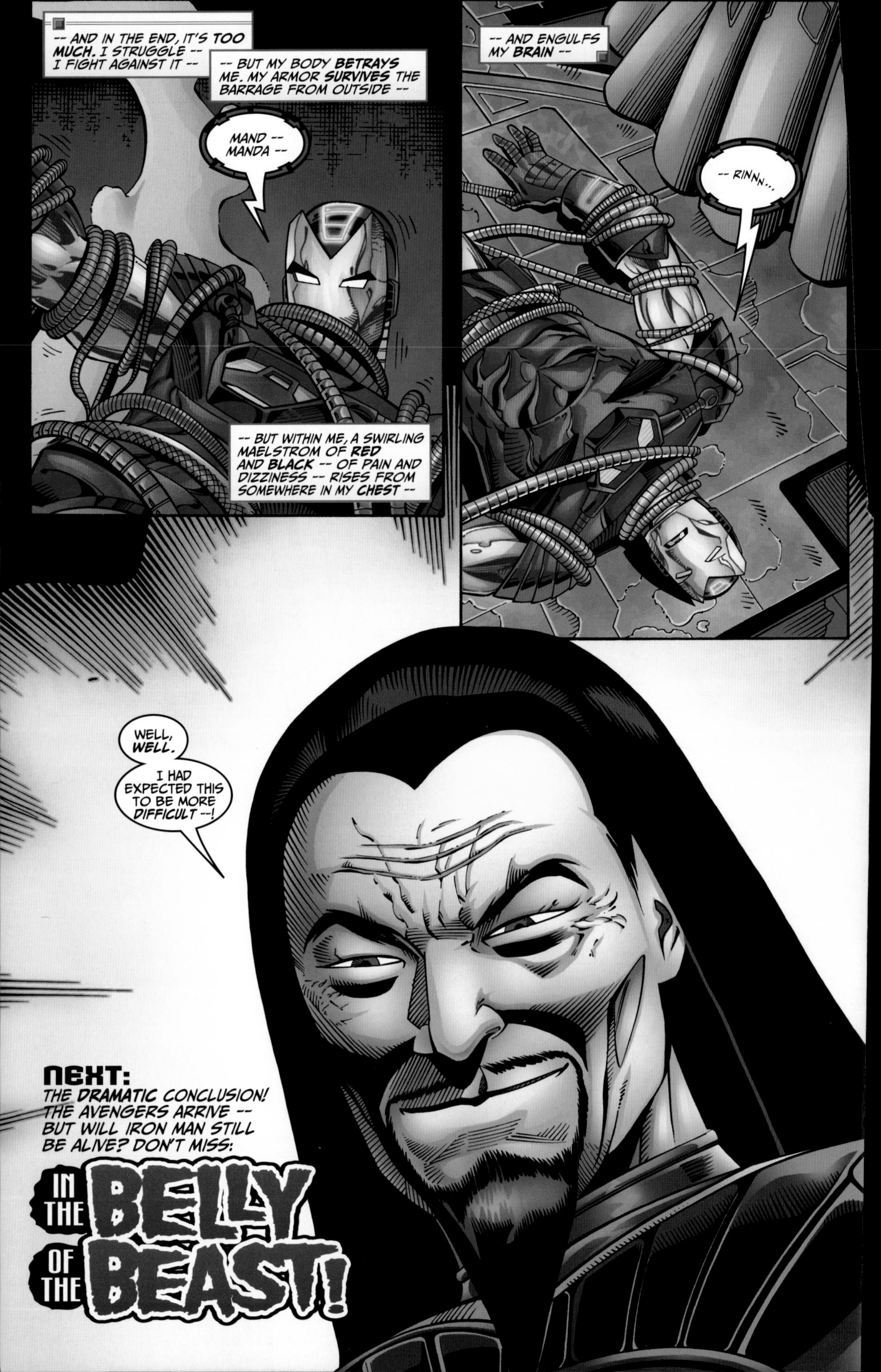
-- AND IN THE END, IT'S TOO MUCH. I STRUGGLE -- I FIGHT AGAINST IT --
-- BUT MY BODY BETRAYS ME. MY ARMOR SURVIVES THE BARRAGE FROM OUTSIDE --
MAND -- MANDA --
-- BUT WITHIN ME, A SWIRLING MAELSTROM OF RED AND BLACK -- OF PAIN AND DIZZINESS -- RISES FROM SOMEWHERE IN MY CHEST --
-- AND ENGULFS MY BRAIN --
-- RINNN...
WELL, WELL.
I HAD EXPECTED THIS TO BE MORE DIFFICULT --!
NEXT:
THE DRAMATIC CONCLUSION! THE AVENGERS ARRIVE -- BUT WILL IRON MAN STILL BE ALIVE? DON'T MISS:
IN THE BELLY OF THE BEAST!

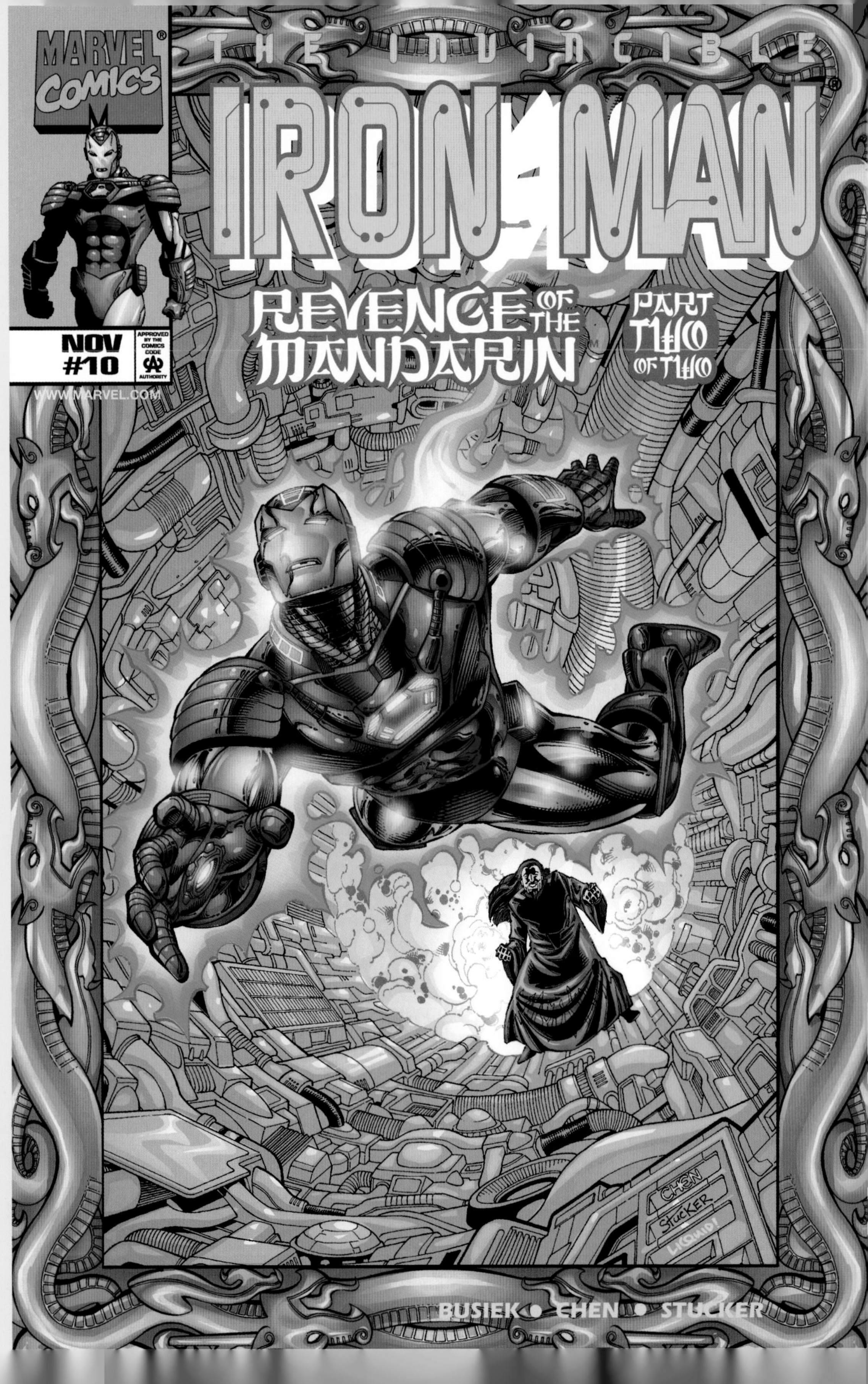
MARVEL COMICS
THE INVINCIBLE
IRON MAN
REVENGE OF THE MANDARIN
PART TWO OF TWO
NOV #10
APPROVED BY THE COMICS CODE AUTHORITY
WWW.MARVEL.COM
CHEN
STUCKER
BUSIEK • CHEN • STUCKER

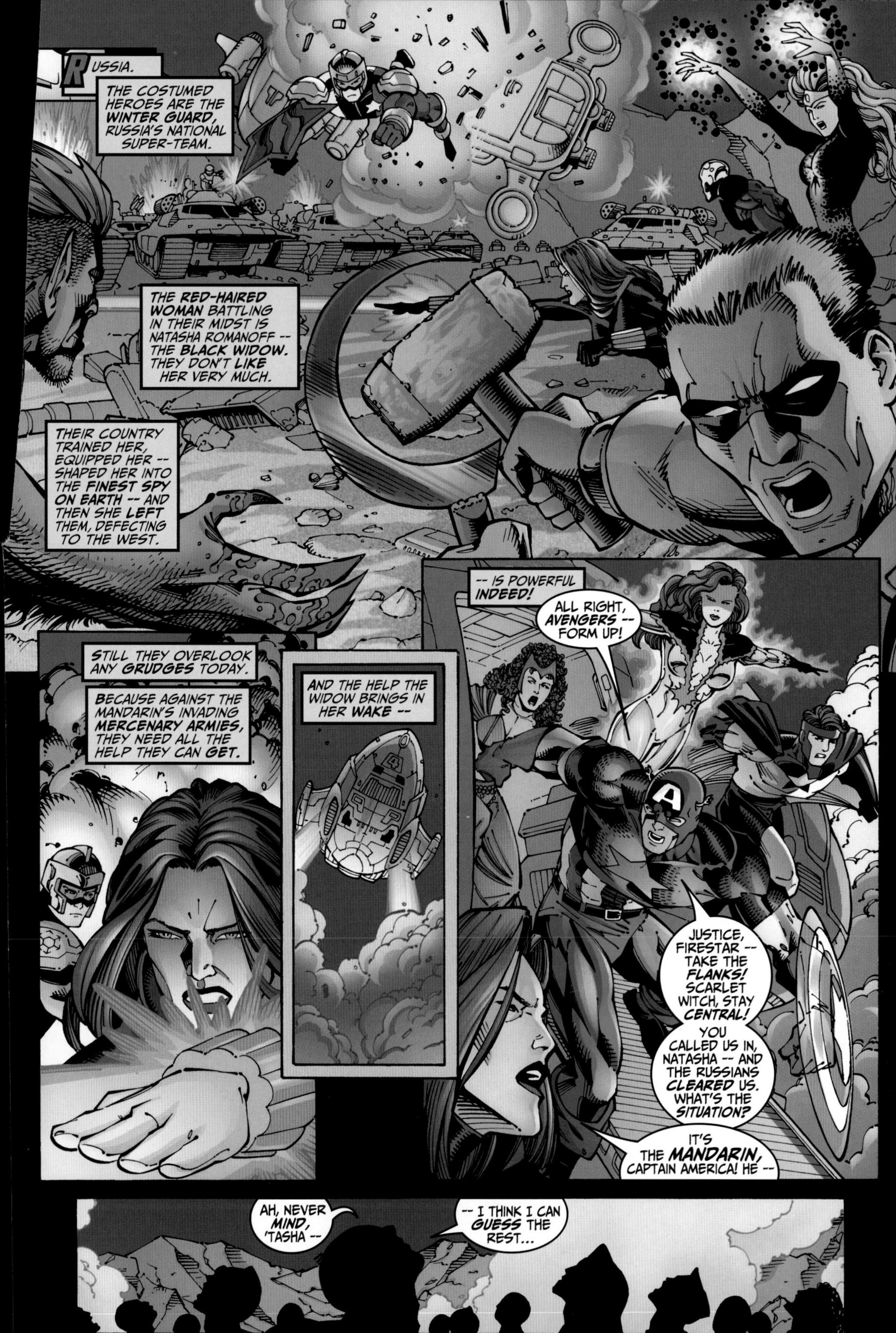
RUSSIA.
THE COSTUMED HEROES ARE THE WINTER GUARD, RUSSIA'S NATIONAL SUPER-TEAM.
THE RED-HAIRED WOMAN BATTLING IN THEIR MIDST IS NATASHA ROMANOFF -- THE BLACK WIDOW. THEY DON'T LIKE HER VERY MUCH.
THEIR COUNTRY TRAINED HER, EQUIPPED HER -- SHAPED HER INTO THE FINEST SPY ON EARTH -- AND THEN SHE LEFT THEM, DEFECTING TO THE WEST.
STILL THEY OVERLOOK ANY GRUDGES TODAY.
BECAUSE AGAINST THE MANDARIN'S INVADING MERCENARY ARMIES, THEY NEED ALL THE HELP THEY CAN GET.
AND THE HELP THE WIDOW BRINGS IN HER WAKE --
-- IS POWERFUL INDEED!
ALL RIGHT, AVENGERS -- FORM UP!
JUSTICE, FIRESTAR -- TAKE THE FLANKS! SCARLET WITCH, STAY CENTRAL!
YOU CALLED US IN, NATASHA -- AND THE RUSSIANS CLEARED US. WHAT'S THE SITUATION?
IT'S THE MANDARIN, CAPTAIN AMERICA! HE --
AH, NEVER MIND, 'TASHA --
-- I THINK I CAN GUESS THE REST...

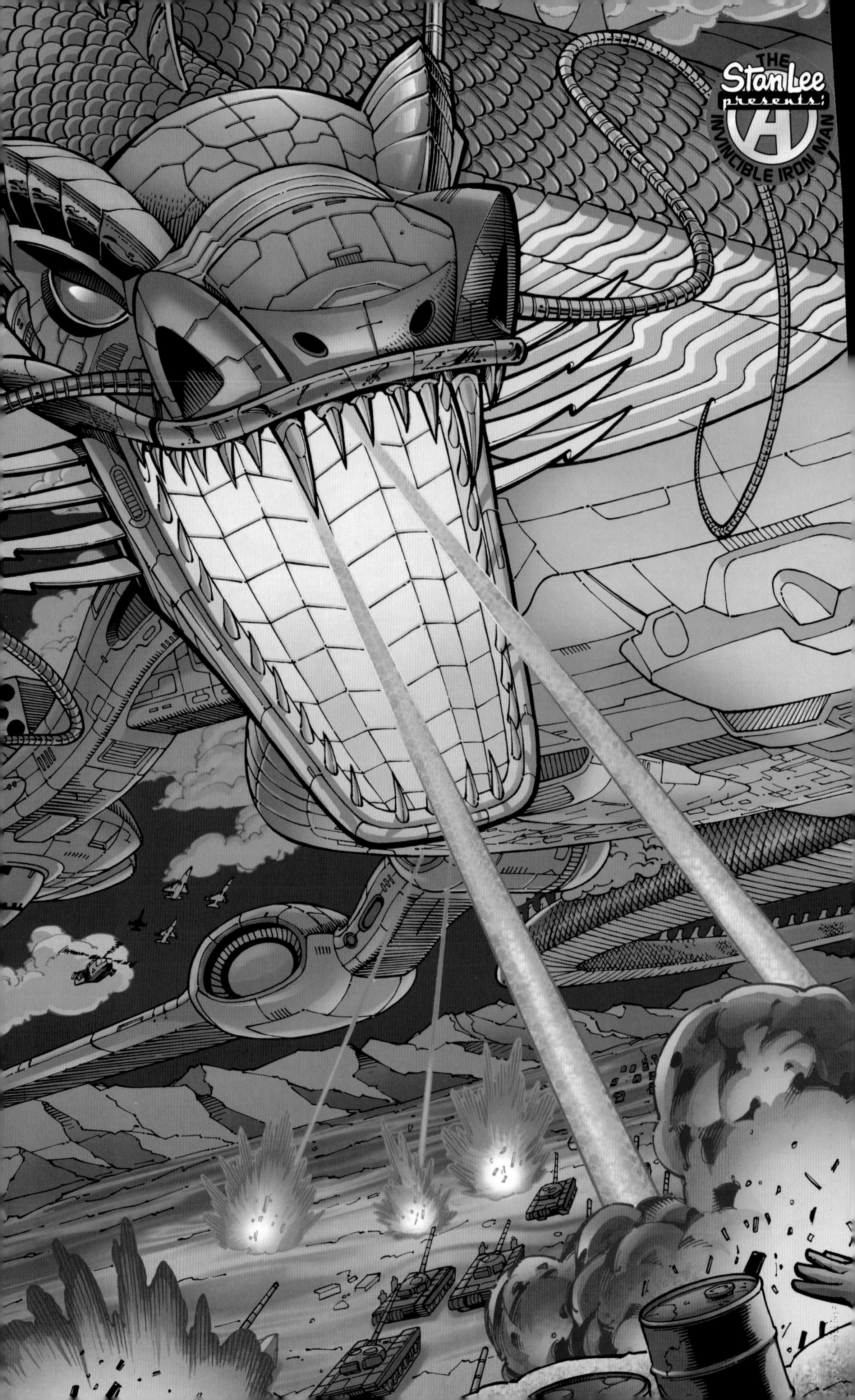
THE
Stan Lee
presents:
INVINCIBLE IRON MAN

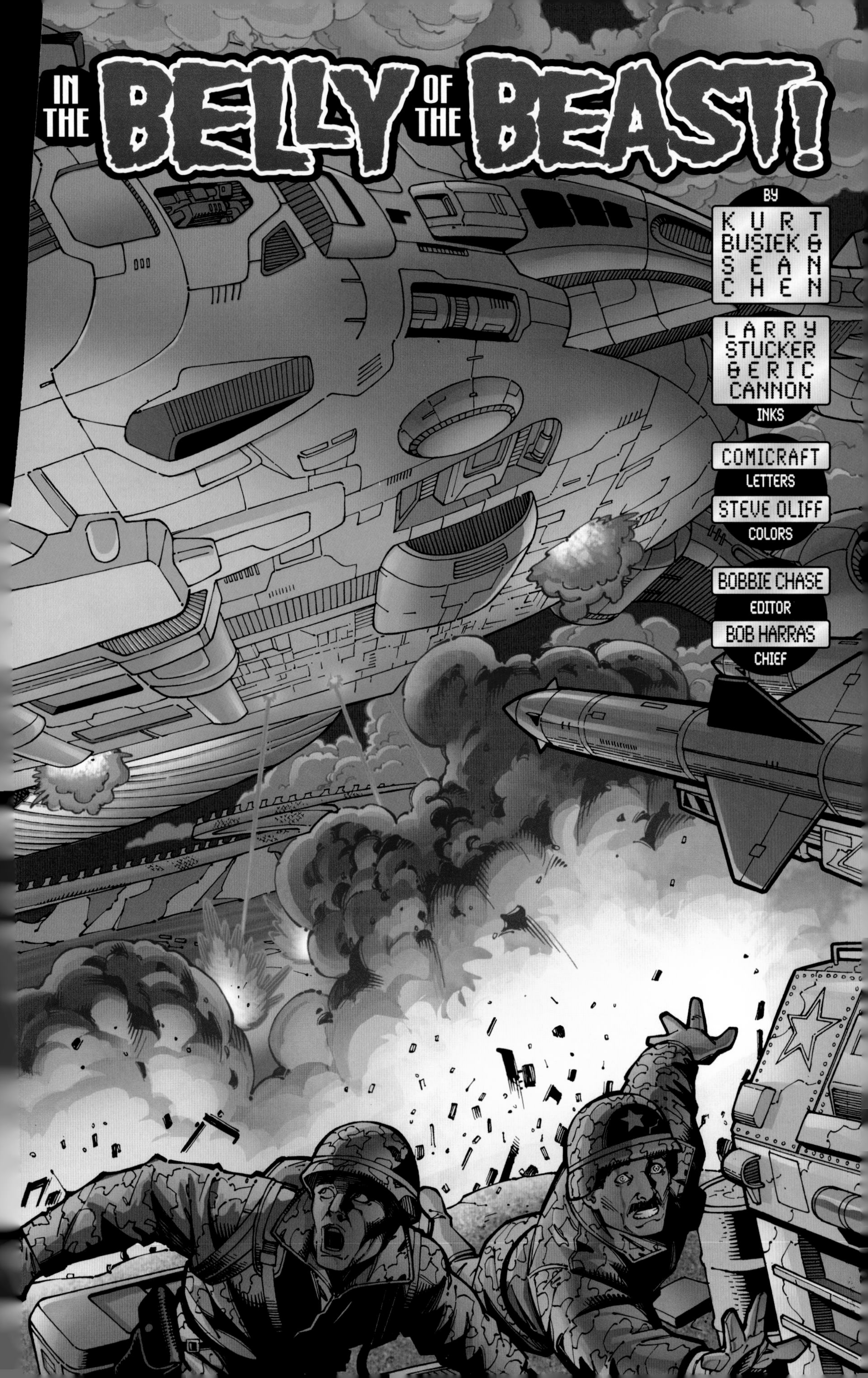
IN THE BELLY OF THE BEAST!
BY
KURT BUSIEK & SEAN CHEN
LARRY STUCKER & ERIC CANNON
INKS
COMICRAFT
LETTERS
STEVE OLIFF
COLORS
BOBBIE CHASE
EDITOR
BOB HARRAS
CHIEF

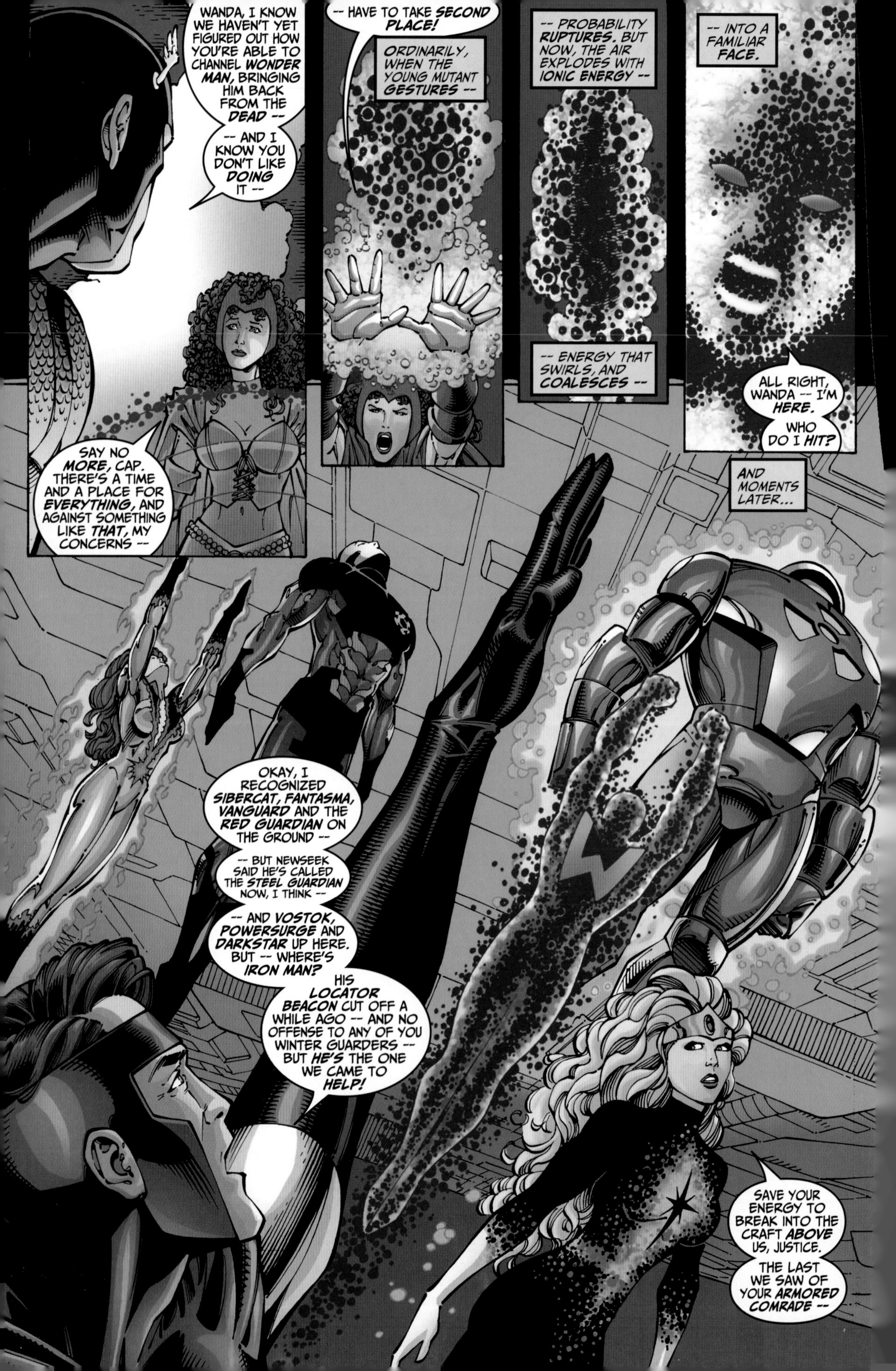
WANDA, I KNOW WE HAVEN'T YET FIGURED OUT HOW YOU'RE ABLE TO CHANNEL WONDER MAN, BRINGING HIM BACK FROM THE DEAD --
-- AND I KNOW YOU DON'T LIKE DOING IT --
SAY NO MORE, CAP. THERE'S A TIME AND A PLACE FOR EVERYTHING, AND AGAINST SOMETHING LIKE THAT, MY CONCERNS --
-- HAVE TO TAKE SECOND PLACE!
ORDINARILY, WHEN THE YOUNG MUTANT GESTURES --
-- PROBABILITY RUPTURES. BUT NOW, THE AIR EXPLODES WITH IONIC ENERGY --
-- ENERGY THAT SWIRLS, AND COALESCES --
-- INTO A FAMILIAR FACE.
ALL RIGHT, WANDA -- I'M HERE.
WHO DO I HIT?
AND MOMENTS LATER...
OKAY, I RECOGNIZED SIBERCAT, FANTASMA, VANGUARD AND THE RED GUARDIAN ON THE GROUND --
-- BUT NEWSEEK SAID HE'S CALLED THE STEEL GUARDIAN NOW, I THINK --
-- AND VOSTOK, POWERSURGE AND DARKSTAR UP HERE. BUT -- WHERE'S IRON MAN?
HIS LOCATOR BEACON CUT OFF A WHILE AGO -- AND NO OFFENSE TO ANY OF YOU WINTER GUARDERS -- BUT HE'S THE ONE WE CAME TO HELP!
SAVE YOUR ENERGY TO BREAK INTO THE CRAFT ABOVE US, JUSTICE.
THE LAST WE SAW OF YOUR ARMORED COMRADE --

"-- THAT IS WHERE HE WAS *HEADED!*"

OUUALH!

IT'S GETTING SO I HATE WAKING UP.

OF COURSE, GETTING BEATEN TO A PULP BY THE SPYMASTER'S *ESPIONAGE ELITE,* WITHOUT BENEFIT OF MY *ARMOR**--

-- AND GETTING SLAMMED AROUND BY THE MANDARIN'S *"DRAGON OF HEAVEN"* WILL DO THAT TO A GUY.**

MY ARMOR -- PUMPING *COLD AIR* AT MY FACE, ALL AROUND ME -- JOLTING ME ALERT WITH AN *AGONIZING* START. BUT HOW --

MY HEAD SWIMS, AND I HAVE A HARD TIME *FOCUSING.* I KNOW I'VE GOT BROKEN *RIBS,* AND WHAT FEELS LIKE SERIOUS *INTERNAL INJURIES* --

-- AND I'VE BARELY REGAINED *CONSCIOUSNESS* WHEN I FEEL MYSELF SLIPPING BACK INTO SOFT VELVET *BLACKNESS.*

*IN #8.
**LAST ISSUE -- BOBBIE

M-MANDARIN --?

A THOUSAND *PARDONS,* OLD FOE.

BUT I WAS GROWING *BORED* WITH WATCHING YOU *LOLL* ABOUT LIKE AN *INSENSATE* THING --

-- AND I COULD THINK OF NO BETTER WAY TO *ROUSE* YOU.

NOR TO *DEMONSTRATE,* AS WELL, THAT YOUR ARMOR IS COMPLETELY UNDER THE CONTROL OF MY NEW *COMMAND RINGS* --

-- AS, INDEED, IS *EVERYTHING* ABOARD THE *DRAGON OF HEAVEN.*

B-BUT --

AH, BUT I FORGET MY *MANNERS,* DON'T I? DO FORGIVE ME.

HAVE I TOLD YOU HOW I *SURVIVED* OUR LAST ENCOUNTER? *NO?*

PLEASE -- INDULGE AN OLD MAN'S RAMBLINGS, AS I *CORRECT* THAT MOST GRIEVOUS OVERSIGHT...

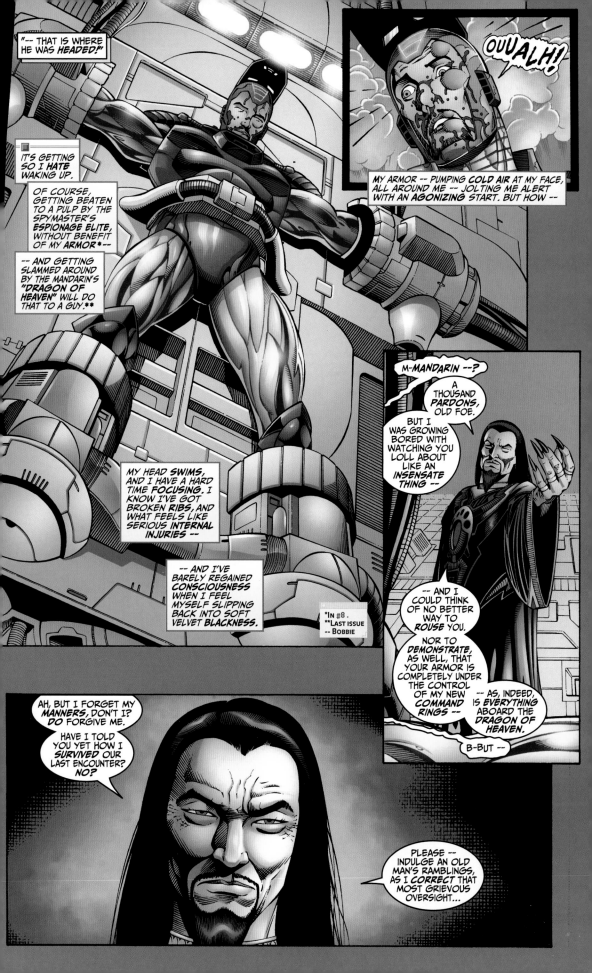

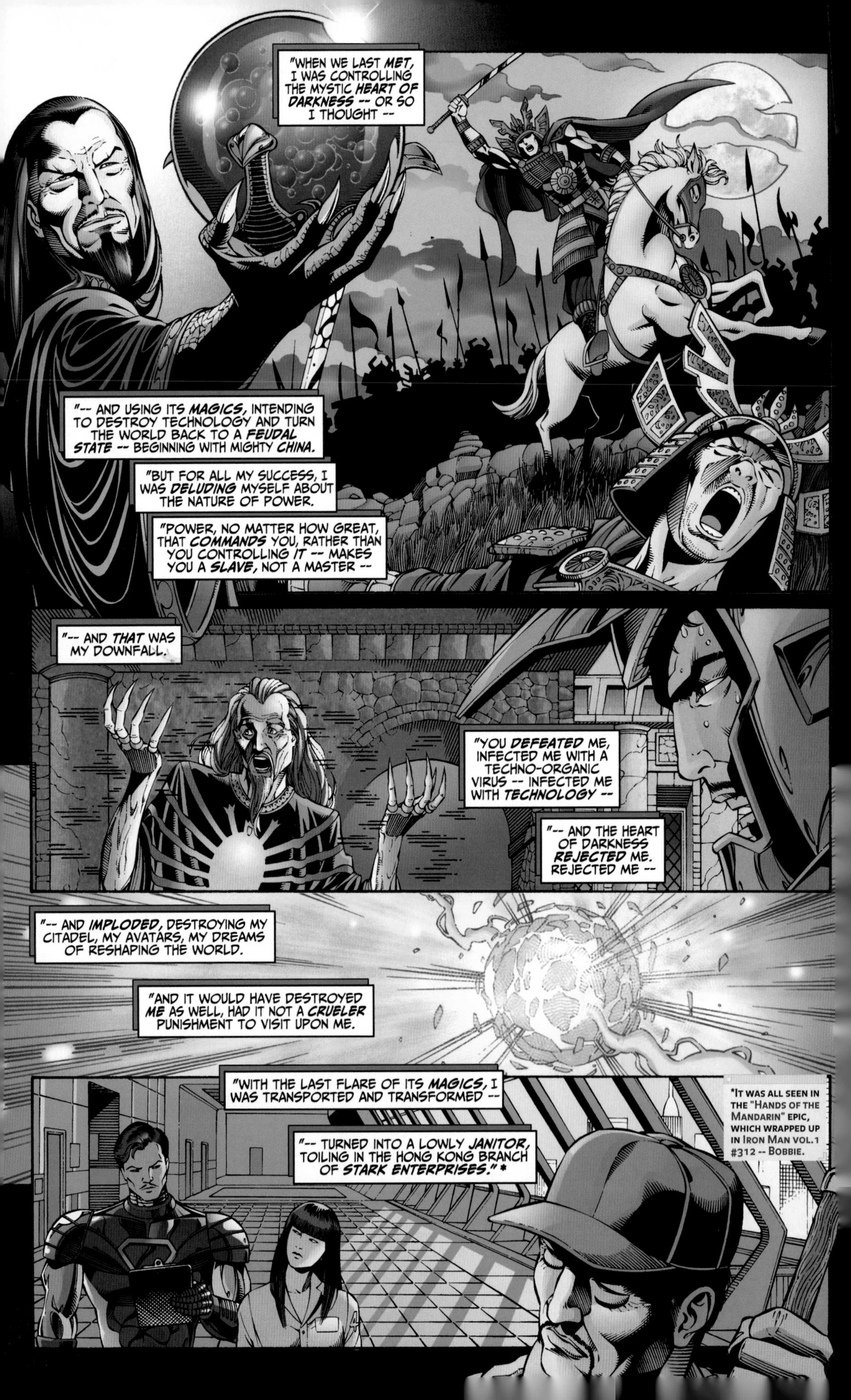
"WHEN WE LAST MET, I WAS CONTROLLING THE MYSTIC HEART OF DARKNESS -- OR SO I THOUGHT --
"-- AND USING ITS MAGICS, INTENDING TO DESTROY TECHNOLOGY AND TURN THE WORLD BACK TO A FEUDAL STATE -- BEGINNING WITH MIGHTY CHINA.
"BUT FOR ALL MY SUCCESS, I WAS DELUDING MYSELF ABOUT THE NATURE OF POWER.
"POWER, NO MATTER HOW GREAT, THAT COMMANDS YOU, RATHER THAN YOU CONTROLLING IT -- MAKES YOU A SLAVE, NOT A MASTER --
"-- AND THAT WAS MY DOWNFALL.
"YOU DEFEATED ME, INFECTED ME WITH A TECHNO-ORGANIC VIRUS -- INFECTED ME WITH TECHNOLOGY --
"-- AND THE HEART OF DARKNESS REJECTED ME. REJECTED ME --
"-- AND IMPLODED, DESTROYING MY CITADEL, MY AVATARS, MY DREAMS OF RESHAPING THE WORLD.
"AND IT WOULD HAVE DESTROYED ME AS WELL, HAD IT NOT A CRUELER PUNISHMENT TO VISIT UPON ME.
"WITH THE LAST FLARE OF ITS MAGICS, I WAS TRANSPORTED AND TRANSFORMED --
"-- TURNED INTO A LOWLY JANITOR, TOILING IN THE HONG KONG BRANCH OF STARK ENTERPRISES." *
*IT WAS ALL SEEN IN THE "HANDS OF THE MANDARIN" EPIC, WHICH WRAPPED UP IN IRON MAN VOL.1 #312 -- BOBBIE.

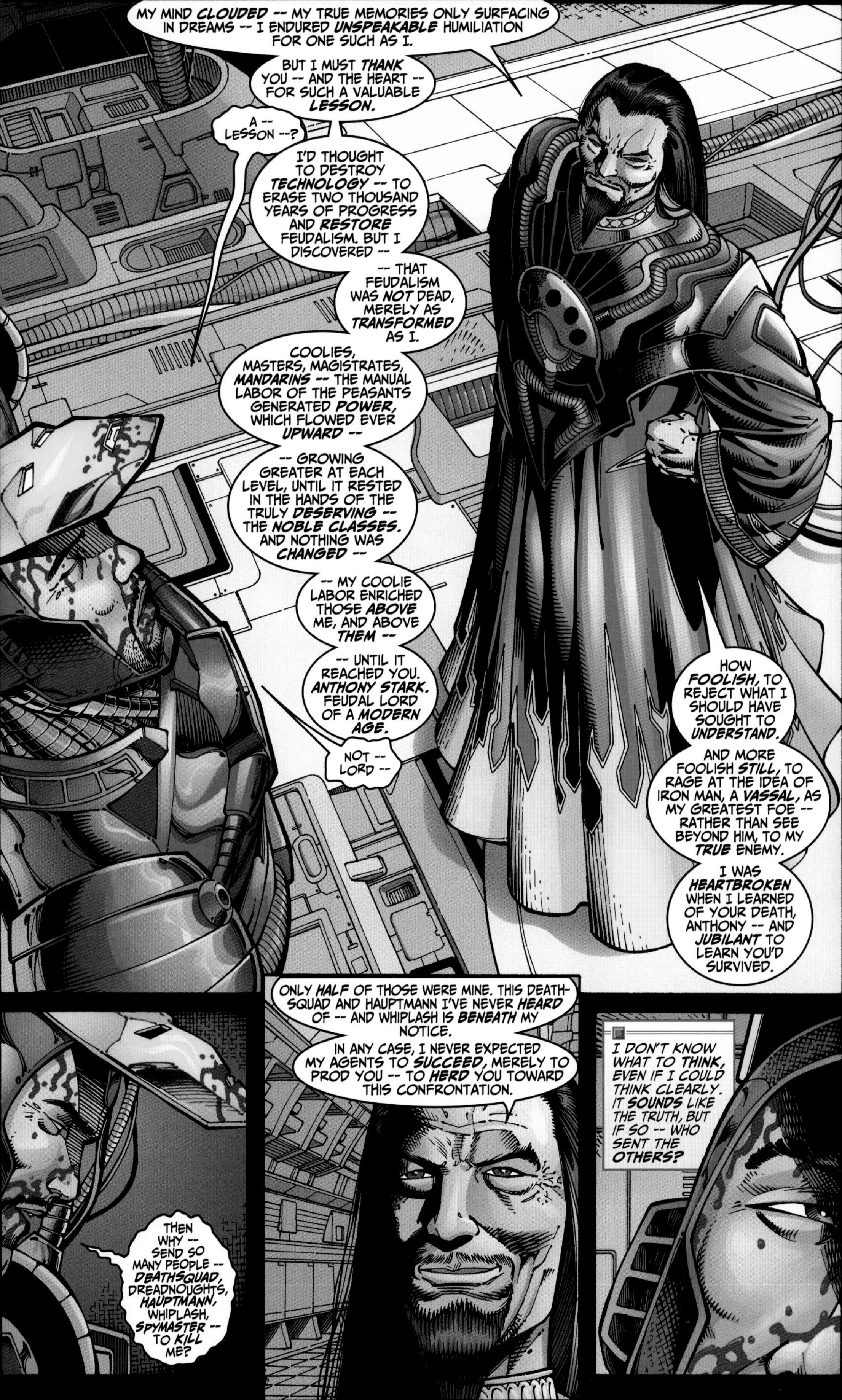

MY MIND CLOUDED -- MY TRUE MEMORIES ONLY SURFACING IN DREAMS -- I ENDURED UNSPEAKABLE HUMILIATION FOR ONE SUCH AS I.
BUT I MUST THANK YOU -- AND THE HEART -- FOR SUCH A VALUABLE LESSON.
A -- LESSON --?
I'D THOUGHT TO DESTROY TECHNOLOGY -- TO ERASE TWO THOUSAND YEARS OF PROGRESS AND RESTORE FEUDALISM. BUT I DISCOVERED --
-- THAT FEUDALISM WAS NOT DEAD, MERELY AS TRANSFORMED AS I.
COOLIES, MASTERS, MAGISTRATES, MANDARINS -- THE MANUAL LABOR OF THE PEASANTS GENERATED POWER, WHICH FLOWED EVER UPWARD --
-- GROWING GREATER AT EACH LEVEL, UNTIL IT RESTED IN THE HANDS OF THE TRULY DESERVING -- THE NOBLE CLASSES. AND NOTHING WAS CHANGED --
-- MY COOLIE LABOR ENRICHED THOSE ABOVE ME, AND ABOVE THEM --
-- UNTIL IT REACHED YOU. ANTHONY STARK. FEUDAL LORD OF A MODERN AGE.
NOT -- LORD --
HOW FOOLISH, TO REJECT WHAT I SHOULD HAVE SOUGHT TO UNDERSTAND.
AND MORE FOOLISH STILL, TO RAGE AT THE IDEA OF IRON MAN, A VASSAL, AS MY GREATEST FOE -- RATHER THAN SEE BEYOND HIM, TO MY TRUE ENEMY.
I WAS HEARTBROKEN WHEN I LEARNED OF YOUR DEATH, ANTHONY -- AND JUBILANT TO LEARN YOU'D SURVIVED.
THEN WHY -- SEND SO MANY PEOPLE -- DEATHSQUAD, DREADNOUGHTS, HAUPTMANN, WHIPLASH, SPYMASTER -- TO KILL ME?
ONLY HALF OF THOSE WERE MINE. THIS DEATH-SQUAD AND HAUPTMANN I'VE NEVER HEARD OF -- AND WHIPLASH IS BENEATH MY NOTICE.
IN ANY CASE, I NEVER EXPECTED MY AGENTS TO SUCCEED, MERELY TO PROD YOU -- TO HERD YOU TOWARD THIS CONFRONTATION.
I DON'T KNOW WHAT TO THINK, EVEN IF I COULD THINK CLEARLY. IT SOUNDS LIKE THE TRUTH, BUT IF SO -- WHO SENT THE OTHERS?

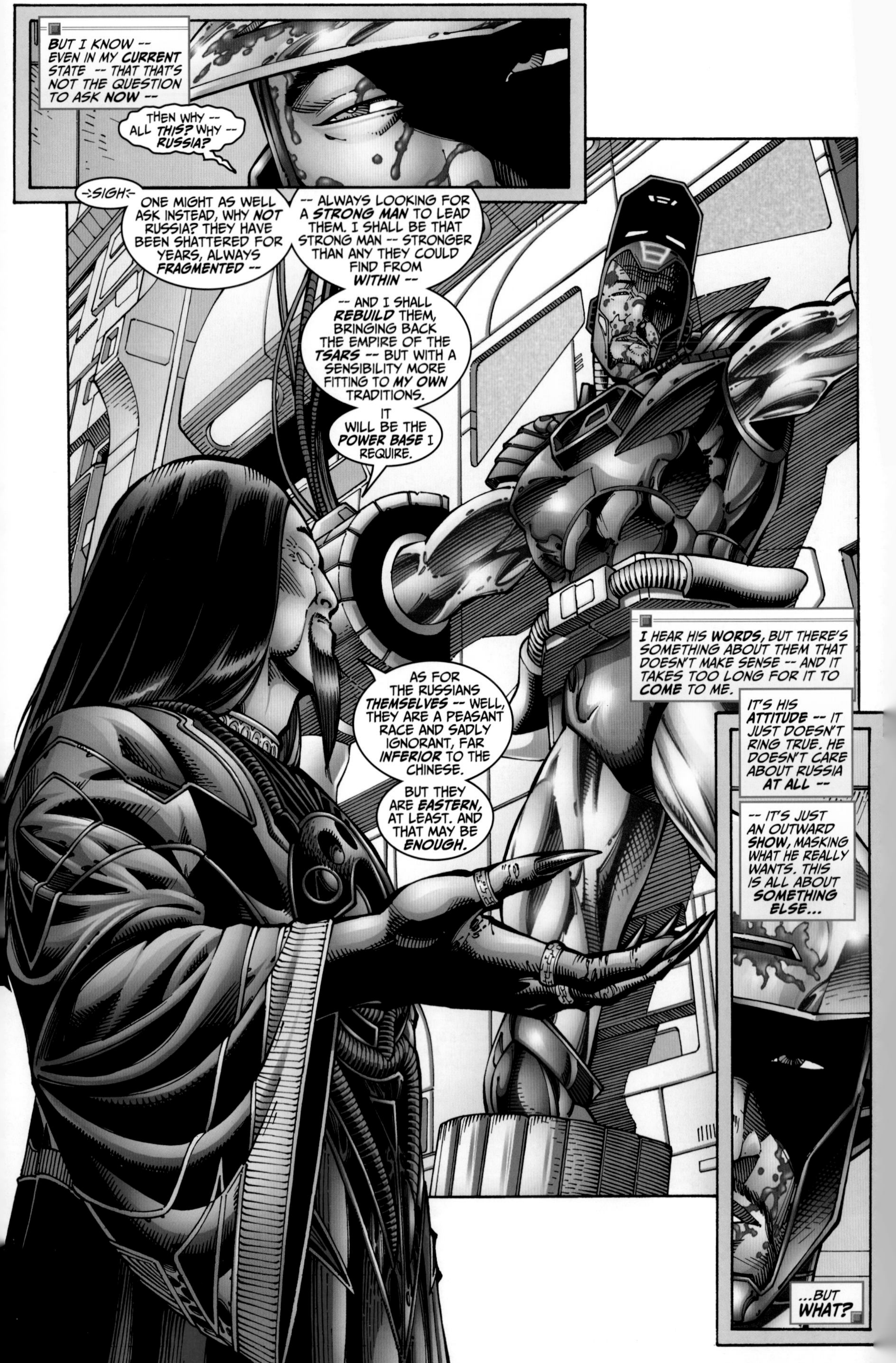
BUT I KNOW -- EVEN IN MY CURRENT STATE -- THAT THAT'S NOT THE QUESTION TO ASK NOW --
THEN WHY -- ALL THIS? WHY -- RUSSIA?
-SIGH-
ONE MIGHT AS WELL ASK INSTEAD, WHY NOT RUSSIA? THEY HAVE BEEN SHATTERED FOR YEARS, ALWAYS FRAGMENTED --
-- ALWAYS LOOKING FOR A STRONG MAN TO LEAD THEM. I SHALL BE THAT STRONG MAN -- STRONGER THAN ANY THEY COULD FIND FROM WITHIN --
-- AND I SHALL REBUILD THEM, BRINGING BACK THE EMPIRE OF THE TSARS -- BUT WITH A SENSIBILITY MORE FITTING TO MY OWN TRADITIONS.
IT WILL BE THE POWER BASE I REQUIRE.
AS FOR THE RUSSIANS THEMSELVES -- WELL, THEY ARE A PEASANT RACE AND SADLY IGNORANT, FAR INFERIOR TO THE CHINESE.
BUT THEY ARE EASTERN, AT LEAST. AND THAT MAY BE ENOUGH.
I HEAR HIS WORDS, BUT THERE'S SOMETHING ABOUT THEM THAT DOESN'T MAKE SENSE -- AND IT TAKES TOO LONG FOR IT TO COME TO ME.
IT'S HIS ATTITUDE -- IT JUST DOESN'T RING TRUE. HE DOESN'T CARE ABOUT RUSSIA AT ALL --
-- IT'S JUST AN OUTWARD SHOW, MASKING WHAT HE REALLY WANTS. THIS IS ALL ABOUT SOMETHING ELSE...
...BUT WHAT?

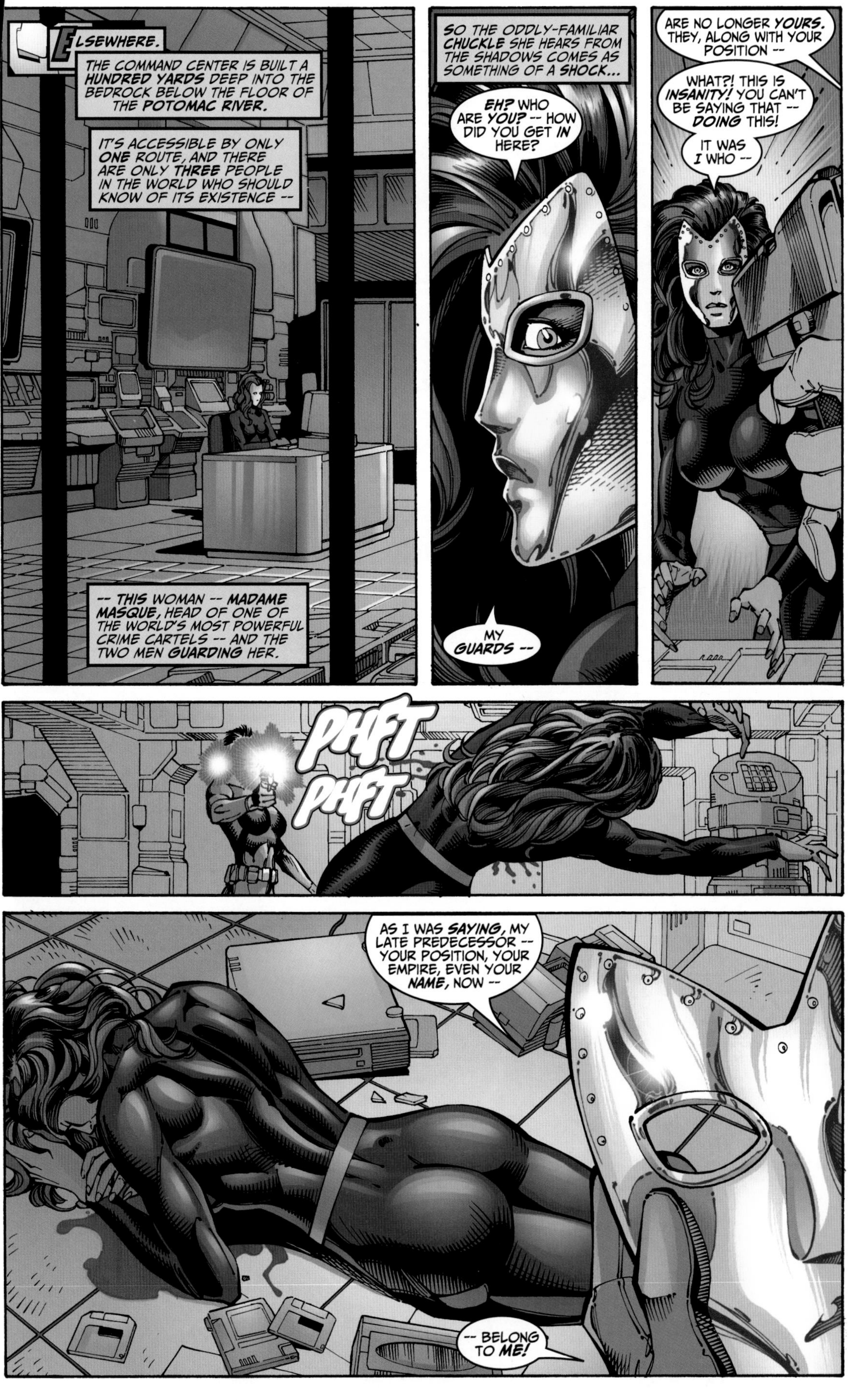
ELSEWHERE.
THE COMMAND CENTER IS BUILT A HUNDRED YARDS DEEP INTO THE BEDROCK BELOW THE FLOOR OF THE POTOMAC RIVER.
IT'S ACCESSIBLE BY ONLY ONE ROUTE, AND THERE ARE ONLY THREE PEOPLE IN THE WORLD WHO SHOULD KNOW OF ITS EXISTENCE --
-- THIS WOMAN -- MADAME MASQUE, HEAD OF ONE OF THE WORLD'S MOST POWERFUL CRIME CARTELS -- AND THE TWO MEN GUARDING HER.
SO THE ODDLY-FAMILIAR CHUCKLE SHE HEARS FROM THE SHADOWS COMES AS SOMETHING OF A SHOCK...
EH? WHO ARE YOU? -- HOW DID YOU GET IN HERE?
MY GUARDS --
ARE NO LONGER YOURS. THEY, ALONG WITH YOUR POSITION --
WHAT?! THIS IS INSANITY! YOU CAN'T BE SAYING THAT -- DOING THIS!
IT WAS I WHO --
PHFT
PHFT
AS I WAS SAYING, MY LATE PREDECESSOR -- YOUR POSITION, YOUR EMPIRE, EVEN YOUR NAME, NOW --
-- BELONG TO ME!

AND, BACK IN RUSSIA...

‹MANY HAVE INVADED RUSSIAN SOIL, INVADERS -- FROM NAPOLEON TO HITLER!›

‹NONE HAVE SUCCEEDED!›

WATCH IT, STEEL GUARDIAN!

KSSH

POONT

ZAKKT

‹PUSH THEM BACK! BACK!›

I SAW THAT YOU *HAD* THEM, CAPTAIN AMERICA. MY *THANKS*.

BUT YOU SOUND AS FRUSTRATED AS *I*, AT BEING LIMITED TO THIS ROLE.

WE'RE SAVING *LIVES*, GUARDIAN. THAT'S WHAT *MATTERS*.

I *AGREE*, CAPTAIN. STILL, TRUE AS THAT MAY BE, WE *BOTH* KNOW THAT WE ARE MERELY SUPPORTING THE EFFORTS OF THOSE *ABOVE* US --

"-- THOSE WHO FIGHT THE *TRUE* BATTLE!"

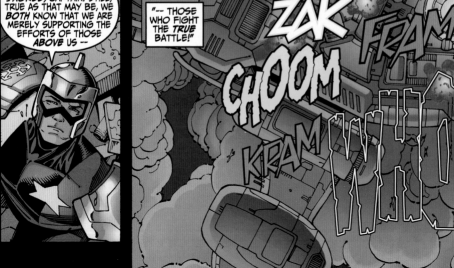

ZAK CHOOM FRAM BAM KRAM WHOOM

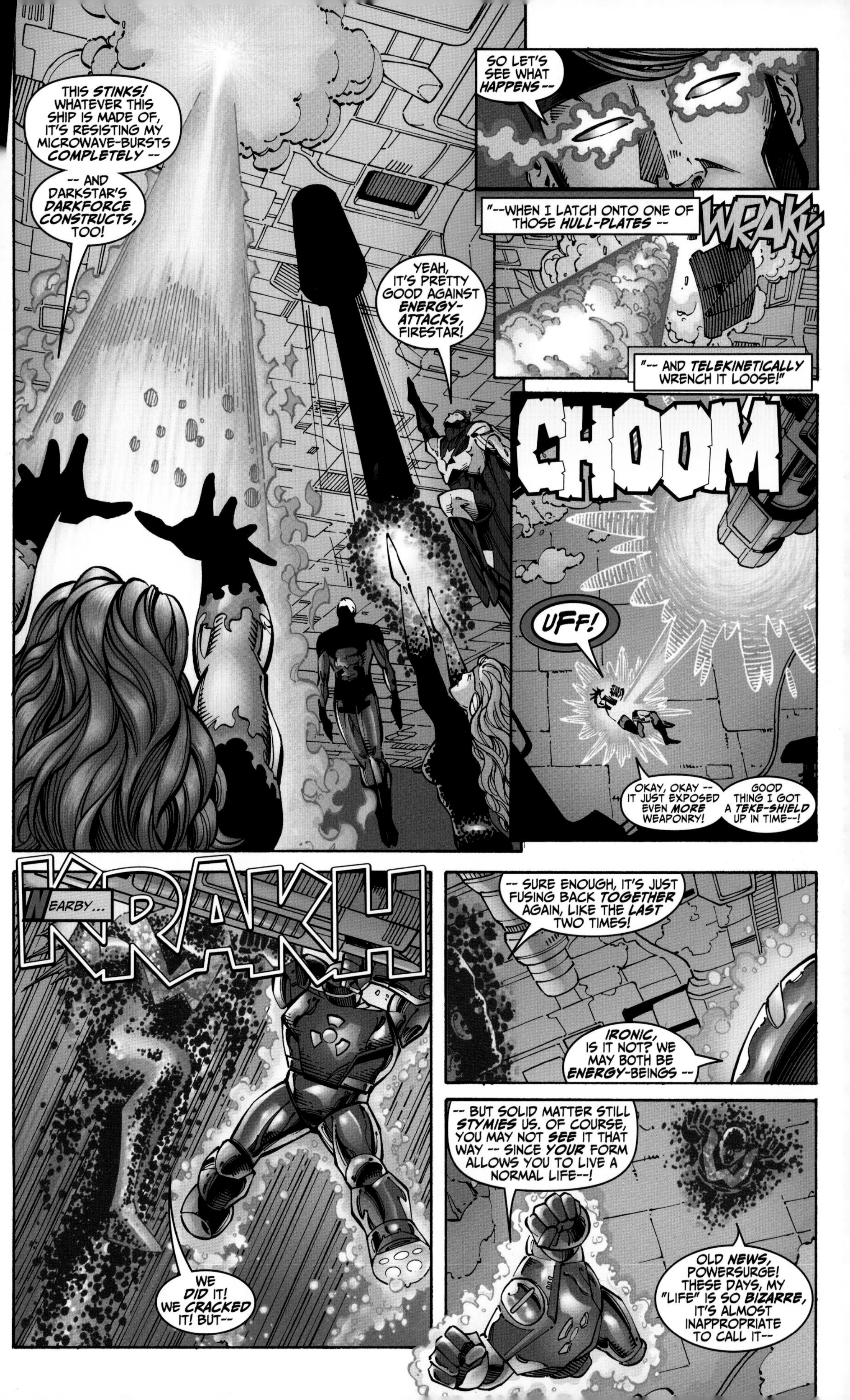
THIS STINKS! WHATEVER THIS SHIP IS MADE OF, IT'S RESISTING MY MICROWAVE-BURSTS COMPLETELY --
-- AND DARKSTAR'S DARKFORCE CONSTRUCTS, TOO!
YEAH, IT'S PRETTY GOOD AGAINST ENERGY-ATTACKS, FIRESTAR!
SO LET'S SEE WHAT HAPPENS --
"--WHEN I LATCH ONTO ONE OF THOSE HULL-PLATES --
WRAKK
"-- AND TELEKINETICALLY WRENCH IT LOOSE!"
CHOOM
UFF!
OKAY, OKAY -- IT JUST EXPOSED EVEN MORE WEAPONRY!
GOOD THING I GOT A TEKE-SHIELD UP IN TIME--!
NEARBY...
KRAKH
WE DID IT! WE CRACKED IT! BUT--
-- SURE ENOUGH, IT'S JUST FUSING BACK TOGETHER AGAIN, LIKE THE LAST TWO TIMES!
IRONIC, IS IT NOT? WE MAY BOTH BE ENERGY-BEINGS --
-- BUT SOLID MATTER STILL STYMIES US. OF COURSE, YOU MAY NOT SEE IT THAT WAY -- SINCE YOUR FORM ALLOWS YOU TO LIVE A NORMAL LIFE--!
OLD NEWS, POWERSURGE! THESE DAYS, MY "LIFE" IS SO BIZARRE, IT'S ALMOST INAPPROPRIATE TO CALL IT--

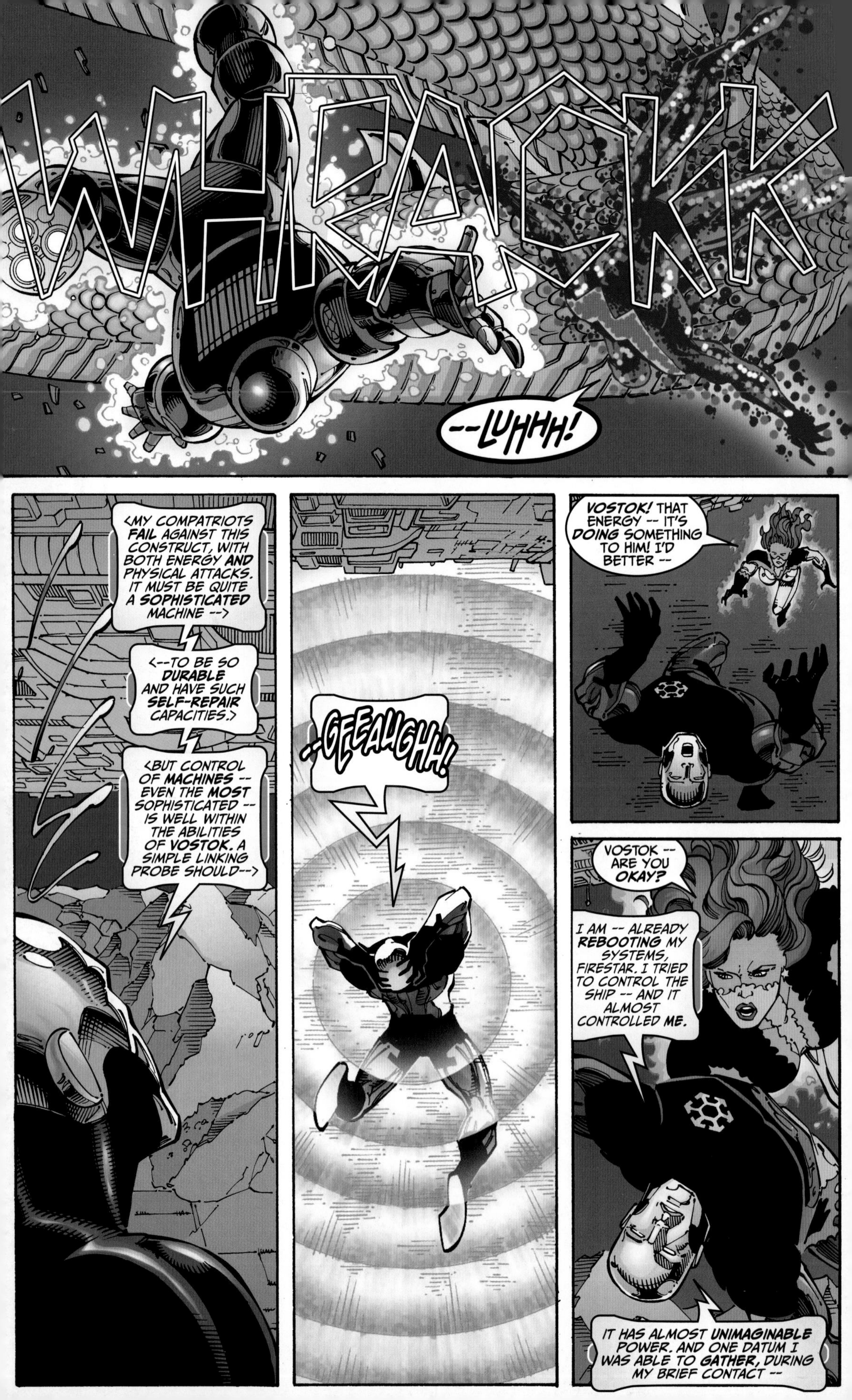
WHRACKK
--LUHHH!
<MY COMPATRIOTS FAIL AGAINST THIS CONSTRUCT, WITH BOTH ENERGY AND PHYSICAL ATTACKS. IT MUST BE QUITE A SOPHISTICATED MACHINE -->
<--TO BE SO DURABLE AND HAVE SUCH SELF-REPAIR CAPACITIES.>
<BUT CONTROL OF MACHINES -- EVEN THE MOST SOPHISTICATED -- IS WELL WITHIN THE ABILITIES OF VOSTOK. A SIMPLE LINKING PROBE SHOULD-->
--GLEEAUGHH!
VOSTOK! THAT ENERGY -- IT'S DOING SOMETHING TO HIM! I'D BETTER --
VOSTOK -- ARE YOU OKAY?
I AM -- ALREADY REBOOTING MY SYSTEMS, FIRESTAR. I TRIED TO CONTROL THE SHIP -- AND IT ALMOST CONTROLLED ME.
IT HAS ALMOST UNIMAGINABLE POWER. AND ONE DATUM I WAS ABLE TO GATHER, DURING MY BRIEF CONTACT --

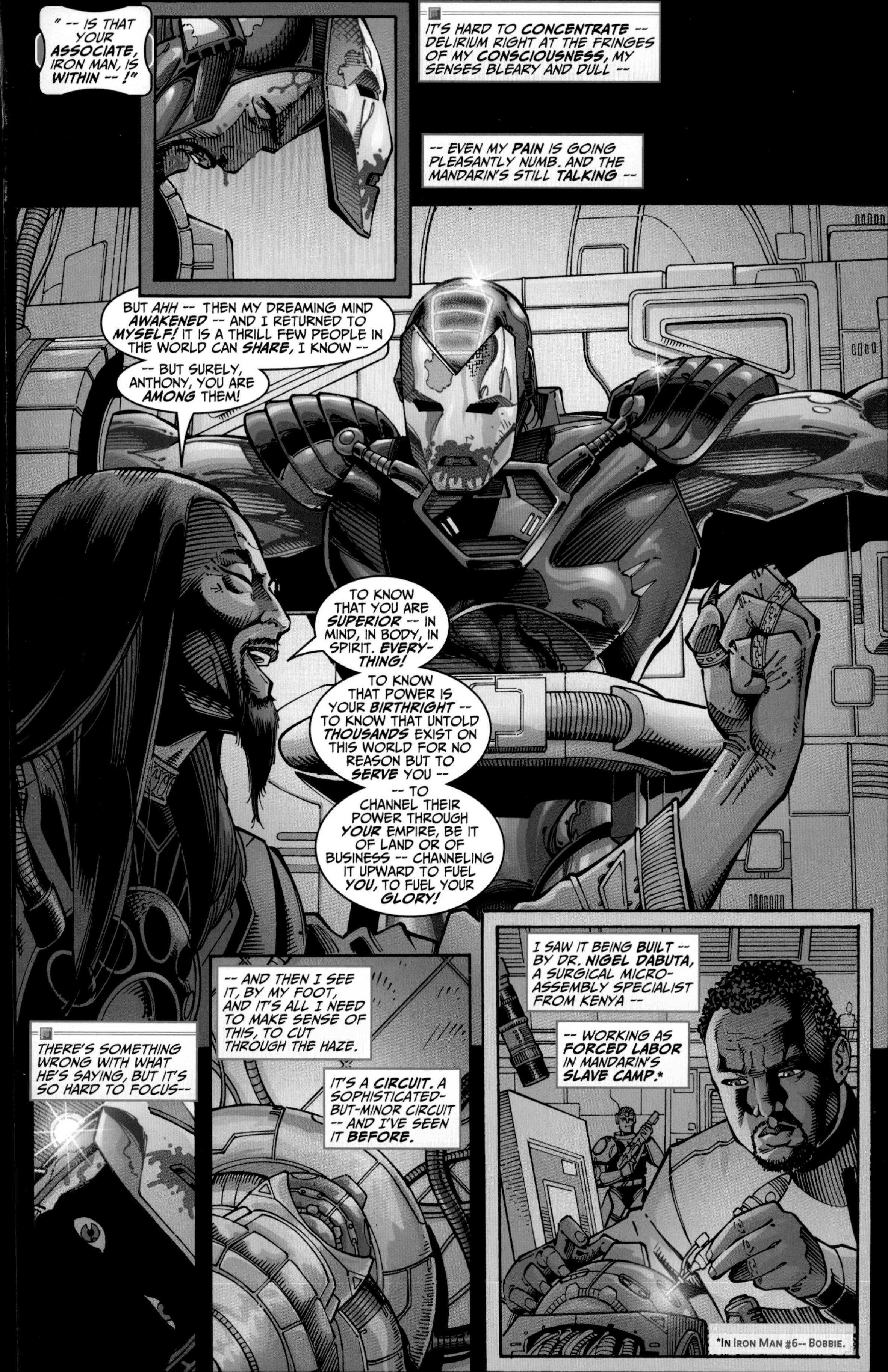
" -- IS THAT YOUR ASSOCIATE, IRON MAN, IS WITHIN -- !"
IT'S HARD TO CONCENTRATE -- DELIRIUM RIGHT AT THE FRINGES OF MY CONSCIOUSNESS, MY SENSES BLEARY AND DULL --
-- EVEN MY PAIN IS GOING PLEASANTLY NUMB. AND THE MANDARIN'S STILL TALKING --
BUT AHH -- THEN MY DREAMING MIND AWAKENED -- AND I RETURNED TO MYSELF! IT IS A THRILL FEW PEOPLE IN THE WORLD CAN SHARE, I KNOW --
-- BUT SURELY, ANTHONY, YOU ARE AMONG THEM!
TO KNOW THAT YOU ARE SUPERIOR -- IN MIND, IN BODY, IN SPIRIT. EVERY-THING!
TO KNOW THAT POWER IS YOUR BIRTHRIGHT -- TO KNOW THAT UNTOLD THOUSANDS EXIST ON THIS WORLD FOR NO REASON BUT TO SERVE YOU --
-- TO CHANNEL THEIR POWER THROUGH YOUR EMPIRE, BE IT OF LAND OR OF BUSINESS -- CHANNELING IT UPWARD TO FUEL YOU, TO FUEL YOUR GLORY!
THERE'S SOMETHING WRONG WITH WHAT HE'S SAYING, BUT IT'S SO HARD TO FOCUS--
-- AND THEN I SEE IT, BY MY FOOT, AND IT'S ALL I NEED TO MAKE SENSE OF THIS, TO CUT THROUGH THE HAZE.
IT'S A CIRCUIT. A SOPHISTICATED-BUT-MINOR CIRCUIT -- AND I'VE SEEN IT BEFORE.
I SAW IT BEING BUILT -- BY DR. NIGEL DABUTA, A SURGICAL MICRO-ASSEMBLY SPECIALIST FROM KENYA --
-- WORKING AS FORCED LABOR IN MANDARIN'S SLAVE CAMP.*
*IN IRON MAN #6-- BOBBIE.

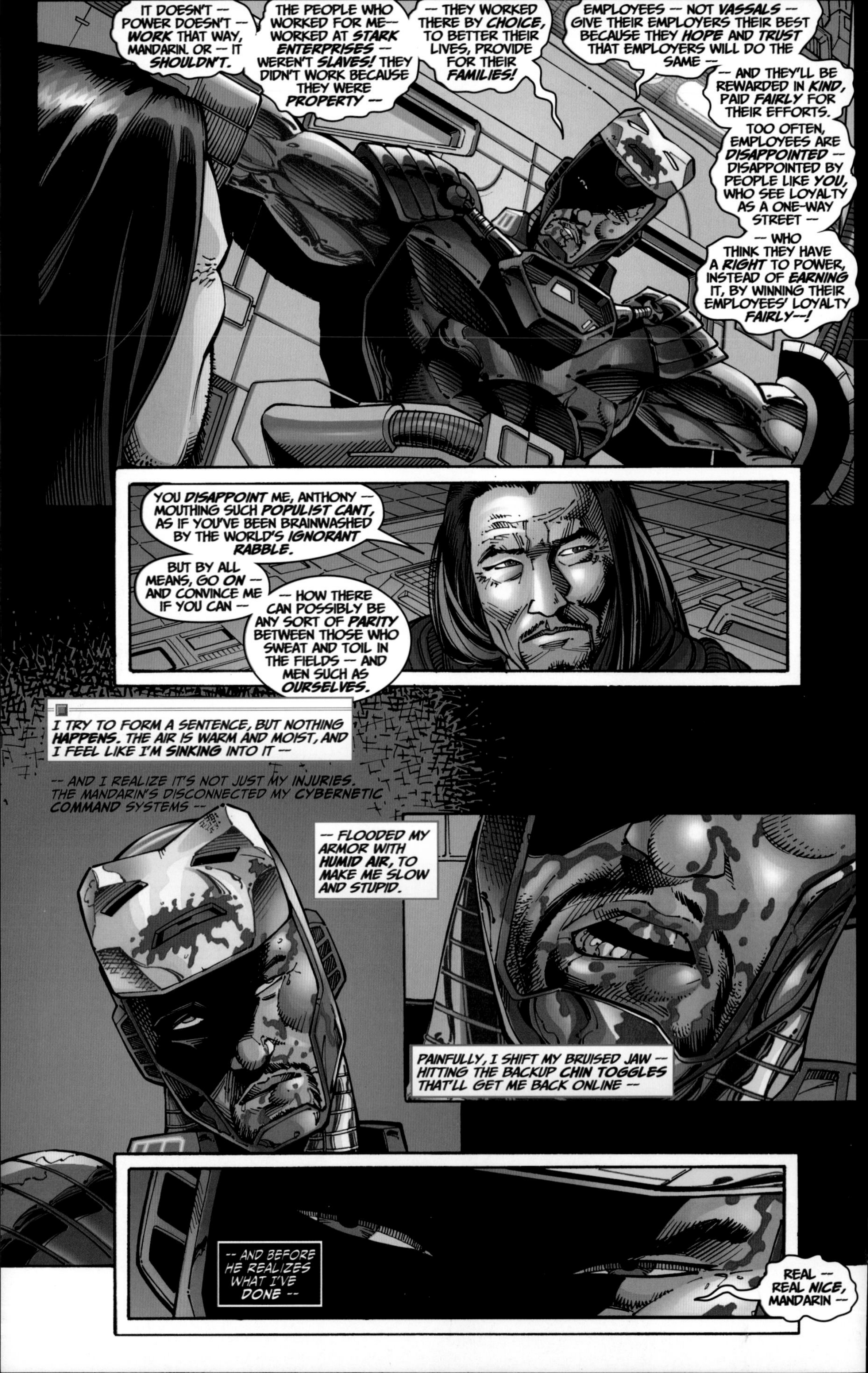
IT DOESN'T -- POWER DOESN'T -- WORK THAT WAY, MANDARIN. OR -- IT SHOULDN'T.
THE PEOPLE WHO WORKED FOR ME-- WORKED AT STARK ENTERPRISES -- WEREN'T SLAVES! THEY DIDN'T WORK BECAUSE THEY WERE PROPERTY --
-- THEY WORKED THERE BY CHOICE, TO BETTER THEIR LIVES, PROVIDE FOR THEIR FAMILIES!
EMPLOYEES -- NOT VASSALS -- GIVE THEIR EMPLOYERS THEIR BEST BECAUSE THEY HOPE AND TRUST THAT EMPLOYERS WILL DO THE SAME --
-- AND THEY'LL BE REWARDED IN KIND, PAID FAIRLY FOR THEIR EFFORTS.
TOO OFTEN, EMPLOYEES ARE DISAPPOINTED -- DISAPPOINTED BY PEOPLE LIKE YOU, WHO SEE LOYALTY AS A ONE-WAY STREET --
-- WHO THINK THEY HAVE A RIGHT TO POWER, INSTEAD OF EARNING IT, BY WINNING THEIR EMPLOYEES' LOYALTY FAIRLY--!
YOU DISAPPOINT ME, ANTHONY -- MOUTHING SUCH POPULIST CANT, AS IF YOU'VE BEEN BRAINWASHED BY THE WORLD'S IGNORANT RABBLE.
BUT BY ALL MEANS, GO ON -- AND CONVINCE ME IF YOU CAN --
-- HOW THERE CAN POSSIBLY BE ANY SORT OF PARITY BETWEEN THOSE WHO SWEAT AND TOIL IN THE FIELDS -- AND MEN SUCH AS OURSELVES.
I TRY TO FORM A SENTENCE, BUT NOTHING HAPPENS. THE AIR IS WARM AND MOIST, AND I FEEL LIKE I'M SINKING INTO IT --
-- AND I REALIZE IT'S NOT JUST MY INJURIES. THE MANDARIN'S DISCONNECTED MY CYBERNETIC COMMAND SYSTEMS --
-- FLOODED MY ARMOR WITH HUMID AIR, TO MAKE ME SLOW AND STUPID.
PAINFULLY, I SHIFT MY BRUISED JAW -- HITTING THE BACKUP CHIN TOGGLES THAT'LL GET ME BACK ONLINE --
-- AND BEFORE HE REALIZES WHAT I'VE DONE --
REAL -- REAL NICE, MANDARIN --

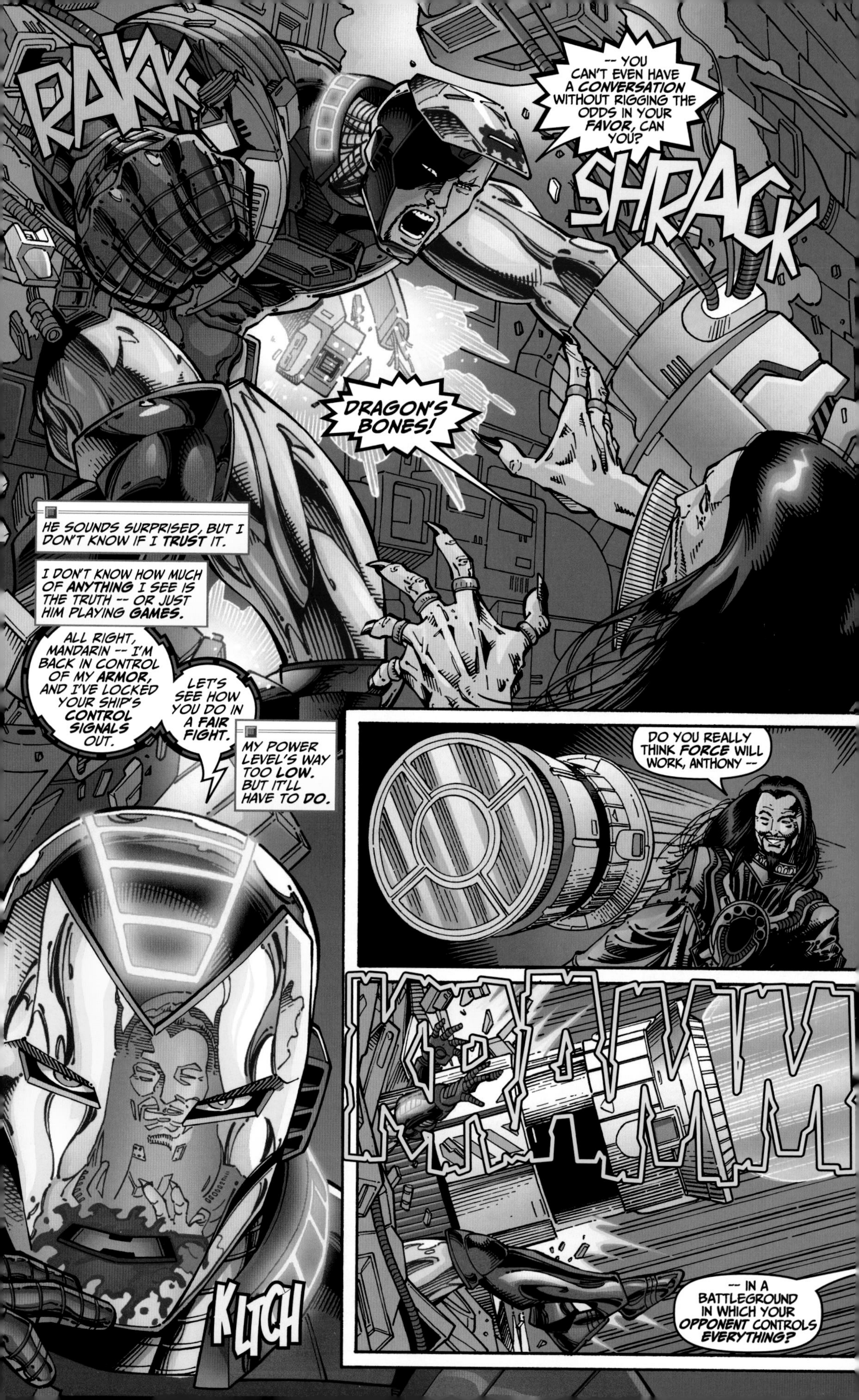
RAKK
-- YOU CAN'T EVEN HAVE A CONVERSATION WITHOUT RIGGING THE ODDS IN YOUR FAVOR, CAN YOU?
SHRACK
DRAGON'S BONES!
HE SOUNDS SURPRISED, BUT I DON'T KNOW IF I TRUST IT.
I DON'T KNOW HOW MUCH OF ANYTHING I SEE IS THE TRUTH -- OR JUST HIM PLAYING GAMES.
ALL RIGHT, MANDARIN -- I'M BACK IN CONTROL OF MY ARMOR, AND I'VE LOCKED YOUR SHIP'S CONTROL SIGNALS OUT.
LET'S SEE HOW YOU DO IN A FAIR FIGHT.
MY POWER LEVEL'S WAY TOO LOW. BUT IT'LL HAVE TO DO.
KLTCH
DO YOU REALLY THINK FORCE WILL WORK, ANTHONY --
-- IN A BATTLEGROUND IN WHICH YOUR OPPONENT CONTROLS EVERYTHING?

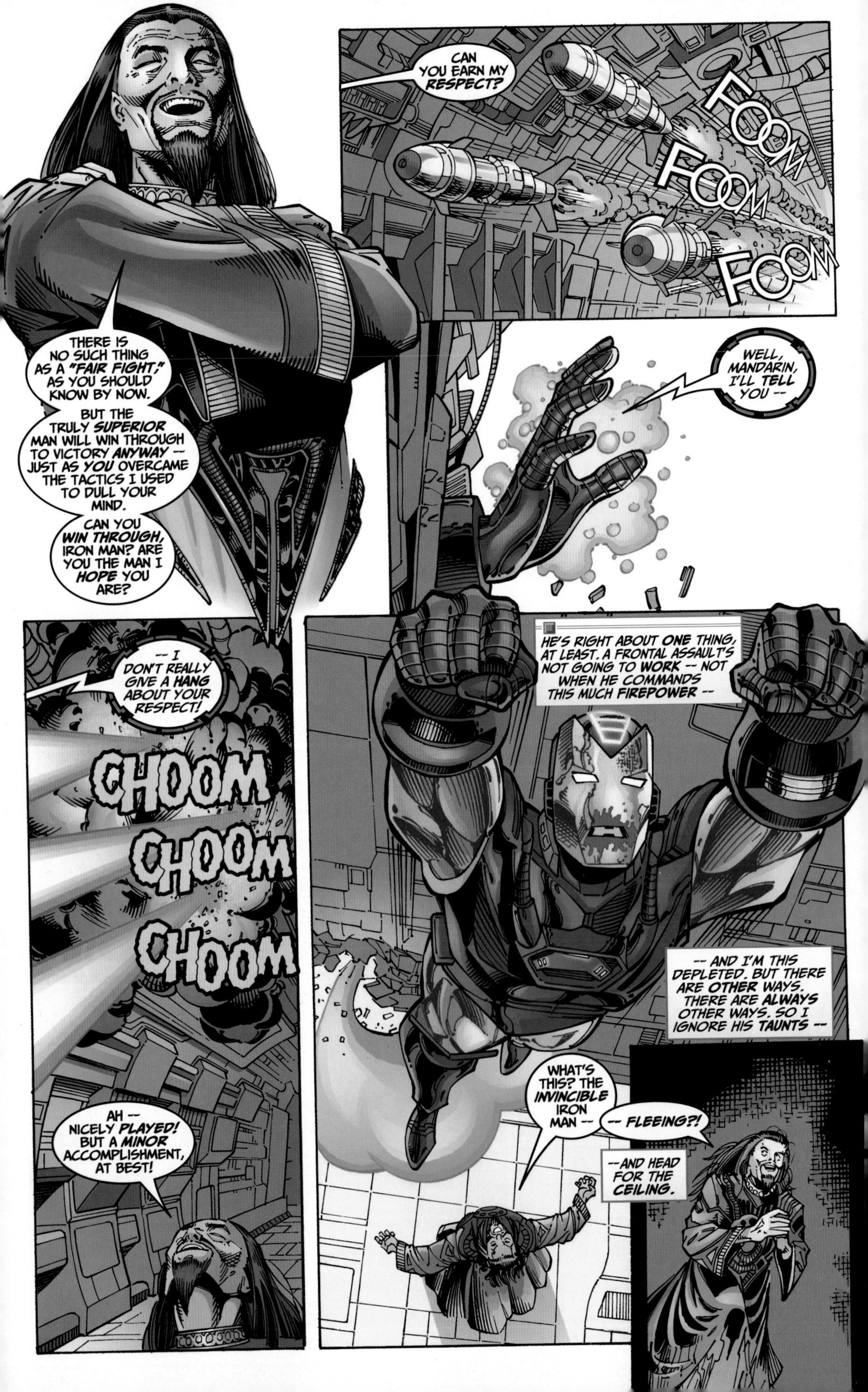

CAN YOU EARN MY RESPECT?
FOOM
FOOM
FOOM
THERE IS NO SUCH THING AS A "FAIR FIGHT," AS YOU SHOULD KNOW BY NOW.
BUT THE TRULY SUPERIOR MAN WILL WIN THROUGH TO VICTORY ANYWAY -- JUST AS YOU OVERCAME THE TACTICS I USED TO DULL YOUR MIND.
CAN YOU WIN THROUGH, IRON MAN? ARE YOU THE MAN I HOPE YOU ARE?
WELL, MANDARIN, I'LL TELL YOU --
-- I DON'T REALLY GIVE A HANG ABOUT YOUR RESPECT!
CHOOM
CHOOM
CHOOM
AH -- NICELY PLAYED! BUT A MINOR ACCOMPLISHMENT, AT BEST!
HE'S RIGHT ABOUT ONE THING, AT LEAST. A FRONTAL ASSAULT'S NOT GOING TO WORK -- NOT WHEN HE COMMANDS THIS MUCH FIREPOWER --
-- AND I'M THIS DEPLETED. BUT THERE ARE OTHER WAYS. THERE ARE ALWAYS OTHER WAYS. SO I IGNORE HIS TAUNTS --
WHAT'S THIS? THE INVINCIBLE IRON MAN --
-- FLEEING?!
--AND HEAD FOR THE CEILING.

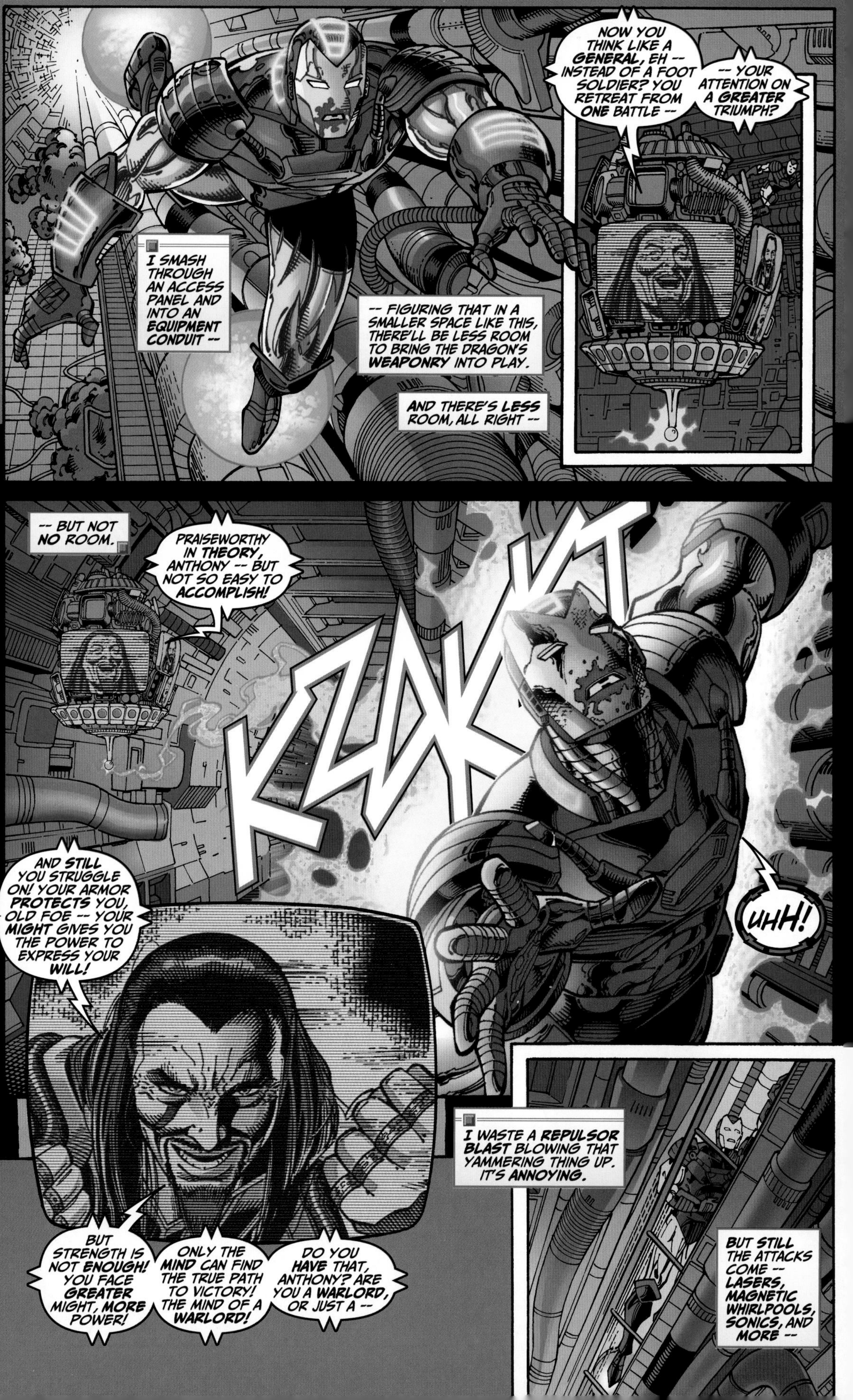

I SMASH THROUGH AN ACCESS PANEL AND INTO AN EQUIPMENT CONDUIT --
-- FIGURING THAT IN A SMALLER SPACE LIKE THIS, THERE'LL BE LESS ROOM TO BRING THE DRAGON'S WEAPONRY INTO PLAY.
AND THERE'S LESS ROOM, ALL RIGHT --
NOW YOU THINK LIKE A GENERAL, EH -- INSTEAD OF A FOOT SOLDIER? YOU RETREAT FROM ONE BATTLE --
-- YOUR ATTENTION ON A GREATER TRIUMPH?
-- BUT NOT NO ROOM.
PRAISEWORTHY IN THEORY, ANTHONY -- BUT NOT SO EASY TO ACCOMPLISH!
KZOKT
UHH!
AND STILL YOU STRUGGLE ON! YOUR ARMOR PROTECTS YOU, OLD FOE -- YOUR MIGHT GIVES YOU THE POWER TO EXPRESS YOUR WILL!
BUT STRENGTH IS NOT ENOUGH! YOU FACE GREATER MIGHT, MORE POWER!
ONLY THE MIND CAN FIND THE TRUE PATH TO VICTORY! THE MIND OF A WARLORD!
DO YOU HAVE THAT, ANTHONY? ARE YOU A WARLORD, OR JUST A --
I WASTE A REPULSOR BLAST BLOWING THAT YAMMERING THING UP. IT'S ANNOYING.
BUT STILL THE ATTACKS COME -- LASERS, MAGNETIC WHIRLPOOLS, SONICS, AND MORE --

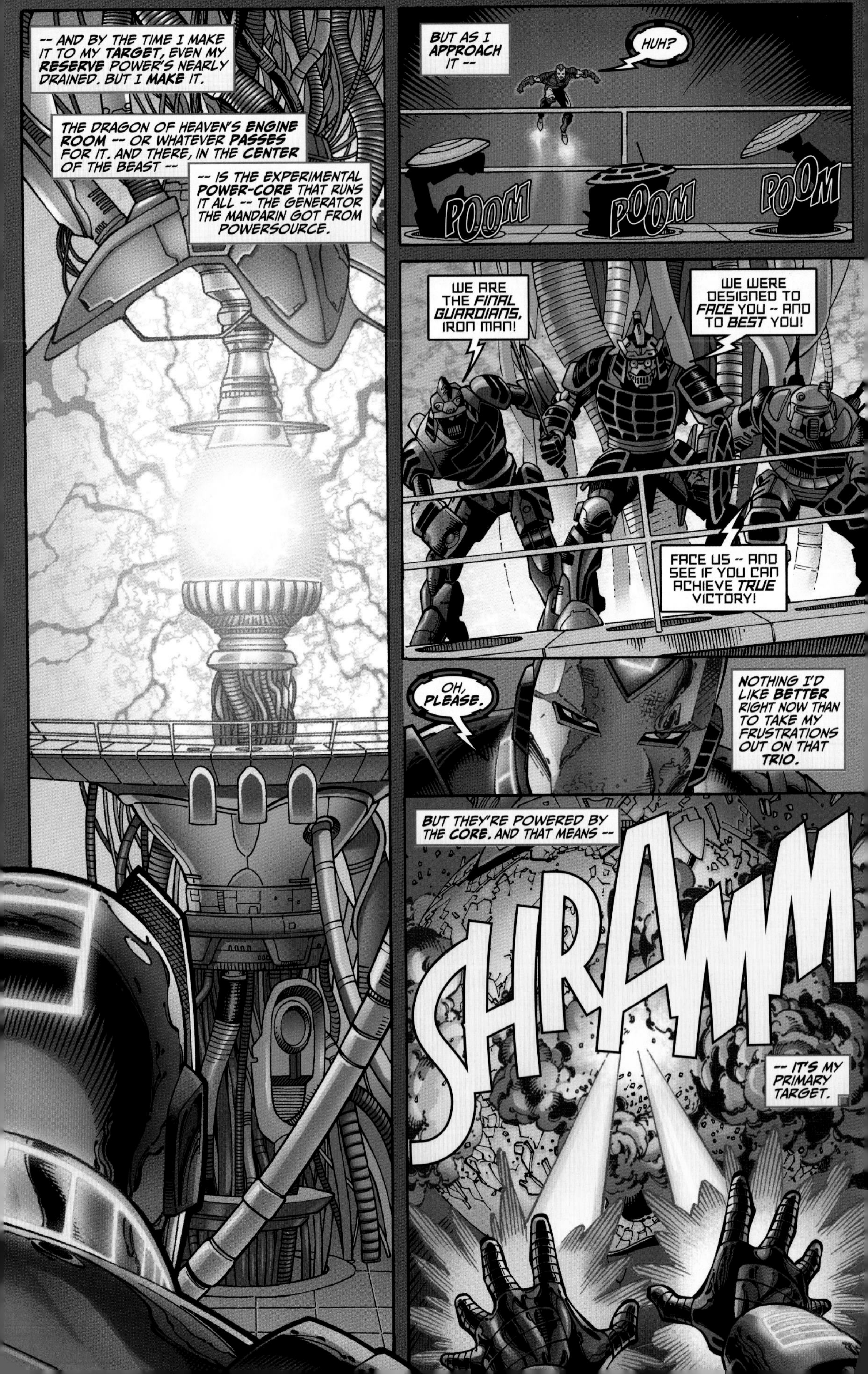
-- AND BY THE TIME I MAKE IT TO MY TARGET, EVEN MY RESERVE POWER'S NEARLY DRAINED. BUT I MAKE IT.
THE DRAGON OF HEAVEN'S ENGINE ROOM -- OR WHATEVER PASSES FOR IT. AND THERE, IN THE CENTER OF THE BEAST --
-- IS THE EXPERIMENTAL POWER-CORE THAT RUNS IT ALL -- THE GENERATOR THE MANDARIN GOT FROM POWERSOURCE.
BUT AS I APPROACH IT --
HUH?
POOM
POOM
POOM
WE ARE THE FINAL GUARDIANS, IRON MAN!
WE WERE DESIGNED TO FACE YOU -- AND TO BEST YOU!
FACE US -- AND SEE IF YOU CAN ACHIEVE TRUE VICTORY!
OH, PLEASE.
NOTHING I'D LIKE BETTER RIGHT NOW THAN TO TAKE MY FRUSTRATIONS OUT ON THAT TRIO.
BUT THEY'RE POWERED BY THE CORE. AND THAT MEANS --
SHRAMM
-- IT'S MY PRIMARY TARGET.

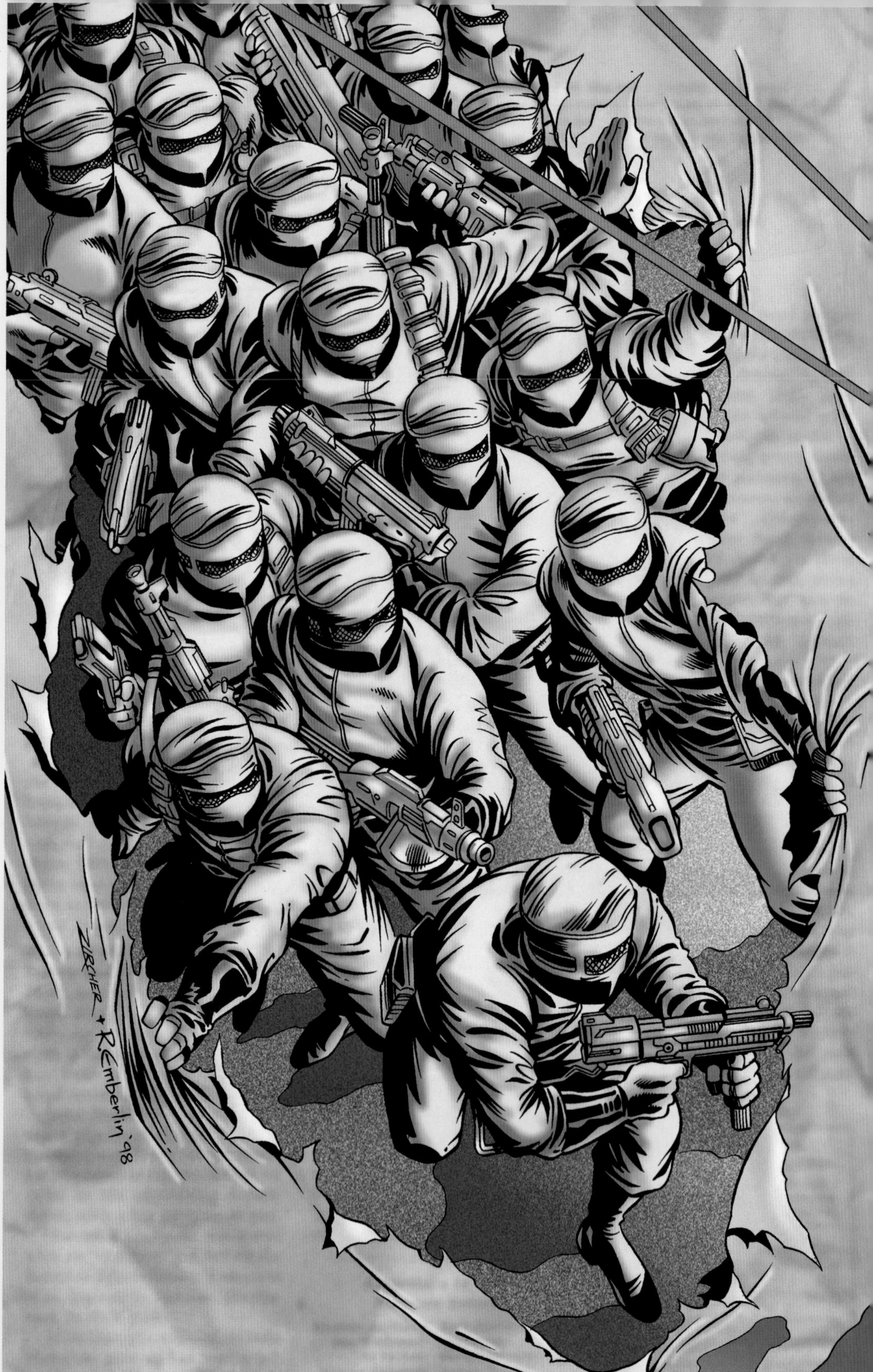
ZIRCHER
R.Emberlin '98

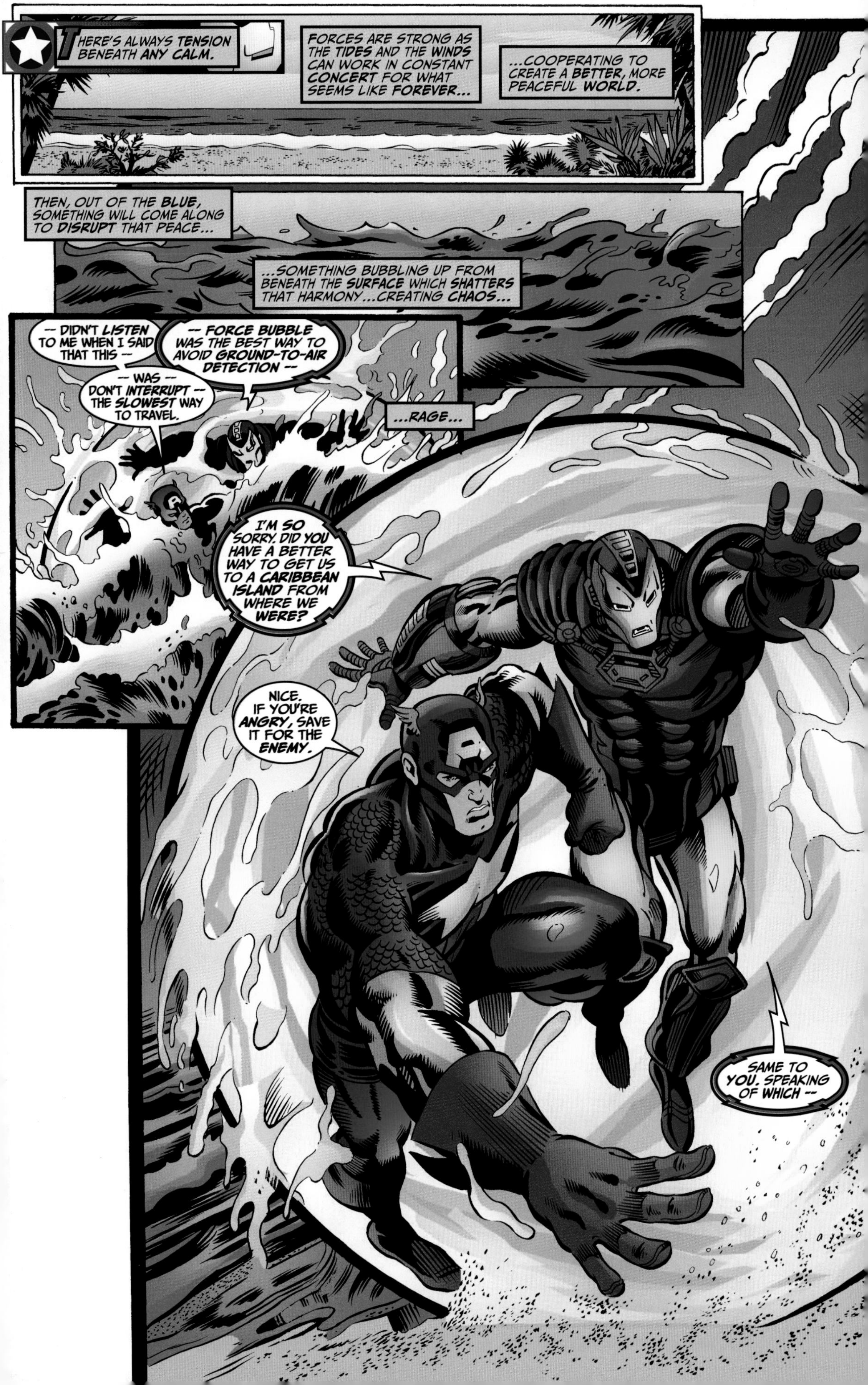
THERE'S ALWAYS TENSION BENEATH ANY CALM.
FORCES ARE STRONG AS THE TIDES AND THE WINDS CAN WORK IN CONSTANT CONCERT FOR WHAT SEEMS LIKE FOREVER...
...COOPERATING TO CREATE A BETTER, MORE PEACEFUL WORLD.
THEN, OUT OF THE BLUE, SOMETHING WILL COME ALONG TO DISRUPT THAT PEACE...
...SOMETHING BUBBLING UP FROM BENEATH THE SURFACE WHICH SHATTERS THAT HARMONY...CREATING CHAOS...
-- DIDN'T LISTEN TO ME WHEN I SAID THAT THIS --
-- FORCE BUBBLE WAS THE BEST WAY TO AVOID GROUND-TO-AIR DETECTION --
-- WAS -- DON'T INTERRUPT -- THE SLOWEST WAY TO TRAVEL.
...RAGE...
I'M SO SORRY. DID YOU HAVE A BETTER WAY TO GET US TO A CARIBBEAN ISLAND FROM WHERE WE WERE?
NICE. IF YOU'RE ANGRY, SAVE IT FOR THE ENEMY.
SAME TO YOU. SPEAKING OF WHICH --

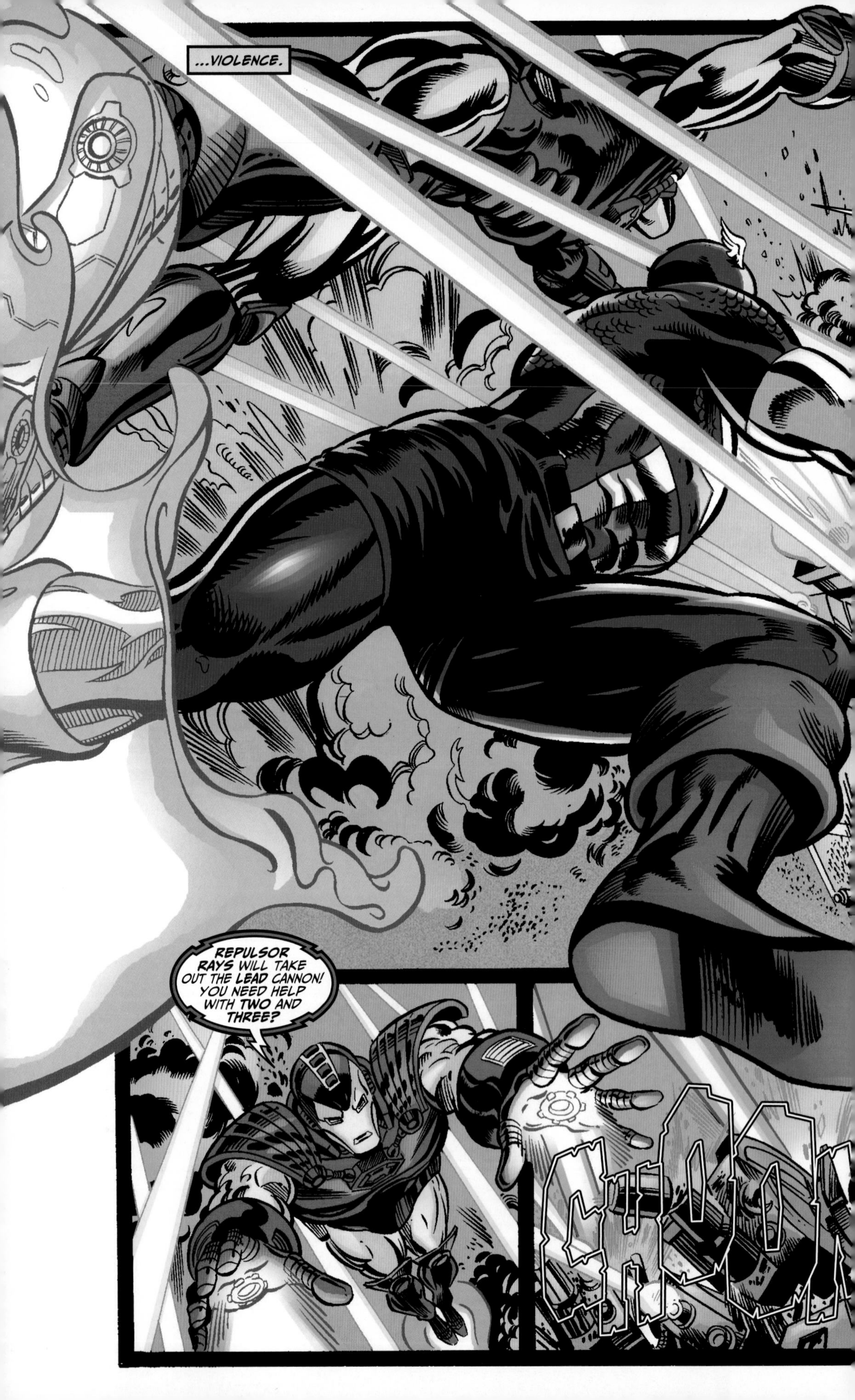
...VIOLENCE.
REPULSOR RAYS WILL TAKE OUT THE LEAD CANNON! YOU NEED HELP WITH TWO AND THREE?

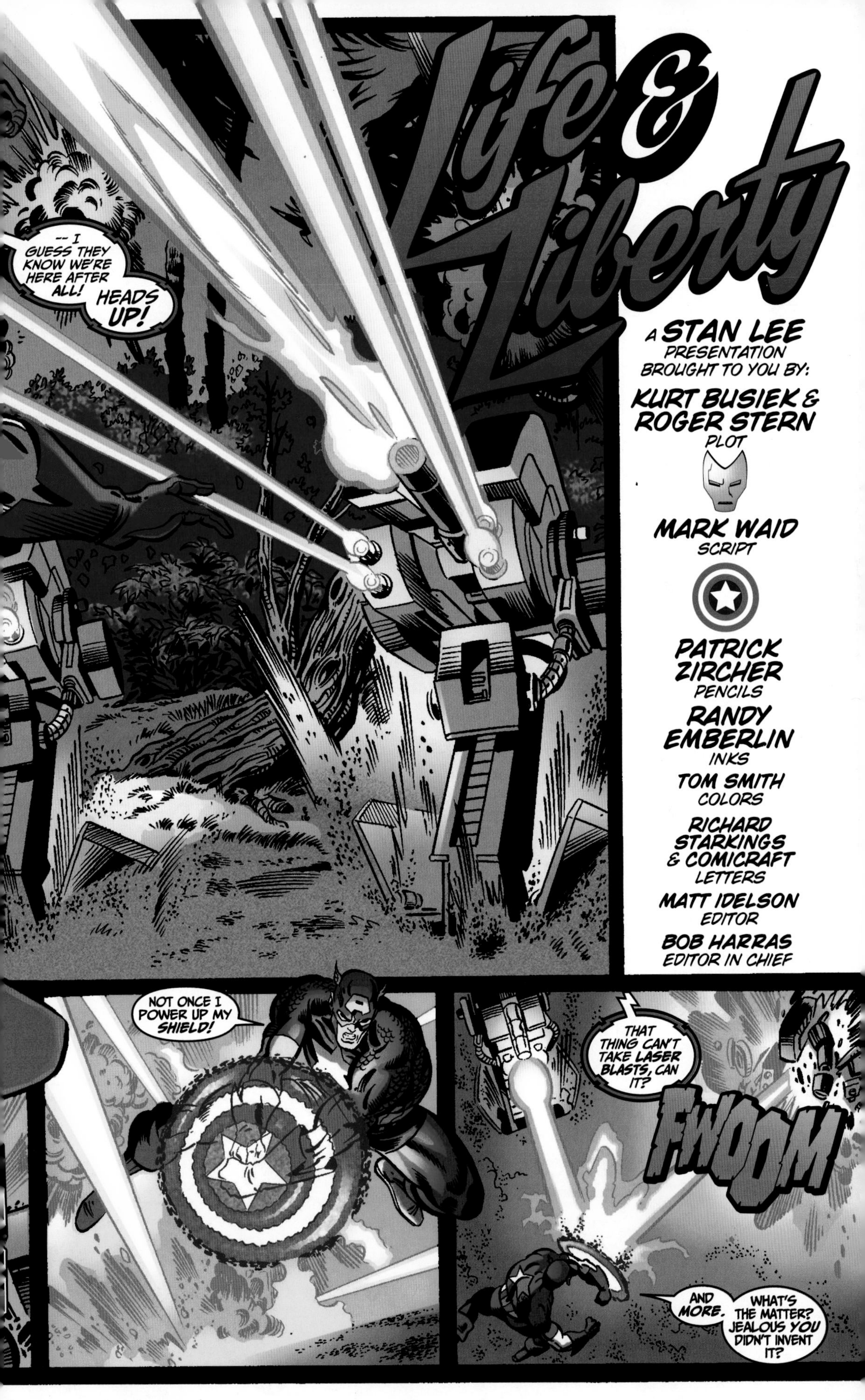
Life & Liberty
-- I GUESS THEY KNOW WE'RE HERE AFTER ALL!
HEADS UP!
A STAN LEE PRESENTATION BROUGHT TO YOU BY:
KURT BUSIEK & ROGER STERN
PLOT
MARK WAID
SCRIPT
PATRICK ZIRCHER
PENCILS
RANDY EMBERLIN
INKS
TOM SMITH
COLORS
RICHARD STARKINGS & COMICRAFT
LETTERS
MATT IDELSON
EDITOR
BOB HARRAS
EDITOR IN CHIEF
NOT ONCE I POWER UP MY SHIELD!
THAT THING CAN'T TAKE LASER BLASTS, CAN IT?
FWOOM
AND MORE.
WHAT'S THE MATTER? JEALOUS YOU DIDN'T INVENT IT?

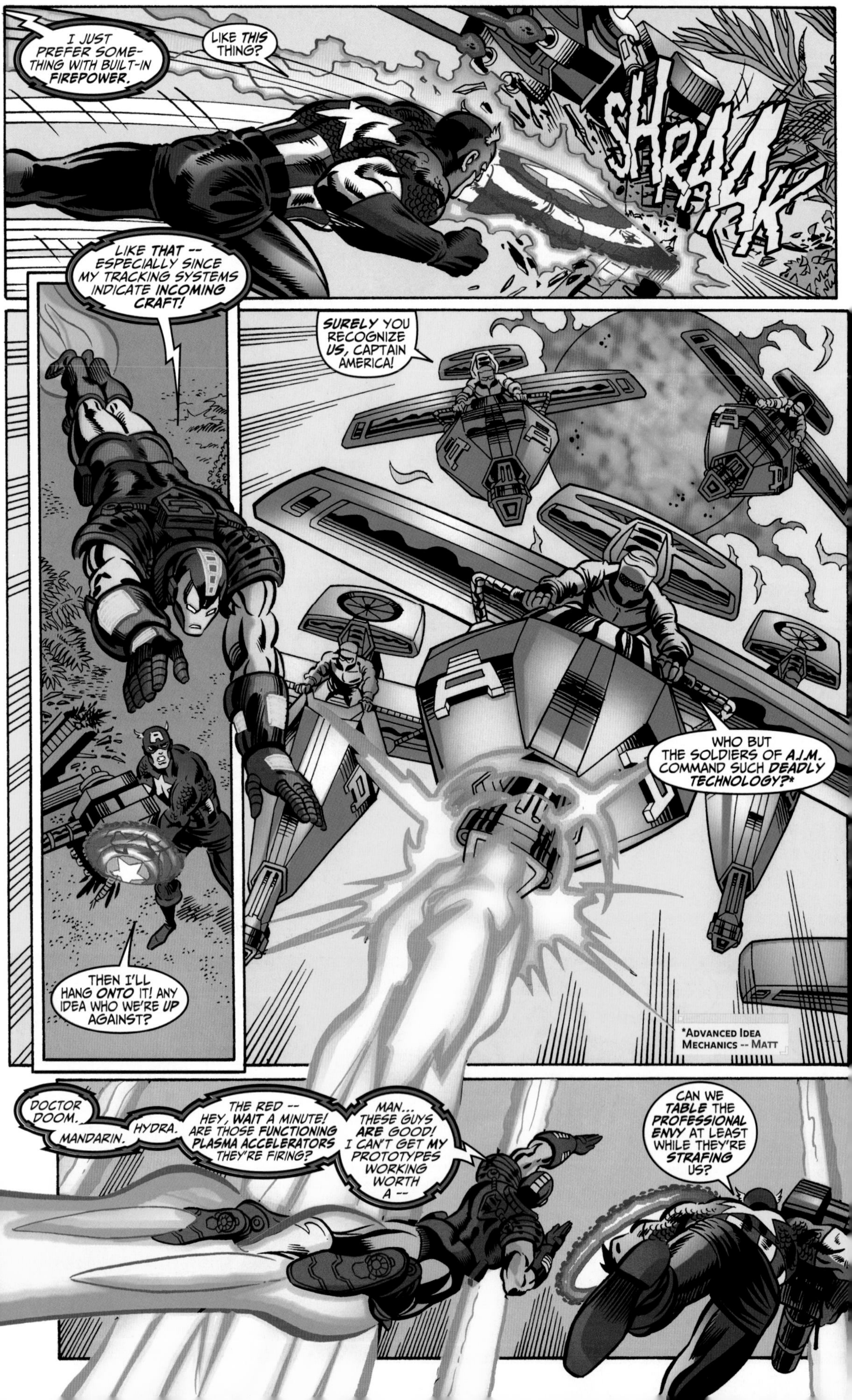

I JUST PREFER SOMETHING WITH BUILT-IN FIREPOWER.
LIKE THIS THING?
SHRAAKK
LIKE THAT -- ESPECIALLY SINCE MY TRACKING SYSTEMS INDICATE INCOMING CRAFT!
THEN I'LL HANG ONTO IT! ANY IDEA WHO WE'RE UP AGAINST?
SURELY YOU RECOGNIZE US, CAPTAIN AMERICA!
WHO BUT THE SOLDIERS OF A.I.M. COMMAND SUCH DEADLY TECHNOLOGY?*
*ADVANCED IDEA MECHANICS -- MATT
DOCTOR DOOM.
MANDARIN.
HYDRA.
THE RED -- HEY, WAIT A MINUTE! ARE THOSE FUNCTIONING PLASMA ACCELERATORS THEY'RE FIRING?
MAN... THESE GUYS ARE GOOD! I CAN'T GET MY PROTOTYPES WORKING WORTH A --
CAN WE TABLE THE PROFESSIONAL ENVY AT LEAST WHILE THEY'RE STRAFING US?

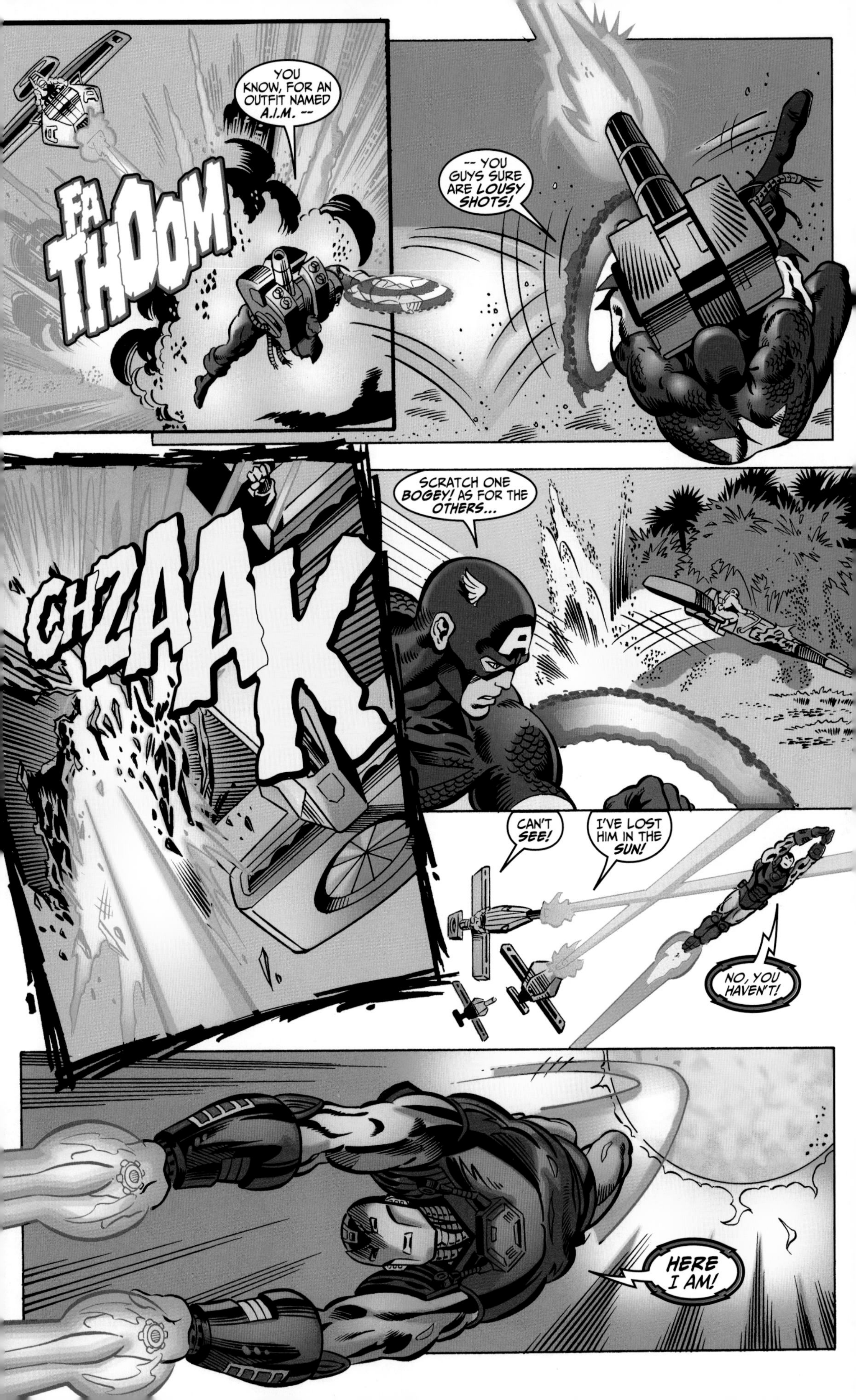
YOU KNOW, FOR AN OUTFIT NAMED A.I.M. --
FA THOOM
-- YOU GUYS SURE ARE LOUSY SHOTS!
CHZAAK
SCRATCH ONE BOGEY! AS FOR THE OTHERS...
CAN'T SEE!
I'VE LOST HIM IN THE SUN!
NO, YOU HAVEN'T!
HERE I AM!

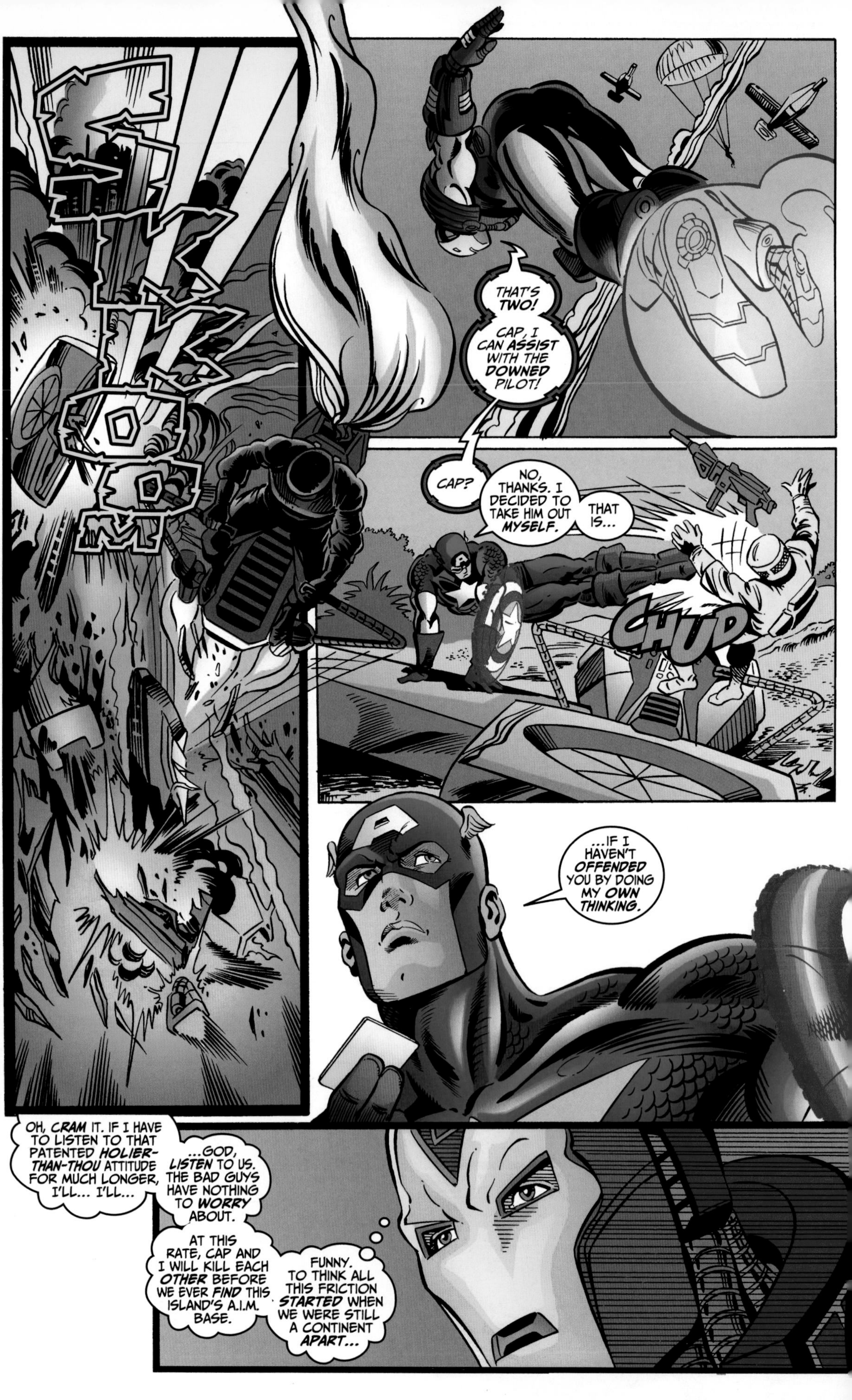
THAT'S TWO!
CAP, I CAN ASSIST WITH THE DOWNED PILOT!
CAP?
NO, THANKS. I DECIDED TO TAKE HIM OUT MYSELF.
THAT IS...
CHUD
...IF I HAVEN'T OFFENDED YOU BY DOING MY OWN THINKING.
OH, CRAM IT. IF I HAVE TO LISTEN TO THAT PATENTED HOLIER-THAN-THOU ATTITUDE FOR MUCH LONGER, I'LL... I'LL...
...GOD, LISTEN TO US. THE BAD GUYS HAVE NOTHING TO WORRY ABOUT.
AT THIS RATE, CAP AND I WILL KILL EACH OTHER BEFORE WE EVER FIND THIS ISLAND'S A.I.M. BASE.
FUNNY. TO THINK ALL THIS FRICTION STARTED WHEN WE WERE STILL A CONTINENT APART...

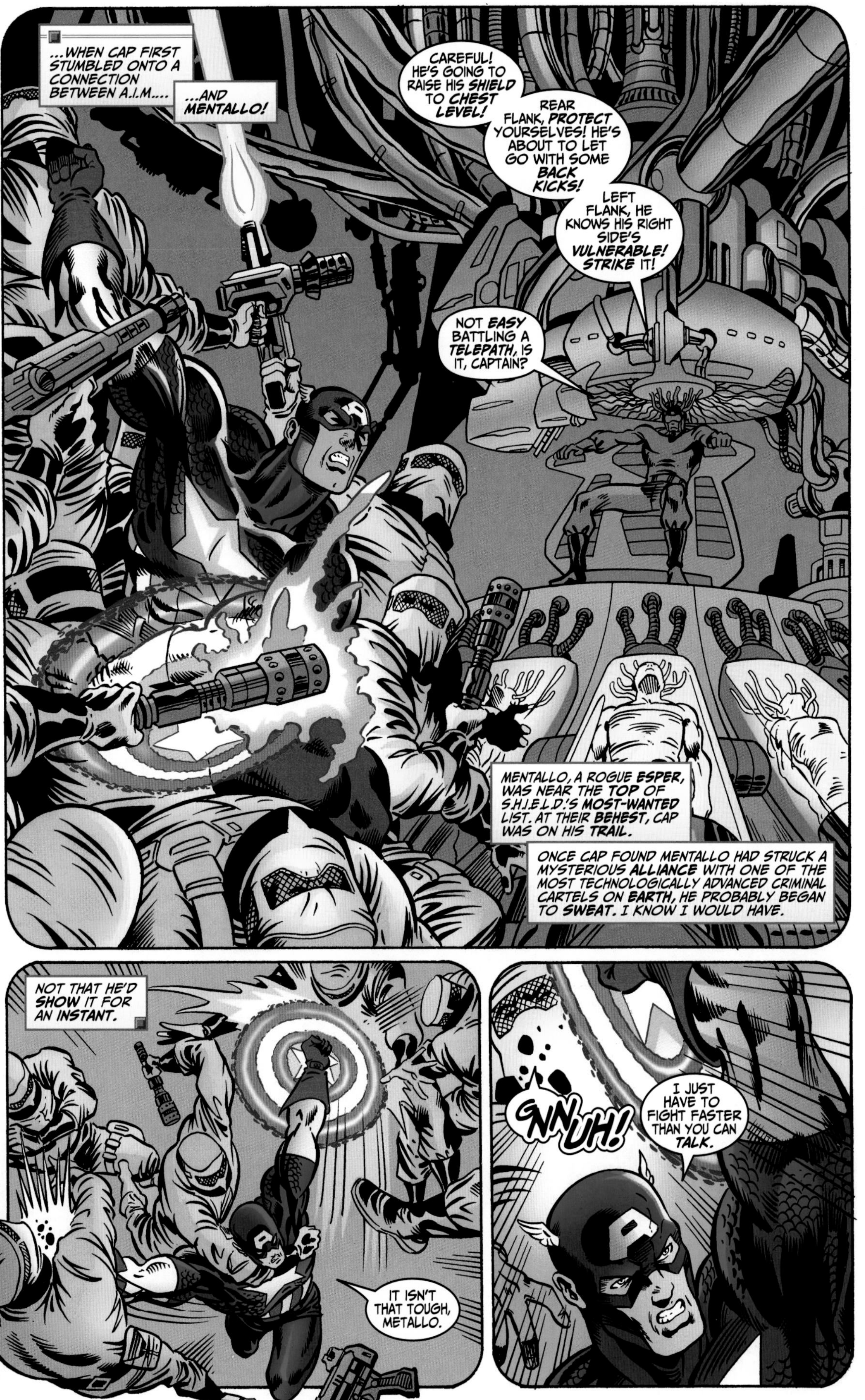
...WHEN CAP FIRST STUMBLED ONTO A CONNECTION BETWEEN A.I.M....
...AND MENTALLO!
CAREFUL! HE'S GOING TO RAISE HIS SHIELD TO CHEST LEVEL!
REAR FLANK, PROTECT YOURSELVES! HE'S ABOUT TO LET GO WITH SOME BACK KICKS!
LEFT FLANK, HE KNOWS HIS RIGHT SIDE'S VULNERABLE! STRIKE IT!
NOT EASY BATTLING A TELEPATH, IS IT, CAPTAIN?
MENTALLO, A ROGUE ESPER, WAS NEAR THE TOP OF S.H.I.E.L.D.'S MOST-WANTED LIST. AT THEIR BEHEST, CAP WAS ON HIS TRAIL.
ONCE CAP FOUND MENTALLO HAD STRUCK A MYSTERIOUS ALLIANCE WITH ONE OF THE MOST TECHNOLOGICALLY ADVANCED CRIMINAL CARTELS ON EARTH, HE PROBABLY BEGAN TO SWEAT. I KNOW I WOULD HAVE.
NOT THAT HE'D SHOW IT FOR AN INSTANT.
IT ISN'T THAT TOUGH, METALLO.
GNNUH!
I JUST HAVE TO FIGHT FASTER THAN YOU CAN TALK.

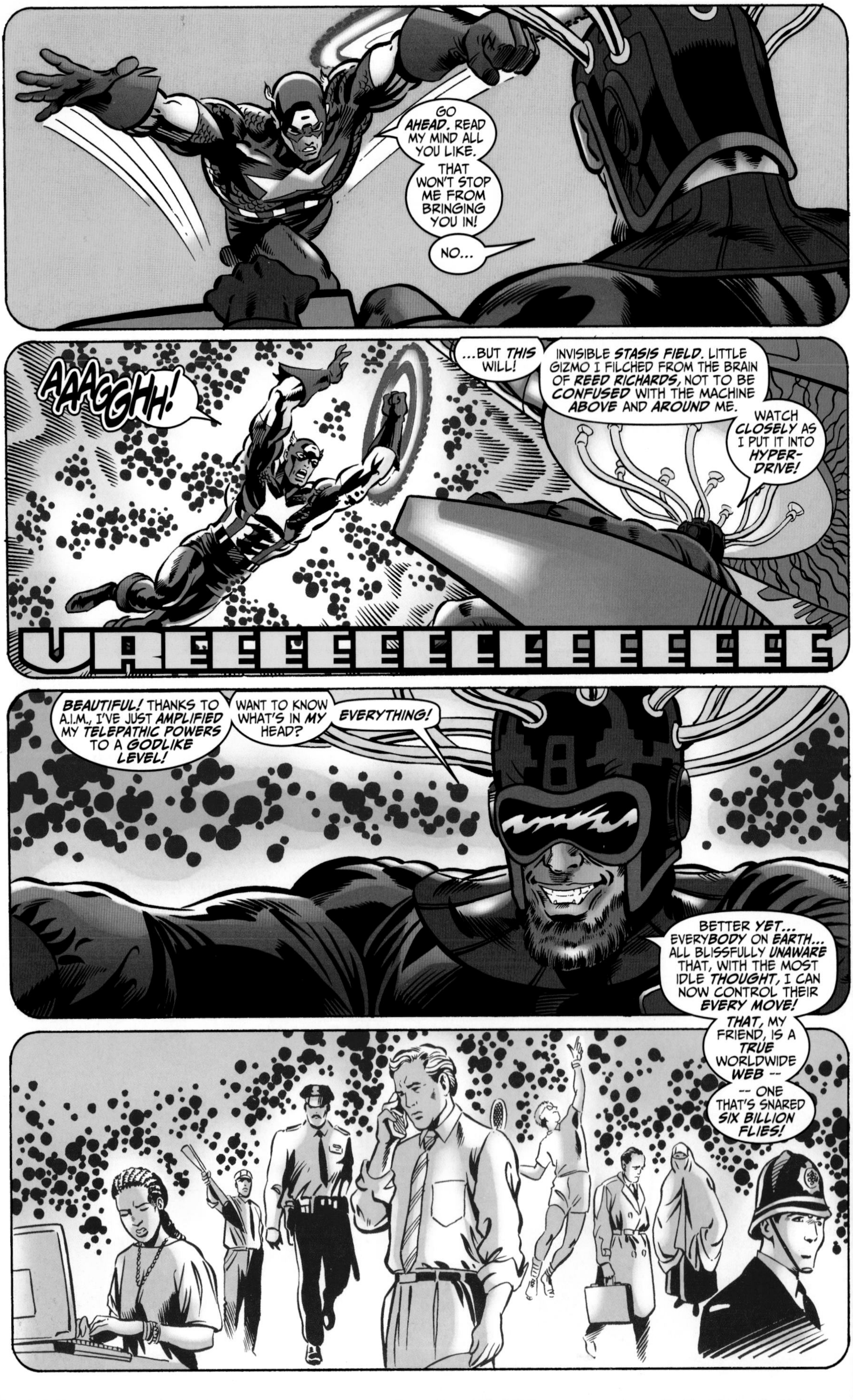
GO AHEAD. READ MY MIND ALL YOU LIKE.
THAT WON'T STOP ME FROM BRINGING YOU IN!
NO...
...BUT THIS WILL!
INVISIBLE STASIS FIELD. LITTLE GIZMO I FILCHED FROM THE BRAIN OF REED RICHARDS, NOT TO BE CONFUSED WITH THE MACHINE ABOVE AND AROUND ME.
WATCH CLOSELY AS I PUT IT INTO HYPER-DRIVE!
AAAGGHH!
VREEEEEEEEEEEEE
BEAUTIFUL! THANKS TO A.I.M., I'VE JUST AMPLIFIED MY TELEPATHIC POWERS TO A GODLIKE LEVEL!
WANT TO KNOW WHAT'S IN MY HEAD?
EVERYTHING!
BETTER YET... EVERYBODY ON EARTH... ALL BLISSFULLY UNAWARE THAT, WITH THE MOST IDLE THOUGHT, I CAN NOW CONTROL THEIR EVERY MOVE!
THAT, MY FRIEND, IS A TRUE WORLDWIDE WEB --
-- ONE THAT'S SNARED SIX BILLION FLIES!

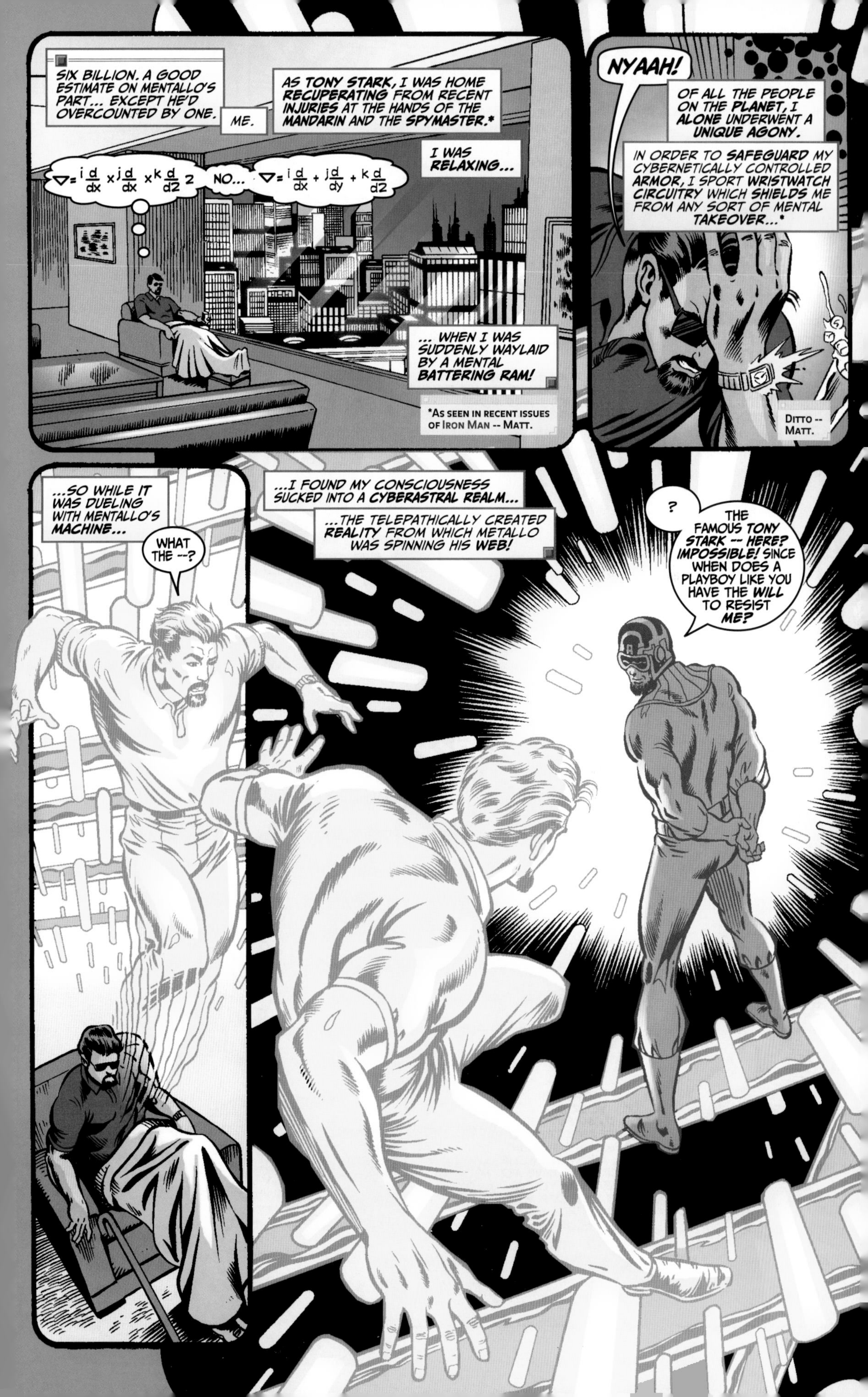
SIX BILLION. A GOOD ESTIMATE ON MENTALLO'S PART... EXCEPT HE'D OVERCOUNTED BY ONE.
ME.
AS TONY STARK, I WAS HOME RECUPERATING FROM RECENT INJURIES AT THE HANDS OF THE MANDARIN AND THE SPYMASTER.*
I WAS RELAXING...
$\nabla = i\frac{d}{dx} \times j\frac{d}{dx} \times k\frac{d}{d2}$ 2 NO... $\nabla = i\frac{d}{dx} + j\frac{d}{dy} + k\frac{d}{d2}$
... WHEN I WAS SUDDENLY WAYLAID BY A MENTAL BATTERING RAM!
*AS SEEN IN RECENT ISSUES OF IRON MAN -- MATT.
NYAAH!
OF ALL THE PEOPLE ON THE PLANET, I ALONE UNDERWENT A UNIQUE AGONY.
IN ORDER TO SAFEGUARD MY CYBERNETICALLY CONTROLLED ARMOR, I SPORT WRISTWATCH CIRCUITRY WHICH SHIELDS ME FROM ANY SORT OF MENTAL TAKEOVER...*
DITTO -- MATT.
...SO WHILE IT WAS DUELING WITH MENTALLO'S MACHINE...
WHAT THE --?
...I FOUND MY CONSCIOUSNESS SUCKED INTO A CYBERASTRAL REALM...
...THE TELEPATHICALLY CREATED REALITY FROM WHICH METALLO WAS SPINNING HIS WEB!
?
THE FAMOUS TONY STARK -- HERE? IMPOSSIBLE! SINCE WHEN DOES A PLAYBOY LIKE YOU HAVE THE WILL TO RESIST ME?

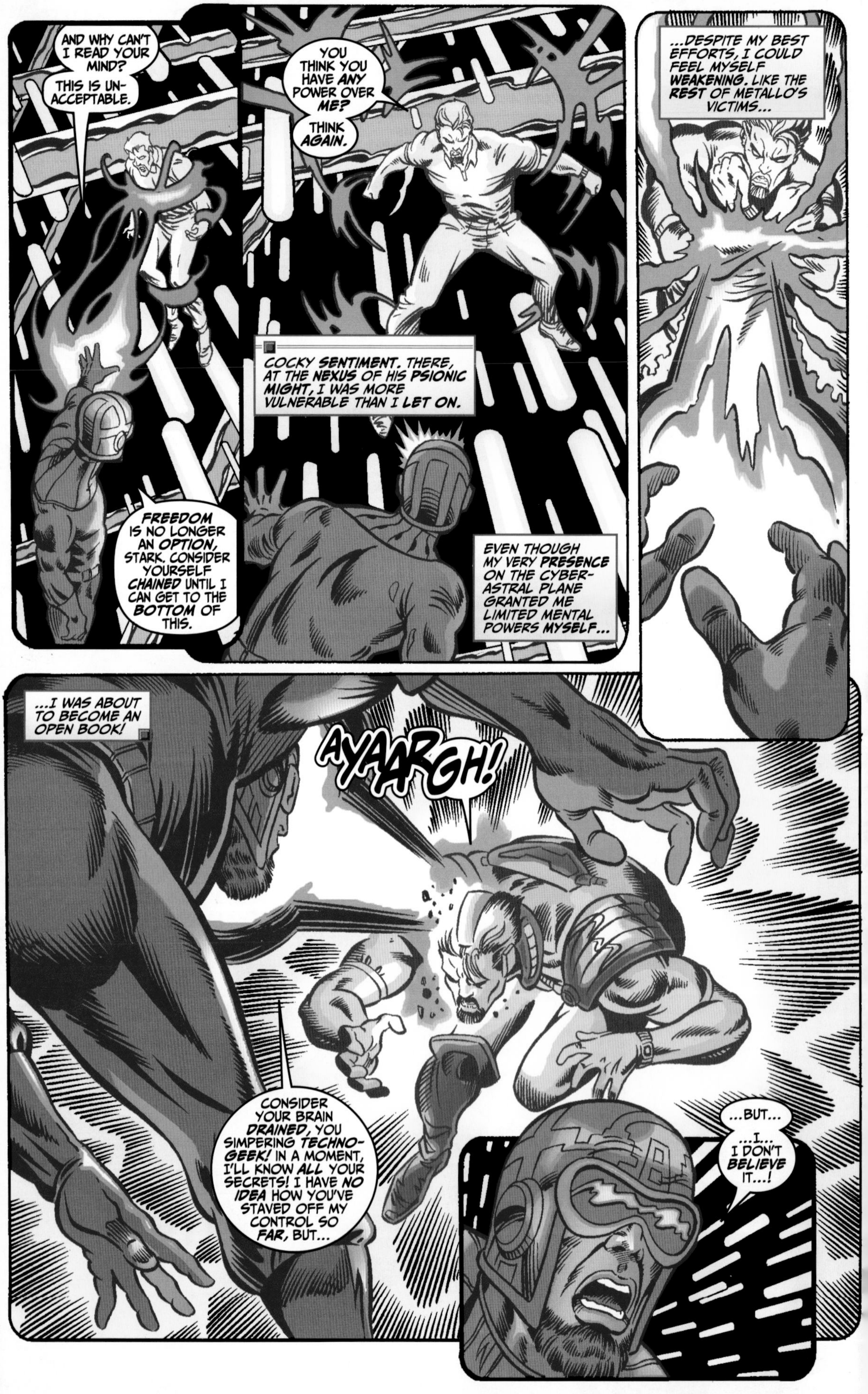
AND WHY CAN'T I READ YOUR MIND?
THIS IS UN-ACCEPTABLE.
FREEDOM IS NO LONGER AN OPTION, STARK. CONSIDER YOURSELF CHAINED UNTIL I CAN GET TO THE BOTTOM OF THIS.
YOU THINK YOU HAVE ANY POWER OVER ME?
THINK AGAIN.
COCKY SENTIMENT. THERE, AT THE NEXUS OF HIS PSIONIC MIGHT, I WAS MORE VULNERABLE THAN I LET ON.
EVEN THOUGH MY VERY PRESENCE ON THE CYBER-ASTRAL PLANE GRANTED ME LIMITED MENTAL POWERS MYSELF...
...DESPITE MY BEST EFFORTS, I COULD FEEL MYSELF WEAKENING. LIKE THE REST OF METALLO'S VICTIMS...
...I WAS ABOUT TO BECOME AN OPEN BOOK!
AYAARGH!
CONSIDER YOUR BRAIN DRAINED, YOU SIMPERING TECHNO-GEEK! IN A MOMENT, I'LL KNOW ALL YOUR SECRETS! I HAVE NO IDEA HOW YOU'VE STAVED OFF MY CONTROL SO FAR, BUT...
...BUT... ...I... I DON'T BELIEVE IT...!

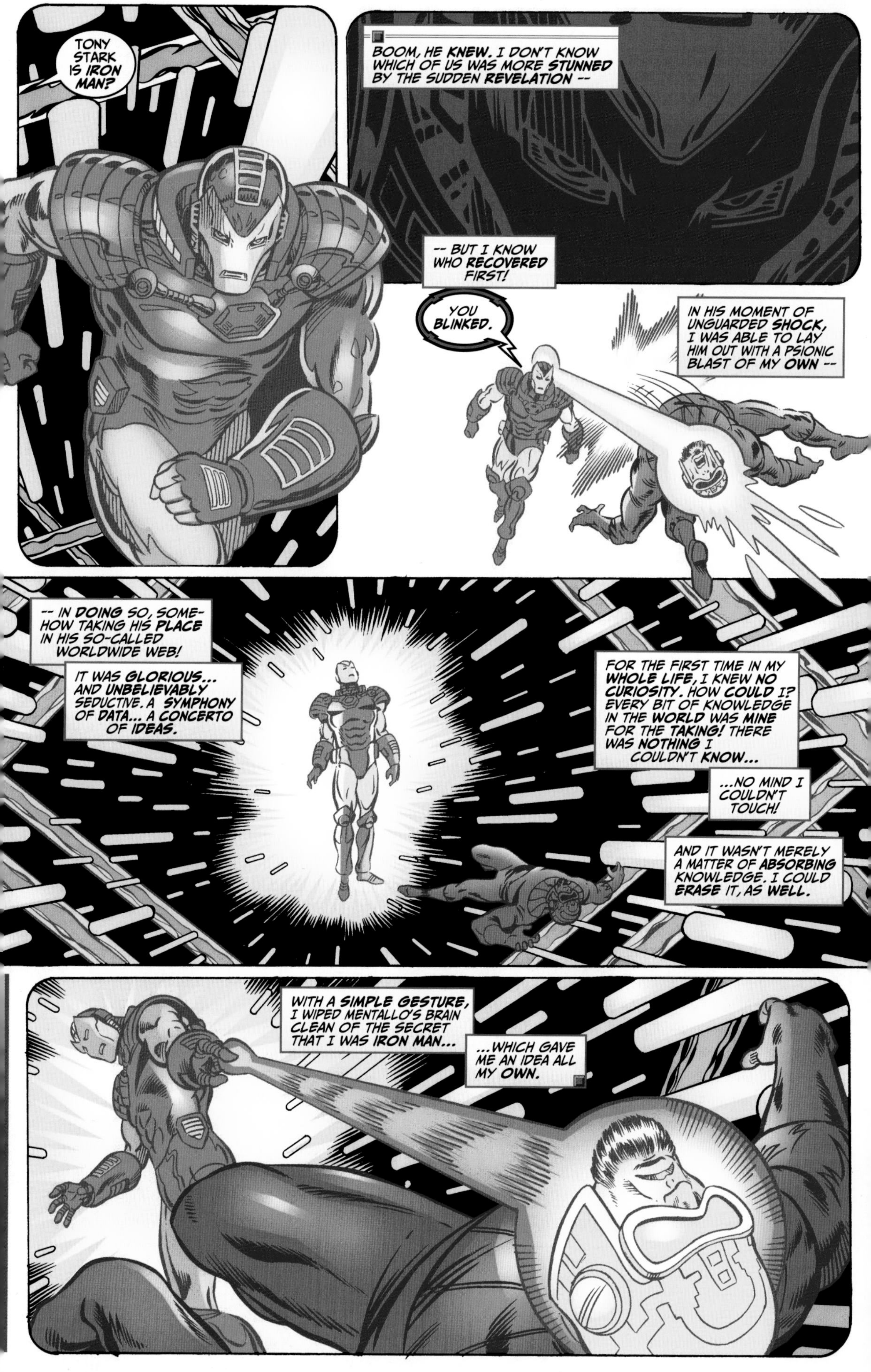
TONY STARK IS IRON MAN?
BOOM, HE KNEW. I DON'T KNOW WHICH OF US WAS MORE STUNNED BY THE SUDDEN REVELATION --
-- BUT I KNOW WHO RECOVERED FIRST!
YOU BLINKED.
IN HIS MOMENT OF UNGUARDED SHOCK, I WAS ABLE TO LAY HIM OUT WITH A PSIONIC BLAST OF MY OWN --
-- IN DOING SO, SOMEHOW TAKING HIS PLACE IN HIS SO-CALLED WORLDWIDE WEB!
IT WAS GLORIOUS... AND UNBELIEVABLY SEDUCTIVE. A SYMPHONY OF DATA... A CONCERTO OF IDEAS.
FOR THE FIRST TIME IN MY WHOLE LIFE, I KNEW NO CURIOSITY. HOW COULD I? EVERY BIT OF KNOWLEDGE IN THE WORLD WAS MINE FOR THE TAKING! THERE WAS NOTHING I COULDN'T KNOW...
...NO MIND I COULDN'T TOUCH!
AND IT WASN'T MERELY A MATTER OF ABSORBING KNOWLEDGE. I COULD ERASE IT, AS WELL.
WITH A SIMPLE GESTURE, I WIPED MENTALLO'S BRAIN CLEAN OF THE SECRET THAT I WAS IRON MAN...
...WHICH GAVE ME AN IDEA ALL MY OWN.

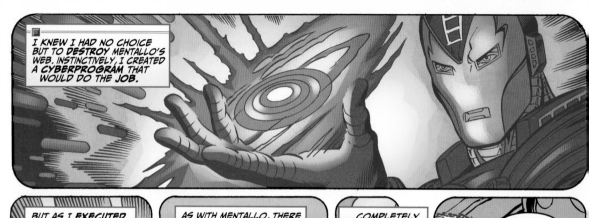

I KNEW I HAD NO CHOICE BUT TO **DESTROY** MENTALLO'S WEB. INSTINCTIVELY, I CREATED A **CYBERPROGRAM** THAT WOULD DO THE **JOB.**

BUT AS I **EXECUTED** IT, I GAVE IT A **SECONDARY** FUNCTION.

AS WITH MENTALLO, THERE WERE MANY... TOO MANY... PEOPLE OVER THE YEARS WHO'D LEARNED MY SECRET IDENTITY.

SPYMASTER.

THE CONTROLLER.

MOLECULE MAN. MACHINESMITH. OTHERS.

EVEN AS THE WEB UNRAVELED, MY PROGRAM ERADICATED THAT BIT OF INFORMATION FROM THEIR **MINDS...**

...COMPLETELY.

:UNNFF!:

FALLING --? WHAT HAPPENED TO --

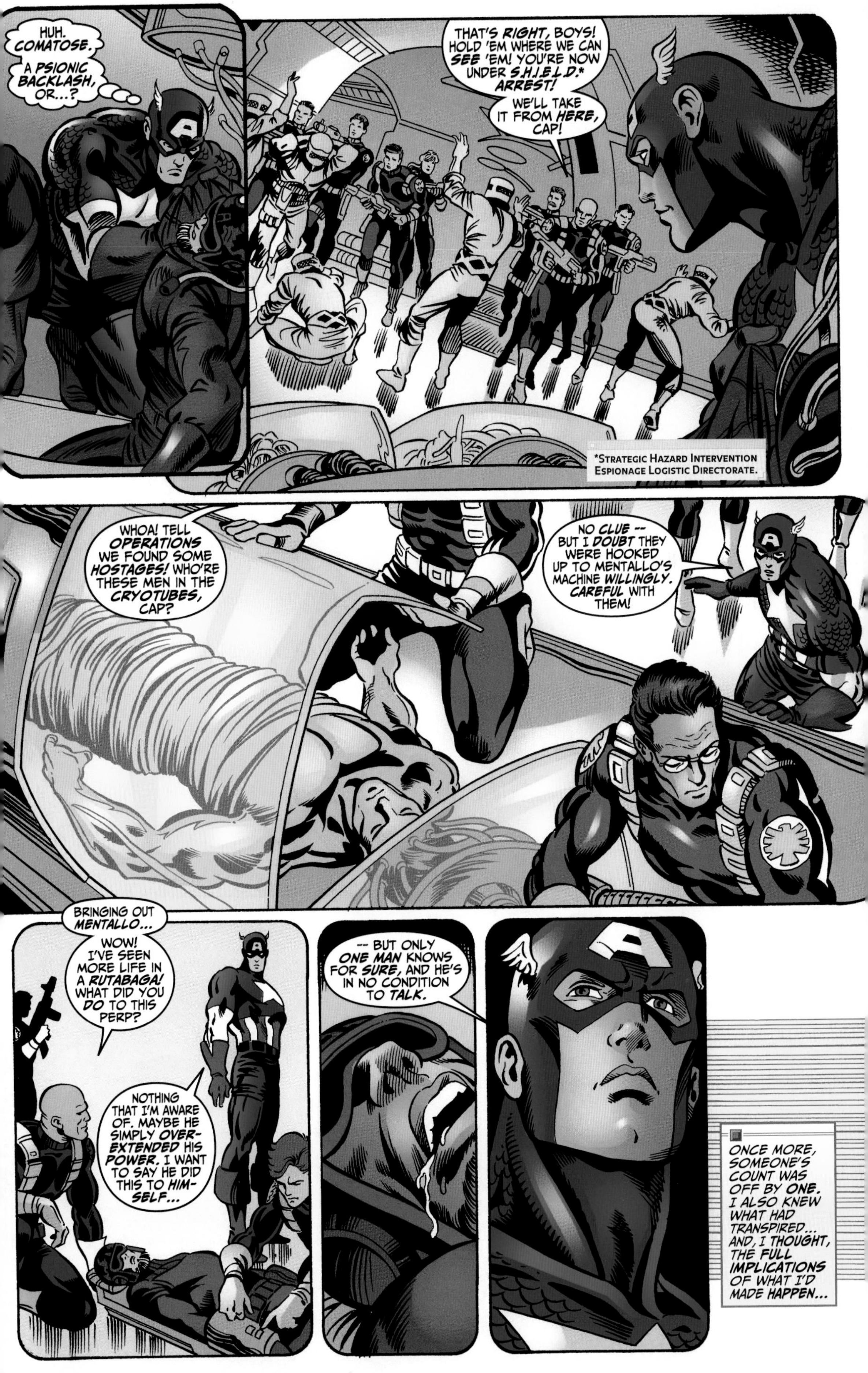
HUH. COMATOSE. A PSIONIC BACKLASH, OR...?
THAT'S RIGHT, BOYS! HOLD 'EM WHERE WE CAN SEE 'EM! YOU'RE NOW UNDER S.H.I.E.L.D.* ARREST!
WE'LL TAKE IT FROM HERE, CAP!
*STRATEGIC HAZARD INTERVENTION ESPIONAGE LOGISTIC DIRECTORATE.
WHOA! TELL OPERATIONS WE FOUND SOME HOSTAGES! WHO'RE THESE MEN IN THE CRYOTUBES, CAP?
NO CLUE -- BUT I DOUBT THEY WERE HOOKED UP TO MENTALLO'S MACHINE WILLINGLY. CAREFUL WITH THEM!
BRINGING OUT MENTALLO...
WOW! I'VE SEEN MORE LIFE IN A RUTABAGA! WHAT DID YOU DO TO THIS PERP?
NOTHING THAT I'M AWARE OF. MAYBE HE SIMPLY OVER-EXTENDED HIS POWER. I WANT TO SAY HE DID THIS TO HIM-SELF...
-- BUT ONLY ONE MAN KNOWS FOR SURE, AND HE'S IN NO CONDITION TO TALK.
ONCE MORE, SOMEONE'S COUNT WAS OFF BY ONE. I ALSO KNEW WHAT HAD TRANSPIRED... AND, I THOUGHT, THE FULL IMPLICATIONS OF WHAT I'D MADE HAPPEN...

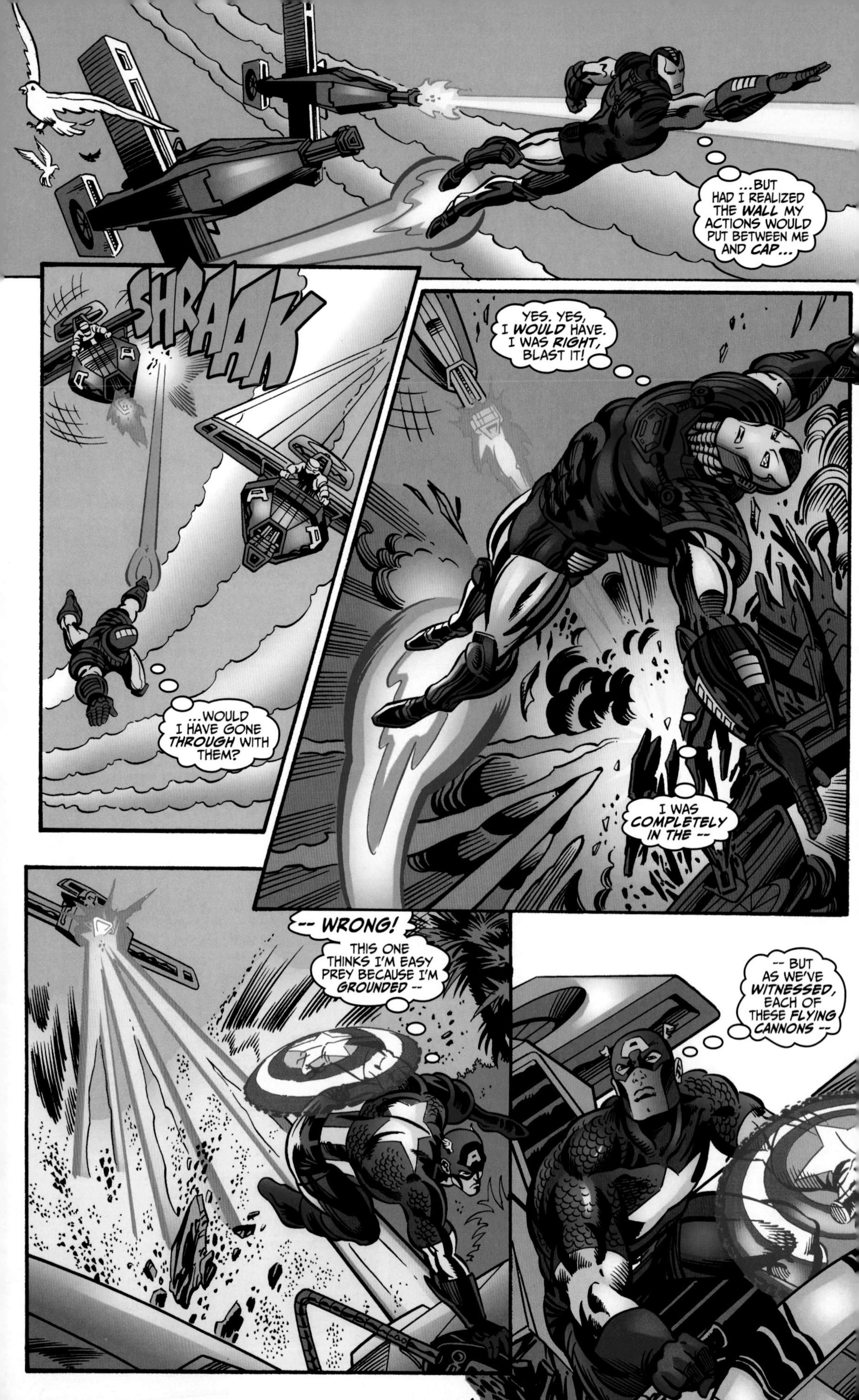
...BUT HAD I REALIZED THE WALL MY ACTIONS WOULD PUT BETWEEN ME AND CAP...
SHRAAK
...WOULD I HAVE GONE THROUGH WITH THEM?
YES. YES, I WOULD HAVE. I WAS RIGHT, BLAST IT!
I WAS COMPLETELY IN THE --
-- WRONG!
THIS ONE THINKS I'M EASY PREY BECAUSE I'M GROUNDED --
-- BUT AS WE'VE WITNESSED, EACH OF THESE FLYING CANNONS --

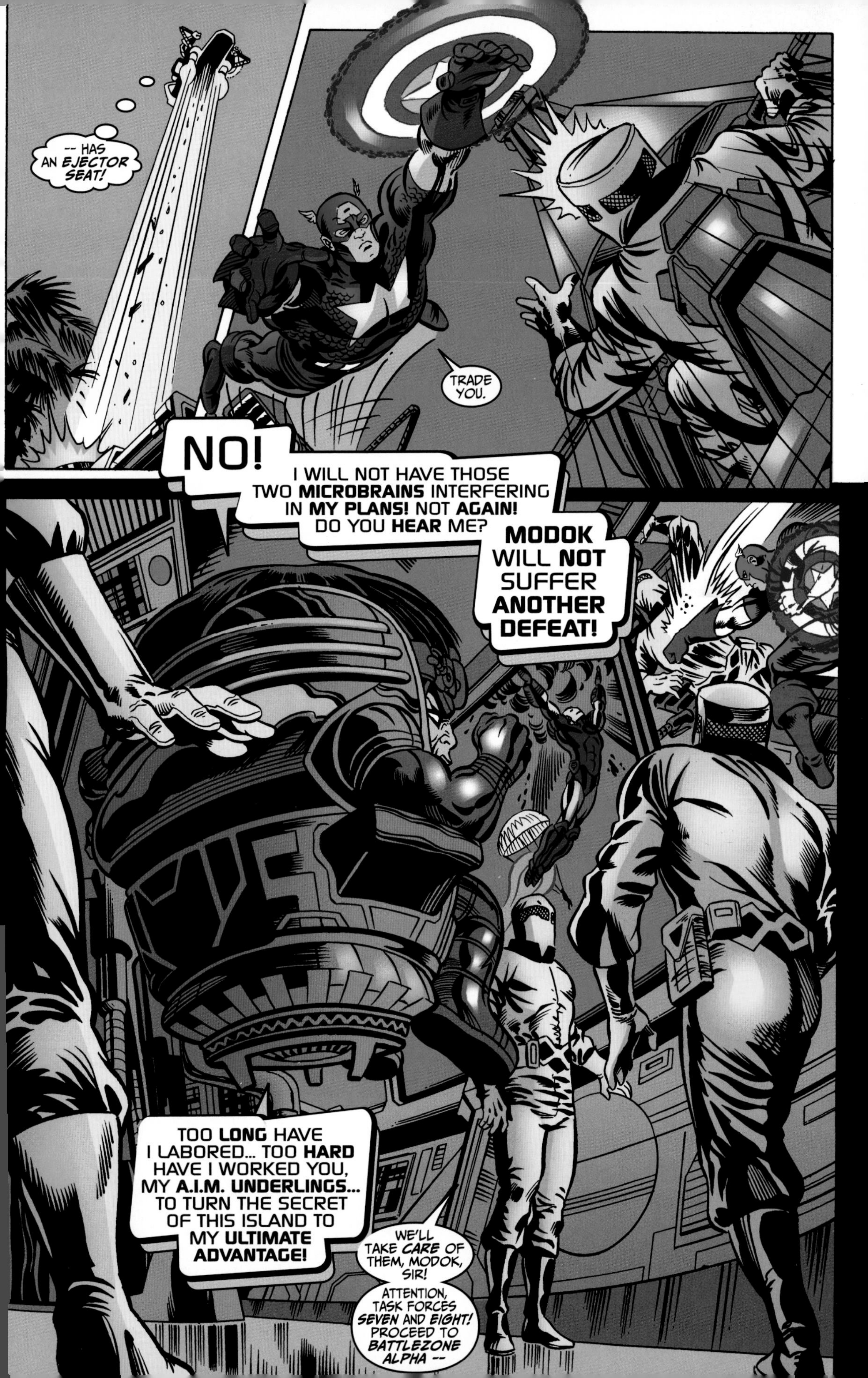
-- HAS AN EJECTOR SEAT!
TRADE YOU.
NO!
I WILL NOT HAVE THOSE TWO MICROBRAINS INTERFERING IN MY PLANS! NOT AGAIN! DO YOU HEAR ME?
MODOK WILL NOT SUFFER ANOTHER DEFEAT!
TOO LONG HAVE I LABORED... TOO HARD HAVE I WORKED YOU, MY A.I.M. UNDERLINGS... TO TURN THE SECRET OF THIS ISLAND TO MY ULTIMATE ADVANTAGE!
WE'LL TAKE CARE OF THEM, MODOK, SIR!
ATTENTION, TASK FORCES SEVEN AND EIGHT! PROCEED TO BATTLEZONE ALPHA --

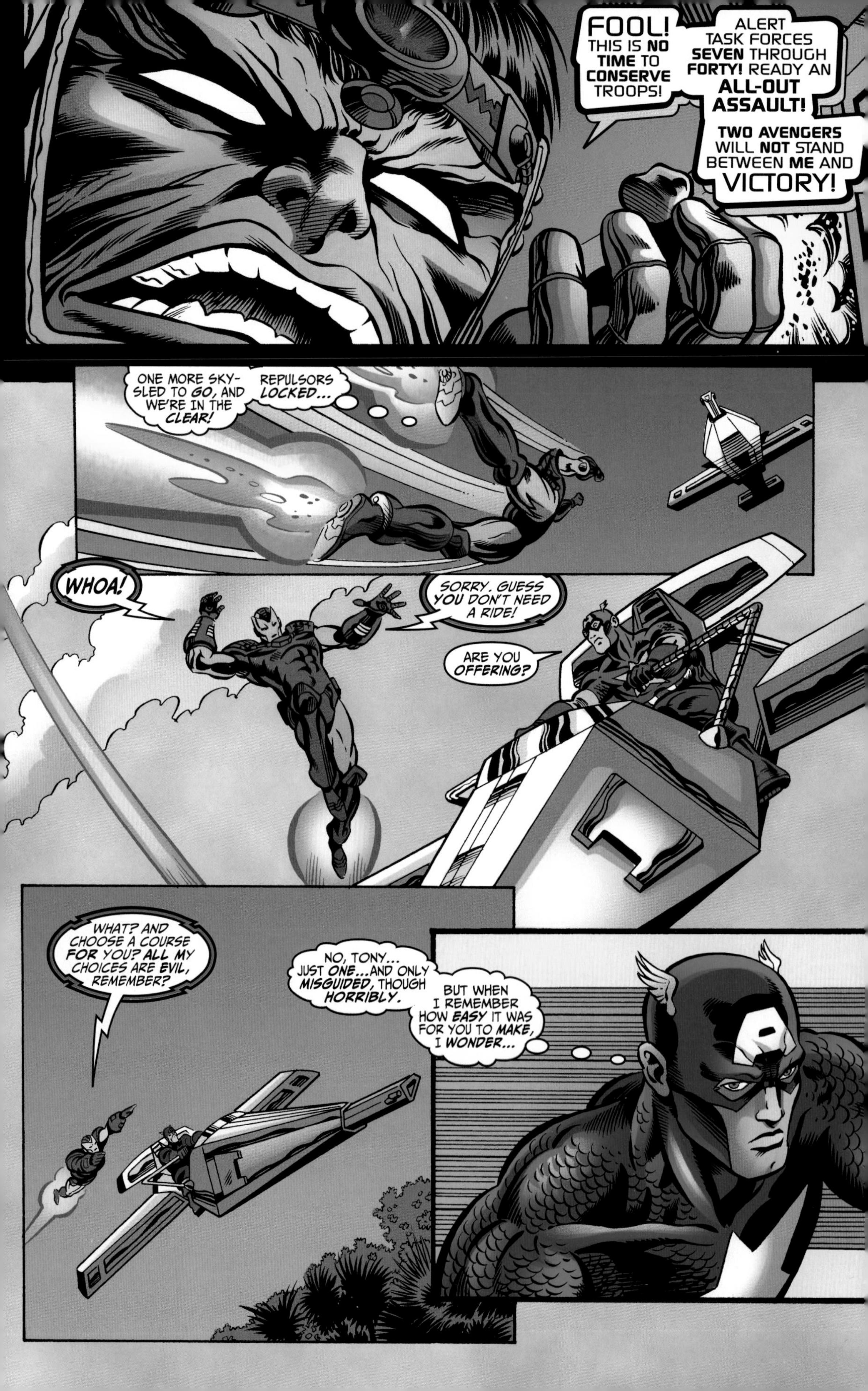
FOOL! THIS IS NO TIME TO CONSERVE TROOPS!
ALERT TASK FORCES SEVEN THROUGH FORTY! READY AN ALL-OUT ASSAULT!
TWO AVENGERS WILL NOT STAND BETWEEN ME AND VICTORY!
ONE MORE SKY-SLED TO GO, AND WE'RE IN THE CLEAR!
REPULSORS LOCKED...
WHOA!
SORRY. GUESS YOU DON'T NEED A RIDE!
ARE YOU OFFERING?
WHAT? AND CHOOSE A COURSE FOR YOU? ALL MY CHOICES ARE EVIL, REMEMBER?
NO, TONY... JUST ONE...AND ONLY MISGUIDED, THOUGH HORRIBLY.
BUT WHEN I REMEMBER HOW EASY IT WAS FOR YOU TO MAKE, I WONDER...

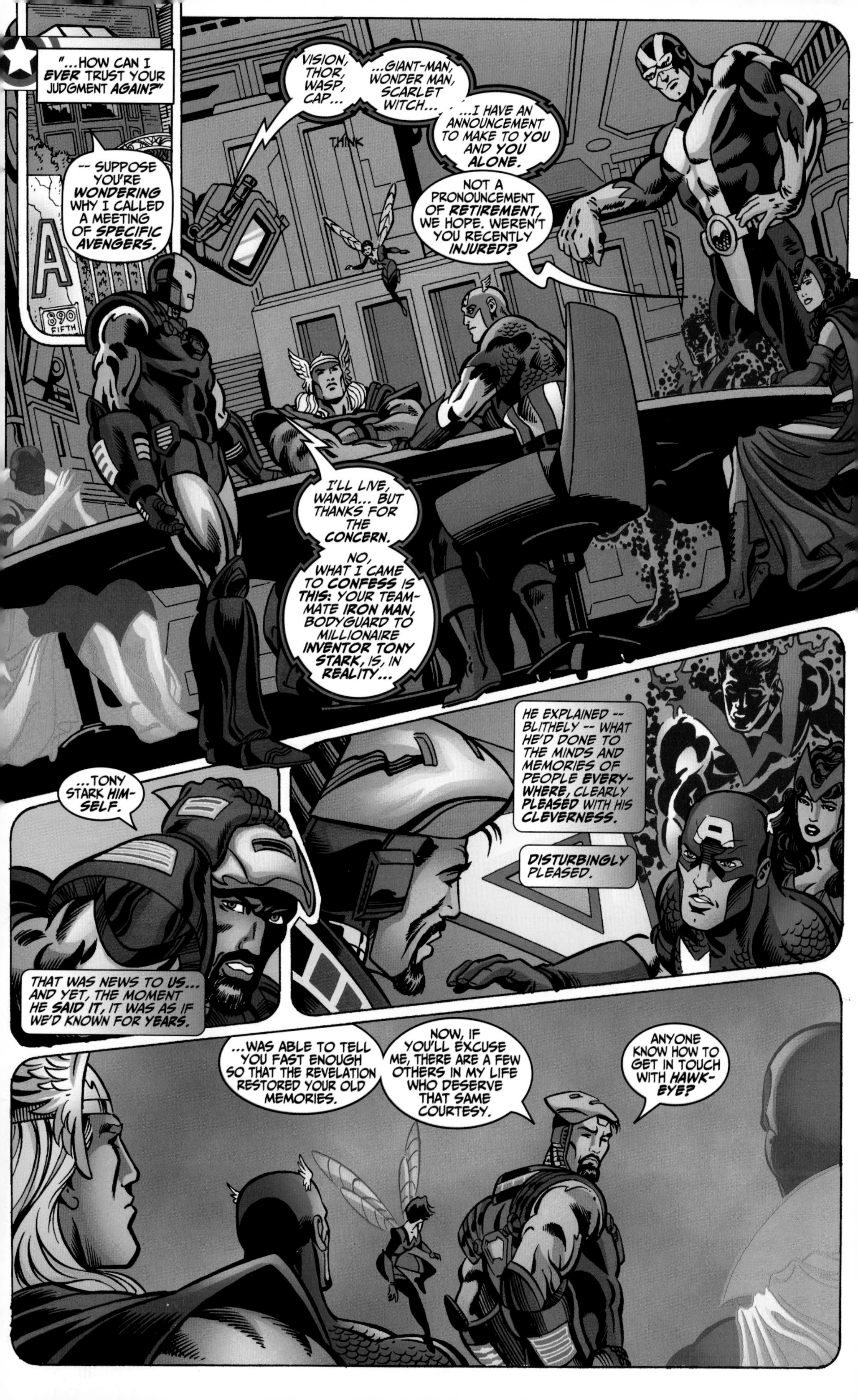
"...HOW CAN I EVER TRUST YOUR JUDGMENT AGAIN?"
-- SUPPOSE YOU'RE WONDERING WHY I CALLED A MEETING OF SPECIFIC AVENGERS.
VISION, THOR, WASP, CAP...
...GIANT-MAN, WONDER MAN, SCARLET WITCH...
...I HAVE AN ANNOUNCEMENT TO MAKE TO YOU AND YOU ALONE.
NOT A PRONOUNCEMENT OF RETIREMENT, WE HOPE. WEREN'T YOU RECENTLY INJURED?
I'LL LIVE, WANDA... BUT THANKS FOR THE CONCERN.
NO, WHAT I CAME TO CONFESS IS THIS: YOUR TEAMMATE IRON MAN, BODYGUARD TO MILLIONAIRE INVENTOR TONY STARK, IS, IN REALITY...
...TONY STARK HIMSELF.
THAT WAS NEWS TO US... AND YET, THE MOMENT HE SAID IT, IT WAS AS IF WE'D KNOWN FOR YEARS.
HE EXPLAINED -- BLITHELY -- WHAT HE'D DONE TO THE MINDS AND MEMORIES OF PEOPLE EVERYWHERE, CLEARLY PLEASED WITH HIS CLEVERNESS.
DISTURBINGLY PLEASED.
...WAS ABLE TO TELL YOU FAST ENOUGH SO THAT THE REVELATION RESTORED YOUR OLD MEMORIES.
NOW, IF YOU'LL EXCUSE ME, THERE ARE A FEW OTHERS IN MY LIFE WHO DESERVE THAT SAME COURTESY.
ANYONE KNOW HOW TO GET IN TOUCH WITH HAWKEYE?

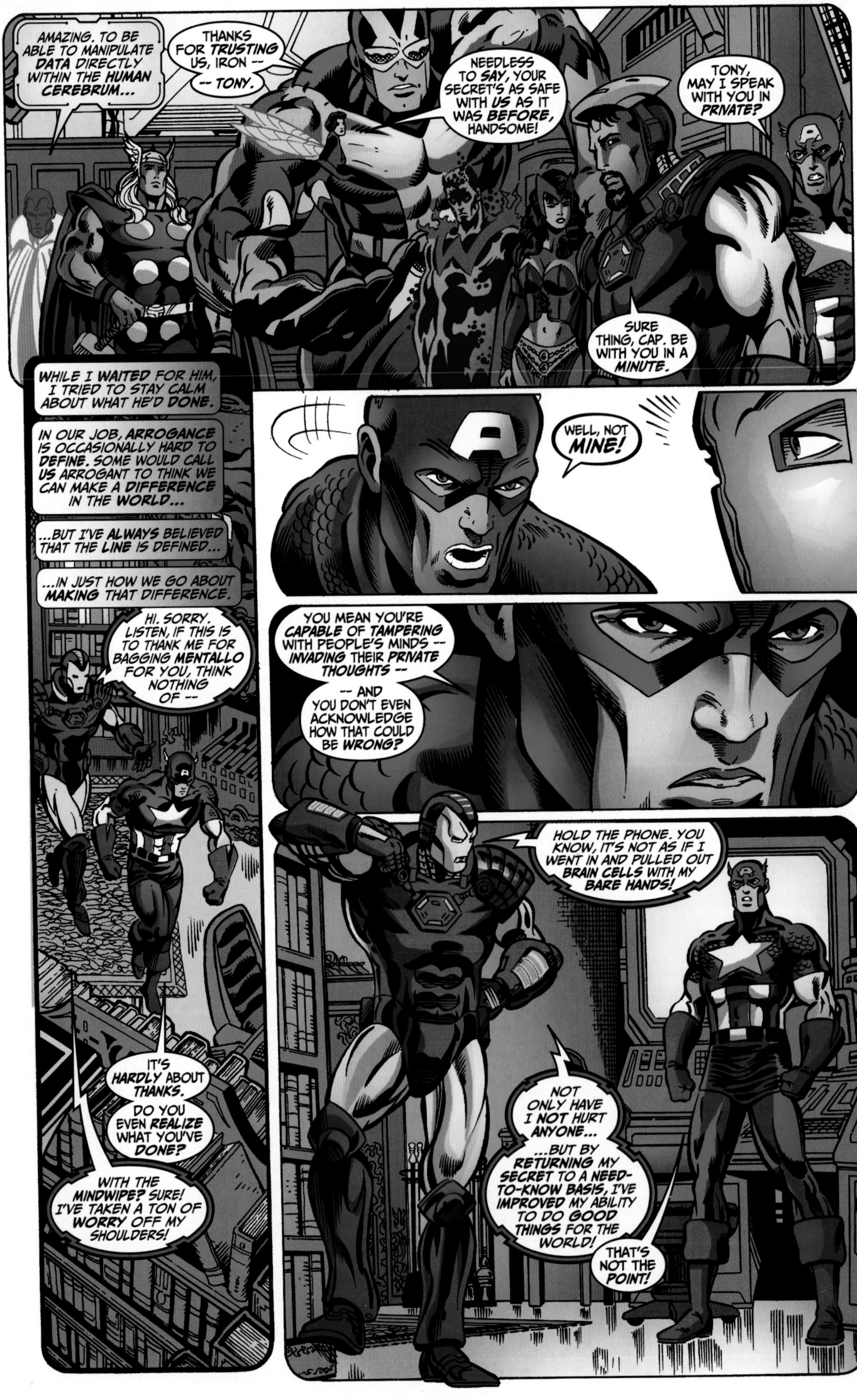
AMAZING. TO BE ABLE TO MANIPULATE DATA DIRECTLY WITHIN THE HUMAN CEREBRUM...
THANKS FOR TRUSTING US, IRON --
-- TONY.
NEEDLESS TO SAY, YOUR SECRET'S AS SAFE WITH US AS IT WAS BEFORE, HANDSOME!
TONY, MAY I SPEAK WITH YOU IN PRIVATE?
SURE THING, CAP. BE WITH YOU IN A MINUTE.
WHILE I WAITED FOR HIM, I TRIED TO STAY CALM ABOUT WHAT HE'D DONE.
IN OUR JOB, ARROGANCE IS OCCASIONALLY HARD TO DEFINE. SOME WOULD CALL US ARROGANT TO THINK WE CAN MAKE A DIFFERENCE IN THE WORLD...
...BUT I'VE ALWAYS BELIEVED THAT THE LINE IS DEFINED...
...IN JUST HOW WE GO ABOUT MAKING THAT DIFFERENCE.
HI. SORRY. LISTEN, IF THIS IS TO THANK ME FOR BAGGING MENTALLO FOR YOU, THINK NOTHING OF --
IT'S HARDLY ABOUT THANKS.
DO YOU EVEN REALIZE WHAT YOU'VE DONE?
WITH THE MINDWIPE? SURE! I'VE TAKEN A TON OF WORRY OFF MY SHOULDERS!
WELL, NOT MINE!
YOU MEAN YOU'RE CAPABLE OF TAMPERING WITH PEOPLE'S MINDS -- INVADING THEIR PRIVATE THOUGHTS --
-- AND YOU DON'T EVEN ACKNOWLEDGE HOW THAT COULD BE WRONG?
HOLD THE PHONE. YOU KNOW, IT'S NOT AS IF I WENT IN AND PULLED OUT BRAIN CELLS WITH MY BARE HANDS!
NOT ONLY HAVE I NOT HURT ANYONE...
...BUT BY RETURNING MY SECRET TO A NEED-TO-KNOW BASIS, I'VE IMPROVED MY ABILITY TO DO GOOD THINGS FOR THE WORLD!
THAT'S NOT THE POINT!

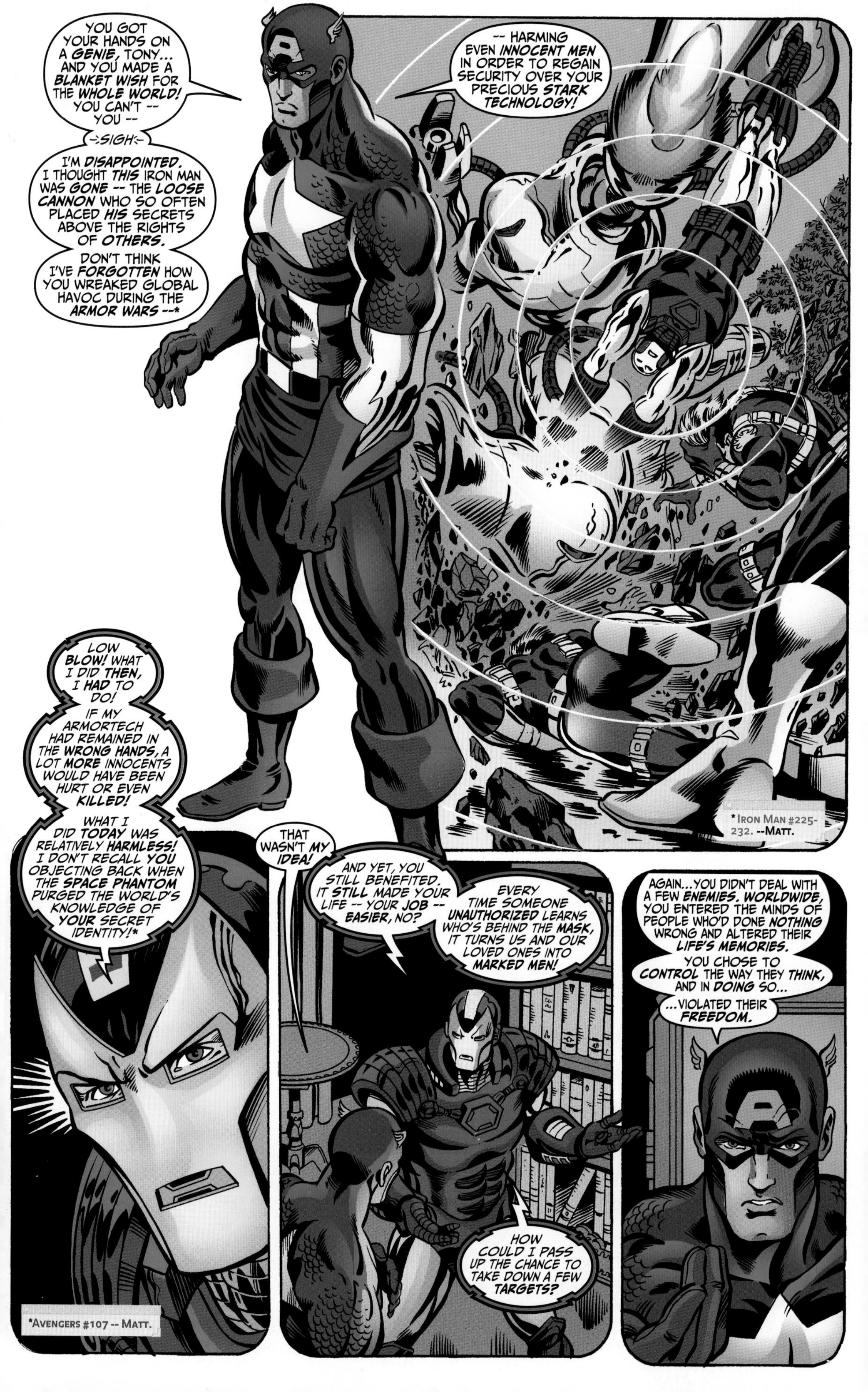
YOU GOT YOUR HANDS ON A GENIE, TONY... AND YOU MADE A BLANKET WISH FOR THE WHOLE WORLD! YOU CAN'T -- YOU --
SIGH
I'M DISAPPOINTED. I THOUGHT THIS IRON MAN WAS GONE -- THE LOOSE CANNON WHO SO OFTEN PLACED HIS SECRETS ABOVE THE RIGHTS OF OTHERS.
DON'T THINK I'VE FORGOTTEN HOW YOU WREAKED GLOBAL HAVOC DURING THE ARMOR WARS --*
-- HARMING EVEN INNOCENT MEN IN ORDER TO REGAIN SECURITY OVER YOUR PRECIOUS STARK TECHNOLOGY!
*IRON MAN #225-232. --MATT.
LOW BLOW! WHAT I DID THEN, I HAD TO DO!
IF MY ARMORTECH HAD REMAINED IN THE WRONG HANDS, A LOT MORE INNOCENTS WOULD HAVE BEEN HURT OR EVEN KILLED!
WHAT I DID TODAY WAS RELATIVELY HARMLESS! I DON'T RECALL YOU OBJECTING BACK WHEN THE SPACE PHANTOM PURGED THE WORLD'S KNOWLEDGE OF YOUR SECRET IDENTITY!*
*AVENGERS #107 -- MATT.
THAT WASN'T MY IDEA!
AND YET, YOU STILL BENEFITED. IT STILL MADE YOUR LIFE -- YOUR JOB -- EASIER, NO?
EVERY TIME SOMEONE UNAUTHORIZED LEARNS WHO'S BEHIND THE MASK, IT TURNS US AND OUR LOVED ONES INTO MARKED MEN!
HOW COULD I PASS UP THE CHANCE TO TAKE DOWN A FEW TARGETS?
AGAIN...YOU DIDN'T DEAL WITH A FEW ENEMIES. WORLDWIDE, YOU ENTERED THE MINDS OF PEOPLE WHO'D DONE NOTHING WRONG AND ALTERED THEIR LIFE'S MEMORIES.
YOU CHOSE TO CONTROL THE WAY THEY THINK, AND IN DOING SO...
...VIOLATED THEIR FREEDOM.

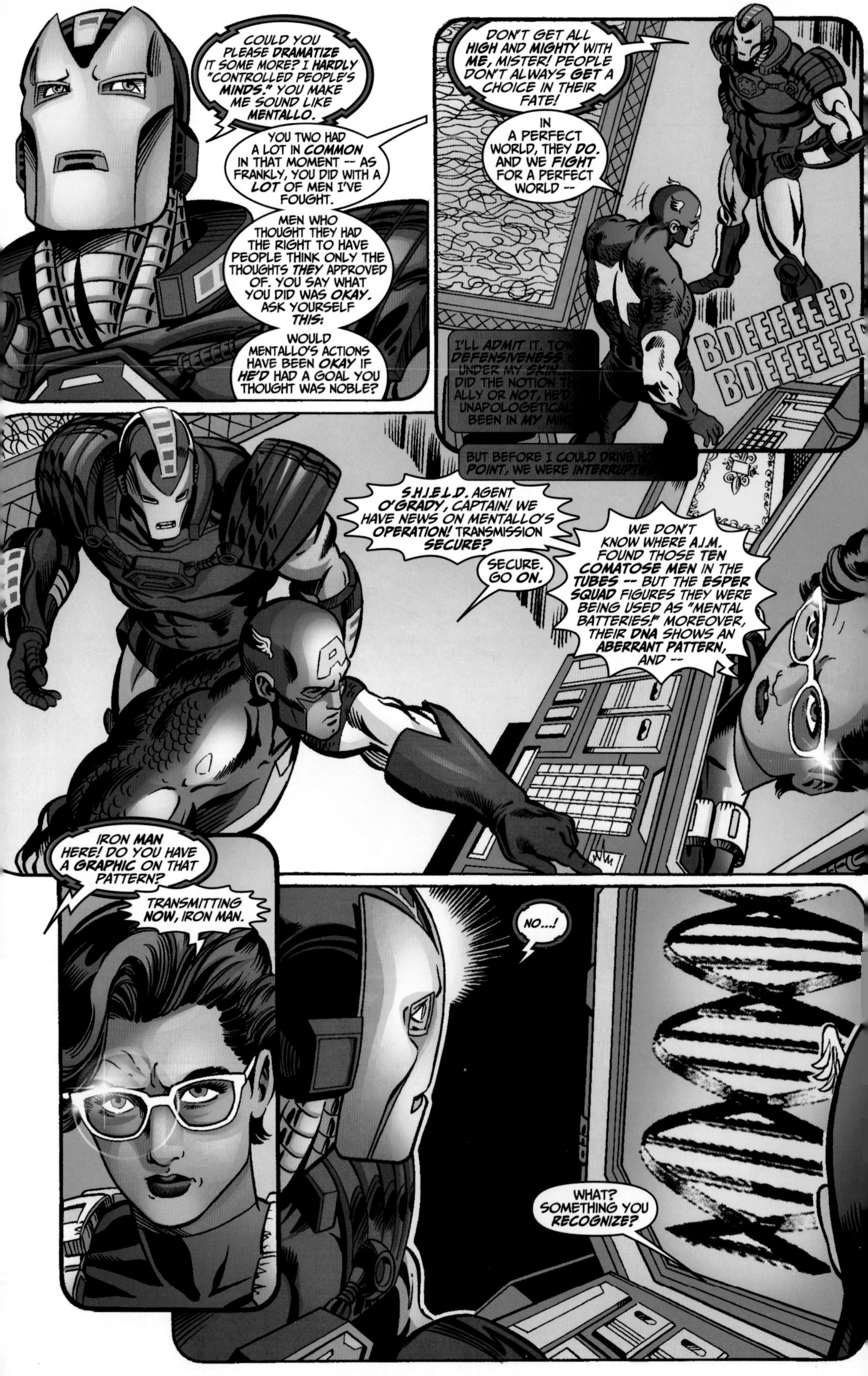

COULD YOU PLEASE DRAMATIZE IT SOME MORE? I HARDLY "CONTROLLED PEOPLE'S MINDS." YOU MAKE ME SOUND LIKE MENTALLO.
YOU TWO HAD A LOT IN COMMON IN THAT MOMENT -- AS FRANKLY, YOU DID WITH A LOT OF MEN I'VE FOUGHT.
MEN WHO THOUGHT THEY HAD THE RIGHT TO HAVE PEOPLE THINK ONLY THE THOUGHTS THEY APPROVED OF. YOU SAY WHAT YOU DID WAS OKAY. ASK YOURSELF THIS:
WOULD MENTALLO'S ACTIONS HAVE BEEN OKAY IF HE'D HAD A GOAL YOU THOUGHT WAS NOBLE?
DON'T GET ALL HIGH AND MIGHTY WITH ME, MISTER! PEOPLE DON'T ALWAYS GET A CHOICE IN THEIR FATE!
IN A PERFECT WORLD, THEY DO. AND WE FIGHT FOR A PERFECT WORLD --
BDEEEEEEP
BDEEEEEEE
I'LL ADMIT IT. TO DEFENSIVENESS UNDER MY SKIN... DID THE NOTION ALLY OR NOT, HE UNAPOLOGETICA BEEN IN MY MI
BUT BEFORE I COULD DRIVE POINT, WE WERE INTERRUPT
S.H.I.E.L.D. AGENT O'GRADY, CAPTAIN! WE HAVE NEWS ON MENTALLO'S OPERATION! TRANSMISSION SECURE?
SECURE. GO ON.
WE DON'T KNOW WHERE A.I.M. FOUND THOSE TEN COMATOSE MEN IN THE TUBES -- BUT THE ESPER SQUAD FIGURES THEY WERE BEING USED AS "MENTAL BATTERIES!" MOREOVER, THEIR DNA SHOWS AN ABERRANT PATTERN, AND --
IRON MAN HERE! DO YOU HAVE A GRAPHIC ON THAT PATTERN?
TRANSMITTING NOW, IRON MAN.
NO...!
WHAT? SOMETHING YOU RECOGNIZE?

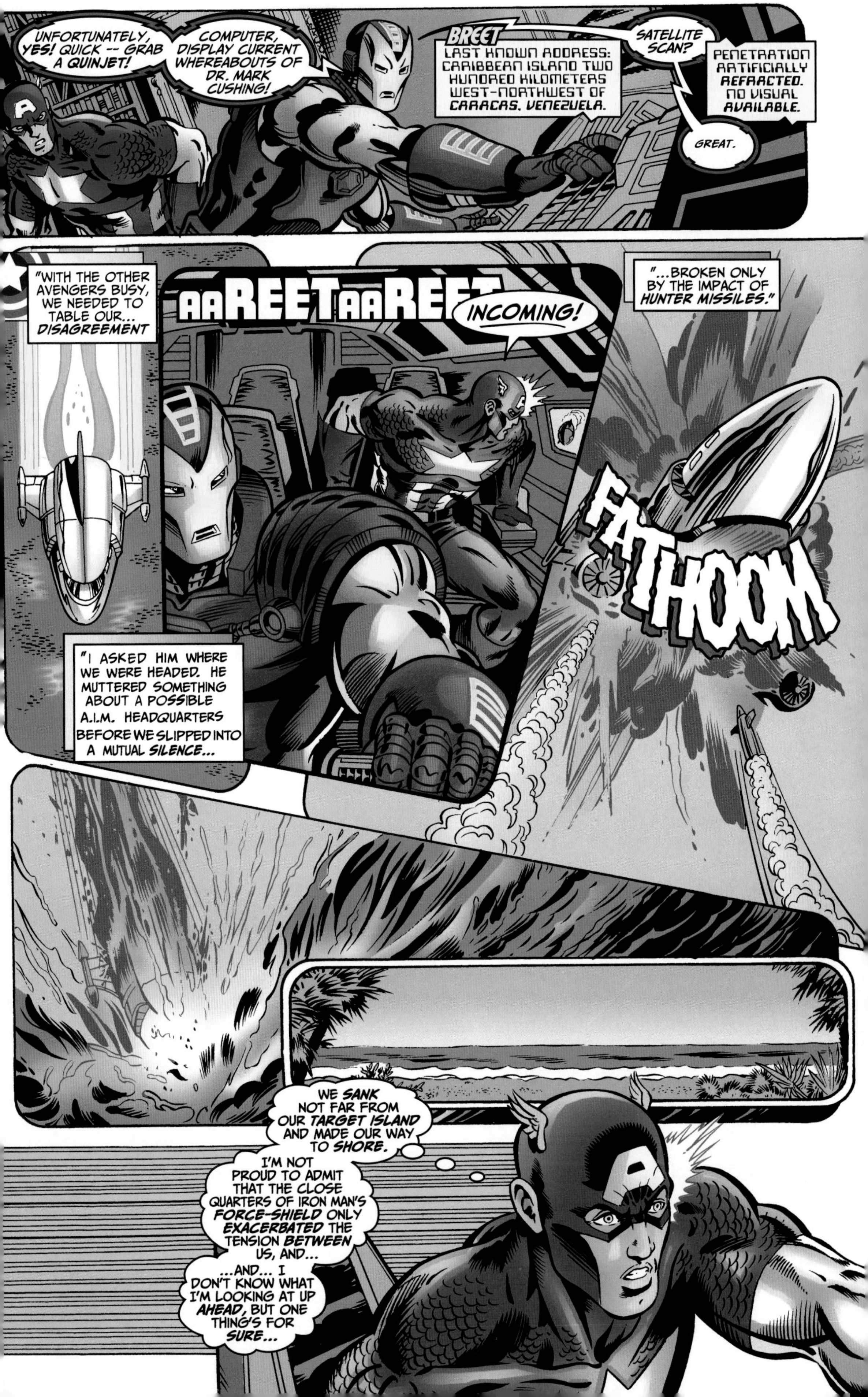
UNFORTUNATELY, YES! QUICK -- GRAB A QUINJET!
COMPUTER, DISPLAY CURRENT WHEREABOUTS OF DR. MARK CUSHING!
BREET
LAST KNOWN ADDRESS: CARIBBEAN ISLAND TWO HUNDRED KILOMETERS WEST-NORTHWEST OF CARACAS, VENEZUELA.
SATELLITE SCAN?
PENETRATION ARTIFICIALLY REFRACTED. NO VISUAL AVAILABLE.
GREAT.
"WITH THE OTHER AVENGERS BUSY, WE NEEDED TO TABLE OUR... DISAGREEMENT
AAREETAAREET
INCOMING!
"I ASKED HIM WHERE WE WERE HEADED. HE MUTTERED SOMETHING ABOUT A POSSIBLE A.I.M. HEADQUARTERS BEFORE WE SLIPPED INTO A MUTUAL SILENCE...
"...BROKEN ONLY BY THE IMPACT OF HUNTER MISSILES."
FATHOOM
WE SANK NOT FAR FROM OUR TARGET ISLAND AND MADE OUR WAY TO SHORE.
I'M NOT PROUD TO ADMIT THAT THE CLOSE QUARTERS OF IRON MAN'S FORCE-SHIELD ONLY EXACERBATED THE TENSION BETWEEN US, AND...
...AND... I DON'T KNOW WHAT I'M LOOKING AT UP AHEAD, BUT ONE THING'S FOR SURE...

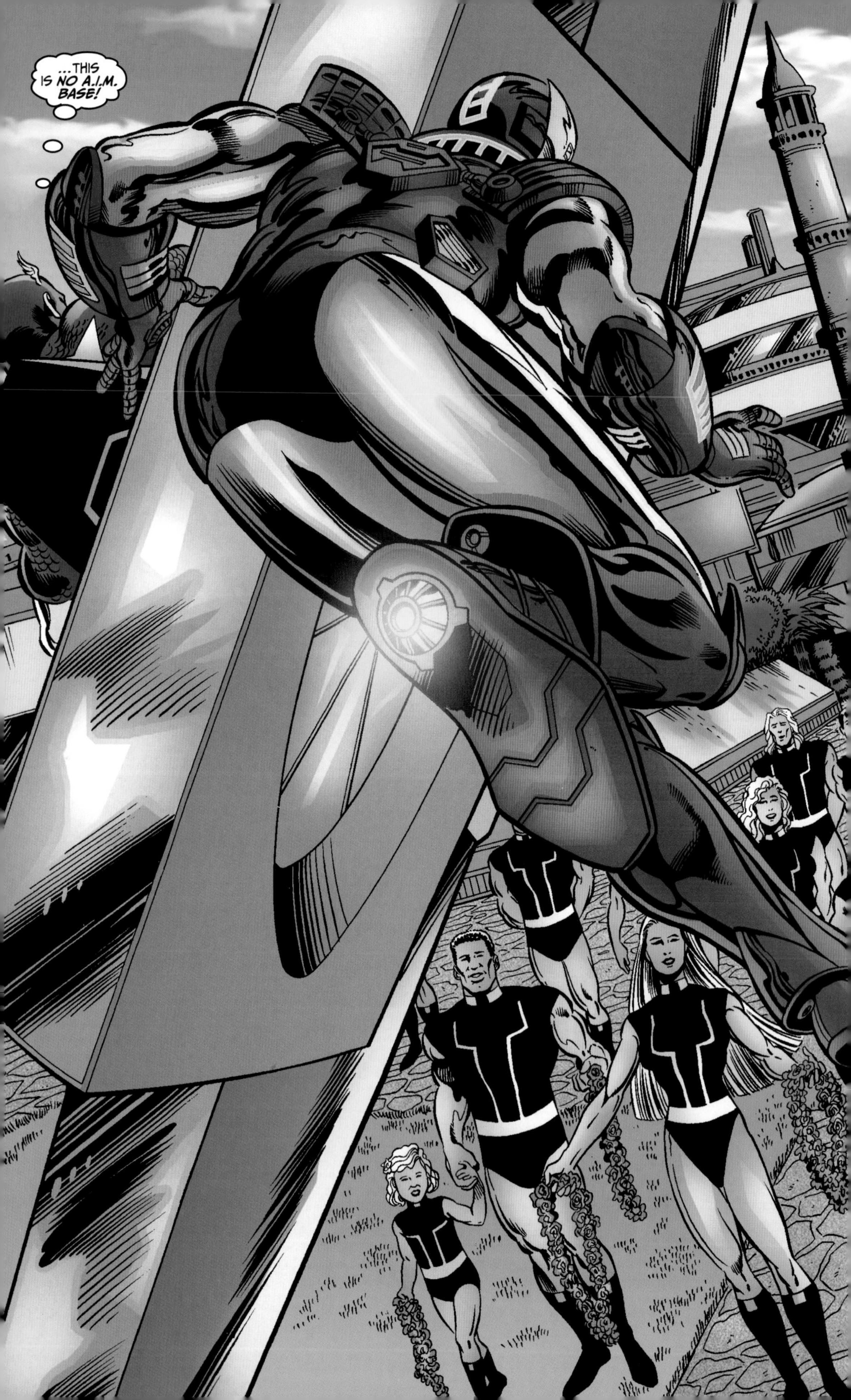

...THIS IS NO A.I.M. BASE!

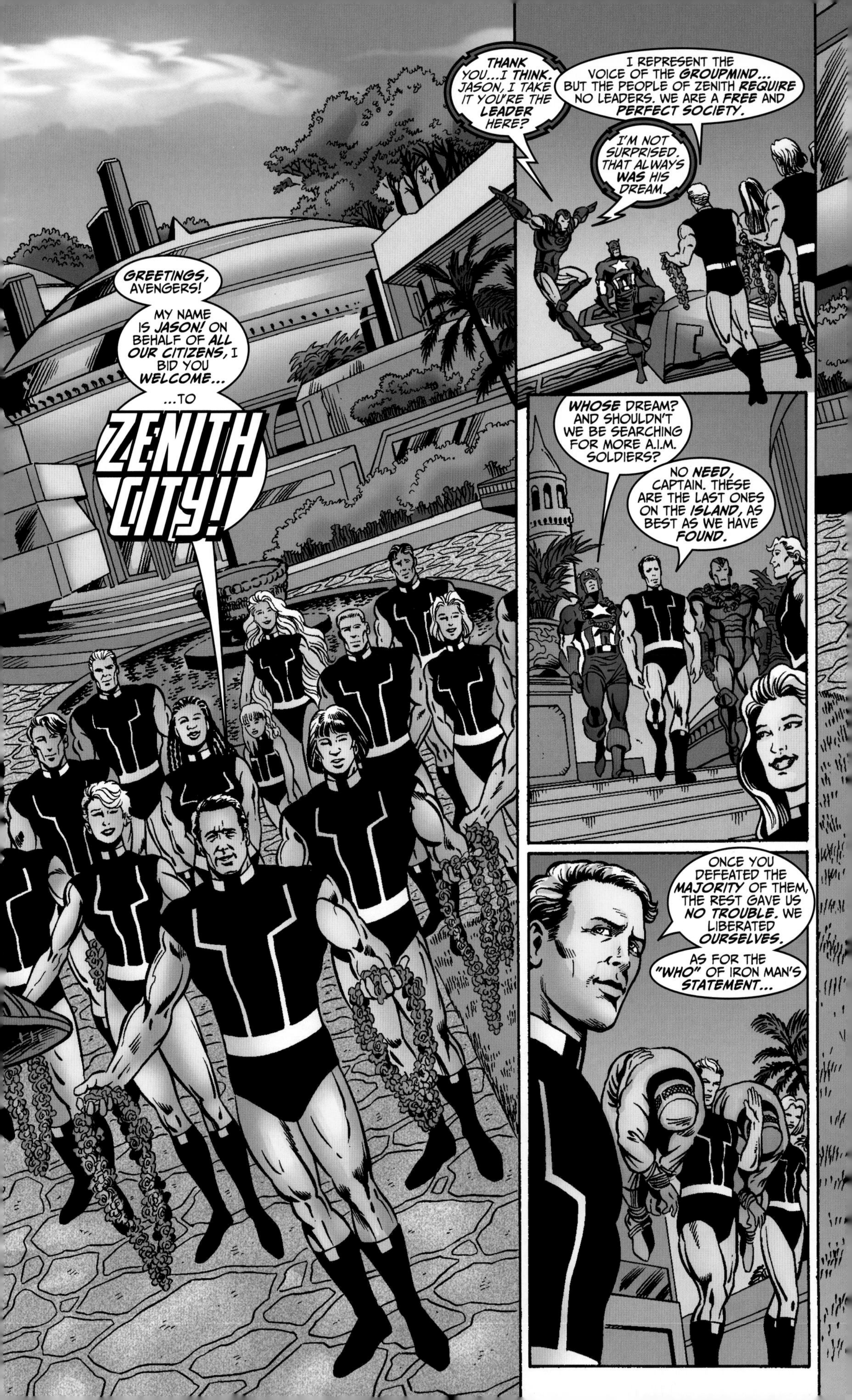
GREETINGS, AVENGERS!
MY NAME IS JASON! ON BEHALF OF ALL OUR CITIZENS, I BID YOU WELCOME...
...TO
ZENITH CITY!
THANK YOU...I THINK. JASON, I TAKE IT YOU'RE THE LEADER HERE?
I REPRESENT THE VOICE OF THE GROUPMIND... BUT THE PEOPLE OF ZENITH REQUIRE NO LEADERS. WE ARE A FREE AND PERFECT SOCIETY.
I'M NOT SURPRISED. THAT ALWAYS WAS HIS DREAM.
WHOSE DREAM? AND SHOULDN'T WE BE SEARCHING FOR MORE A.I.M. SOLDIERS?
NO NEED, CAPTAIN. THESE ARE THE LAST ONES ON THE ISLAND, AS BEST AS WE HAVE FOUND.
ONCE YOU DEFEATED THE MAJORITY OF THEM, THE REST GAVE US NO TROUBLE. WE LIBERATED OURSELVES.
AS FOR THE "WHO" OF IRON MAN'S STATEMENT...

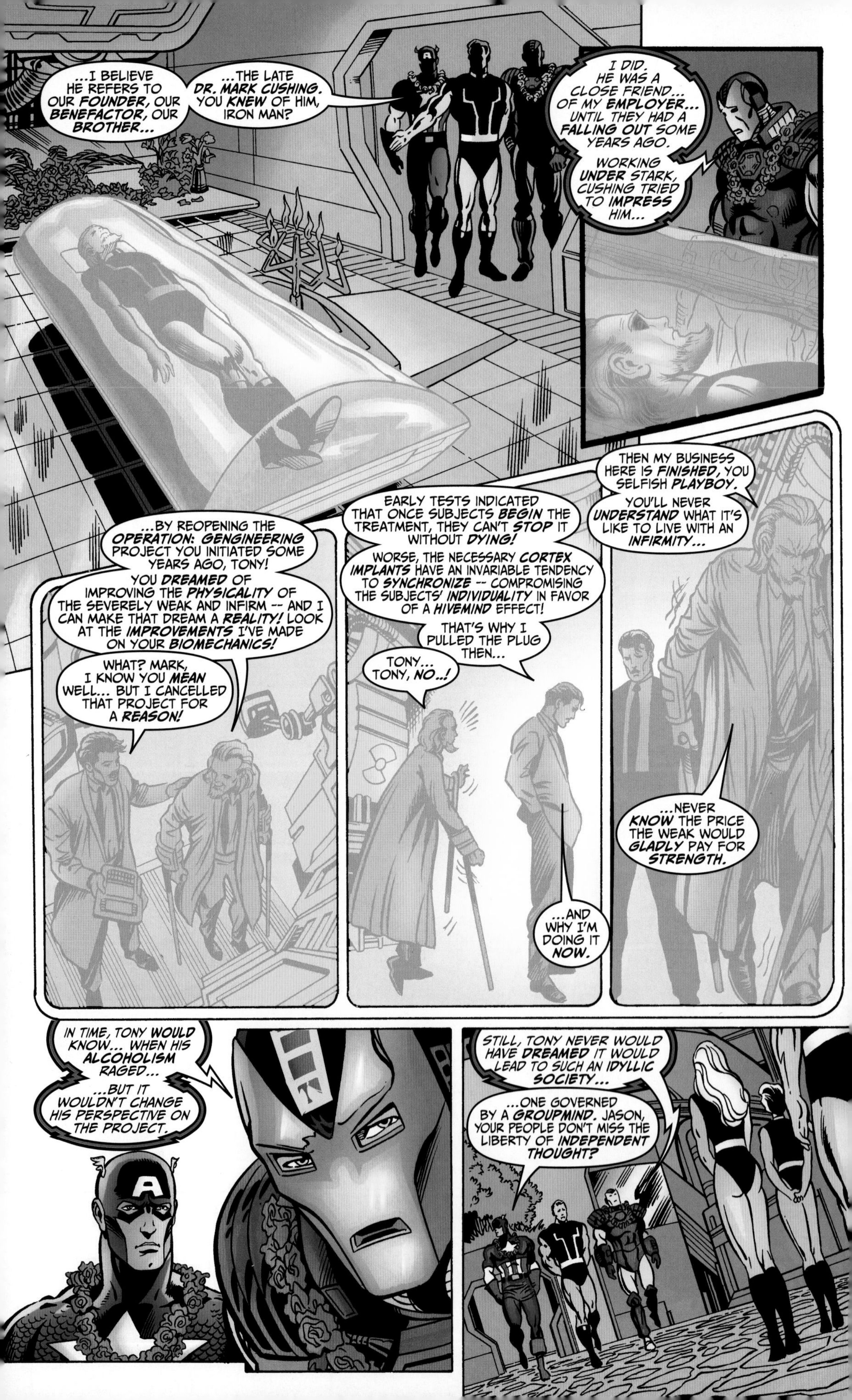
...I BELIEVE HE REFERS TO OUR FOUNDER, OUR BENEFACTOR, OUR BROTHER...
...THE LATE DR. MARK CUSHING. YOU KNEW OF HIM, IRON MAN?
I DID. HE WAS A CLOSE FRIEND... OF MY EMPLOYER... UNTIL THEY HAD A FALLING OUT SOME YEARS AGO.
WORKING UNDER STARK, CUSHING TRIED TO IMPRESS HIM...
...BY REOPENING THE OPERATION: GENGINEERING PROJECT YOU INITIATED SOME YEARS AGO, TONY!
YOU DREAMED OF IMPROVING THE PHYSICALITY OF THE SEVERELY WEAK AND INFIRM -- AND I CAN MAKE THAT DREAM A REALITY! LOOK AT THE IMPROVEMENTS I'VE MADE ON YOUR BIOMECHANICS!
WHAT? MARK, I KNOW YOU MEAN WELL... BUT I CANCELLED THAT PROJECT FOR A REASON!
EARLY TESTS INDICATED THAT ONCE SUBJECTS BEGIN THE TREATMENT, THEY CAN'T STOP IT WITHOUT DYING!
WORSE, THE NECESSARY CORTEX IMPLANTS HAVE AN INVARIABLE TENDENCY TO SYNCHRONIZE -- COMPROMISING THE SUBJECTS' INDIVIDUALITY IN FAVOR OF A HIVEMIND EFFECT!
THAT'S WHY I PULLED THE PLUG THEN...
TONY... TONY, NO...!
...AND WHY I'M DOING IT NOW.
THEN MY BUSINESS HERE IS FINISHED, YOU SELFISH PLAYBOY.
YOU'LL NEVER UNDERSTAND WHAT IT'S LIKE TO LIVE WITH AN INFIRMITY...
...NEVER KNOW THE PRICE THE WEAK WOULD GLADLY PAY FOR STRENGTH.
IN TIME, TONY WOULD KNOW... WHEN HIS ALCOHOLISM RAGED...
...BUT IT WOULDN'T CHANGE HIS PERSPECTIVE ON THE PROJECT.
STILL, TONY NEVER WOULD HAVE DREAMED IT WOULD LEAD TO SUCH AN IDYLLIC SOCIETY...
...ONE GOVERNED BY A GROUPMIND. JASON, YOUR PEOPLE DON'T MISS THE LIBERTY OF INDEPENDENT THOUGHT?

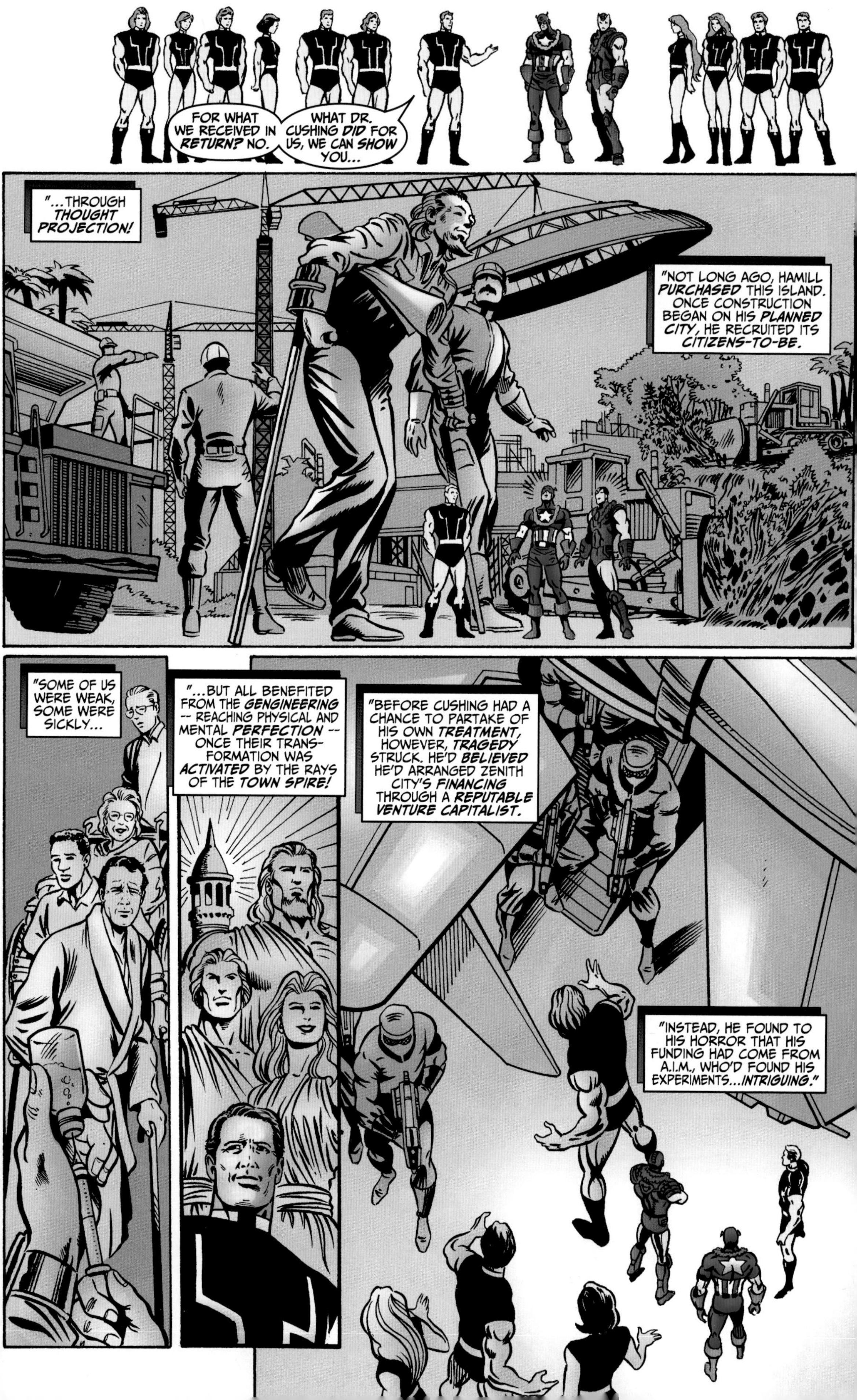

FOR WHAT WE RECEIVED IN RETURN? NO.
WHAT DR. CUSHING DID FOR US, WE CAN SHOW YOU...
"...THROUGH THOUGHT PROJECTION!
"NOT LONG AGO, HAMILL PURCHASED THIS ISLAND. ONCE CONSTRUCTION BEGAN ON HIS PLANNED CITY, HE RECRUITED ITS CITIZENS-TO-BE.
"SOME OF US WERE WEAK, SOME WERE SICKLY...
"...BUT ALL BENEFITED FROM THE GENGINEERING -- REACHING PHYSICAL AND MENTAL PERFECTION -- ONCE THEIR TRANS-FORMATION WAS ACTIVATED BY THE RAYS OF THE TOWN SPIRE!
"BEFORE CUSHING HAD A CHANCE TO PARTAKE OF HIS OWN TREATMENT, HOWEVER, TRAGEDY STRUCK. HE'D BELIEVED HE'D ARRANGED ZENITH CITY'S FINANCING THROUGH A REPUTABLE VENTURE CAPITALIST.
"INSTEAD, HE FOUND TO HIS HORROR THAT HIS FUNDING HAD COME FROM A.I.M., WHO'D FOUND HIS EXPERIMENTS...INTRIGUING."

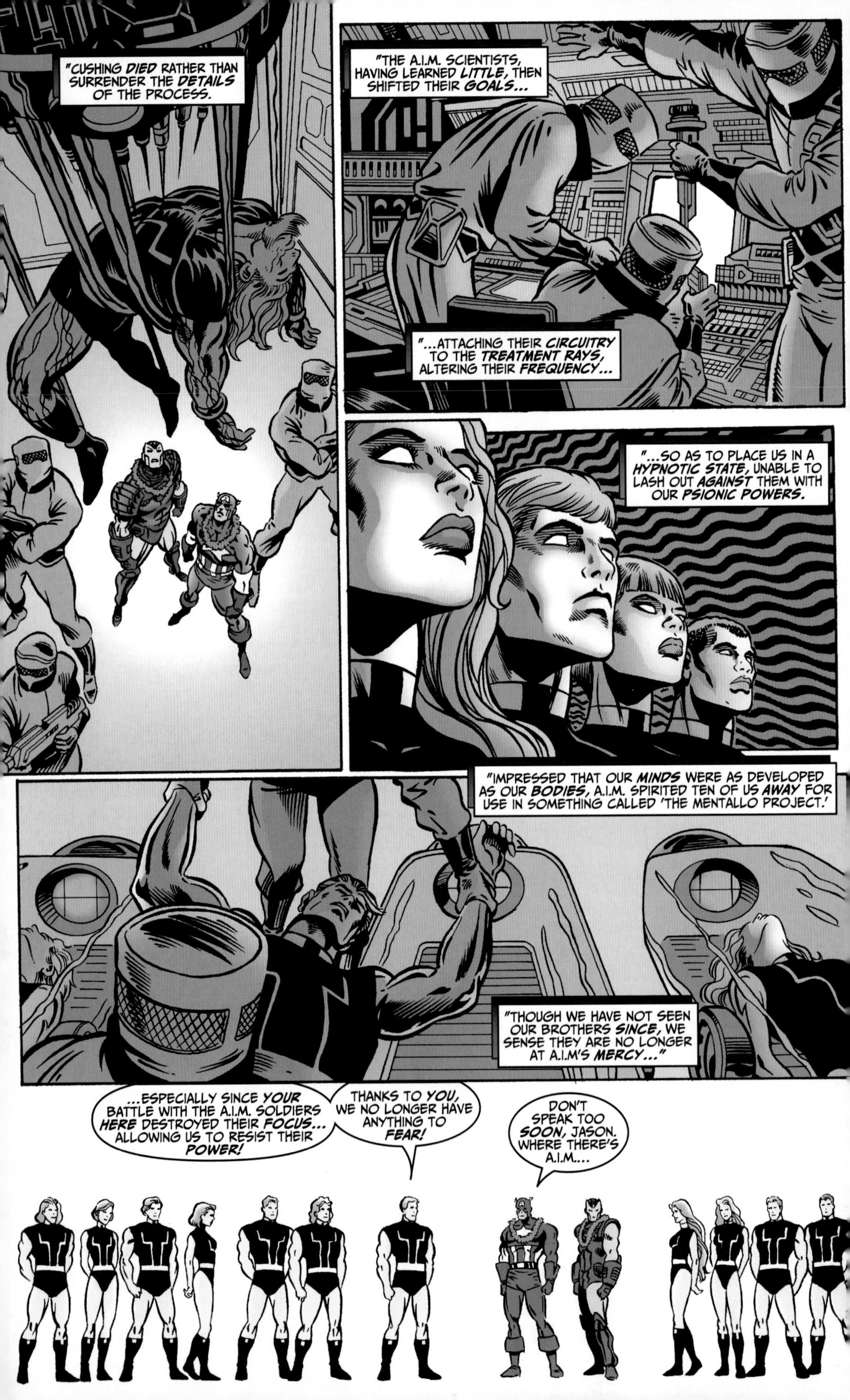
"CUSHING DIED RATHER THAN SURRENDER THE DETAILS OF THE PROCESS.
"THE A.I.M. SCIENTISTS, HAVING LEARNED LITTLE, THEN SHIFTED THEIR GOALS...
"...ATTACHING THEIR CIRCUITRY TO THE TREATMENT RAYS, ALTERING THEIR FREQUENCY...
"...SO AS TO PLACE US IN A HYPNOTIC STATE, UNABLE TO LASH OUT AGAINST THEM WITH OUR PSIONIC POWERS.
"IMPRESSED THAT OUR MINDS WERE AS DEVELOPED AS OUR BODIES, A.I.M. SPIRITED TEN OF US AWAY FOR USE IN SOMETHING CALLED 'THE MENTALLO PROJECT.'
"THOUGH WE HAVE NOT SEEN OUR BROTHERS SINCE, WE SENSE THEY ARE NO LONGER AT A.I.M'S MERCY..."
...ESPECIALLY SINCE YOUR BATTLE WITH THE A.I.M. SOLDIERS HERE DESTROYED THEIR FOCUS... ALLOWING US TO RESIST THEIR POWER!
THANKS TO YOU, WE NO LONGER HAVE ANYTHING TO FEAR!
DON'T SPEAK TOO SOON, JASON. WHERE THERE'S A.I.M...

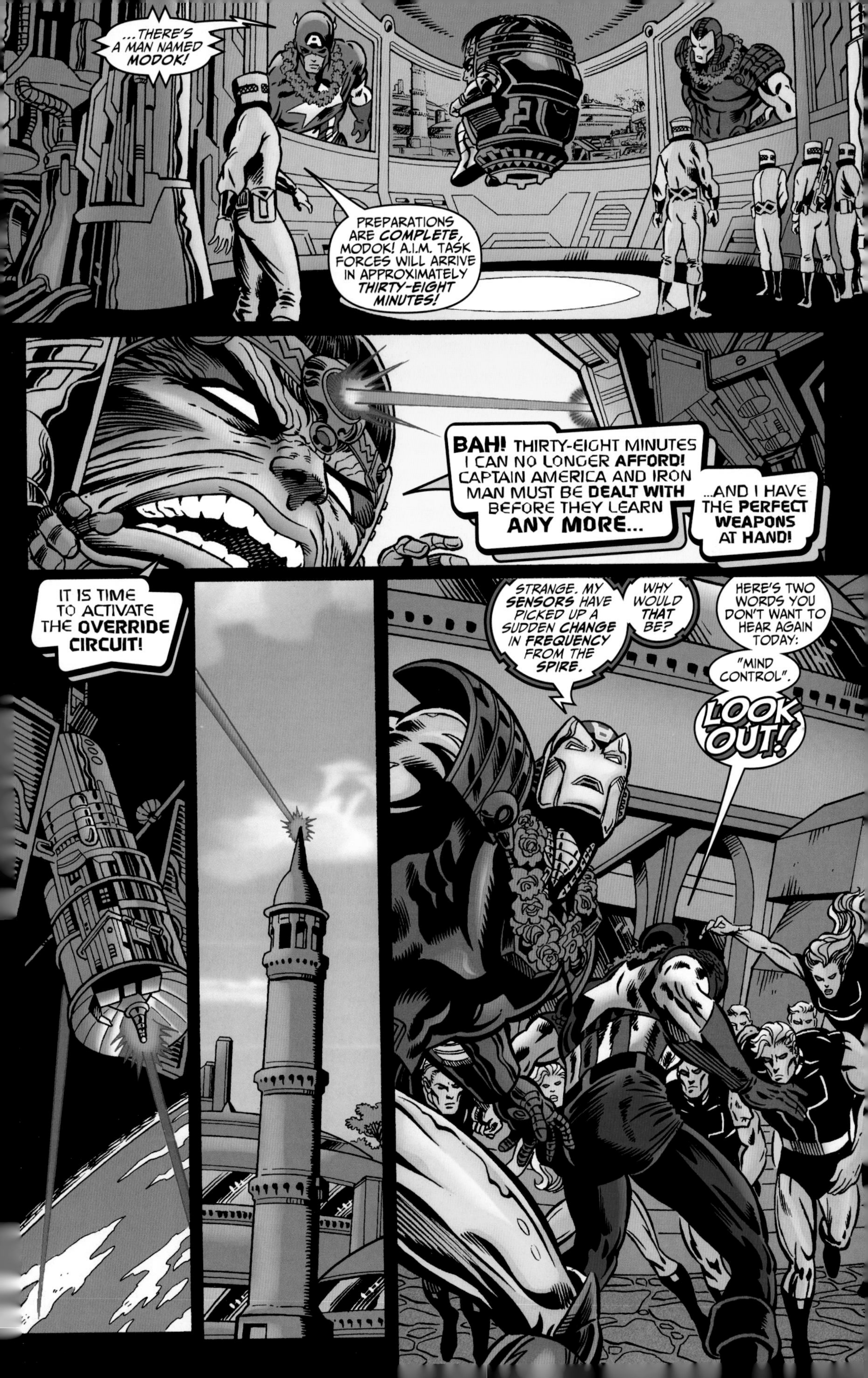
...THERE'S A MAN NAMED MODOK!
PREPARATIONS ARE COMPLETE, MODOK! A.I.M. TASK FORCES WILL ARRIVE IN APPROXIMATELY THIRTY-EIGHT MINUTES!
BAH! THIRTY-EIGHT MINUTES I CAN NO LONGER AFFORD! CAPTAIN AMERICA AND IRON MAN MUST BE DEALT WITH BEFORE THEY LEARN ANY MORE...
...AND I HAVE THE PERFECT WEAPONS AT HAND!
IT IS TIME TO ACTIVATE THE OVERRIDE CIRCUIT!
STRANGE. MY SENSORS HAVE PICKED UP A SUDDEN CHANGE IN FREQUENCY FROM THE SPIRE.
WHY WOULD THAT BE?
HERE'S TWO WORDS YOU DON'T WANT TO HEAR AGAIN TODAY:
"MIND CONTROL".
LOOK OUT!

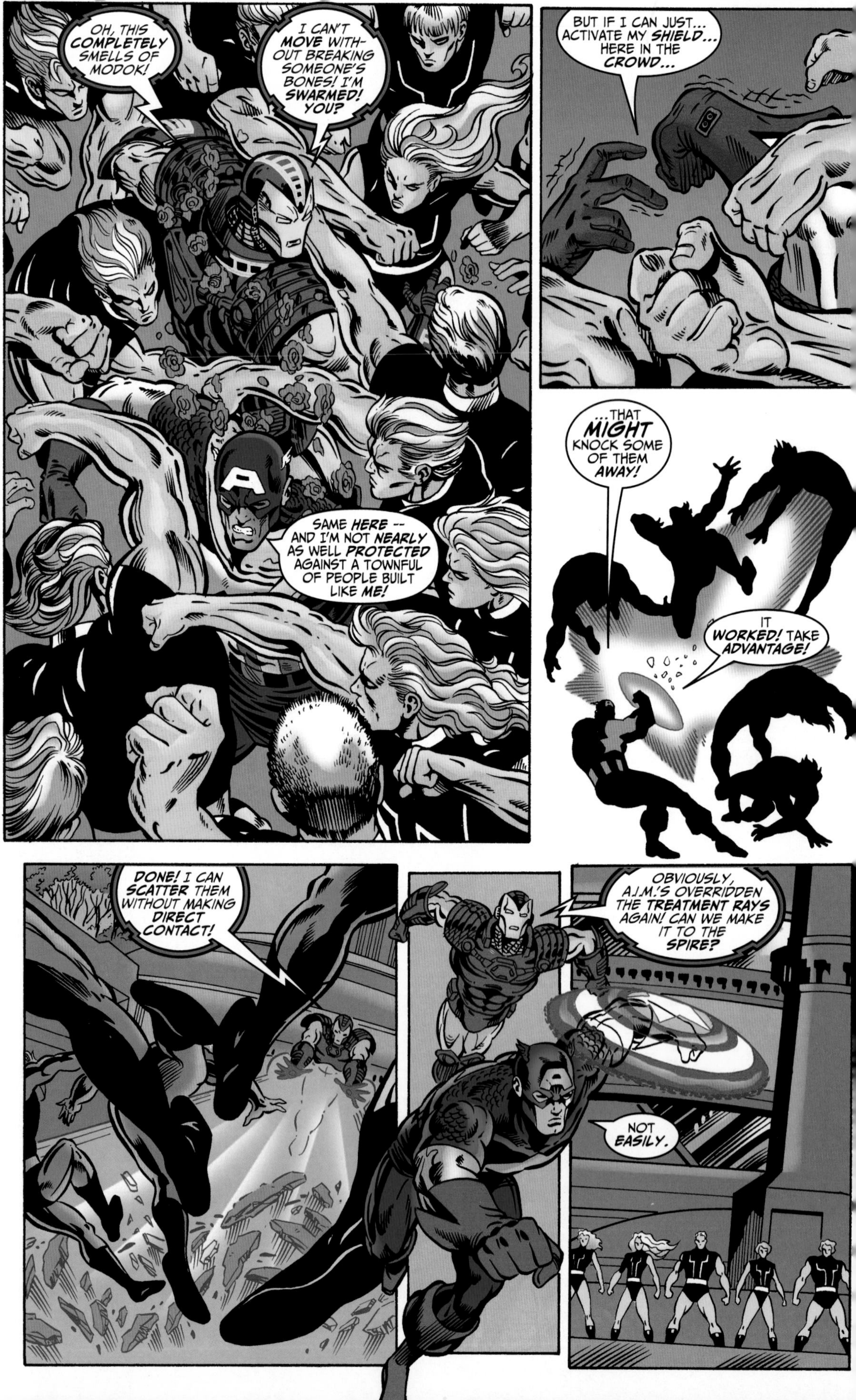
OH, THIS COMPLETELY SMELLS OF MODOK!
I CAN'T MOVE WITHOUT BREAKING SOMEONE'S BONES! I'M SWARMED! YOU?
SAME HERE -- AND I'M NOT NEARLY AS WELL PROTECTED AGAINST A TOWNFUL OF PEOPLE BUILT LIKE ME!
BUT IF I CAN JUST... ACTIVATE MY SHIELD... HERE IN THE CROWD...
...THAT MIGHT KNOCK SOME OF THEM AWAY!
IT WORKED! TAKE ADVANTAGE!
DONE! I CAN SCATTER THEM WITHOUT MAKING DIRECT CONTACT!
OBVIOUSLY, A.I.M.'S OVERRIDDEN THE TREATMENT RAYS AGAIN! CAN WE MAKE IT TO THE SPIRE?
NOT EASILY.

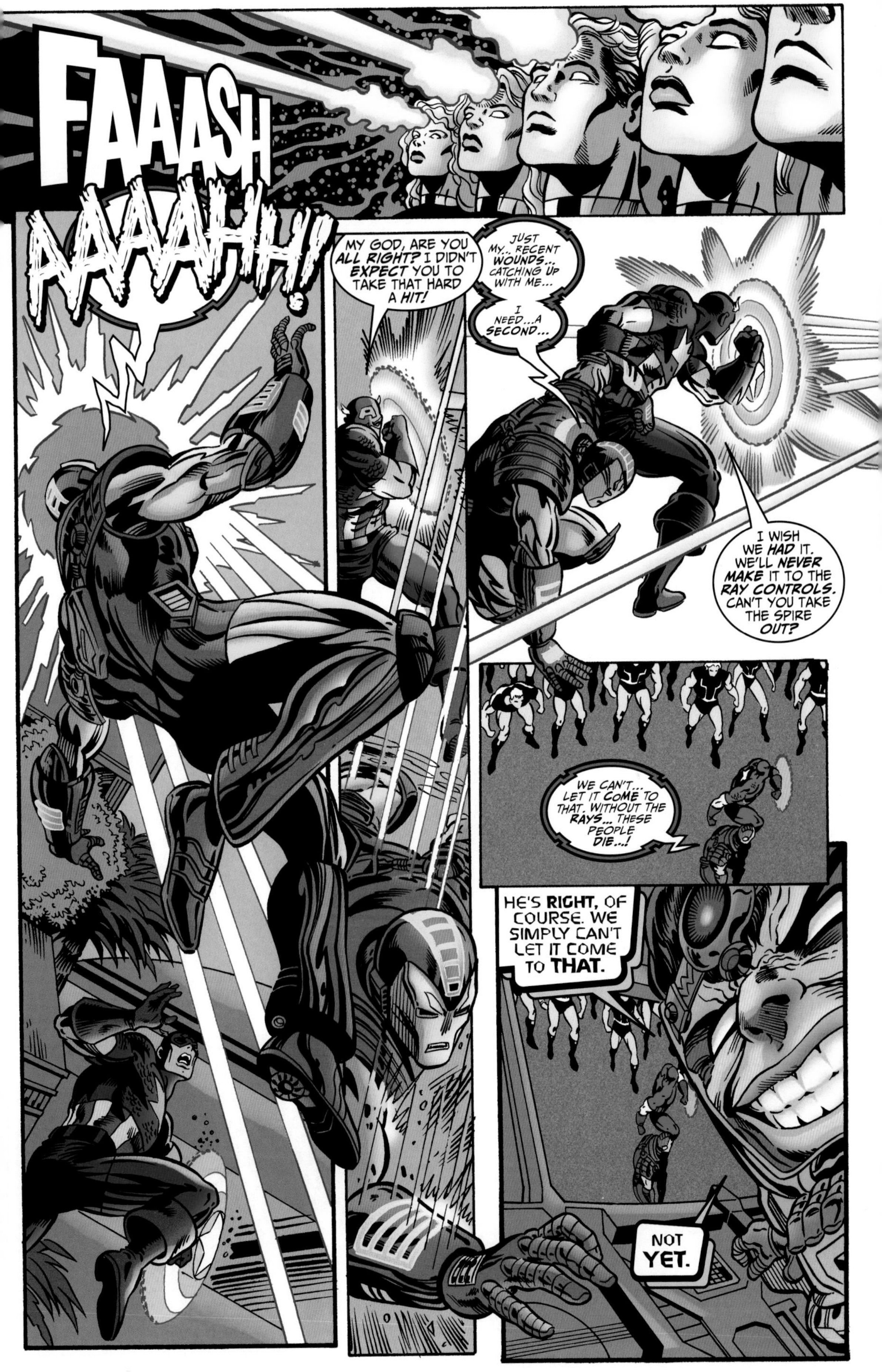
FAAASH
AAAAHH!
MY GOD, ARE YOU ALL RIGHT? I DIDN'T EXPECT YOU TO TAKE THAT HARD A HIT!
JUST MY... RECENT WOUNDS... CATCHING UP WITH ME...
I NEED...A SECOND...
I WISH WE HAD IT. WE'LL NEVER MAKE IT TO THE RAY CONTROLS. CAN'T YOU TAKE THE SPIRE OUT?
WE CAN'T... LET IT COME TO THAT. WITHOUT THE RAYS... THESE PEOPLE DIE...!
HE'S RIGHT, OF COURSE. WE SIMPLY CAN'T LET IT COME TO THAT.
NOT YET.

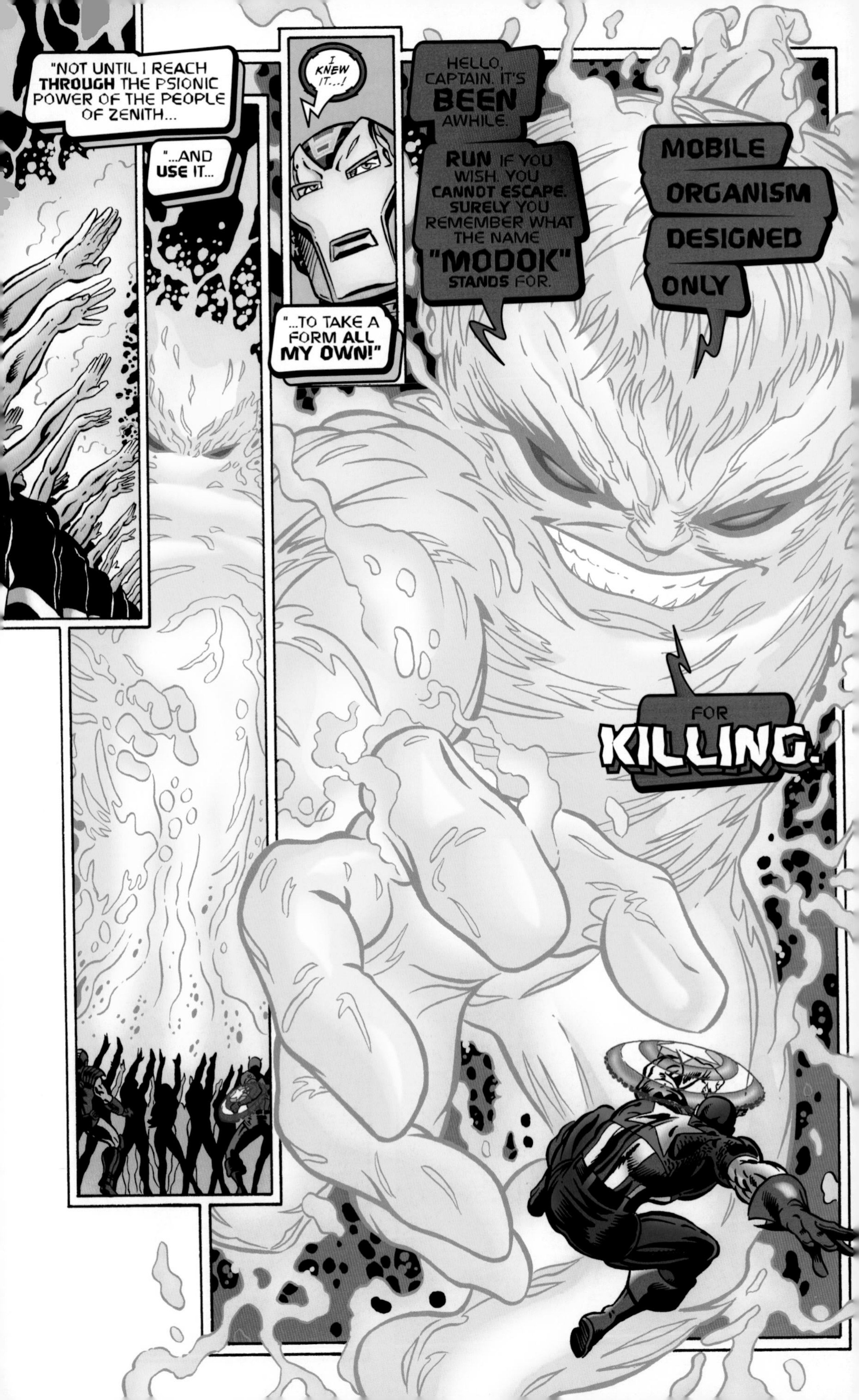
"NOT UNTIL I REACH THROUGH THE PSIONIC POWER OF THE PEOPLE OF ZENITH...
"...AND USE IT...
I KNEW IT...!
"...TO TAKE A FORM ALL MY OWN!"
HELLO, CAPTAIN. IT'S BEEN AWHILE.
RUN IF YOU WISH. YOU CANNOT ESCAPE. SURELY YOU REMEMBER WHAT THE NAME "MODOK" STANDS FOR.
MOBILE ORGANISM DESIGNED ONLY
FOR KILLING.

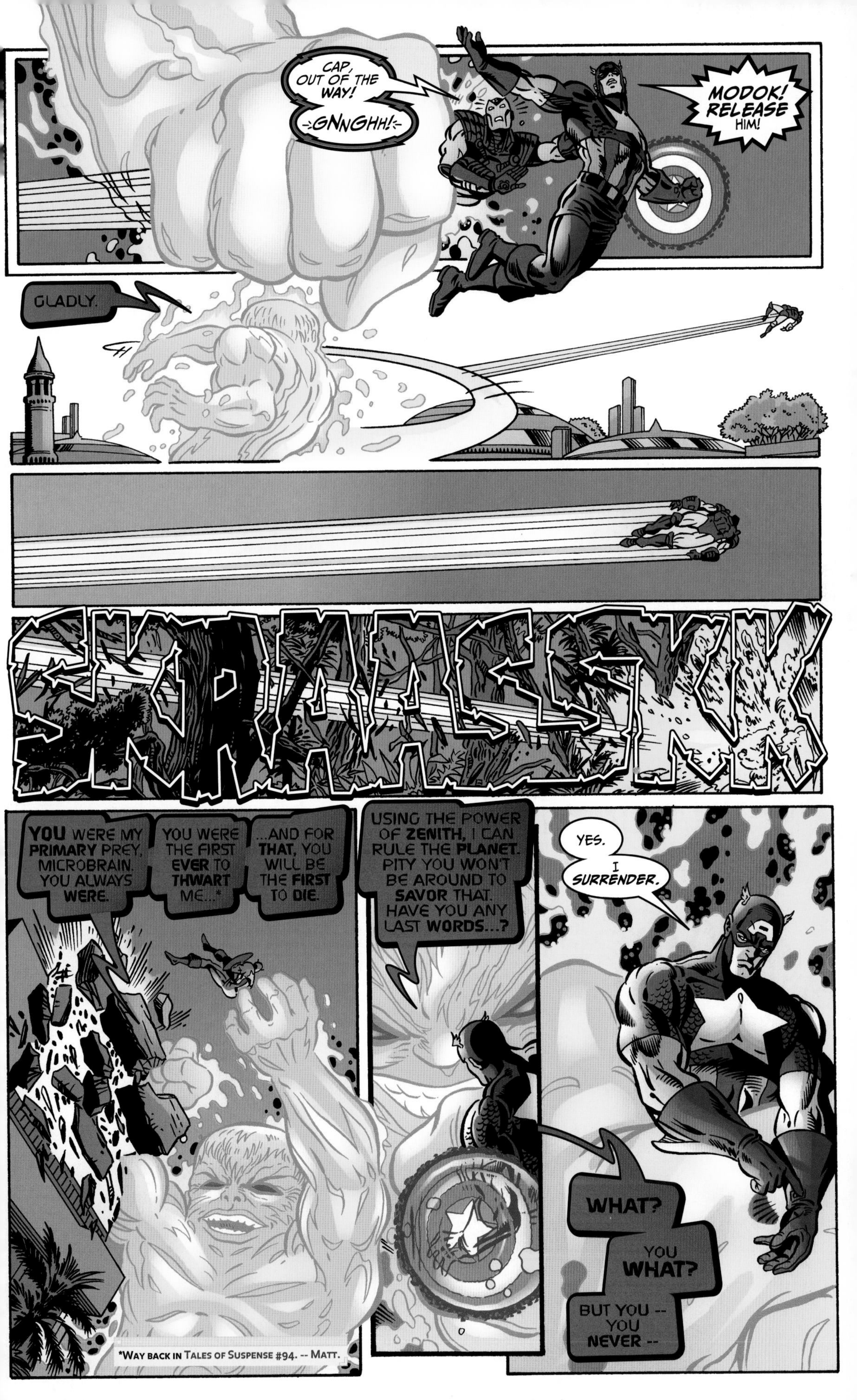
CAP, OUT OF THE WAY!
-GNNGHH!-
MODOK! RELEASE HIM!
GLADLY.
SKRAKSSHK
YOU WERE MY PRIMARY PREY, MICROBRAIN. YOU ALWAYS WERE.
YOU WERE THE FIRST EVER TO THWART ME...*
...AND FOR THAT, YOU WILL BE THE FIRST TO DIE.
USING THE POWER OF ZENITH, I CAN RULE THE PLANET. PITY YOU WON'T BE AROUND TO SAVOR THAT. HAVE YOU ANY LAST WORDS...?
YES.
I SURRENDER.
WHAT?
YOU WHAT?
BUT YOU -- YOU NEVER --
*WAY BACK IN TALES OF SUSPENSE #94. -- MATT.

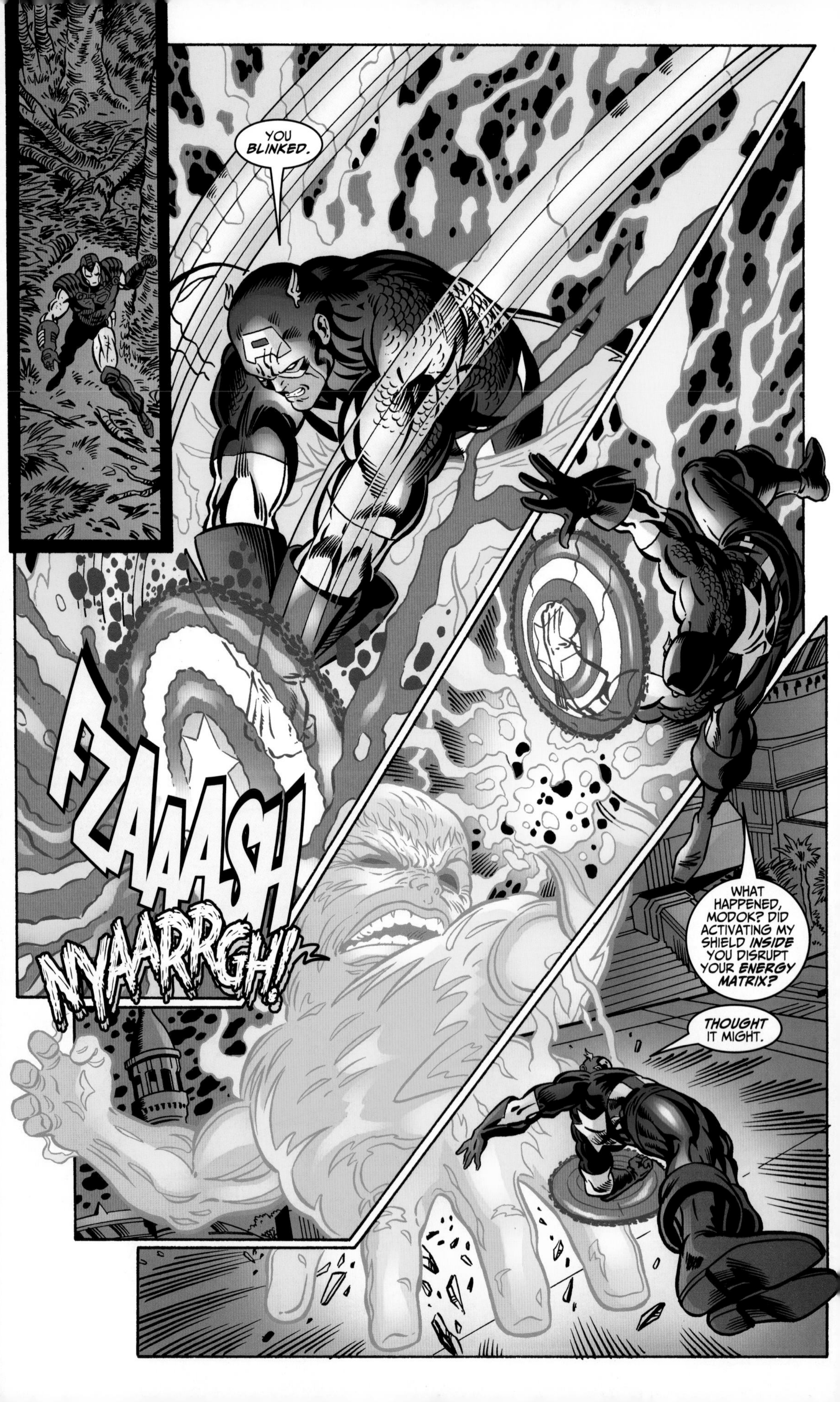
YOU BLINKED.
FZAAASH
NYAARRGH!
WHAT HAPPENED, MODOK? DID ACTIVATING MY SHIELD INSIDE YOU DISRUPT YOUR ENERGY MATRIX?
THOUGHT IT MIGHT.

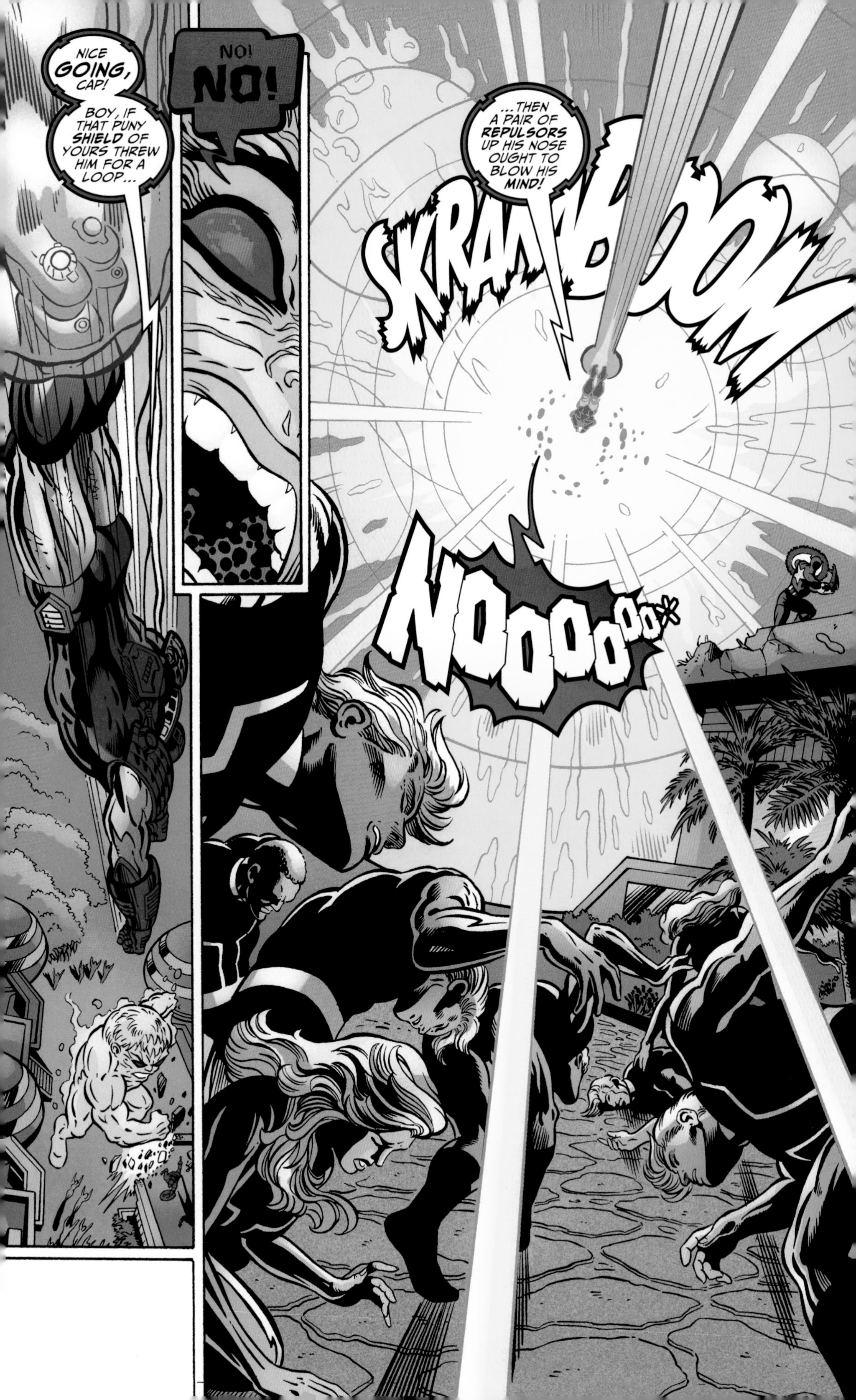
NICE GOING, CAP!
BOY, IF THAT PUNY SHIELD OF YOURS THREW HIM FOR A LOOP...
NO! NO!
...THEN A PAIR OF REPULSORS UP HIS NOSE OUGHT TO BLOW HIS MIND!
SKRAAABOOM
NOOOOOO*

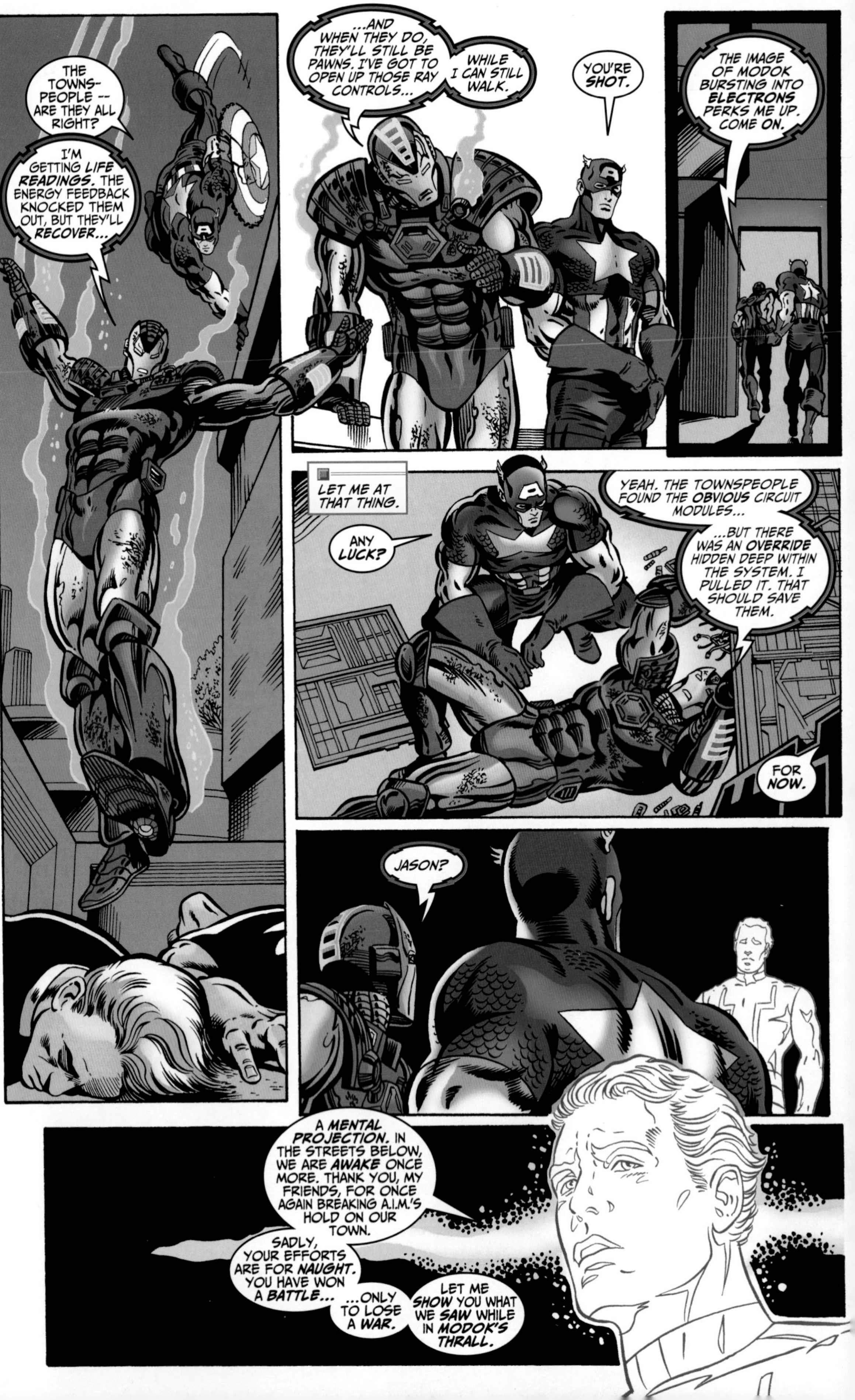
THE TOWNS-PEOPLE -- ARE THEY ALL RIGHT?
I'M GETTING **LIFE READINGS.** THE ENERGY FEEDBACK KNOCKED THEM OUT, BUT THEY'LL **RECOVER...**
...AND WHEN THEY DO, THEY'LL STILL BE PAWNS. I'VE GOT TO OPEN UP THOSE RAY CONTROLS...
WHILE I CAN STILL WALK.
YOU'RE **SHOT.**
THE IMAGE OF MODOK BURSTING INTO **ELECTRONS** PERKS ME UP. COME **ON.**
LET ME AT THAT THING.
ANY **LUCK?**
YEAH. THE TOWNSPEOPLE FOUND THE **OBVIOUS** CIRCUIT MODULES...
...BUT THERE WAS AN **OVERRIDE** HIDDEN DEEP WITHIN THE SYSTEM. I PULLED IT. THAT SHOULD SAVE THEM.
FOR **NOW.**
JASON?
A **MENTAL PROJECTION.** IN THE STREETS BELOW, WE ARE **AWAKE** ONCE MORE. THANK YOU, MY FRIENDS, FOR ONCE AGAIN BREAKING A.I.M.'S HOLD ON OUR TOWN.
SADLY, YOUR EFFORTS ARE FOR **NAUGHT.** YOU HAVE WON A **BATTLE...**
...ONLY TO LOSE A **WAR.**
LET ME **SHOW** YOU WHAT WE **SAW** WHILE IN **MODOK'S THRALL.**

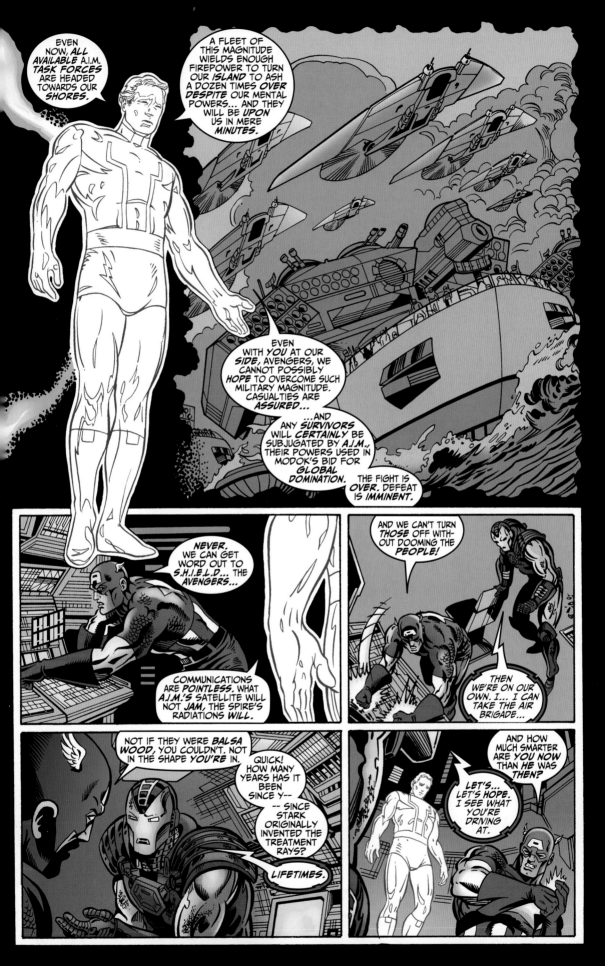

EVEN NOW, *ALL AVAILABLE A.I.M. TASK FORCES* ARE HEADED TOWARDS OUR *SHORES.*

A FLEET OF THIS MAGNITUDE WIELDS ENOUGH FIREPOWER TO TURN OUR *ISLAND* TO ASH A DOZEN TIMES *OVER* DESPITE OUR MENTAL POWERS... AND THEY WILL BE *UPON* US IN MERE *MINUTES.*

EVEN WITH *YOU* AT OUR *SIDE,* AVENGERS, WE CANNOT POSSIBLY *HOPE* TO OVERCOME SUCH MILITARY MAGNITUDE. CASUALTIES ARE *ASSURED...*

...AND ANY *SURVIVORS* WILL *CERTAINLY* BE SUBJUGATED BY *A.I.M.,* THEIR POWERS USED IN MODOK'S BID FOR *GLOBAL DOMINATION.*

THE FIGHT IS *OVER.* DEFEAT IS *IMMINENT.*

NEVER. WE CAN GET WORD OUT TO S.H.I.E.L.D... THE *AVENGERS...*

COMMUNICATIONS ARE *POINTLESS.* WHAT *A.I.M.'S* SATELLITE WILL NOT *JAM,* THE SPIRE'S RADIATIONS *WILL.*

AND WE CAN'T TURN *THOSE* OFF WITH-OUT DOOMING THE *PEOPLE!*

THEN WE'RE ON OUR *OWN.* I... I CAN TAKE THE AIR *BRIGADE...*

NOT IF THEY WERE *BALSA WOOD,* YOU COULDN'T. NOT IN THE SHAPE *YOU'RE* IN.

QUICK! HOW MANY YEARS HAS IT BEEN Y--

-- SINCE STARK ORIGINALLY INVENTED THE TREATMENT RAYS?

LIFETIMES.

AND HOW MUCH SMARTER ARE *YOU* NOW THAN *HE* WAS *THEN?*

LET'S... LET'S *HOPE.* I SEE WHAT YOU'RE DRIVING AT.

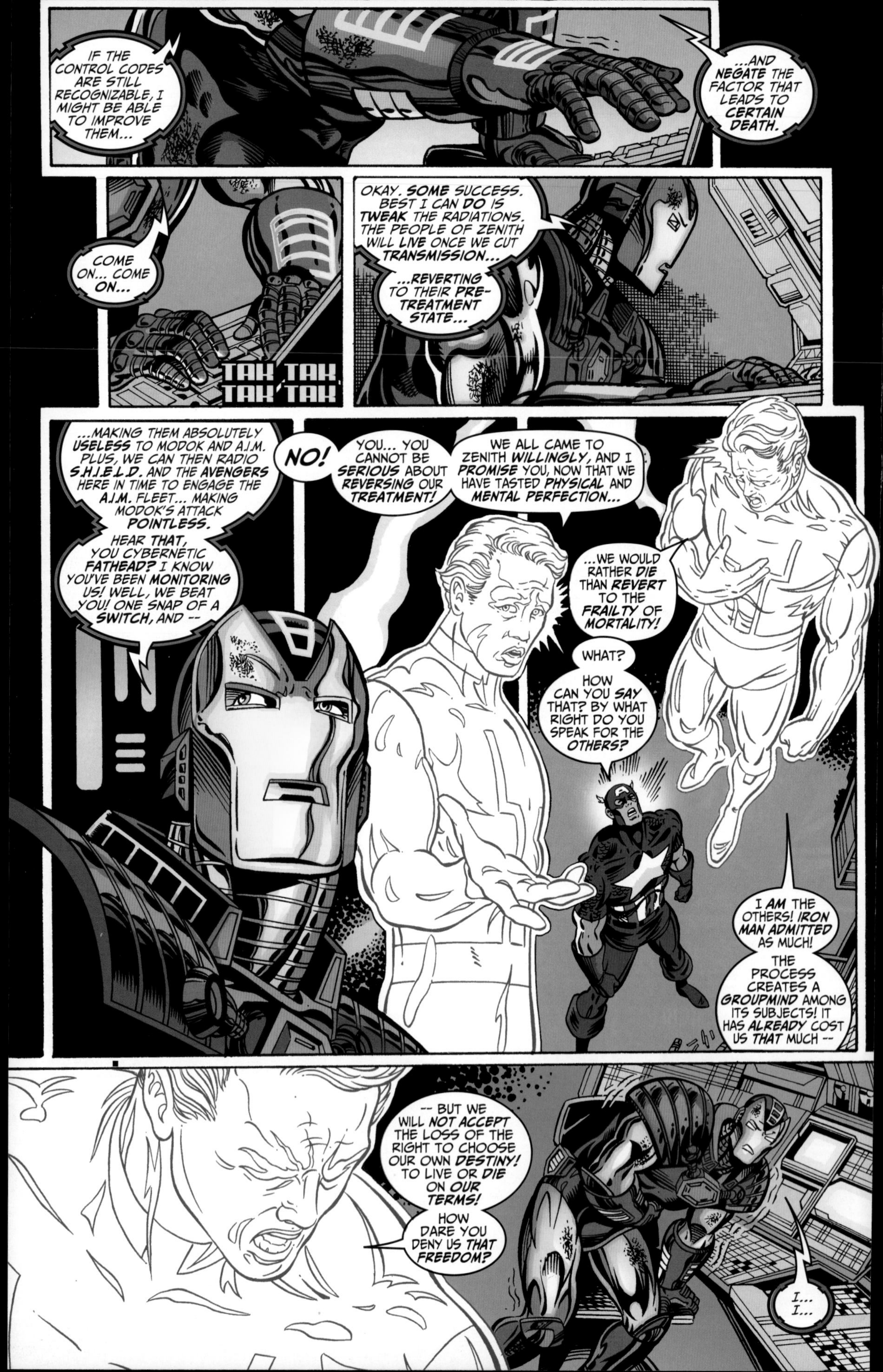

IF THE CONTROL CODES ARE STILL RECOGNIZABLE, I MIGHT BE ABLE TO IMPROVE THEM...
...AND NEGATE THE FACTOR THAT LEADS TO CERTAIN DEATH.
COME ON... COME ON...
TAK TAK TAK TAK
OKAY. SOME SUCCESS. BEST I CAN DO IS TWEAK THE RADIATIONS. THE PEOPLE OF ZENITH WILL LIVE ONCE WE CUT TRANSMISSION...
...REVERTING TO THEIR PRE-TREATMENT STATE...
...MAKING THEM ABSOLUTELY USELESS TO MODOK AND A.I.M. PLUS, WE CAN THEN RADIO S.H.I.E.L.D. AND THE AVENGERS HERE IN TIME TO ENGAGE THE A.I.M. FLEET... MAKING MODOK'S ATTACK POINTLESS.
HEAR THAT, YOU CYBERNETIC FATHEAD? I KNOW YOU'VE BEEN MONITORING US! WELL, WE BEAT YOU! ONE SNAP OF A SWITCH, AND --
NO!
YOU... YOU CANNOT BE SERIOUS ABOUT REVERSING OUR TREATMENT!
WE ALL CAME TO ZENITH WILLINGLY, AND I PROMISE YOU, NOW THAT WE HAVE TASTED PHYSICAL AND MENTAL PERFECTION...
...WE WOULD RATHER DIE THAN REVERT TO THE FRAILTY OF MORTALITY!
WHAT?
HOW CAN YOU SAY THAT? BY WHAT RIGHT DO YOU SPEAK FOR THE OTHERS?
I AM THE OTHERS! IRON MAN ADMITTED AS MUCH!
THE PROCESS CREATES A GROUPMIND AMONG ITS SUBJECTS! IT HAS ALREADY COST US THAT MUCH --
-- BUT WE WILL NOT ACCEPT THE LOSS OF THE RIGHT TO CHOOSE OUR OWN DESTINY! TO LIVE OR DIE ON OUR TERMS!
HOW DARE YOU DENY US THAT FREEDOM?
I... I...

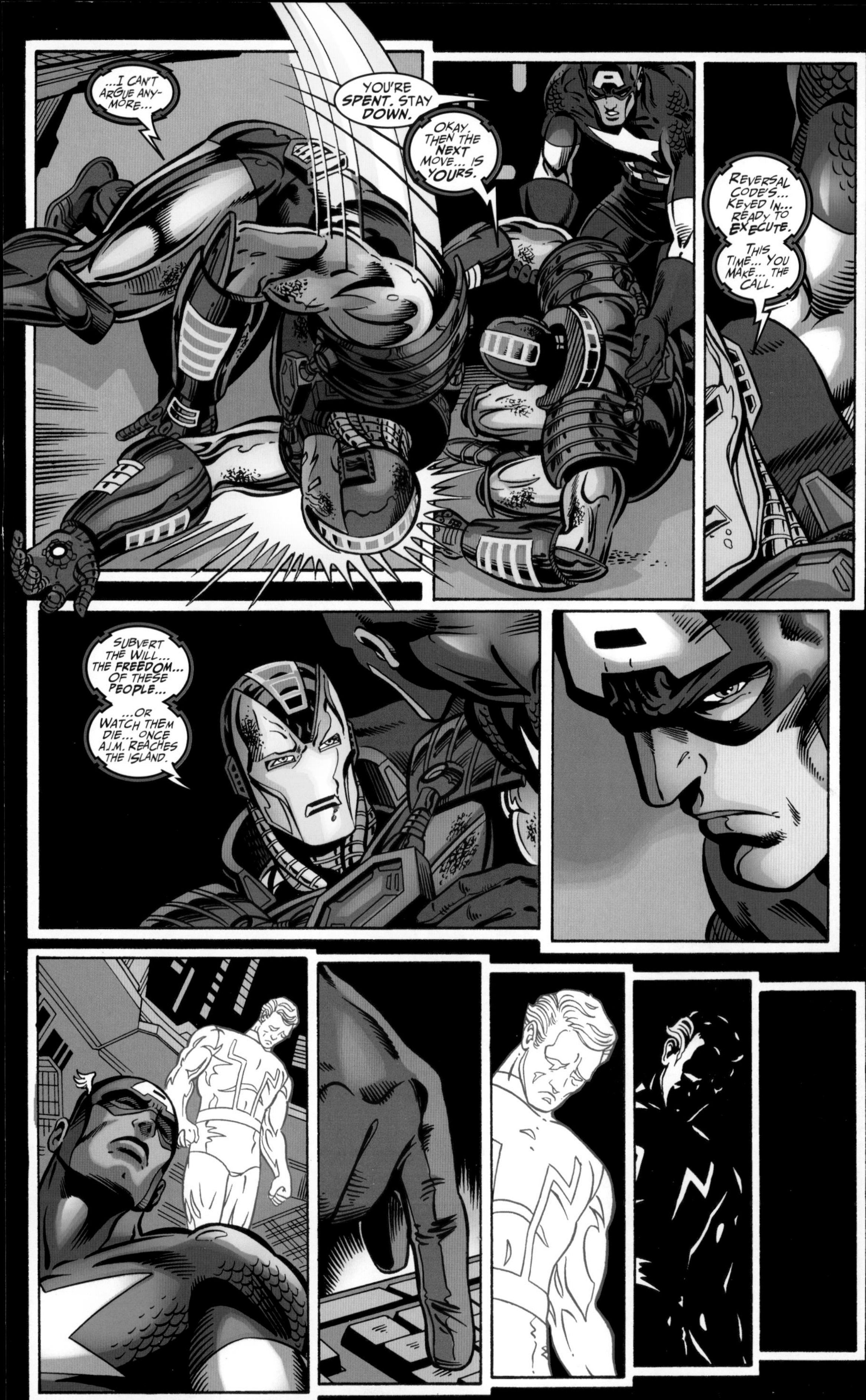

...I CAN'T ARGUE ANYMORE...
YOU'RE SPENT. STAY DOWN.
OKAY, THEN THE NEXT MOVE... IS YOURS.
REVERSAL CODE'S... KEYED IN... READY TO EXECUTE.
THIS TIME... YOU MAKE... THE CALL.
SUBVERT THE WILL... THE FREEDOM... OF THESE PEOPLE...
...OR WATCH THEM DIE... ONCE A.I.M. REACHES THE ISLAND.

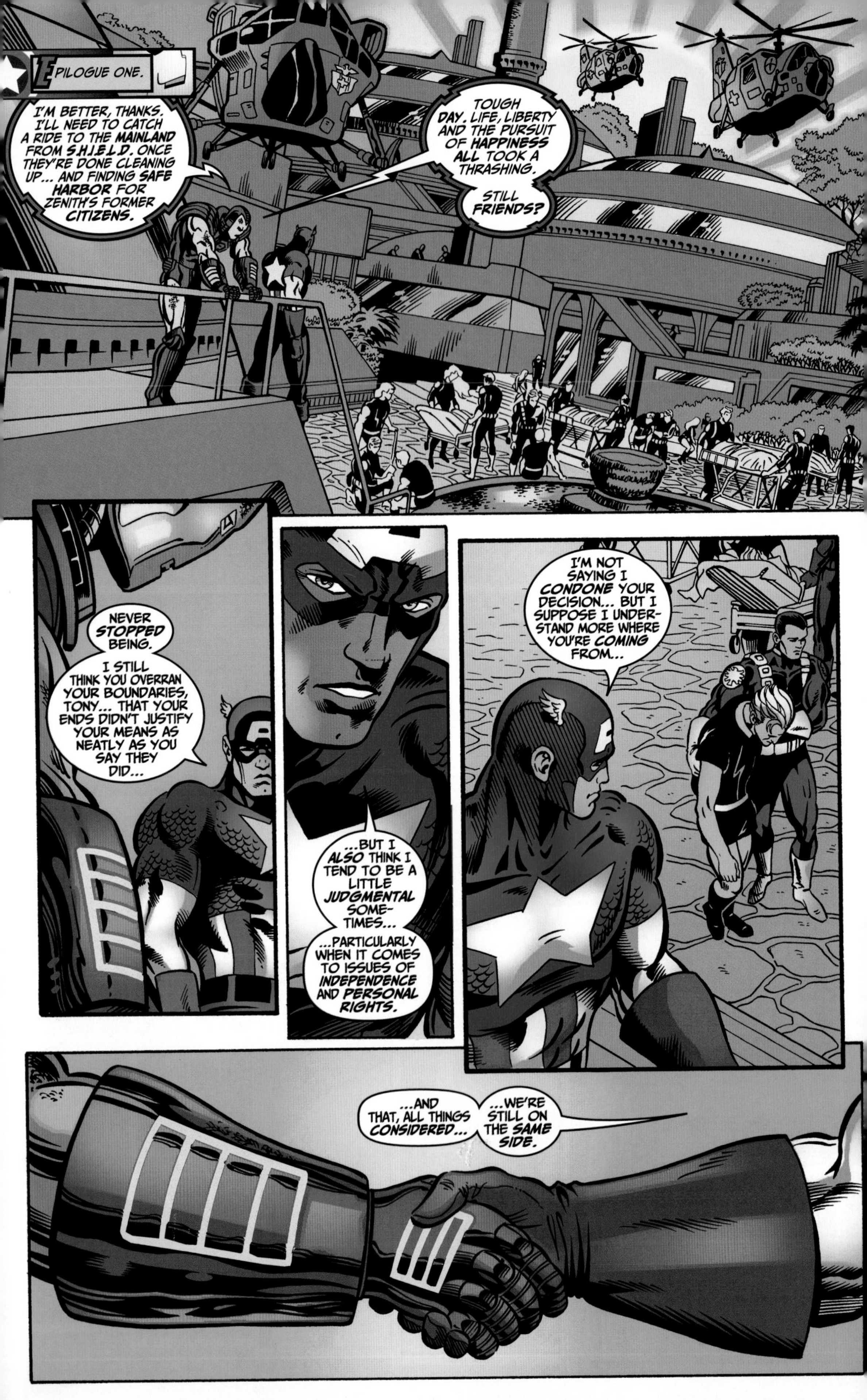

EPILOGUE ONE.
I'M BETTER, THANKS. I'LL NEED TO CATCH A RIDE TO THE MAINLAND FROM S.H.I.E.L.D. ONCE THEY'RE DONE CLEANING UP... AND FINDING SAFE HARBOR FOR ZENITH'S FORMER CITIZENS.
TOUGH DAY. LIFE, LIBERTY AND THE PURSUIT OF HAPPINESS ALL TOOK A THRASHING.
STILL FRIENDS?
NEVER STOPPED BEING.
I STILL THINK YOU OVERRAN YOUR BOUNDARIES, TONY... THAT YOUR ENDS DIDN'T JUSTIFY YOUR MEANS AS NEATLY AS YOU SAY THEY DID...
...BUT I ALSO THINK I TEND TO BE A LITTLE JUDGMENTAL SOME-TIMES...
...PARTICULARLY WHEN IT COMES TO ISSUES OF INDEPENDENCE AND PERSONAL RIGHTS.
I'M NOT SAYING I CONDONE YOUR DECISION... BUT I SUPPOSE I UNDER-STAND MORE WHERE YOU'RE COMING FROM...
...AND THAT, ALL THINGS CONSIDERED...
...WE'RE STILL ON THE SAME SIDE.

PILOGUE TWO.

YOU WANTED TO SEE US, BOSS?

YES. PEPPER... HAPPY... YOU TWO HAVE BEEN WITH ME A *LONG* TIME. WE'VE SHARED A *LOT*.

IN FACT... MORE THAN YOU REMEMBER.

TONY, DO YOU NEED MORE *MEDICATION?* YOU'RE NOT MAKING A WHOLE LOT OF SENSE.

MAYBE A *VISUAL AID* WILL HELP.

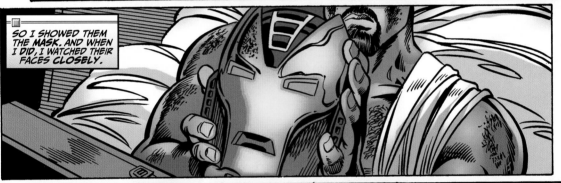

SO I SHOWED THEM THE MASK. AND WHEN I DID, I WATCHED THEIR FACES CLOSELY.

AS WITH THE AVENGERS, I SAW RECOGNITION AND DAWNING *REALIZATION* AS THEIR MEMORIES RETURNED.

BUT THIS TIME, WHEN I *EXPLAINED* MYSELF, I NOTICED SOMETHING *ELSE* FLIT ACROSS THEIR GAZE.

A TINY WINCE OF BETRAYAL.

A BRIEF LOOK OF DISAPPOINTMENT THAT WILL FOREVER *COLOR* MY OUTLOOK ON THE SANCTITY OF PERSONAL PRIVACY... ON PEOPLE'S RIGHT TO CHOOSE FOR THEMSELVES RATHER THAN HAVE CHOICE THRUST UPON THEM.

LIKE IT OR NOT... I SUDDENLY UNDER-STOOD BETTER WHERE *CAP* WAS COMING FROM, TOO.

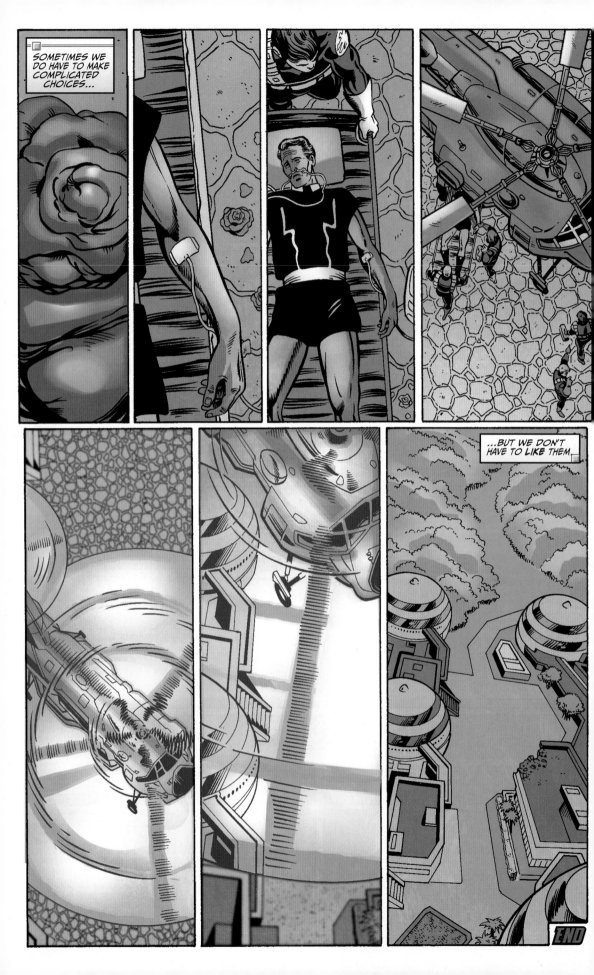

SOMETIMES WE DO HAVE TO MAKE COMPLICATED CHOICES...

...BUT WE DON'T HAVE TO LIKE THEM.

END

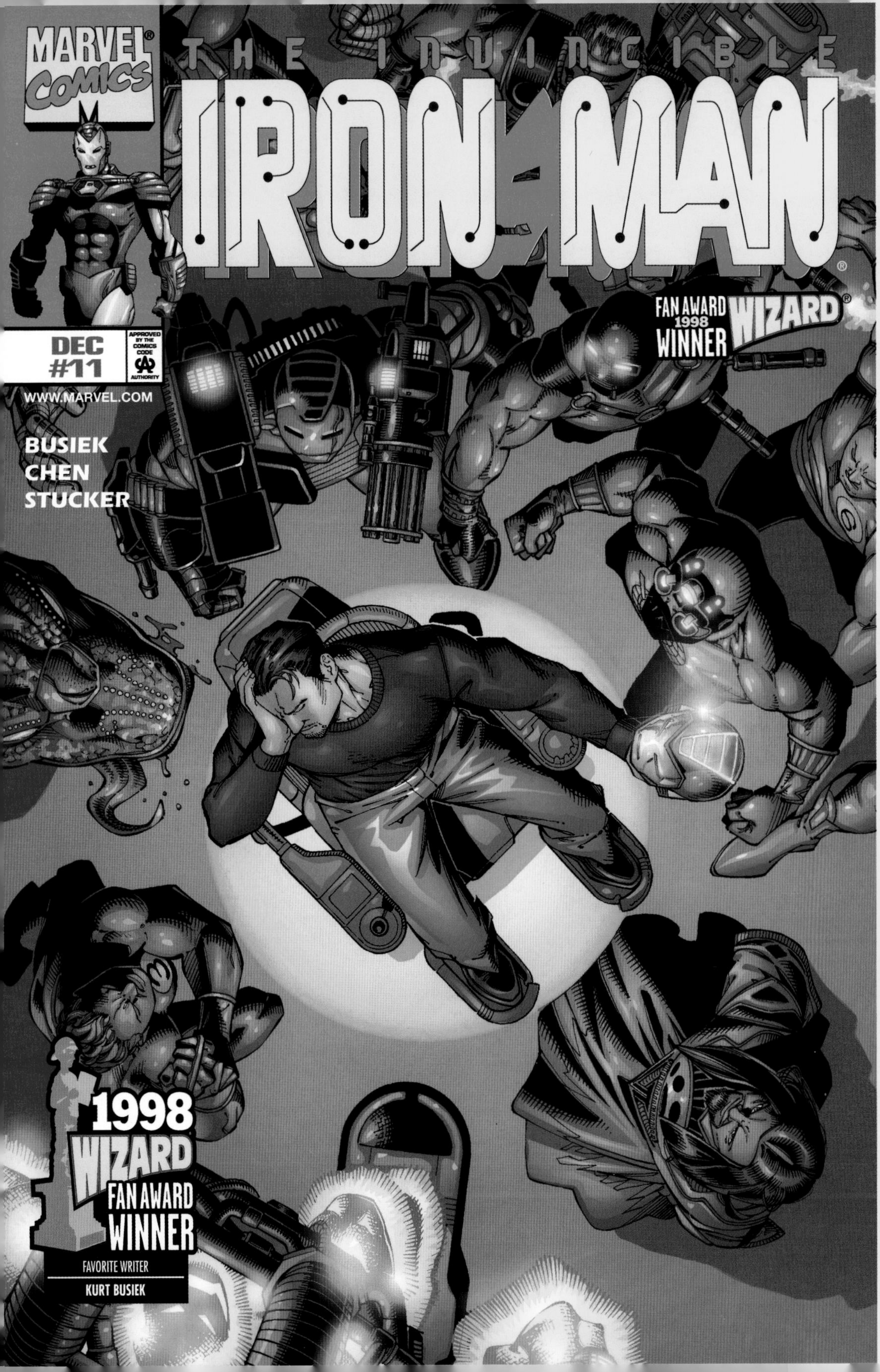
MARVEL COMICS
THE INVINCIBLE
IRON MAN
DEC #11
APPROVED BY THE COMICS CODE AUTHORITY
WWW.MARVEL.COM
BUSIEK
CHEN
STUCKER
FAN AWARD 1998 WINNER WIZARD
1998
WIZARD
FAN AWARD
WINNER
FAVORITE WRITER
KURT BUSIEK

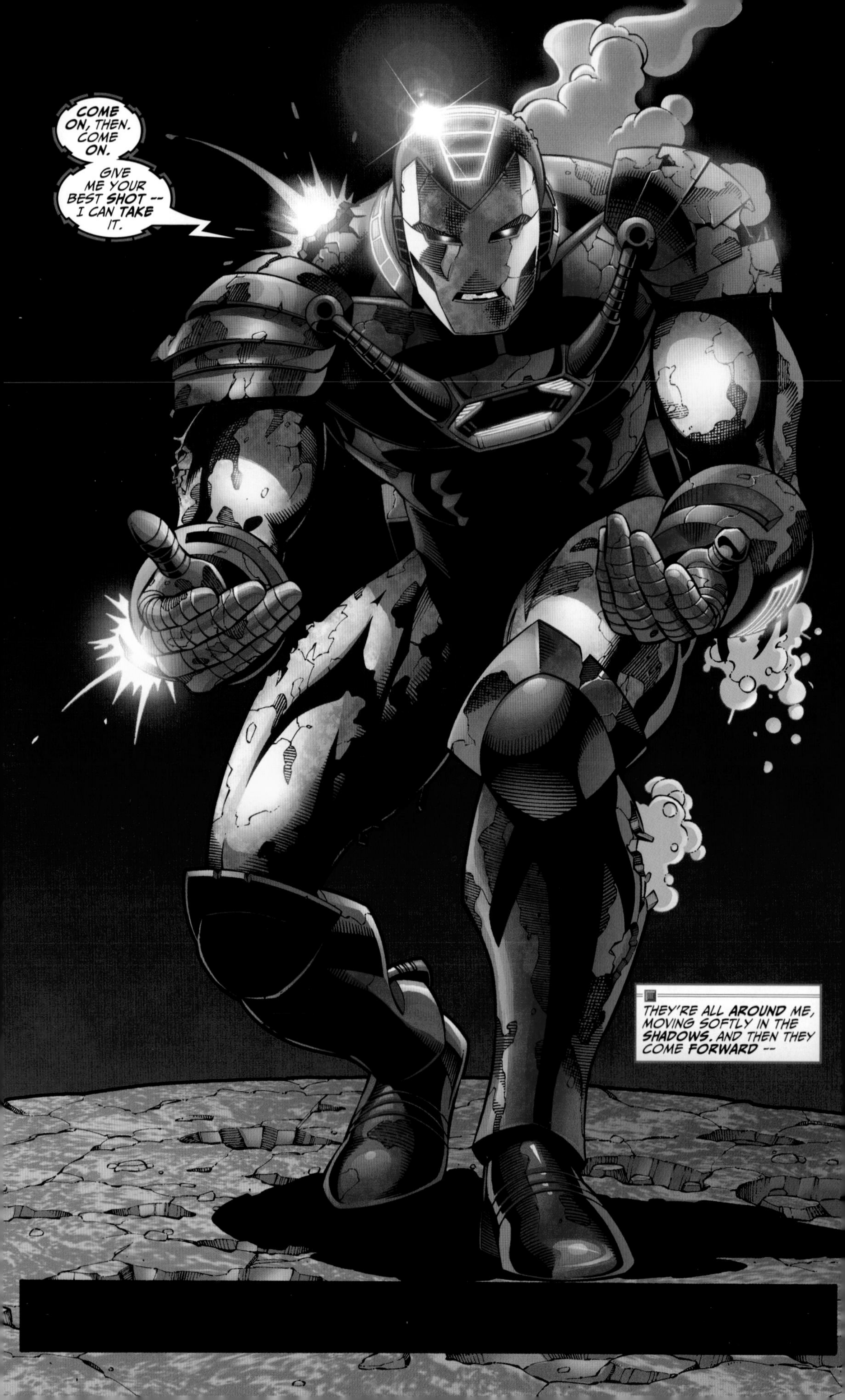
COME ON, THEN. COME ON.
GIVE ME YOUR BEST SHOT -- I CAN TAKE IT.
THEY'RE ALL AROUND ME, MOVING SOFTLY IN THE SHADOWS. AND THEN THEY COME FORWARD --
[redacted]

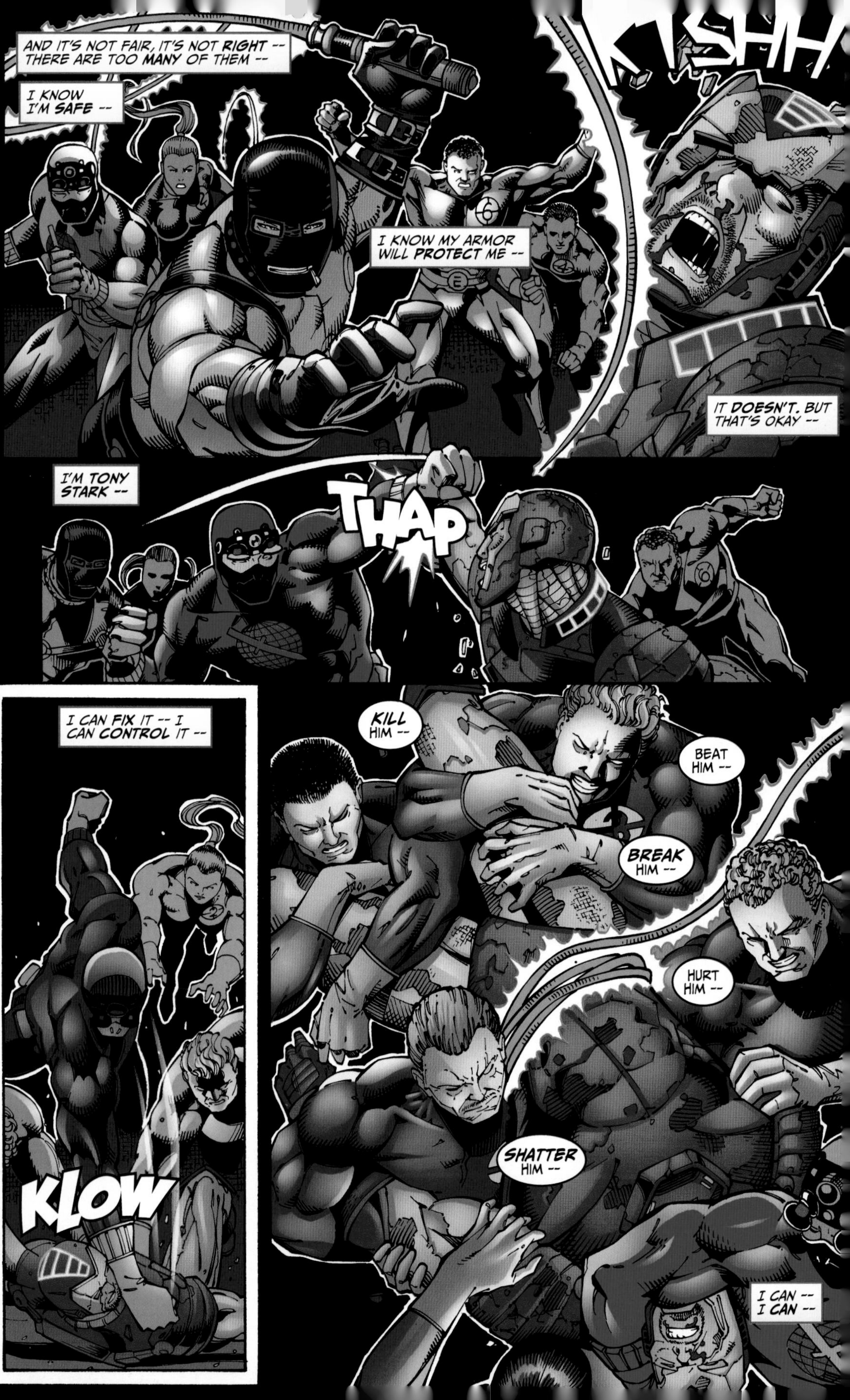
AND IT'S NOT FAIR, IT'S NOT RIGHT -- THERE ARE TOO MANY OF THEM --
I KNOW I'M SAFE --
I KNOW MY ARMOR WILL PROTECT ME --
KKSHH
IT DOESN'T. BUT THAT'S OKAY --
I'M TONY STARK --
THAP
I CAN FIX IT -- I CAN CONTROL IT --
KLOW
KILL HIM --
BEAT HIM --
BREAK HIM --
HURT HIM --
SHATTER HIM --
I CAN -- I CAN --

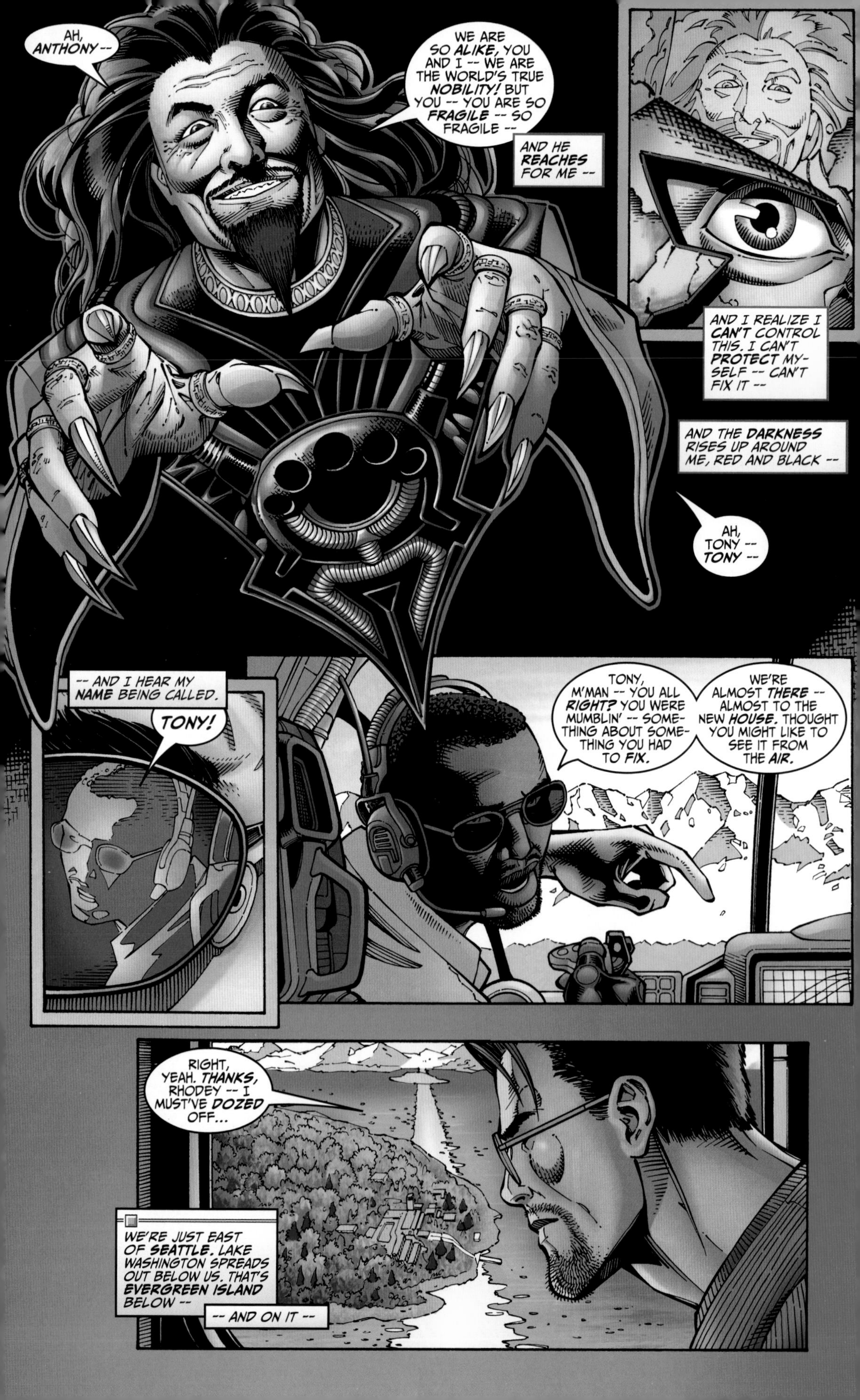
AH, ANTHONY --
WE ARE SO ALIKE, YOU AND I -- WE ARE THE WORLD'S TRUE NOBILITY! BUT YOU -- YOU ARE SO FRAGILE -- SO FRAGILE --
AND HE REACHES FOR ME --
AND I REALIZE I CAN'T CONTROL THIS. I CAN'T PROTECT MYSELF -- CAN'T FIX IT --
AND THE DARKNESS RISES UP AROUND ME, RED AND BLACK --
AH, TONY -- TONY --
-- AND I HEAR MY NAME BEING CALLED.
TONY!
TONY, M'MAN -- YOU ALL RIGHT? YOU WERE MUMBLIN' -- SOMETHING ABOUT SOMETHING YOU HAD TO FIX.
WE'RE ALMOST THERE -- ALMOST TO THE NEW HOUSE. THOUGHT YOU MIGHT LIKE TO SEE IT FROM THE AIR.
RIGHT, YEAH. THANKS, RHODEY -- I MUST'VE DOZED OFF...
WE'RE JUST EAST OF SEATTLE. LAKE WASHINGTON SPREADS OUT BELOW US. THAT'S EVERGREEN ISLAND BELOW --
-- AND ON IT --

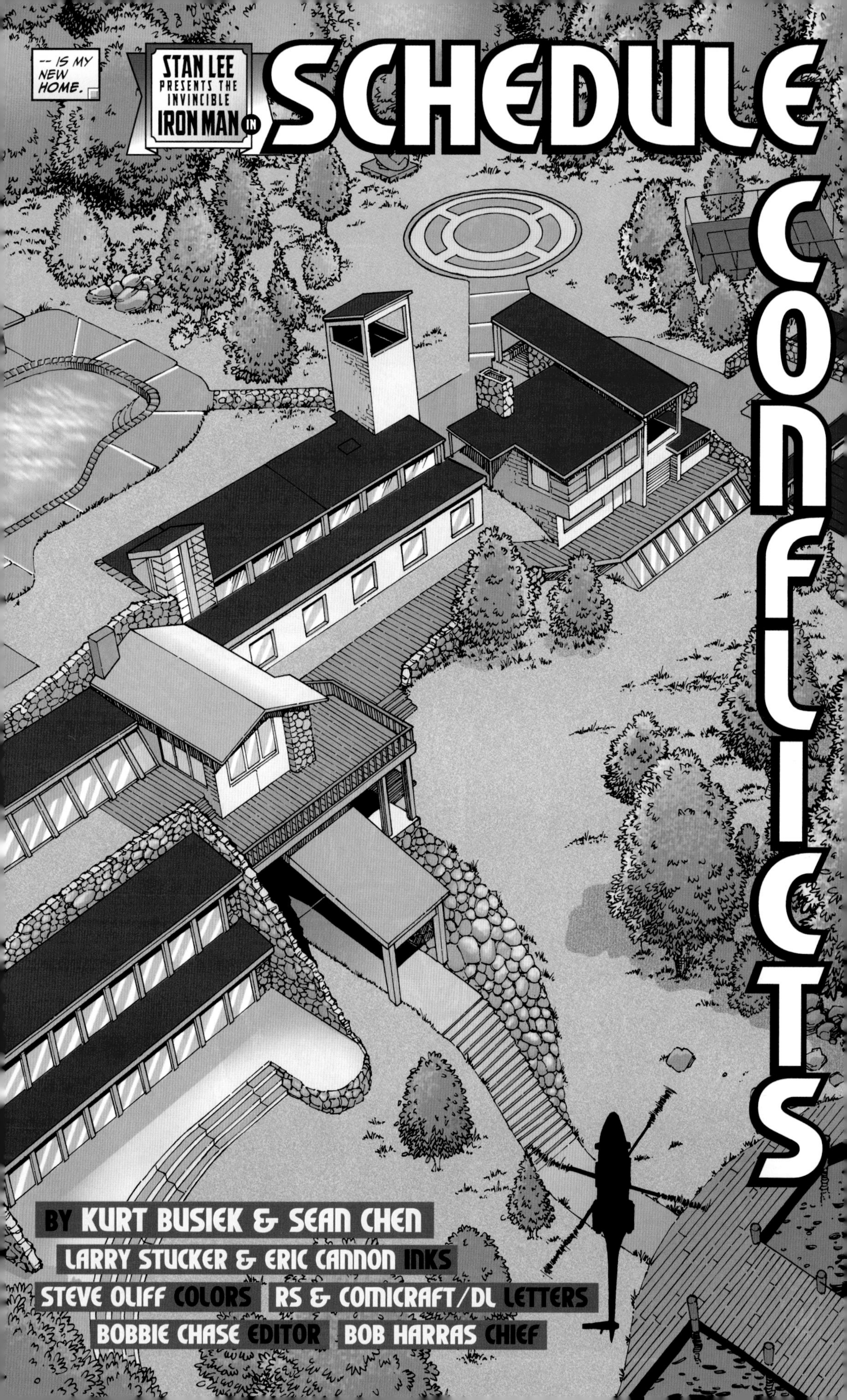
-- IS MY NEW HOME.
STAN LEE PRESENTS THE INVINCIBLE IRON MAN IN
SCHEDULE CONFLICTS
BY KURT BUSIEK & SEAN CHEN
LARRY STUCKER & ERIC CANNON INKS
STEVE OLIFF COLORS
RS & COMICRAFT/DL LETTERS
BOBBIE CHASE EDITOR
BOB HARRAS CHIEF

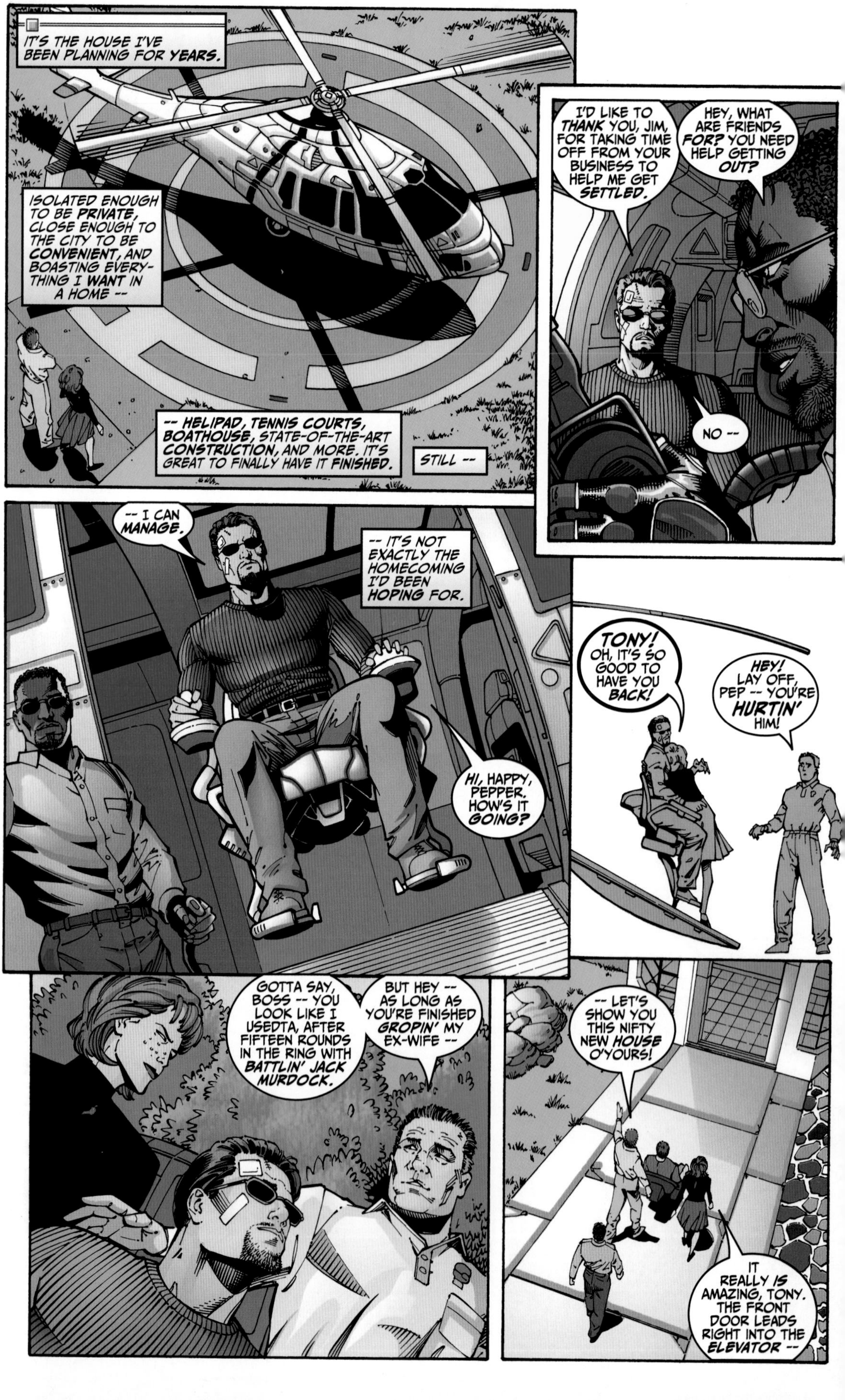
IT'S THE HOUSE I'VE BEEN PLANNING FOR YEARS.
ISOLATED ENOUGH TO BE PRIVATE, CLOSE ENOUGH TO THE CITY TO BE CONVENIENT, AND BOASTING EVERY-THING I WANT IN A HOME --
-- HELIPAD, TENNIS COURTS, BOATHOUSE, STATE-OF-THE-ART CONSTRUCTION, AND MORE. IT'S GREAT TO FINALLY HAVE IT FINISHED.
STILL --
I'D LIKE TO THANK YOU, JIM, FOR TAKING TIME OFF FROM YOUR BUSINESS TO HELP ME GET SETTLED.
HEY, WHAT ARE FRIENDS FOR? YOU NEED HELP GETTING OUT?
NO --
-- I CAN MANAGE.
-- IT'S NOT EXACTLY THE HOMECOMING I'D BEEN HOPING FOR.
HI, HAPPY, PEPPER. HOW'S IT GOING?
TONY! OH, IT'S SO GOOD TO HAVE YOU BACK!
HEY! LAY OFF, PEP -- YOU'RE HURTIN' HIM!
GOTTA SAY, BOSS -- YOU LOOK LIKE I USEDTA, AFTER FIFTEEN ROUNDS IN THE RING WITH BATTLIN' JACK MURDOCK.
BUT HEY -- AS LONG AS YOU'RE FINISHED GROPIN' MY EX-WIFE --
-- LET'S SHOW YOU THIS NIFTY NEW HOUSE O'YOURS!
IT REALLY IS AMAZING, TONY. THE FRONT DOOR LEADS RIGHT INTO THE ELEVATOR --

-- AND ONCE YOU'RE INSIDE, THE HOUSE *AUTOMATICALLY REACTS* TO YOUR PRESENCE, ADJUSTING THINGS TO BE THE WAY YOU *LIKE* THEM.

WE TOOK THE LIBERTY OF PRE-PROGRAMMING THIS *PIN* FOR YOU --

-- IT'LL LET THE HOUSE COMPUTERS KNOW WHAT LEVEL OF *AIR CONDITIONING* YOU WANT, HOW YOU LIKE THE *LIGHTS*, THE *MUSIC* --

-- IT'LL EVEN GIVE YOU IMMEDIATE *COMPUTER ACCESS* FROM ANY ROOM.

AS WE *DESCEND* INTO THE HOUSE, *VIVALDI* BEGINS TO PLAY. THE FOUR SEASONS -- ITS TONES *PRECISE*, CLEAR AND PURE.

HE *KNOWS*, PEP, HE KNOWS -- HE DESIGNED MOST OF IT *HIM-SELF*, REMEMBER? BESIDES, I DON'T SEE WHAT'S SO *GREAT* ABOUT IT --

-- EVERY TIME YOU WALK IN, IT INTERRUPTS MY *ELLINGTON* AN' *DORSEY* WITH THAT *BACKSTREET BOYS* JUNK.

WELL, *EXCUSE* ME FOR LIKING SOMETHING THAT WASN'T RECORDED BEFORE I WAS *BORN!*

BUT SOMEHOW, IT SOUNDS *HOLLOW.* THIS HOUSE WAS SUPPOSED TO BE A *CELEBRATION*, A PLACE OF RELAXATION AND COMFORT. BUT INSTEAD --

-- IT FEELS LIKE A *REFUGE*, A PLACE TO HIDE AFTER ALL THAT'S HAPPENED. OR MAYBE THAT'S JUST BECAUSE I KNOW WHERE WE'RE HEADED.

WE BYPASS THE *OFFICES*, THE LIVING *QUARTERS*, THE KITCHEN, THE GYM FACILITIES, THEATER -- AND WIND UP --

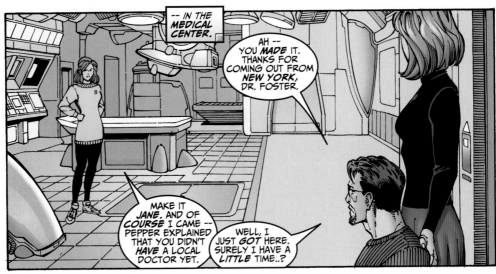

-- IN THE *MEDICAL CENTER.*

AH -- YOU *MADE* IT. THANKS FOR COMING OUT FROM *NEW YORK*, DR. FOSTER.

MAKE IT *JANE.* AND OF *COURSE* I CAME -- PEPPER EXPLAINED THAT YOU DIDN'T *HAVE* A LOCAL DOCTOR YET.

WELL, I JUST *GOT* HERE. SURELY I HAVE A *LITTLE* TIME..?

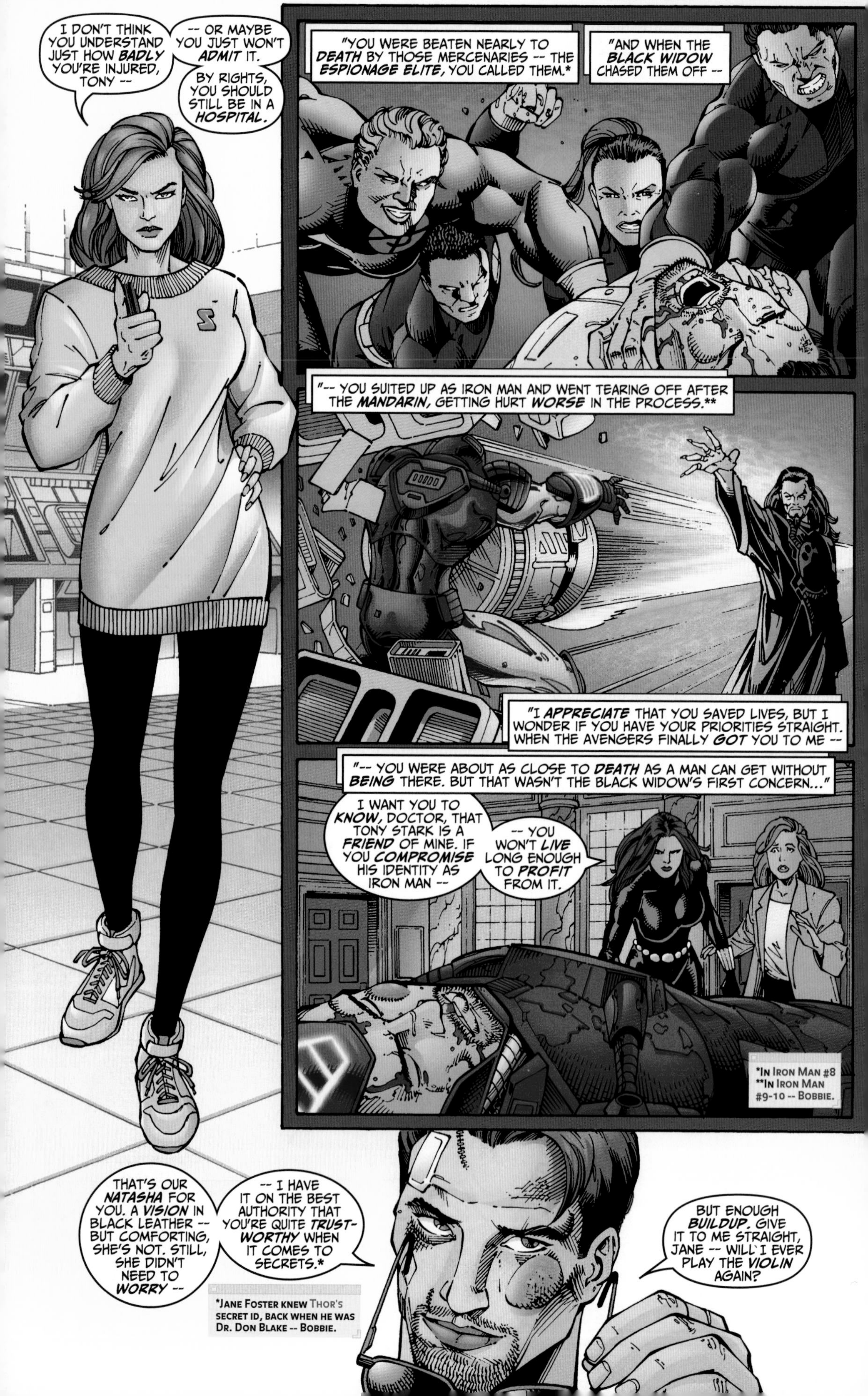

I DON'T THINK YOU UNDERSTAND JUST HOW BADLY YOU'RE INJURED, TONY --
-- OR MAYBE YOU JUST WON'T ADMIT IT.
BY RIGHTS, YOU SHOULD STILL BE IN A HOSPITAL.
"YOU WERE BEATEN NEARLY TO DEATH BY THOSE MERCENARIES -- THE ESPIONAGE ELITE, YOU CALLED THEM.*
"AND WHEN THE BLACK WIDOW CHASED THEM OFF --
"-- YOU SUITED UP AS IRON MAN AND WENT TEARING OFF AFTER THE MANDARIN, GETTING HURT WORSE IN THE PROCESS.**
"I APPRECIATE THAT YOU SAVED LIVES, BUT I WONDER IF YOU HAVE YOUR PRIORITIES STRAIGHT. WHEN THE AVENGERS FINALLY GOT YOU TO ME --
"-- YOU WERE ABOUT AS CLOSE TO DEATH AS A MAN CAN GET WITHOUT BEING THERE. BUT THAT WASN'T THE BLACK WIDOW'S FIRST CONCERN..."
I WANT YOU TO KNOW, DOCTOR, THAT TONY STARK IS A FRIEND OF MINE. IF YOU COMPROMISE HIS IDENTITY AS IRON MAN --
-- YOU WON'T LIVE LONG ENOUGH TO PROFIT FROM IT.
*IN IRON MAN #8 **IN IRON MAN #9-10 -- BOBBIE.
THAT'S OUR NATASHA FOR YOU. A VISION IN BLACK LEATHER -- BUT COMFORTING, SHE'S NOT. STILL, SHE DIDN'T NEED TO WORRY --
-- I HAVE IT ON THE BEST AUTHORITY THAT YOU'RE QUITE TRUST-WORTHY WHEN IT COMES TO SECRETS.*
*JANE FOSTER KNEW THOR'S SECRET ID, BACK WHEN HE WAS DR. DON BLAKE -- BOBBIE.
BUT ENOUGH BUILDUP. GIVE IT TO ME STRAIGHT, JANE -- WILL I EVER PLAY THE VIOLIN AGAIN?

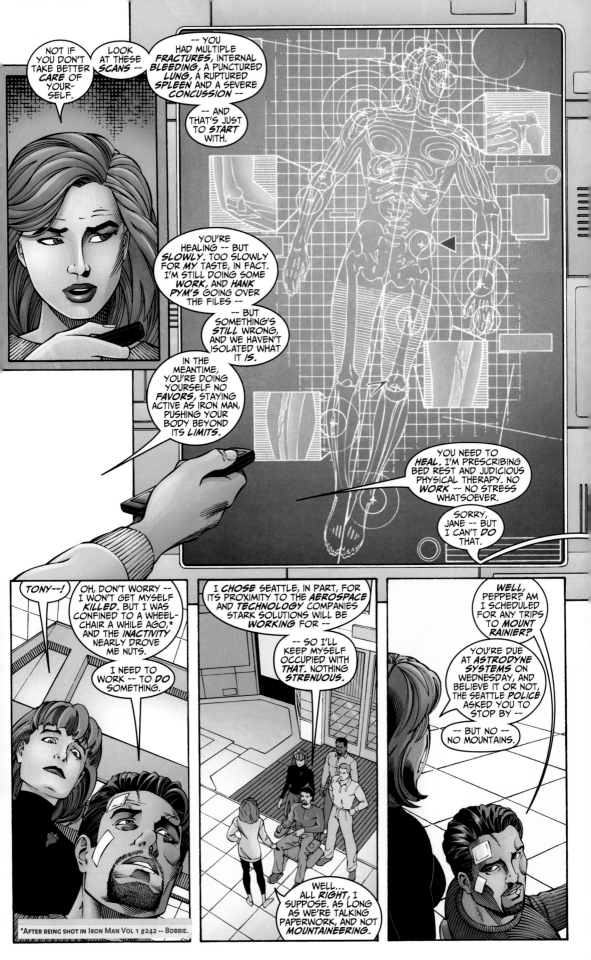

NOT IF YOU DON'T TAKE BETTER *CARE* OF YOURSELF.

LOOK AT THESE *SCANS* --

-- YOU HAD MULTIPLE *FRACTURES*, INTERNAL *BLEEDING*, A PUNCTURED *LUNG*, A RUPTURED *SPLEEN* AND A SEVERE *CONCUSSION* --

-- AND THAT'S JUST TO *START* WITH.

YOU'RE *HEALING* -- BUT *SLOWLY*. TOO SLOWLY FOR *MY* TASTE, IN FACT. I'M STILL DOING SOME *WORK*, AND *HANK PYM'S* GOING OVER THE FILES --

-- BUT SOMETHING'S *STILL* WRONG, AND WE HAVEN'T *ISOLATED* WHAT IT *IS*.

IN THE MEANTIME, YOU'RE DOING YOURSELF NO *FAVORS*, STAYING ACTIVE AS IRON MAN, PUSHING YOUR BODY BEYOND ITS *LIMITS*.

YOU NEED TO *HEAL*. I'M PRESCRIBING BED REST AND JUDICIOUS PHYSICAL THERAPY. NO *WORK* -- NO STRESS WHATSOEVER.

SORRY, JANE -- BUT I CAN'T *DO* THAT.

TONY--!

OH, DON'T WORRY -- I WON'T GET MYSELF *KILLED*. BUT I WAS CONFINED TO A WHEEL-CHAIR A WHILE AGO,* AND THE *INACTIVITY* NEARLY DROVE ME NUTS.

I NEED TO *WORK* -- TO *DO* SOMETHING.

I *CHOSE* SEATTLE, IN PART, FOR ITS PROXIMITY TO THE *AEROSPACE* AND *TECHNOLOGY* COMPANIES STARK SOLUTIONS WILL BE *WORKING* FOR --

-- SO I'LL KEEP MYSELF OCCUPIED WITH *THAT*. NOTHING *STRENUOUS*.

WELL... ALL *RIGHT*, I SUPPOSE. AS LONG AS WE'RE TALKING PAPERWORK, AND NOT *MOUNTAINEERING*.

WELL, PEPPER? AM I SCHEDULED FOR ANY TRIPS TO *MOUNT RAINIER*?

YOU'RE DUE AT *ASTRODYNE SYSTEMS* ON WEDNESDAY, AND BELIEVE IT OR NOT, THE SEATTLE *POLICE* ASKED YOU TO STOP BY --

-- BUT NO -- NO MOUNTAINS.

*AFTER BEING SHOT IN IRON MAN VOL 1 #242 -- BOBBIE.

KWHOOM KWHOOM KWHOOM

MEANWHILE, SOME DISTANCE SOUTH AND WEST OF EVERGREEN ISLAND...

...AT THE COPORATE HEADQUARTERS OF BAINTRONICS, INC....

HMM. FIRE-CONTROL'S GOOD...

-- BUT WE'LL HAVE TO WORK ON RESPONSE TIME.

EH? BILMES?

PARDON ME, MS. BAIN -- BUT YOU SAID YOU WANTED TO HEAR THE MOMENT STARK SOLUTIONS RESPONDED TO OUR REQUEST.

THEY SAID NO -- THAT MR. STARK'S GOT NO ROOM IN HIS SCHEDULE AT THE MOMENT.

SO... HE'S MOVED TO THE AREA, BUT LITTLE TONY'S STILL BASHFUL AROUND HIS OLD PAL SUNSET. THAT'LL NEVER DO.

BUT THERE ARE FEW PROBLEMS --

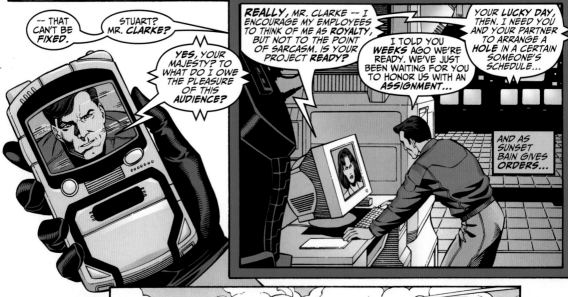

-- THAT CAN'T BE FIXED.

STUART? MR. CLARKE?

YES, YOUR MAJESTY? TO WHAT DO I OWE THE PLEASURE OF THIS AUDIENCE?

REALLY, MR. CLARKE -- I ENCOURAGE MY EMPLOYEES TO THINK OF ME AS ROYALTY, BUT NOT TO THE POINT OF SARCASM. IS YOUR PROJECT READY?

I TOLD YOU WEEKS AGO WE'RE READY. WE'VE JUST BEEN WAITING FOR YOU TO HONOR US WITH AN ASSIGNMENT...

YOUR LUCKY DAY, THEN. I NEED YOU AND YOUR PARTNER TO ARRANGE A HOLE IN A CERTAIN SOMEONE'S SCHEDULE...

AND AS SUNSET BAIN GIVES ORDERS...

...WE SHIFT OUR ATTENTION TO THE NEXT DAY, AND TO A STREAK OF LIGHT THAT SWOOPS AND GAMBOLS OVER THE SEATTLE SKYLINE...

...LIKE A COMET WITH A MIND OF ITS OWN.

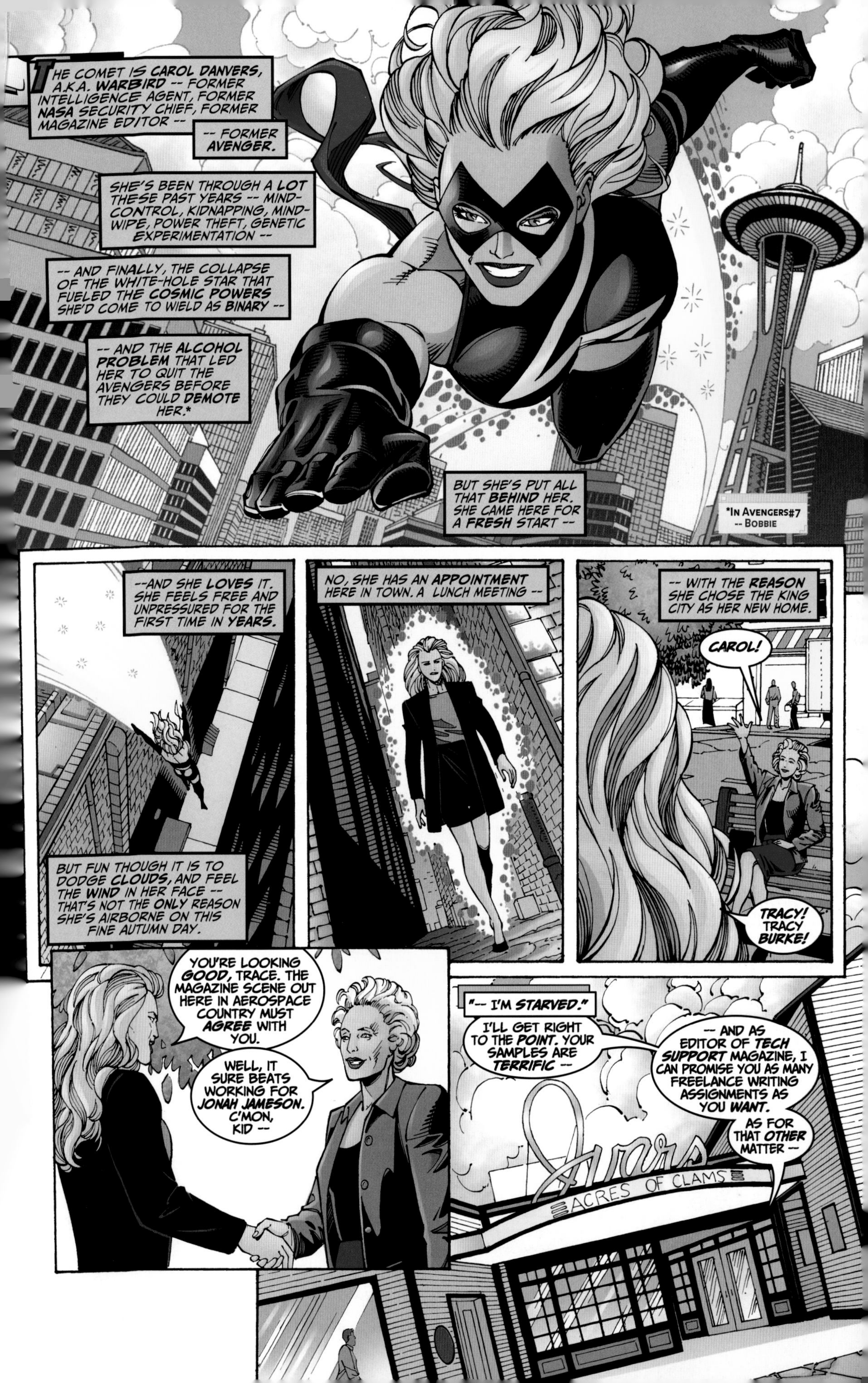
THE COMET IS CAROL DANVERS, A.K.A. WARBIRD -- FORMER INTELLIGENCE AGENT, FORMER NASA SECURITY CHIEF, FORMER MAGAZINE EDITOR --
-- FORMER AVENGER.
SHE'S BEEN THROUGH A LOT THESE PAST YEARS -- MIND-CONTROL, KIDNAPPING, MIND-WIPE, POWER THEFT, GENETIC EXPERIMENTATION --
-- AND FINALLY, THE COLLAPSE OF THE WHITE-HOLE STAR THAT FUELED THE COSMIC POWERS SHE'D COME TO WIELD AS BINARY --
-- AND THE ALCOHOL PROBLEM THAT LED HER TO QUIT THE AVENGERS BEFORE THEY COULD DEMOTE HER.*
BUT SHE'S PUT ALL THAT BEHIND HER. SHE CAME HERE FOR A FRESH START --
*IN AVENGERS#7 -- BOBBIE
--AND SHE LOVES IT. SHE FEELS FREE AND UNPRESSURED FOR THE FIRST TIME IN YEARS.
BUT FUN THOUGH IT IS TO DODGE CLOUDS, AND FEEL THE WIND IN HER FACE -- THAT'S NOT THE ONLY REASON SHE'S AIRBORNE ON THIS FINE AUTUMN DAY.
NO, SHE HAS AN APPOINTMENT HERE IN TOWN. A LUNCH MEETING --
-- WITH THE REASON SHE CHOSE THE KING CITY AS HER NEW HOME.
CAROL!
TRACY! TRACY BURKE!
YOU'RE LOOKING GOOD, TRACE. THE MAGAZINE SCENE OUT HERE IN AEROSPACE COUNTRY MUST AGREE WITH YOU.
WELL, IT SURE BEATS WORKING FOR JONAH JAMESON. C'MON, KID --
"-- I'M STARVED."
I'LL GET RIGHT TO THE POINT. YOUR SAMPLES ARE TERRIFIC --
-- AND AS EDITOR OF TECH SUPPORT MAGAZINE, I CAN PROMISE YOU AS MANY FREELANCE WRITING ASSIGNMENTS AS YOU WANT.
AS FOR THAT OTHER MATTER --
Ivar's
ACRES OF CLAMS

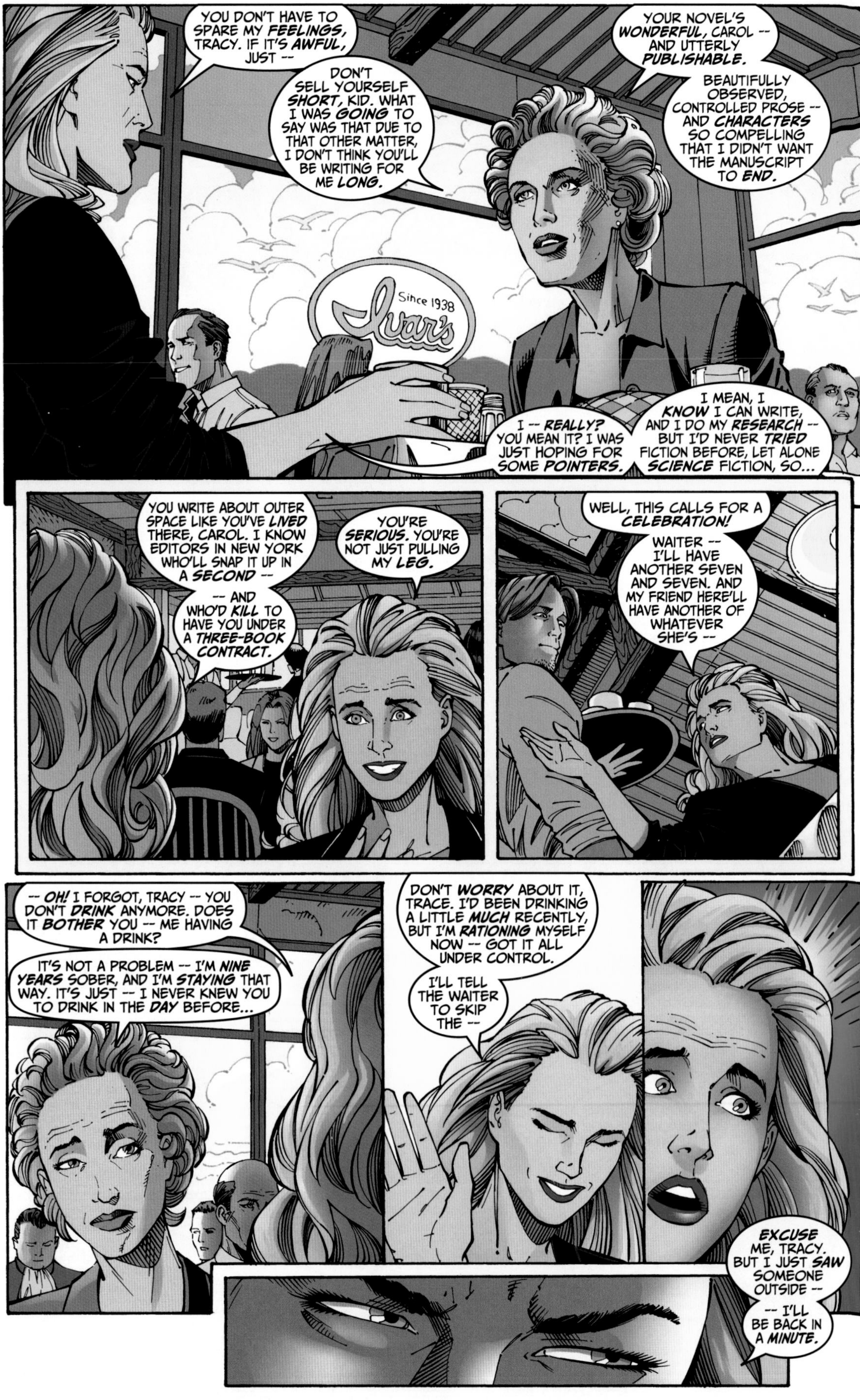
YOU DON'T HAVE TO SPARE MY FEELINGS, TRACY. IF IT'S AWFUL, JUST --
DON'T SELL YOURSELF SHORT, KID. WHAT I WAS GOING TO SAY WAS THAT DUE TO THAT OTHER MATTER, I DON'T THINK YOU'LL BE WRITING FOR ME LONG.
YOUR NOVEL'S WONDERFUL, CAROL -- AND UTTERLY PUBLISHABLE.
BEAUTIFULLY OBSERVED, CONTROLLED PROSE -- AND CHARACTERS SO COMPELLING THAT I DIDN'T WANT THE MANUSCRIPT TO END.
Since 1938
Ivar's
I -- REALLY? YOU MEAN IT? I WAS JUST HOPING FOR SOME POINTERS.
I MEAN, I KNOW I CAN WRITE, AND I DO MY RESEARCH -- BUT I'D NEVER TRIED FICTION BEFORE, LET ALONE SCIENCE FICTION, SO...
YOU WRITE ABOUT OUTER SPACE LIKE YOU'VE LIVED THERE, CAROL. I KNOW EDITORS IN NEW YORK WHO'LL SNAP IT UP IN A SECOND --
YOU'RE SERIOUS. YOU'RE NOT JUST PULLING MY LEG.
-- AND WHO'D KILL TO HAVE YOU UNDER A THREE-BOOK CONTRACT.
WELL, THIS CALLS FOR A CELEBRATION!
WAITER -- I'LL HAVE ANOTHER SEVEN AND SEVEN. AND MY FRIEND HERE'LL HAVE ANOTHER OF WHATEVER SHE'S --
-- OH! I FORGOT, TRACY -- YOU DON'T DRINK ANYMORE. DOES IT BOTHER YOU -- ME HAVING A DRINK?
IT'S NOT A PROBLEM -- I'M NINE YEARS SOBER, AND I'M STAYING THAT WAY. IT'S JUST -- I NEVER KNEW YOU TO DRINK IN THE DAY BEFORE...
DON'T WORRY ABOUT IT, TRACE. I'D BEEN DRINKING A LITTLE MUCH RECENTLY, BUT I'M RATIONING MYSELF NOW -- GOT IT ALL UNDER CONTROL.
I'LL TELL THE WAITER TO SKIP THE --
EXCUSE ME, TRACY. BUT I JUST SAW SOMEONE OUTSIDE --
-- I'LL BE BACK IN A MINUTE.

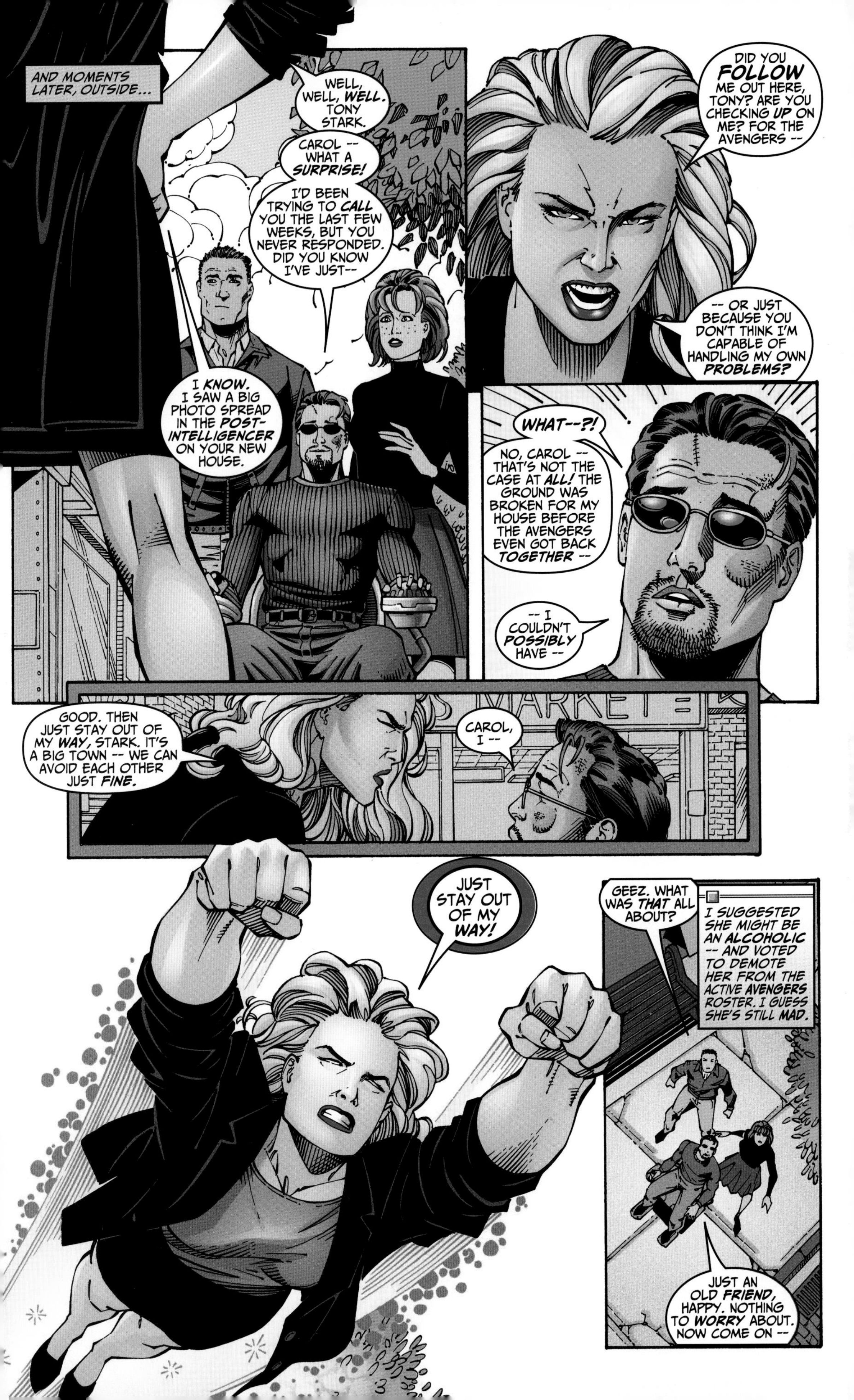
AND MOMENTS LATER, OUTSIDE...
WELL, WELL, WELL. TONY STARK.
CAROL -- WHAT A SURPRISE!
I'D BEEN TRYING TO CALL YOU THE LAST FEW WEEKS, BUT YOU NEVER RESPONDED. DID YOU KNOW I'VE JUST--
I KNOW. I SAW A BIG PHOTO SPREAD IN THE POST-INTELLIGENCER ON YOUR NEW HOUSE.
DID YOU FOLLOW ME OUT HERE, TONY? ARE YOU CHECKING UP ON ME? FOR THE AVENGERS --
-- OR JUST BECAUSE YOU DON'T THINK I'M CAPABLE OF HANDLING MY OWN PROBLEMS?
WHAT--?!
NO, CAROL -- THAT'S NOT THE CASE AT ALL! THE GROUND WAS BROKEN FOR MY HOUSE BEFORE THE AVENGERS EVEN GOT BACK TOGETHER --
-- I COULDN'T POSSIBLY HAVE --
GOOD. THEN JUST STAY OUT OF MY WAY, STARK. IT'S A BIG TOWN -- WE CAN AVOID EACH OTHER JUST FINE.
CAROL, I --
JUST STAY OUT OF MY WAY!
GEEZ. WHAT WAS THAT ALL ABOUT?
I SUGGESTED SHE MIGHT BE AN ALCOHOLIC -- AND VOTED TO DEMOTE HER FROM THE ACTIVE AVENGERS ROSTER. I GUESS SHE'S STILL MAD.
JUST AN OLD FRIEND, HAPPY. NOTHING TO WORRY ABOUT. NOW COME ON --

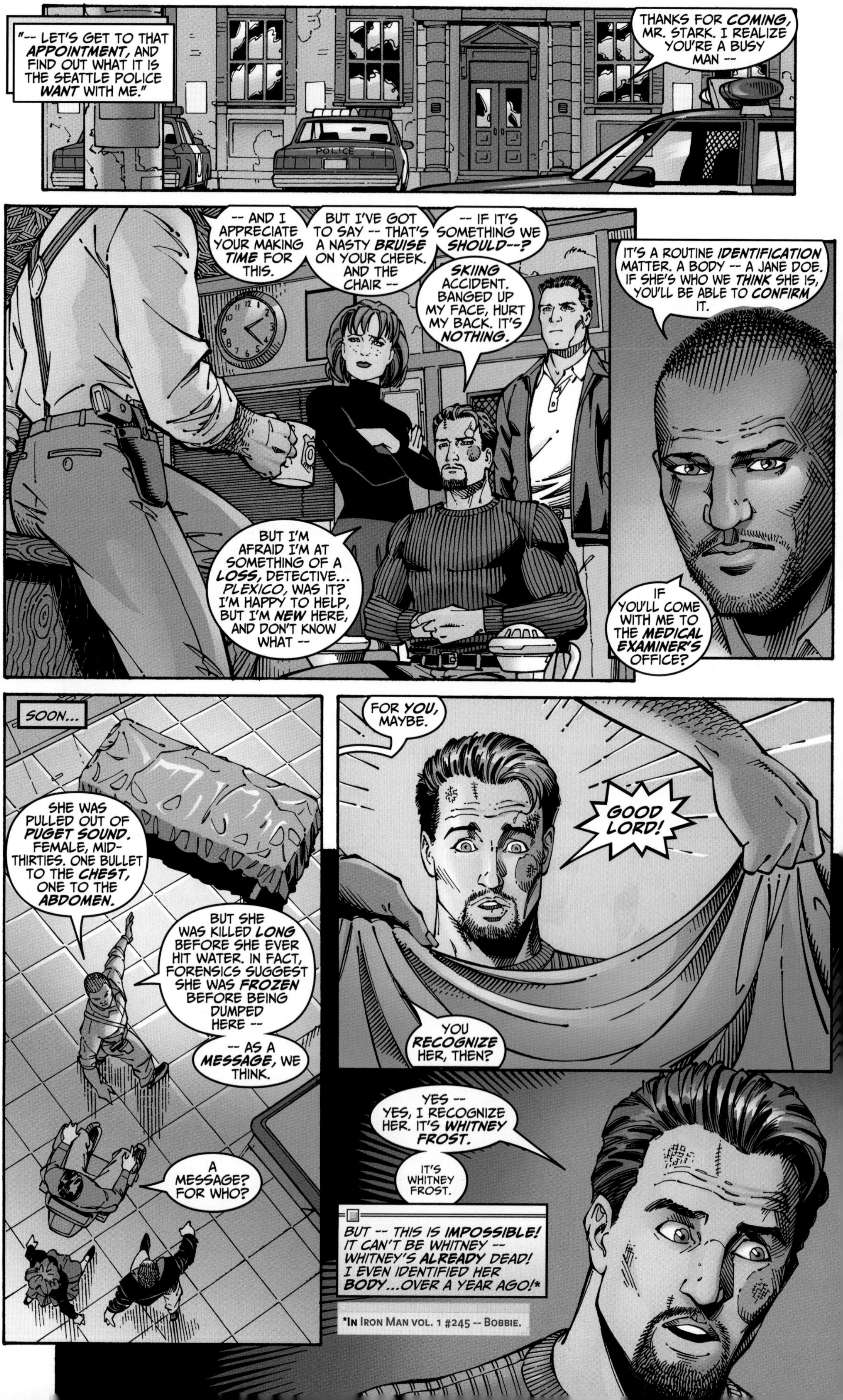
"-- LET'S GET TO THAT APPOINTMENT, AND FIND OUT WHAT IT IS THE SEATTLE POLICE WANT WITH ME."
THANKS FOR COMING, MR. STARK. I REALIZE YOU'RE A BUSY MAN --
POLICE
-- AND I APPRECIATE YOUR MAKING TIME FOR THIS.
BUT I'VE GOT TO SAY -- THAT'S A NASTY BRUISE ON YOUR CHEEK. AND THE CHAIR --
-- IF IT'S SOMETHING WE SHOULD--?
SKIING ACCIDENT. BANGED UP MY FACE, HURT MY BACK. IT'S NOTHING.
BUT I'M AFRAID I'M AT SOMETHING OF A LOSS, DETECTIVE... PLEXICO, WAS IT? I'M HAPPY TO HELP, BUT I'M NEW HERE, AND DON'T KNOW WHAT --
IT'S A ROUTINE IDENTIFICATION MATTER. A BODY -- A JANE DOE. IF SHE'S WHO WE THINK SHE IS, YOU'LL BE ABLE TO CONFIRM IT.
IF YOU'LL COME WITH ME TO THE MEDICAL EXAMINER'S OFFICE?
SOON...
SHE WAS PULLED OUT OF PUGET SOUND. FEMALE, MID-THIRTIES. ONE BULLET TO THE CHEST, ONE TO THE ABDOMEN.
BUT SHE WAS KILLED LONG BEFORE SHE EVER HIT WATER. IN FACT, FORENSICS SUGGEST SHE WAS FROZEN BEFORE BEING DUMPED HERE --
-- AS A MESSAGE, WE THINK.
A MESSAGE? FOR WHO?
FOR YOU, MAYBE.
GOOD LORD!
YOU RECOGNIZE HER, THEN?
YES -- YES, I RECOGNIZE HER. IT'S WHITNEY FROST.
IT'S WHITNEY FROST.
BUT -- THIS IS IMPOSSIBLE! IT CAN'T BE WHITNEY -- WHITNEY'S ALREADY DEAD! I EVEN IDENTIFIED HER BODY...OVER A YEAR AGO!*
*IN IRON MAN VOL. 1 #245 -- BOBBIE.

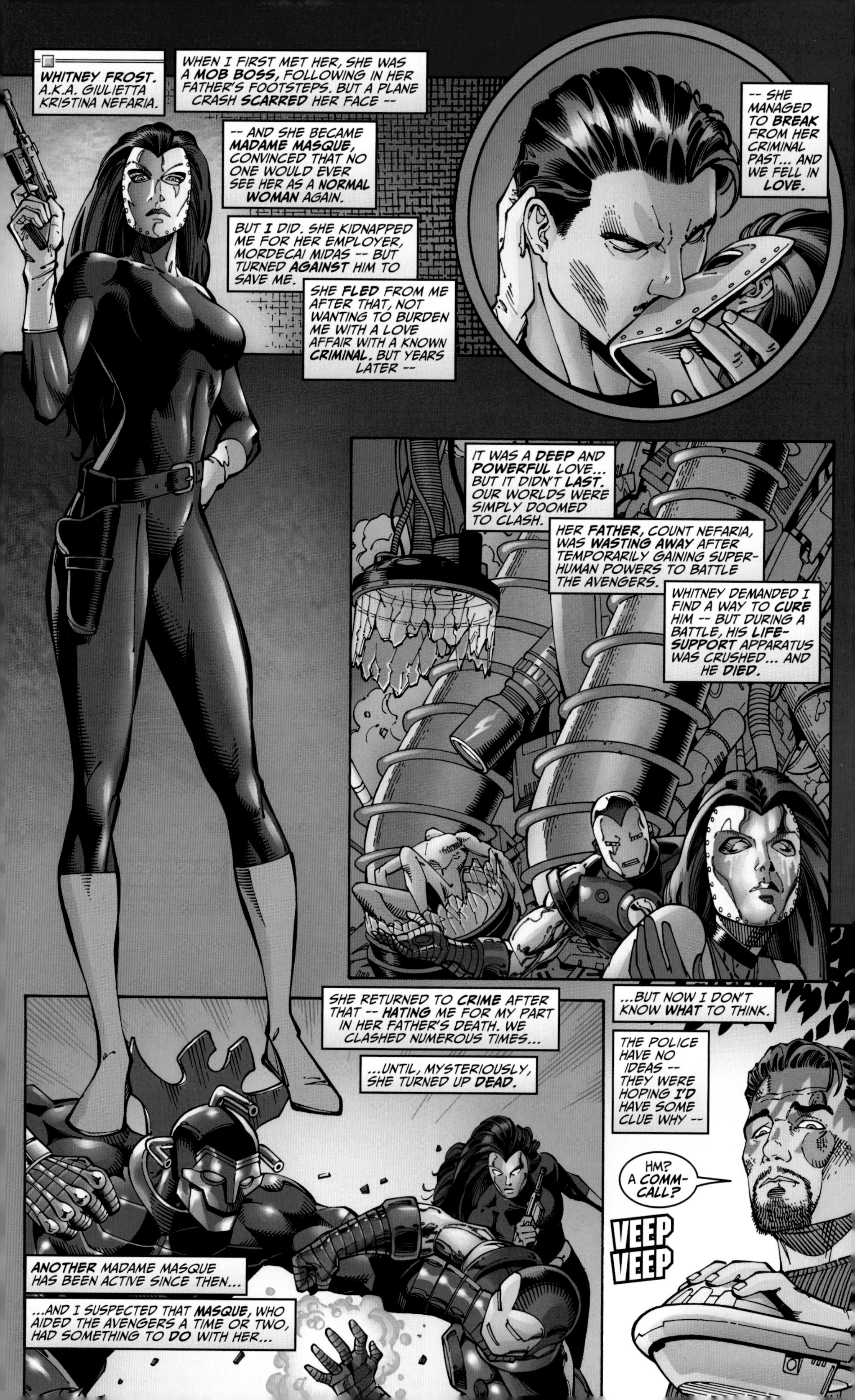
WHITNEY FROST. A.K.A. GIULIETTA KRISTINA NEFARIA.
WHEN I FIRST MET HER, SHE WAS A MOB BOSS, FOLLOWING IN HER FATHER'S FOOTSTEPS. BUT A PLANE CRASH SCARRED HER FACE --
-- AND SHE BECAME MADAME MASQUE, CONVINCED THAT NO ONE WOULD EVER SEE HER AS A NORMAL WOMAN AGAIN.
BUT I DID. SHE KIDNAPPED ME FOR HER EMPLOYER, MORDECAI MIDAS -- BUT TURNED AGAINST HIM TO SAVE ME.
SHE FLED FROM ME AFTER THAT, NOT WANTING TO BURDEN ME WITH A LOVE AFFAIR WITH A KNOWN CRIMINAL. BUT YEARS LATER --
-- SHE MANAGED TO BREAK FROM HER CRIMINAL PAST... AND WE FELL IN LOVE.
IT WAS A DEEP AND POWERFUL LOVE... BUT IT DIDN'T LAST. OUR WORLDS WERE SIMPLY DOOMED TO CLASH.
HER FATHER, COUNT NEFARIA, WAS WASTING AWAY AFTER TEMPORARILY GAINING SUPER-HUMAN POWERS TO BATTLE THE AVENGERS.
WHITNEY DEMANDED I FIND A WAY TO CURE HIM -- BUT DURING A BATTLE, HIS LIFE-SUPPORT APPARATUS WAS CRUSHED... AND HE DIED.
SHE RETURNED TO CRIME AFTER THAT -- HATING ME FOR MY PART IN HER FATHER'S DEATH. WE CLASHED NUMEROUS TIMES...
...UNTIL, MYSTERIOUSLY, SHE TURNED UP DEAD.
ANOTHER MADAME MASQUE HAS BEEN ACTIVE SINCE THEN...
...AND I SUSPECTED THAT MASQUE, WHO AIDED THE AVENGERS A TIME OR TWO, HAD SOMETHING TO DO WITH HER...
...BUT NOW I DON'T KNOW WHAT TO THINK.
THE POLICE HAVE NO IDEAS -- THEY WERE HOPING I'D HAVE SOME CLUE WHY --
HM? A COMM-CALL?
VEEP VEEP

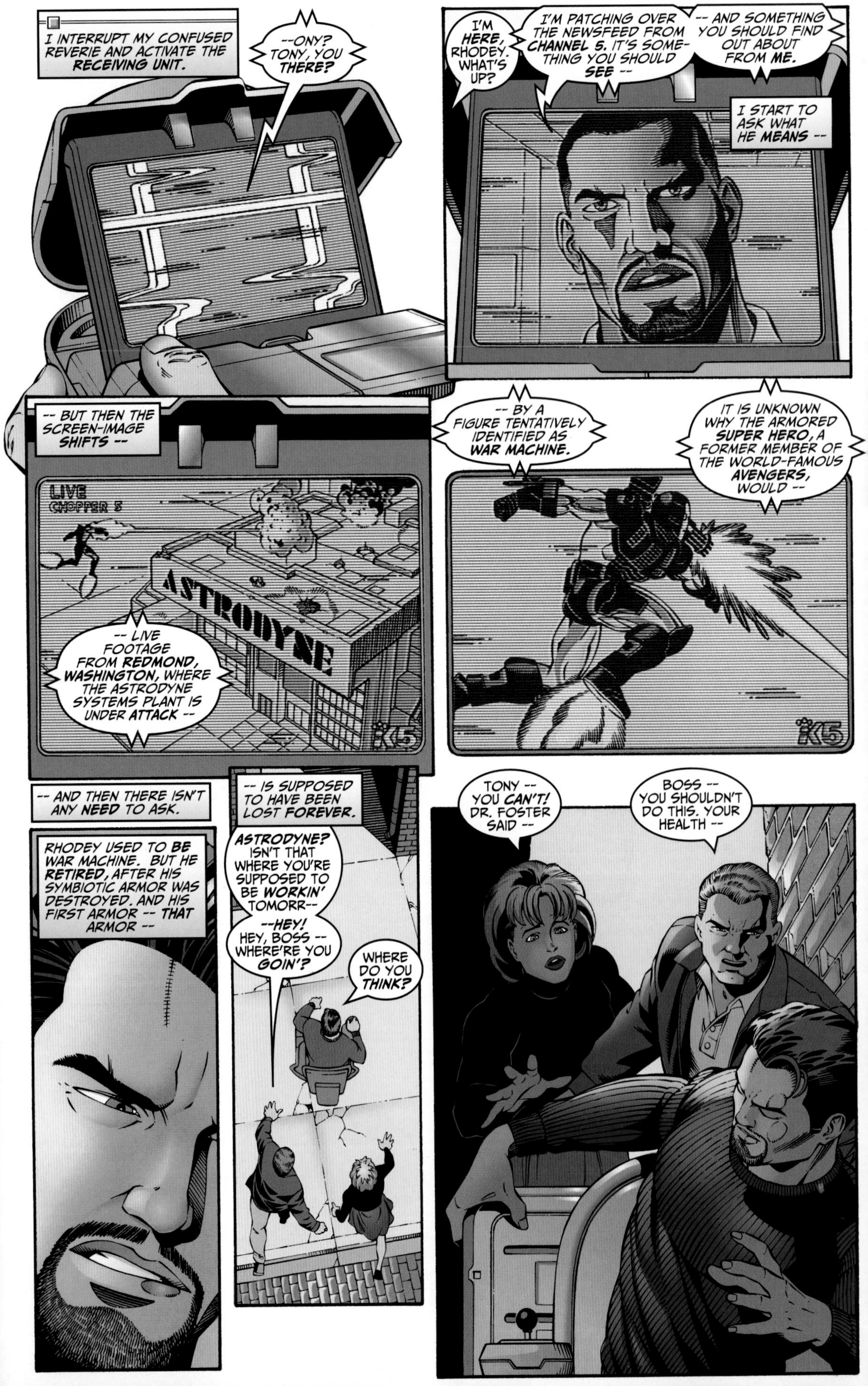
I INTERRUPT MY CONFUSED REVERIE AND ACTIVATE THE RECEIVING UNIT.
--ONY? TONY, YOU THERE?
I'M HERE, RHODEY. WHAT'S UP?
I'M PATCHING OVER THE NEWSFEED FROM CHANNEL 5. IT'S SOMETHING YOU SHOULD SEE --
-- AND SOMETHING YOU SHOULD FIND OUT ABOUT FROM ME.
I START TO ASK WHAT HE MEANS --
-- BUT THEN THE SCREEN-IMAGE SHIFTS --
LIVE
CHOPPER 5
ASTRODYNE
-- LIVE FOOTAGE FROM REDMOND, WASHINGTON, WHERE THE ASTRODYNE SYSTEMS PLANT IS UNDER ATTACK --
K5
-- BY A FIGURE TENTATIVELY IDENTIFIED AS WAR MACHINE.
IT IS UNKNOWN WHY THE ARMORED SUPER HERO, A FORMER MEMBER OF THE WORLD-FAMOUS AVENGERS, WOULD --
K5
-- AND THEN THERE ISN'T ANY NEED TO ASK.
RHODEY USED TO BE WAR MACHINE. BUT HE RETIRED, AFTER HIS SYMBIOTIC ARMOR WAS DESTROYED. AND HIS FIRST ARMOR -- THAT ARMOR --
-- IS SUPPOSED TO HAVE BEEN LOST FOREVER.
ASTRODYNE? ISN'T THAT WHERE YOU'RE SUPPOSED TO BE WORKIN' TOMORR--
--HEY! HEY, BOSS -- WHERE'RE YOU GOIN'?
WHERE DO YOU THINK?
TONY -- YOU CAN'T! DR. FOSTER SAID --
BOSS -- YOU SHOULDN'T DO THIS. YOUR HEALTH --

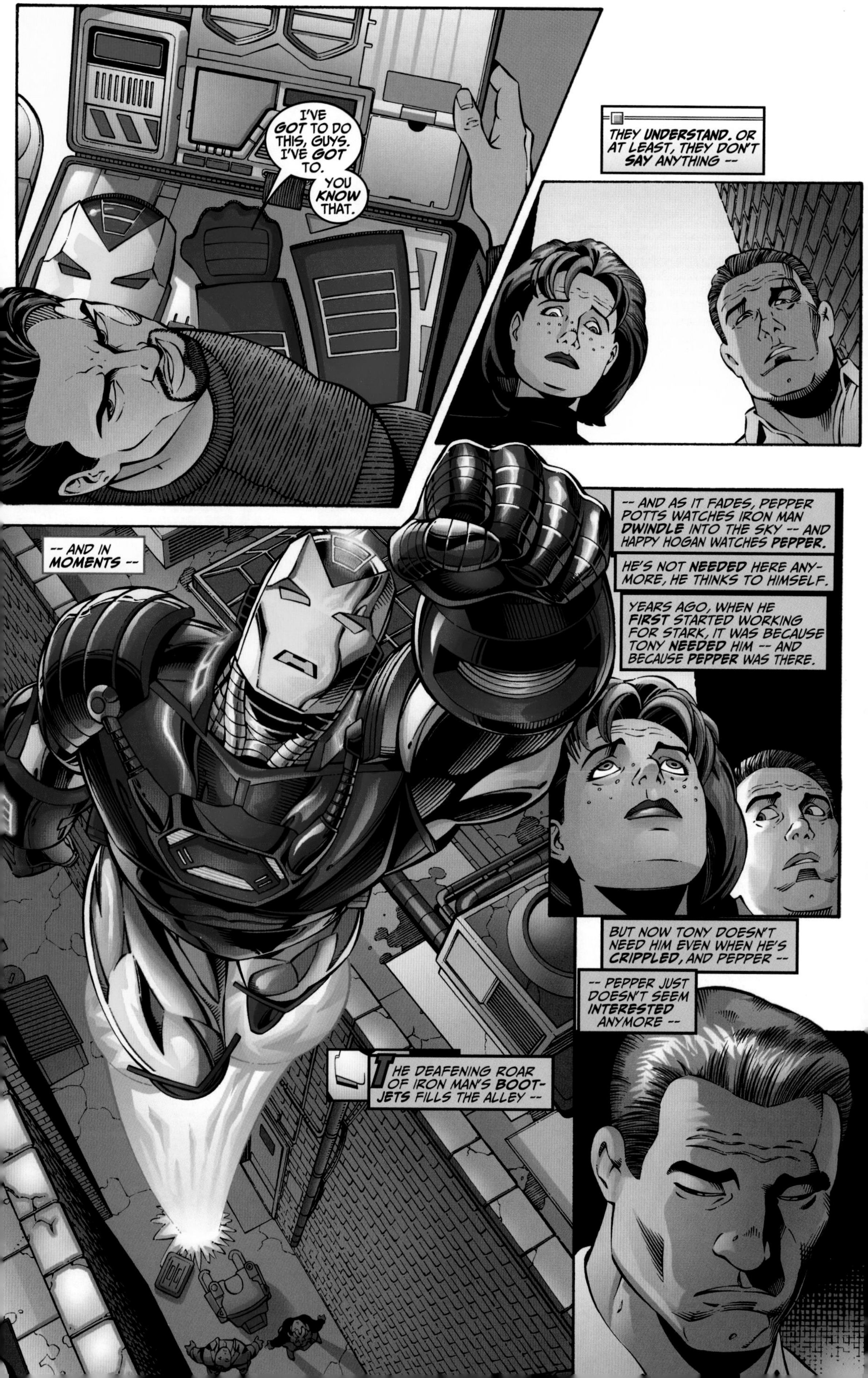
I'VE GOT TO DO THIS, GUYS. I'VE GOT TO.
YOU KNOW THAT.
THEY UNDERSTAND. OR AT LEAST, THEY DON'T SAY ANYTHING --
THE DEAFENING ROAR OF IRON MAN'S BOOT-JETS FILLS THE ALLEY --
-- AND IN MOMENTS --
-- AND AS IT FADES, PEPPER POTTS WATCHES IRON MAN DWINDLE INTO THE SKY -- AND HAPPY HOGAN WATCHES PEPPER.
HE'S NOT NEEDED HERE ANYMORE, HE THINKS TO HIMSELF.
YEARS AGO, WHEN HE FIRST STARTED WORKING FOR STARK, IT WAS BECAUSE TONY NEEDED HIM -- AND BECAUSE PEPPER WAS THERE.
BUT NOW TONY DOESN'T NEED HIM EVEN WHEN HE'S CRIPPLED, AND PEPPER --
-- PEPPER JUST DOESN'T SEEM INTERESTED ANYMORE --

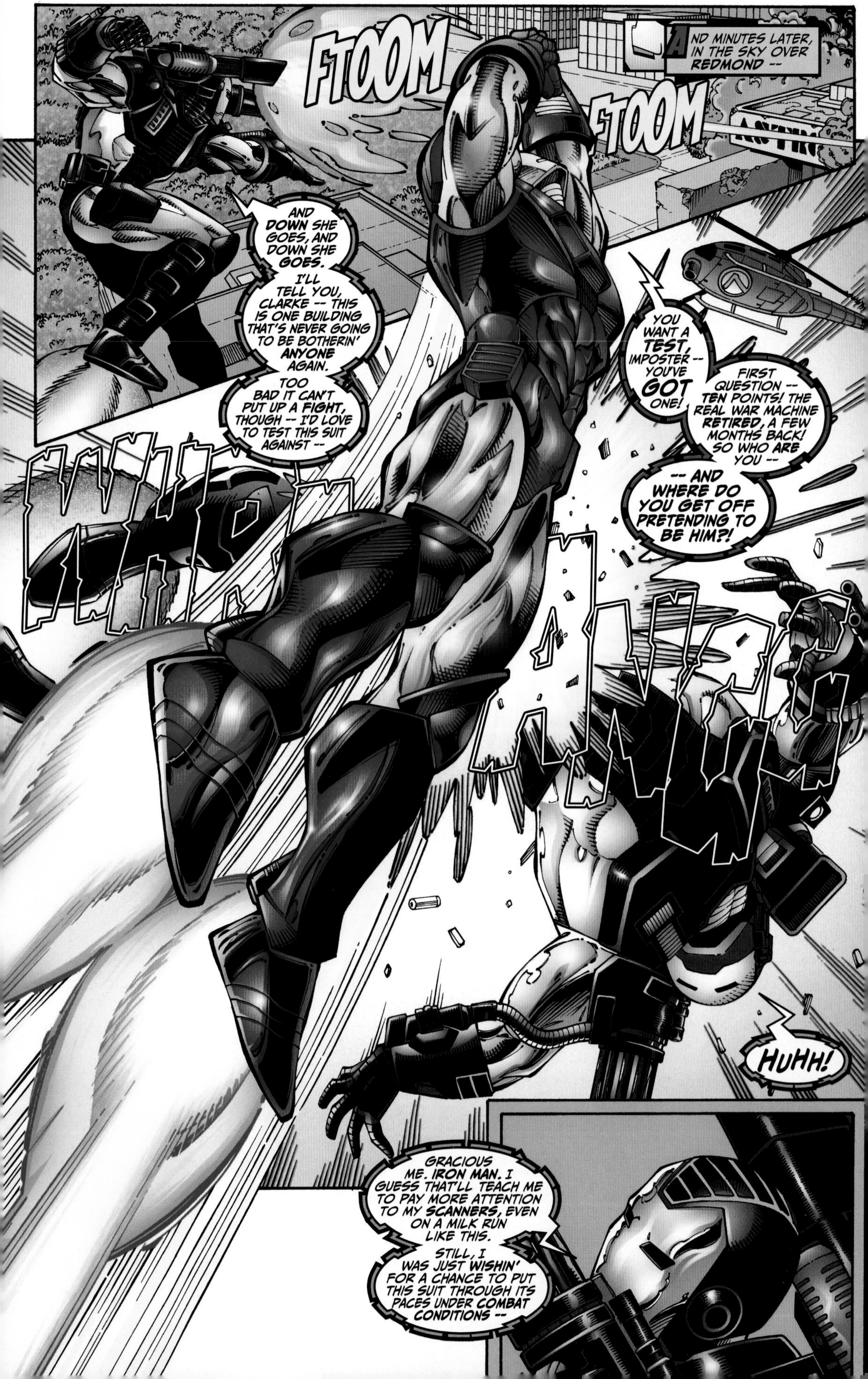

AND MINUTES LATER, IN THE SKY OVER REDMOND --
FTOOM
FTOOM
AND DOWN SHE GOES, AND DOWN SHE GOES.
I'LL TELL YOU, CLARKE -- THIS IS ONE BUILDING THAT'S NEVER GOING TO BE BOTHERIN' ANYONE AGAIN.
TOO BAD IT CAN'T PUT UP A FIGHT, THOUGH -- I'D LOVE TO TEST THIS SUIT AGAINST --
YOU WANT A TEST, IMPOSTER -- YOU'VE GOT ONE!
FIRST QUESTION -- TEN POINTS! THE REAL WAR MACHINE RETIRED, A FEW MONTHS BACK! SO WHO ARE YOU --
-- AND WHERE DO YOU GET OFF PRETENDING TO BE HIM?!
HUHH!
GRACIOUS ME. IRON MAN. I GUESS THAT'LL TEACH ME TO PAY MORE ATTENTION TO MY SCANNERS, EVEN ON A MILK RUN LIKE THIS.
STILL, I WAS JUST WISHIN' FOR A CHANCE TO PUT THIS SUIT THROUGH ITS PACES UNDER COMBAT CONDITIONS --

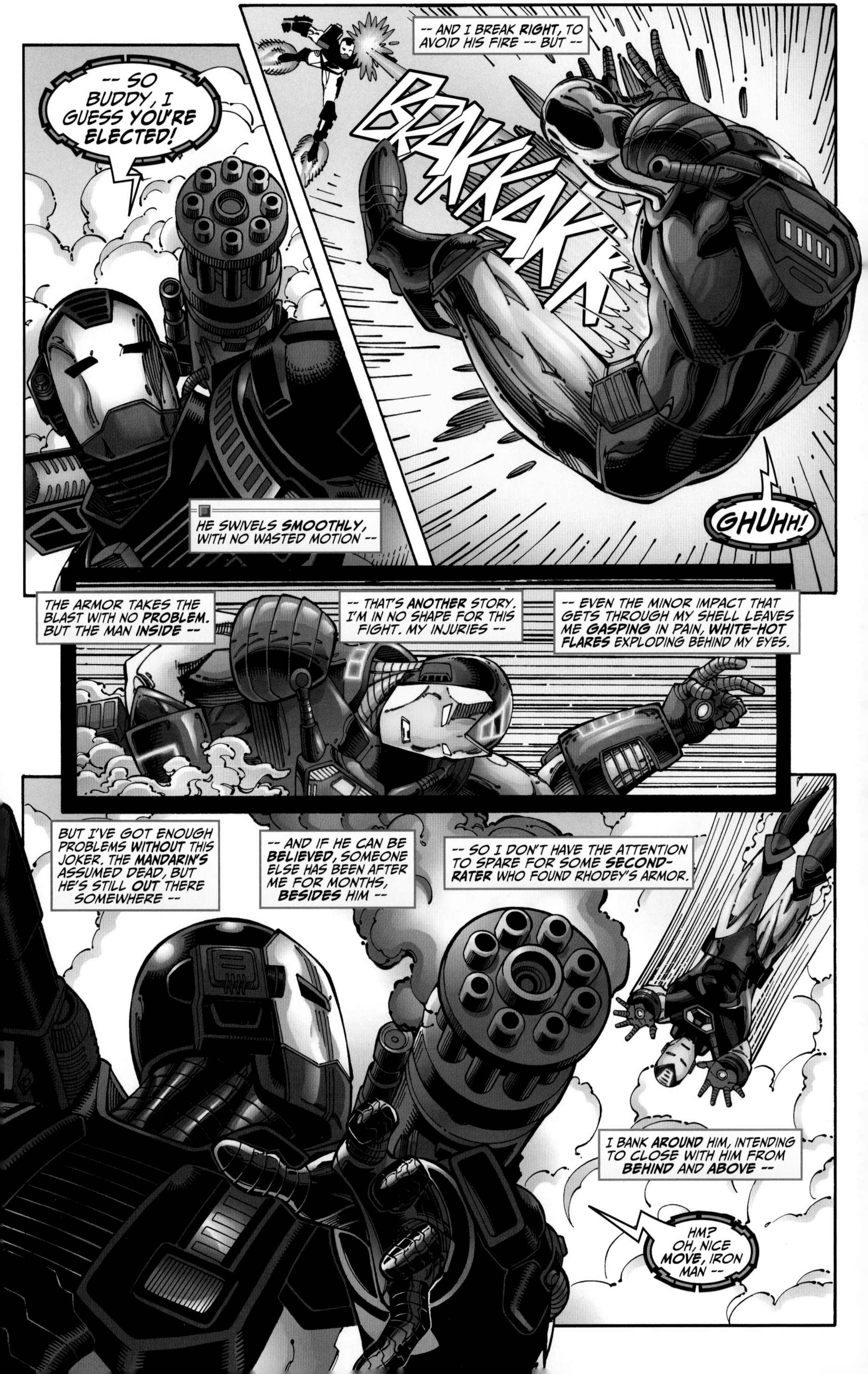
-- SO BUDDY, I GUESS YOU'RE ELECTED!
-- AND I BREAK RIGHT, TO AVOID HIS FIRE -- BUT --
BRAKKAKKK
HE SWIVELS SMOOTHLY, WITH NO WASTED MOTION --
GHUHH!
THE ARMOR TAKES THE BLAST WITH NO PROBLEM. BUT THE MAN INSIDE --
-- THAT'S ANOTHER STORY. I'M IN NO SHAPE FOR THIS FIGHT. MY INJURIES --
-- EVEN THE MINOR IMPACT THAT GETS THROUGH MY SHELL LEAVES ME GASPING IN PAIN, WHITE-HOT FLARES EXPLODING BEHIND MY EYES.
BUT I'VE GOT ENOUGH PROBLEMS WITHOUT THIS JOKER. THE MANDARIN'S ASSUMED DEAD, BUT HE'S STILL OUT THERE SOMEWHERE --
-- AND IF HE CAN BE BELIEVED, SOMEONE ELSE HAS BEEN AFTER ME FOR MONTHS, BESIDES HIM --
-- SO I DON'T HAVE THE ATTENTION TO SPARE FOR SOME SECOND-RATER WHO FOUND RHODEY'S ARMOR.
I BANK AROUND HIM, INTENDING TO CLOSE WITH HIM FROM BEHIND AND ABOVE --
HM? OH, NICE MOVE, IRON MAN --

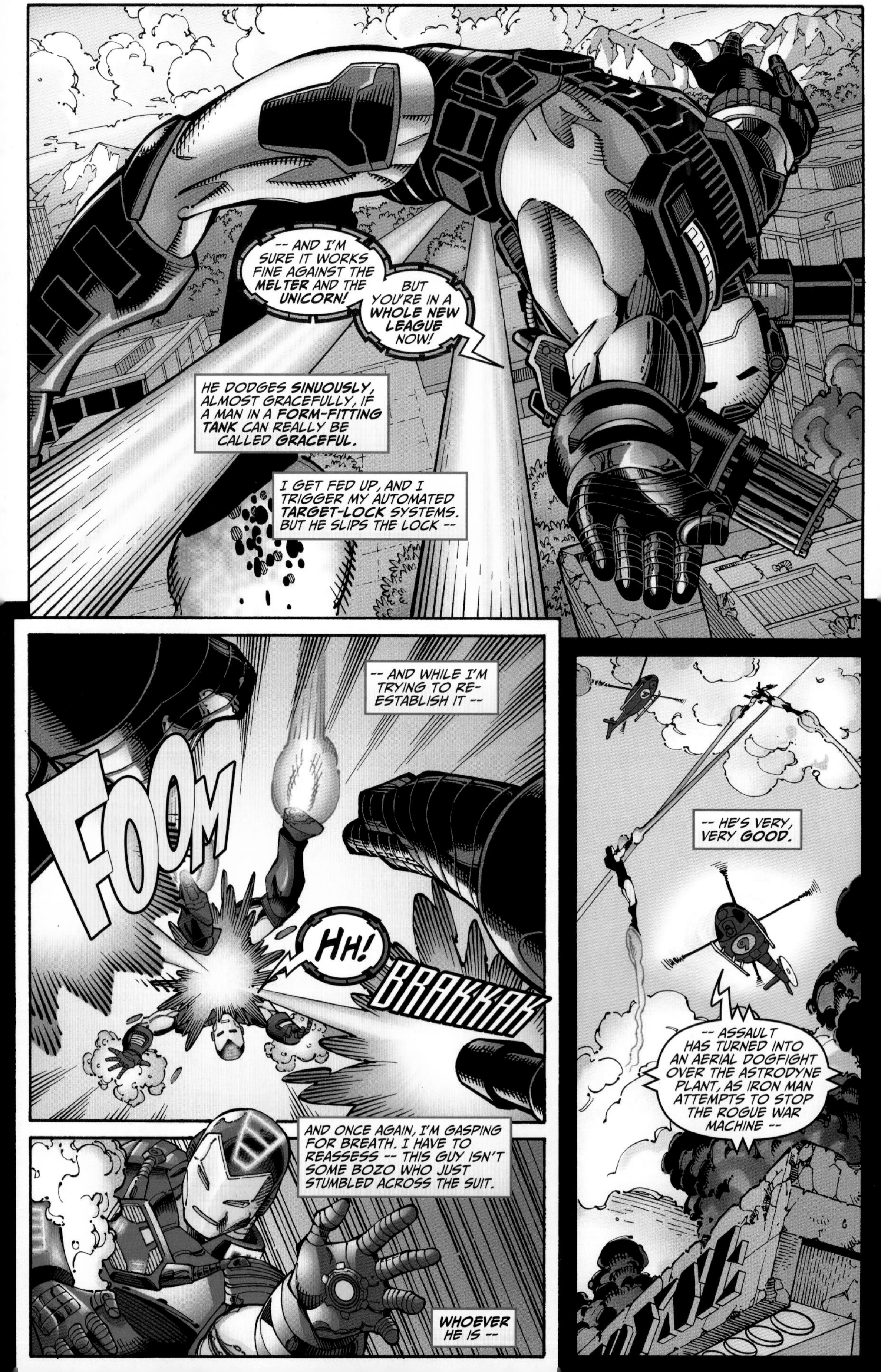
-- AND I'M SURE IT WORKS FINE AGAINST THE MELTER AND THE UNICORN!
BUT YOU'RE IN A WHOLE NEW LEAGUE NOW!
HE DODGES SINUOUSLY, ALMOST GRACEFULLY, IF A MAN IN A FORM-FITTING TANK CAN REALLY BE CALLED GRACEFUL.
I GET FED UP, AND I TRIGGER MY AUTOMATED TARGET-LOCK SYSTEMS. BUT HE SLIPS THE LOCK --
-- AND WHILE I'M TRYING TO RE-ESTABLISH IT --
FOOM
HH!
BRAKKAK
AND ONCE AGAIN, I'M GASPING FOR BREATH. I HAVE TO REASSESS -- THIS GUY ISN'T SOME BOZO WHO JUST STUMBLED ACROSS THE SUIT.
WHOEVER HE IS --
-- HE'S VERY, VERY GOOD.
-- ASSAULT HAS TURNED INTO AN AERIAL DOGFIGHT OVER THE ASTRODYNE PLANT, AS IRON MAN ATTEMPTS TO STOP THE ROGUE WAR MACHINE --

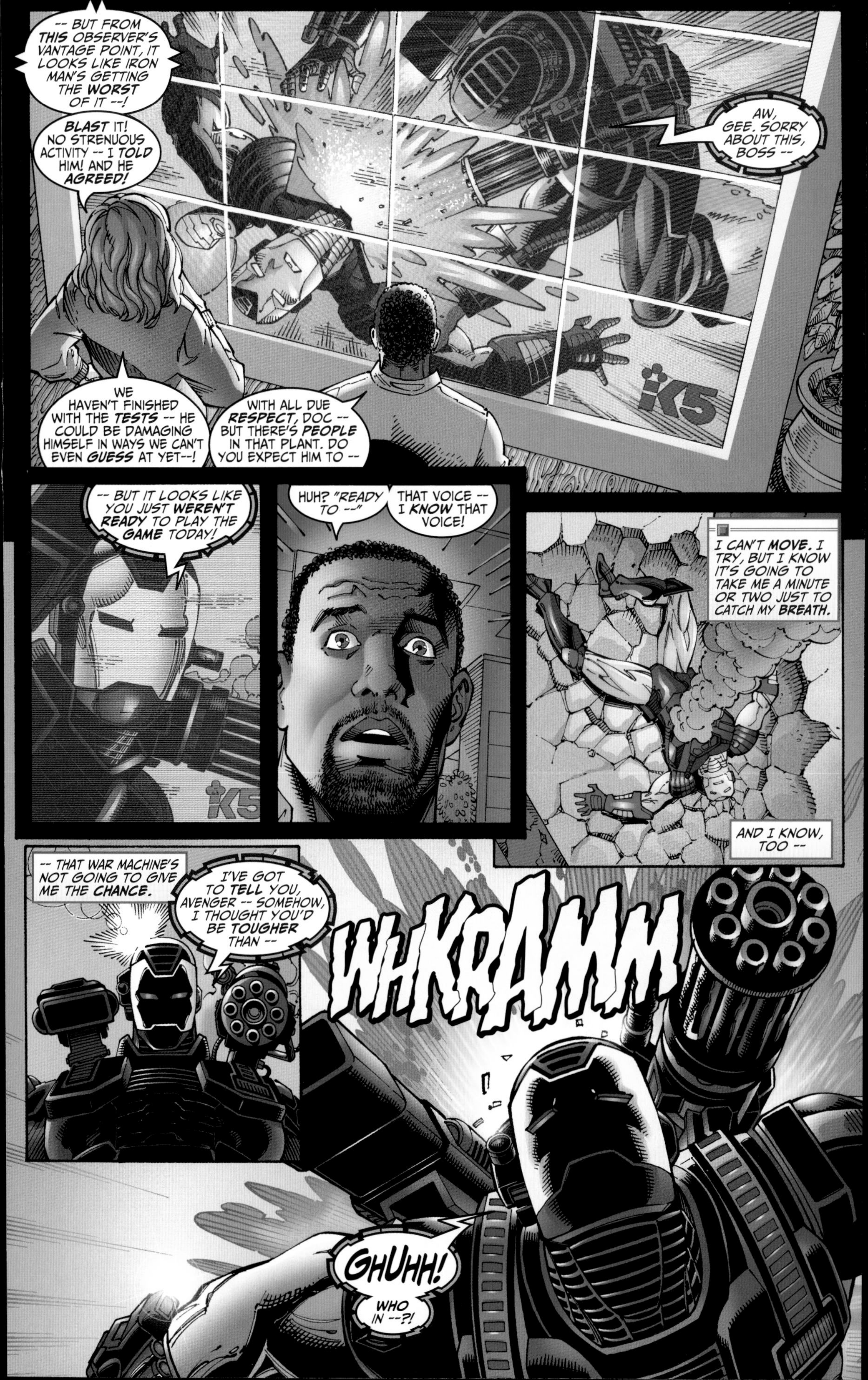
-- BUT FROM THIS OBSERVER'S VANTAGE POINT, IT LOOKS LIKE IRON MAN'S GETTING THE WORST OF IT --!
BLAST IT! NO STRENUOUS ACTIVITY -- I TOLD HIM! AND HE AGREED!
AW, GEE. SORRY ABOUT THIS, BOSS --
WE HAVEN'T FINISHED WITH THE TESTS -- HE COULD BE DAMAGING HIMSELF IN WAYS WE CAN'T EVEN GUESS AT YET--!
WITH ALL DUE RESPECT, DOC -- BUT THERE'S PEOPLE IN THAT PLANT. DO YOU EXPECT HIM TO --
K5
-- BUT IT LOOKS LIKE YOU JUST WEREN'T READY TO PLAY THE GAME TODAY!
K5
HUH? "READY TO --"
THAT VOICE -- I KNOW THAT VOICE!
I CAN'T MOVE. I TRY, BUT I KNOW IT'S GOING TO TAKE ME A MINUTE OR TWO JUST TO CATCH MY BREATH.
AND I KNOW, TOO --
-- THAT WAR MACHINE'S NOT GOING TO GIVE ME THE CHANCE.
I'VE GOT TO TELL YOU, AVENGER -- SOMEHOW, I THOUGHT YOU'D BE TOUGHER THAN --
WHKRAMM
GHUHH!
WHO IN --?!

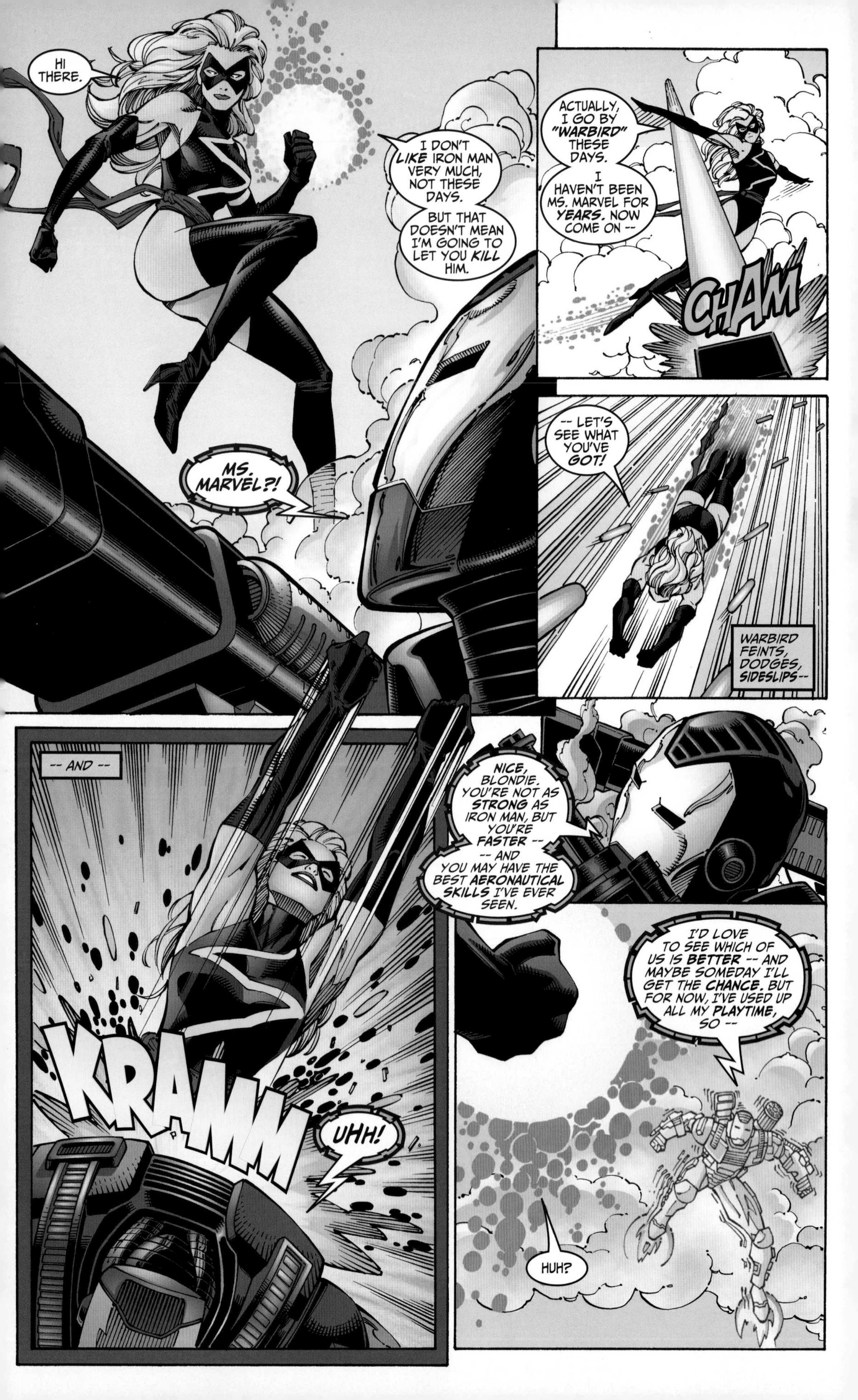
HI THERE.
I DON'T LIKE IRON MAN VERY MUCH, NOT THESE DAYS.
BUT THAT DOESN'T MEAN I'M GOING TO LET YOU KILL HIM.
MS. MARVEL?!
ACTUALLY, I GO BY "WARBIRD" THESE DAYS.
I HAVEN'T BEEN MS. MARVEL FOR YEARS. NOW COME ON --
CHAM
-- LET'S SEE WHAT YOU'VE GOT!
WARBIRD FEINTS, DODGES, SIDESLIPS--
-- AND --
NICE, BLONDIE. YOU'RE NOT AS STRONG AS IRON MAN, BUT YOU'RE FASTER --
-- AND YOU MAY HAVE THE BEST AERONAUTICAL SKILLS I'VE EVER SEEN.
KRAMM
UHH!
I'D LOVE TO SEE WHICH OF US IS BETTER -- AND MAYBE SOMEDAY I'LL GET THE CHANCE. BUT FOR NOW, I'VE USED UP ALL MY PLAYTIME, SO --
HUH?

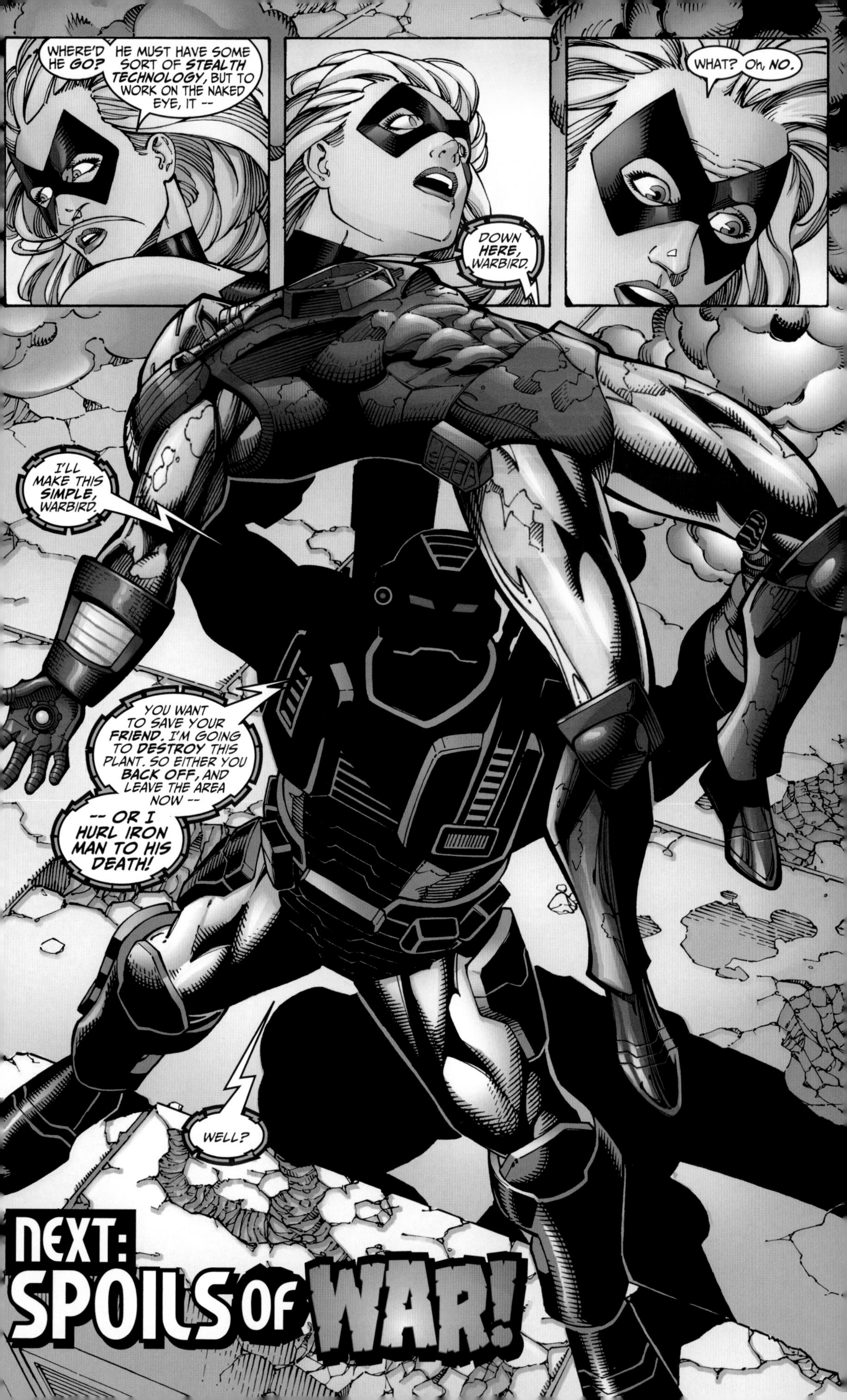

WHERE'D HE GO?
HE MUST HAVE SOME SORT OF STEALTH TECHNOLOGY, BUT TO WORK ON THE NAKED EYE, IT --
DOWN HERE, WARBIRD.
WHAT? Oh, NO.
I'LL MAKE THIS SIMPLE, WARBIRD.
YOU WANT TO SAVE YOUR FRIEND. I'M GOING TO DESTROY THIS PLANT. SO EITHER YOU BACK OFF, AND LEAVE THE AREA NOW --
-- OR I HURL IRON MAN TO HIS DEATH!
WELL?
NEXT: SPOILS OF WAR!

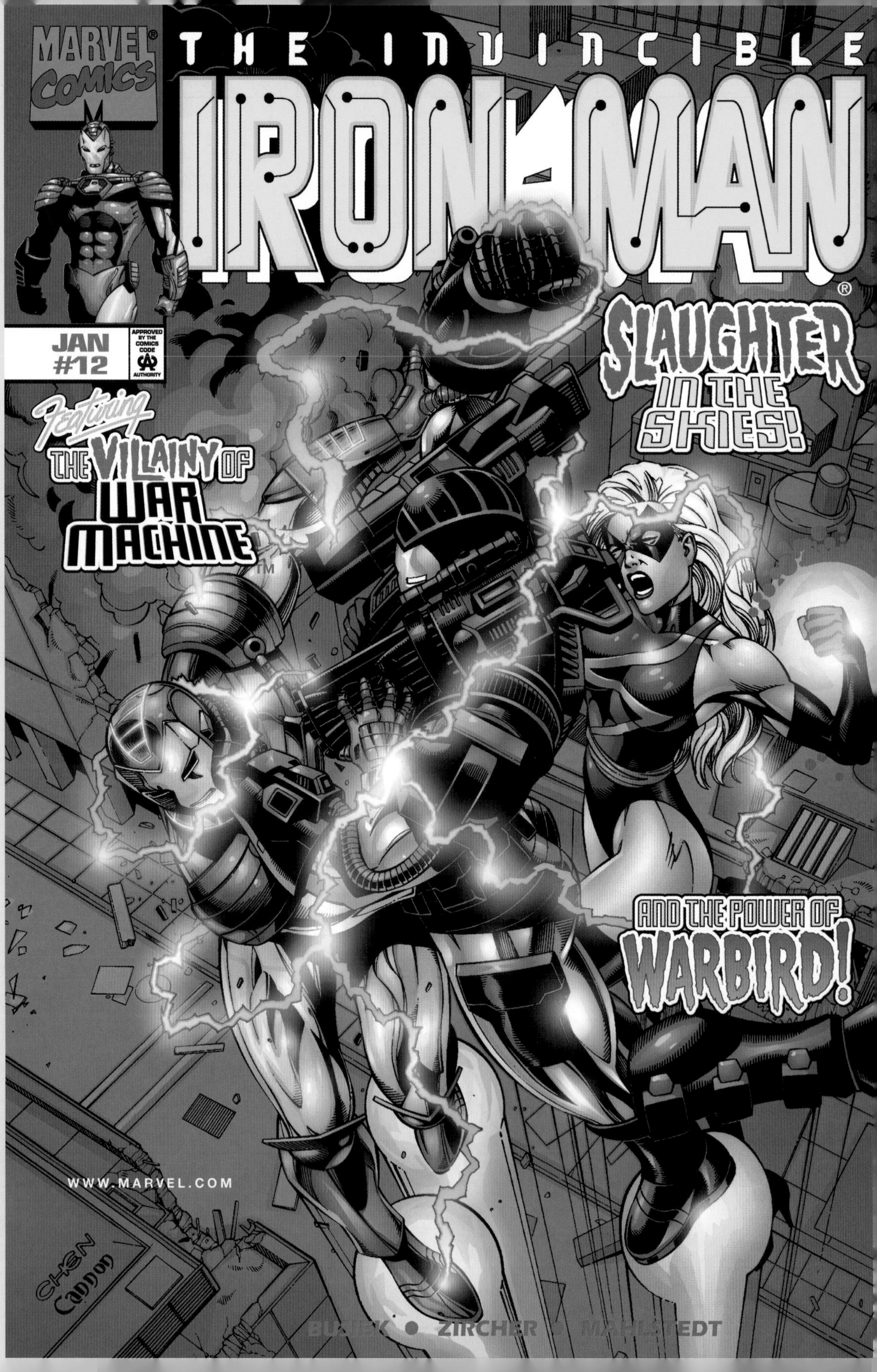
MARVEL® COMICS
THE INVINCIBLE
IRON MAN®
JAN #12
APPROVED BY THE COMICS CODE AUTHORITY
SLAUGHTER IN THE SKIES!
Featuring THE VILLAINY OF WAR MACHINE™
AND THE POWER OF WARBIRD!
WWW.MARVEL.COM
BUSIEK • ZIRCHER • MAHLSTEDT

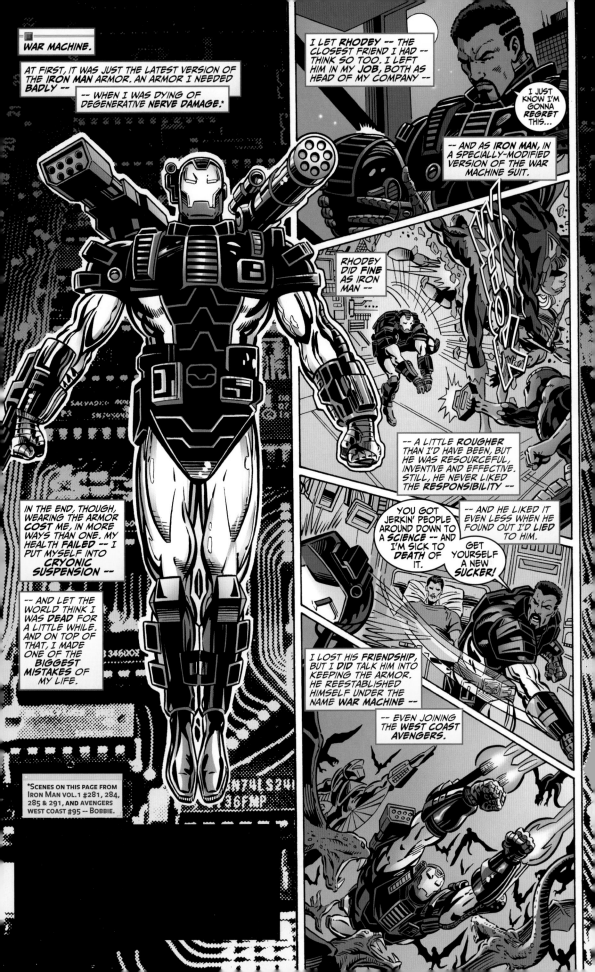

WAR MACHINE.

AT FIRST, IT WAS JUST THE LATEST VERSION OF THE IRON MAN ARMOR. AN ARMOR I NEEDED BADLY --

-- WHEN I WAS DYING OF DEGENERATIVE NERVE DAMAGE.*

IN THE END, THOUGH, WEARING THE ARMOR COST ME, IN MORE WAYS THAN ONE. MY HEALTH FAILED -- I PUT MYSELF INTO CRYONIC SUSPENSION --

-- AND LET THE WORLD THINK I WAS DEAD FOR A LITTLE WHILE. AND ON TOP OF THAT, I MADE ONE OF THE BIGGEST MISTAKES OF MY LIFE.

*SCENES ON THIS PAGE FROM IRON MAN VOL.1 #281, 284, 285 & 291, AND AVENGERS WEST COAST #95 -- BOBBIE.

I LET RHODEY -- THE CLOSEST FRIEND I HAD -- THINK SO TOO. I LEFT HIM IN MY JOB, BOTH AS HEAD OF MY COMPANY --

I JUST KNOW I'M GONNA REGRET THIS...

-- AND AS IRON MAN, IN A SPECIALLY-MODIFIED VERSION OF THE WAR MACHINE SUIT.

RHODEY DID FINE AS IRON MAN --

-- A LITTLE ROUGHER THAN I'D HAVE BEEN, BUT HE WAS RESOURCEFUL, INVENTIVE AND EFFECTIVE. STILL, HE NEVER LIKED THE RESPONSIBILITY --

YOU GOT JERKIN' PEOPLE AROUND DOWN TO A SCIENCE -- AND I'M SICK TO DEATH OF IT.

-- AND HE LIKED IT EVEN LESS WHEN HE FOUND OUT I'D LIED TO HIM.

GET YOURSELF A NEW SUCKER!

I LOST HIS FRIENDSHIP, BUT I DID TALK HIM INTO KEEPING THE ARMOR. HE REESTABLISHED HIMSELF UNDER THE NAME WAR MACHINE --

-- EVEN JOINING THE WEST COAST AVENGERS.

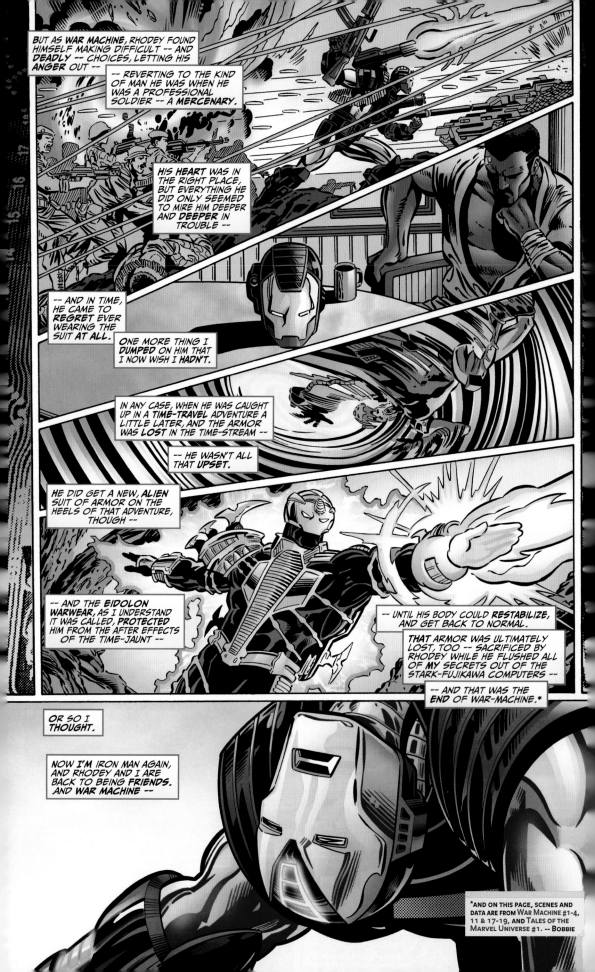

BUT AS WAR MACHINE, RHODEY FOUND HIMSELF MAKING DIFFICULT -- AND DEADLY -- CHOICES, LETTING HIS ANGER OUT --

-- REVERTING TO THE KIND OF MAN HE WAS WHEN HE WAS A PROFESSIONAL SOLDIER -- A MERCENARY.

HIS HEART WAS IN THE RIGHT PLACE, BUT EVERYTHING HE DID ONLY SEEMED TO MIRE HIM DEEPER AND DEEPER IN TROUBLE --

-- AND IN TIME, HE CAME TO REGRET EVER WEARING THE SUIT AT ALL.

ONE MORE THING I DUMPED ON HIM THAT I NOW WISH I HADN'T.

IN ANY CASE, WHEN HE WAS CAUGHT UP IN A TIME-TRAVEL ADVENTURE A LITTLE LATER, AND THE ARMOR WAS LOST IN THE TIME-STREAM --

-- HE WASN'T ALL THAT UPSET.

HE DID GET A NEW, ALIEN SUIT OF ARMOR ON THE HEELS OF THAT ADVENTURE, THOUGH --

-- AND THE EIDOLON WARWEAR, AS I UNDERSTAND IT WAS CALLED, PROTECTED HIM FROM THE AFTER EFFECTS OF THE TIME-JAUNT --

-- UNTIL HIS BODY COULD RESTABILIZE, AND GET BACK TO NORMAL.

THAT ARMOR WAS ULTIMATELY LOST, TOO -- SACRIFICED BY RHODEY WHILE HE FLUSHED ALL OF MY SECRETS OUT OF THE STARK-FUJIKAWA COMPUTERS --

-- AND THAT WAS THE END OF WAR-MACHINE.*

OR SO I THOUGHT.

NOW I'M IRON MAN AGAIN, AND RHODEY AND I ARE BACK TO BEING FRIENDS. AND WAR MACHINE --

*AND ON THIS PAGE, SCENES AND DATA ARE FROM WAR MACHINE #1-4, 11 & 17-19, AND TALES OF THE MARVEL UNIVERSE #1. -- BOBBIE

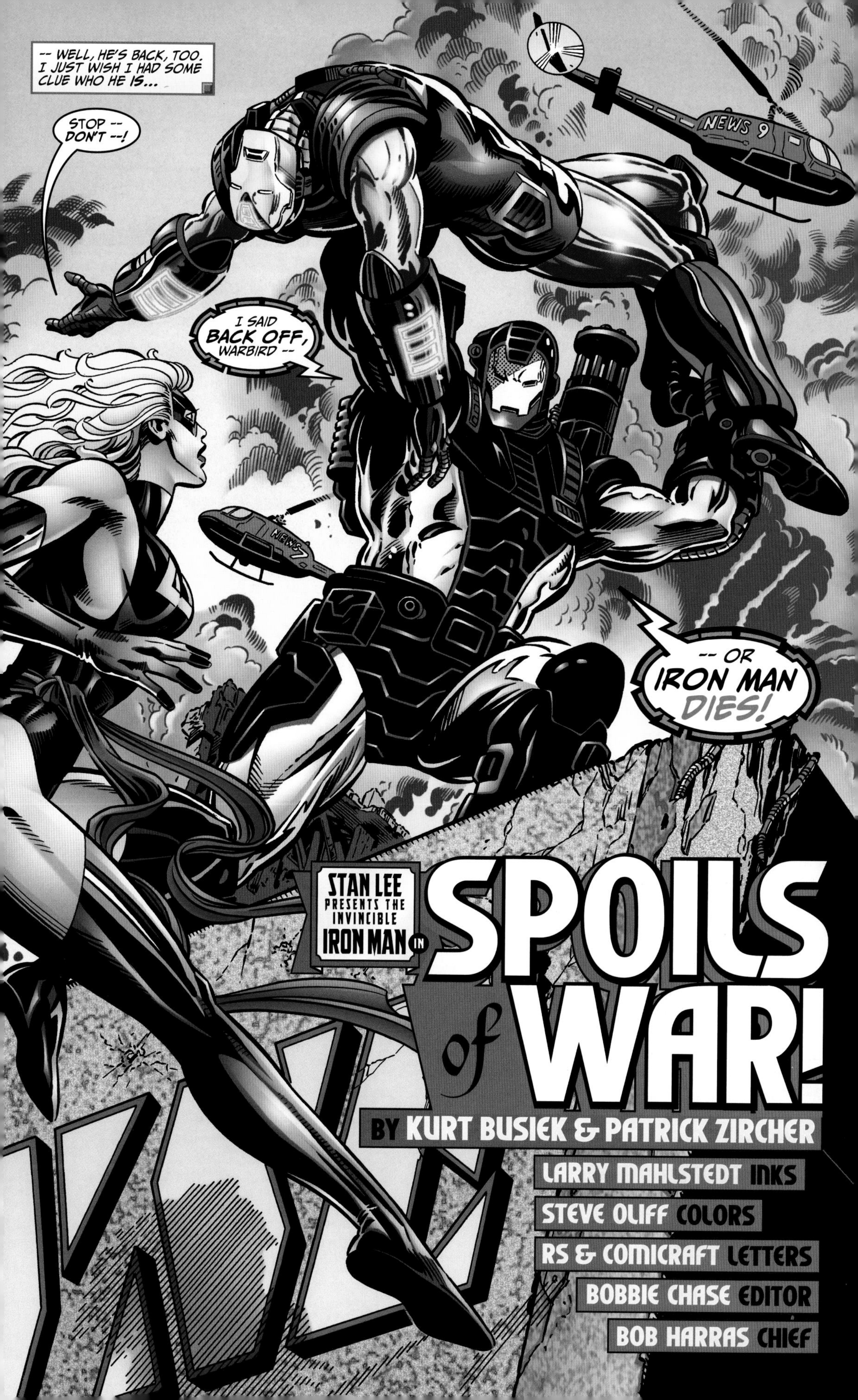
-- WELL, HE'S BACK, TOO. I JUST WISH I HAD SOME CLUE WHO HE IS...
STOP -- DON'T --!
NEWS 9
I SAID BACK OFF, WARBIRD --
NEWS 7
-- OR IRON MAN DIES!
STAN LEE PRESENTS THE INVINCIBLE IRON MAN IN
SPOILS of WAR!
BY KURT BUSIEK & PATRICK ZIRCHER
LARRY MAHLSTEDT INKS
STEVE OLIFF COLORS
RS & COMICRAFT LETTERS
BOBBIE CHASE EDITOR
BOB HARRAS CHIEF

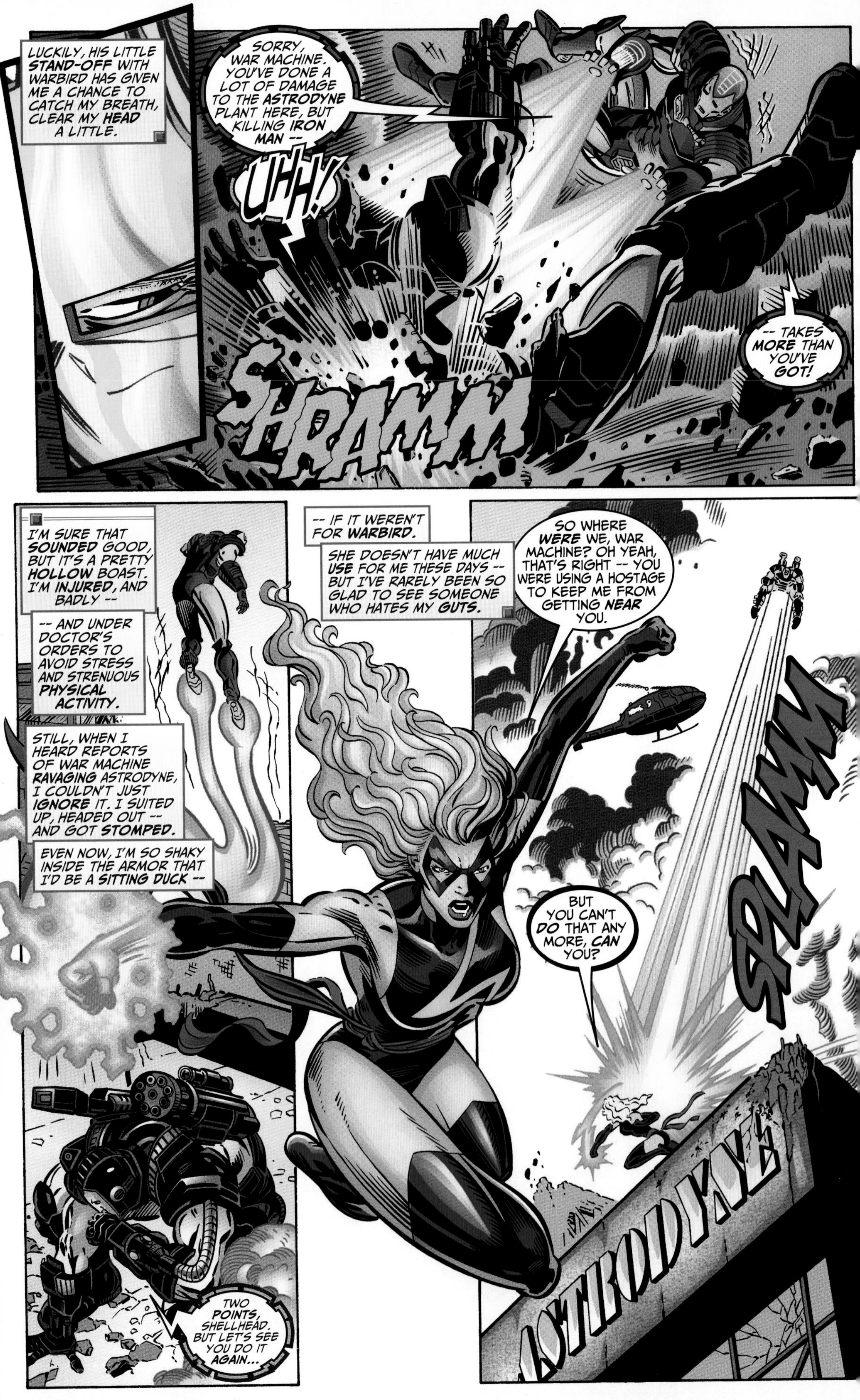

LUCKILY, HIS LITTLE STAND-OFF WITH WARBIRD HAS GIVEN ME A CHANCE TO CATCH MY BREATH, CLEAR MY HEAD A LITTLE.
SORRY, WAR MACHINE. YOU'VE DONE A LOT OF DAMAGE TO THE ASTRODYNE PLANT HERE, BUT KILLING IRON MAN --
UHH!
SHRAMM
-- TAKES MORE THAN YOU'VE GOT!
I'M SURE THAT SOUNDED GOOD, BUT IT'S A PRETTY HOLLOW BOAST. I'M INJURED, AND BADLY --
-- AND UNDER DOCTOR'S ORDERS TO AVOID STRESS AND STRENUOUS PHYSICAL ACTIVITY.
STILL, WHEN I HEARD REPORTS OF WAR MACHINE RAVAGING ASTRODYNE, I COULDN'T JUST IGNORE IT. I SUITED UP, HEADED OUT -- AND GOT STOMPED.
EVEN NOW, I'M SO SHAKY INSIDE THE ARMOR THAT I'D BE A SITTING DUCK --
-- IF IT WEREN'T FOR WARBIRD.
SHE DOESN'T HAVE MUCH USE FOR ME THESE DAYS -- BUT I'VE RARELY BEEN SO GLAD TO SEE SOMEONE WHO HATES MY GUTS.
TWO POINTS, SHELLHEAD. BUT LET'S SEE YOU DO IT AGAIN...
SO WHERE WERE WE, WAR MACHINE? OH YEAH, THAT'S RIGHT -- YOU WERE USING A HOSTAGE TO KEEP ME FROM GETTING NEAR YOU.
BUT YOU CAN'T DO THAT ANY MORE, CAN YOU?
SPLAMM
ASTRODYNE

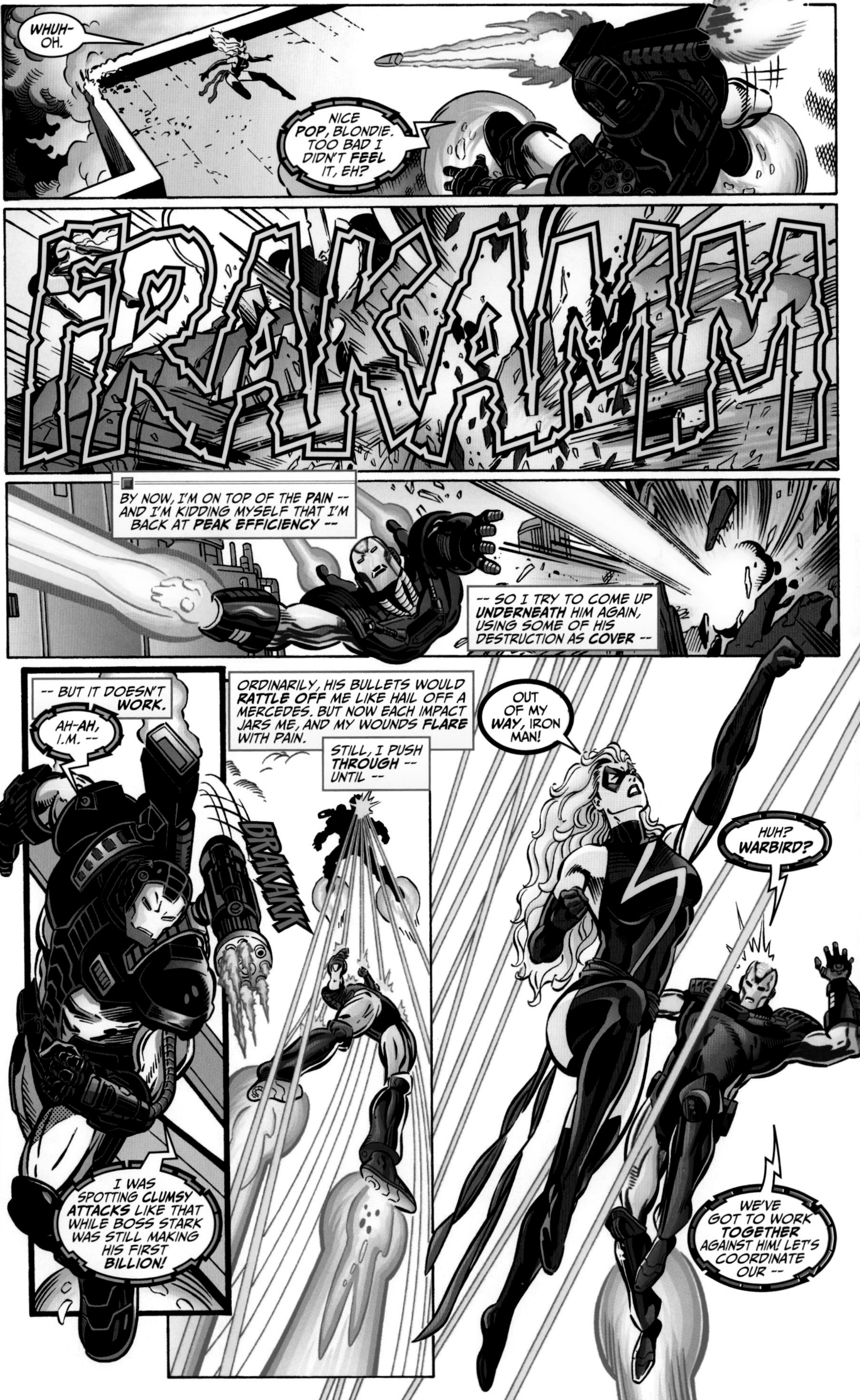
WHUH-OH.
NICE POP, BLONDIE. TOO BAD I DIDN'T FEEL IT, EH?
FRAKAMM
BY NOW, I'M ON TOP OF THE PAIN -- AND I'M KIDDING MYSELF THAT I'M BACK AT PEAK EFFICIENCY --
-- SO I TRY TO COME UP UNDERNEATH HIM AGAIN, USING SOME OF HIS DESTRUCTION AS COVER --
-- BUT IT DOESN'T WORK.
AH-AH, I.M. --
BRAKAKK
I WAS SPOTTING CLUMSY ATTACKS LIKE THAT WHILE BOSS STARK WAS STILL MAKING HIS FIRST BILLION!
ORDINARILY, HIS BULLETS WOULD RATTLE OFF ME LIKE HAIL OFF A MERCEDES. BUT NOW EACH IMPACT JARS ME, AND MY WOUNDS FLARE WITH PAIN.
STILL, I PUSH THROUGH -- UNTIL --
OUT OF MY WAY, IRON MAN!
HUH? WARBIRD?
WE'VE GOT TO WORK TOGETHER AGAINST HIM! LET'S COORDINATE OUR --

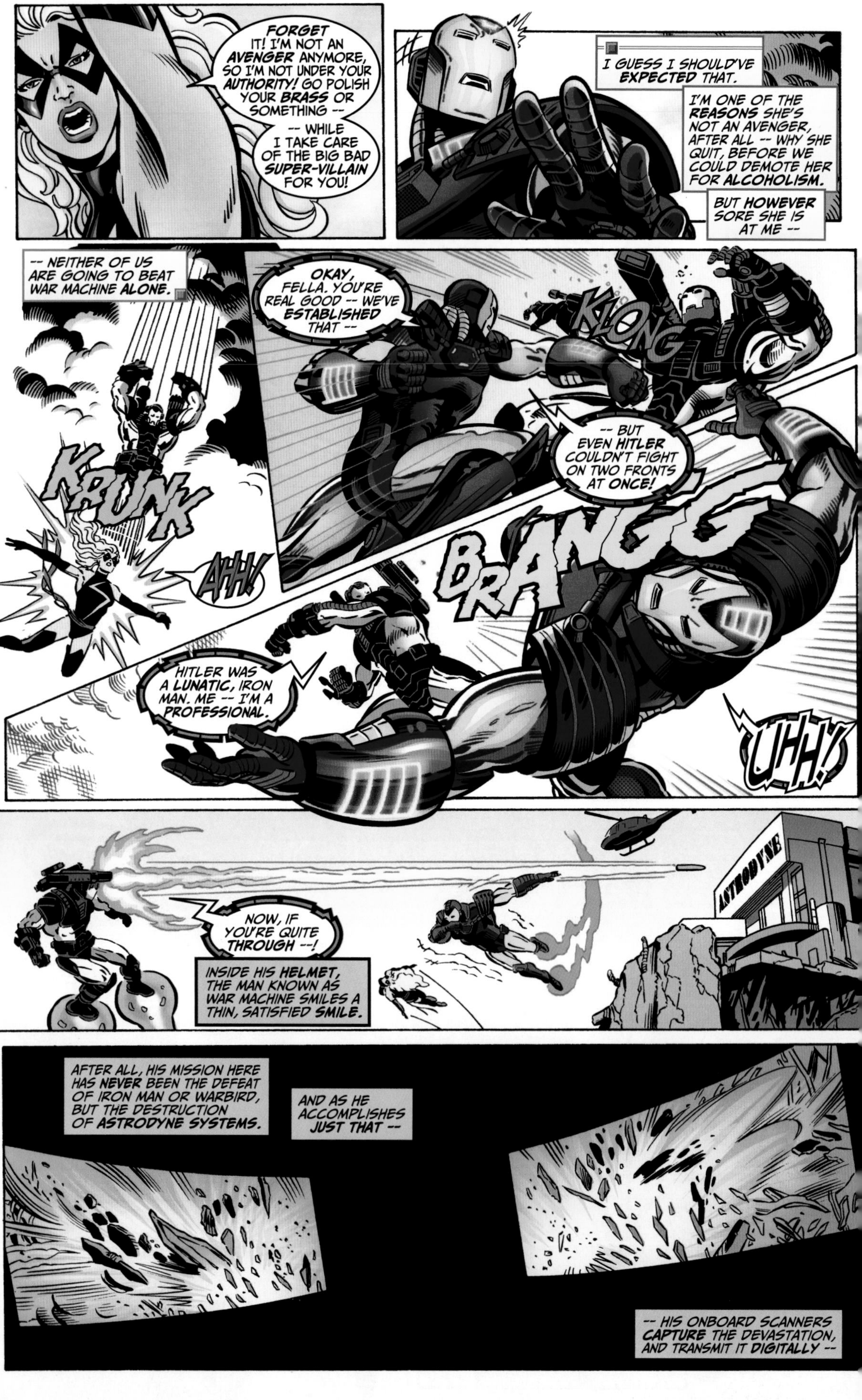
FORGET IT! I'M NOT AN AVENGER ANYMORE, SO I'M NOT UNDER YOUR AUTHORITY! GO POLISH YOUR BRASS OR SOMETHING --
-- WHILE I TAKE CARE OF THE BIG BAD SUPER-VILLAIN FOR YOU!
I GUESS I SHOULD'VE EXPECTED THAT.
I'M ONE OF THE REASONS SHE'S NOT AN AVENGER, AFTER ALL -- WHY SHE QUIT, BEFORE WE COULD DEMOTE HER FOR ALCOHOLISM.
BUT HOWEVER SORE SHE IS AT ME --
-- NEITHER OF US ARE GOING TO BEAT WAR MACHINE ALONE.
OKAY, FELLA. YOU'RE REAL GOOD -- WE'VE ESTABLISHED THAT --
KLONG
-- BUT EVEN HITLER COULDN'T FIGHT ON TWO FRONTS AT ONCE!
KRUNK
AHH!
BRANGG
HITLER WAS A LUNATIC, IRON MAN. ME -- I'M A PROFESSIONAL.
UHH!
ASTRODYNE
NOW, IF YOU'RE QUITE THROUGH --!
INSIDE HIS HELMET, THE MAN KNOWN AS WAR MACHINE SMILES A THIN, SATISFIED SMILE.
AFTER ALL, HIS MISSION HERE HAS NEVER BEEN THE DEFEAT OF IRON MAN OR WARBIRD, BUT THE DESTRUCTION OF ASTRODYNE SYSTEMS.
AND AS HE ACCOMPLISHES JUST THAT --
-- HIS ONBOARD SCANNERS CAPTURE THE DEVASTATION, AND TRANSMIT IT DIGITALLY --

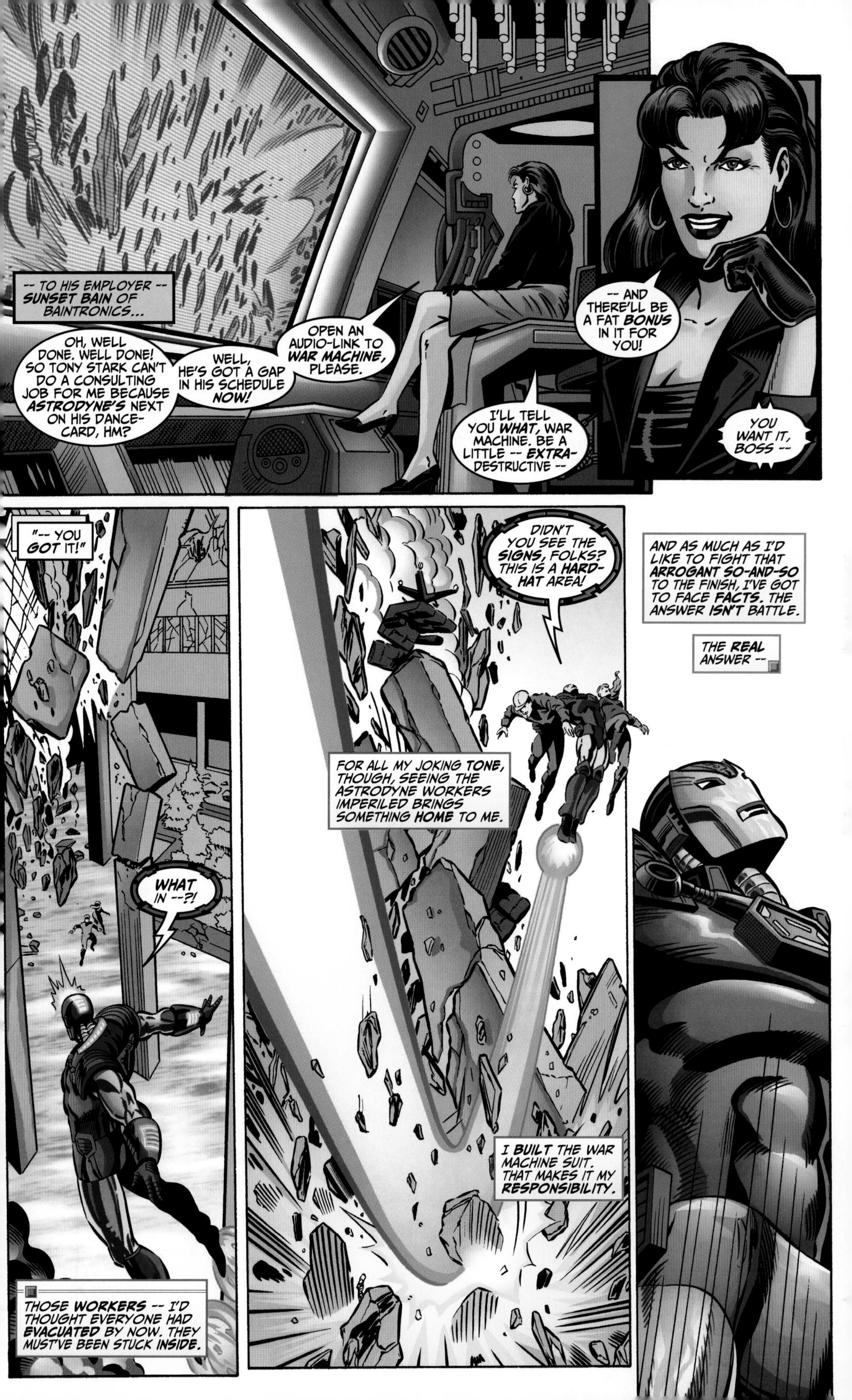
-- TO HIS EMPLOYER -- SUNSET BAIN OF BAINTRONICS...
OH, WELL DONE. WELL DONE! SO TONY STARK CAN'T DO A CONSULTING JOB FOR ME BECAUSE ASTRODYNE'S NEXT ON HIS DANCE-CARD, HM?
WELL, HE'S GOT A GAP IN HIS SCHEDULE NOW!
OPEN AN AUDIO-LINK TO WAR MACHINE, PLEASE.
-- AND THERE'LL BE A FAT BONUS IN IT FOR YOU!
I'LL TELL YOU WHAT, WAR MACHINE. BE A LITTLE -- EXTRA-DESTRUCTIVE --
YOU WANT IT, BOSS --
"-- YOU GOT IT!"
WHAT IN --?!
THOSE WORKERS -- I'D THOUGHT EVERYONE HAD EVACUATED BY NOW. THEY MUST'VE BEEN STUCK INSIDE.
DIDN'T YOU SEE THE SIGNS, FOLKS? THIS IS A HARD-HAT AREA!
FOR ALL MY JOKING TONE, THOUGH, SEEING THE ASTRODYNE WORKERS IMPERILED BRINGS SOMETHING HOME TO ME.
I BUILT THE WAR MACHINE SUIT. THAT MAKES IT MY RESPONSIBILITY.
AND AS MUCH AS I'D LIKE TO FIGHT THAT ARROGANT SO-AND-SO TO THE FINISH, I'VE GOT TO FACE FACTS. THE ANSWER ISN'T BATTLE.
THE REAL ANSWER --

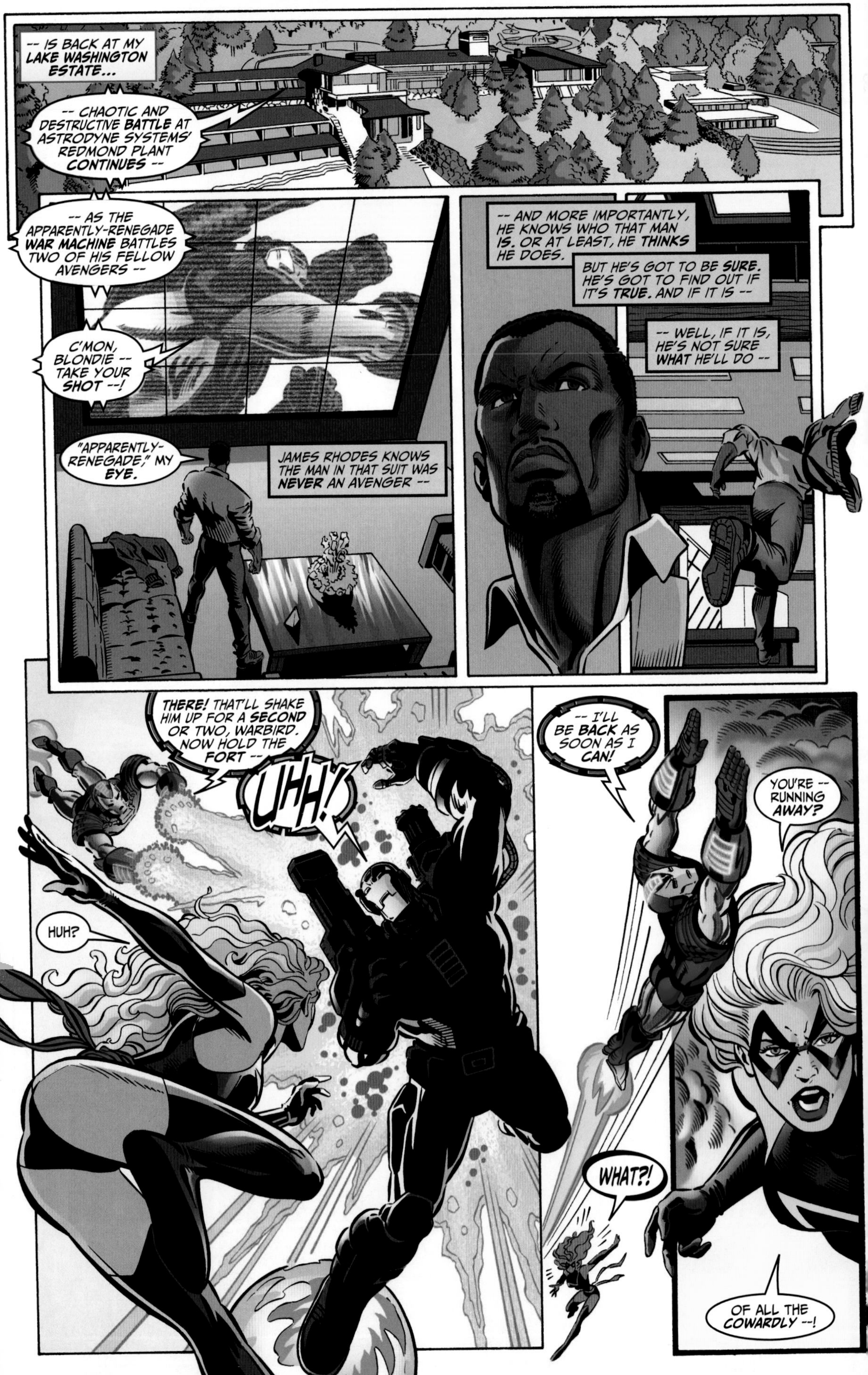

-- IS BACK AT MY LAKE WASHINGTON ESTATE...
-- CHAOTIC AND DESTRUCTIVE BATTLE AT ASTRODYNE SYSTEMS' REDMOND PLANT CONTINUES --
-- AS THE APPARENTLY-RENEGADE WAR MACHINE BATTLES TWO OF HIS FELLOW AVENGERS --
C'MON, BLONDIE -- TAKE YOUR SHOT --!
"APPARENTLY-RENEGADE," MY EYE.
JAMES RHODES KNOWS THE MAN IN THAT SUIT WAS NEVER AN AVENGER --
-- AND MORE IMPORTANTLY, HE KNOWS WHO THAT MAN IS. OR AT LEAST, HE THINKS HE DOES.
BUT HE'S GOT TO BE SURE. HE'S GOT TO FIND OUT IF IT'S TRUE. AND IF IT IS --
-- WELL, IF IT IS, HE'S NOT SURE WHAT HE'LL DO --
THERE! THAT'LL SHAKE HIM UP FOR A SECOND OR TWO, WARBIRD. NOW HOLD THE FORT --
UHH!
HUH?
-- I'LL BE BACK AS SOON AS I CAN!
YOU'RE -- RUNNING AWAY?
WHAT?!
OF ALL THE COWARDLY --!

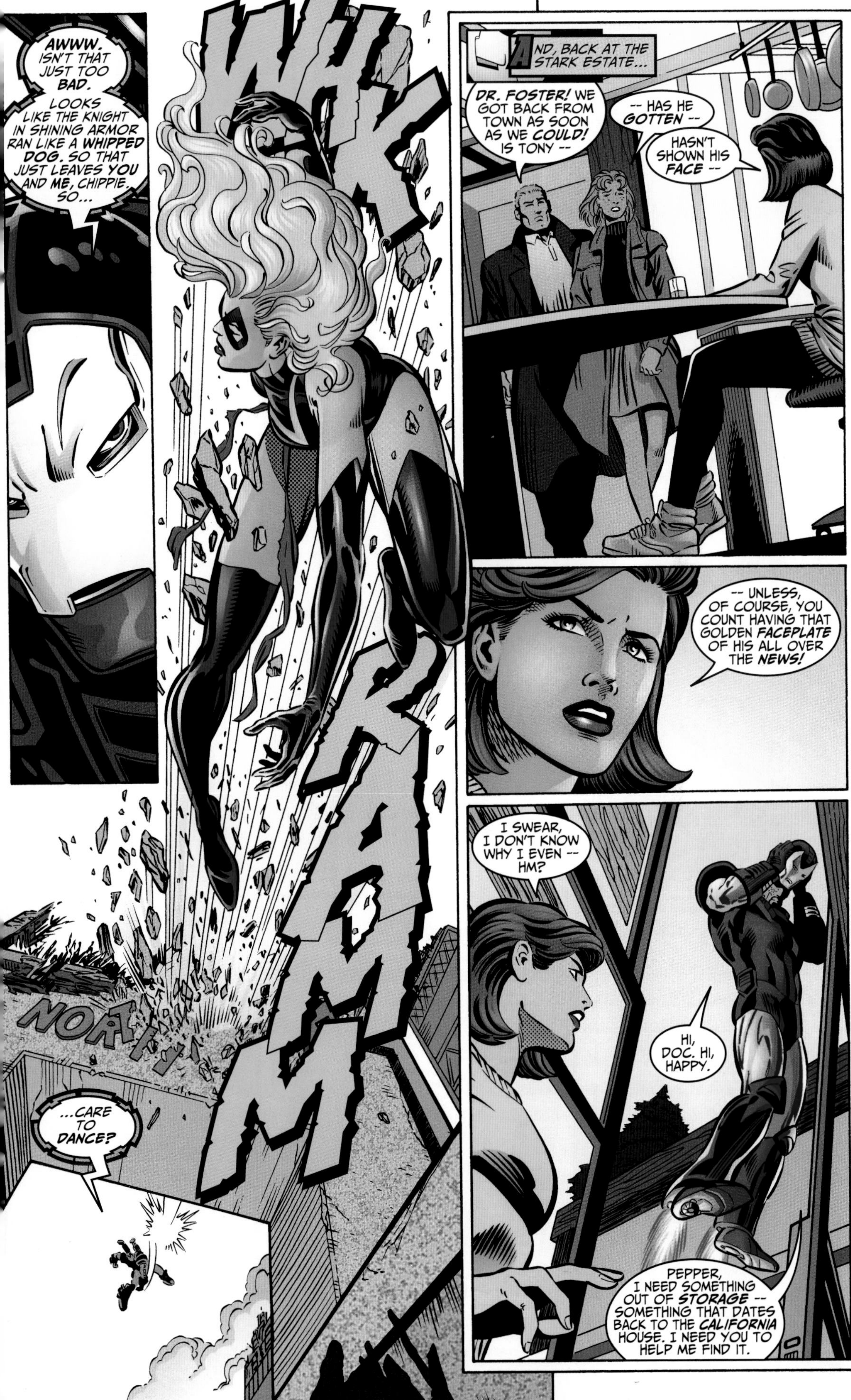
AWWW. ISN'T THAT JUST TOO BAD.
LOOKS LIKE THE KNIGHT IN SHINING ARMOR RAN LIKE A WHIPPED DOG. SO THAT JUST LEAVES YOU AND ME, CHIPPIE. SO...
WHK
KRAKMM
NOR
...CARE TO DANCE?
AND, BACK AT THE STARK ESTATE...
DR. FOSTER! WE GOT BACK FROM TOWN AS SOON AS WE COULD! IS TONY --
-- HAS HE GOTTEN --
HASN'T SHOWN HIS FACE --
-- UNLESS, OF COURSE, YOU COUNT HAVING THAT GOLDEN FACEPLATE OF HIS ALL OVER THE NEWS!
I SWEAR, I DON'T KNOW WHY I EVEN -- HM?
HI, DOC. HI, HAPPY.
PEPPER, I NEED SOMETHING OUT OF STORAGE -- SOMETHING THAT DATES BACK TO THE CALIFORNIA HOUSE. I NEED YOU TO HELP ME FIND IT.

YOU JUST HOLD IT *RIGHT THERE*, MISTER.

I TOLD YOU NO *STRESS*. I TOLD YOU NO RUNNING AROUND IN THAT *SUIT*. I DON'T THINK YOU REALIZE THE *DANGER* YOU COULD BE IN --

-- I'VE BEEN GOING OVER YOUR *TEST DATA* WITH *HENRY PYM*, AND --

I'M *SORRY*, JANE --

-- BUT THERE ARE *OTHER* LIVES AT STAKE RIGHT NOW, AND I DON'T HAVE ANY *TIME.*

BUT --!

TONY, MAYBE YOU *SHOULD* --

PEPPER, I *NEED* THIS. *NOW.*

BING BONG

BING BONG

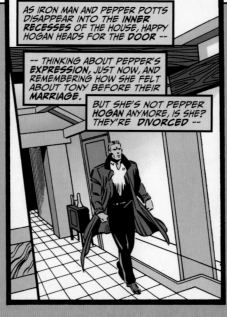

OKAY, OKAY.

BUT IF YOU WIND UP *KILLING* YOURSELF, I'M NEVER *SPEAKING* TO YOU AGAIN. HAPPY, COULD YOU GET THE *DOOR?*

AS IRON MAN AND PEPPER POTTS DISAPPEAR INTO THE *INNER RECESSES* OF THE HOUSE, HAPPY HOGAN HEADS FOR THE *DOOR* --

-- THINKING ABOUT PEPPER'S *EXPRESSION*, JUST NOW, AND REMEMBERING HOW SHE FELT ABOUT TONY BEFORE THEIR *MARRIAGE.*

BUT SHE'S NOT PEPPER HOGAN ANYMORE, IS SHE? THEY'RE *DIVORCED* --

-- AND HE'S ABOUT AS MUCH *USE* AROUND HERE AS A *JOCKSTRAP* ON A *MAILBOX.*

HE'LL STICK AROUND 'TIL THIS CURRENT CRISIS IS OVER, HE FIGURES. JUST UNTIL THEN --

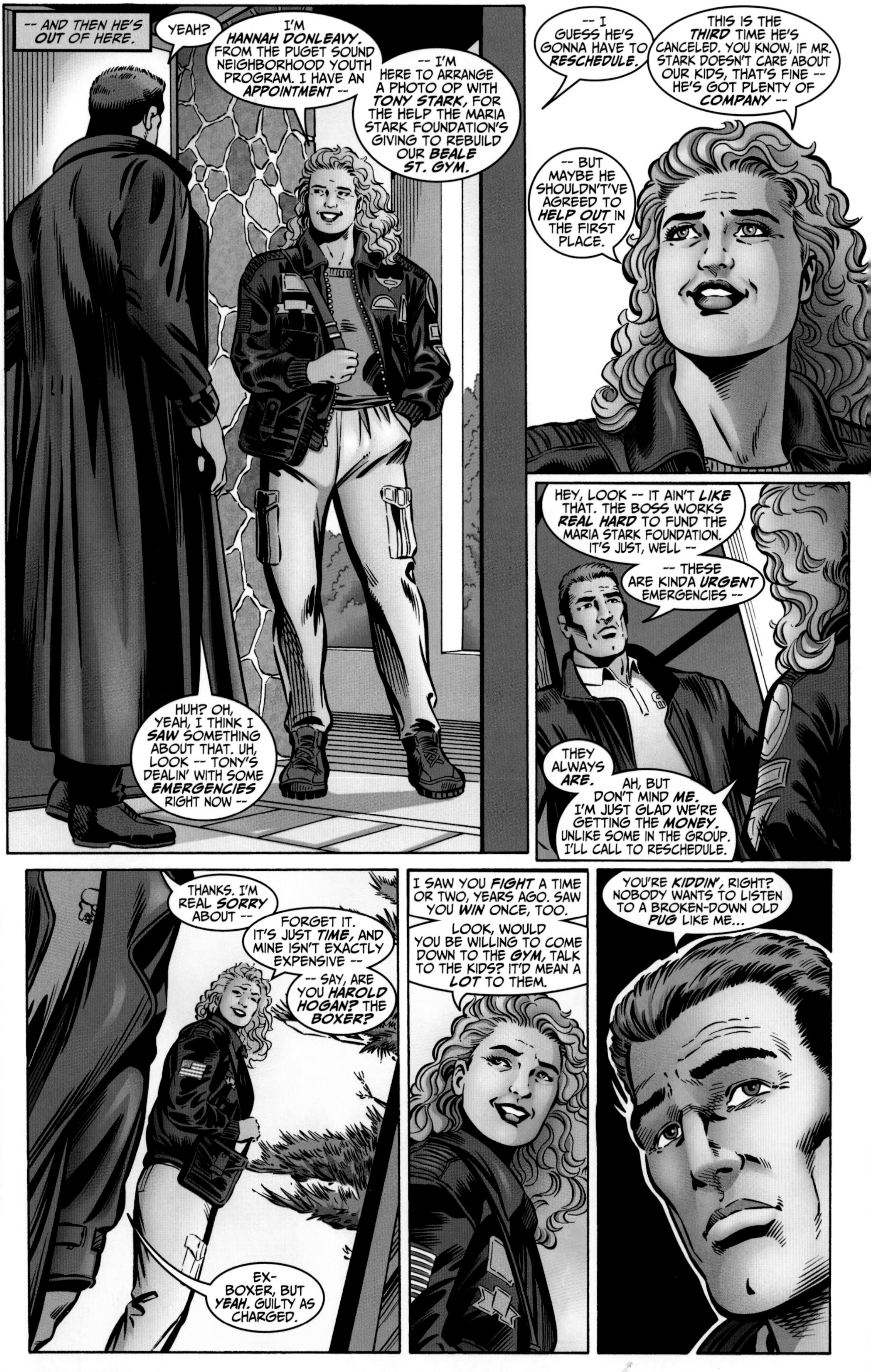
-- AND THEN HE'S OUT OF HERE.
YEAH?
I'M HANNAH DONLEAVY. FROM THE PUGET SOUND NEIGHBORHOOD YOUTH PROGRAM. I HAVE AN APPOINTMENT --
-- I'M HERE TO ARRANGE A PHOTO OP WITH TONY STARK, FOR THE HELP THE MARIA STARK FOUNDATION'S GIVING TO REBUILD OUR BEALE ST. GYM.
HUH? OH, YEAH, I THINK I SAW SOMETHING ABOUT THAT. UH, LOOK -- TONY'S DEALIN' WITH SOME EMERGENCIES RIGHT NOW --
-- I GUESS HE'S GONNA HAVE TO RESCHEDULE.
THIS IS THE THIRD TIME HE'S CANCELED. YOU KNOW, IF MR. STARK DOESN'T CARE ABOUT OUR KIDS, THAT'S FINE -- HE'S GOT PLENTY OF COMPANY --
-- BUT MAYBE HE SHOULDN'T'VE AGREED TO HELP OUT IN THE FIRST PLACE.
HEY, LOOK -- IT AIN'T LIKE THAT. THE BOSS WORKS REAL HARD TO FUND THE MARIA STARK FOUNDATION. IT'S JUST, WELL --
-- THESE ARE KINDA URGENT EMERGENCIES --
THEY ALWAYS ARE.
AH, BUT DON'T MIND ME. I'M JUST GLAD WE'RE GETTING THE MONEY. UNLIKE SOME IN THE GROUP. I'LL CALL TO RESCHEDULE.
THANKS. I'M REAL SORRY ABOUT --
FORGET IT. IT'S JUST TIME, AND MINE ISN'T EXACTLY EXPENSIVE --
-- SAY, ARE YOU HAROLD HOGAN? THE BOXER?
EX-BOXER, BUT YEAH. GUILTY AS CHARGED.
I SAW YOU FIGHT A TIME OR TWO, YEARS AGO. SAW YOU WIN ONCE, TOO.
LOOK, WOULD YOU BE WILLING TO COME DOWN TO THE GYM, TALK TO THE KIDS? IT'D MEAN A LOT TO THEM.
YOU'RE KIDDIN', RIGHT? NOBODY WANTS TO LISTEN TO A BROKEN-DOWN OLD PUG LIKE ME...

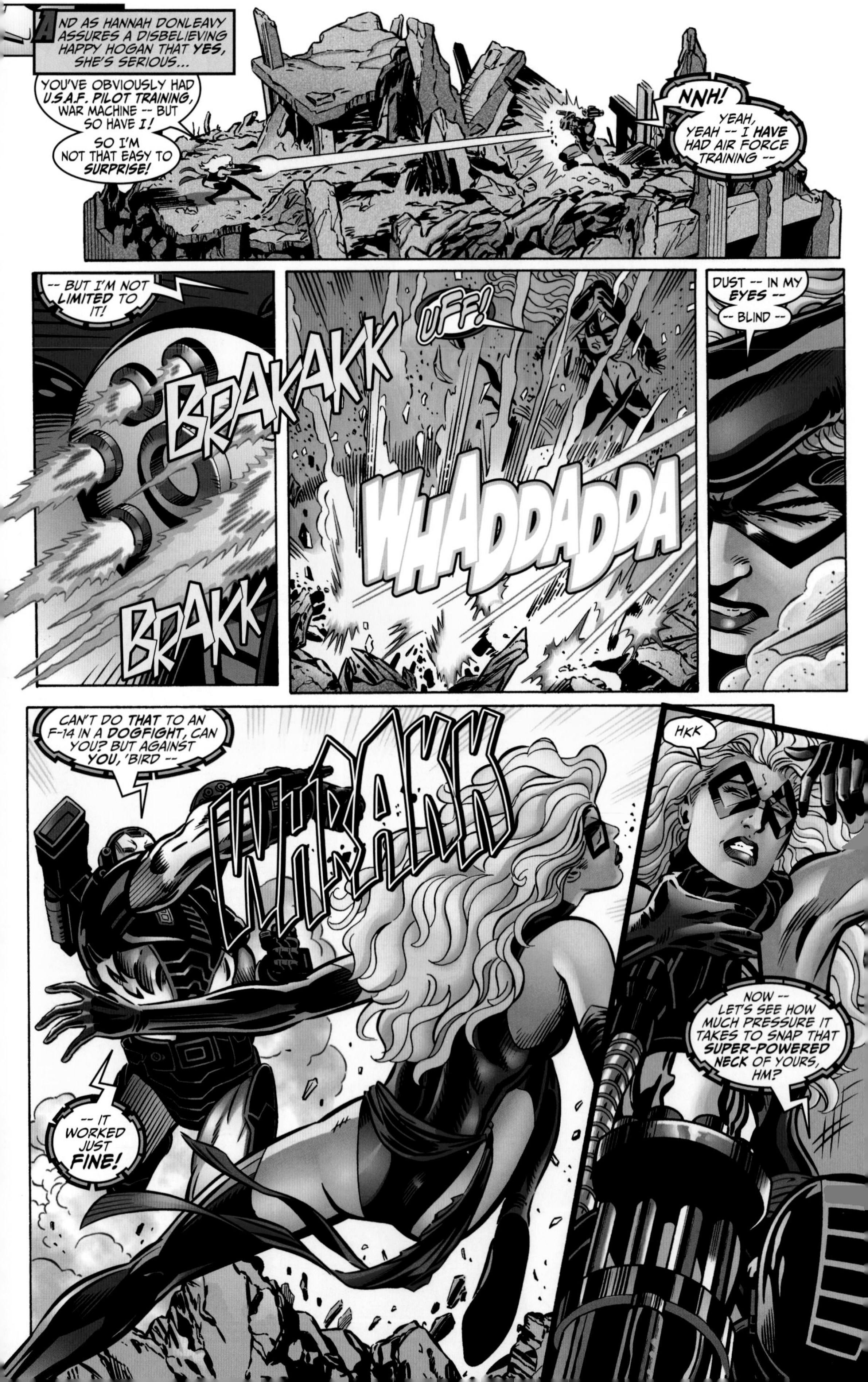
AND AS HANNAH DONLEAVY ASSURES A DISBELIEVING HAPPY HOGAN THAT YES, SHE'S SERIOUS...
YOU'VE OBVIOUSLY HAD U.S.A.F. PILOT TRAINING, WAR MACHINE -- BUT SO HAVE I!
SO I'M NOT THAT EASY TO SURPRISE!
NNH!
YEAH, YEAH -- I HAVE HAD AIR FORCE TRAINING --
-- BUT I'M NOT LIMITED TO IT!
BRAKAKK
BRAKK
UFF!
WHADDADDA
DUST -- IN MY EYES --
-- BLIND --
CAN'T DO THAT TO AN F-14 IN A DOGFIGHT, CAN YOU? BUT AGAINST YOU, 'BIRD --
WRAKK
-- IT WORKED JUST FINE!
HKK
NOW -- LET'S SEE HOW MUCH PRESSURE IT TAKES TO SNAP THAT SUPER-POWERED NECK OF YOURS, HM?

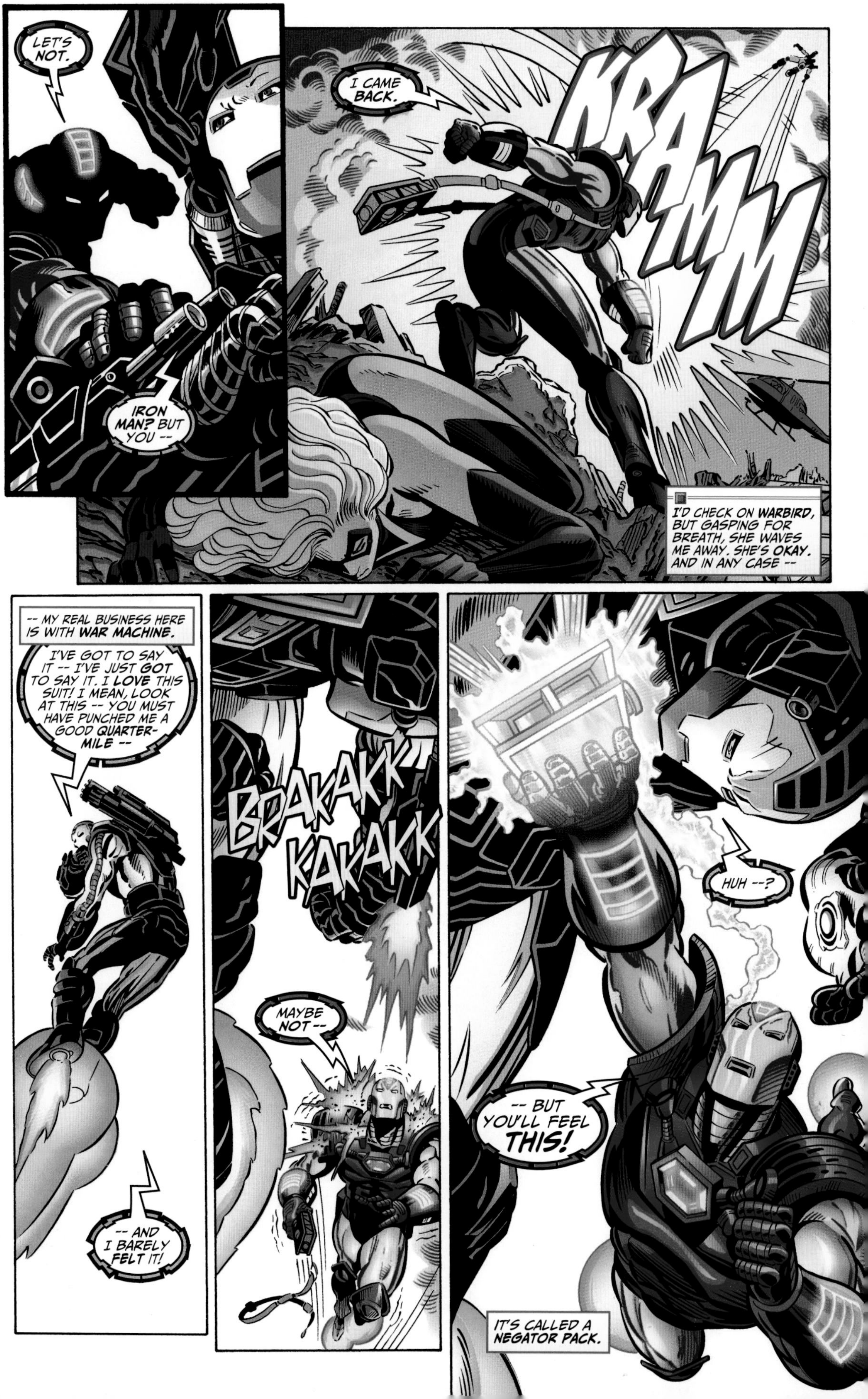
LET'S NOT.
IRON MAN? BUT YOU --
I CAME BACK.
KRAMMM
I'D CHECK ON WARBIRD, BUT GASPING FOR BREATH, SHE WAVES ME AWAY. SHE'S OKAY. AND IN ANY CASE --
-- MY REAL BUSINESS HERE IS WITH WAR MACHINE.
I'VE GOT TO SAY IT -- I'VE JUST GOT TO SAY IT. I LOVE THIS SUIT! I MEAN, LOOK AT THIS -- YOU MUST HAVE PUNCHED ME A GOOD QUARTER-MILE --
-- AND I BARELY FELT IT!
BRAKAKK KAKAKK
MAYBE NOT --
HUH --?
-- BUT YOU'LL FEEL THIS!
IT'S CALLED A NEGATOR PACK.

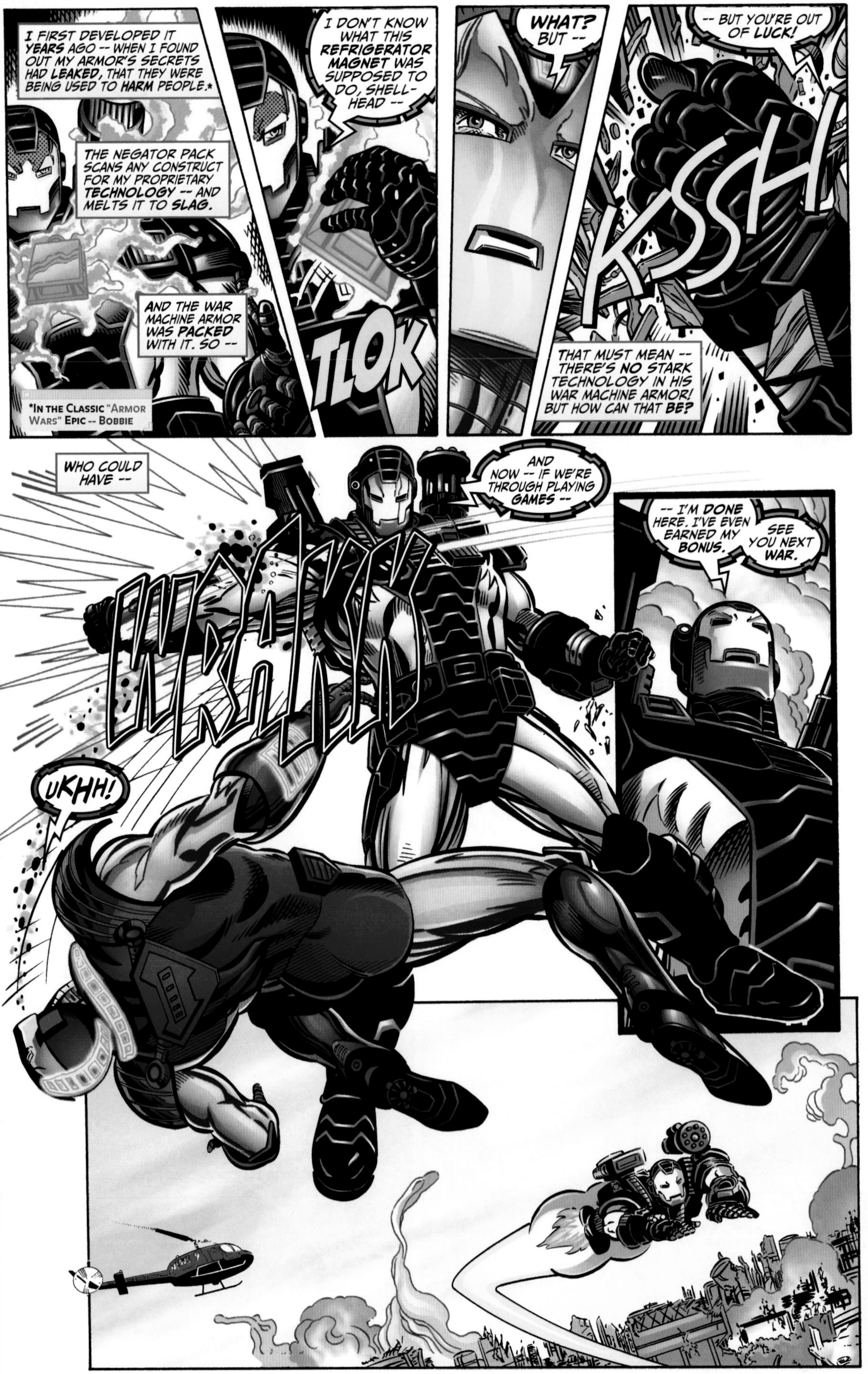
I FIRST DEVELOPED IT YEARS AGO -- WHEN I FOUND OUT MY ARMOR'S SECRETS HAD LEAKED, THAT THEY WERE BEING USED TO HARM PEOPLE.*
THE NEGATOR PACK SCANS ANY CONSTRUCT FOR MY PROPRIETARY TECHNOLOGY -- AND MELTS IT TO SLAG.
AND THE WAR MACHINE ARMOR WAS PACKED WITH IT. SO --
*IN THE CLASSIC "ARMOR WARS" EPIC -- BOBBIE
I DON'T KNOW WHAT THIS REFRIGERATOR MAGNET WAS SUPPOSED TO DO, SHELL-HEAD --
TLOK
WHAT? BUT --
-- BUT YOU'RE OUT OF LUCK!
KSSH
THAT MUST MEAN -- THERE'S NO STARK TECHNOLOGY IN HIS WAR MACHINE ARMOR! BUT HOW CAN THAT BE?
WHO COULD HAVE --
AND NOW -- IF WE'RE THROUGH PLAYING GAMES --
UKHH!
-- I'M DONE HERE. I'VE EVEN EARNED MY BONUS.
SEE YOU NEXT WAR.

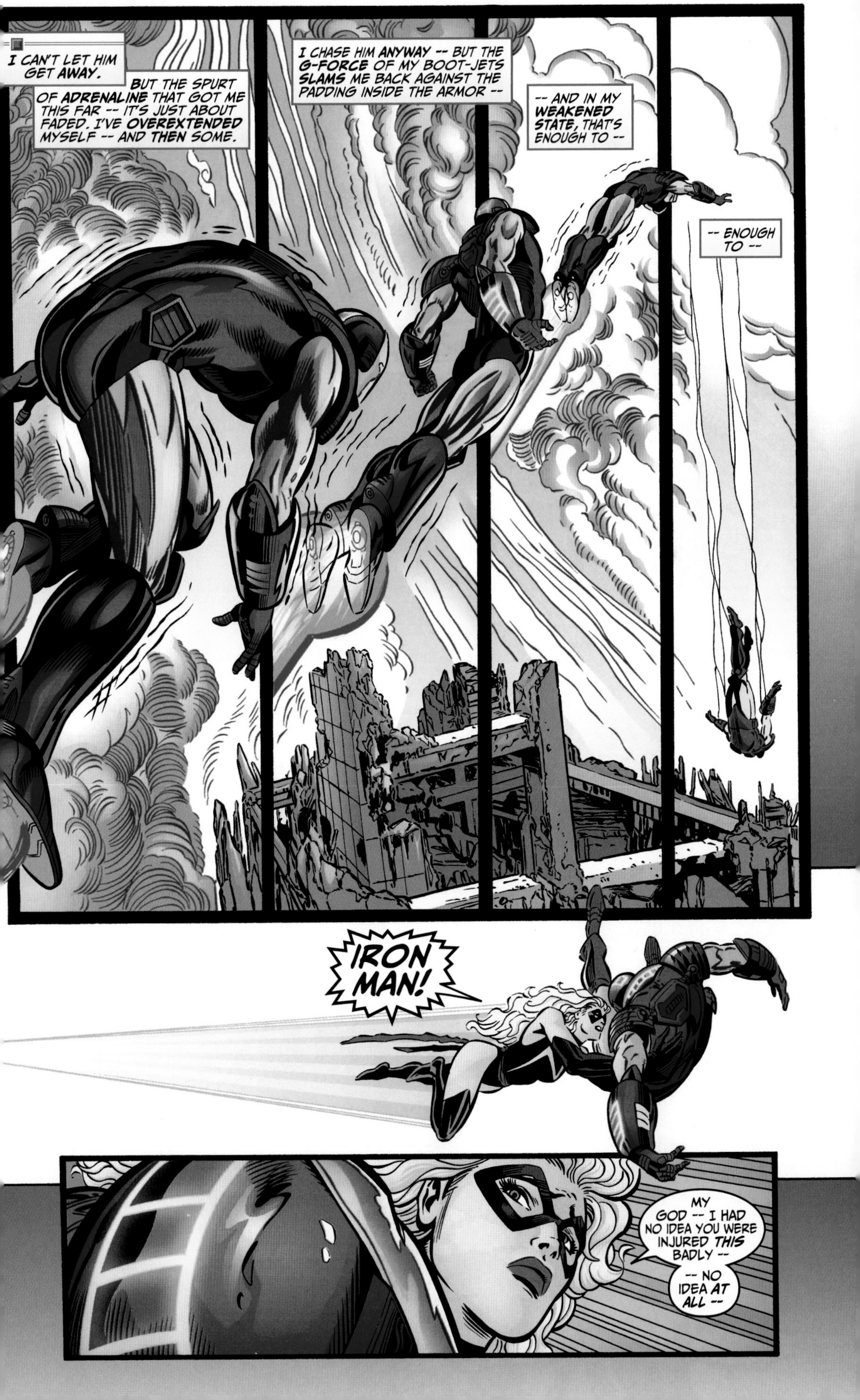
I CAN'T LET HIM GET AWAY.
BUT THE SPURT OF ADRENALINE THAT GOT ME THIS FAR -- IT'S JUST ABOUT FADED. I'VE OVEREXTENDED MYSELF -- AND THEN SOME.
I CHASE HIM ANYWAY -- BUT THE G-FORCE OF MY BOOT-JETS SLAMS ME BACK AGAINST THE PADDING INSIDE THE ARMOR --
-- AND IN MY WEAKENED STATE, THAT'S ENOUGH TO --
-- ENOUGH TO --
IRON MAN!
MY GOD -- I HAD NO IDEA YOU WERE INJURED THIS BADLY --
-- NO IDEA AT ALL --

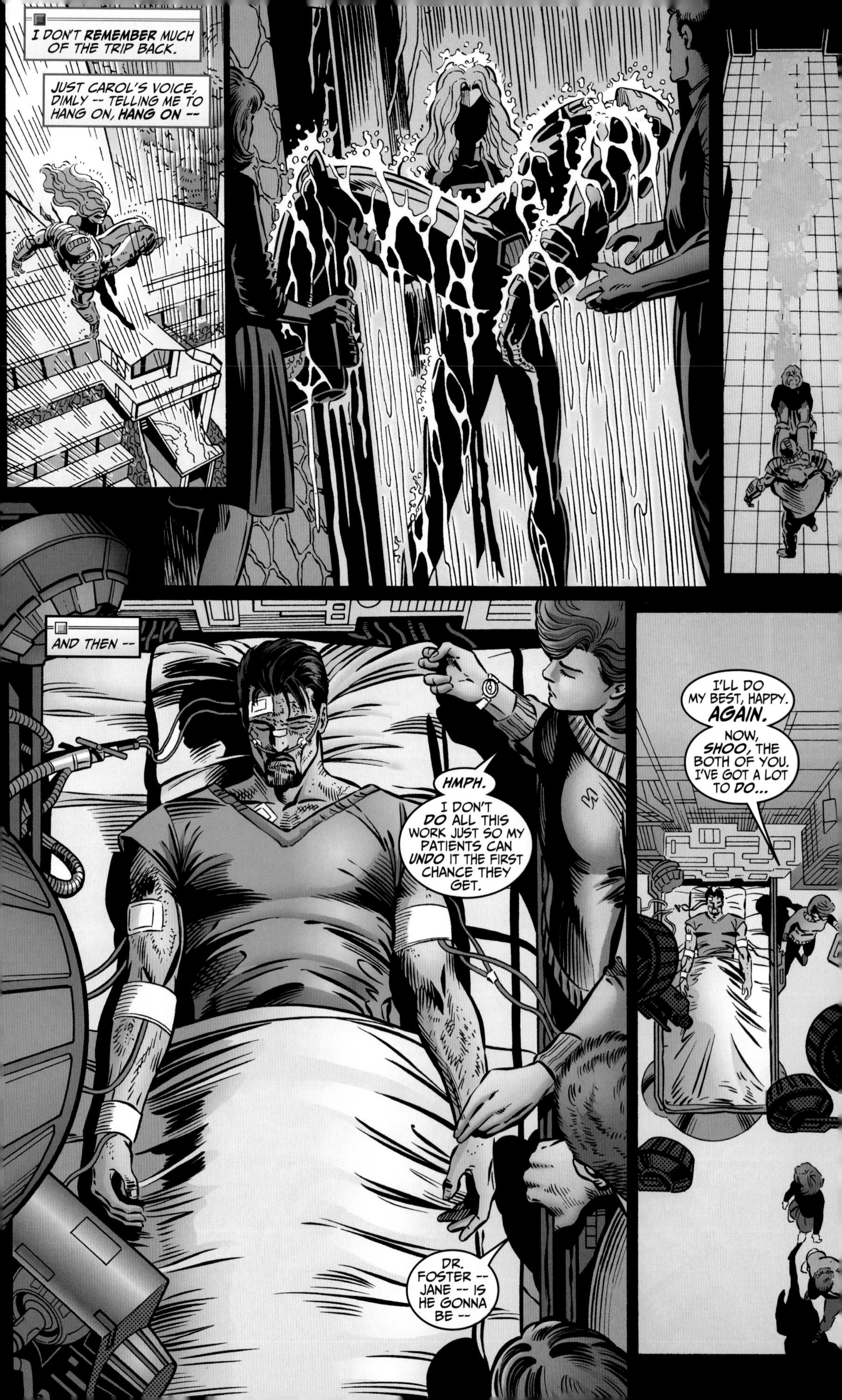
I DON'T REMEMBER MUCH OF THE TRIP BACK.
JUST CAROL'S VOICE, DIMLY -- TELLING ME TO HANG ON, HANG ON --
AND THEN --
HMPH.
I DON'T DO ALL THIS WORK JUST SO MY PATIENTS CAN UNDO IT THE FIRST CHANCE THEY GET.
DR. FOSTER -- JANE -- IS HE GONNA BE --
I'LL DO MY BEST, HAPPY. AGAIN.
NOW, SHOO, THE BOTH OF YOU. I'VE GOT A LOT TO DO...

THE NEXT MORNING.

I CAN BARELY *MOVE.* I'M THINKING ABOUT *ASTRODYNE* --

-- ABOUT THE SEVEN PEOPLE WHO *DIED* THERE, DESPITE *WARBIRD'S* AND MY BEST EFFORTS.

AND ABOUT *MADAME MASQUE* AND THE *MANDARIN* AND WHOEVER IT IS WHO'S BEEN TRYING TO KILL ME -- WHEN --

VEEP VEEP

OPEN *PHONE* CONNECTION. *STARK* HERE.

HI, *TONES.* IT'S *SUNSET.*

I WAS JUST READING THE NEWS ABOUT THAT *AWFUL* DISASTER AT *ASTRODYNE,* AND HOW THEY'RE CLOSING THEIR DOORS FOR *REPAIRS* --

-- AND I *REMEMBERED* -- WEREN'T YOU ABOUT TO START A *CONSULTING JOB* FOR THEM?

AND, WELL -- I KNOW HOW *IMPORTANT* YOUR CHARITY WORK IS TO YOU --

-- HOW YOU WANT TO KEEP GENERATING MONEY FOR THE MARIA STARK FOUNDATION. SO I THOUGHT, FOR OLD TIME'S SAKE, IF NOTHING ELSE --

-- I'D OFFER TO *FILL* THAT HOLE IN YOUR *SCHEDULE* --

TONY? ARE YOU STILL *THERE* --?

I'LL -- I'LL GET *BACK* TO YOU, SUNSET.

IT WAS *HER.*

SHE DID IT. SHE HIRED *WAR MACHINE.* AND ALL TO -- ALL TO GET ME TO --

BUT IT'S JUST A *HUNCH* -- IT'S NOTHING I CAN PROVE --

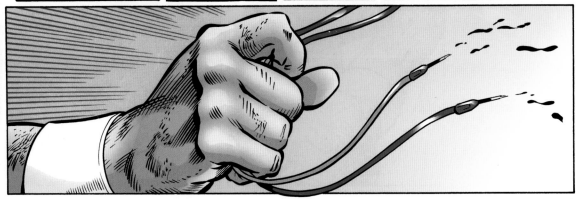

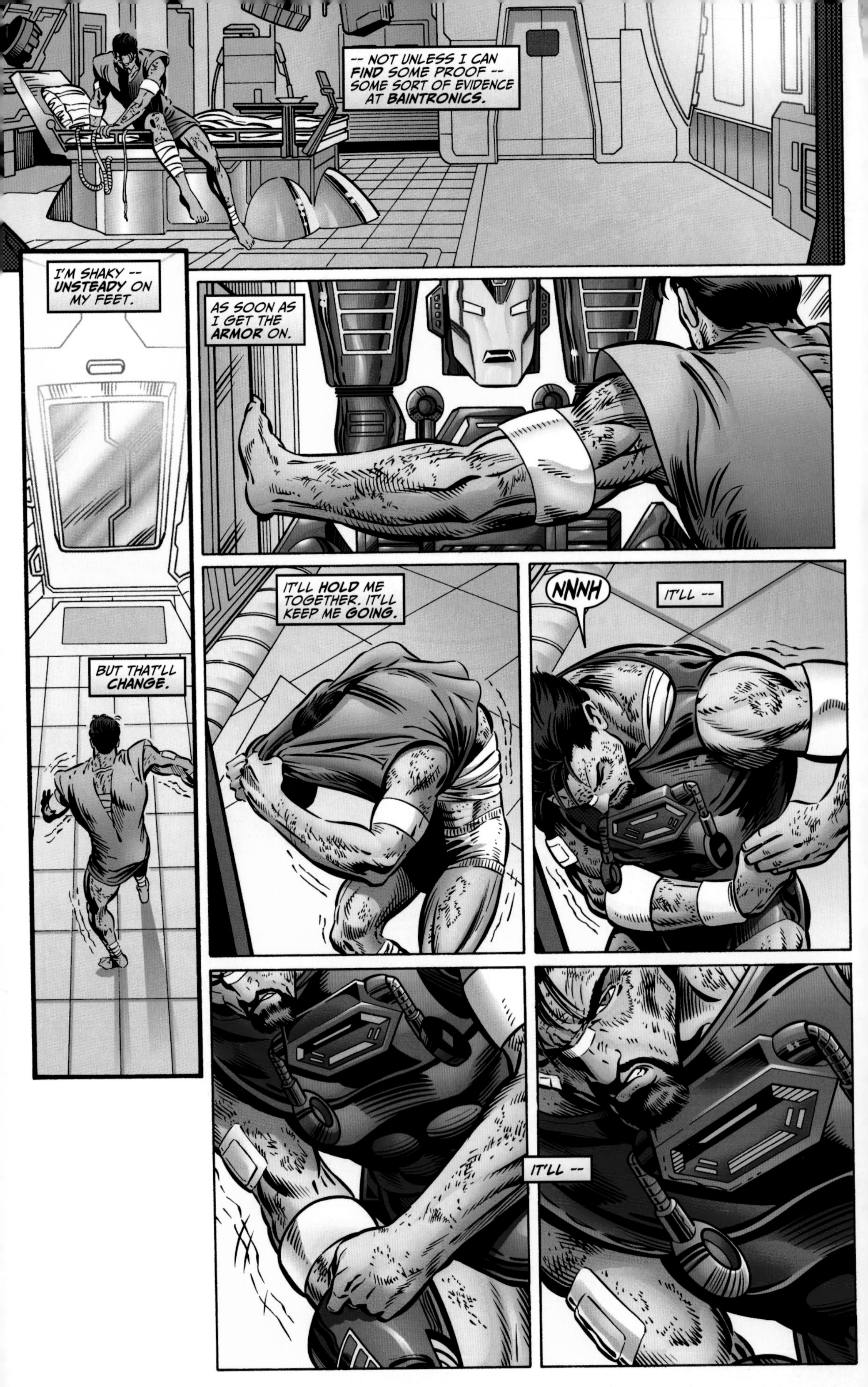
-- NOT UNLESS I CAN FIND SOME PROOF -- SOME SORT OF EVIDENCE AT BAINTRONICS.
I'M SHAKY -- UNSTEADY ON MY FEET.
BUT THAT'LL CHANGE.
AS SOON AS I GET THE ARMOR ON.
IT'LL HOLD ME TOGETHER. IT'LL KEEP ME GOING.
NNNH
IT'LL --
IT'LL --

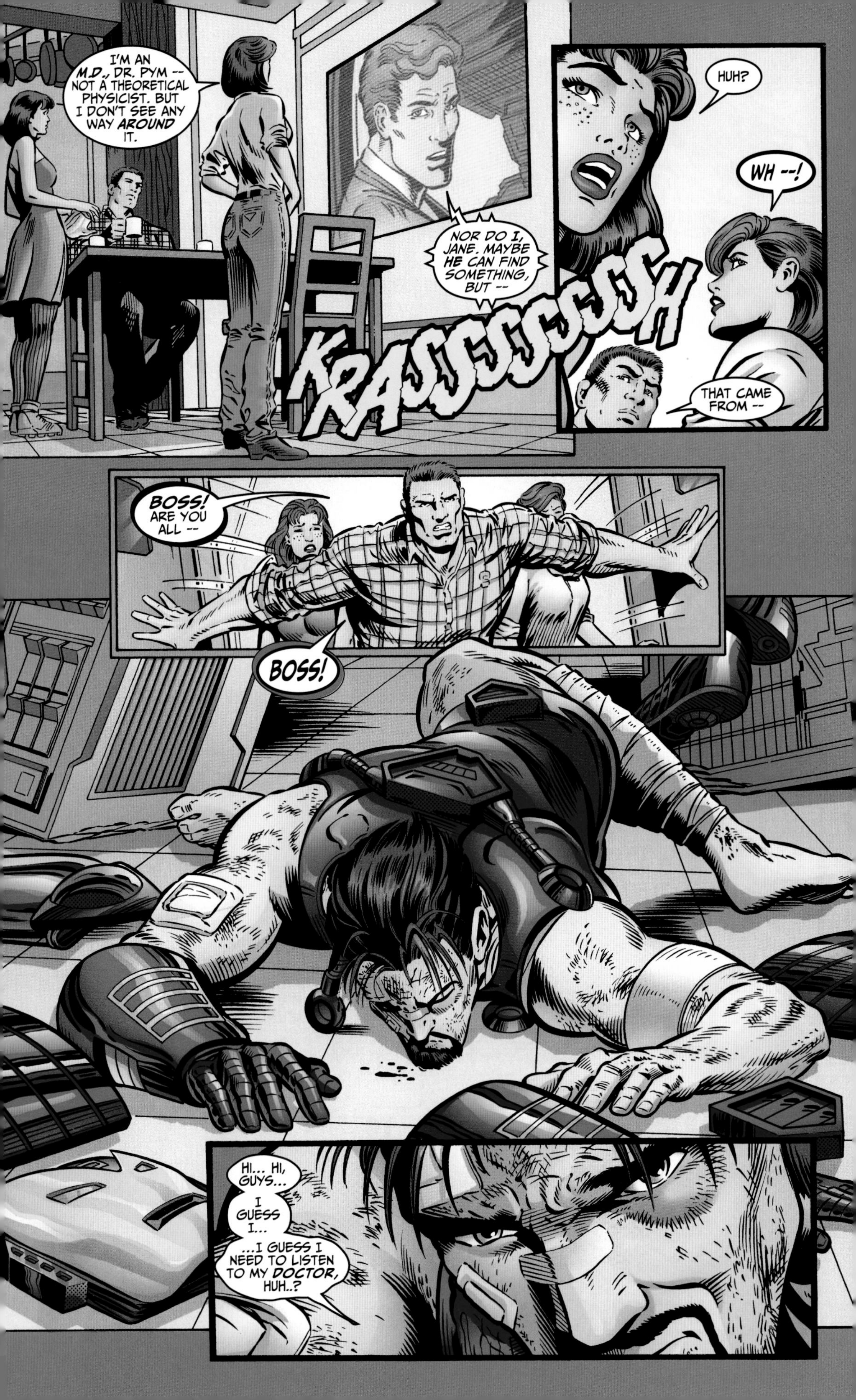
I'M AN M.D., DR. PYM -- NOT A THEORETICAL PHYSICIST. BUT I DON'T SEE ANY WAY AROUND IT.
NOR DO I, JANE. MAYBE HE CAN FIND SOMETHING, BUT --
KRASSSSSSH
HUH?
WH --!
THAT CAME FROM --
BOSS! ARE YOU ALL --
BOSS!
HI... HI, GUYS...
I GUESS I...
...I GUESS I NEED TO LISTEN TO MY DOCTOR, HUH..?

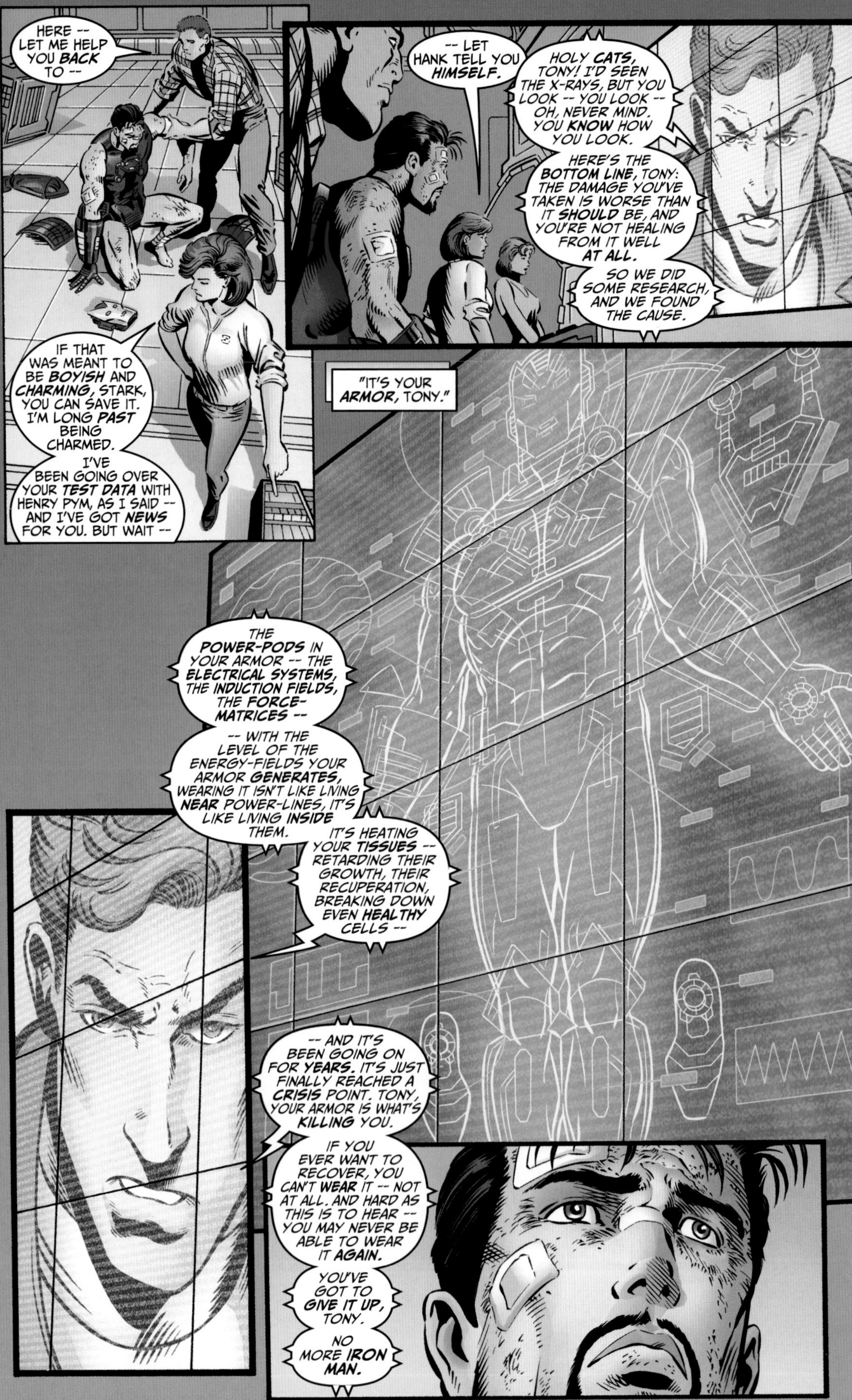
HERE -- LET ME HELP YOU BACK TO --
-- LET HANK TELL YOU HIMSELF.
HOLY CATS, TONY! I'D SEEN THE X-RAYS, BUT YOU LOOK -- YOU LOOK -- OH, NEVER MIND. YOU KNOW HOW YOU LOOK.
HERE'S THE BOTTOM LINE, TONY: THE DAMAGE YOU'VE TAKEN IS WORSE THAN IT SHOULD BE, AND YOU'RE NOT HEALING FROM IT WELL AT ALL.
SO WE DID SOME RESEARCH, AND WE FOUND THE CAUSE.
IF THAT WAS MEANT TO BE BOYISH AND CHARMING, STARK, YOU CAN SAVE IT. I'M LONG PAST BEING CHARMED.
I'VE BEEN GOING OVER YOUR TEST DATA WITH HENRY PYM, AS I SAID -- AND I'VE GOT NEWS FOR YOU. BUT WAIT --
"IT'S YOUR ARMOR, TONY."
THE POWER-PODS IN YOUR ARMOR -- THE ELECTRICAL SYSTEMS, THE INDUCTION FIELDS, THE FORCE-MATRICES --
-- WITH THE LEVEL OF THE ENERGY-FIELDS YOUR ARMOR GENERATES, WEARING IT ISN'T LIKE LIVING NEAR POWER-LINES, IT'S LIKE LIVING INSIDE THEM.
IT'S HEATING YOUR TISSUES -- RETARDING THEIR GROWTH, THEIR RECUPERATION, BREAKING DOWN EVEN HEALTHY CELLS --
-- AND IT'S BEEN GOING ON FOR YEARS. IT'S JUST FINALLY REACHED A CRISIS POINT. TONY, YOUR ARMOR IS WHAT'S KILLING YOU.
IF YOU EVER WANT TO RECOVER, YOU CAN'T WEAR IT -- NOT AT ALL. AND HARD AS THIS IS TO HEAR -- YOU MAY NEVER BE ABLE TO WEAR IT AGAIN.
YOU'VE GOT TO GIVE IT UP, TONY.
NO MORE IRON MAN.

THAT NIGHT, I SPEND SOME TIME TRYING TO GET *USED* TO THE IDEA. NOT THAT IT *WORKS.* BUT AFTER AN HOUR OR TWO --

HM?

HI, TONY. I LEFT A CONTACT NUMBER WITH *PEPPER,* AND SHE CALLED ME. SAID YOU MIGHT LIKE TO TALK TO SOMEONE WHO'D *UNDERSTAND.*

YOU TOLD PEPPER WHO YOU REALLY *ARE?*

YOU'VE TRUSTED ME WITH *YOUR* SECRET IDENTITY -- *TWICE.** IF YOU THINK SHE'S TRUSTWORTHY, THAT'S ENOUGH FOR *ME.* SO -- HOW *ARE* YOU?

*IN #7 AND IN THE WAKE OF IRON MAN/CAP'98 -- BOBBIE

I CAN'T BE TRUSTED TO STAY AWAY FROM THE *ARMOR,* IT SEEMS.

THEY'RE PACKING ME OFF TO THE *BASEL STRESS CLINIC* FOR RECUPERATION -- A TOP-NOTCH CLINIC, RECOMMENDED BY *HALF* THE *A.M.A.*

I'LL STAY THERE UNTIL I'M *WELL.* NO CONSULTING, NO AVENGING, NO WORK, NO *NOTHING.* I LEAVE *TOMORROW.*

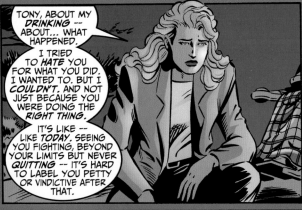

TONY, ABOUT MY *DRINKING* -- ABOUT... WHAT HAPPENED.

I TRIED TO *HATE* YOU FOR WHAT YOU DID. I WANTED TO. BUT I *COULDN'T.* AND NOT JUST BECAUSE YOU WERE DOING THE *RIGHT THING.*

IT'S LIKE -- LIKE *TODAY.* SEEING YOU FIGHTING, BEYOND YOUR LIMITS BUT NEVER *QUITTING* -- IT'S HARD TO LABEL YOU PETTY OR VINDICTIVE AFTER THAT.

I KNOW YOU WERE TRYING TO *HELP* ME. AND I APOLOGIZE FOR LASHING OUT.

AND WHAT'S MORE -- I KNOW YOU CAN BEAT *THIS.* YOU'RE STRONG ENOUGH TO DO *ANYTHING.*

A REGULAR *IRON MAN,* THAT'S ME. BUT HOW ARE *YOU* DOING?

MANAGING.

I HAVE A PROBLEM, I *KNOW* THAT. BUT I CAN LICK IT -- *I'M* PRETTY STRONG, TOO. AND HEY, WHEN YOU'RE BACK IN *TOWN* --

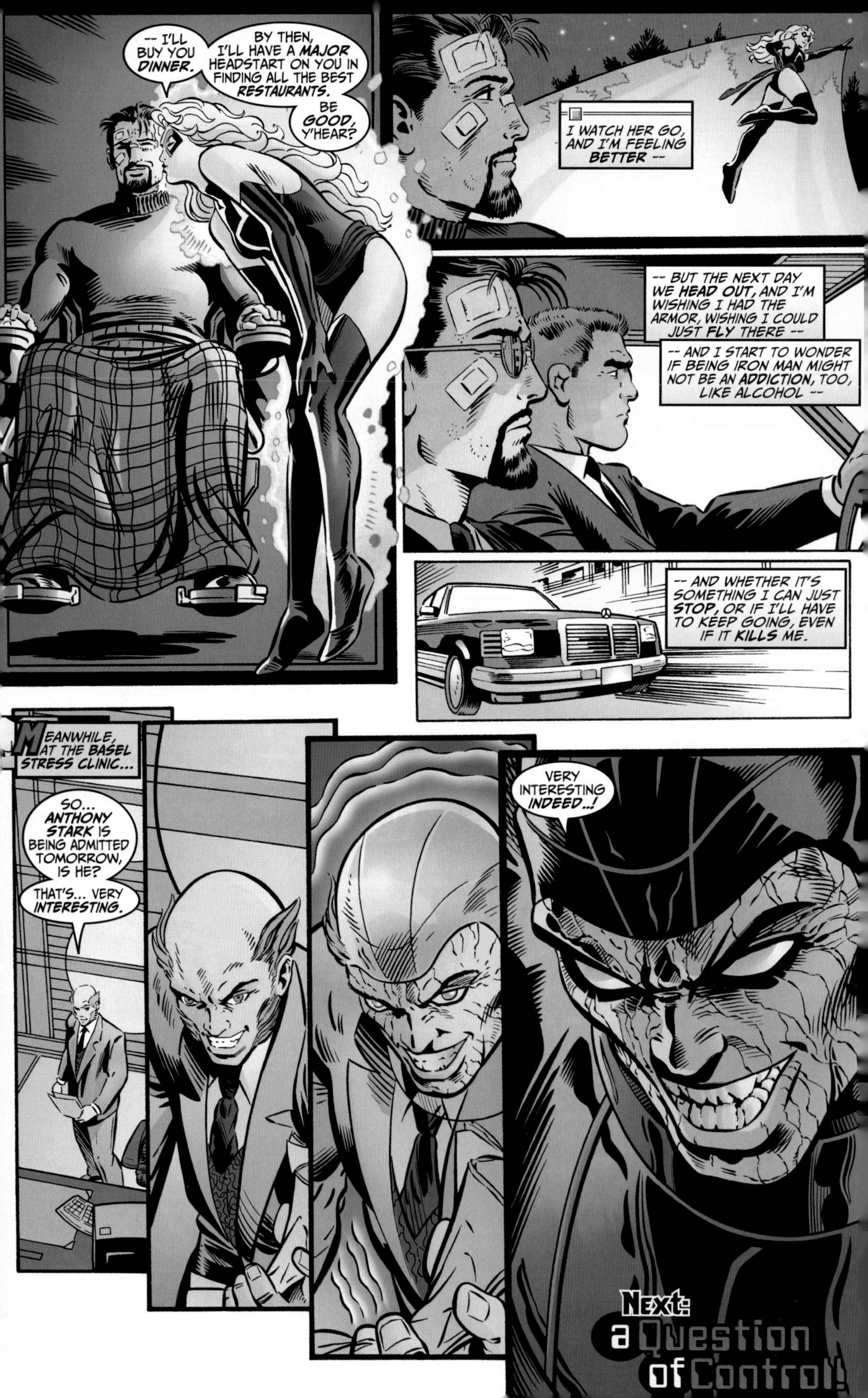
-- I'LL BUY YOU DINNER.
BY THEN, I'LL HAVE A MAJOR HEADSTART ON YOU IN FINDING ALL THE BEST RESTAURANTS.
BE GOOD, Y'HEAR?
I WATCH HER GO, AND I'M FEELING BETTER --
-- BUT THE NEXT DAY WE HEAD OUT, AND I'M WISHING I HAD THE ARMOR, WISHING I COULD JUST FLY THERE --
-- AND I START TO WONDER IF BEING IRON MAN MIGHT NOT BE AN ADDICTION, TOO, LIKE ALCOHOL --
-- AND WHETHER IT'S SOMETHING I CAN JUST STOP, OR IF I'LL HAVE TO KEEP GOING, EVEN IF IT KILLS ME.
MEANWHILE, AT THE BASEL STRESS CLINIC...
SO... ANTHONY STARK IS BEING ADMITTED TOMORROW, IS HE?
THAT'S... VERY INTERESTING.
VERY INTERESTING INDEED..!
Next: a Question of Control!

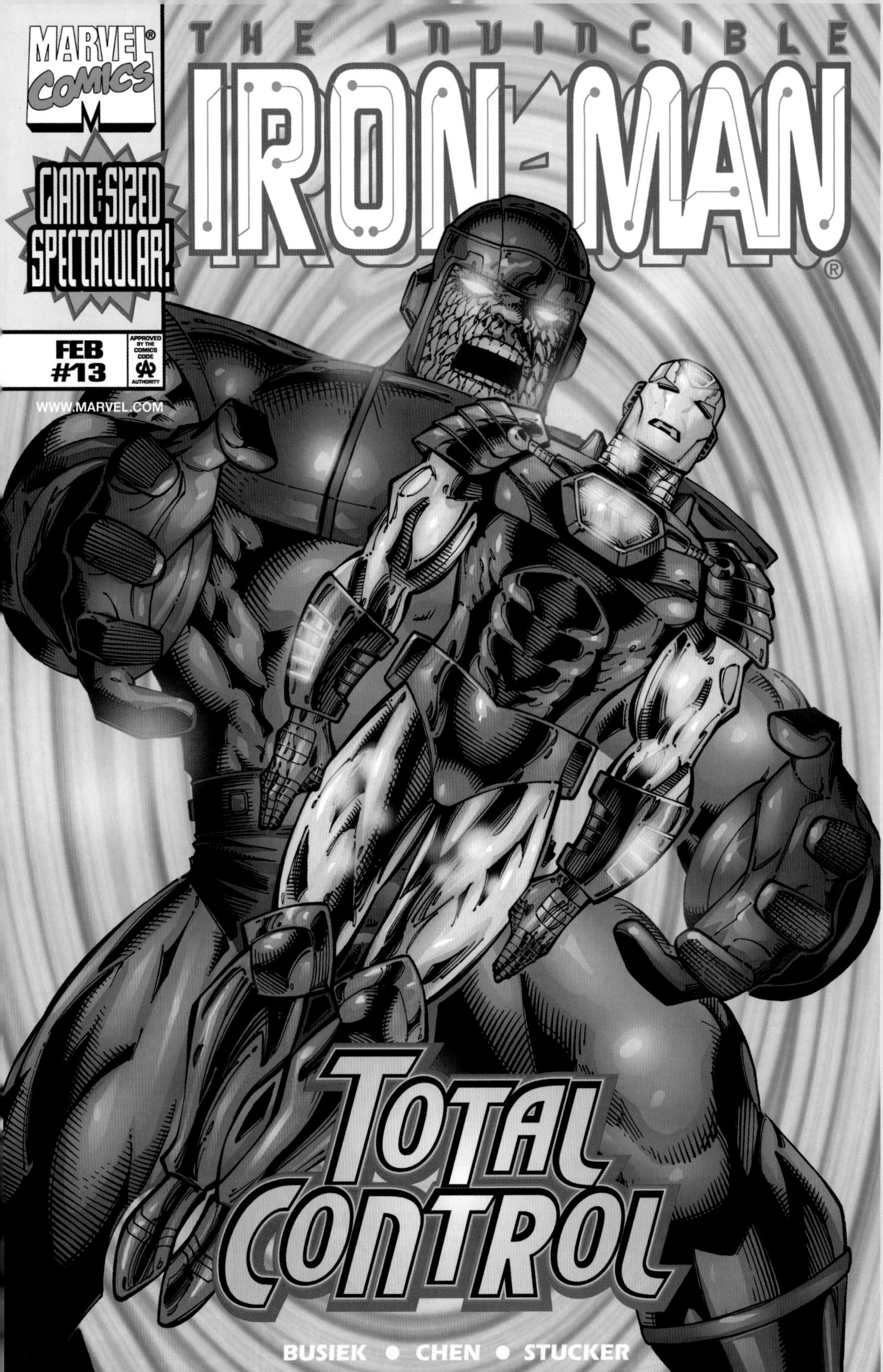
MARVEL COMICS
THE INVINCIBLE
IRON MAN
GIANT-SIZED SPECTACULAR!
FEB #13
APPROVED BY THE COMICS CODE AUTHORITY
WWW.MARVEL.COM
TOTAL CONTROL
BUSIEK • CHEN • STUCKER

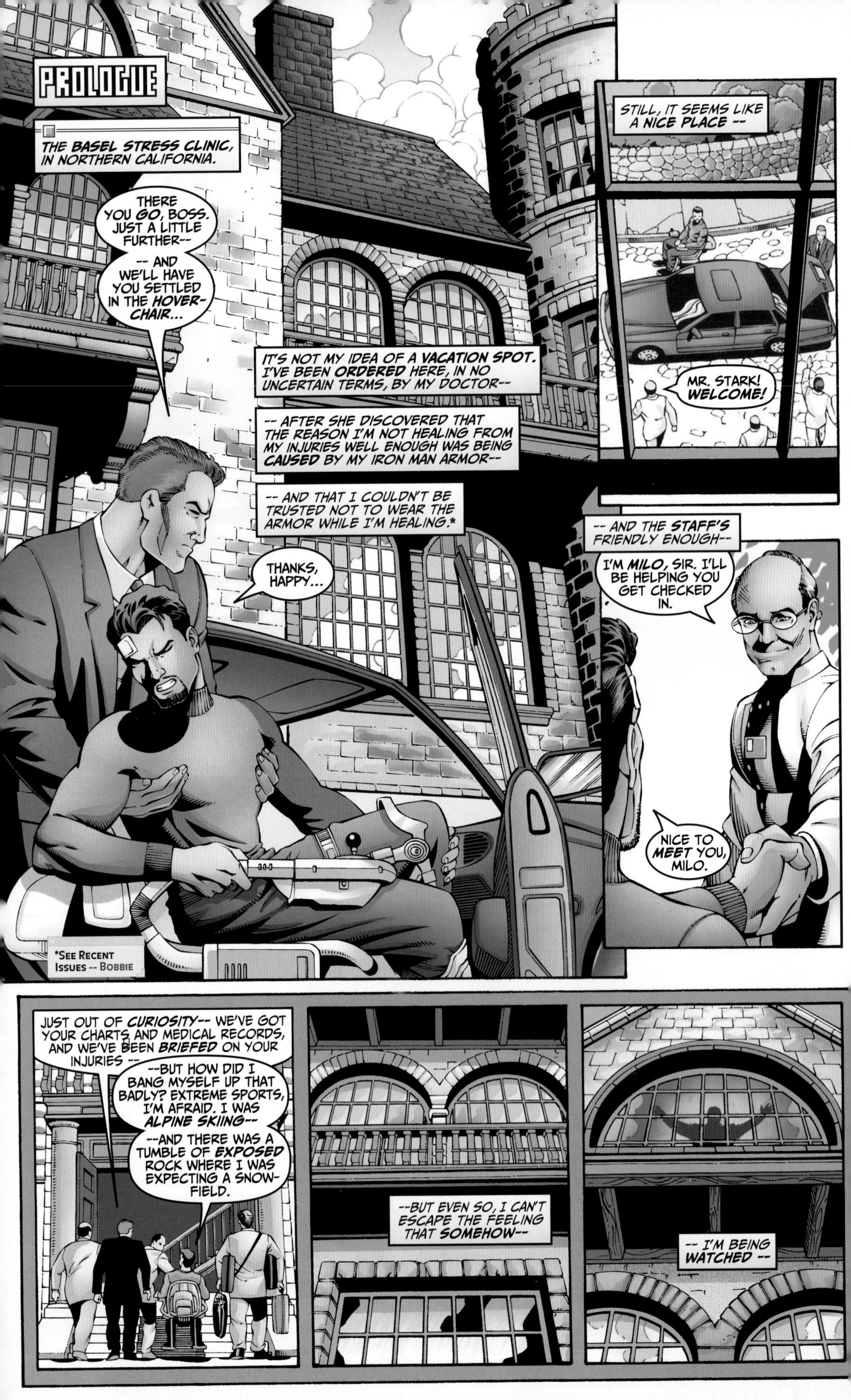
PROLOGUE
THE BASEL STRESS CLINIC, IN NORTHERN CALIFORNIA.
THERE YOU GO, BOSS. JUST A LITTLE FURTHER--
-- AND WE'LL HAVE YOU SETTLED IN THE HOVER-CHAIR...
IT'S NOT MY IDEA OF A VACATION SPOT. I'VE BEEN ORDERED HERE, IN NO UNCERTAIN TERMS, BY MY DOCTOR--
-- AFTER SHE DISCOVERED THAT THE REASON I'M NOT HEALING FROM MY INJURIES WELL ENOUGH WAS BEING CAUSED BY MY IRON MAN ARMOR--
-- AND THAT I COULDN'T BE TRUSTED NOT TO WEAR THE ARMOR WHILE I'M HEALING.*
THANKS, HAPPY...
*SEE RECENT ISSUES -- BOBBIE
STILL, IT SEEMS LIKE A NICE PLACE --
MR. STARK! WELCOME!
-- AND THE STAFF'S FRIENDLY ENOUGH--
I'M MILO, SIR. I'LL BE HELPING YOU GET CHECKED IN.
NICE TO MEET YOU, MILO.
JUST OUT OF CURIOSITY-- WE'VE GOT YOUR CHARTS AND MEDICAL RECORDS, AND WE'VE BEEN BRIEFED ON YOUR INJURIES --
--BUT HOW DID I BANG MYSELF UP THAT BADLY? EXTREME SPORTS, I'M AFRAID. I WAS ALPINE SKIING--
--AND THERE WAS A TUMBLE OF EXPOSED ROCK WHERE I WAS EXPECTING A SNOW-FIELD.
--BUT EVEN SO, I CAN'T ESCAPE THE FEELING THAT SOMEHOW--
-- I'M BEING WATCHED --

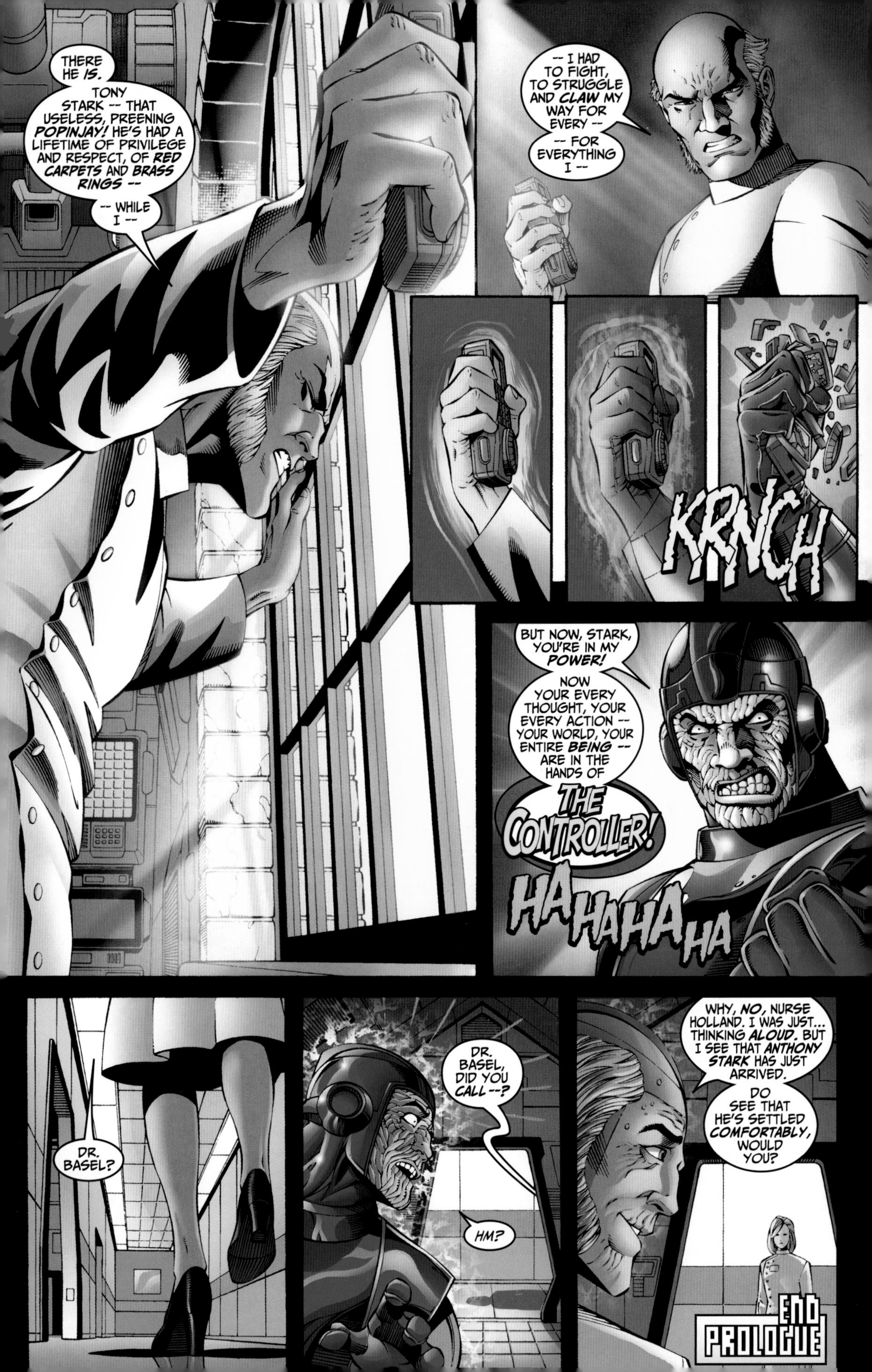
THERE HE IS.
TONY STARK -- THAT USELESS, PREENING POPINJAY! HE'S HAD A LIFETIME OF PRIVILEGE AND RESPECT, OF RED CARPETS AND BRASS RINGS --
-- WHILE I --
-- I HAD TO FIGHT, TO STRUGGLE AND CLAW MY WAY FOR EVERY --
-- FOR EVERYTHING I --
KRNCH
BUT NOW, STARK, YOU'RE IN MY POWER!
NOW YOUR EVERY THOUGHT, YOUR EVERY ACTION -- YOUR WORLD, YOUR ENTIRE BEING -- ARE IN THE HANDS OF
THE CONTROLLER!
HA HAHAHA HA
DR. BASEL?
DR. BASEL, DID YOU CALL --?
HM?
WHY, NO, NURSE HOLLAND. I WAS JUST... THINKING ALOUD. BUT I SEE THAT ANTHONY STARK HAS JUST ARRIVED.
DO SEE THAT HE'S SETTLED COMFORTABLY, WOULD YOU?
END PROLOGUE

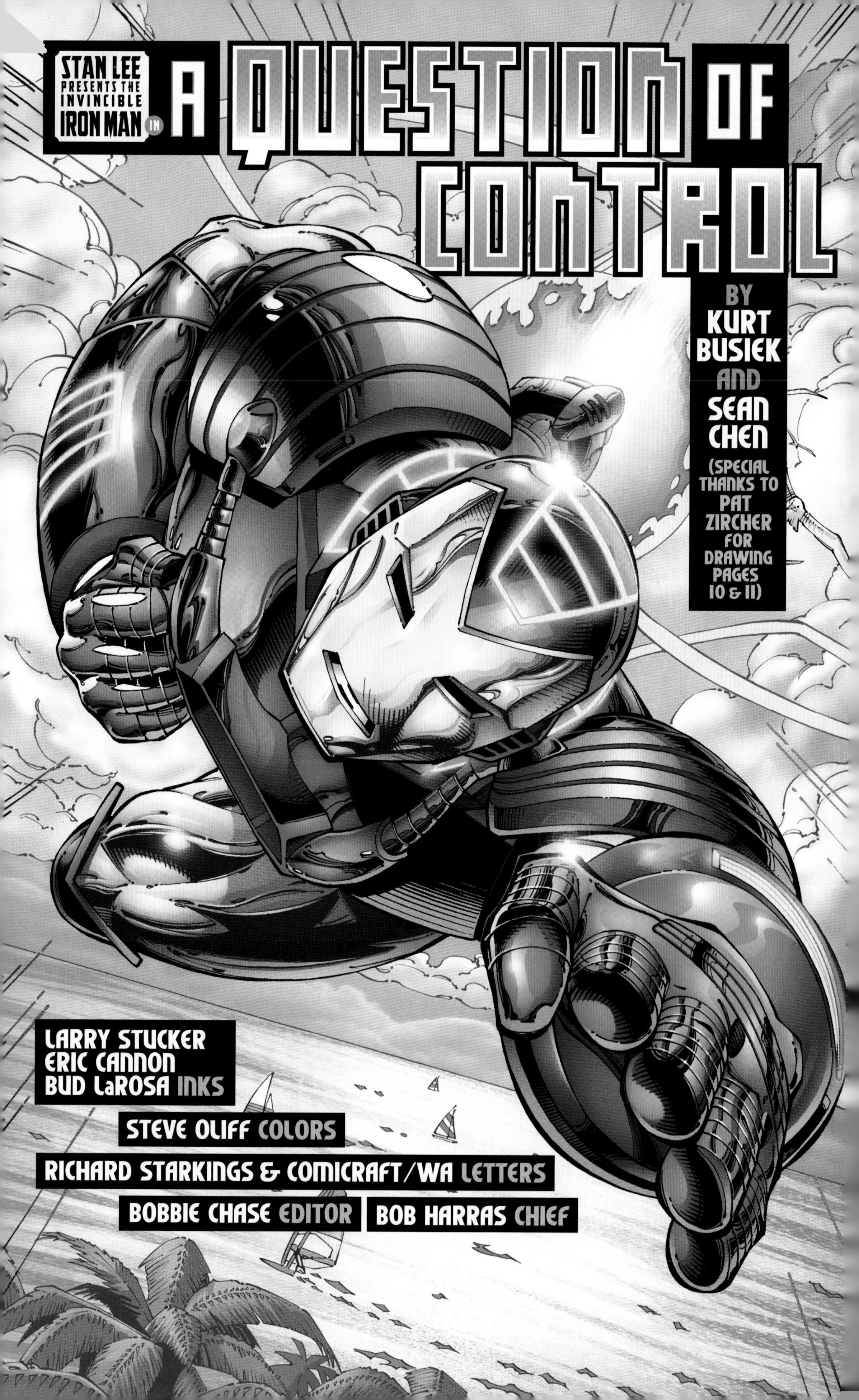

STAN LEE PRESENTS THE INVINCIBLE IRON MAN IN
A QUESTION OF CONTROL
BY KURT BUSIEK AND SEAN CHEN
(SPECIAL THANKS TO PAT ZIRCHER FOR DRAWING PAGES 10 & 11)
LARRY STUCKER
ERIC CANNON
BUD LaROSA INKS
STEVE OLIFF COLORS
RICHARD STARKINGS & COMICRAFT/WA LETTERS
BOBBIE CHASE EDITOR
BOB HARRAS CHIEF

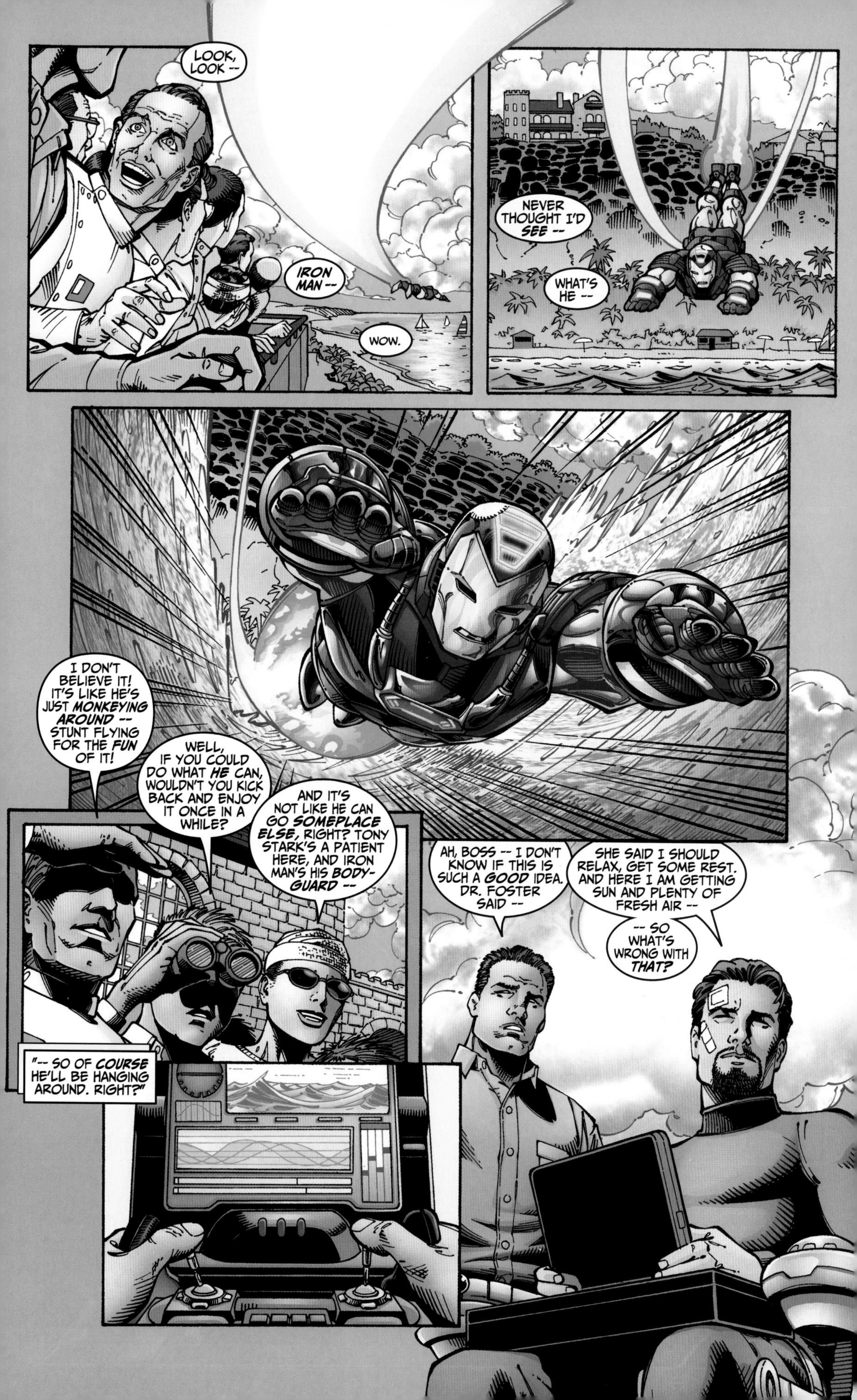
LOOK, LOOK --
IRON MAN --
WOW.
NEVER THOUGHT I'D SEE --
WHAT'S HE --
I DON'T BELIEVE IT! IT'S LIKE HE'S JUST MONKEYING AROUND -- STUNT FLYING FOR THE FUN OF IT!
WELL, IF YOU COULD DO WHAT HE CAN, WOULDN'T YOU KICK BACK AND ENJOY IT ONCE IN A WHILE?
AND IT'S NOT LIKE HE CAN GO SOMEPLACE ELSE, RIGHT? TONY STARK'S A PATIENT HERE, AND IRON MAN'S HIS BODY-GUARD --
"-- SO OF COURSE HE'LL BE HANGING AROUND. RIGHT?"
AH, BOSS -- I DON'T KNOW IF THIS IS SUCH A GOOD IDEA. DR. FOSTER SAID --
SHE SAID I SHOULD RELAX, GET SOME REST. AND HERE I AM GETTING SUN AND PLENTY OF FRESH AIR --
-- SO WHAT'S WRONG WITH THAT?

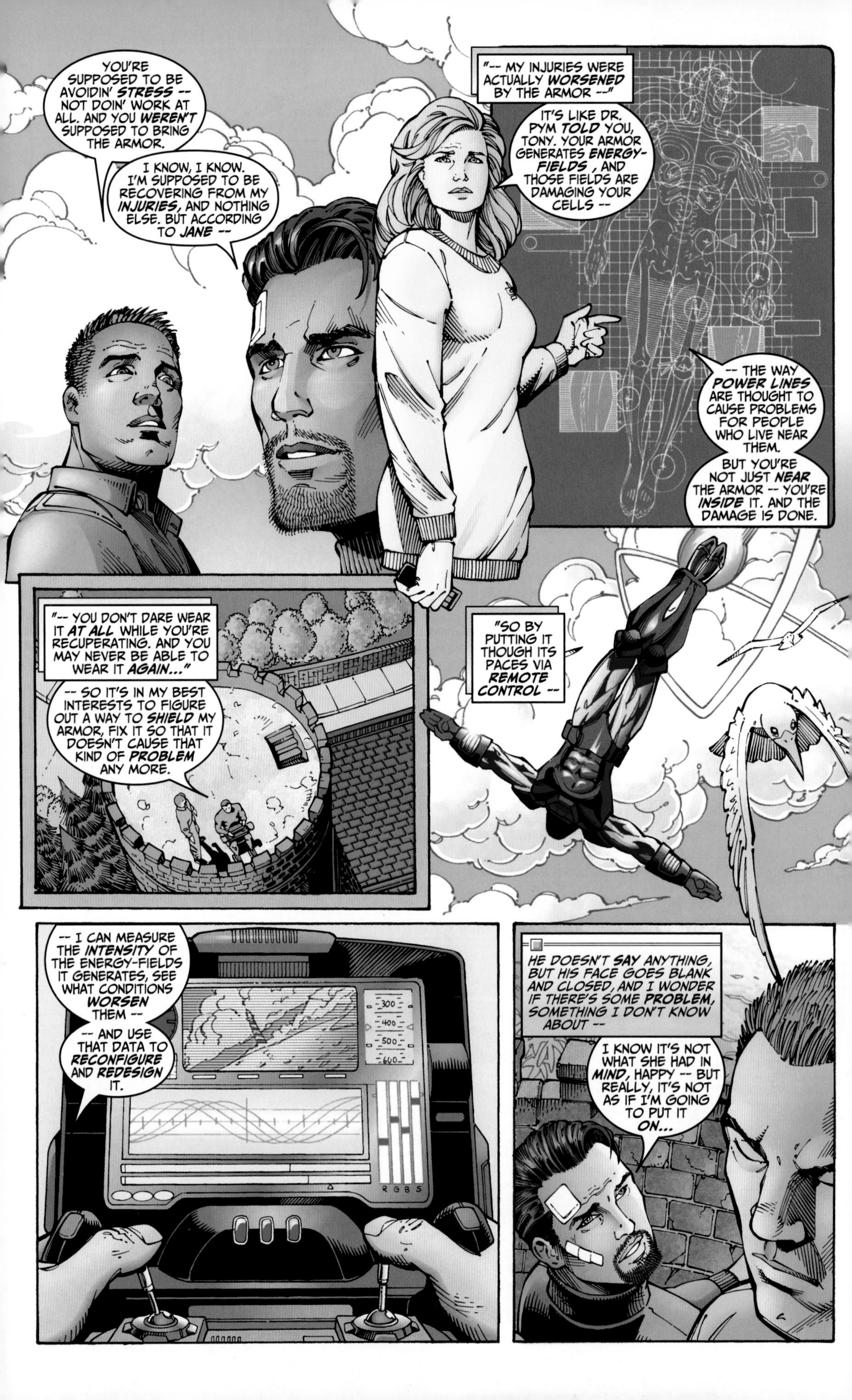
YOU'RE SUPPOSED TO BE AVOIDIN' STRESS -- NOT DOIN' WORK AT ALL. AND YOU WEREN'T SUPPOSED TO BRING THE ARMOR.
I KNOW, I KNOW. I'M SUPPOSED TO BE RECOVERING FROM MY INJURIES, AND NOTHING ELSE. BUT ACCORDING TO JANE --
"-- MY INJURIES WERE ACTUALLY WORSENED BY THE ARMOR --"
IT'S LIKE DR. PYM TOLD YOU, TONY. YOUR ARMOR GENERATES ENERGY-FIELDS , AND THOSE FIELDS ARE DAMAGING YOUR CELLS --
-- THE WAY POWER LINES ARE THOUGHT TO CAUSE PROBLEMS FOR PEOPLE WHO LIVE NEAR THEM.
BUT YOU'RE NOT JUST NEAR THE ARMOR -- YOU'RE INSIDE IT. AND THE DAMAGE IS DONE.
"-- YOU DON'T DARE WEAR IT AT ALL WHILE YOU'RE RECUPERATING. AND YOU MAY NEVER BE ABLE TO WEAR IT AGAIN..."
-- SO IT'S IN MY BEST INTERESTS TO FIGURE OUT A WAY TO SHIELD MY ARMOR, FIX IT SO THAT IT DOESN'T CAUSE THAT KIND OF PROBLEM ANY MORE.
"SO BY PUTTING IT THOUGH ITS PACES VIA REMOTE CONTROL --
-- I CAN MEASURE THE INTENSITY OF THE ENERGY-FIELDS IT GENERATES, SEE WHAT CONDITIONS WORSEN THEM --
-- AND USE THAT DATA TO RECONFIGURE AND REDESIGN IT.
300
400
500
600
R G B S
HE DOESN'T SAY ANYTHING, BUT HIS FACE GOES BLANK AND CLOSED, AND I WONDER IF THERE'S SOME PROBLEM, SOMETHING I DON'T KNOW ABOUT --
I KNOW IT'S NOT WHAT SHE HAD IN MIND, HAPPY -- BUT REALLY, IT'S NOT AS IF I'M GOING TO PUT IT ON...

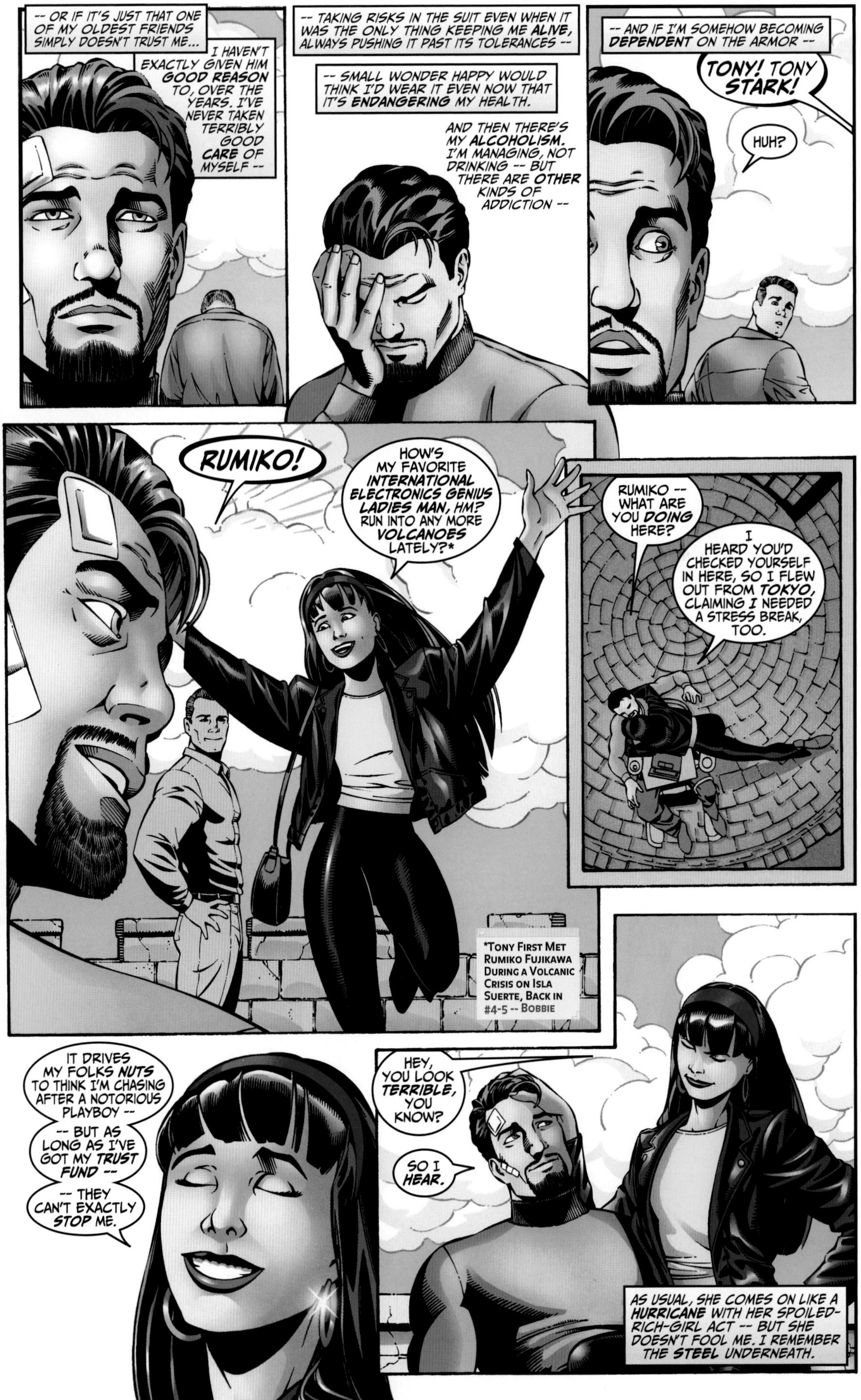
-- OR IF IT'S JUST THAT ONE OF MY OLDEST FRIENDS SIMPLY DOESN'T TRUST ME...
I HAVEN'T EXACTLY GIVEN HIM GOOD REASON TO, OVER THE YEARS. I'VE NEVER TAKEN TERRIBLY GOOD CARE OF MYSELF --
-- TAKING RISKS IN THE SUIT EVEN WHEN IT WAS THE ONLY THING KEEPING ME ALIVE, ALWAYS PUSHING IT PAST ITS TOLERANCES --
-- SMALL WONDER HAPPY WOULD THINK I'D WEAR IT EVEN NOW THAT IT'S ENDANGERING MY HEALTH.
AND THEN THERE'S MY ALCOHOLISM. I'M MANAGING, NOT DRINKING -- BUT THERE ARE OTHER KINDS OF ADDICTION --
-- AND IF I'M SOMEHOW BECOMING DEPENDENT ON THE ARMOR --
TONY! TONY STARK!
HUH?
RUMIKO!
HOW'S MY FAVORITE INTERNATIONAL ELECTRONICS GENIUS LADIES MAN, HM? RUN INTO ANY MORE VOLCANOES LATELY?*
*TONY FIRST MET RUMIKO FUJIKAWA DURING A VOLCANIC CRISIS ON ISLA SUERTE, BACK IN #4-5 -- BOBBIE
RUMIKO -- WHAT ARE YOU DOING HERE?
I HEARD YOU'D CHECKED YOURSELF IN HERE, SO I FLEW OUT FROM TOKYO, CLAIMING I NEEDED A STRESS BREAK, TOO.
IT DRIVES MY FOLKS NUTS TO THINK I'M CHASING AFTER A NOTORIOUS PLAYBOY --
-- BUT AS LONG AS I'VE GOT MY TRUST FUND --
-- THEY CAN'T EXACTLY STOP ME.
HEY, YOU LOOK TERRIBLE, YOU KNOW?
SO I HEAR.
AS USUAL, SHE COMES ON LIKE A HURRICANE WITH HER SPOILED-RICH-GIRL ACT -- BUT SHE DOESN'T FOOL ME. I REMEMBER THE STEEL UNDERNEATH.

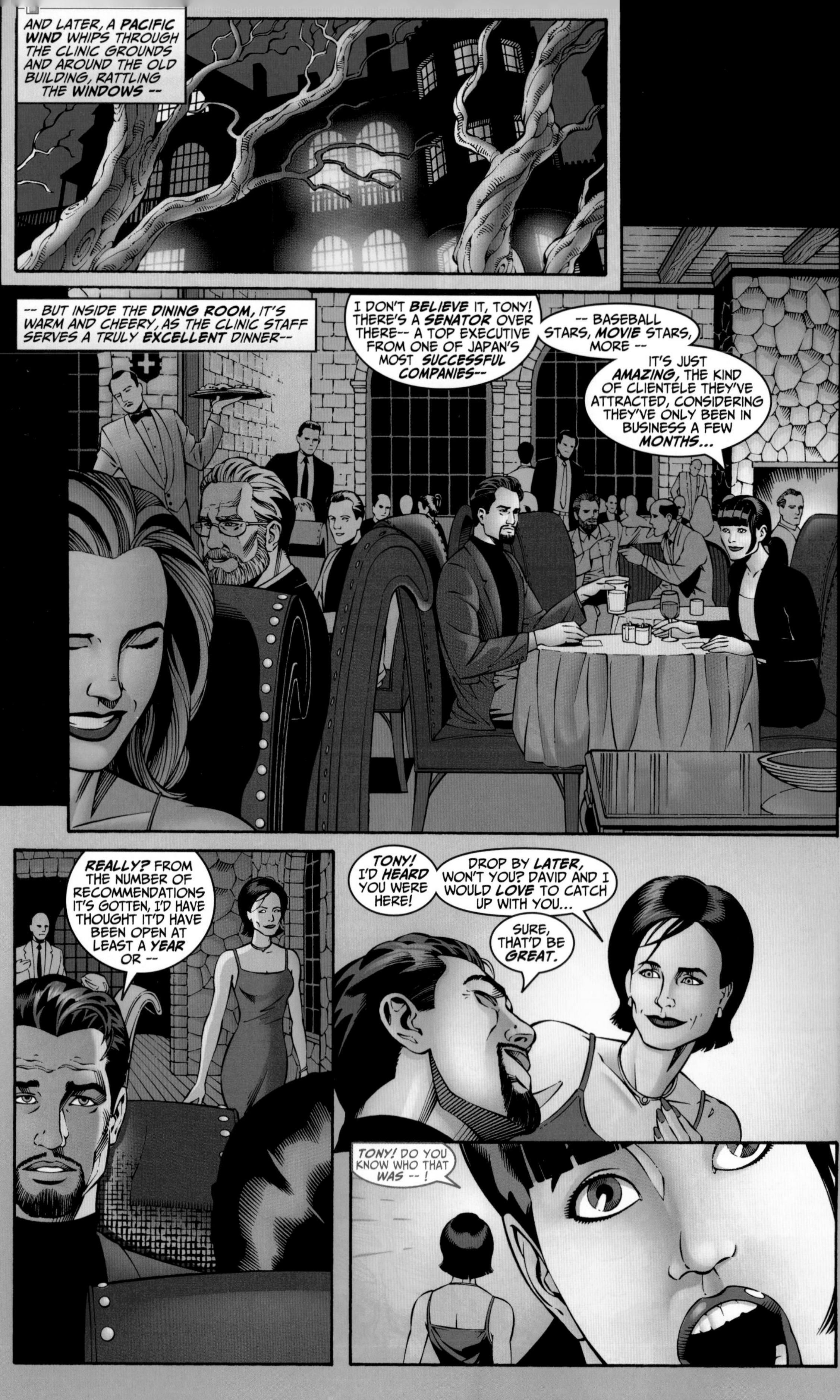
AND LATER, A PACIFIC WIND WHIPS THROUGH THE CLINIC GROUNDS AND AROUND THE OLD BUILDING, RATTLING THE WINDOWS --
-- BUT INSIDE THE DINING ROOM, IT'S WARM AND CHEERY, AS THE CLINIC STAFF SERVES A TRULY EXCELLENT DINNER--
I DON'T BELIEVE IT, TONY! THERE'S A SENATOR OVER THERE-- A TOP EXECUTIVE FROM ONE OF JAPAN'S MOST SUCCESSFUL COMPANIES--
-- BASEBALL STARS, MOVIE STARS, MORE --
IT'S JUST AMAZING, THE KIND OF CLIENTÈLE THEY'VE ATTRACTED, CONSIDERING THEY'VE ONLY BEEN IN BUSINESS A FEW MONTHS...
REALLY? FROM THE NUMBER OF RECOMMENDATIONS IT'S GOTTEN, I'D HAVE THOUGHT IT'D HAVE BEEN OPEN AT LEAST A YEAR OR --
TONY! I'D HEARD YOU WERE HERE!
DROP BY LATER, WON'T YOU? DAVID AND I WOULD LOVE TO CATCH UP WITH YOU...
SURE, THAT'D BE GREAT.
TONY! DO YOU KNOW WHO THAT WAS -- !

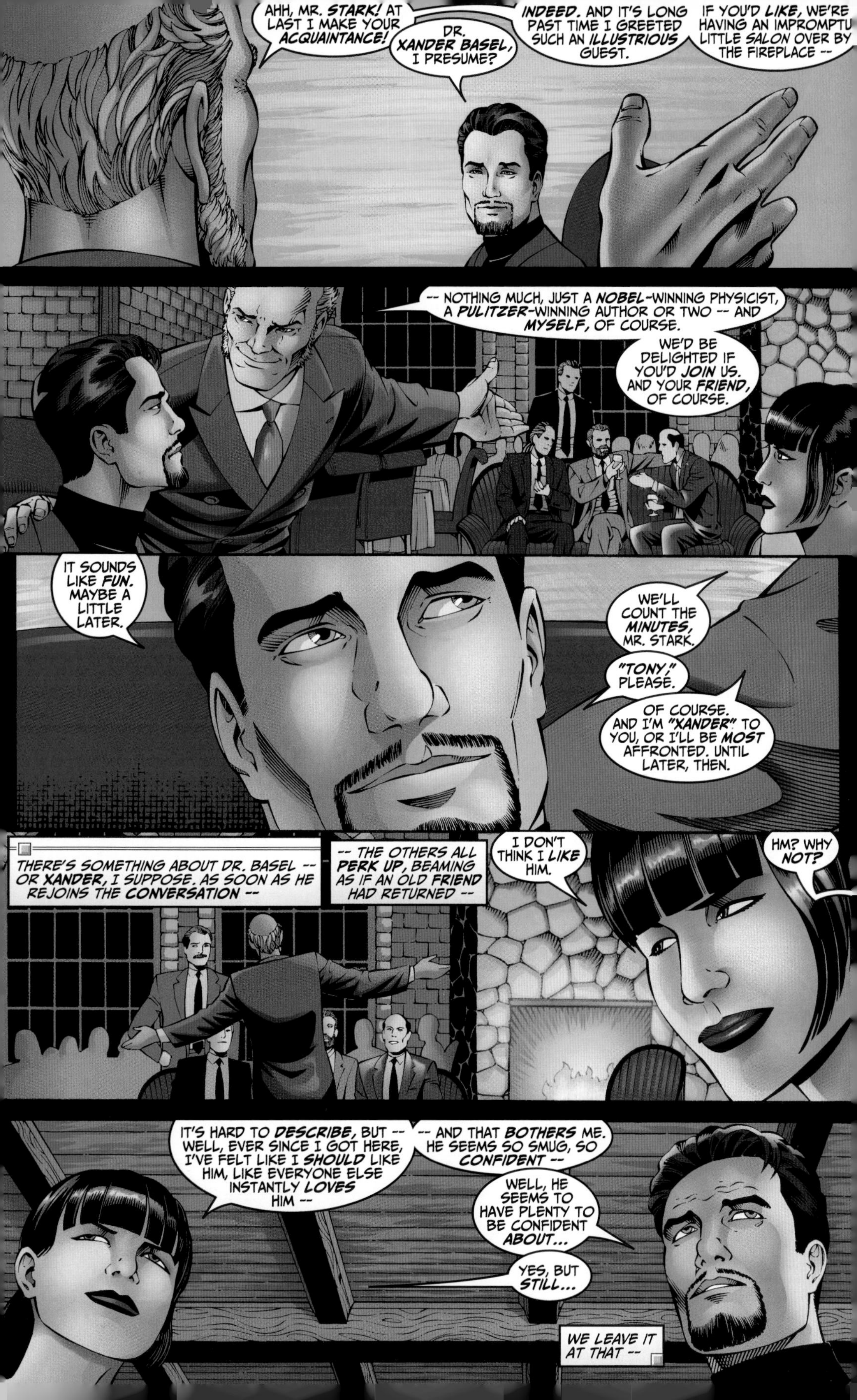
AHH, MR. STARK! AT LAST I MAKE YOUR ACQUAINTANCE!
DR. XANDER BASEL, I PRESUME?
INDEED. AND IT'S LONG PAST TIME I GREETED SUCH AN ILLUSTRIOUS GUEST.
IF YOU'D LIKE, WE'RE HAVING AN IMPROMPTU LITTLE SALON OVER BY THE FIREPLACE --
-- NOTHING MUCH, JUST A NOBEL-WINNING PHYSICIST, A PULITZER-WINNING AUTHOR OR TWO -- AND MYSELF, OF COURSE.
WE'D BE DELIGHTED IF YOU'D JOIN US. AND YOUR FRIEND, OF COURSE.
IT SOUNDS LIKE FUN. MAYBE A LITTLE LATER.
WE'LL COUNT THE MINUTES, MR. STARK.
"TONY," PLEASE.
OF COURSE. AND I'M "XANDER" TO YOU, OR I'LL BE MOST AFFRONTED. UNTIL LATER, THEN.
THERE'S SOMETHING ABOUT DR. BASEL -- OR XANDER, I SUPPOSE. AS SOON AS HE REJOINS THE CONVERSATION --
-- THE OTHERS ALL PERK UP, BEAMING AS IF AN OLD FRIEND HAD RETURNED --
I DON'T THINK I LIKE HIM.
HM? WHY NOT?
IT'S HARD TO DESCRIBE, BUT -- WELL, EVER SINCE I GOT HERE, I'VE FELT LIKE I SHOULD LIKE HIM, LIKE EVERYONE ELSE INSTANTLY LOVES HIM --
-- AND THAT BOTHERS ME. HE SEEMS SO SMUG, SO CONFIDENT --
WELL, HE SEEMS TO HAVE PLENTY TO BE CONFIDENT ABOUT...
YES, BUT STILL...
WE LEAVE IT AT THAT --

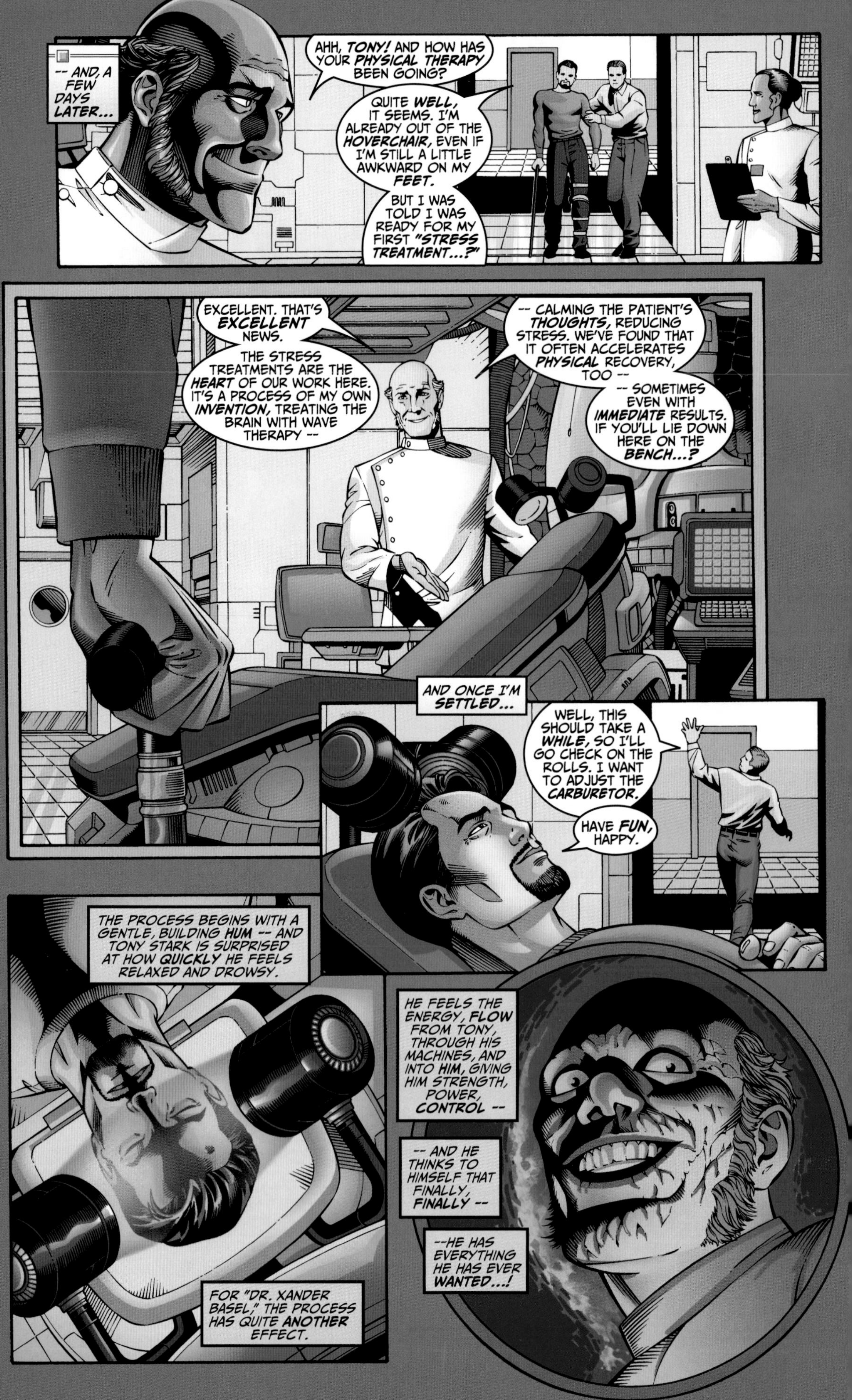
-- AND, A FEW DAYS LATER...
AHH, TONY! AND HOW HAS YOUR PHYSICAL THERAPY BEEN GOING?
QUITE WELL, IT SEEMS. I'M ALREADY OUT OF THE HOVERCHAIR, EVEN IF I'M STILL A LITTLE AWKWARD ON MY FEET.
BUT I WAS TOLD I WAS READY FOR MY FIRST "STRESS TREATMENT...?"
EXCELLENT. THAT'S EXCELLENT NEWS.
THE STRESS TREATMENTS ARE THE HEART OF OUR WORK HERE. IT'S A PROCESS OF MY OWN INVENTION, TREATING THE BRAIN WITH WAVE THERAPY --
-- CALMING THE PATIENT'S THOUGHTS, REDUCING STRESS. WE'VE FOUND THAT IT OFTEN ACCELERATES PHYSICAL RECOVERY, TOO --
-- SOMETIMES EVEN WITH IMMEDIATE RESULTS. IF YOU'LL LIE DOWN HERE ON THE BENCH...?
AND ONCE I'M SETTLED...
WELL, THIS SHOULD TAKE A WHILE, SO I'LL GO CHECK ON THE ROLLS. I WANT TO ADJUST THE CARBURETOR.
HAVE FUN, HAPPY.
THE PROCESS BEGINS WITH A GENTLE, BUILDING HUM -- AND TONY STARK IS SURPRISED AT HOW QUICKLY HE FEELS RELAXED AND DROWSY.
FOR "DR. XANDER BASEL," THE PROCESS HAS QUITE ANOTHER EFFECT.
HE FEELS THE ENERGY, FLOW FROM TONY, THROUGH HIS MACHINES, AND INTO HIM, GIVING HIM STRENGTH, POWER, CONTROL --
-- AND HE THINKS TO HIMSELF THAT FINALLY, FINALLY --
--HE HAS EVERYTHING HE HAS EVER WANTED...!

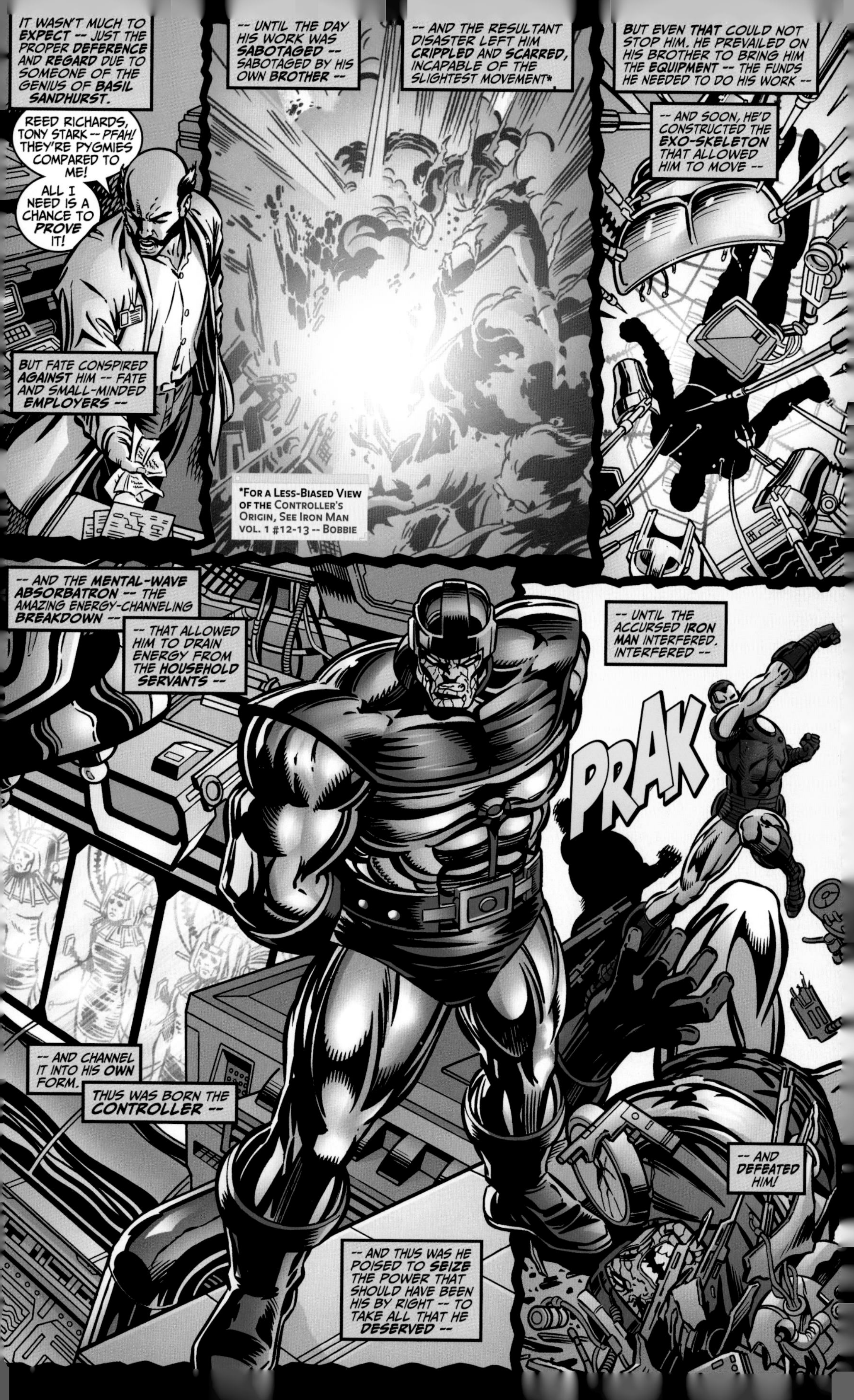
IT WASN'T MUCH TO EXPECT -- JUST THE PROPER DEFERENCE AND REGARD DUE TO SOMEONE OF THE GENIUS OF BASIL SANDHURST.
REED RICHARDS, TONY STARK -- PFAH! THEY'RE PYGMIES COMPARED TO ME!
ALL I NEED IS A CHANCE TO PROVE IT!
BUT FATE CONSPIRED AGAINST HIM -- FATE AND SMALL-MINDED EMPLOYERS --
-- UNTIL THE DAY HIS WORK WAS SABOTAGED -- SABOTAGED BY HIS OWN BROTHER --
-- AND THE RESULTANT DISASTER LEFT HIM CRIPPLED AND SCARRED, INCAPABLE OF THE SLIGHTEST MOVEMENT*.
*FOR A LESS-BIASED VIEW OF THE CONTROLLER'S ORIGIN, SEE IRON MAN VOL. 1 #12-13 -- BOBBIE
BUT EVEN THAT COULD NOT STOP HIM. HE PREVAILED ON HIS BROTHER TO BRING HIM THE EQUIPMENT -- THE FUNDS HE NEEDED TO DO HIS WORK --
-- AND SOON, HE'D CONSTRUCTED THE EXO-SKELETON THAT ALLOWED HIM TO MOVE --
-- AND THE MENTAL-WAVE ABSORBATRON -- THE AMAZING ENERGY-CHANNELING BREAKDOWN --
-- THAT ALLOWED HIM TO DRAIN ENERGY FROM THE HOUSEHOLD SERVANTS --
-- AND CHANNEL IT INTO HIS OWN FORM.
THUS WAS BORN THE CONTROLLER --
-- AND THUS WAS HE POISED TO SEIZE THE POWER THAT SHOULD HAVE BEEN HIS BY RIGHT -- TO TAKE ALL THAT HE DESERVED --
-- UNTIL THE ACCURSED IRON MAN INTERFERED. INTERFERED --
PRAK
-- AND DEFEATED HIM!

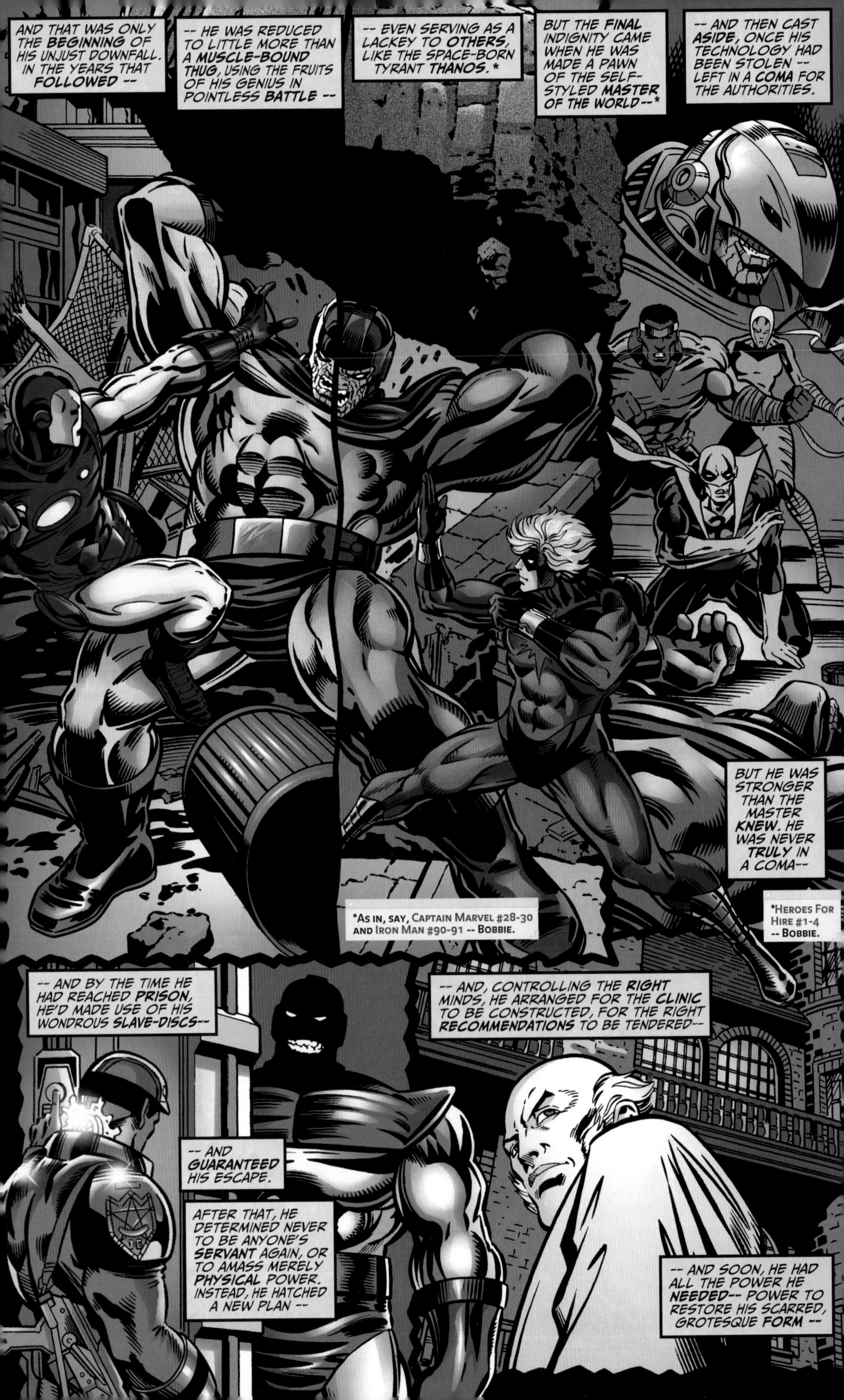
AND THAT WAS ONLY THE BEGINNING OF HIS UNJUST DOWNFALL. IN THE YEARS THAT FOLLOWED --
-- HE WAS REDUCED TO LITTLE MORE THAN A MUSCLE-BOUND THUG, USING THE FRUITS OF HIS GENIUS IN POINTLESS BATTLE --
-- EVEN SERVING AS A LACKEY TO OTHERS, LIKE THE SPACE-BORN TYRANT THANOS.*
BUT THE FINAL INDIGNITY CAME WHEN HE WAS MADE A PAWN OF THE SELF-STYLED MASTER OF THE WORLD--*
-- AND THEN CAST ASIDE, ONCE HIS TECHNOLOGY HAD BEEN STOLEN -- LEFT IN A COMA FOR THE AUTHORITIES.
BUT HE WAS STRONGER THAN THE MASTER KNEW. HE WAS NEVER TRULY IN A COMA--
*As in, say, Captain Marvel #28-30 and Iron Man #90-91 -- Bobbie.
*Heroes For Hire #1-4 -- Bobbie.
-- AND BY THE TIME HE HAD REACHED PRISON, HE'D MADE USE OF HIS WONDROUS SLAVE-DISCS--
-- AND GUARANTEED HIS ESCAPE.
AFTER THAT, HE DETERMINED NEVER TO BE ANYONE'S SERVANT AGAIN, OR TO AMASS MERELY PHYSICAL POWER. INSTEAD, HE HATCHED A NEW PLAN --
-- AND, CONTROLLING THE RIGHT MINDS, HE ARRANGED FOR THE CLINIC TO BE CONSTRUCTED, FOR THE RIGHT RECOMMENDATIONS TO BE TENDERED--
-- AND SOON, HE HAD ALL THE POWER HE NEEDED-- POWER TO RESTORE HIS SCARRED, GROTESQUE FORM --

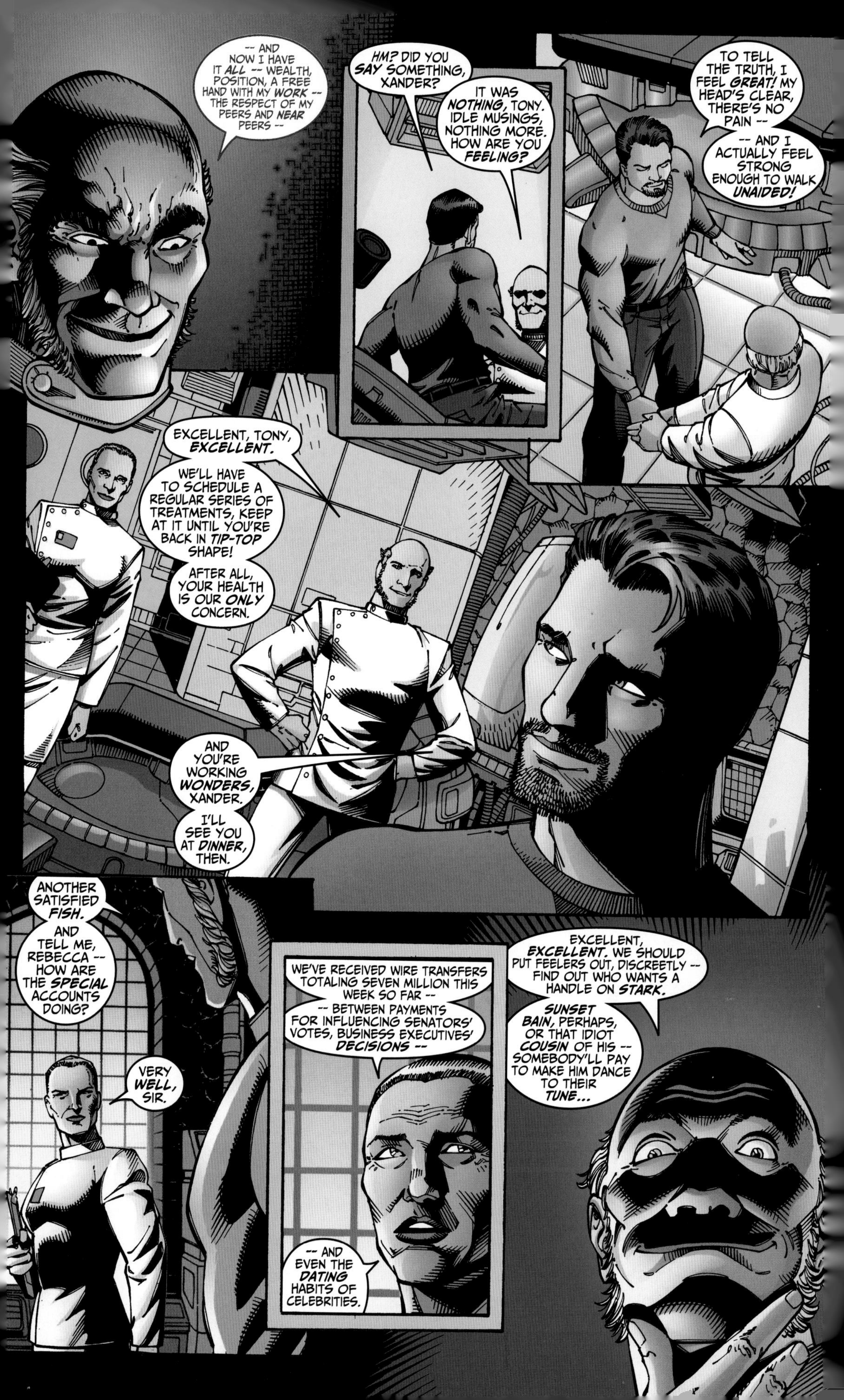
-- AND NOW I HAVE IT ALL -- WEALTH, POSITION, A FREE HAND WITH MY WORK -- THE RESPECT OF MY PEERS AND NEAR PEERS --
HM? DID YOU SAY SOMETHING, XANDER?
IT WAS NOTHING, TONY. IDLE MUSINGS, NOTHING MORE. HOW ARE YOU FEELING?
TO TELL THE TRUTH, I FEEL GREAT! MY HEAD'S CLEAR, THERE'S NO PAIN --
-- AND I ACTUALLY FEEL STRONG ENOUGH TO WALK UNAIDED!
EXCELLENT, TONY, EXCELLENT.
WE'LL HAVE TO SCHEDULE A REGULAR SERIES OF TREATMENTS, KEEP AT IT UNTIL YOU'RE BACK IN TIP-TOP SHAPE!
AFTER ALL, YOUR HEALTH IS OUR ONLY CONCERN.
AND YOU'RE WORKING WONDERS, XANDER.
I'LL SEE YOU AT DINNER, THEN.
ANOTHER SATISFIED FISH.
AND TELL ME, REBECCA -- HOW ARE THE SPECIAL ACCOUNTS DOING?
VERY WELL, SIR.
WE'VE RECEIVED WIRE TRANSFERS TOTALING SEVEN MILLION THIS WEEK SO FAR --
-- BETWEEN PAYMENTS FOR INFLUENCING SENATORS' VOTES, BUSINESS EXECUTIVES' DECISIONS --
-- AND EVEN THE DATING HABITS OF CELEBRITIES.
EXCELLENT, EXCELLENT. WE SHOULD PUT FEELERS OUT, DISCREETLY -- FIND OUT WHO WANTS A HANDLE ON STARK.
SUNSET BAIN, PERHAPS, OR THAT IDIOT COUSIN OF HIS -- SOMEBODY'LL PAY TO MAKE HIM DANCE TO THEIR TUNE...

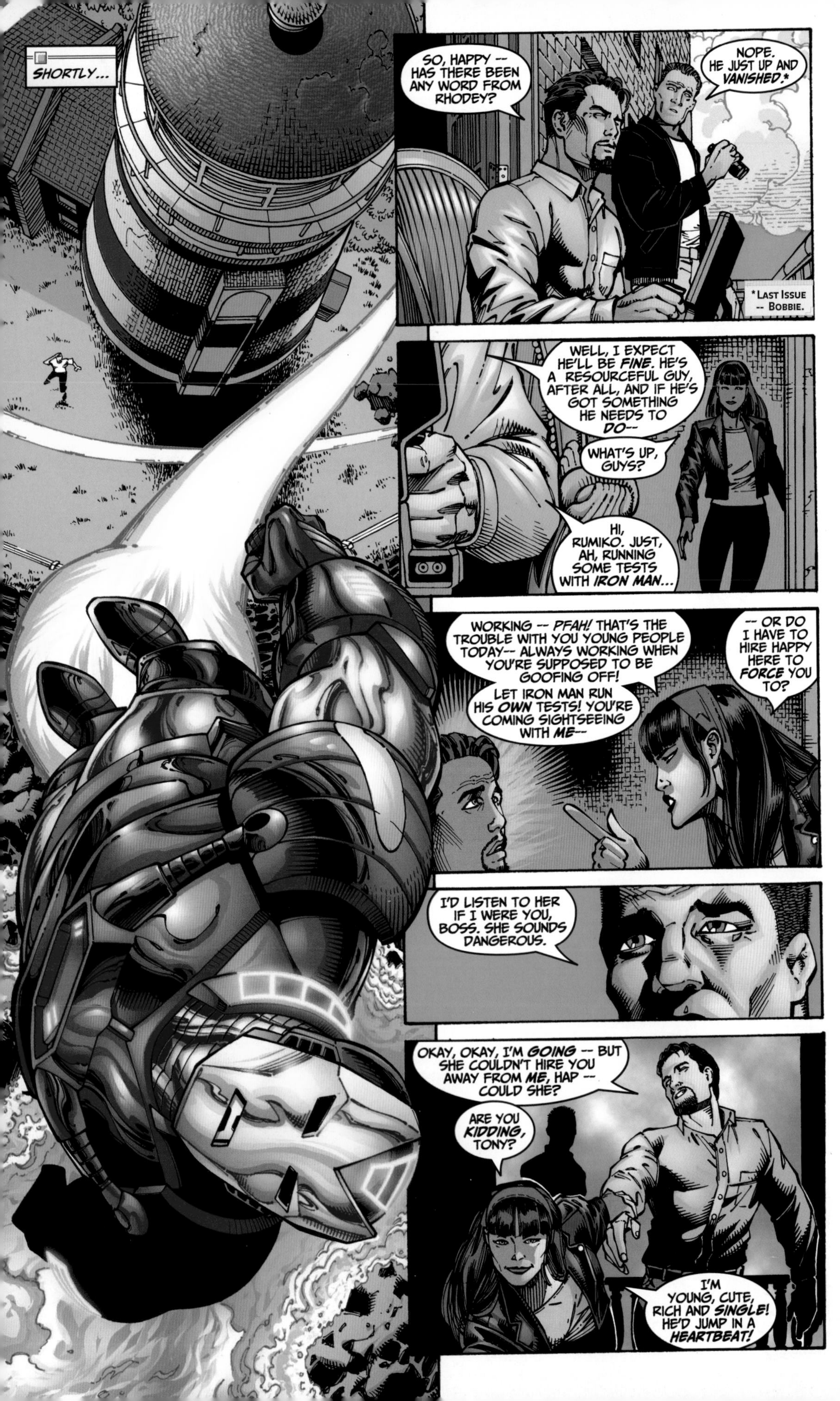

SHORTLY...
SO, HAPPY -- HAS THERE BEEN ANY WORD FROM RHODEY?
NOPE. HE JUST UP AND VANISHED.*
*LAST ISSUE -- BOBBIE.
WELL, I EXPECT HE'LL BE FINE. HE'S A RESOURCEFUL GUY, AFTER ALL, AND IF HE'S GOT SOMETHING HE NEEDS TO DO--
WHAT'S UP, GUYS?
HI, RUMIKO. JUST, AH, RUNNING SOME TESTS WITH IRON MAN...
WORKING -- PFAH! THAT'S THE TROUBLE WITH YOU YOUNG PEOPLE TODAY-- ALWAYS WORKING WHEN YOU'RE SUPPOSED TO BE GOOFING OFF!
LET IRON MAN RUN HIS OWN TESTS! YOU'RE COMING SIGHTSEEING WITH ME--
-- OR DO I HAVE TO HIRE HAPPY HERE TO FORCE YOU TO?
I'D LISTEN TO HER IF I WERE YOU, BOSS. SHE SOUNDS DANGEROUS.
OKAY, OKAY, I'M GOING -- BUT SHE COULDN'T HIRE YOU AWAY FROM ME, HAP -- COULD SHE?
ARE YOU KIDDING, TONY?
I'M YOUNG, CUTE, RICH AND SINGLE! HE'D JUMP IN A HEARTBEAT!

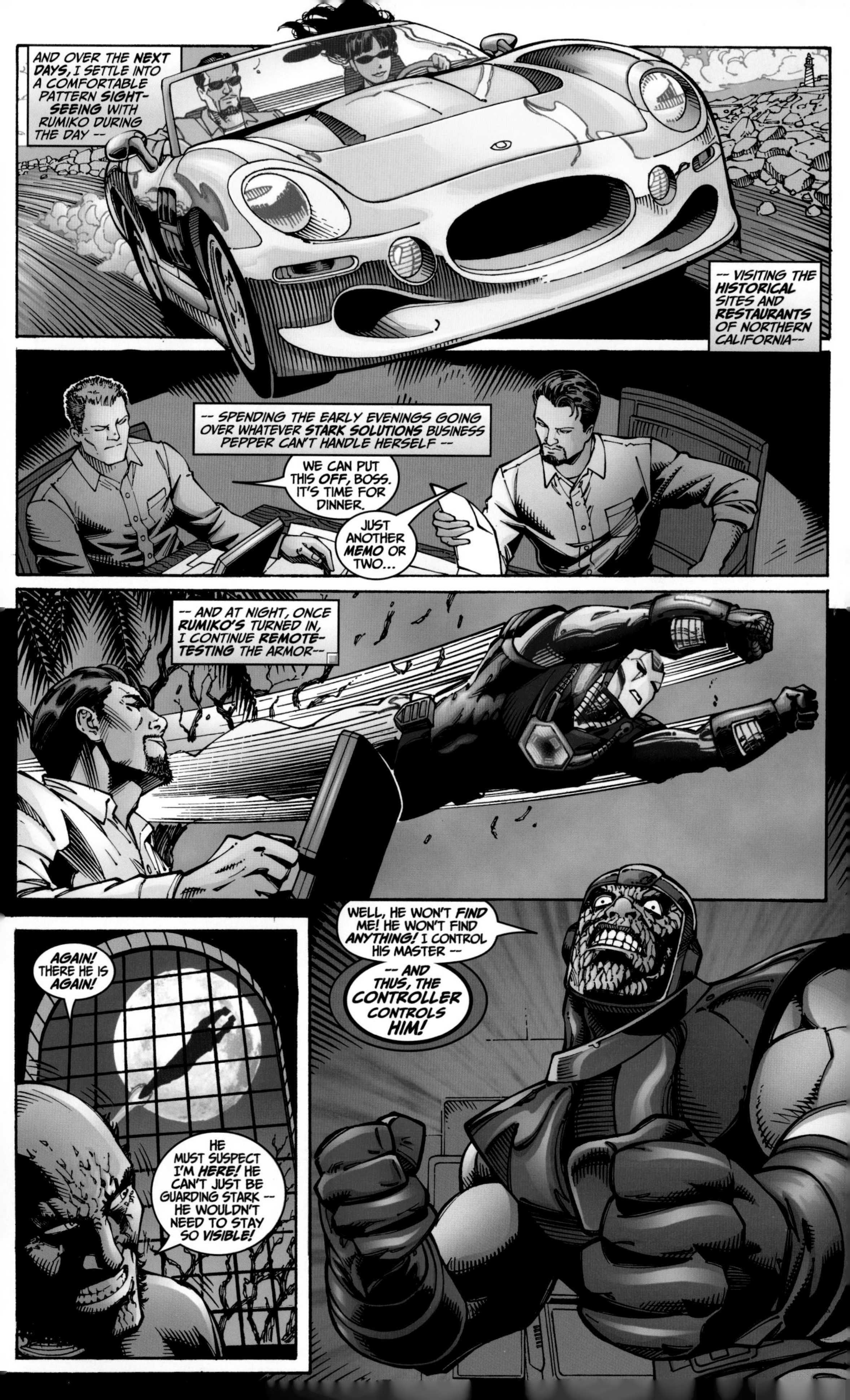
AND OVER THE NEXT DAYS, I SETTLE INTO A COMFORTABLE PATTERN SIGHT-SEEING WITH RUMIKO DURING THE DAY --
-- VISITING THE HISTORICAL SITES AND RESTAURANTS OF NORTHERN CALIFORNIA--
-- SPENDING THE EARLY EVENINGS GOING OVER WHATEVER STARK SOLUTIONS BUSINESS PEPPER CAN'T HANDLE HERSELF --
WE CAN PUT THIS OFF, BOSS. IT'S TIME FOR DINNER.
JUST ANOTHER MEMO OR TWO...
-- AND AT NIGHT, ONCE RUMIKO'S TURNED IN, I CONTINUE REMOTE-TESTING THE ARMOR--
AGAIN! THERE HE IS AGAIN!
HE MUST SUSPECT I'M HERE! HE CAN'T JUST BE GUARDING STARK -- HE WOULDN'T NEED TO STAY SO VISIBLE!
WELL, HE WON'T FIND ME! HE WON'T FIND ANYTHING! I CONTROL HIS MASTER --
-- AND THUS, THE CONTROLLER CONTROLS HIM!

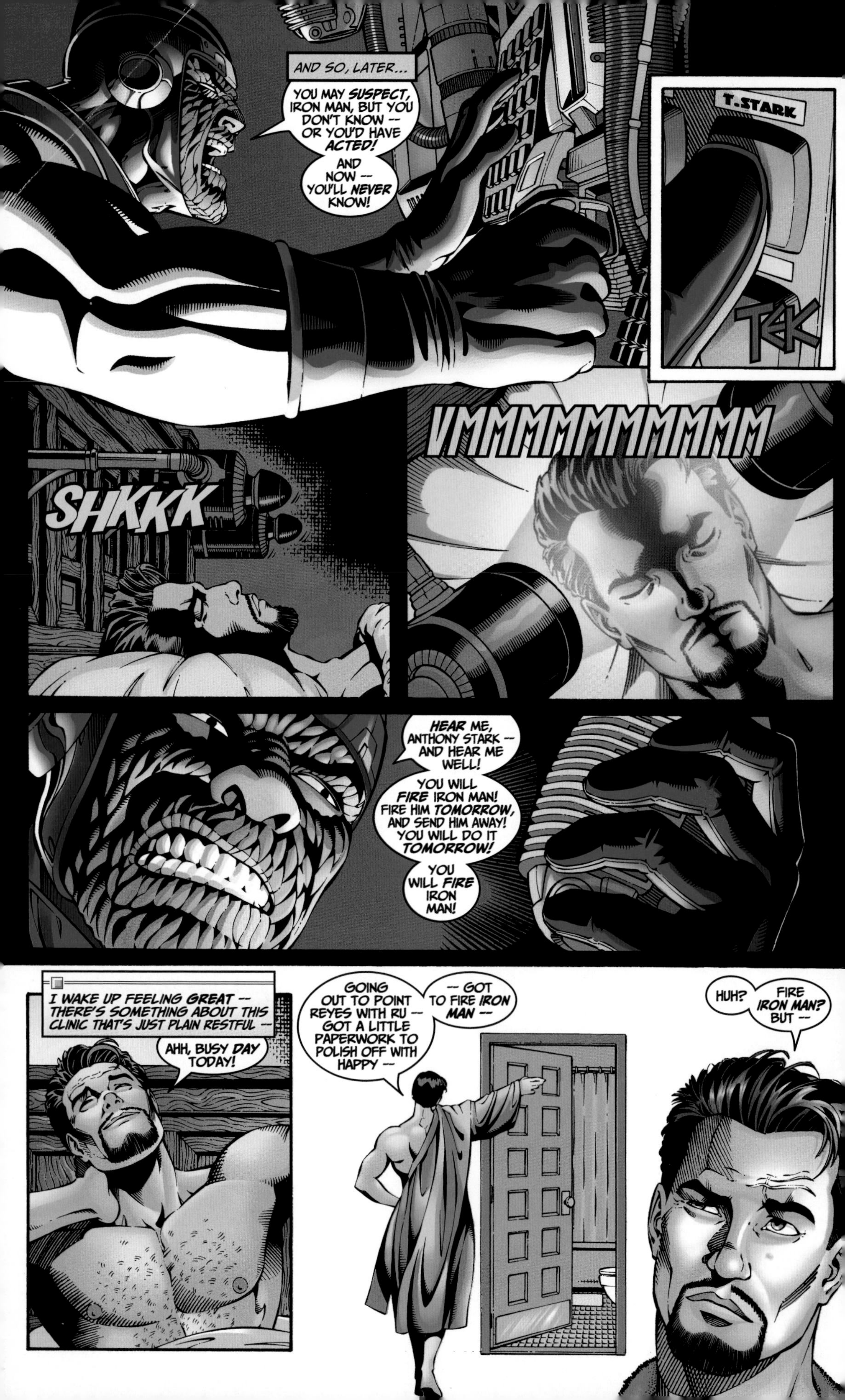
AND SO, LATER...
YOU MAY SUSPECT, IRON MAN, BUT YOU DON'T KNOW -- OR YOU'D HAVE ACTED!
AND NOW -- YOU'LL NEVER KNOW!
T. STARK
TEK
SHKKK
VMMMMMMMMMMMM
HEAR ME, ANTHONY STARK -- AND HEAR ME WELL!
YOU WILL FIRE IRON MAN! FIRE HIM TOMORROW, AND SEND HIM AWAY! YOU WILL DO IT TOMORROW!
YOU WILL FIRE IRON MAN!
I WAKE UP FEELING GREAT -- THERE'S SOMETHING ABOUT THIS CLINIC THAT'S JUST PLAIN RESTFUL --
AHH, BUSY DAY TODAY!
GOING OUT TO POINT REYES WITH RU -- GOT A LITTLE PAPERWORK TO POLISH OFF WITH HAPPY --
-- GOT TO FIRE IRON MAN --
HUH?
FIRE IRON MAN? BUT --

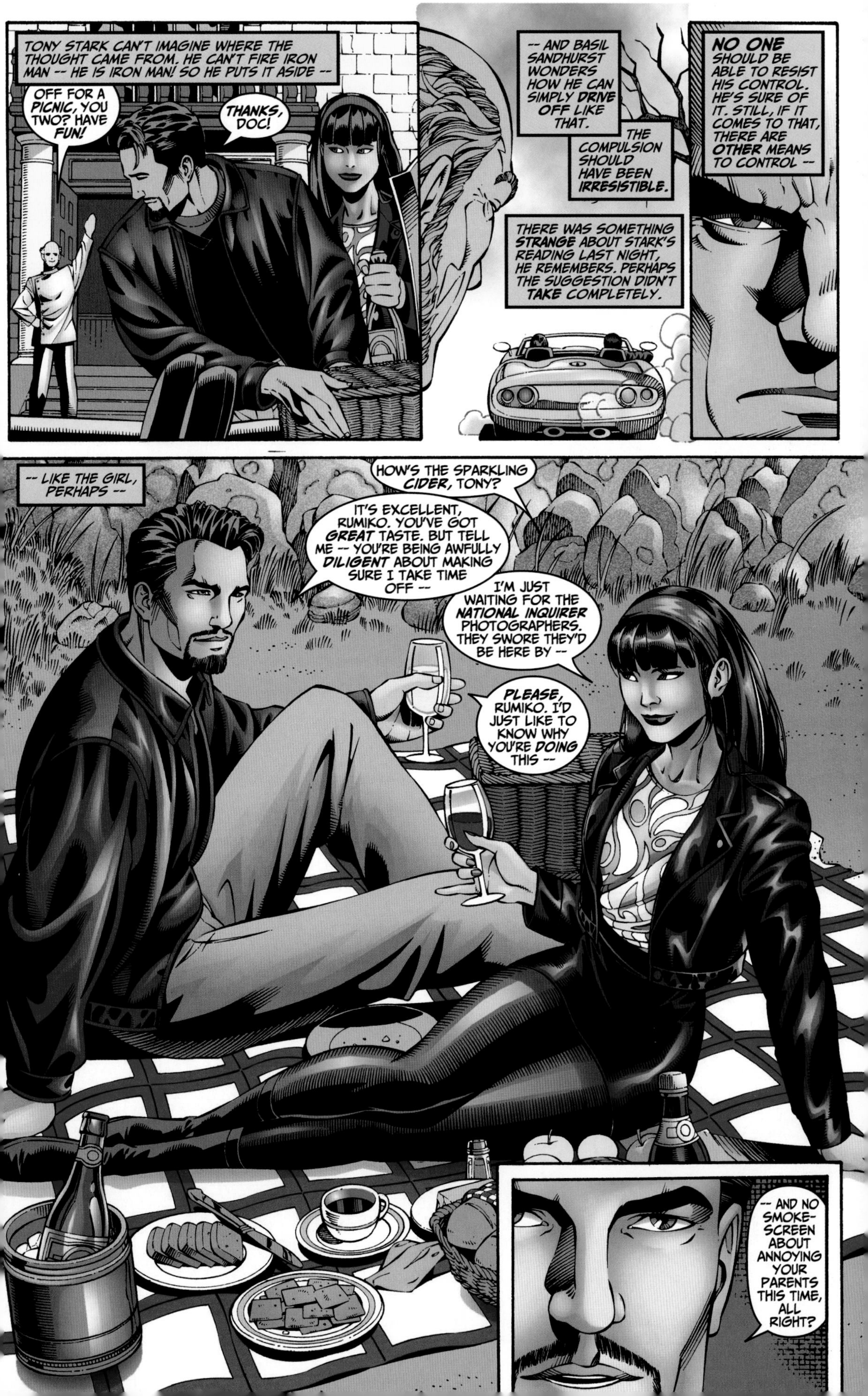
TONY STARK CAN'T IMAGINE WHERE THE THOUGHT CAME FROM. HE CAN'T FIRE IRON MAN -- HE IS IRON MAN! SO HE PUTS IT ASIDE --
OFF FOR A PICNIC, YOU TWO? HAVE FUN!
THANKS, DOC!
-- AND BASIL SANDHURST WONDERS HOW HE CAN SIMPLY DRIVE OFF LIKE THAT.
THE COMPULSION SHOULD HAVE BEEN IRRESISTIBLE.
THERE WAS SOMETHING STRANGE ABOUT STARK'S READING LAST NIGHT, HE REMEMBERS. PERHAPS THE SUGGESTION DIDN'T TAKE COMPLETELY.
NO ONE SHOULD BE ABLE TO RESIST HIS CONTROL. HE'S SURE OF IT. STILL, IF IT COMES TO THAT, THERE ARE OTHER MEANS TO CONTROL --
-- LIKE THE GIRL, PERHAPS --
HOW'S THE SPARKLING CIDER, TONY?
IT'S EXCELLENT, RUMIKO. YOU'VE GOT GREAT TASTE. BUT TELL ME -- YOU'RE BEING AWFULLY DILIGENT ABOUT MAKING SURE I TAKE TIME OFF --
I'M JUST WAITING FOR THE NATIONAL INQUIRER PHOTOGRAPHERS. THEY SWORE THEY'D BE HERE BY --
PLEASE, RUMIKO. I'D JUST LIKE TO KNOW WHY YOU'RE DOING THIS --
-- AND NO SMOKE-SCREEN ABOUT ANNOYING YOUR PARENTS THIS TIME, ALL RIGHT?

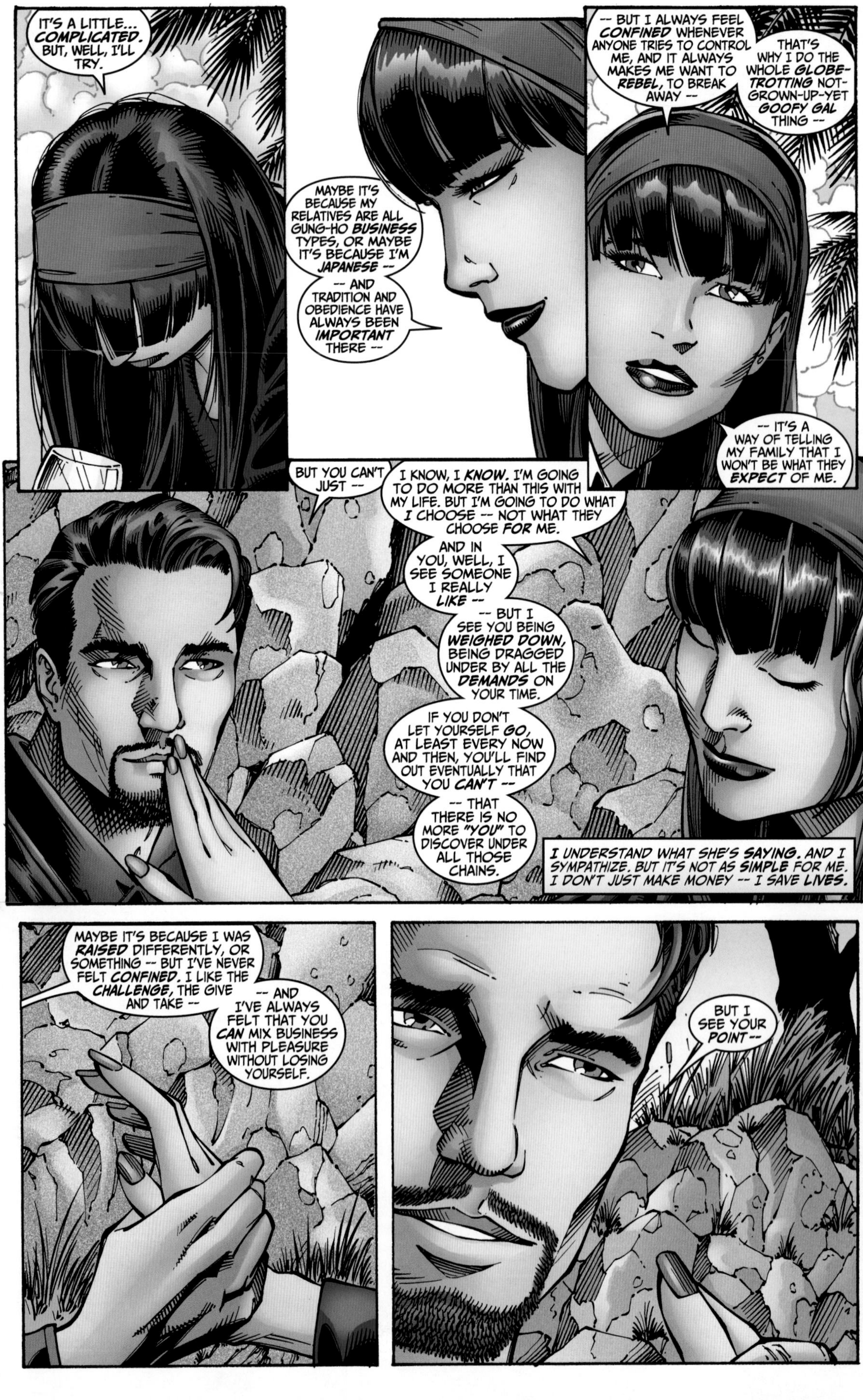

IT'S A LITTLE... COMPLICATED. BUT, WELL, I'LL TRY.
MAYBE IT'S BECAUSE MY RELATIVES ARE ALL GUNG-HO BUSINESS TYPES, OR MAYBE IT'S BECAUSE I'M JAPANESE --
-- AND TRADITION AND OBEDIENCE HAVE ALWAYS BEEN IMPORTANT THERE --
-- BUT I ALWAYS FEEL CONFINED WHENEVER ANYONE TRIES TO CONTROL ME, AND IT ALWAYS MAKES ME WANT TO REBEL, TO BREAK AWAY --
THAT'S WHY I DO THE WHOLE GLOBE-TROTTING NOT-GROWN-UP-YET GOOFY GAL THING --
-- IT'S A WAY OF TELLING MY FAMILY THAT I WON'T BE WHAT THEY EXPECT OF ME.
BUT YOU CAN'T JUST --
I KNOW, I KNOW. I'M GOING TO DO MORE THAN THIS WITH MY LIFE. BUT I'M GOING TO DO WHAT I CHOOSE -- NOT WHAT THEY CHOOSE FOR ME.
AND IN YOU, WELL, I SEE SOMEONE I REALLY LIKE --
-- BUT I SEE YOU BEING WEIGHED DOWN, BEING DRAGGED UNDER BY ALL THE DEMANDS ON YOUR TIME.
IF YOU DON'T LET YOURSELF GO, AT LEAST EVERY NOW AND THEN, YOU'LL FIND OUT EVENTUALLY THAT YOU CAN'T --
-- THAT THERE IS NO MORE "YOU" TO DISCOVER UNDER ALL THOSE CHAINS.
I UNDERSTAND WHAT SHE'S SAYING. AND I SYMPATHIZE. BUT IT'S NOT AS SIMPLE FOR ME. I DON'T JUST MAKE MONEY -- I SAVE LIVES.
MAYBE IT'S BECAUSE I WAS RAISED DIFFERENTLY, OR SOMETHING -- BUT I'VE NEVER FELT CONFINED. I LIKE THE CHALLENGE, THE GIVE AND TAKE --
-- AND I'VE ALWAYS FELT THAT YOU CAN MIX BUSINESS WITH PLEASURE WITHOUT LOSING YOURSELF.
BUT I SEE YOUR POINT --

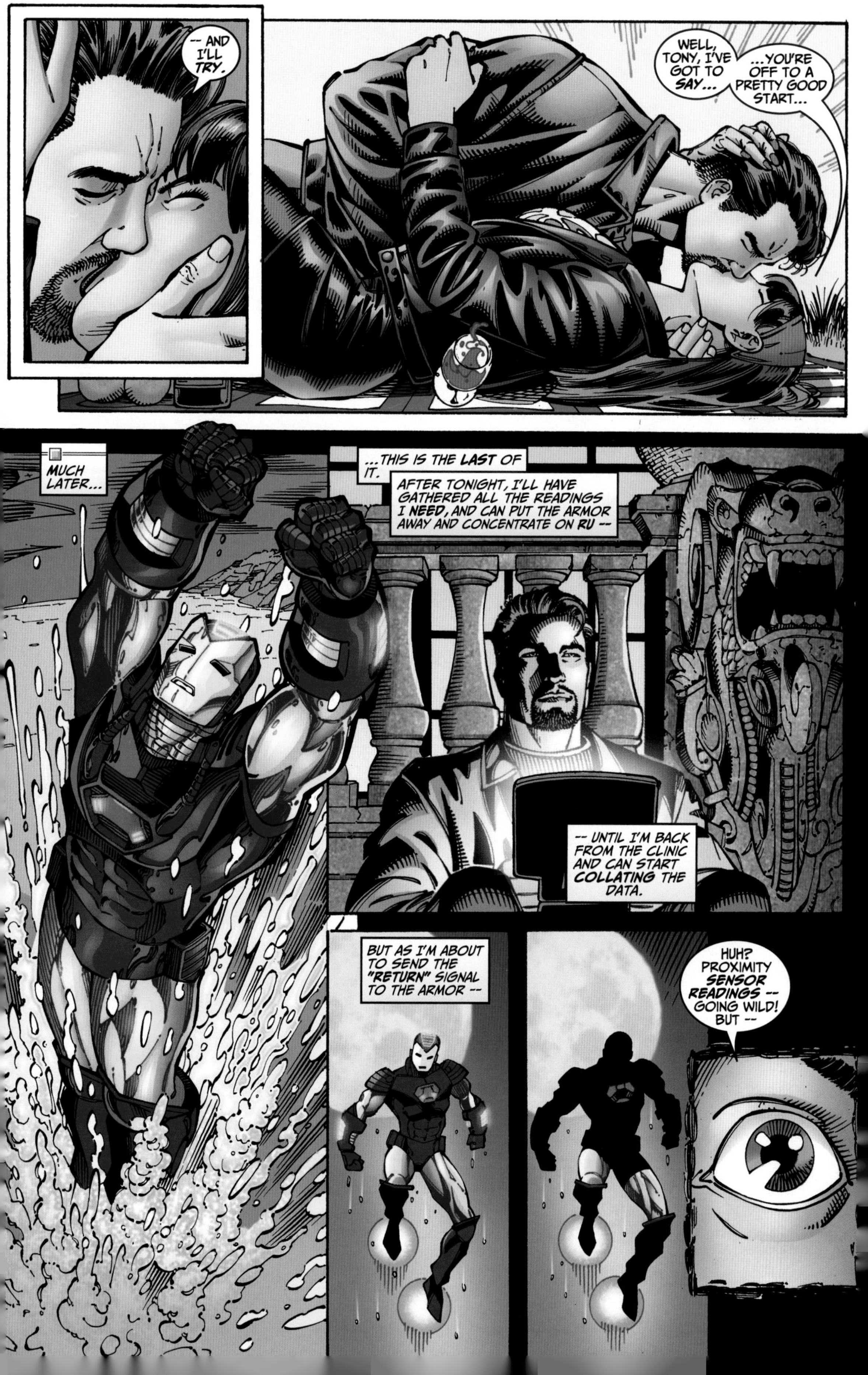
-- AND I'LL TRY.
WELL, TONY, I'VE GOT TO SAY...
...YOU'RE OFF TO A PRETTY GOOD START...
MUCH LATER...
...THIS IS THE LAST OF IT.
AFTER TONIGHT, I'LL HAVE GATHERED ALL THE READINGS I NEED, AND CAN PUT THE ARMOR AWAY AND CONCENTRATE ON RU --
-- UNTIL I'M BACK FROM THE CLINIC AND CAN START COLLATING THE DATA.
BUT AS I'M ABOUT TO SEND THE "RETURN" SIGNAL TO THE ARMOR --
HUH? PROXIMITY SENSOR READINGS -- GOING WILD! BUT --

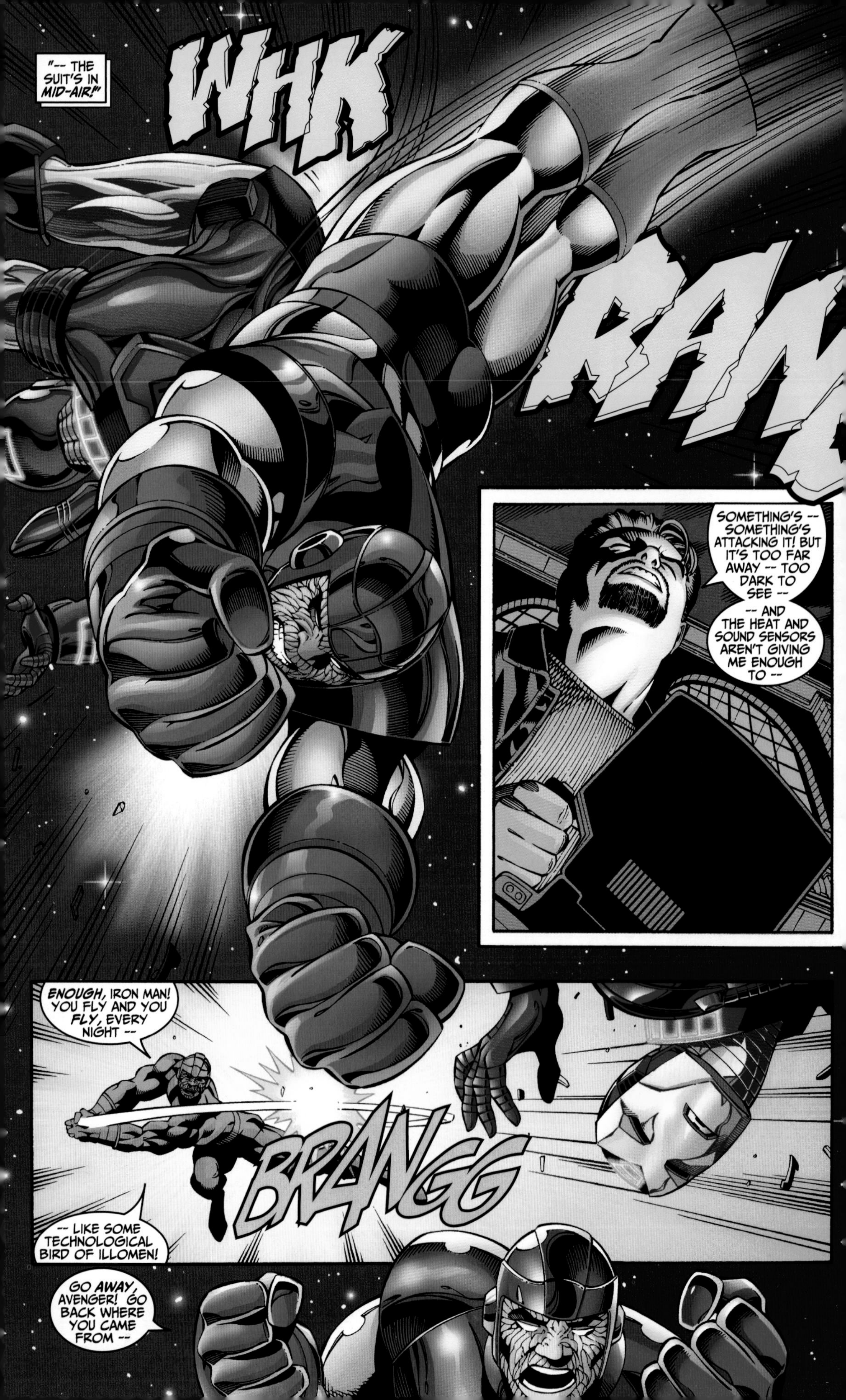
"-- THE SUIT'S IN MID-AIR!"
WHK
RAM
SOMETHING'S -- SOMETHING'S ATTACKING IT! BUT IT'S TOO FAR AWAY -- TOO DARK TO SEE --
-- AND THE HEAT AND SOUND SENSORS AREN'T GIVING ME ENOUGH TO --
ENOUGH, IRON MAN! YOU FLY AND YOU FLY, EVERY NIGHT --
BRANGG
-- LIKE SOME TECHNOLOGICAL BIRD OF ILLOMEN!
GO AWAY, AVENGER! GO BACK WHERE YOU CAME FROM --

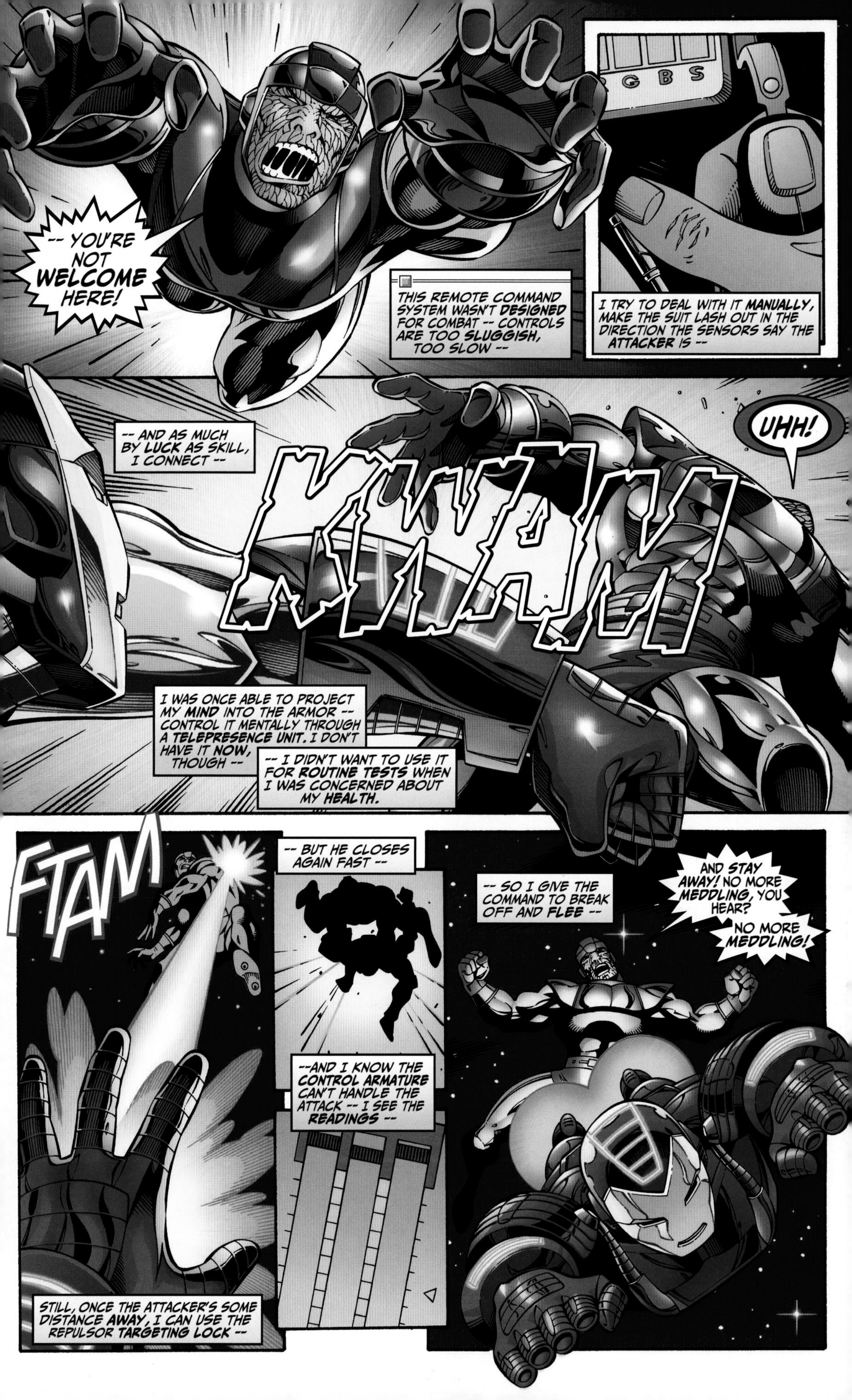
RGBS
-- YOU'RE NOT WELCOME HERE!
THIS REMOTE COMMAND SYSTEM WASN'T DESIGNED FOR COMBAT -- CONTROLS ARE TOO SLUGGISH, TOO SLOW --
I TRY TO DEAL WITH IT MANUALLY, MAKE THE SUIT LASH OUT IN THE DIRECTION THE SENSORS SAY THE ATTACKER IS --
-- AND AS MUCH BY LUCK AS SKILL, I CONNECT --
KWAM
UHH!
I WAS ONCE ABLE TO PROJECT MY MIND INTO THE ARMOR -- CONTROL IT MENTALLY THROUGH A TELEPRESENCE UNIT. I DON'T HAVE IT NOW, THOUGH --
-- I DIDN'T WANT TO USE IT FOR ROUTINE TESTS WHEN I WAS CONCERNED ABOUT MY HEALTH.
FTAM
STILL, ONCE THE ATTACKER'S SOME DISTANCE AWAY, I CAN USE THE REPULSOR TARGETING LOCK --
-- BUT HE CLOSES AGAIN FAST --
--AND I KNOW THE CONTROL ARMATURE CAN'T HANDLE THE ATTACK -- I SEE THE READINGS --
-- SO I GIVE THE COMMAND TO BREAK OFF AND FLEE --
AND STAY AWAY! NO MORE MEDDLING, YOU HEAR?
NO MORE MEDDLING!

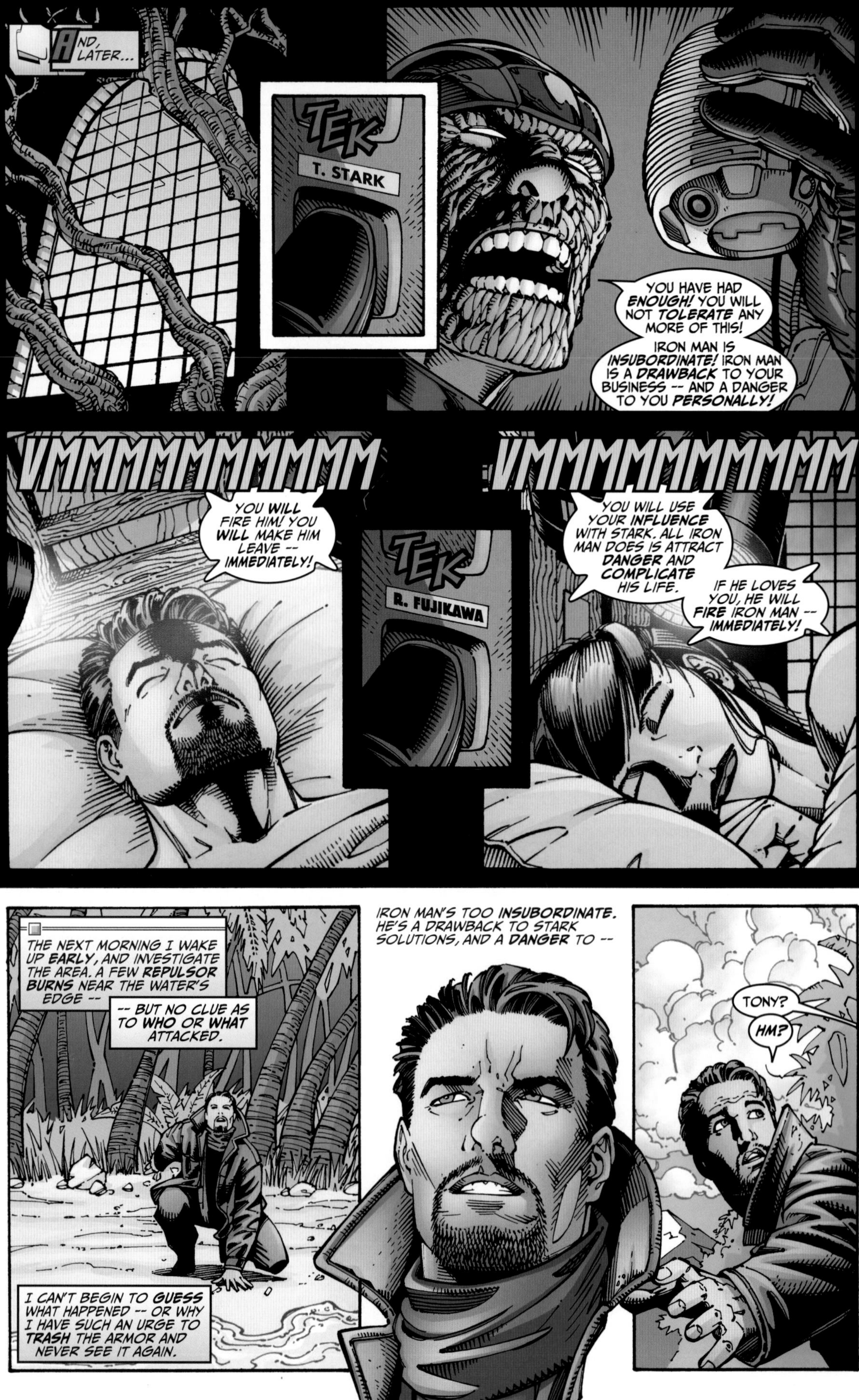
AND, LATER...
TEK
T. STARK
YOU HAVE HAD ENOUGH! YOU WILL NOT TOLERATE ANY MORE OF THIS!
IRON MAN IS INSUBORDINATE! IRON MAN IS A DRAWBACK TO YOUR BUSINESS -- AND A DANGER TO YOU PERSONALLY!
VMMMMMMMMMMM
YOU WILL FIRE HIM! YOU WILL MAKE HIM LEAVE -- IMMEDIATELY!
TEK
R. FUJIKAWA
VMMMMMMMMMMM
YOU WILL USE YOUR INFLUENCE WITH STARK. ALL IRON MAN DOES IS ATTRACT DANGER AND COMPLICATE HIS LIFE.
IF HE LOVES YOU, HE WILL FIRE IRON MAN -- IMMEDIATELY!
THE NEXT MORNING I WAKE UP EARLY, AND INVESTIGATE THE AREA. A FEW REPULSOR BURNS NEAR THE WATER'S EDGE --
-- BUT NO CLUE AS TO WHO OR WHAT ATTACKED.
I CAN'T BEGIN TO GUESS WHAT HAPPENED -- OR WHY I HAVE SUCH AN URGE TO TRASH THE ARMOR AND NEVER SEE IT AGAIN.
IRON MAN'S TOO INSUBORDINATE. HE'S A DRAWBACK TO STARK SOLUTIONS, AND A DANGER TO --
TONY?
HM?

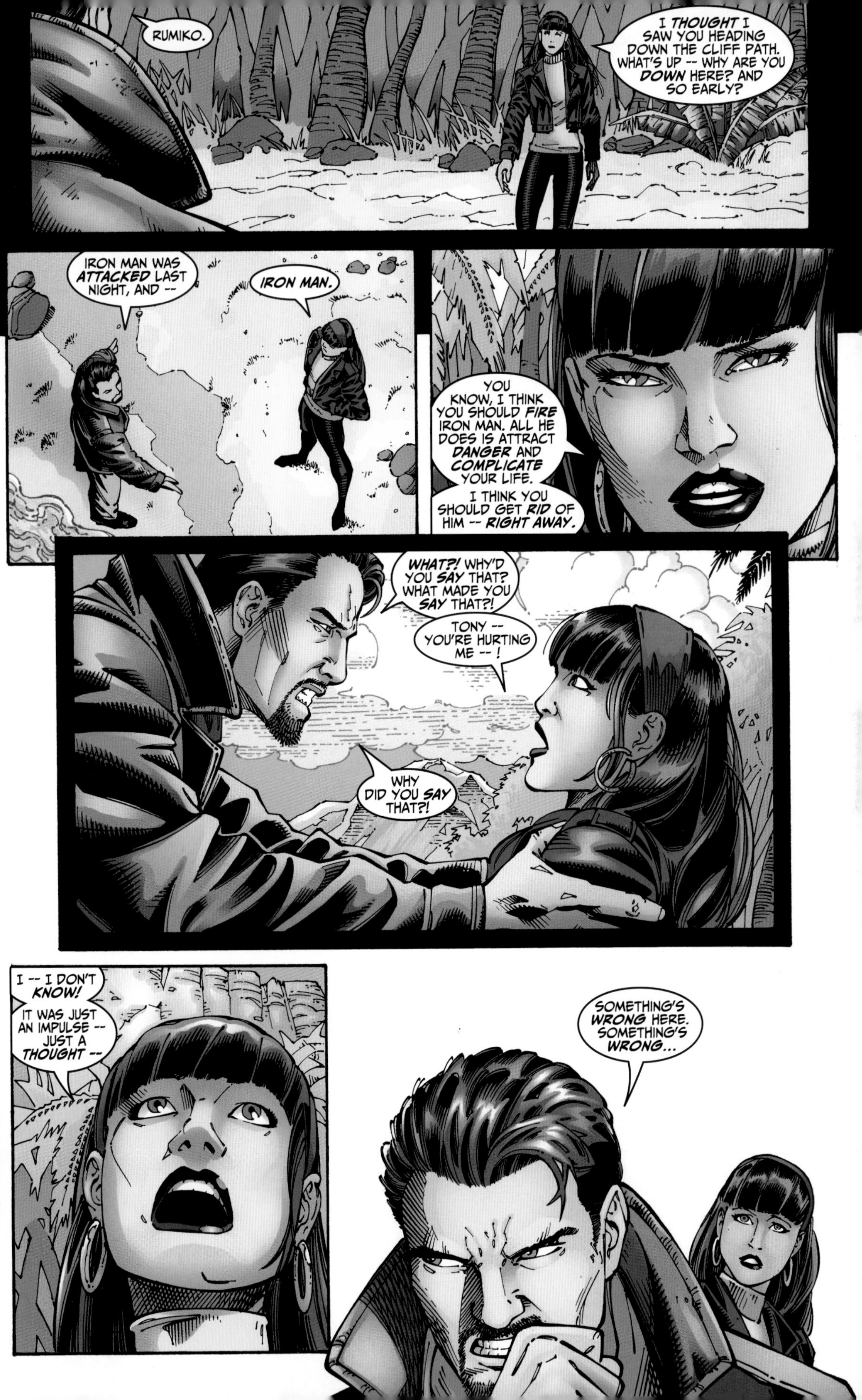
RUMIKO.
I *THOUGHT* I SAW YOU HEADING DOWN THE CLIFF PATH. WHAT'S UP -- WHY ARE YOU *DOWN* HERE? AND SO EARLY?
IRON MAN WAS *ATTACKED* LAST NIGHT, AND --
IRON MAN.
YOU KNOW, I THINK YOU SHOULD *FIRE* IRON MAN. ALL HE DOES IS ATTRACT *DANGER* AND *COMPLICATE* YOUR LIFE.
I THINK YOU SHOULD GET *RID* OF HIM -- *RIGHT AWAY.*
WHAT?! WHY'D YOU *SAY* THAT? WHAT MADE YOU *SAY* THAT?!
TONY -- YOU'RE HURTING ME -- !
WHY DID YOU *SAY* THAT?!
I -- I DON'T *KNOW!*
IT WAS JUST AN IMPULSE -- JUST A *THOUGHT* --
SOMETHING'S *WRONG* HERE. SOMETHING'S *WRONG*...

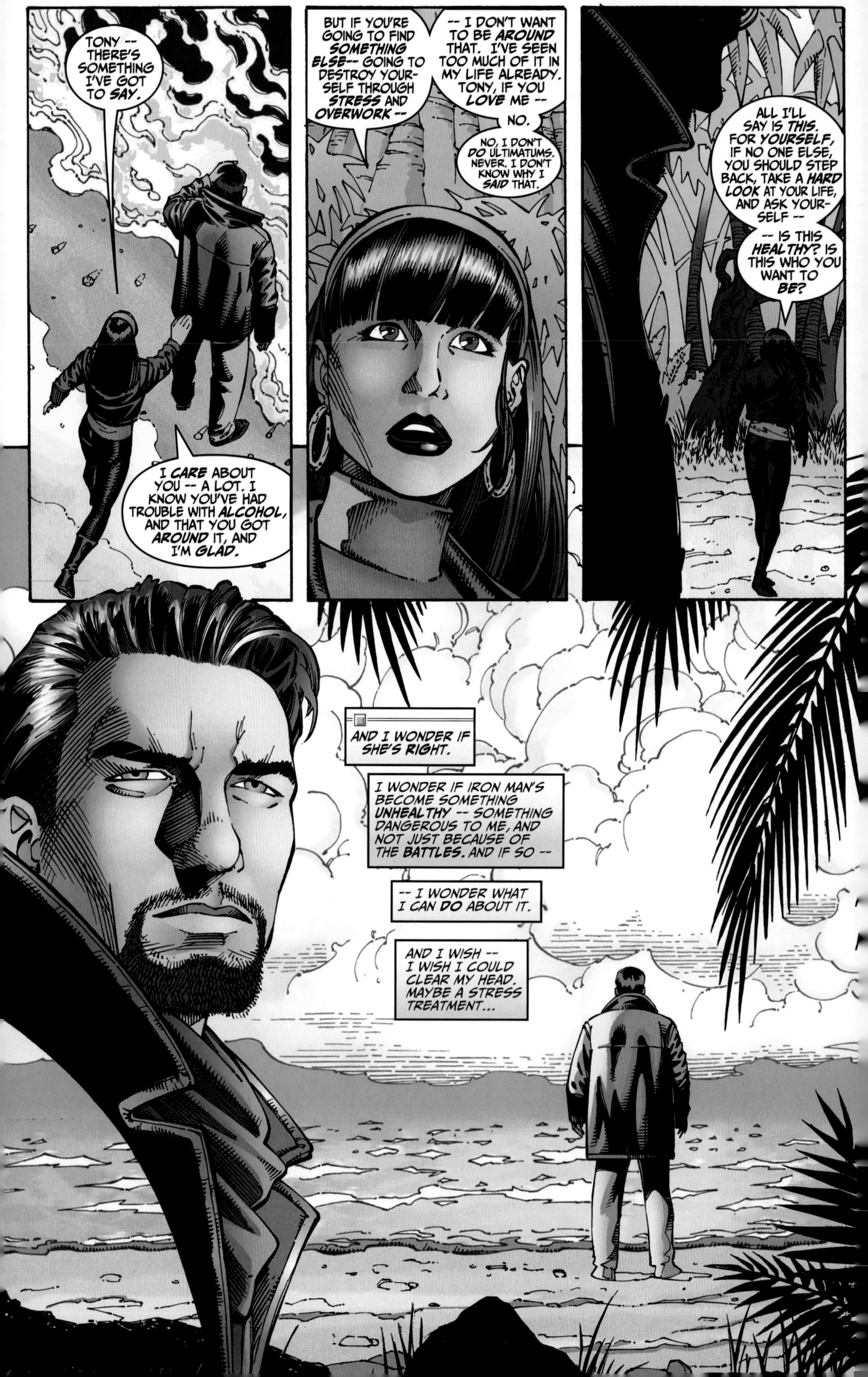
TONY -- THERE'S SOMETHING I'VE GOT TO SAY.
I CARE ABOUT YOU -- A LOT. I KNOW YOU'VE HAD TROUBLE WITH ALCOHOL, AND THAT YOU GOT AROUND IT, AND I'M GLAD.
BUT IF YOU'RE GOING TO FIND SOMETHING ELSE-- GOING TO DESTROY YOURSELF THROUGH STRESS AND OVERWORK --
-- I DON'T WANT TO BE AROUND THAT. I'VE SEEN TOO MUCH OF IT IN MY LIFE ALREADY. TONY, IF YOU LOVE ME --
NO.
NO, I DON'T DO ULTIMATUMS. NEVER. I DON'T KNOW WHY I SAID THAT.
ALL I'LL SAY IS THIS. FOR YOURSELF, IF NO ONE ELSE, YOU SHOULD STEP BACK, TAKE A HARD LOOK AT YOUR LIFE, AND ASK YOURSELF --
-- IS THIS HEALTHY? IS THIS WHO YOU WANT TO BE?
AND I WONDER IF SHE'S RIGHT.
I WONDER IF IRON MAN'S BECOME SOMETHING UNHEALTHY -- SOMETHING DANGEROUS TO ME, AND NOT JUST BECAUSE OF THE BATTLES. AND IF SO --
-- I WONDER WHAT I CAN DO ABOUT IT.
AND I WISH -- I WISH I COULD CLEAR MY HEAD. MAYBE A STRESS TREATMENT...

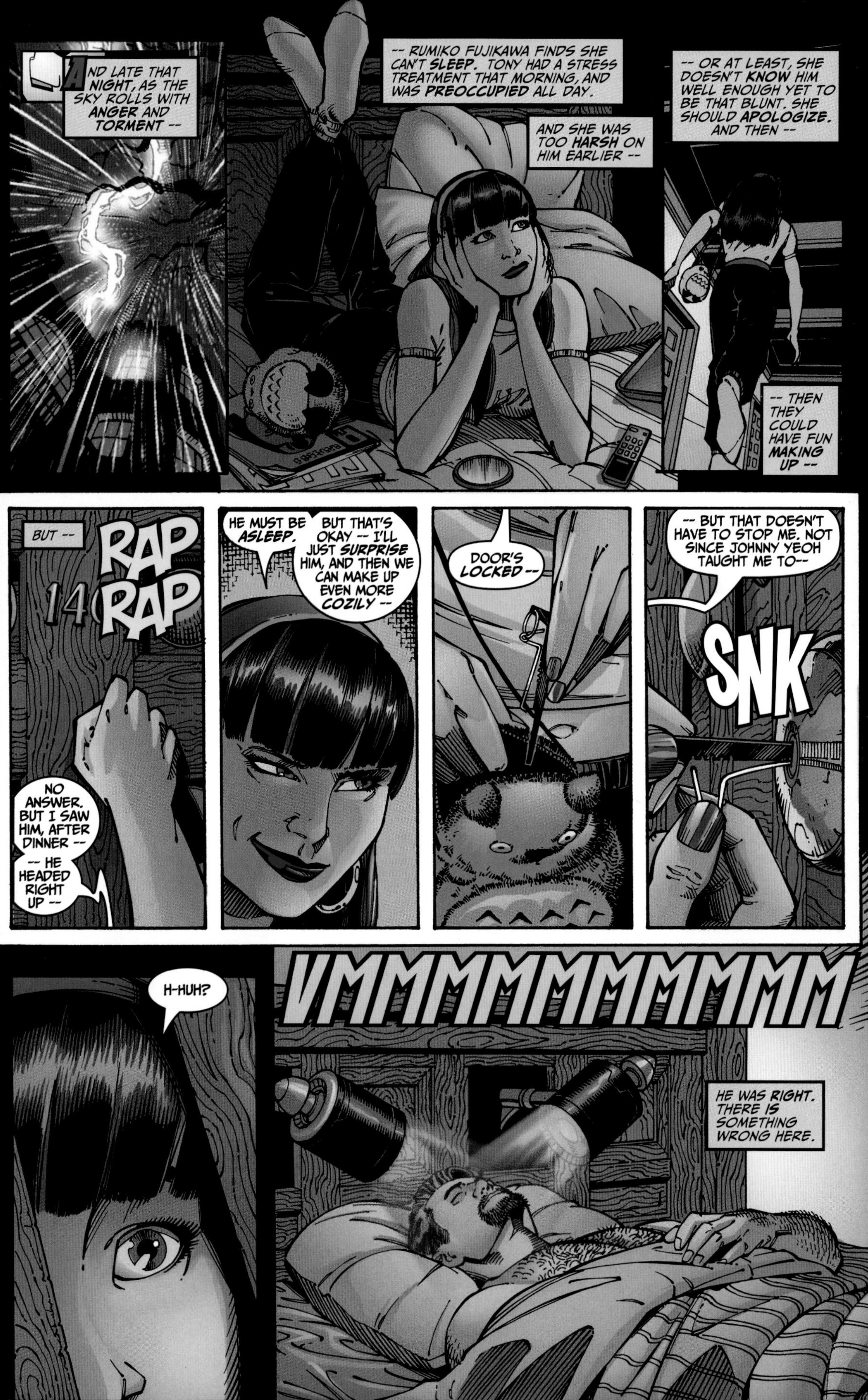
AND LATE THAT NIGHT, AS THE SKY ROLLS WITH ANGER AND TORMENT --
-- RUMIKO FUJIKAWA FINDS SHE CAN'T SLEEP. TONY HAD A STRESS TREATMENT THAT MORNING, AND WAS PREOCCUPIED ALL DAY.
AND SHE WAS TOO HARSH ON HIM EARLIER --
-- OR AT LEAST, SHE DOESN'T KNOW HIM WELL ENOUGH YET TO BE THAT BLUNT. SHE SHOULD APOLOGIZE. AND THEN --
-- THEN THEY COULD HAVE FUN MAKING UP --
BUT --
RAP RAP
14
NO ANSWER. BUT I SAW HIM, AFTER DINNER --
-- HE HEADED RIGHT UP --
HE MUST BE ASLEEP.
BUT THAT'S OKAY -- I'LL JUST SURPRISE HIM, AND THEN WE CAN MAKE UP EVEN MORE COZILY --
DOOR'S LOCKED --
-- BUT THAT DOESN'T HAVE TO STOP ME. NOT SINCE JOHNNY YEOH TAUGHT ME TO--
SNK
H-HUH?
VMMMMMMMMMMMM
HE WAS RIGHT. THERE IS SOMETHING WRONG HERE.

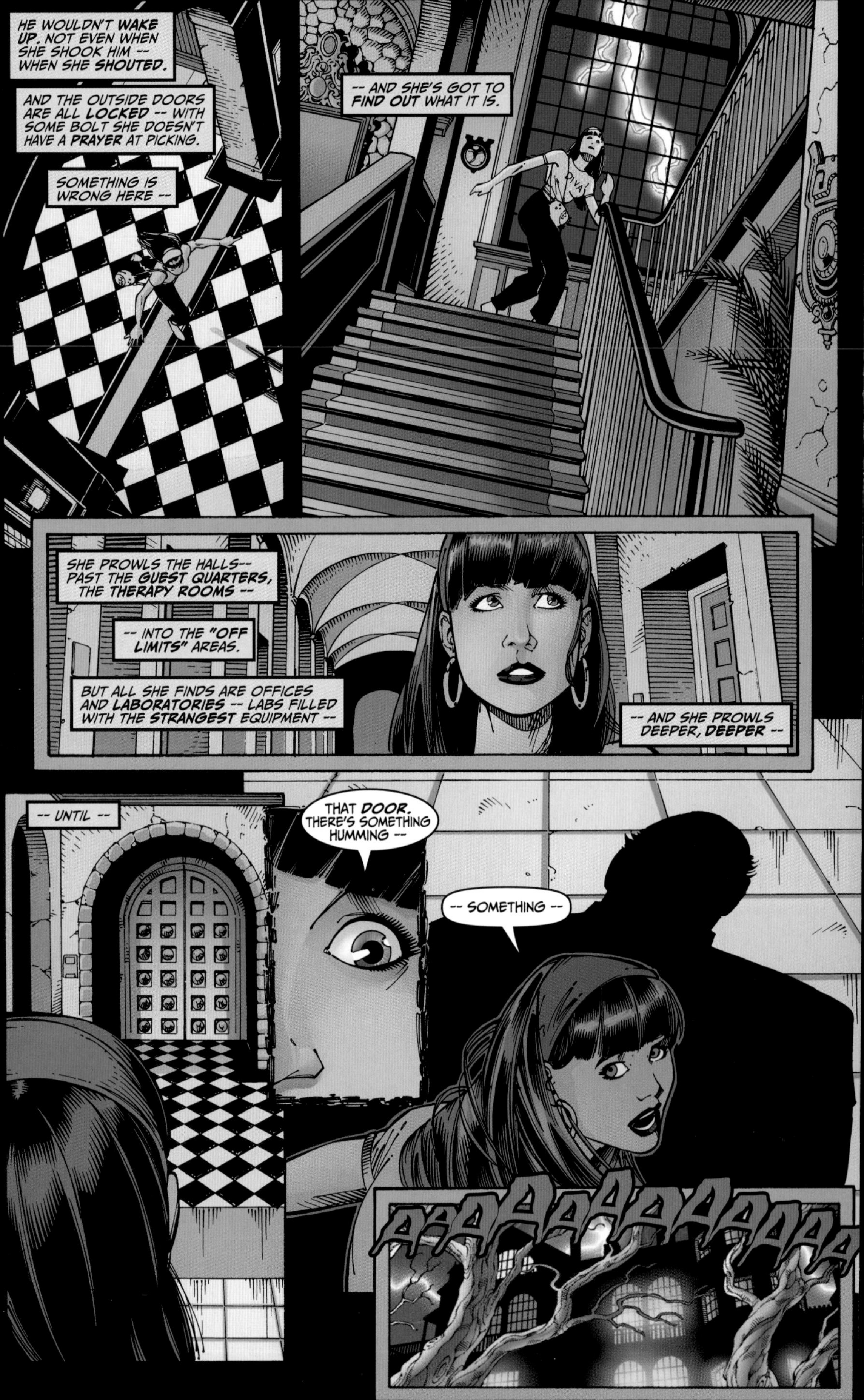
HE WOULDN'T WAKE UP. NOT EVEN WHEN SHE SHOOK HIM -- WHEN SHE SHOUTED.
AND THE OUTSIDE DOORS ARE ALL LOCKED -- WITH SOME BOLT SHE DOESN'T HAVE A PRAYER AT PICKING.
SOMETHING IS WRONG HERE --
-- AND SHE'S GOT TO FIND OUT WHAT IT IS.
SHE PROWLS THE HALLS-- PAST THE GUEST QUARTERS, THE THERAPY ROOMS --
-- INTO THE "OFF LIMITS" AREAS.
BUT ALL SHE FINDS ARE OFFICES AND LABORATORIES -- LABS FILLED WITH THE STRANGEST EQUIPMENT --
-- AND SHE PROWLS DEEPER, DEEPER --
-- UNTIL --
THAT DOOR. THERE'S SOMETHING HUMMING --
-- SOMETHING --
AAAAAAAAAAAAA

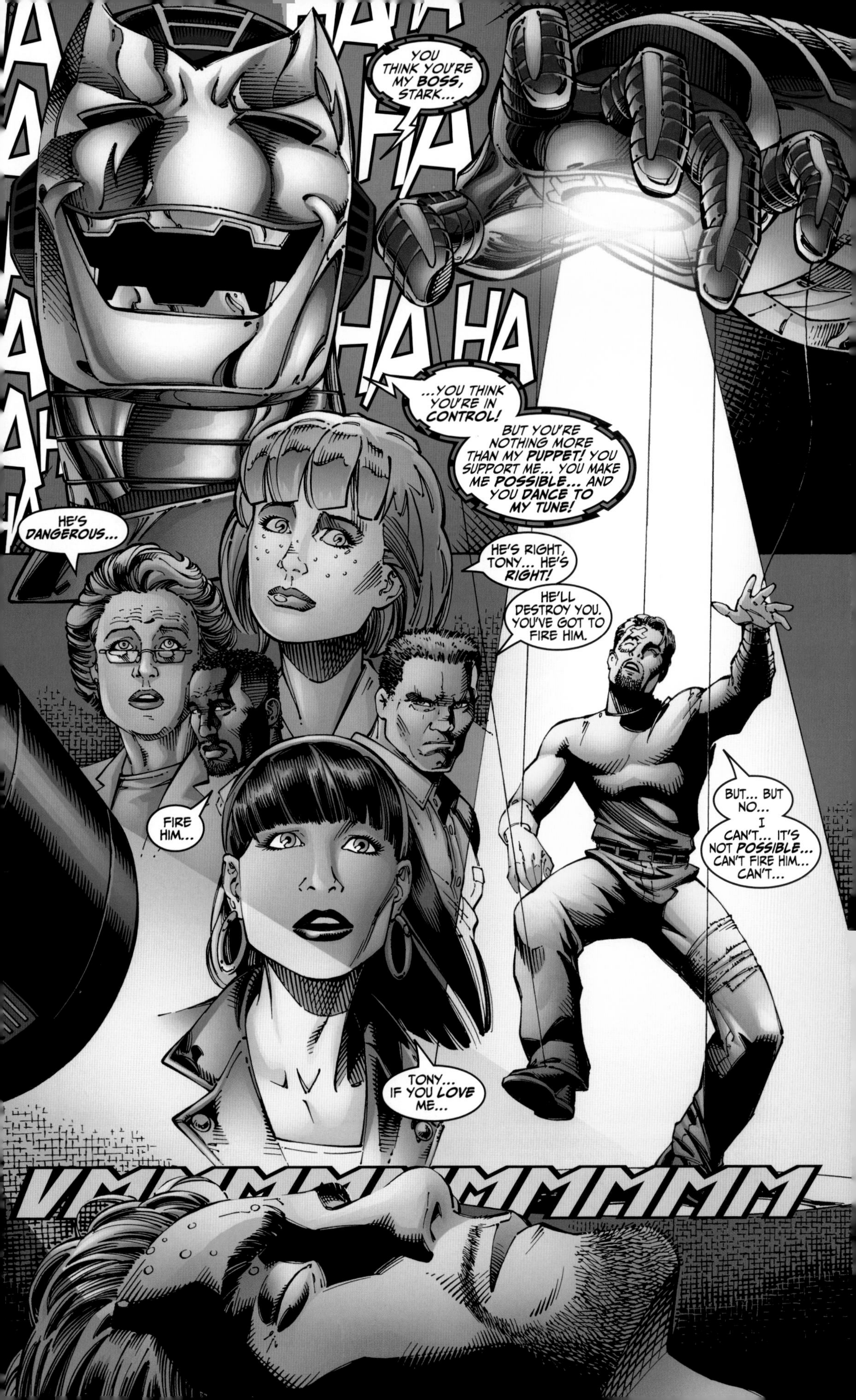
HA HA HA HA
YOU THINK YOU'RE MY BOSS, STARK...
HA
HA HA
...YOU THINK YOU'RE IN CONTROL!
BUT YOU'RE NOTHING MORE THAN MY PUPPET! YOU SUPPORT ME... YOU MAKE ME POSSIBLE... AND YOU DANCE TO MY TUNE!
HE'S DANGEROUS...
HE'S RIGHT, TONY... HE'S RIGHT!
HE'LL DESTROY YOU. YOU'VE GOT TO FIRE HIM.
FIRE HIM...
BUT... BUT NO... I CAN'T... IT'S NOT POSSIBLE... CAN'T FIRE HIM... CAN'T...
TONY... IF YOU LOVE ME...
VMMMMMMMMMMM

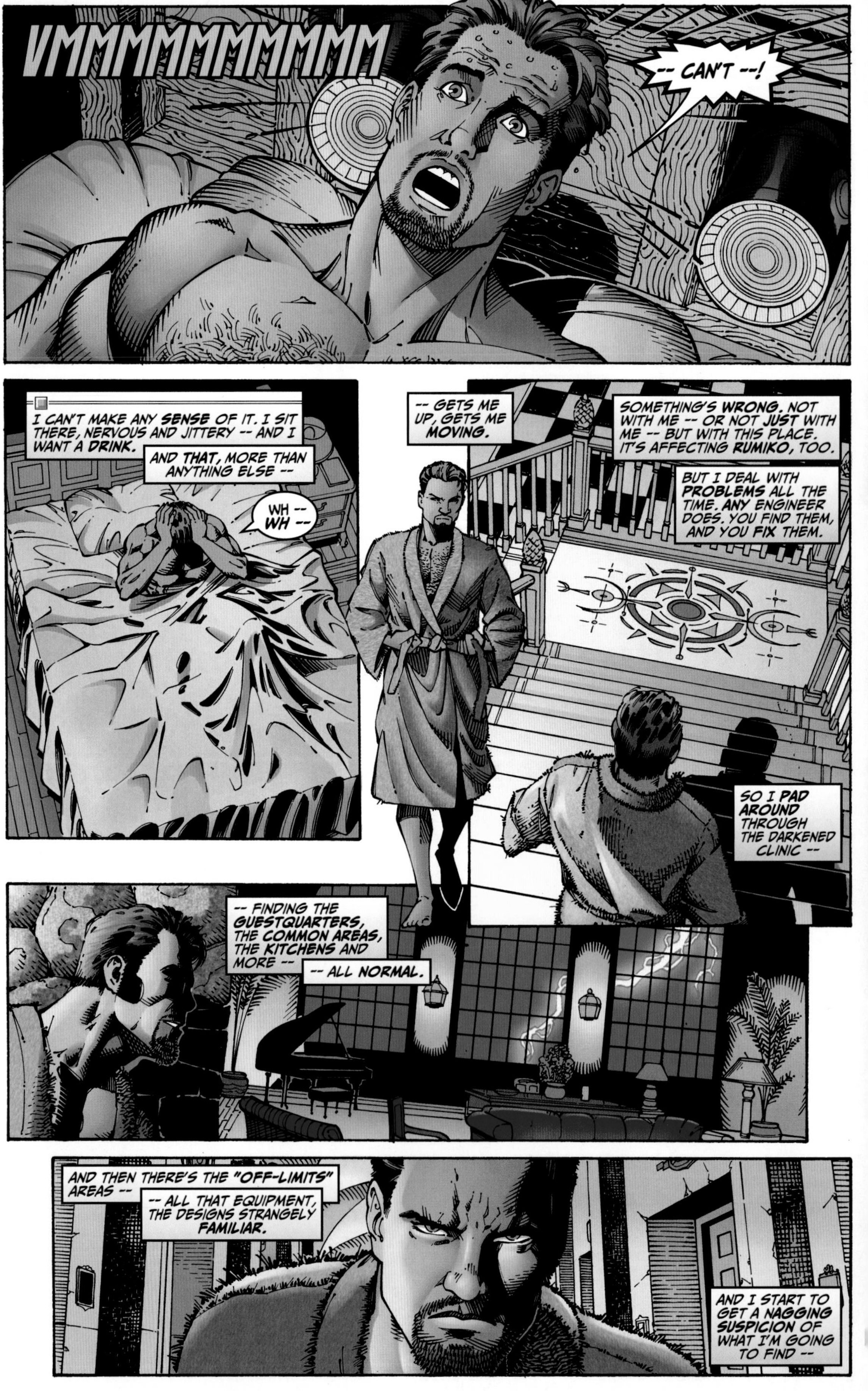
VMMMMMMMMMMM
-- CAN'T --!
I CAN'T MAKE ANY SENSE OF IT. I SIT THERE, NERVOUS AND JITTERY -- AND I WANT A DRINK.
AND THAT, MORE THAN ANYTHING ELSE --
WH -- WH --
-- GETS ME UP, GETS ME MOVING.
SOMETHING'S WRONG. NOT WITH ME -- OR NOT JUST WITH ME -- BUT WITH THIS PLACE. IT'S AFFECTING RUMIKO, TOO.
BUT I DEAL WITH PROBLEMS ALL THE TIME. ANY ENGINEER DOES. YOU FIND THEM, AND YOU FIX THEM.
SO I PAD AROUND THROUGH THE DARKENED CLINIC --
-- FINDING THE GUESTQUARTERS, THE COMMON AREAS, THE KITCHENS AND MORE --
-- ALL NORMAL.
AND THEN THERE'S THE "OFF-LIMITS" AREAS --
-- ALL THAT EQUIPMENT, THE DESIGNS STRANGELY FAMILIAR.
AND I START TO GET A NAGGING SUSPICION OF WHAT I'M GOING TO FIND --

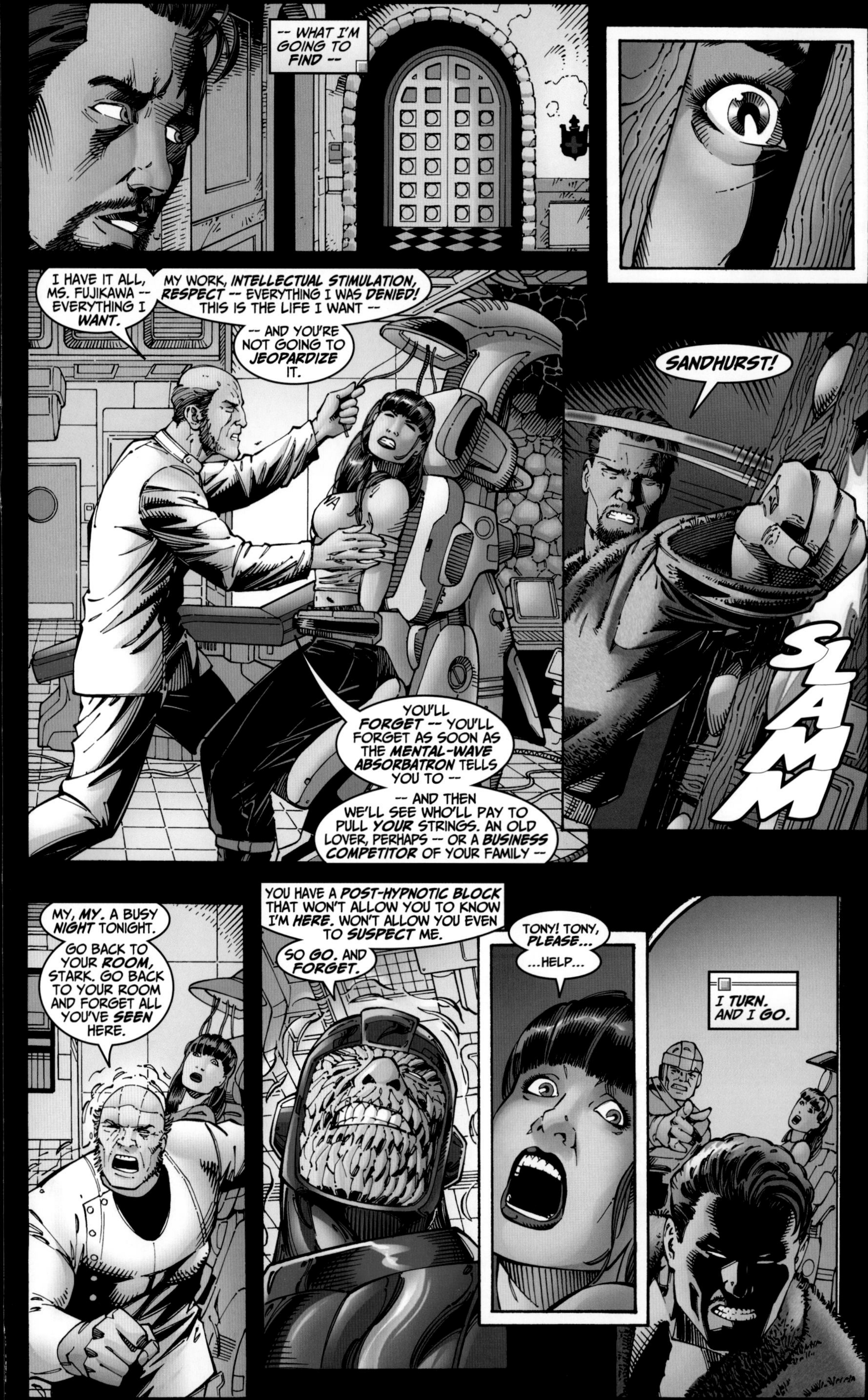
-- WHAT I'M GOING TO FIND --
I HAVE IT ALL, MS. FUJIKAWA -- EVERYTHING I WANT.
MY WORK, INTELLECTUAL STIMULATION, RESPECT -- EVERYTHING I WAS DENIED! THIS IS THE LIFE I WANT --
-- AND YOU'RE NOT GOING TO JEOPARDIZE IT.
YOU'LL FORGET -- YOU'LL FORGET AS SOON AS THE MENTAL-WAVE ABSORBATRON TELLS YOU TO --
-- AND THEN WE'LL SEE WHO'LL PAY TO PULL YOUR STRINGS. AN OLD LOVER, PERHAPS -- OR A BUSINESS COMPETITOR OF YOUR FAMILY --
SANDHURST!
SLAMM
MY, MY. A BUSY NIGHT TONIGHT.
GO BACK TO YOUR ROOM, STARK. GO BACK TO YOUR ROOM AND FORGET ALL YOU'VE SEEN HERE.
YOU HAVE A POST-HYPNOTIC BLOCK THAT WON'T ALLOW YOU TO KNOW I'M HERE. WON'T ALLOW YOU EVEN TO SUSPECT ME.
SO GO. AND FORGET.
TONY! TONY, PLEASE...
...HELP...
I TURN. AND I GO.

AND THE CONTROLLER'S LAUGHTER FOLLOWS ME DOWN THE HALLWAY.

I'VE GOT A SPECIAL *CIRCUITRY* -- IN MY ARMOR, IN MY WRISTWATCH -- EVEN IN THE *TRAVEL CLOCK* THAT SITS ON MY NIGHTSTAND.

IT GUARDS AGAINST ATTEMPTS AT *MENTAL TAKEOVER.*

APPARENTLY, IT'S NOT AS GOOD AT *SLEEP SUGGESTION* AS I'D LIKE IT TO BE. BUT IT WAS AT LEAST *PARTIALLY* EFFECTIVE. I SEND THE COMMAND.

THE ARMOR COMES.

LIKE LIVING INSIDE *POWER LINES*, THEY SAID.

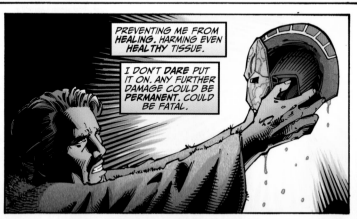

PREVENTING ME FROM *HEALING.* HARMING EVEN *HEALTHY* TISSUE.

I DON'T *DARE* PUT IT ON. ANY FURTHER DAMAGE COULD BE *PERMANENT.* COULD BE FATAL.

I DON'T *DARE* PUT IT ON.

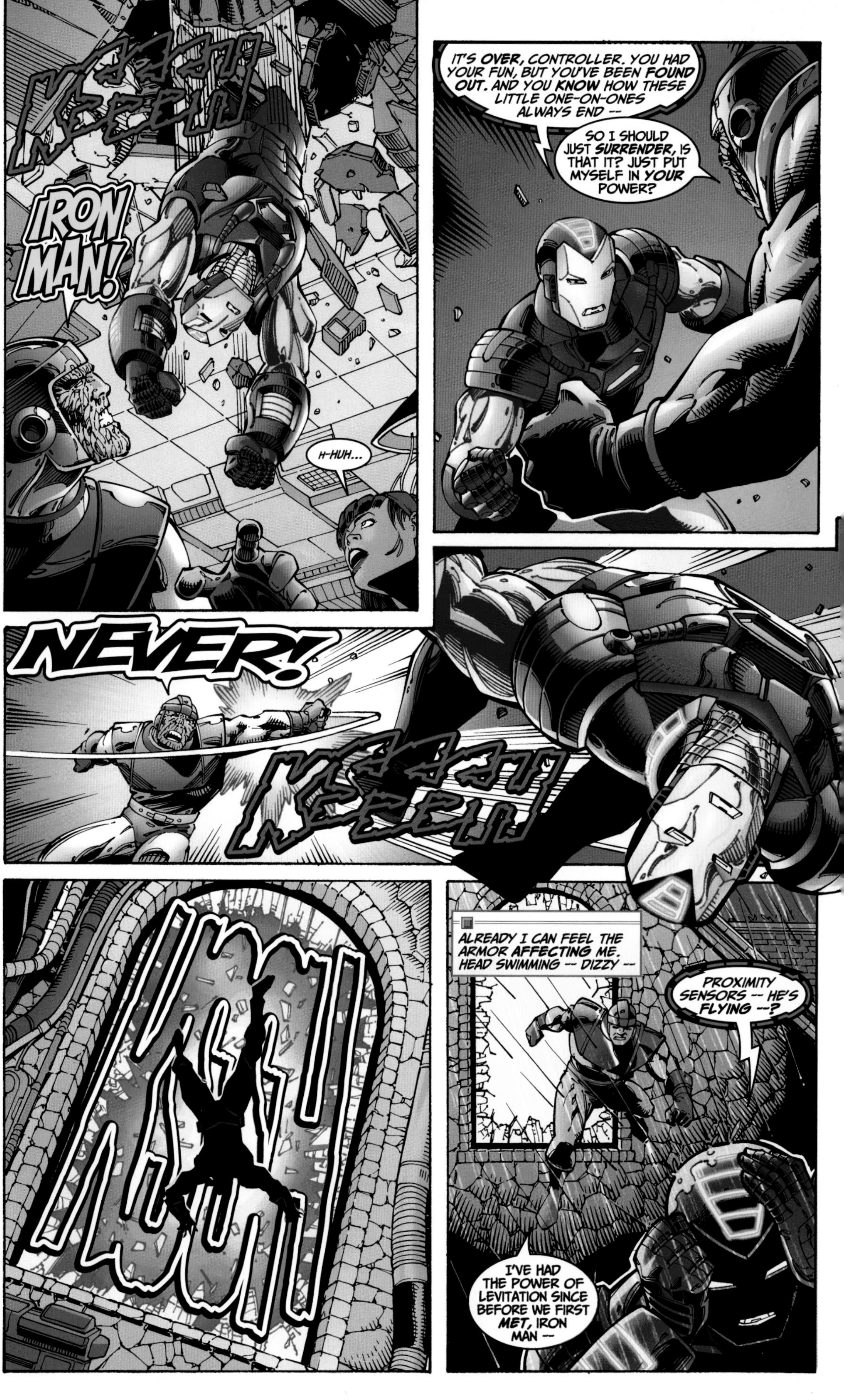

IRON MAN!
H-HUH...
IT'S OVER, CONTROLLER. YOU HAD YOUR FUN, BUT YOU'VE BEEN FOUND OUT. AND YOU KNOW HOW THESE LITTLE ONE-ON-ONES ALWAYS END --
SO I SHOULD JUST SURRENDER, IS THAT IT? JUST PUT MYSELF IN YOUR POWER?
NEVER!
ALREADY I CAN FEEL THE ARMOR AFFECTING ME. HEAD SWIMMING -- DIZZY --
PROXIMITY SENSORS -- HE'S FLYING --?
I'VE HAD THE POWER OF LEVITATION SINCE BEFORE WE FIRST MET, IRON MAN --

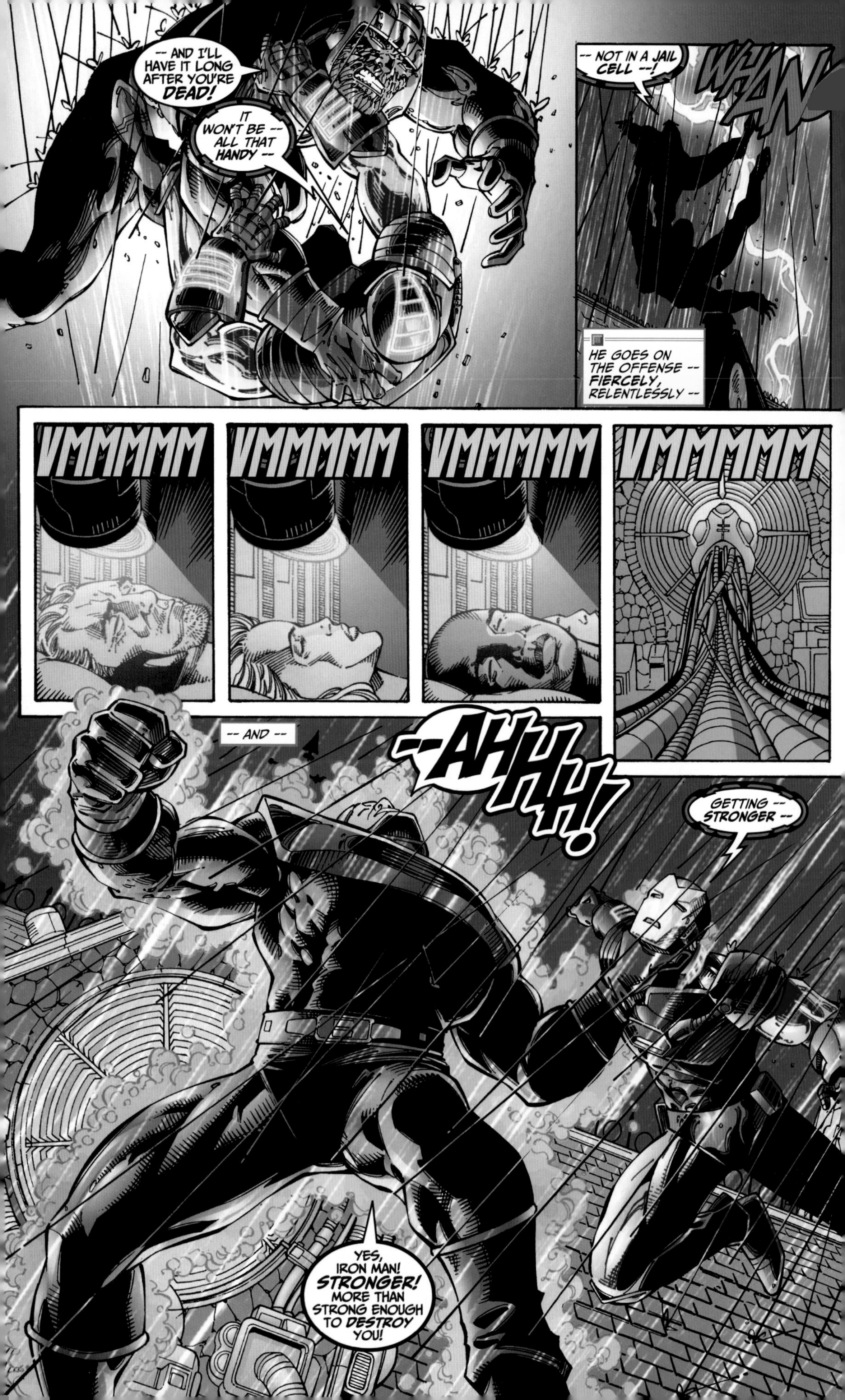
-- AND I'LL HAVE IT LONG AFTER YOU'RE DEAD!
IT WON'T BE -- ALL THAT HANDY --
-- NOT IN A JAIL CELL --!
WHAN
HE GOES ON THE OFFENSE -- FIERCELY, RELENTLESSLY --
VMMMMM
VMMMMM
VMMMMM
VMMMMM
-- AND --
--AHHHH!
GETTING -- STRONGER --
YES, IRON MAN! STRONGER! MORE THAN STRONG ENOUGH TO DESTROY YOU!

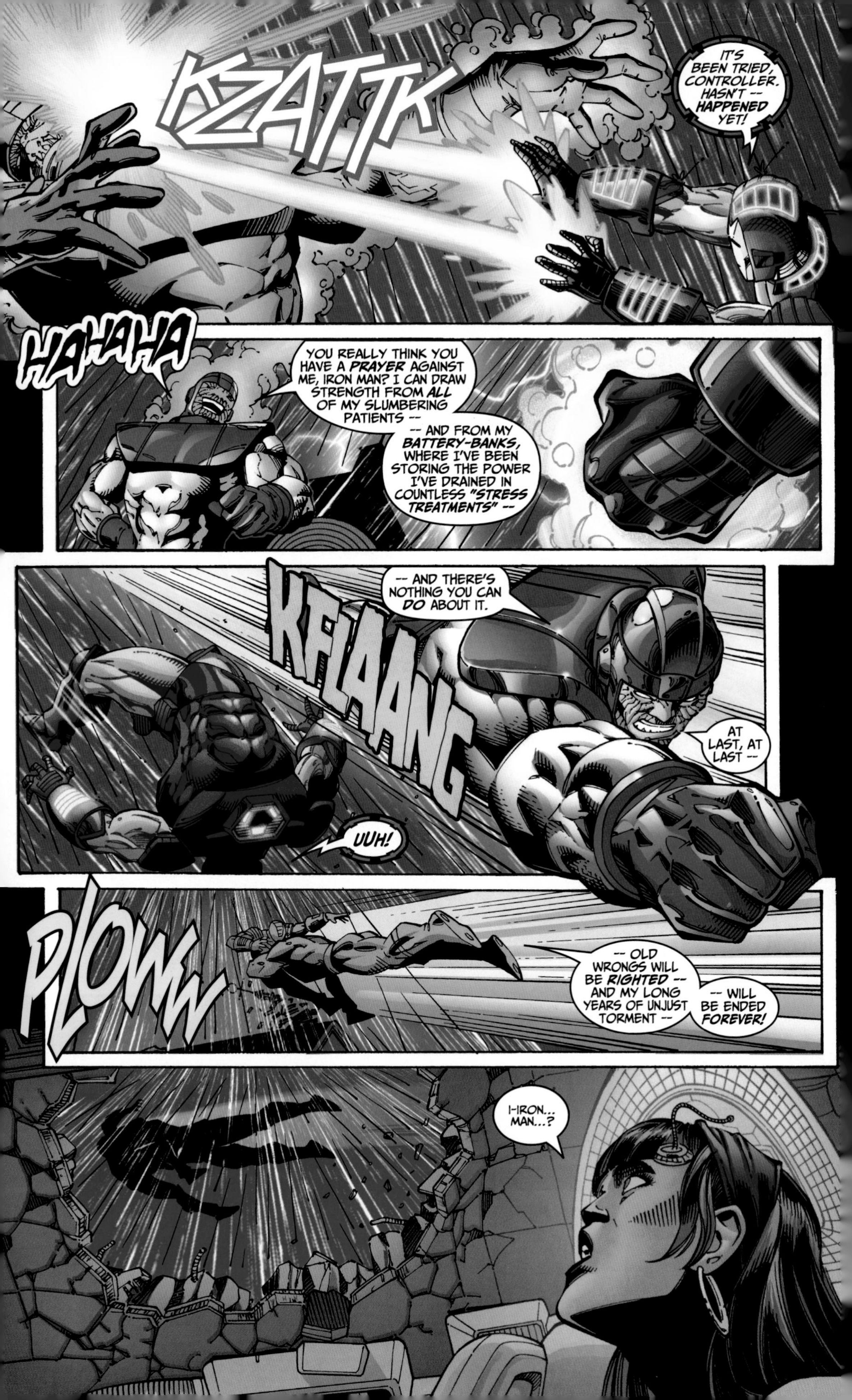
KZATTK
IT'S BEEN TRIED, CONTROLLER. HASN'T -- HAPPENED YET!
HAHAHA
YOU REALLY THINK YOU HAVE A PRAYER AGAINST ME, IRON MAN? I CAN DRAW STRENGTH FROM ALL OF MY SLUMBERING PATIENTS --
-- AND FROM MY BATTERY-BANKS, WHERE I'VE BEEN STORING THE POWER I'VE DRAINED IN COUNTLESS "STRESS TREATMENTS" --
-- AND THERE'S NOTHING YOU CAN DO ABOUT IT.
KFLAANG
AT LAST, AT LAST --
UUH!
PLOWW
-- OLD WRONGS WILL BE RIGHTED -- AND MY LONG YEARS OF UNJUST TORMENT --
-- WILL BE ENDED FOREVER!
I-IRON... MAN...?

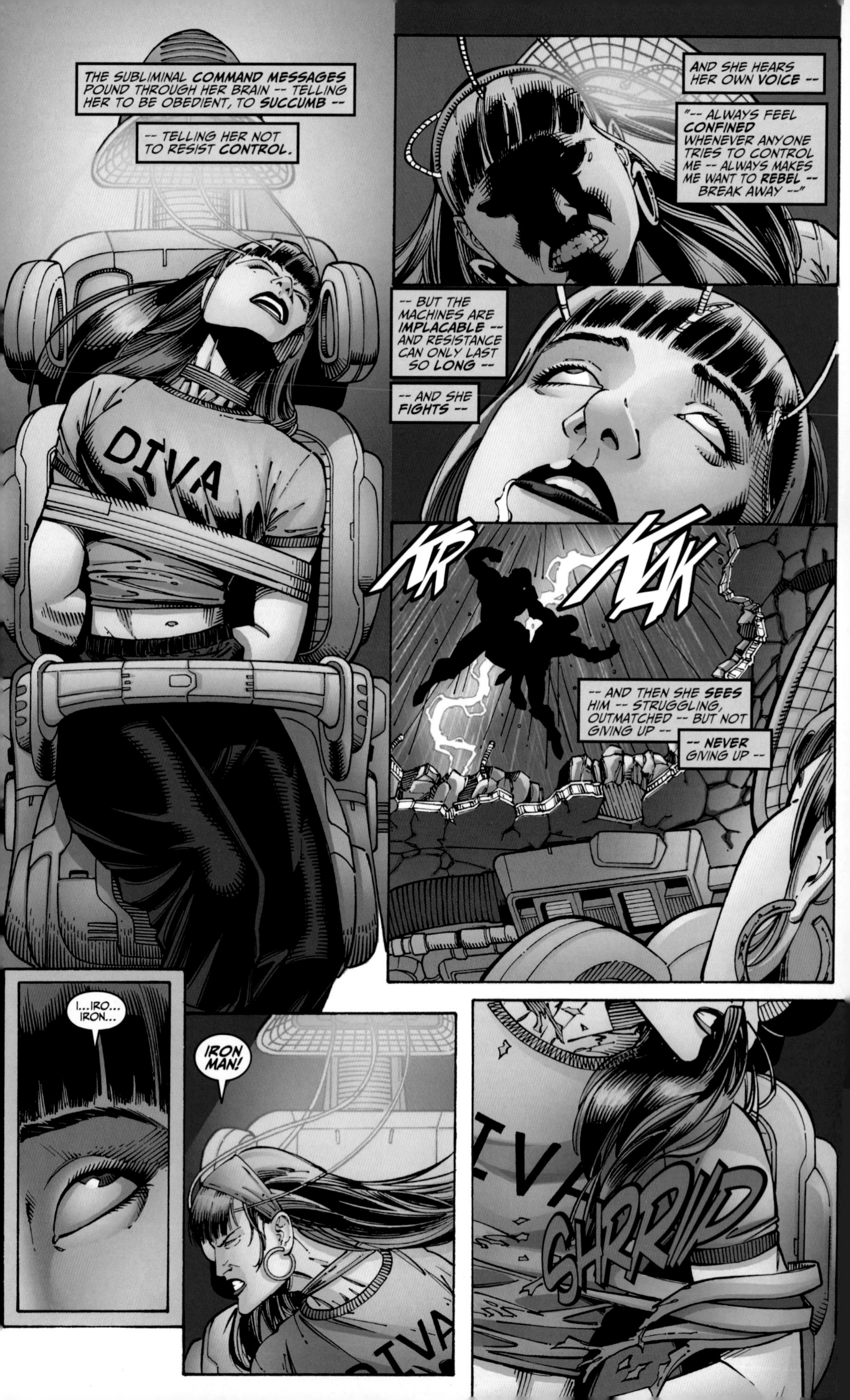
THE SUBLIMINAL COMMAND MESSAGES POUND THROUGH HER BRAIN -- TELLING HER TO BE OBEDIENT, TO SUCCUMB --
-- TELLING HER NOT TO RESIST CONTROL.
AND SHE HEARS HER OWN VOICE --
"-- ALWAYS FEEL CONFINED WHENEVER ANYONE TRIES TO CONTROL ME -- ALWAYS MAKES ME WANT TO REBEL -- BREAK AWAY --"
-- BUT THE MACHINES ARE IMPLACABLE -- AND RESISTANCE CAN ONLY LAST SO LONG --
-- AND SHE FIGHTS --
KR
KAK
-- AND THEN SHE SEES HIM -- STRUGGLING, OUTMATCHED -- BUT NOT GIVING UP --
-- NEVER GIVING UP --
I...IRO... IRON...
IRON MAN!
SHRRIP

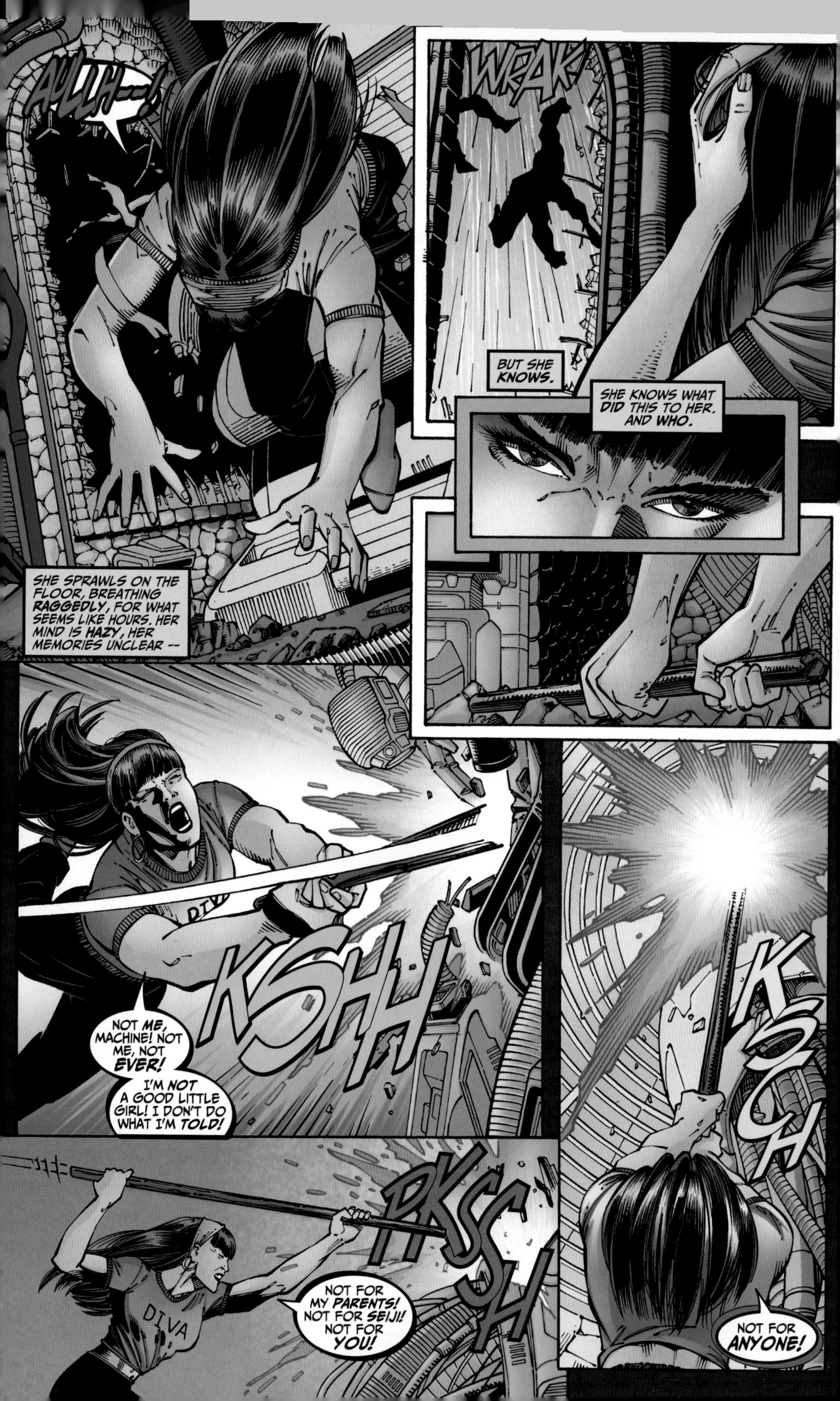
AULLH--!
WRAK!
BUT SHE KNOWS.
SHE KNOWS WHAT DID THIS TO HER. AND WHO.
SHE SPRAWLS ON THE FLOOR, BREATHING RAGGEDLY, FOR WHAT SEEMS LIKE HOURS. HER MIND IS HAZY, HER MEMORIES UNCLEAR --
KSHH
NOT ME, MACHINE! NOT ME, NOT EVER!
I'M NOT A GOOD LITTLE GIRL! I DON'T DO WHAT I'M TOLD!
KSSH
PKSSH
NOT FOR MY PARENTS! NOT FOR SEIJI! NOT FOR YOU!
NOT FOR ANYONE!

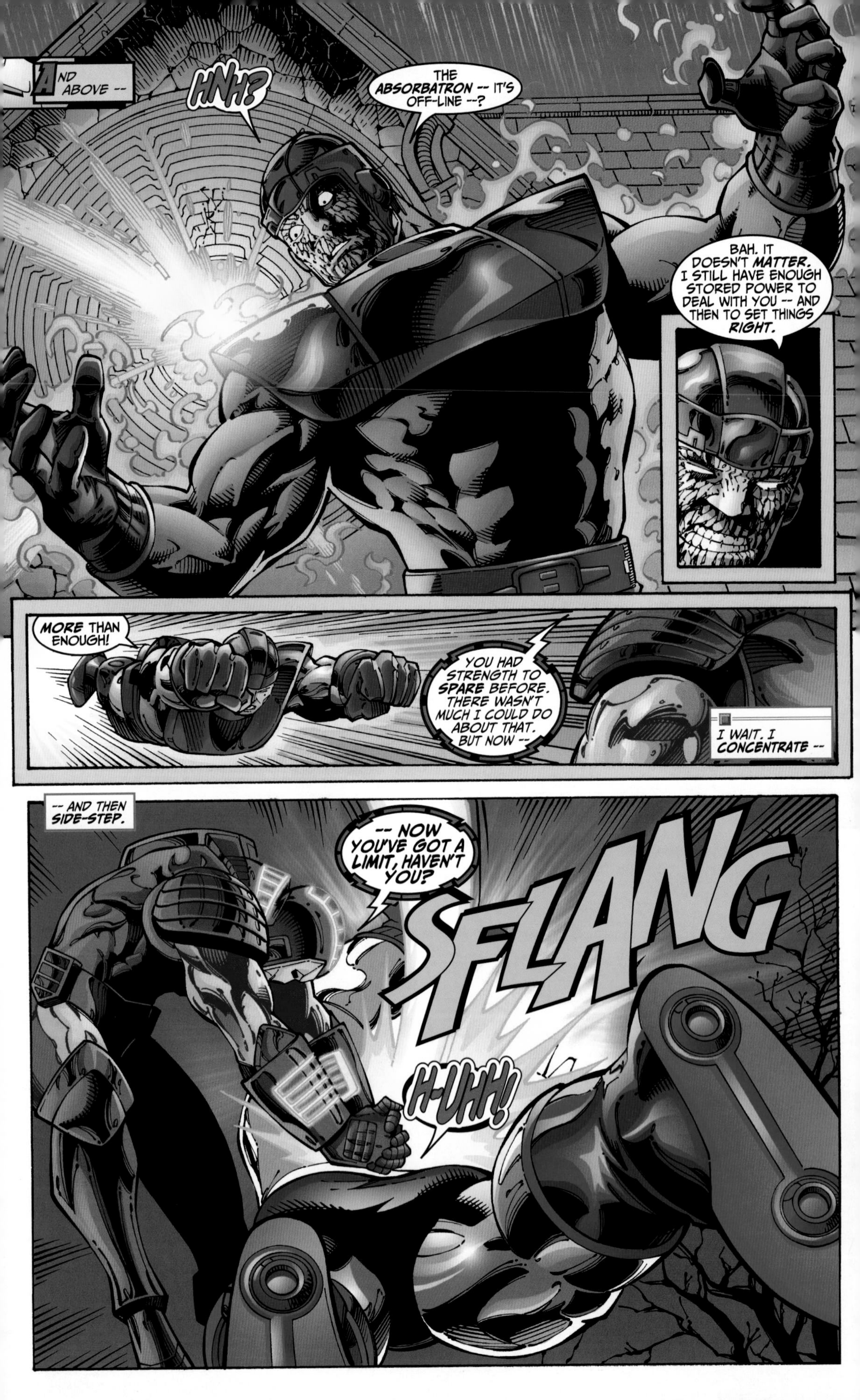
AND ABOVE --
HNH?
THE ABSORBATRON -- IT'S OFF-LINE --?
BAH. IT DOESN'T MATTER. I STILL HAVE ENOUGH STORED POWER TO DEAL WITH YOU -- AND THEN TO SET THINGS RIGHT.
MORE THAN ENOUGH!
YOU HAD STRENGTH TO SPARE BEFORE. THERE WASN'T MUCH I COULD DO ABOUT THAT. BUT NOW --
I WAIT. I CONCENTRATE --
-- AND THEN SIDE-STEP.
-- NOW YOU'VE GOT A LIMIT, HAVEN'T YOU?
SFLANG
H-UHH!

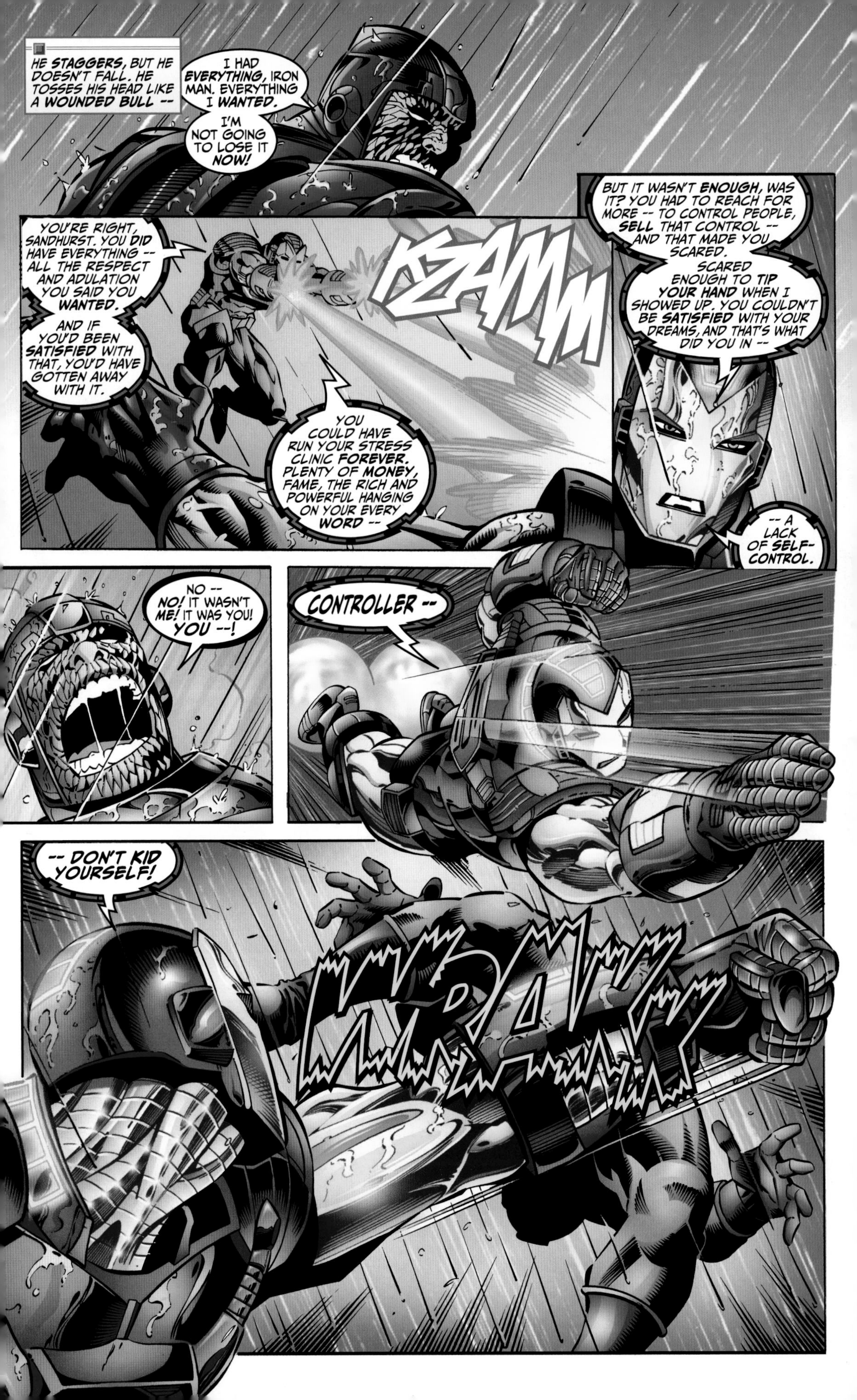
HE STAGGERS, BUT HE DOESN'T FALL. HE TOSSES HIS HEAD LIKE A WOUNDED BULL --
I HAD EVERYTHING, IRON MAN. EVERYTHING I WANTED.
I'M NOT GOING TO LOSE IT NOW!
YOU'RE RIGHT, SANDHURST. YOU DID HAVE EVERYTHING -- ALL THE RESPECT AND ADULATION YOU SAID YOU WANTED.
AND IF YOU'D BEEN SATISFIED WITH THAT, YOU'D HAVE GOTTEN AWAY WITH IT.
KSZAMM
YOU COULD HAVE RUN YOUR STRESS CLINIC FOREVER. PLENTY OF MONEY, FAME, THE RICH AND POWERFUL HANGING ON YOUR EVERY WORD --
BUT IT WASN'T ENOUGH, WAS IT? YOU HAD TO REACH FOR MORE -- TO CONTROL PEOPLE, SELL THAT CONTROL -- AND THAT MADE YOU SCARED.
SCARED ENOUGH TO TIP YOUR HAND WHEN I SHOWED UP. YOU COULDN'T BE SATISFIED WITH YOUR DREAMS, AND THAT'S WHAT DID YOU IN --
-- A LACK OF SELF-CONTROL.
NO -- NO! IT WASN'T ME! IT WAS YOU! YOU --!
CONTROLLER --
-- DON'T KID YOURSELF!
KRAKK

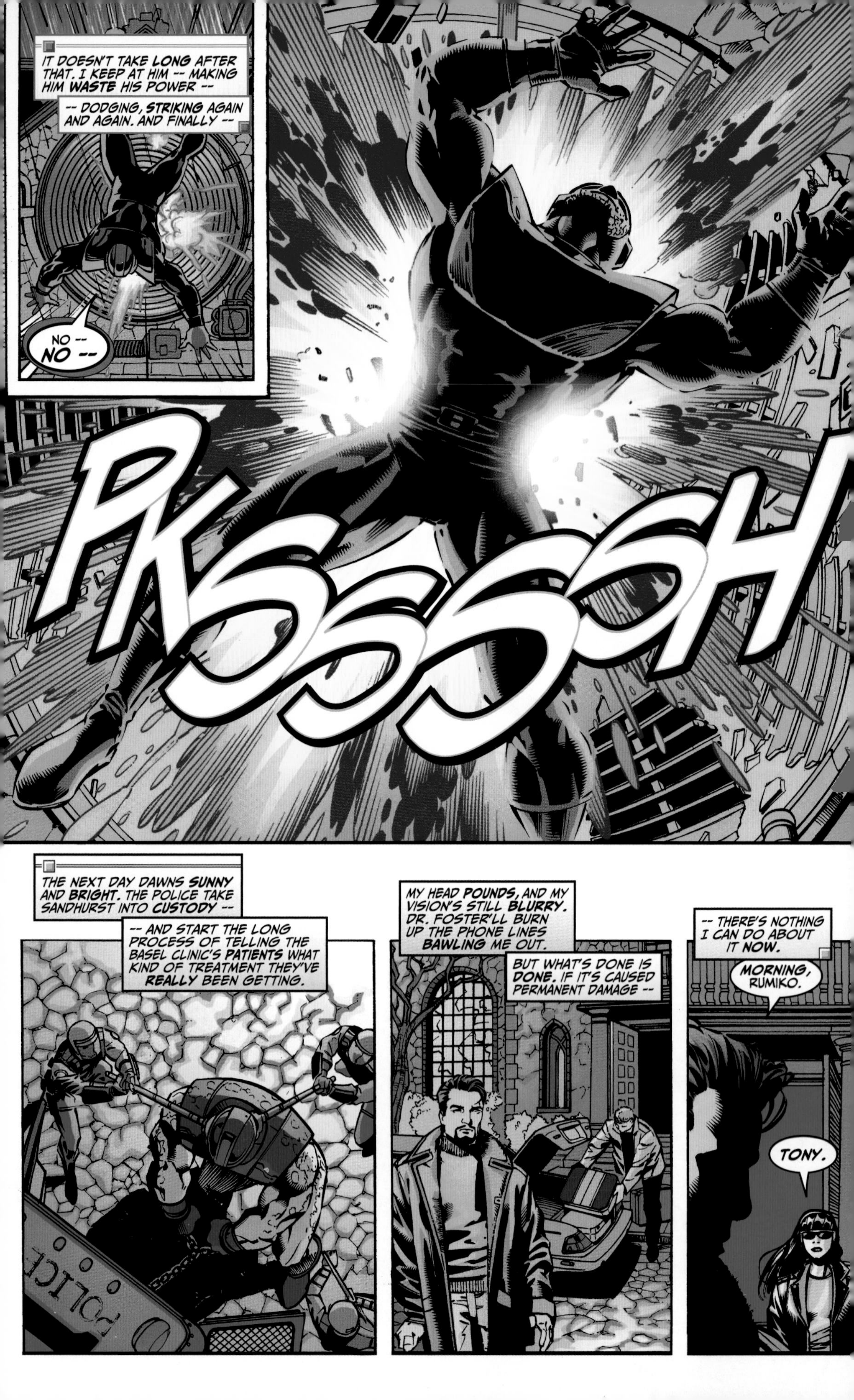
IT DOESN'T TAKE LONG AFTER THAT. I KEEP AT HIM -- MAKING HIM WASTE HIS POWER --
-- DODGING, STRIKING AGAIN AND AGAIN. AND FINALLY --
NO -- NO --
PKSSSSH
THE NEXT DAY DAWNS SUNNY AND BRIGHT. THE POLICE TAKE SANDHURST INTO CUSTODY --
-- AND START THE LONG PROCESS OF TELLING THE BASEL CLINIC'S PATIENTS WHAT KIND OF TREATMENT THEY'VE REALLY BEEN GETTING.
POLICE
MY HEAD POUNDS, AND MY VISION'S STILL BLURRY. DR. FOSTER'LL BURN UP THE PHONE LINES BAWLING ME OUT.
BUT WHAT'S DONE IS DONE. IF IT'S CAUSED PERMANENT DAMAGE --
-- THERE'S NOTHING I CAN DO ABOUT IT NOW.
MORNING, RUMIKO.
TONY.

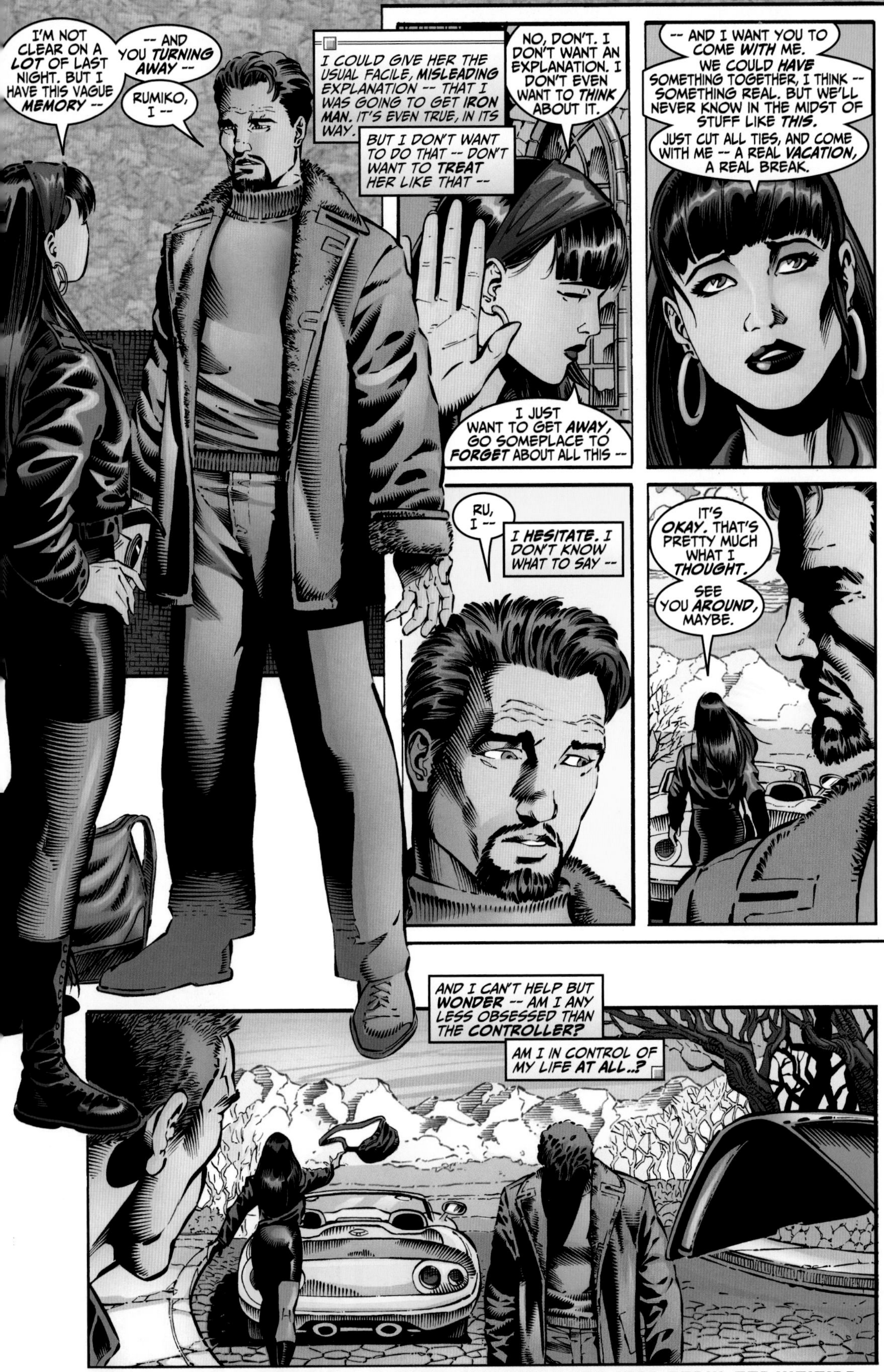

I'M NOT CLEAR ON A LOT OF LAST NIGHT. BUT I HAVE THIS VAGUE MEMORY --
-- AND YOU TURNING AWAY --
RUMIKO, I --
I COULD GIVE HER THE USUAL FACILE, MISLEADING EXPLANATION -- THAT I WAS GOING TO GET IRON MAN. IT'S EVEN TRUE, IN ITS WAY.
BUT I DON'T WANT TO DO THAT -- DON'T WANT TO TREAT HER LIKE THAT --
NO, DON'T. I DON'T WANT AN EXPLANATION. I DON'T EVEN WANT TO THINK ABOUT IT.
I JUST WANT TO GET AWAY, GO SOMEPLACE TO FORGET ABOUT ALL THIS --
-- AND I WANT YOU TO COME WITH ME.
WE COULD HAVE SOMETHING TOGETHER, I THINK -- SOMETHING REAL. BUT WE'LL NEVER KNOW IN THE MIDST OF STUFF LIKE THIS.
JUST CUT ALL TIES, AND COME WITH ME -- A REAL VACATION, A REAL BREAK.
RU, I --
I HESITATE. I DON'T KNOW WHAT TO SAY --
IT'S OKAY. THAT'S PRETTY MUCH WHAT I THOUGHT.
SEE YOU AROUND, MAYBE.
AND I CAN'T HELP BUT WONDER -- AM I ANY LESS OBSESSED THAN THE CONTROLLER?
AM I IN CONTROL OF MY LIFE AT ALL..?

DON'T WORRY, FOLKS -- RUMIKO'LL BE BACK! BUT WHILE YOU (AND TONY) ARE WAITING...
THE FANTASTIC FOUR! RONAN! ROGER STERN! RIGHT HERE IN THIRTY!

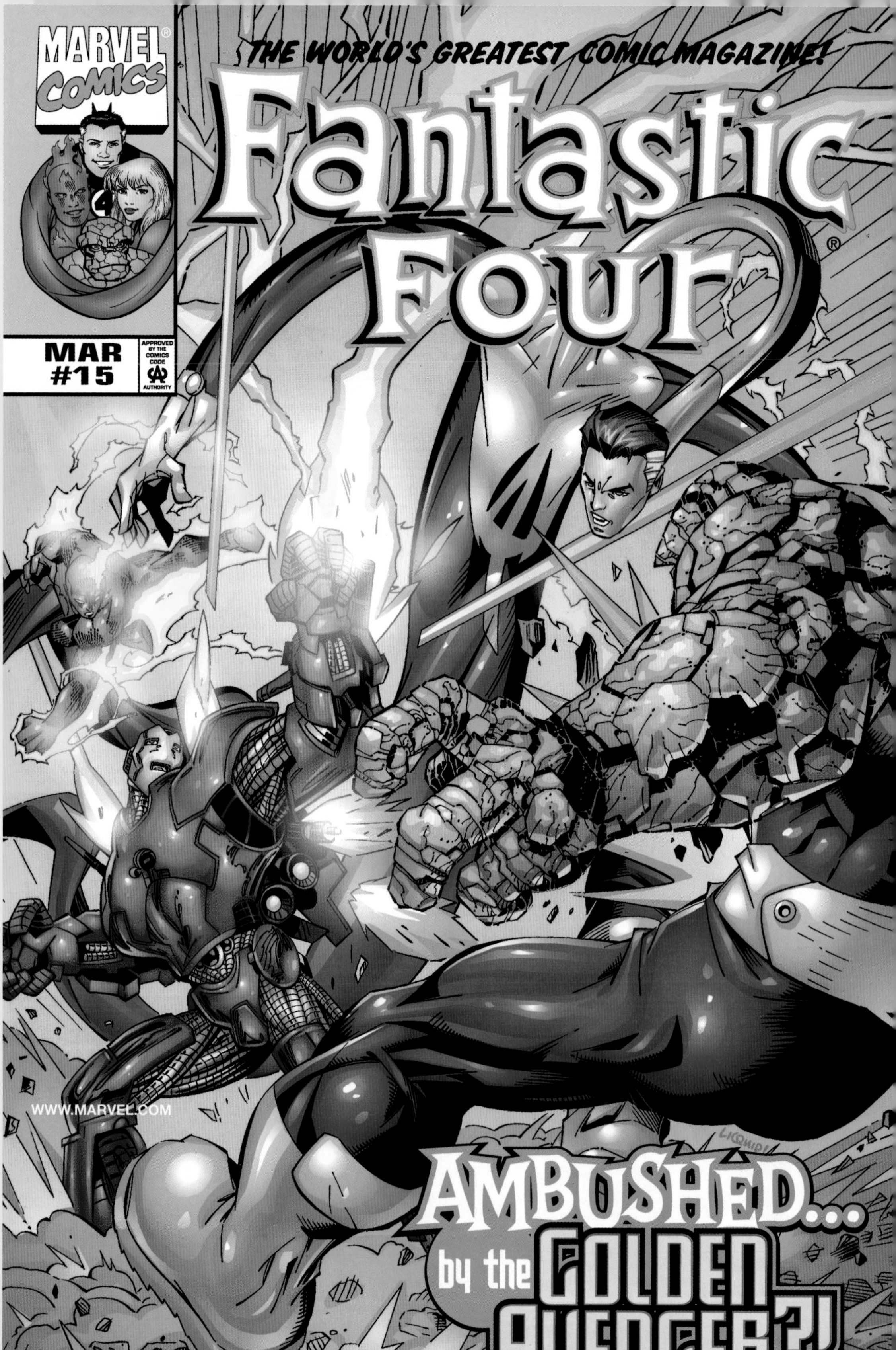
MARVEL COMICS
THE WORLD'S GREATEST COMIC MAGAZINE!
Fantastic Four
MAR #15
APPROVED BY THE COMICS CODE AUTHORITY
WWW.MARVEL.COM
AMBUSHED...
by the GOLDEN AVENGER?!

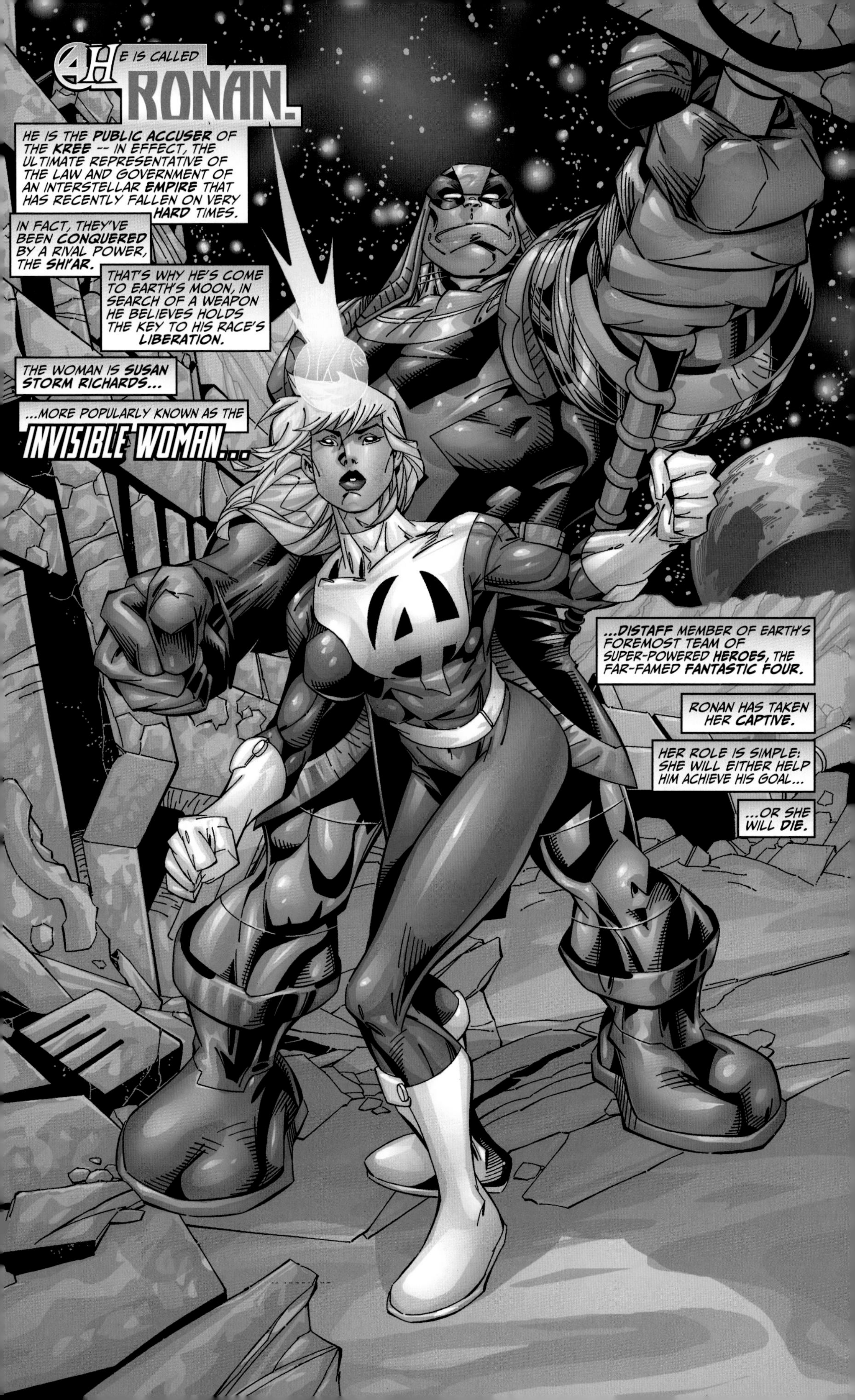
HE IS CALLED
RONAN.
HE IS THE PUBLIC ACCUSER OF THE KREE -- IN EFFECT, THE ULTIMATE REPRESENTATIVE OF THE LAW AND GOVERNMENT OF AN INTERSTELLAR EMPIRE THAT HAS RECENTLY FALLEN ON VERY HARD TIMES.
IN FACT, THEY'VE BEEN CONQUERED BY A RIVAL POWER, THE SHI'AR.
THAT'S WHY HE'S COME TO EARTH'S MOON, IN SEARCH OF A WEAPON HE BELIEVES HOLDS THE KEY TO HIS RACE'S LIBERATION.
THE WOMAN IS SUSAN STORM RICHARDS...
...MORE POPULARLY KNOWN AS THE
INVISIBLE WOMAN...
...DISTAFF MEMBER OF EARTH'S FOREMOST TEAM OF SUPER-POWERED HEROES, THE FAR-FAMED FANTASTIC FOUR.
RONAN HAS TAKEN HER CAPTIVE.
HER ROLE IS SIMPLE: SHE WILL EITHER HELP HIM ACHIEVE HIS GOAL...
...OR SHE WILL DIE.

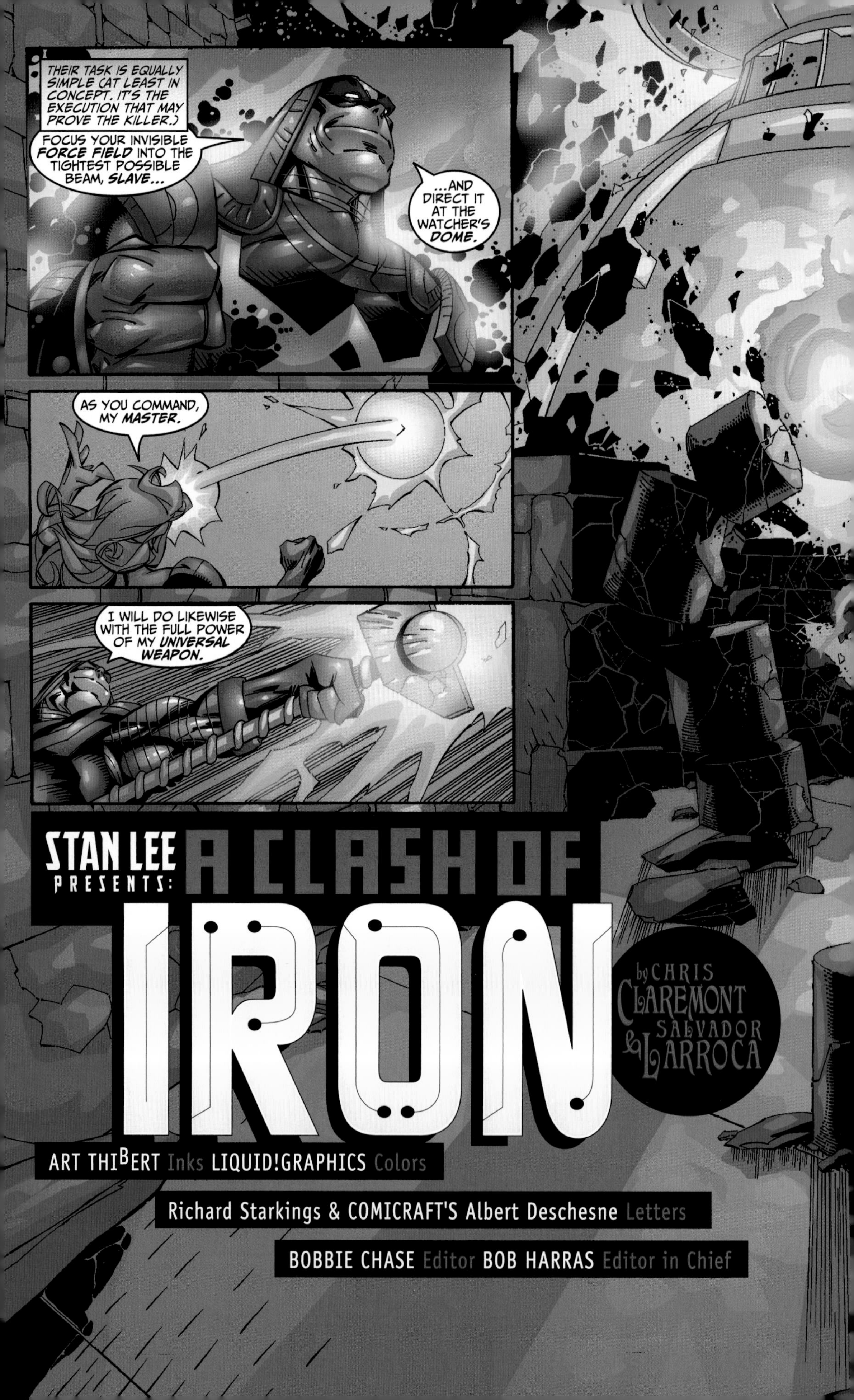
THEIR TASK IS EQUALLY SIMPLE (AT LEAST IN CONCEPT. IT'S THE EXECUTION THAT MAY PROVE THE KILLER.)
FOCUS YOUR INVISIBLE FORCE FIELD INTO THE TIGHTEST POSSIBLE BEAM, SLAVE...
...AND DIRECT IT AT THE WATCHER'S DOME.
AS YOU COMMAND, MY MASTER.
I WILL DO LIKEWISE WITH THE FULL POWER OF MY UNIVERSAL WEAPON.
STAN LEE PRESENTS: A CLASH OF IRON
by CHRIS CLAREMONT & SALVADOR LARROCA
ART THIBERT Inks LIQUID!GRAPHICS Colors
Richard Starkings & COMICRAFT'S Albert Deschesne Letters
BOBBIE CHASE Editor BOB HARRAS Editor in Chief

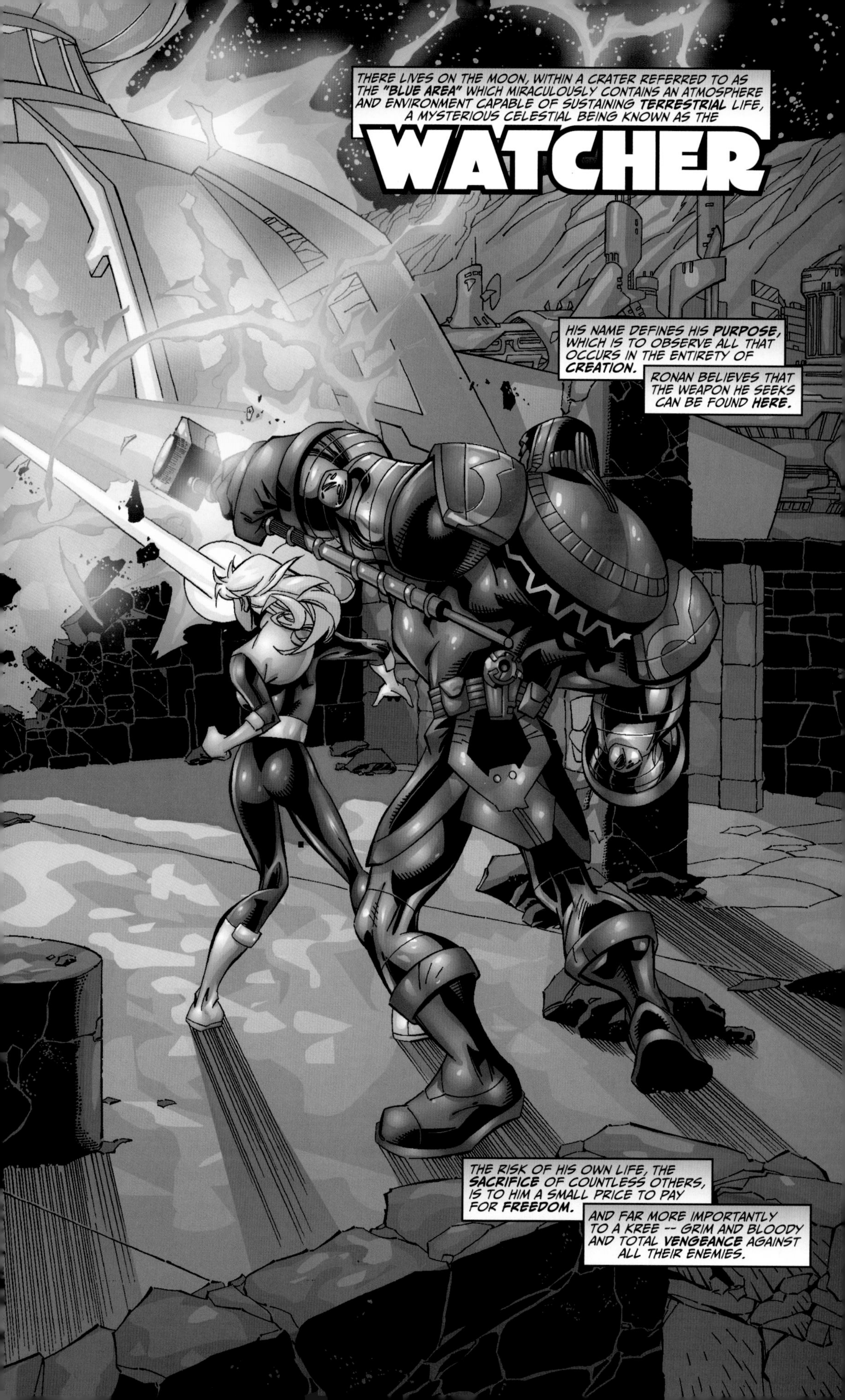
THERE LIVES ON THE MOON, WITHIN A CRATER REFERRED TO AS THE "BLUE AREA" WHICH MIRACULOUSLY CONTAINS AN ATMOSPHERE AND ENVIRONMENT CAPABLE OF SUSTAINING TERRESTRIAL LIFE, A MYSTERIOUS CELESTIAL BEING KNOWN AS THE
WATCHER
HIS NAME DEFINES HIS PURPOSE, WHICH IS TO OBSERVE ALL THAT OCCURS IN THE ENTIRETY OF CREATION.
RONAN BELIEVES THAT THE WEAPON HE SEEKS CAN BE FOUND HERE.
THE RISK OF HIS OWN LIFE, THE SACRIFICE OF COUNTLESS OTHERS, IS TO HIM A SMALL PRICE TO PAY FOR FREEDOM.
AND FAR MORE IMPORTANTLY TO A KREE -- GRIM AND BLOODY AND TOTAL VENGEANCE AGAINST ALL THEIR ENEMIES.

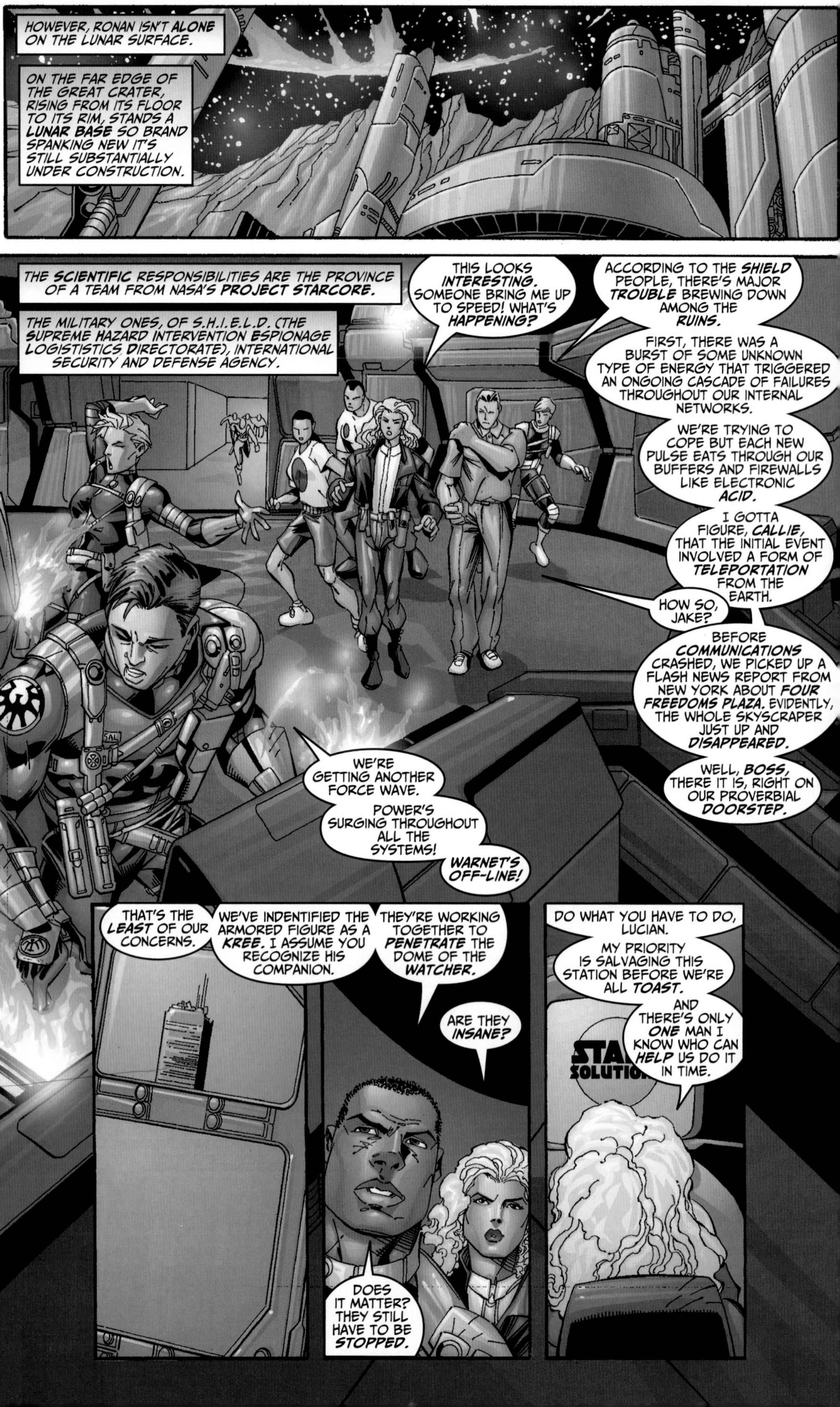
HOWEVER, RONAN ISN'T ALONE ON THE LUNAR SURFACE.
ON THE FAR EDGE OF THE GREAT CRATER, RISING FROM ITS FLOOR TO ITS RIM, STANDS A LUNAR BASE SO BRAND SPANKING NEW IT'S STILL SUBSTANTIALLY UNDER CONSTRUCTION.
THE SCIENTIFIC RESPONSIBILITIES ARE THE PROVINCE OF A TEAM FROM NASA'S PROJECT STARCORE.
THE MILITARY ONES, OF S.H.I.E.L.D. (THE SUPREME HAZARD INTERVENTION ESPIONAGE LOGISTISTICS DIRECTORATE), INTERNATIONAL SECURITY AND DEFENSE AGENCY.
THIS LOOKS INTERESTING. SOMEONE BRING ME UP TO SPEED! WHAT'S HAPPENING?
ACCORDING TO THE SHIELD PEOPLE, THERE'S MAJOR TROUBLE BREWING DOWN AMONG THE RUINS.
FIRST, THERE WAS A BURST OF SOME UNKNOWN TYPE OF ENERGY THAT TRIGGERED AN ONGOING CASCADE OF FAILURES THROUGHOUT OUR INTERNAL NETWORKS.
WE'RE TRYING TO COPE BUT EACH NEW PULSE EATS THROUGH OUR BUFFERS AND FIREWALLS LIKE ELECTRONIC ACID.
I GOTTA FIGURE, CALLIE, THAT THE INITIAL EVENT INVOLVED A FORM OF TELEPORTATION FROM THE EARTH.
HOW SO, JAKE?
BEFORE COMMUNICATIONS CRASHED, WE PICKED UP A FLASH NEWS REPORT FROM NEW YORK ABOUT FOUR FREEDOMS PLAZA. EVIDENTLY, THE WHOLE SKYSCRAPER JUST UP AND DISAPPEARED.
WELL, BOSS, THERE IT IS, RIGHT ON OUR PROVERBIAL DOORSTEP.
WE'RE GETTING ANOTHER FORCE WAVE.
POWER'S SURGING THROUGHOUT ALL THE SYSTEMS!
WARNET'S OFF-LINE!
THAT'S THE LEAST OF OUR CONCERNS.
WE'VE INDENTIFIED THE ARMORED FIGURE AS A KREE. I ASSUME YOU RECOGNIZE HIS COMPANION.
THEY'RE WORKING TOGETHER TO PENETRATE THE DOME OF THE WATCHER.
ARE THEY INSANE?
DOES IT MATTER? THEY STILL HAVE TO BE STOPPED.
DO WHAT YOU HAVE TO DO, LUCIAN.
MY PRIORITY IS SALVAGING THIS STATION BEFORE WE'RE ALL TOAST.
AND THERE'S ONLY ONE MAN I KNOW WHO CAN HELP US DO IT IN TIME.

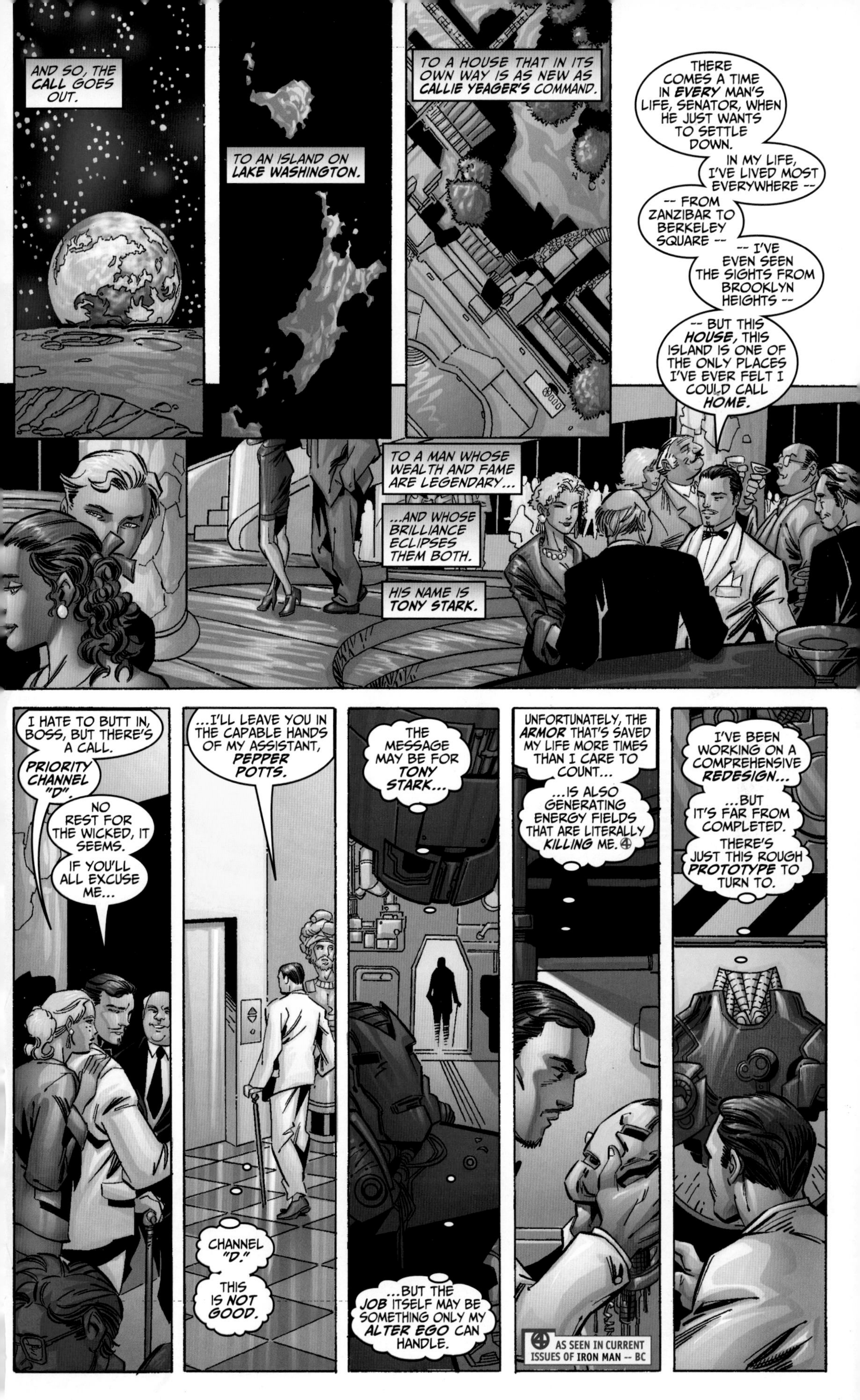
AND SO, THE CALL GOES OUT.
TO AN ISLAND ON LAKE WASHINGTON.
TO A HOUSE THAT IN ITS OWN WAY IS AS NEW AS CALLIE YEAGER'S COMMAND.
THERE COMES A TIME IN EVERY MAN'S LIFE, SENATOR, WHEN HE JUST WANTS TO SETTLE DOWN.
IN MY LIFE, I'VE LIVED MOST EVERYWHERE --
-- FROM ZANZIBAR TO BERKELEY SQUARE --
-- I'VE EVEN SEEN THE SIGHTS FROM BROOKLYN HEIGHTS --
-- BUT THIS HOUSE, THIS ISLAND IS ONE OF THE ONLY PLACES I'VE EVER FELT I COULD CALL HOME.
TO A MAN WHOSE WEALTH AND FAME ARE LEGENDARY...
...AND WHOSE BRILLIANCE ECLIPSES THEM BOTH.
HIS NAME IS TONY STARK.
I HATE TO BUTT IN, BOSS, BUT THERE'S A CALL.
PRIORITY CHANNEL "D".
NO REST FOR THE WICKED, IT SEEMS.
IF YOU'LL ALL EXCUSE ME...
...I'LL LEAVE YOU IN THE CAPABLE HANDS OF MY ASSISTANT, PEPPER POTTS.
CHANNEL "D."
THIS IS NOT GOOD.
THE MESSAGE MAY BE FOR TONY STARK...
...BUT THE JOB ITSELF MAY BE SOMETHING ONLY MY ALTER EGO CAN HANDLE.
UNFORTUNATELY, THE ARMOR THAT'S SAVED MY LIFE MORE TIMES THAN I CARE TO COUNT...
...IS ALSO GENERATING ENERGY FIELDS THAT ARE LITERALLY KILLING ME. 4
4 AS SEEN IN CURRENT ISSUES OF IRON MAN -- BC
I'VE BEEN WORKING ON A COMPREHENSIVE REDESIGN...
...BUT IT'S FAR FROM COMPLETED.
THERE'S JUST THIS ROUGH PROTOTYPE TO TURN TO.

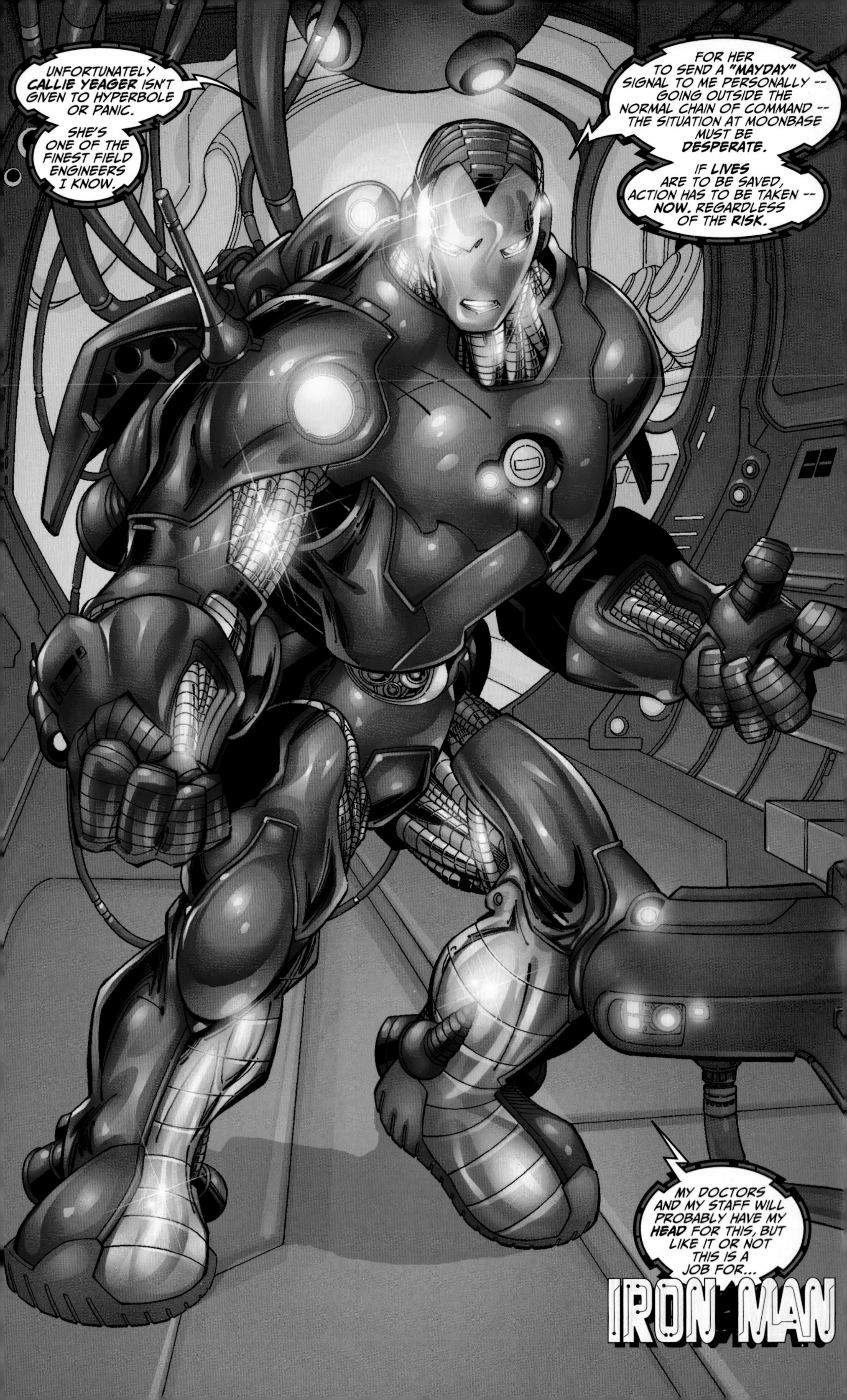
UNFORTUNATELY CALLIE YEAGER ISN'T GIVEN TO HYPERBOLE OR PANIC.
SHE'S ONE OF THE FINEST FIELD ENGINEERS I KNOW.
FOR HER TO SEND A "MAYDAY" SIGNAL TO ME PERSONALLY -- GOING OUTSIDE THE NORMAL CHAIN OF COMMAND -- THE SITUATION AT MOONBASE MUST BE DESPERATE.
IF LIVES ARE TO BE SAVED, ACTION HAS TO BE TAKEN -- NOW. REGARDLESS OF THE RISK.
MY DOCTORS AND MY STAFF WILL PROBABLY HAVE MY HEAD FOR THIS, BUT LIKE IT OR NOT THIS IS A JOB FOR...
IRON MAN

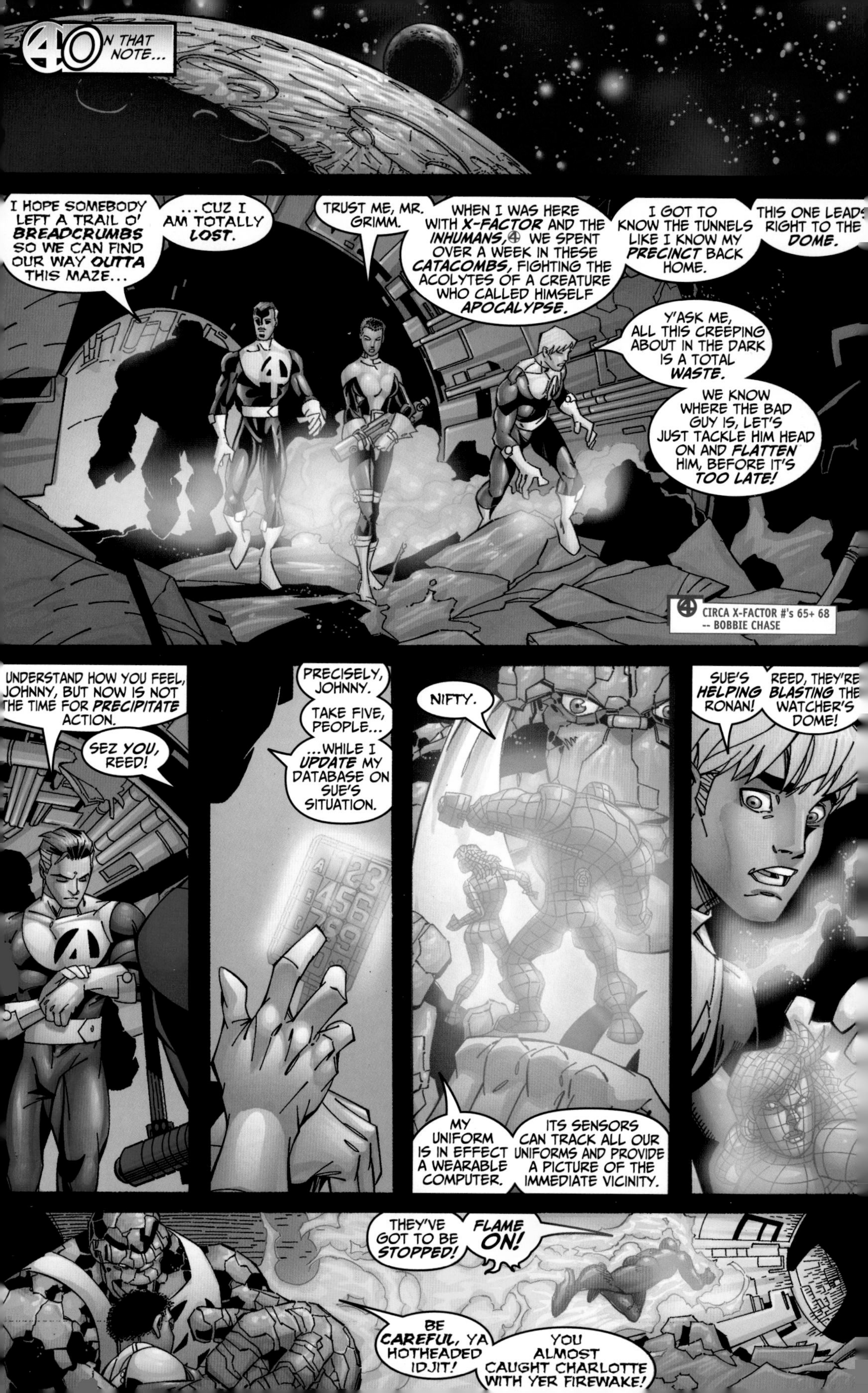
ON THAT NOTE...
I HOPE SOMEBODY LEFT A TRAIL O' BREADCRUMBS SO WE CAN FIND OUR WAY OUTTA THIS MAZE...
...CUZ I AM TOTALLY LOST.
TRUST ME, MR. GRIMM.
WHEN I WAS HERE WITH X-FACTOR AND THE INHUMANS, WE SPENT OVER A WEEK IN THESE CATACOMBS, FIGHTING THE ACOLYTES OF A CREATURE WHO CALLED HIMSELF APOCALYPSE.
I GOT TO KNOW THE TUNNELS LIKE I KNOW MY PRECINCT BACK HOME.
THIS ONE LEADS RIGHT TO THE DOME.
Y'ASK ME, ALL THIS CREEPING ABOUT IN THE DARK IS A TOTAL WASTE.
WE KNOW WHERE THE BAD GUY IS, LET'S JUST TACKLE HIM HEAD ON AND FLATTEN HIM, BEFORE IT'S TOO LATE!
CIRCA X-FACTOR #'s 65+ 68 -- BOBBIE CHASE
UNDERSTAND HOW YOU FEEL, JOHNNY, BUT NOW IS NOT THE TIME FOR PRECIPITATE ACTION.
SEZ YOU, REED!
PRECISELY, JOHNNY.
TAKE FIVE, PEOPLE...
...WHILE I UPDATE MY DATABASE ON SUE'S SITUATION.
NIFTY.
MY UNIFORM IS IN EFFECT A WEARABLE COMPUTER.
ITS SENSORS CAN TRACK ALL OUR UNIFORMS AND PROVIDE A PICTURE OF THE IMMEDIATE VICINITY.
SUE'S HELPING RONAN!
REED, THEY'RE BLASTING THE WATCHER'S DOME!
THEY'VE GOT TO BE STOPPED!
FLAME ON!
BE CAREFUL, YA HOTHEADED IDJIT!
YOU ALMOST CAUGHT CHARLOTTE WITH YER FIREWAKE!

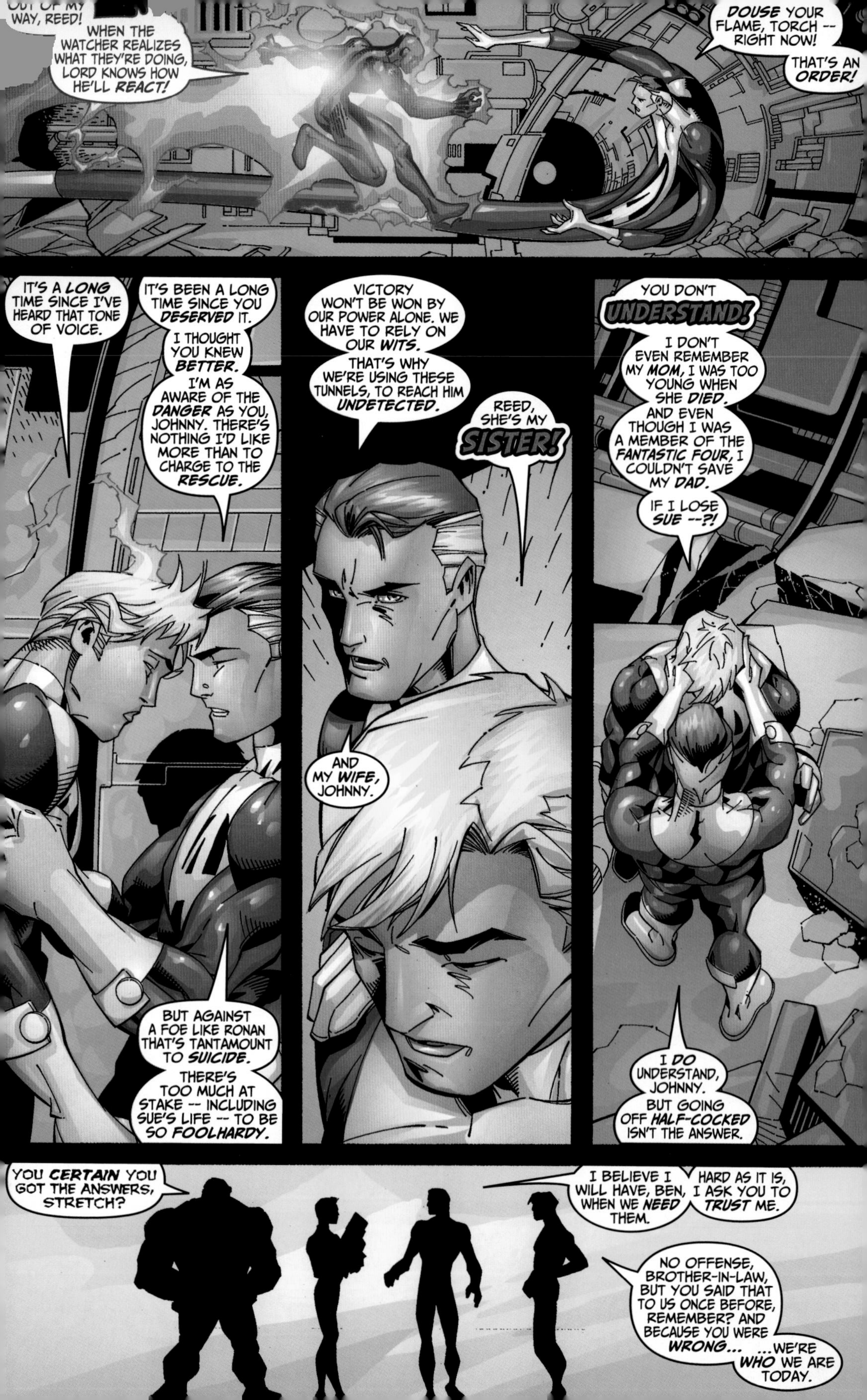

OUT OF MY WAY, REED!
WHEN THE WATCHER REALIZES WHAT THEY'RE DOING, LORD KNOWS HOW HE'LL REACT!
DOUSE YOUR FLAME, TORCH -- RIGHT NOW!
THAT'S AN ORDER!
IT'S A LONG TIME SINCE I'VE HEARD THAT TONE OF VOICE.
IT'S BEEN A LONG TIME SINCE YOU DESERVED IT.
I THOUGHT YOU KNEW BETTER.
I'M AS AWARE OF THE DANGER AS YOU, JOHNNY. THERE'S NOTHING I'D LIKE MORE THAN TO CHARGE TO THE RESCUE.
BUT AGAINST A FOE LIKE RONAN THAT'S TANTAMOUNT TO SUICIDE.
THERE'S TOO MUCH AT STAKE -- INCLUDING SUE'S LIFE -- TO BE SO FOOLHARDY.
VICTORY WON'T BE WON BY OUR POWER ALONE. WE HAVE TO RELY ON OUR WITS.
THAT'S WHY WE'RE USING THESE TUNNELS, TO REACH HIM UNDETECTED.
REED, SHE'S MY SISTER!
AND MY WIFE, JOHNNY.
YOU DON'T UNDERSTAND!
I DON'T EVEN REMEMBER MY MOM, I WAS TOO YOUNG WHEN SHE DIED.
AND EVEN THOUGH I WAS A MEMBER OF THE FANTASTIC FOUR, I COULDN'T SAVE MY DAD.
IF I LOSE SUE --?!
I DO UNDERSTAND, JOHNNY.
BUT GOING OFF HALF-COCKED ISN'T THE ANSWER.
YOU CERTAIN YOU GOT THE ANSWERS, STRETCH?
I BELIEVE I WILL HAVE, BEN, WHEN WE NEED THEM.
HARD AS IT IS, I ASK YOU TO TRUST ME.
NO OFFENSE, BROTHER-IN-LAW, BUT YOU SAID THAT TO US ONCE BEFORE, REMEMBER? AND BECAUSE YOU WERE WRONG...
...WE'RE WHO WE ARE TODAY.

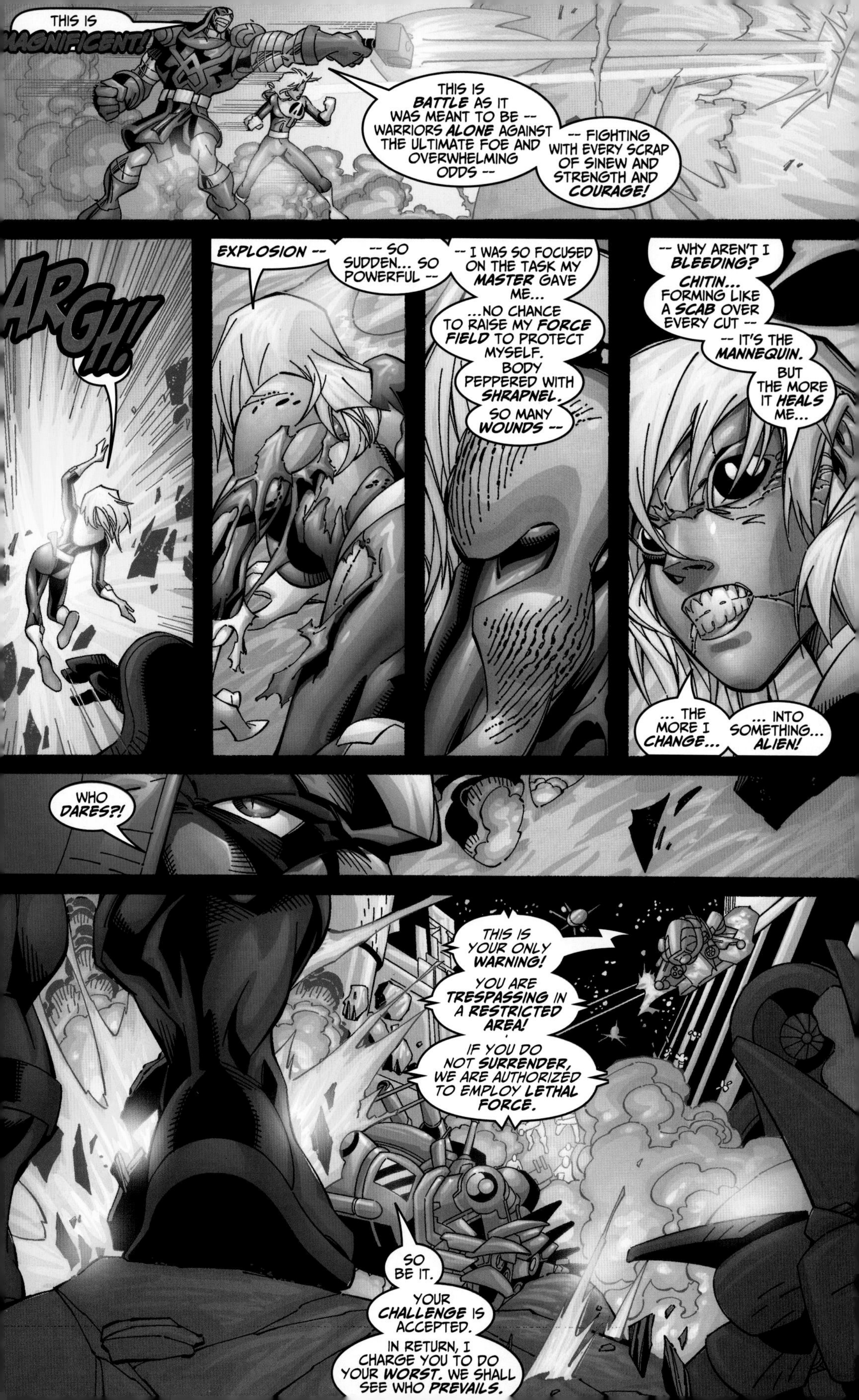

THIS IS MAGNIFICENT!
THIS IS BATTLE AS IT WAS MEANT TO BE -- WARRIORS ALONE AGAINST THE ULTIMATE FOE AND OVERWHELMING ODDS --
-- FIGHTING WITH EVERY SCRAP OF SINEW AND STRENGTH AND COURAGE!
ARGH!
EXPLOSION --
-- SO SUDDEN... SO POWERFUL --
-- I WAS SO FOCUSED ON THE TASK MY MASTER GAVE ME...
...NO CHANCE TO RAISE MY FORCE FIELD TO PROTECT MYSELF.
BODY PEPPERED WITH SHRAPNEL.
SO MANY WOUNDS --
-- WHY AREN'T I BLEEDING?
CHITIN... FORMING LIKE A SCAB OVER EVERY CUT --
-- IT'S THE MANNEQUIN.
BUT THE MORE IT HEALS ME...
... THE MORE I CHANGE...
... INTO SOMETHING... ALIEN!
WHO DARES?!
THIS IS YOUR ONLY WARNING!
YOU ARE TRESPASSING IN A RESTRICTED AREA!
IF YOU DO NOT SURRENDER, WE ARE AUTHORIZED TO EMPLOY LETHAL FORCE.
SO BE IT.
YOUR CHALLENGE IS ACCEPTED.
IN RETURN, I CHARGE YOU TO DO YOUR WORST. WE SHALL SEE WHO PREVAILS.

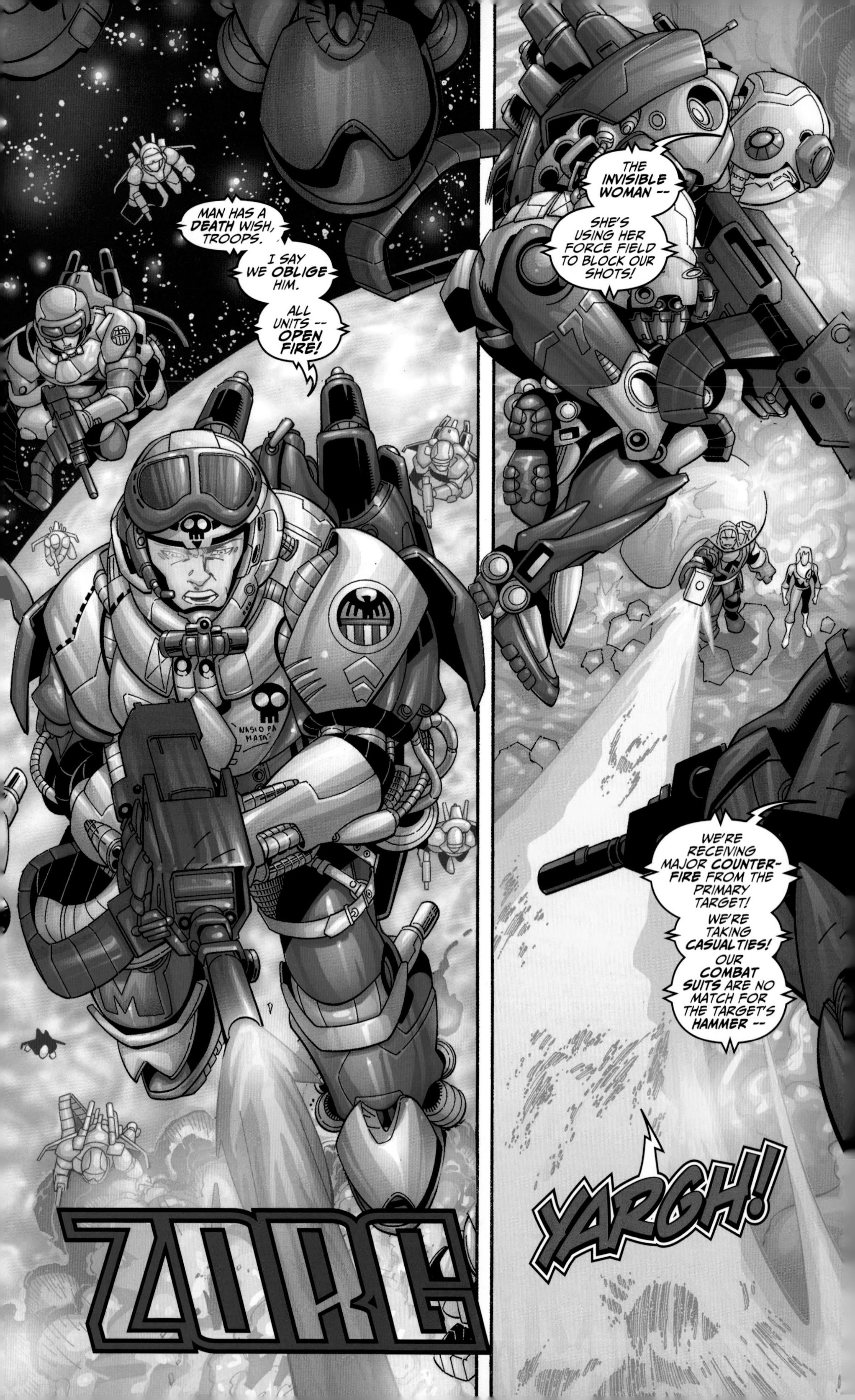
MAN HAS A DEATH WISH, TROOPS.
I SAY WE OBLIGE HIM.
ALL UNITS -- OPEN FIRE!
NASIO PA MATA
ZORT!
THE INVISIBLE WOMAN --
SHE'S USING HER FORCE FIELD TO BLOCK OUR SHOTS!
WE'RE RECEIVING MAJOR COUNTER-FIRE FROM THE PRIMARY TARGET!
WE'RE TAKING CASUALTIES!
OUR COMBAT SUITS ARE NO MATCH FOR THE TARGET'S HAMMER --
YARGH!

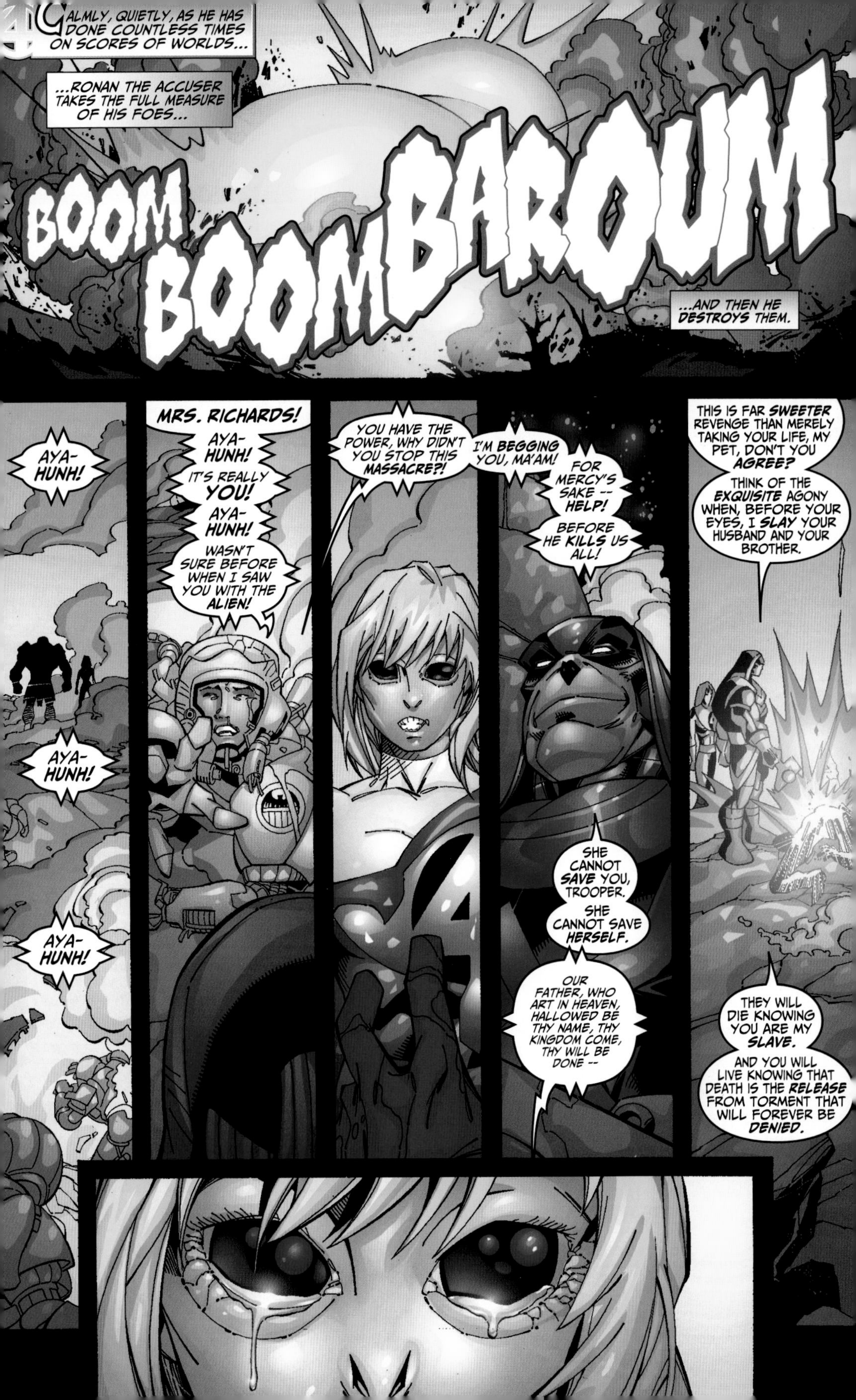
CALMLY, QUIETLY, AS HE HAS DONE COUNTLESS TIMES ON SCORES OF WORLDS...
...RONAN THE ACCUSER TAKES THE FULL MEASURE OF HIS FOES...
BOOM
BOOMBAROUM
...AND THEN HE DESTROYS THEM.
AYA-HUNH!
AYA-HUNH!
AYA-HUNH!
MRS. RICHARDS!
AYA-HUNH!
IT'S REALLY YOU!
AYA-HUNH!
WASN'T SURE BEFORE WHEN I SAW YOU WITH THE ALIEN!
YOU HAVE THE POWER, WHY DIDN'T YOU STOP THIS MASSACRE?!
I'M BEGGING YOU, MA'AM!
FOR MERCY'S SAKE -- HELP!
BEFORE HE KILLS US ALL!
SHE CANNOT SAVE YOU, TROOPER.
SHE CANNOT SAVE HERSELF.
OUR FATHER, WHO ART IN HEAVEN, HALLOWED BE THY NAME, THY KINGDOM COME, THY WILL BE DONE --
THIS IS FAR SWEETER REVENGE THAN MERELY TAKING YOUR LIFE, MY PET, DON'T YOU AGREE?
THINK OF THE EXQUISITE AGONY WHEN, BEFORE YOUR EYES, I SLAY YOUR HUSBAND AND YOUR BROTHER.
THEY WILL DIE KNOWING YOU ARE MY SLAVE.
AND YOU WILL LIVE KNOWING THAT DEATH IS THE RELEASE FROM TORMENT THAT WILL FOREVER BE DENIED.

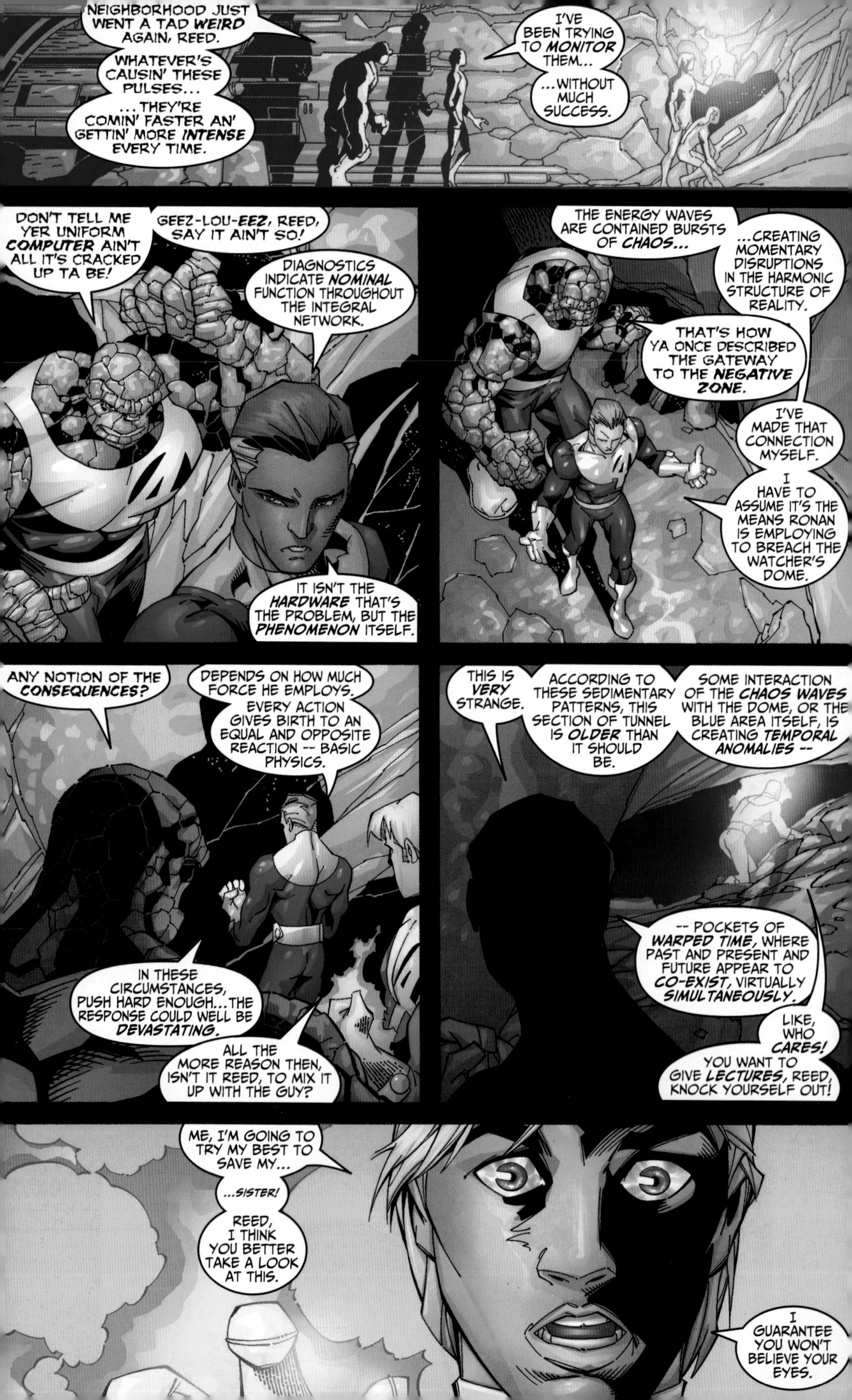
NEIGHBORHOOD JUST WENT A TAD WEIRD AGAIN, REED.
WHATEVER'S CAUSIN' THESE PULSES...
...THEY'RE COMIN' FASTER AN' GETTIN' MORE INTENSE EVERY TIME.
I'VE BEEN TRYING TO MONITOR THEM...
...WITHOUT MUCH SUCCESS.
DON'T TELL ME YER UNIFORM COMPUTER AIN'T ALL IT'S CRACKED UP TA BE!
GEEZ-LOU-EEZ, REED, SAY IT AIN'T SO!
DIAGNOSTICS INDICATE NOMINAL FUNCTION THROUGHOUT THE INTEGRAL NETWORK.
IT ISN'T THE HARDWARE THAT'S THE PROBLEM, BUT THE PHENOMENON ITSELF.
THE ENERGY WAVES ARE CONTAINED BURSTS OF CHAOS...
...CREATING MOMENTARY DISRUPTIONS IN THE HARMONIC STRUCTURE OF REALITY.
THAT'S HOW YA ONCE DESCRIBED THE GATEWAY TO THE NEGATIVE ZONE.
I'VE MADE THAT CONNECTION MYSELF.
I HAVE TO ASSUME IT'S THE MEANS RONAN IS EMPLOYING TO BREACH THE WATCHER'S DOME.
ANY NOTION OF THE CONSEQUENCES?
DEPENDS ON HOW MUCH FORCE HE EMPLOYS.
EVERY ACTION GIVES BIRTH TO AN EQUAL AND OPPOSITE REACTION -- BASIC PHYSICS.
IN THESE CIRCUMSTANCES, PUSH HARD ENOUGH...THE RESPONSE COULD WELL BE DEVASTATING.
ALL THE MORE REASON THEN, ISN'T IT REED, TO MIX IT UP WITH THE GUY?
THIS IS VERY STRANGE.
ACCORDING TO THESE SEDIMENTARY PATTERNS, THIS SECTION OF TUNNEL IS OLDER THAN IT SHOULD BE.
SOME INTERACTION OF THE CHAOS WAVES WITH THE DOME, OR THE BLUE AREA ITSELF, IS CREATING TEMPORAL ANOMALIES --
-- POCKETS OF WARPED TIME, WHERE PAST AND PRESENT AND FUTURE APPEAR TO CO-EXIST, VIRTUALLY SIMULTANEOUSLY.
LIKE, WHO CARES!
YOU WANT TO GIVE LECTURES, REED, KNOCK YOURSELF OUT!
ME, I'M GOING TO TRY MY BEST TO SAVE MY...
...SISTER!
REED, I THINK YOU BETTER TAKE A LOOK AT THIS.
I GUARANTEE YOU WON'T BELIEVE YOUR EYES.

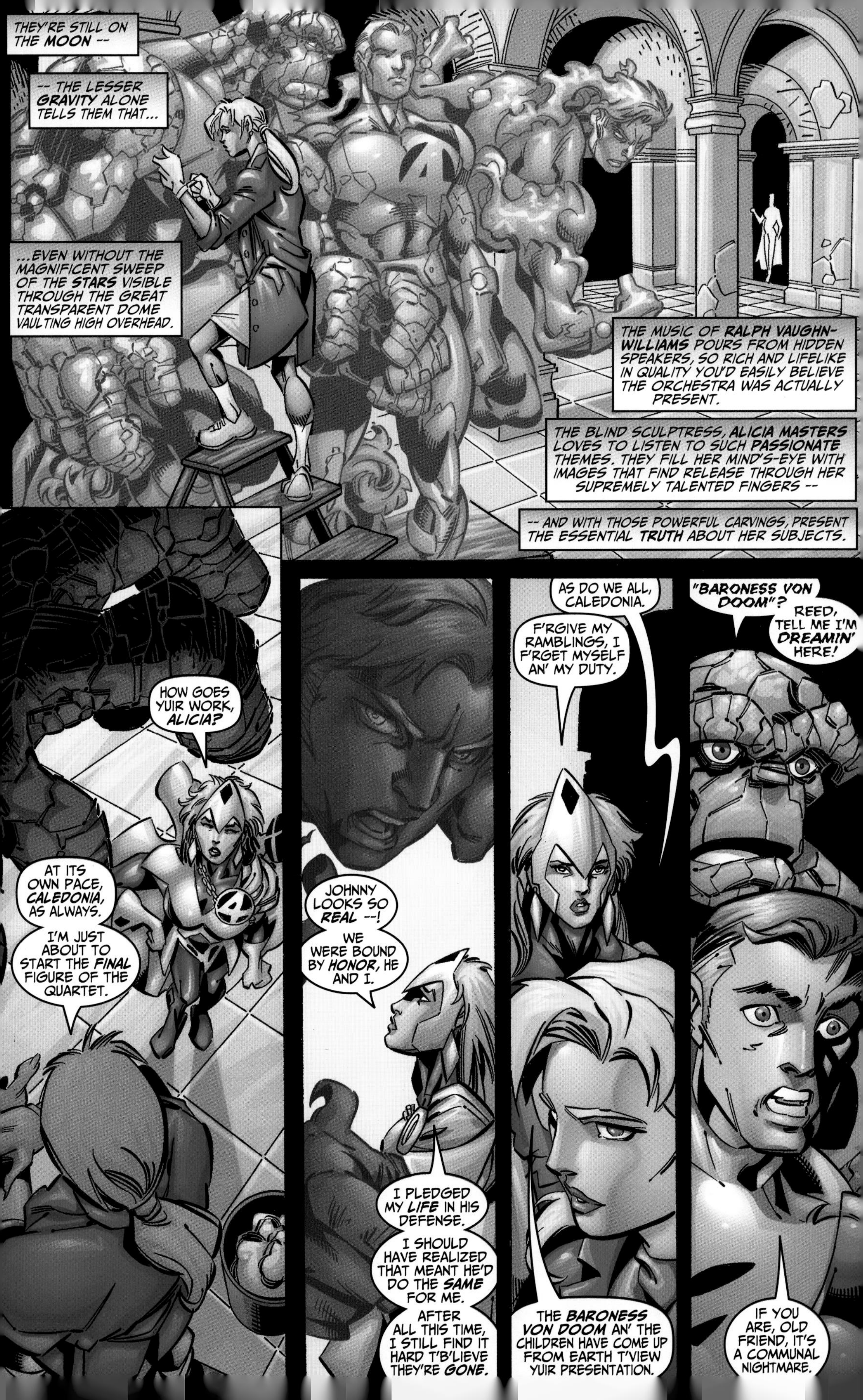
THEY'RE STILL ON THE MOON --
-- THE LESSER GRAVITY ALONE TELLS THEM THAT...
...EVEN WITHOUT THE MAGNIFICENT SWEEP OF THE STARS VISIBLE THROUGH THE GREAT TRANSPARENT DOME VAULTING HIGH OVERHEAD.
THE MUSIC OF RALPH VAUGHN-WILLIAMS POURS FROM HIDDEN SPEAKERS, SO RICH AND LIFELIKE IN QUALITY YOU'D EASILY BELIEVE THE ORCHESTRA WAS ACTUALLY PRESENT.
THE BLIND SCULPTRESS, ALICIA MASTERS LOVES TO LISTEN TO SUCH PASSIONATE THEMES. THEY FILL HER MIND'S-EYE WITH IMAGES THAT FIND RELEASE THROUGH HER SUPREMELY TALENTED FINGERS --
-- AND WITH THOSE POWERFUL CARVINGS, PRESENT THE ESSENTIAL TRUTH ABOUT HER SUBJECTS.
HOW GOES YUIR WORK, ALICIA?
AT ITS OWN PACE, CALEDONIA, AS ALWAYS.
I'M JUST ABOUT TO START THE FINAL FIGURE OF THE QUARTET.
JOHNNY LOOKS SO REAL --!
WE WERE BOUND BY HONOR, HE AND I.
I PLEDGED MY LIFE IN HIS DEFENSE.
I SHOULD HAVE REALIZED THAT MEANT HE'D DO THE SAME FOR ME.
AFTER ALL THIS TIME, I STILL FIND IT HARD T'B'LIEVE THEY'RE GONE.
AS DO WE ALL, CALEDONIA.
F'RGIVE MY RAMBLINGS, I F'RGET MYSELF AN' MY DUTY.
THE BARONESS VON DOOM AN' THE CHILDREN HAVE COME UP FROM EARTH T'VIEW YUIR PRESENTATION.
"BARONESS VON DOOM"?
REED, TELL ME I'M DREAMIN' HERE!
IF YOU ARE, OLD FRIEND, IT'S A COMMUNAL NIGHTMARE.

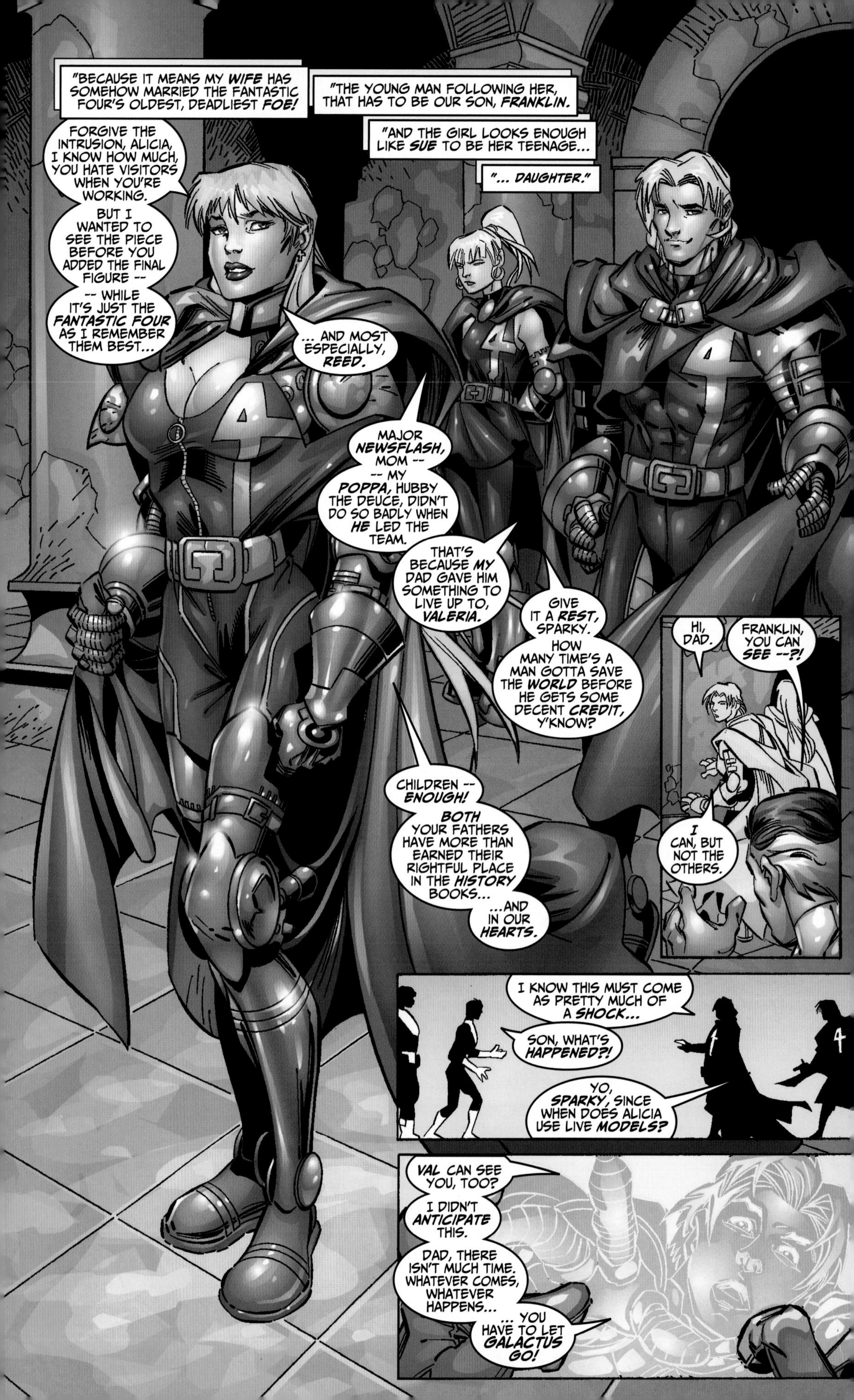

"BECAUSE IT MEANS MY WIFE HAS SOMEHOW MARRIED THE FANTASTIC FOUR'S OLDEST, DEADLIEST FOE!
"THE YOUNG MAN FOLLOWING HER, THAT HAS TO BE OUR SON, FRANKLIN.
"AND THE GIRL LOOKS ENOUGH LIKE SUE TO BE HER TEENAGE...
"... DAUGHTER."
FORGIVE THE INTRUSION, ALICIA, I KNOW HOW MUCH, YOU HATE VISITORS WHEN YOU'RE WORKING.
BUT I WANTED TO SEE THE PIECE BEFORE YOU ADDED THE FINAL FIGURE --
-- WHILE IT'S JUST THE FANTASTIC FOUR AS I REMEMBER THEM BEST...
... AND MOST ESPECIALLY, REED.
MAJOR NEWSFLASH, MOM --
-- MY POPPA, HUBBY THE DEUCE, DIDN'T DO SO BADLY WHEN HE LED THE TEAM.
THAT'S BECAUSE MY DAD GAVE HIM SOMETHING TO LIVE UP TO, VALERIA.
GIVE IT A REST, SPARKY.
HOW MANY TIME'S A MAN GOTTA SAVE THE WORLD BEFORE HE GETS SOME DECENT CREDIT, Y'KNOW?
CHILDREN -- ENOUGH!
BOTH YOUR FATHERS HAVE MORE THAN EARNED THEIR RIGHTFUL PLACE IN THE HISTORY BOOKS...
...AND IN OUR HEARTS.
HI, DAD.
FRANKLIN, YOU CAN SEE --?!
I CAN, BUT NOT THE OTHERS.
I KNOW THIS MUST COME AS PRETTY MUCH OF A SHOCK...
SON, WHAT'S HAPPENED?!
YO, SPARKY, SINCE WHEN DOES ALICIA USE LIVE MODELS?
VAL CAN SEE YOU, TOO?
I DIDN'T ANTICIPATE THIS.
DAD, THERE ISN'T MUCH TIME. WHATEVER COMES, WHATEVER HAPPENS...
... YOU HAVE TO LET GALACTUS GO!

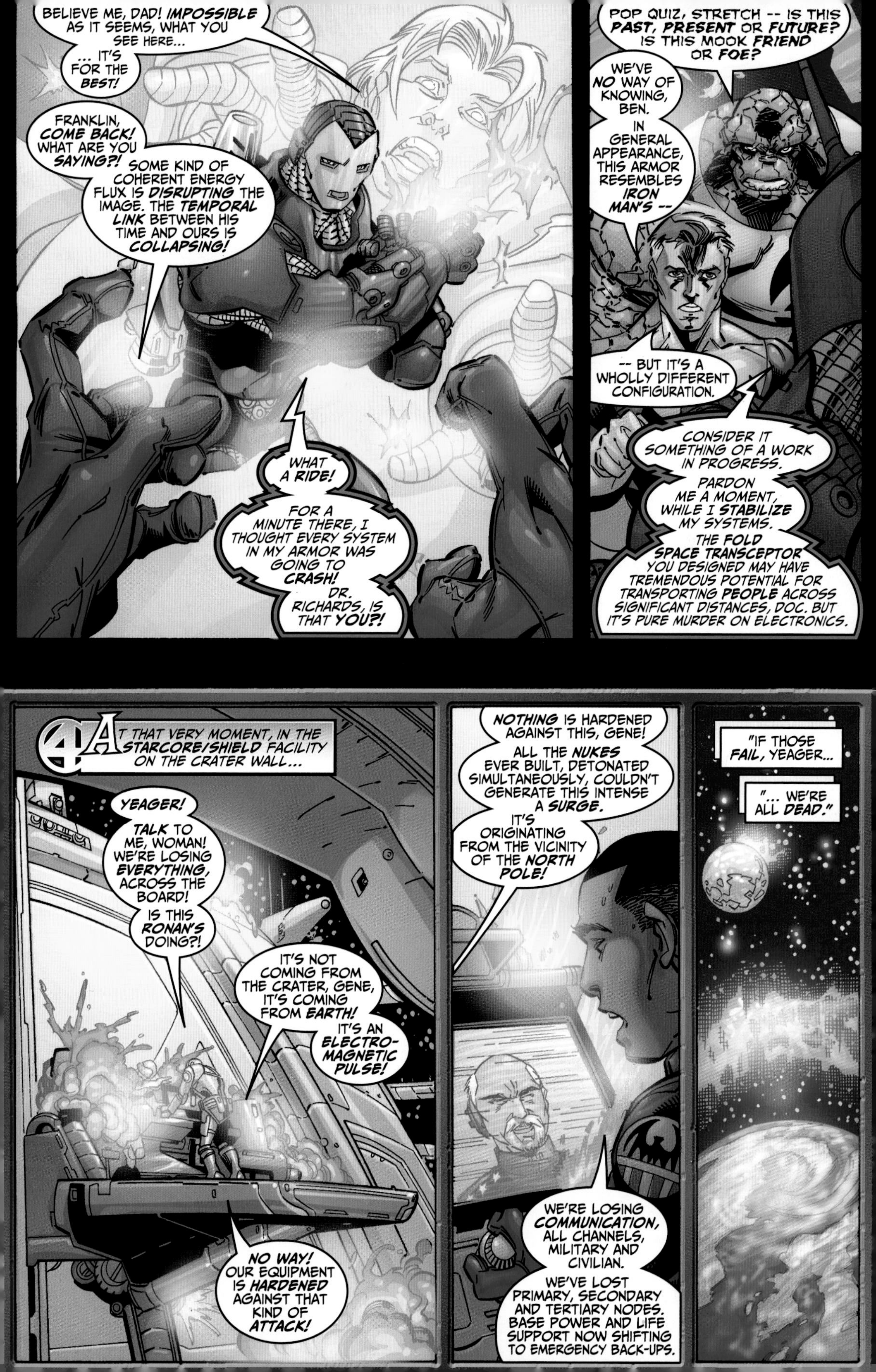
BELIEVE ME, DAD! IMPOSSIBLE AS IT SEEMS, WHAT YOU SEE HERE...
... IT'S FOR THE BEST!
FRANKLIN, COME BACK! WHAT ARE YOU SAYING?!
SOME KIND OF COHERENT ENERGY FLUX IS DISRUPTING THE IMAGE. THE TEMPORAL LINK BETWEEN HIS TIME AND OURS IS COLLAPSING!
WHAT A RIDE!
FOR A MINUTE THERE, I THOUGHT EVERY SYSTEM IN MY ARMOR WAS GOING TO CRASH!
DR. RICHARDS, IS THAT YOU?!
POP QUIZ, STRETCH -- IS THIS PAST, PRESENT OR FUTURE? IS THIS MOOK FRIEND OR FOE?
WE'VE NO WAY OF KNOWING, BEN.
IN GENERAL APPEARANCE, THIS ARMOR RESEMBLES IRON MAN'S --
-- BUT IT'S A WHOLLY DIFFERENT CONFIGURATION.
CONSIDER IT SOMETHING OF A WORK IN PROGRESS.
PARDON ME A MOMENT, WHILE I STABILIZE MY SYSTEMS.
THE FOLD SPACE TRANSCEPTOR YOU DESIGNED MAY HAVE TREMENDOUS POTENTIAL FOR TRANSPORTING PEOPLE ACROSS SIGNIFICANT DISTANCES, DOC. BUT IT'S PURE MURDER ON ELECTRONICS.
AT THAT VERY MOMENT, IN THE STARCORE/SHIELD FACILITY ON THE CRATER WALL...
YEAGER!
TALK TO ME, WOMAN! WE'RE LOSING EVERYTHING, ACROSS THE BOARD!
IS THIS RONAN'S DOING?!
IT'S NOT COMING FROM THE CRATER, GENE, IT'S COMING FROM EARTH!
IT'S AN ELECTRO-MAGNETIC PULSE!
NO WAY! OUR EQUIPMENT IS HARDENED AGAINST THAT KIND OF ATTACK!
NOTHING IS HARDENED AGAINST THIS, GENE!
ALL THE NUKES EVER BUILT, DETONATED SIMULTANEOUSLY, COULDN'T GENERATE THIS INTENSE A SURGE.
IT'S ORIGINATING FROM THE VICINITY OF THE NORTH POLE!
WE'RE LOSING COMMUNICATION, ALL CHANNELS, MILITARY AND CIVILIAN.
WE'VE LOST PRIMARY, SECONDARY AND TERTIARY NODES. BASE POWER AND LIFE SUPPORT NOW SHIFTING TO EMERGENCY BACK-UPS.
"IF THOSE FAIL, YEAGER...
"... WE'RE ALL DEAD."

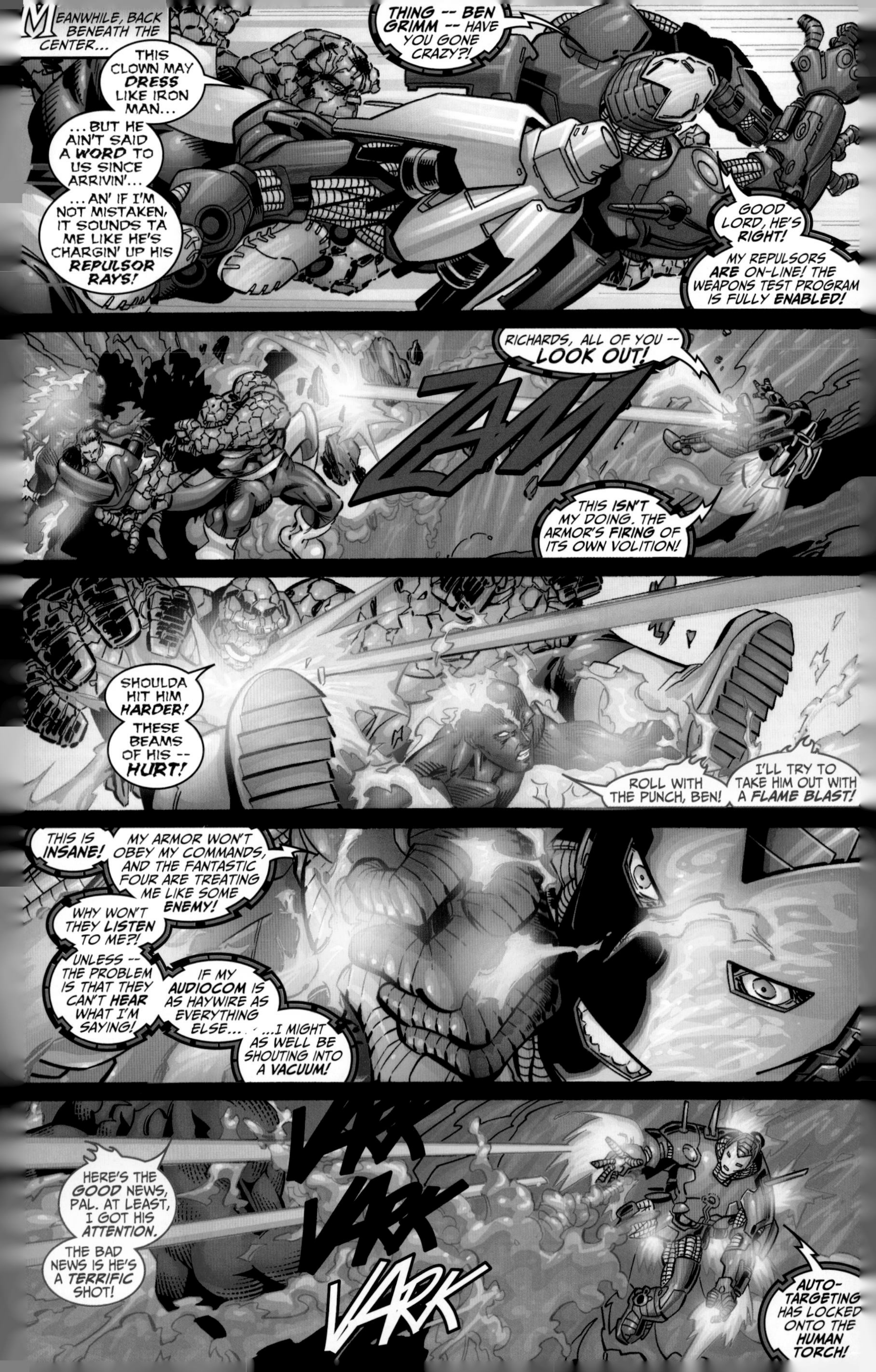
MEANWHILE, BACK BENEATH THE CENTER...
THING -- BEN GRIMM -- HAVE YOU GONE CRAZY?!
THIS CLOWN MAY DRESS LIKE IRON MAN...
...BUT HE AIN'T SAID A WORD TO US SINCE ARRIVIN'...
...AN' IF I'M NOT MISTAKEN, IT SOUNDS TA ME LIKE HE'S CHARGIN' UP HIS REPULSOR RAYS!
GOOD LORD, HE'S RIGHT!
MY REPULSORS ARE ON-LINE! THE WEAPONS TEST PROGRAM IS FULLY ENABLED!
RICHARDS, ALL OF YOU -- LOOK OUT!
ZAM
THIS ISN'T MY DOING. THE ARMOR'S FIRING OF ITS OWN VOLITION!
SHOULDA HIT HIM HARDER!
THESE BEAMS OF HIS -- HURT!
ROLL WITH THE PUNCH, BEN!
I'LL TRY TO TAKE HIM OUT WITH A FLAME BLAST!
THIS IS INSANE!
MY ARMOR WON'T OBEY MY COMMANDS, AND THE FANTASTIC FOUR ARE TREATING ME LIKE SOME ENEMY!
WHY WON'T THEY LISTEN TO ME?!
UNLESS -- THE PROBLEM IS THAT THEY CAN'T HEAR WHAT I'M SAYING!
IF MY AUDIOCOM IS AS HAYWIRE AS EVERYTHING ELSE...
...I MIGHT AS WELL BE SHOUTING INTO A VACUUM!
VARK
VARK
VARK
HERE'S THE GOOD NEWS, PAL. AT LEAST, I GOT HIS ATTENTION.
THE BAD NEWS IS HE'S A TERRIFIC SHOT!
AUTO-TARGETING HAS LOCKED ONTO THE HUMAN TORCH!

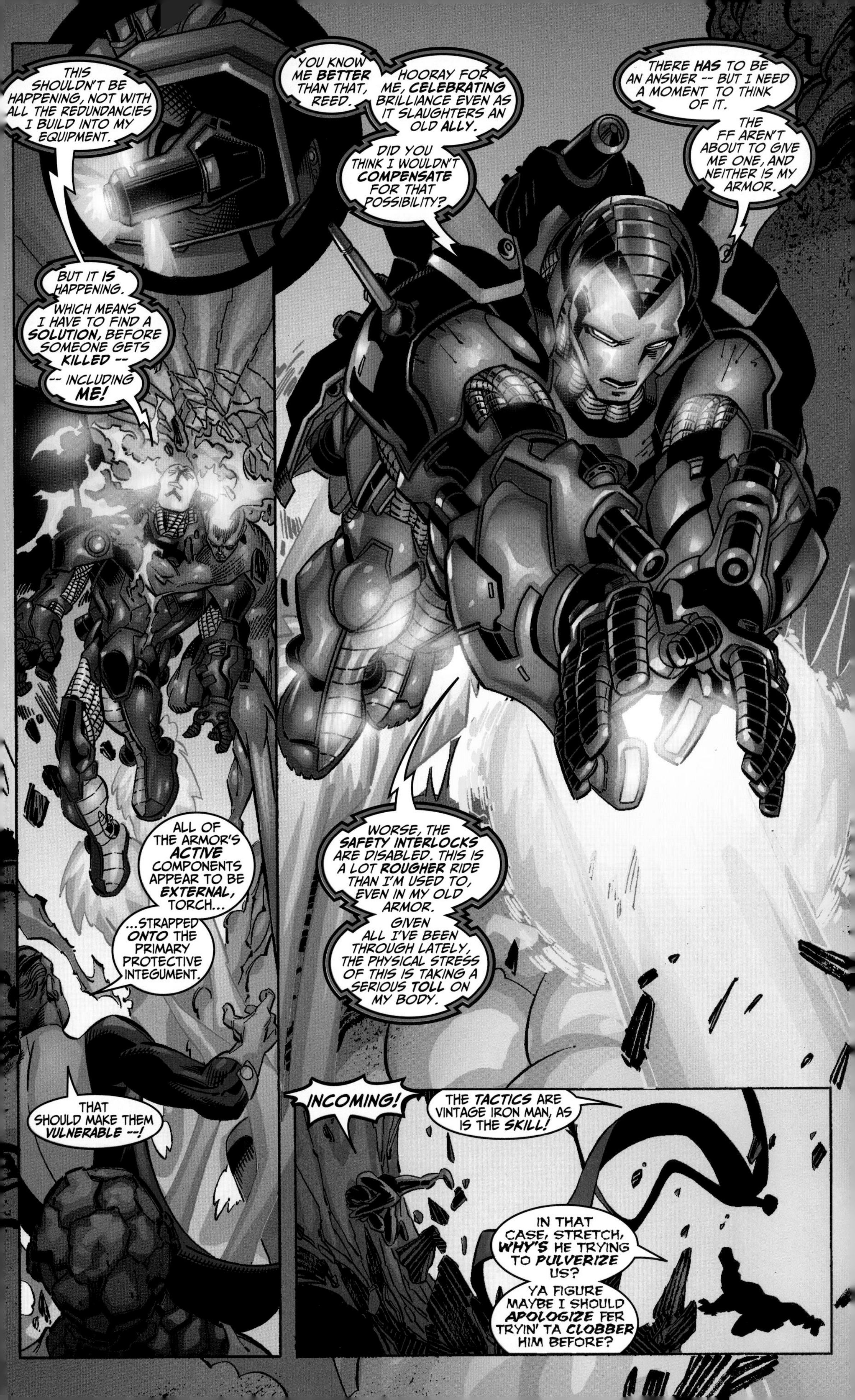

THIS SHOULDN'T BE HAPPENING, NOT WITH ALL THE REDUNDANCIES I BUILD INTO MY EQUIPMENT.
BUT IT IS HAPPENING.
WHICH MEANS I HAVE TO FIND A SOLUTION, BEFORE SOMEONE GETS KILLED --
-- INCLUDING ME!
YOU KNOW ME BETTER THAN THAT, REED.
HOORAY FOR ME, CELEBRATING BRILLIANCE EVEN AS IT SLAUGHTERS AN OLD ALLY.
DID YOU THINK I WOULDN'T COMPENSATE FOR THAT POSSIBILITY?
THERE HAS TO BE AN ANSWER -- BUT I NEED A MOMENT TO THINK OF IT.
THE FF AREN'T ABOUT TO GIVE ME ONE, AND NEITHER IS MY ARMOR.
ALL OF THE ARMOR'S ACTIVE COMPONENTS APPEAR TO BE EXTERNAL, TORCH...
...STRAPPED ONTO THE PRIMARY PROTECTIVE INTEGUMENT.
WORSE, THE SAFETY INTERLOCKS ARE DISABLED. THIS IS A LOT ROUGHER RIDE THAN I'M USED TO, EVEN IN MY OLD ARMOR.
GIVEN ALL I'VE BEEN THROUGH LATELY, THE PHYSICAL STRESS OF THIS IS TAKING A SERIOUS TOLL ON MY BODY.
THAT SHOULD MAKE THEM VULNERABLE --!
INCOMING!
THE TACTICS ARE VINTAGE IRON MAN, AS IS THE SKILL!
IN THAT CASE, STRETCH, WHY'S HE TRYING TO PULVERIZE US?
YA FIGURE MAYBE I SHOULD APOLOGIZE FER TRYIN' TA CLOBBER HIM BEFORE?

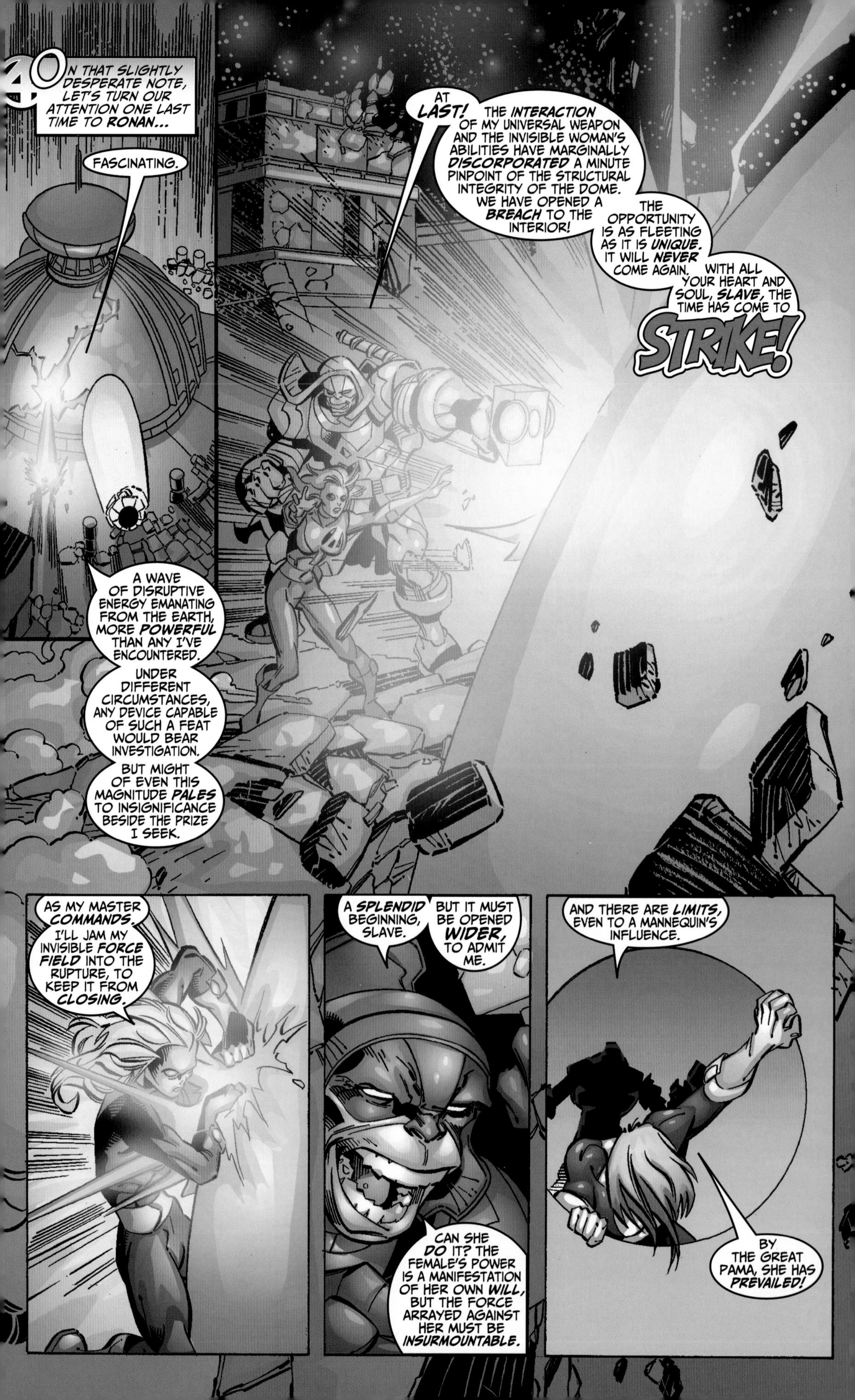
ON THAT SLIGHTLY DESPERATE NOTE, LET'S TURN OUR ATTENTION ONE LAST TIME TO RONAN...
FASCINATING.
A WAVE OF DISRUPTIVE ENERGY EMANATING FROM THE EARTH, MORE POWERFUL THAN ANY I'VE ENCOUNTERED.
UNDER DIFFERENT CIRCUMSTANCES, ANY DEVICE CAPABLE OF SUCH A FEAT WOULD BEAR INVESTIGATION.
BUT MIGHT OF EVEN THIS MAGNITUDE PALES TO INSIGNIFICANCE BESIDE THE PRIZE I SEEK.
AT LAST!
THE INTERACTION OF MY UNIVERSAL WEAPON AND THE INVISIBLE WOMAN'S ABILITIES HAVE MARGINALLY DISCORPORATED A MINUTE PINPOINT OF THE STRUCTURAL INTEGRITY OF THE DOME. WE HAVE OPENED A BREACH TO THE INTERIOR!
THE OPPORTUNITY IS AS FLEETING AS IT IS UNIQUE. IT WILL NEVER COME AGAIN.
WITH ALL YOUR HEART AND SOUL, SLAVE, THE TIME HAS COME TO
STRIKE!
AS MY MASTER COMMANDS.
I'LL JAM MY INVISIBLE FORCE FIELD INTO THE RUPTURE, TO KEEP IT FROM CLOSING.
A SPLENDID BEGINNING, SLAVE.
BUT IT MUST BE OPENED WIDER, TO ADMIT ME.
CAN SHE DO IT? THE FEMALE'S POWER IS A MANIFESTATION OF HER OWN WILL, BUT THE FORCE ARRAYED AGAINST HER MUST BE INSURMOUNTABLE.
AND THERE ARE LIMITS, EVEN TO A MANNEQUIN'S INFLUENCE.
BY THE GREAT PAMA, SHE HAS PREVAILED!

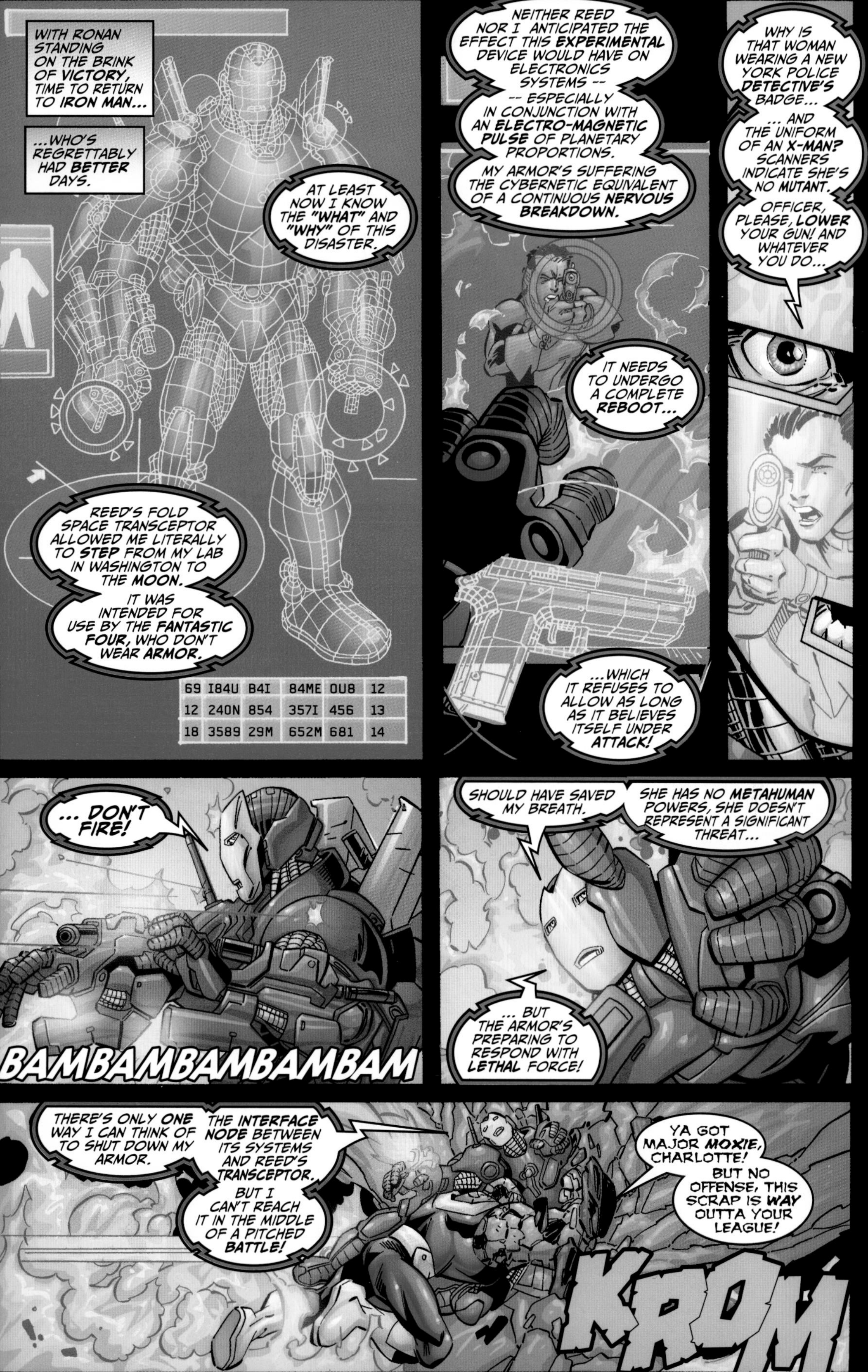

WITH RONAN STANDING ON THE BRINK OF VICTORY, TIME TO RETURN TO IRON MAN...
...WHO'S REGRETTABLY HAD BETTER DAYS.
AT LEAST NOW I KNOW THE "WHAT" AND "WHY" OF THIS DISASTER.
REED'S FOLD SPACE TRANSCEPTOR ALLOWED ME LITERALLY TO STEP FROM MY LAB IN WASHINGTON TO THE MOON.
IT WAS INTENDED FOR USE BY THE FANTASTIC FOUR, WHO DON'T WEAR ARMOR.
69 I84U B4I 84ME OU8 12
12 240N 854 357I 456 13
18 3589 29M 652M 681 14
NEITHER REED NOR I ANTICIPATED THE EFFECT THIS EXPERIMENTAL DEVICE WOULD HAVE ON ELECTRONICS SYSTEMS --
-- ESPECIALLY IN CONJUNCTION WITH AN ELECTRO-MAGNETIC PULSE OF PLANETARY PROPORTIONS.
MY ARMOR'S SUFFERING THE CYBERNETIC EQUIVALENT OF A CONTINUOUS NERVOUS BREAKDOWN.
IT NEEDS TO UNDERGO A COMPLETE REBOOT...
...WHICH IT REFUSES TO ALLOW AS LONG AS IT BELIEVES ITSELF UNDER ATTACK!
WHY IS THAT WOMAN WEARING A NEW YORK POLICE DETECTIVE'S BADGE...
... AND THE UNIFORM OF AN X-MAN? SCANNERS INDICATE SHE'S NO MUTANT.
OFFICER, PLEASE, LOWER YOUR GUN! AND WHATEVER YOU DO...
... DON'T FIRE!
BAMBAMBAMBAMBAM
SHOULD HAVE SAVED MY BREATH.
SHE HAS NO METAHUMAN POWERS, SHE DOESN'T REPRESENT A SIGNIFICANT THREAT...
... BUT THE ARMOR'S PREPARING TO RESPOND WITH LETHAL FORCE!
THERE'S ONLY ONE WAY I CAN THINK OF TO SHUT DOWN MY ARMOR.
THE INTERFACE NODE BETWEEN ITS SYSTEMS AND REED'S TRANSCEPTOR.
BUT I CAN'T REACH IT IN THE MIDDLE OF A PITCHED BATTLE!
YA GOT MAJOR MOXIE, CHARLOTTE!
BUT NO OFFENSE, THIS SCRAP IS WAY OUTTA YOUR LEAGUE!
KROM

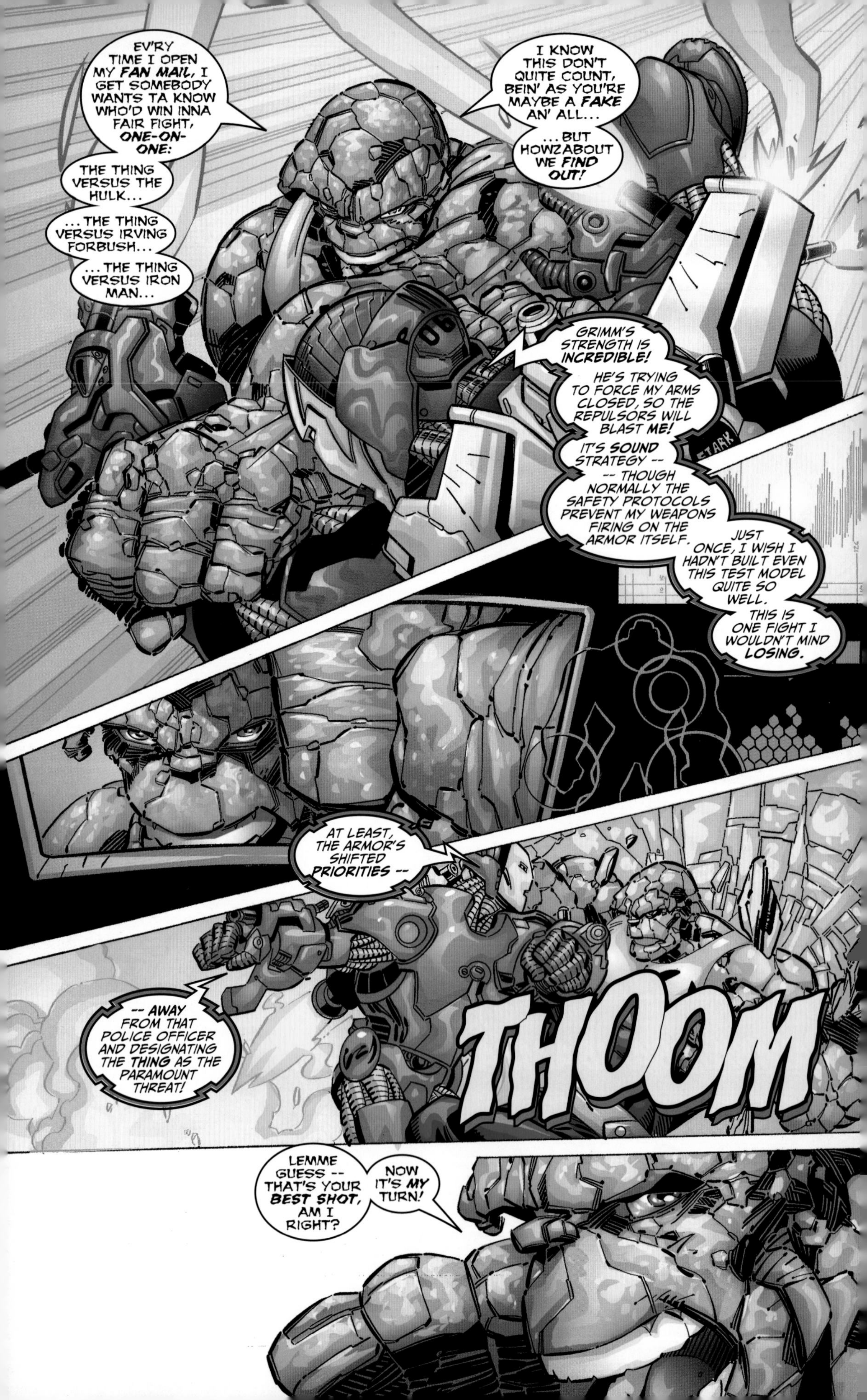
EV'RY TIME I OPEN MY **FAN MAIL,** I GET SOMEBODY WANTS TA KNOW WHO'D WIN INNA FAIR FIGHT, **ONE-ON-ONE:**
THE THING VERSUS THE HULK...
...THE THING VERSUS IRVING FORBUSH...
...THE THING VERSUS IRON MAN...
I KNOW THIS DON'T QUITE COUNT, BEIN' AS YOU'RE MAYBE A **FAKE** AN' ALL...
...BUT HOWZABOUT WE **FIND OUT!**
GRIMM'S STRENGTH IS **INCREDIBLE!**
HE'S TRYING TO FORCE MY ARMS CLOSED, SO THE REPULSORS WILL BLAST **ME!**
IT'S **SOUND** STRATEGY --
-- THOUGH NORMALLY THE SAFETY PROTOCOLS PREVENT MY WEAPONS FIRING ON THE ARMOR ITSELF.
JUST ONCE, I WISH I HADN'T BUILT EVEN THIS TEST MODEL QUITE SO WELL.
THIS IS ONE FIGHT I WOULDN'T MIND **LOSING.**
AT LEAST, THE ARMOR'S SHIFTED **PRIORITIES --**
-- **AWAY** FROM THAT POLICE OFFICER AND DESIGNATING THE **THING** AS THE PARAMOUNT THREAT!
THOOM
LEMME GUESS -- THAT'S YOUR **BEST SHOT,** AM I RIGHT?
NOW IT'S **MY** TURN!

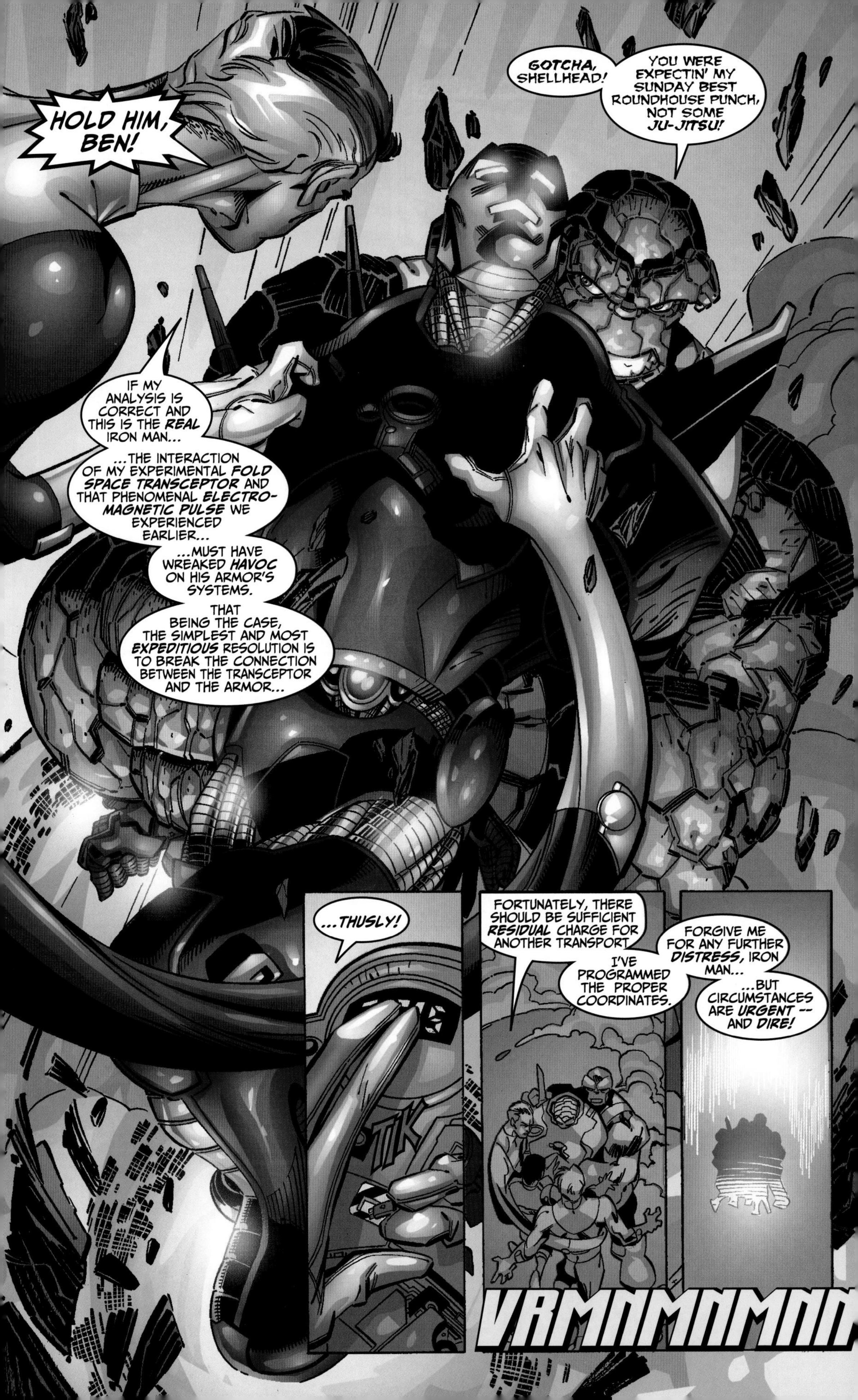

HOLD HIM, BEN!
GOTCHA, SHELLHEAD!
YOU WERE EXPECTIN' MY SUNDAY BEST ROUNDHOUSE PUNCH, NOT SOME JU-JITSU!
IF MY ANALYSIS IS CORRECT AND THIS IS THE REAL IRON MAN...
...THE INTERACTION OF MY EXPERIMENTAL FOLD SPACE TRANSCEPTOR AND THAT PHENOMENAL ELECTRO-MAGNETIC PULSE WE EXPERIENCED EARLIER...
...MUST HAVE WREAKED HAVOC ON HIS ARMOR'S SYSTEMS.
THAT BEING THE CASE, THE SIMPLEST AND MOST EXPEDITIOUS RESOLUTION IS TO BREAK THE CONNECTION BETWEEN THE TRANSCEPTOR AND THE ARMOR...
...THUSLY!
FORTUNATELY, THERE SHOULD BE SUFFICIENT RESIDUAL CHARGE FOR ANOTHER TRANSPORT.
I'VE PROGRAMMED THE PROPER COORDINATES.
FORGIVE ME FOR ANY FURTHER DISTRESS, IRON MAN...
...BUT CIRCUMSTANCES ARE URGENT -- AND DIRE!
VRMNMNMNN

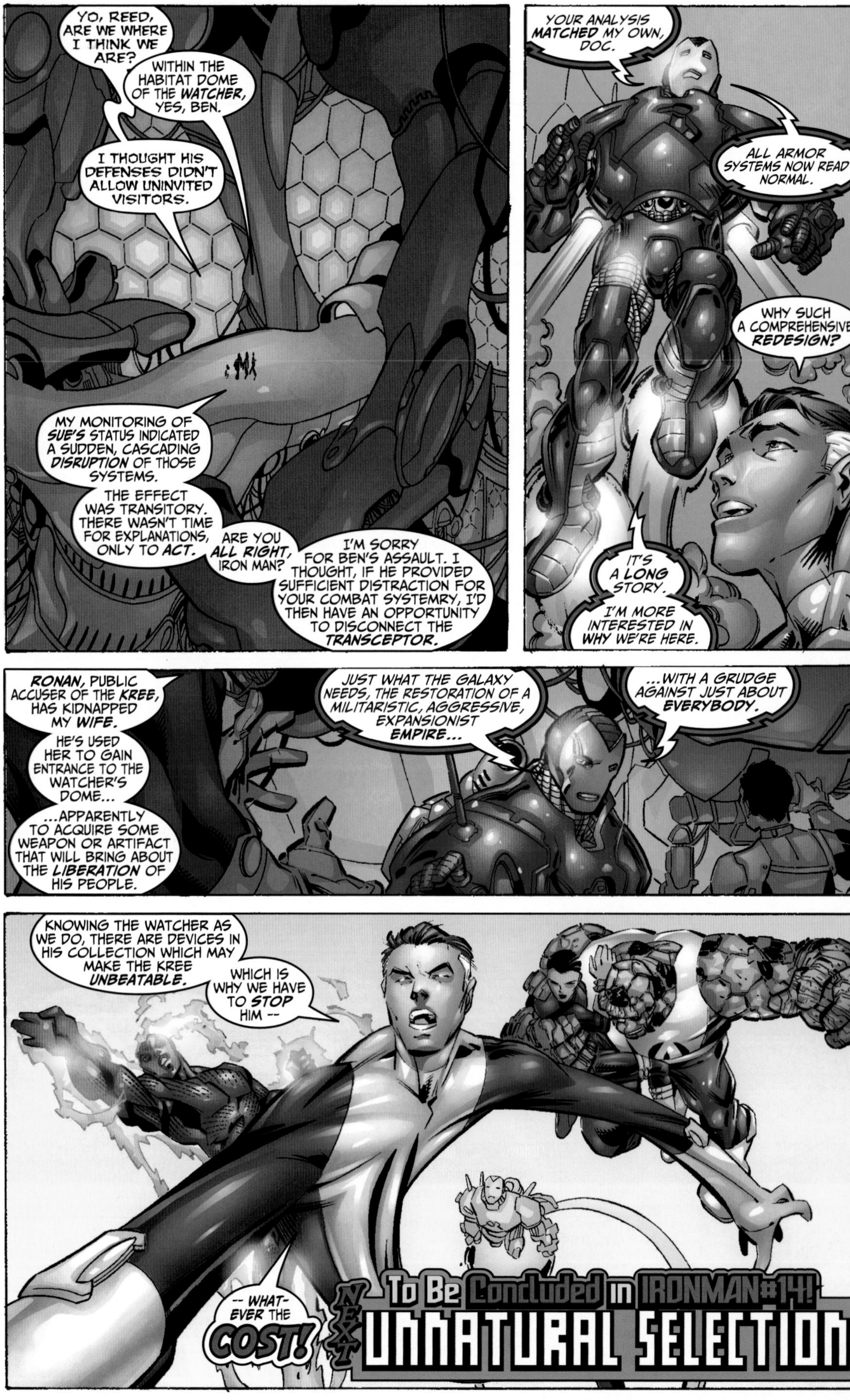
YO, REED, ARE WE WHERE I THINK WE ARE?
WITHIN THE HABITAT DOME OF THE WATCHER, YES, BEN.
I THOUGHT HIS DEFENSES DIDN'T ALLOW UNINVITED VISITORS.
MY MONITORING OF SUE'S STATUS INDICATED A SUDDEN, CASCADING DISRUPTION OF THOSE SYSTEMS.
THE EFFECT WAS TRANSITORY. THERE WASN'T TIME FOR EXPLANATIONS, ONLY TO ACT.
ARE YOU ALL RIGHT, IRON MAN?
I'M SORRY FOR BEN'S ASSAULT. I THOUGHT, IF HE PROVIDED SUFFICIENT DISTRACTION FOR YOUR COMBAT SYSTEMRY, I'D THEN HAVE AN OPPORTUNITY TO DISCONNECT THE TRANSCEPTOR.
YOUR ANALYSIS MATCHED MY OWN, DOC.
ALL ARMOR SYSTEMS NOW READ NORMAL.
WHY SUCH A COMPREHENSIVE REDESIGN?
IT'S A LONG STORY.
I'M MORE INTERESTED IN WHY WE'RE HERE.
RONAN, PUBLIC ACCUSER OF THE KREE, HAS KIDNAPPED MY WIFE.
HE'S USED HER TO GAIN ENTRANCE TO THE WATCHER'S DOME...
...APPARENTLY TO ACQUIRE SOME WEAPON OR ARTIFACT THAT WILL BRING ABOUT THE LIBERATION OF HIS PEOPLE.
JUST WHAT THE GALAXY NEEDS, THE RESTORATION OF A MILITARISTIC, AGGRESSIVE, EXPANSIONIST EMPIRE...
...WITH A GRUDGE AGAINST JUST ABOUT EVERYBODY.
KNOWING THE WATCHER AS WE DO, THERE ARE DEVICES IN HIS COLLECTION WHICH MAY MAKE THE KREE UNBEATABLE.
WHICH IS WHY WE HAVE TO STOP HIM --
-- WHATEVER THE COST!
To Be Concluded in IRONMAN #14!
NEXT
UNNATURAL SELECTION

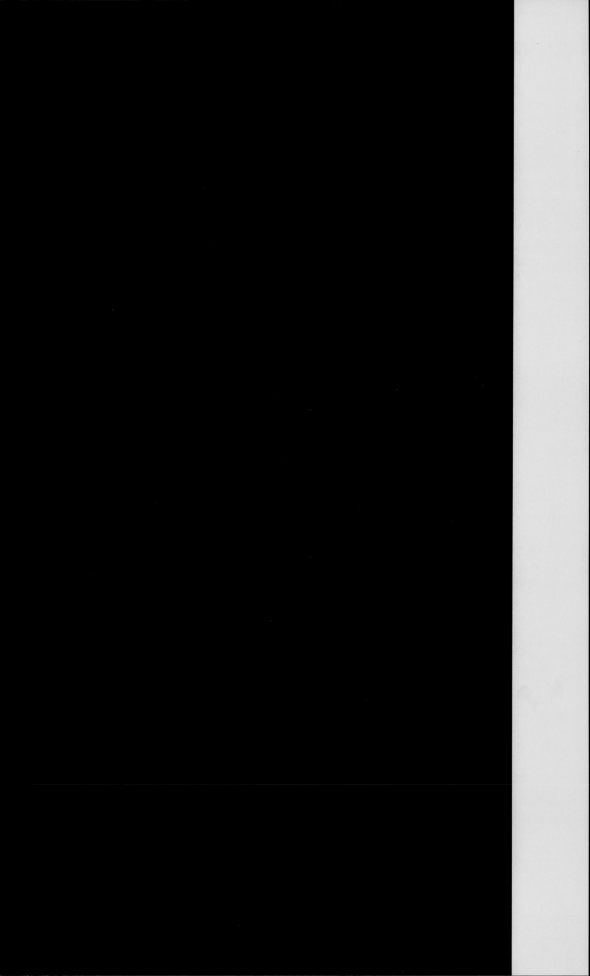

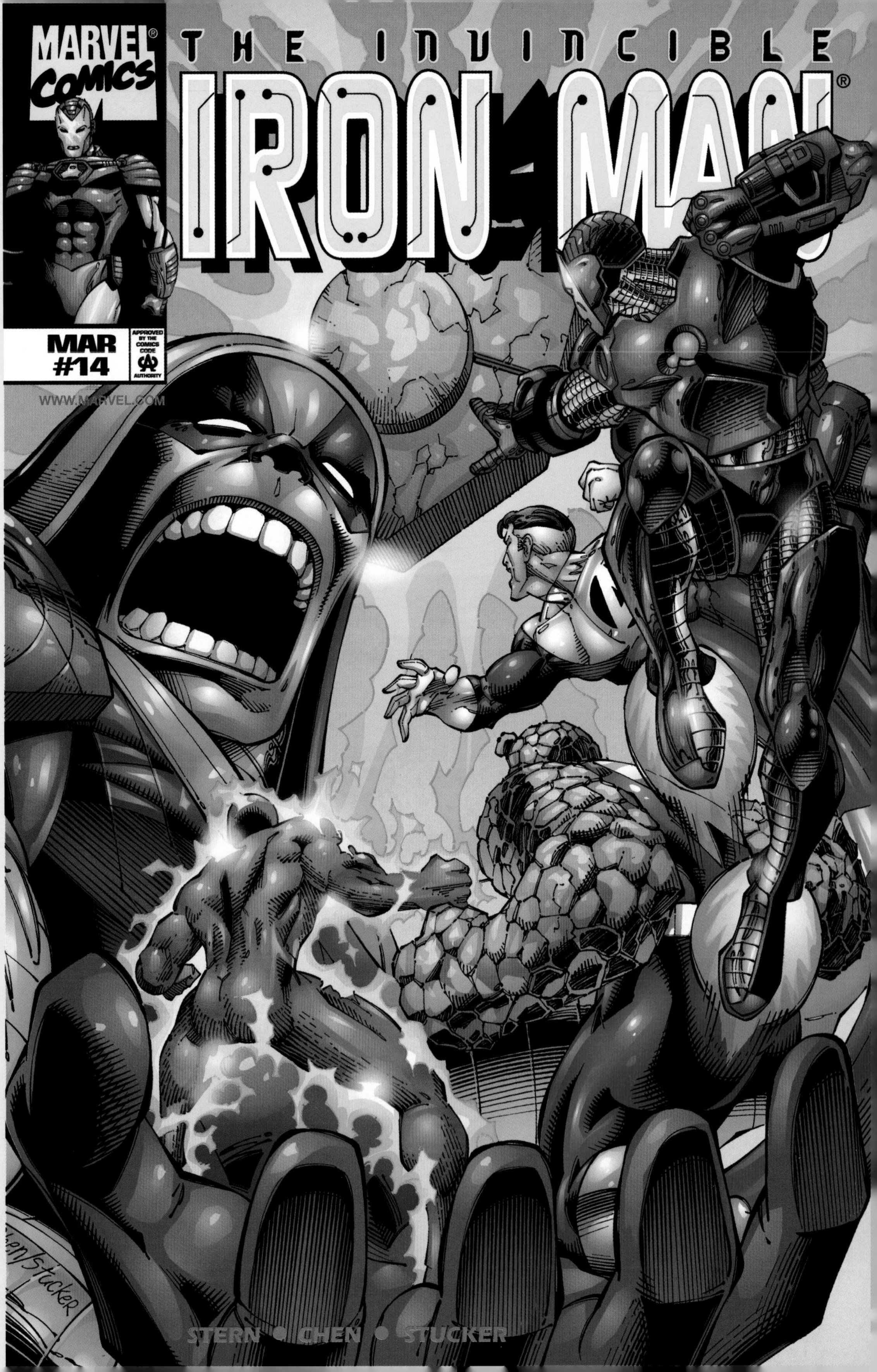
MARVEL COMICS
THE INVINCIBLE
IRON MAN
MAR
#14
APPROVED BY THE COMICS CODE AUTHORITY
WWW.MARVEL.COM
STERN • CHEN • STUCKER

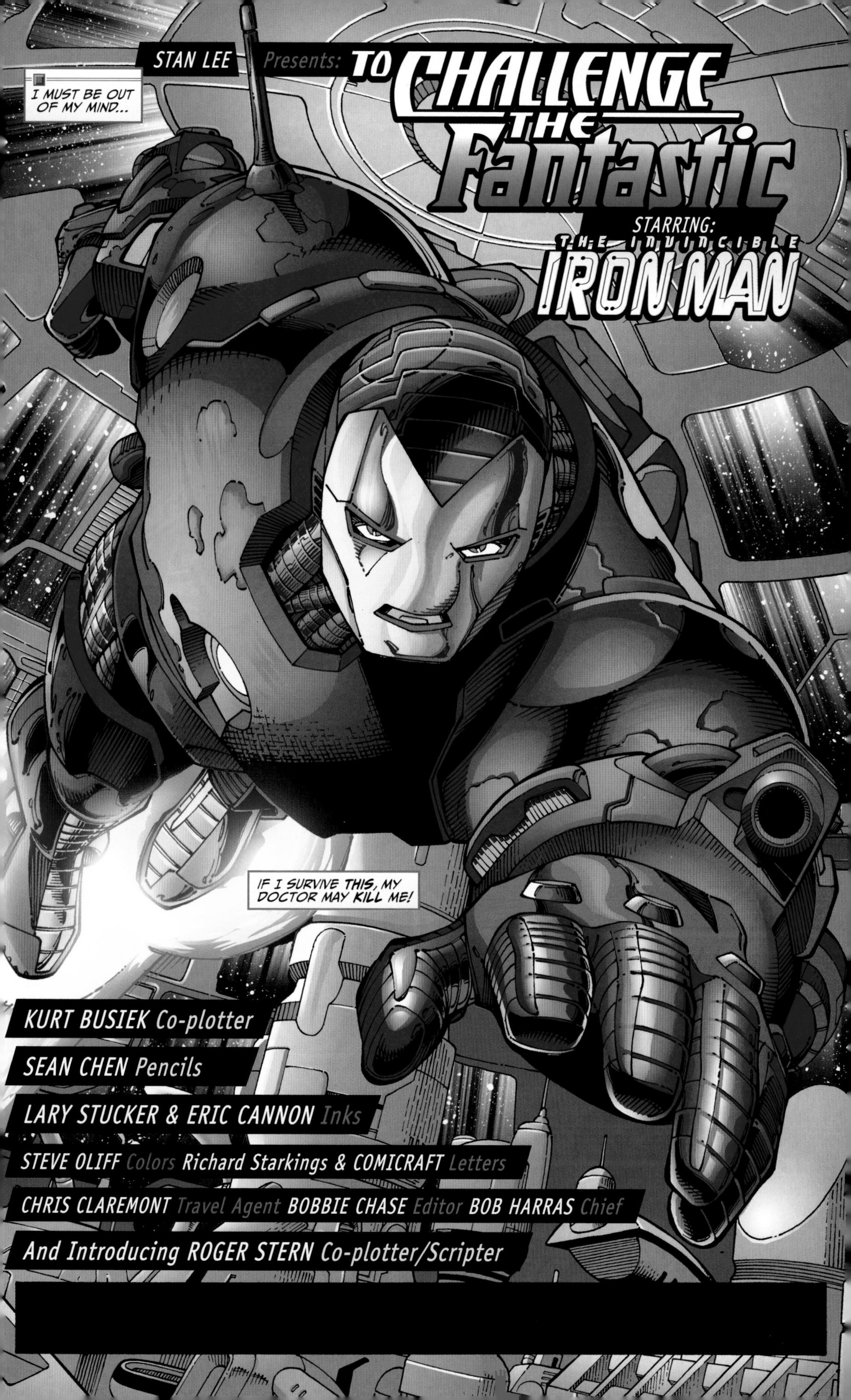
STAN LEE Presents: TO CHALLENGE THE Fantastic
I MUST BE OUT OF MY MIND...
STARRING: THE INVINCIBLE IRON MAN
IF I SURVIVE THIS, MY DOCTOR MAY KILL ME!
KURT BUSIEK Co-plotter
SEAN CHEN Pencils
LARY STUCKER & ERIC CANNON Inks
STEVE OLIFF Colors Richard Starkings & COMICRAFT Letters
CHRIS CLAREMONT Travel Agent BOBBIE CHASE Editor BOB HARRAS Chief
And Introducing ROGER STERN Co-plotter/Scripter
[redacted]

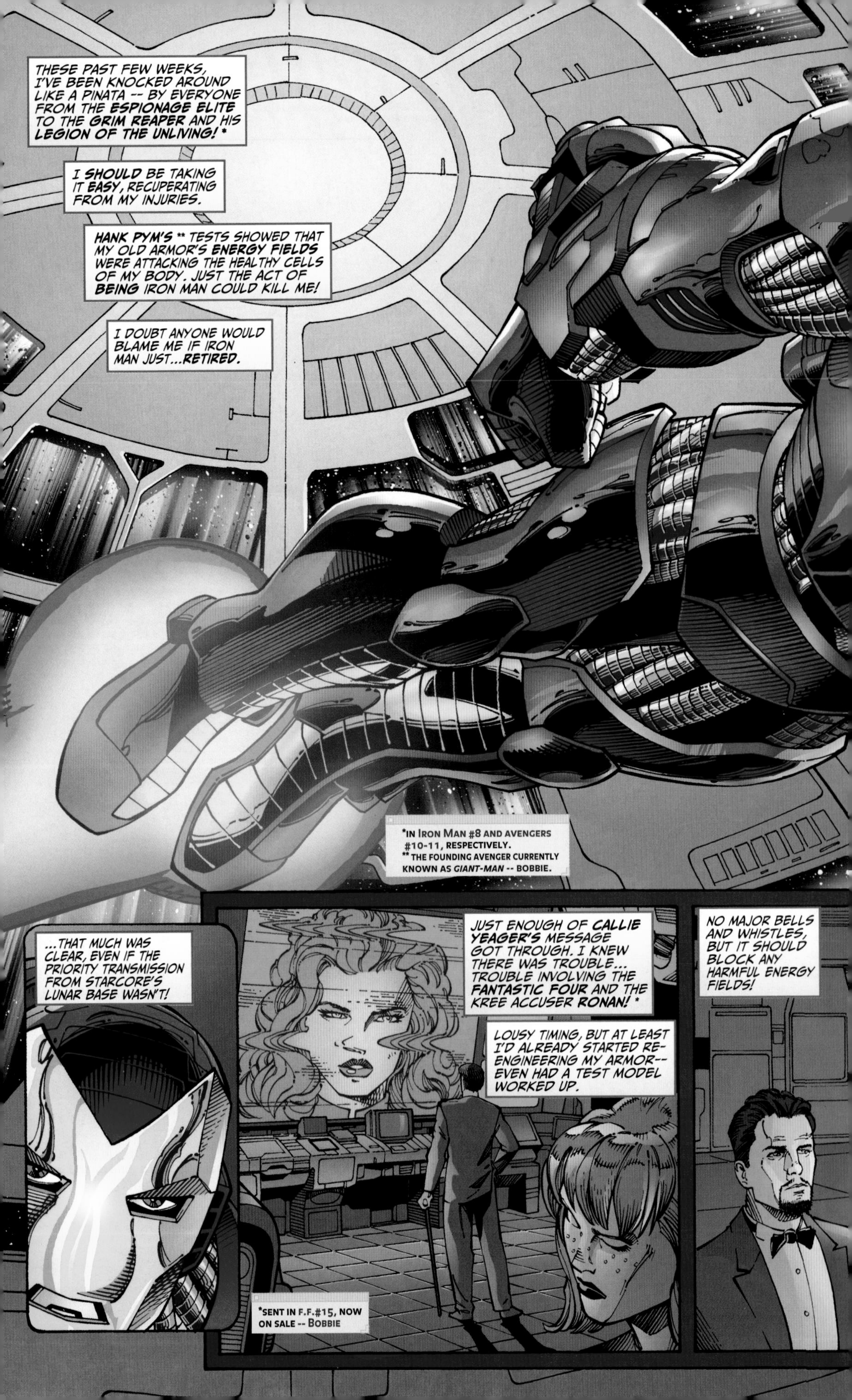
THESE PAST FEW WEEKS, I'VE BEEN KNOCKED AROUND LIKE A PINATA -- BY EVERYONE FROM THE ESPIONAGE ELITE TO THE GRIM REAPER AND HIS LEGION OF THE UNLIVING! *
I SHOULD BE TAKING IT EASY, RECUPERATING FROM MY INJURIES.
HANK PYM'S ** TESTS SHOWED THAT MY OLD ARMOR'S ENERGY FIELDS WERE ATTACKING THE HEALTHY CELLS OF MY BODY. JUST THE ACT OF BEING IRON MAN COULD KILL ME!
I DOUBT ANYONE WOULD BLAME ME IF IRON MAN JUST...RETIRED.
*IN IRON MAN #8 AND AVENGERS #10-11, RESPECTIVELY.
** THE FOUNDING AVENGER CURRENTLY KNOWN AS GIANT-MAN -- BOBBIE.
...THAT MUCH WAS CLEAR, EVEN IF THE PRIORITY TRANSMISSION FROM STARCORE'S LUNAR BASE WASN'T!
JUST ENOUGH OF CALLIE YEAGER'S MESSAGE GOT THROUGH. I KNEW THERE WAS TROUBLE... TROUBLE INVOLVING THE FANTASTIC FOUR AND THE KREE ACCUSER RONAN! *
LOUSY TIMING, BUT AT LEAST I'D ALREADY STARTED RE-ENGINEERING MY ARMOR-- EVEN HAD A TEST MODEL WORKED UP.
*SENT IN F.F.#15, NOW ON SALE -- BOBBIE
NO MAJOR BELLS AND WHISTLES, BUT IT SHOULD BLOCK ANY HARMFUL ENERGY FIELDS!

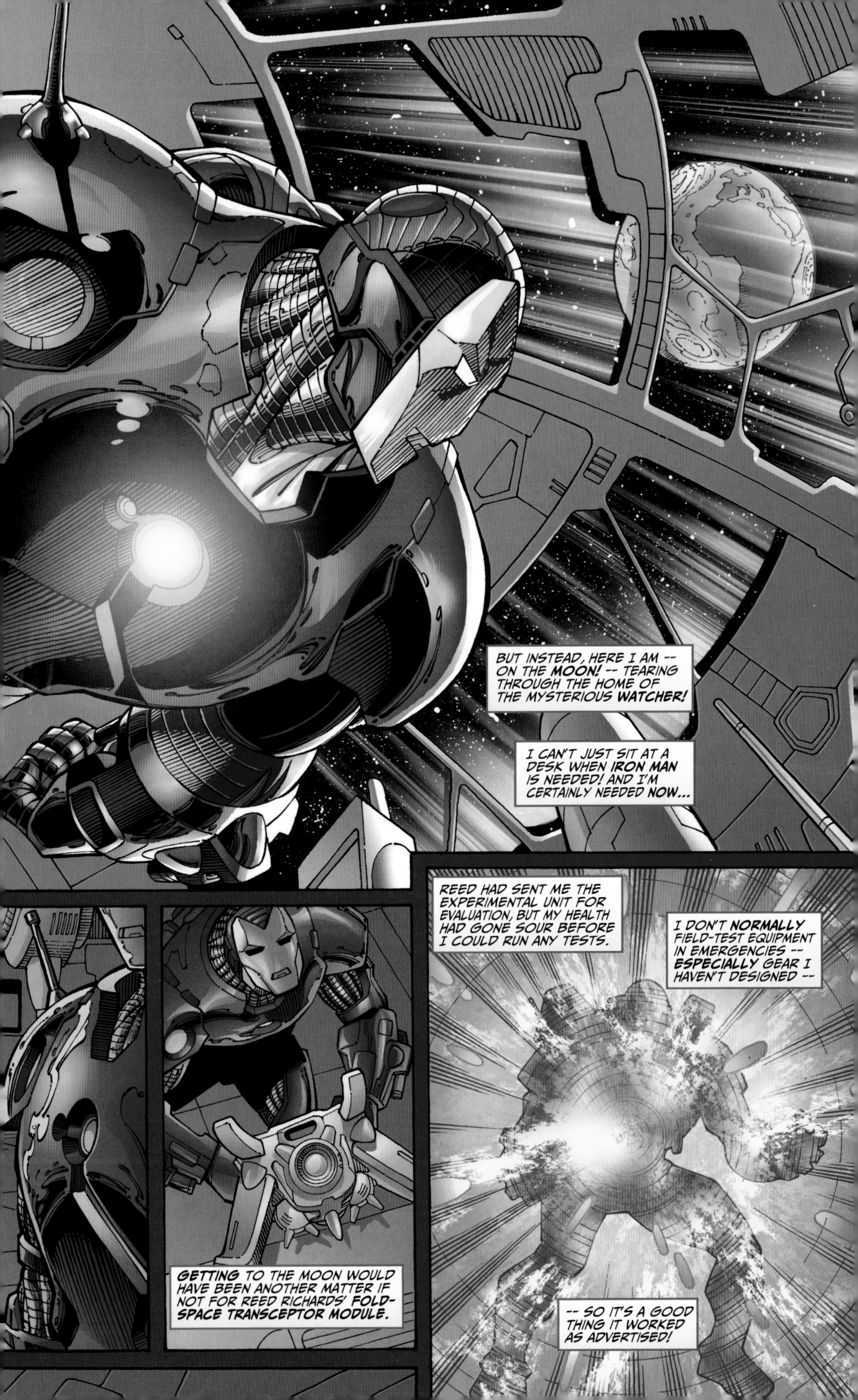
BUT INSTEAD, HERE I AM -- ON THE MOON! -- TEARING THROUGH THE HOME OF THE MYSTERIOUS WATCHER!
I CAN'T JUST SIT AT A DESK WHEN IRON MAN IS NEEDED! AND I'M CERTAINLY NEEDED NOW...
GETTING TO THE MOON WOULD HAVE BEEN ANOTHER MATTER IF NOT FOR REED RICHARDS' FOLD-SPACE TRANSCEPTOR MODULE.
REED HAD SENT ME THE EXPERIMENTAL UNIT FOR EVALUATION, BUT MY HEALTH HAD GONE SOUR BEFORE I COULD RUN ANY TESTS.
I DON'T NORMALLY FIELD-TEST EQUIPMENT IN EMERGENCIES -- ESPECIALLY GEAR I HAVEN'T DESIGNED --
-- SO IT'S A GOOD THING IT WORKED AS ADVERTISED!

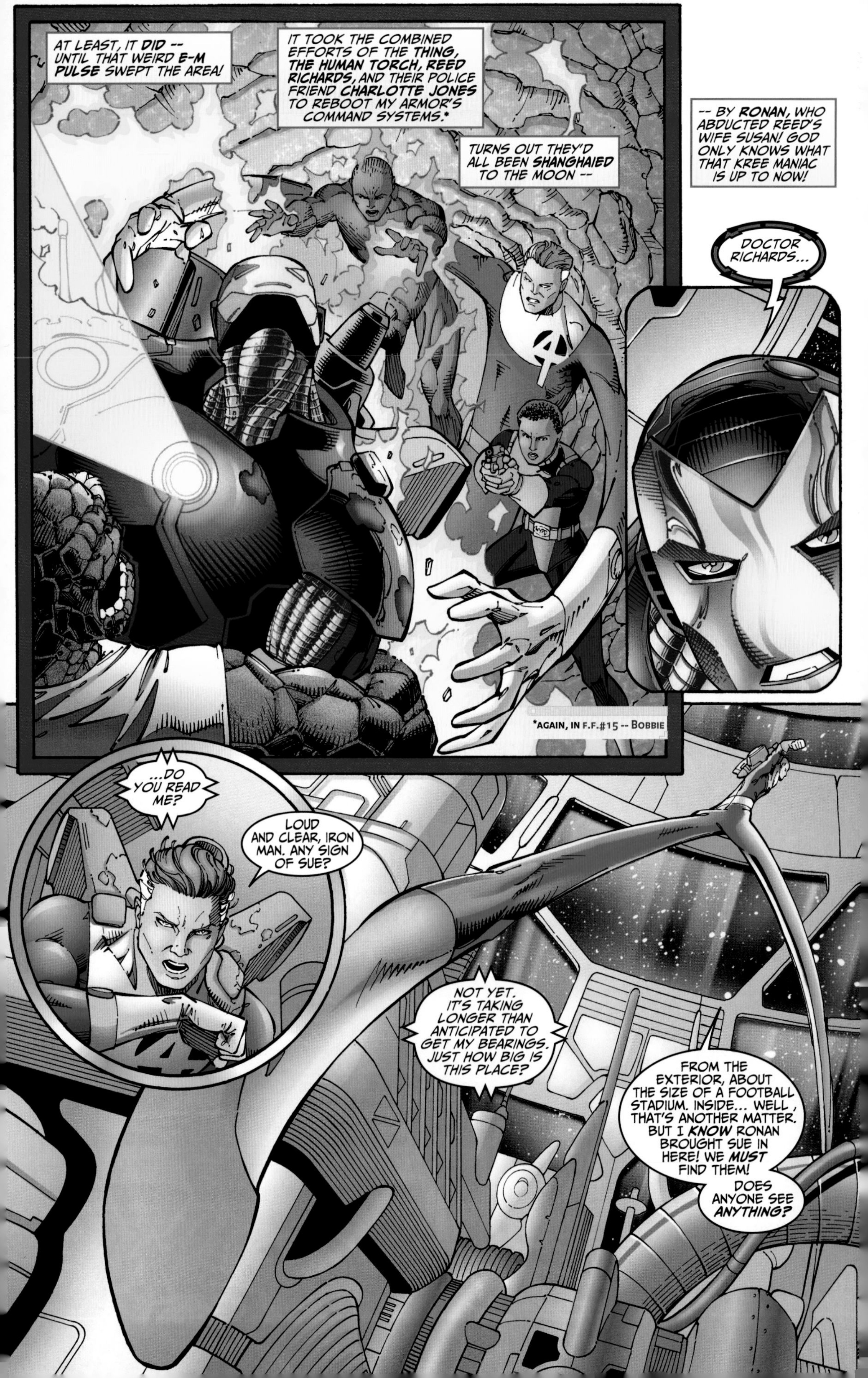

AT LEAST, IT DID -- UNTIL THAT WEIRD E-M PULSE SWEPT THE AREA!
IT TOOK THE COMBINED EFFORTS OF THE THING, THE HUMAN TORCH, REED RICHARDS, AND THEIR POLICE FRIEND CHARLOTTE JONES TO REBOOT MY ARMOR'S COMMAND SYSTEMS.*
TURNS OUT THEY'D ALL BEEN SHANGHAIED TO THE MOON --
-- BY RONAN, WHO ABDUCTED REED'S WIFE SUSAN! GOD ONLY KNOWS WHAT THAT KREE MANIAC IS UP TO NOW!
*AGAIN, IN F.F.#15 -- BOBBIE
DOCTOR RICHARDS...
...DO YOU READ ME?
LOUD AND CLEAR, IRON MAN. ANY SIGN OF SUE?
NOT YET. IT'S TAKING LONGER THAN ANTICIPATED TO GET MY BEARINGS. JUST HOW BIG IS THIS PLACE?
FROM THE EXTERIOR, ABOUT THE SIZE OF A FOOTBALL STADIUM. INSIDE... WELL, THAT'S ANOTHER MATTER. BUT I KNOW RONAN BROUGHT SUE IN HERE! WE MUST FIND THEM!
DOES ANYONE SEE ANYTHING?

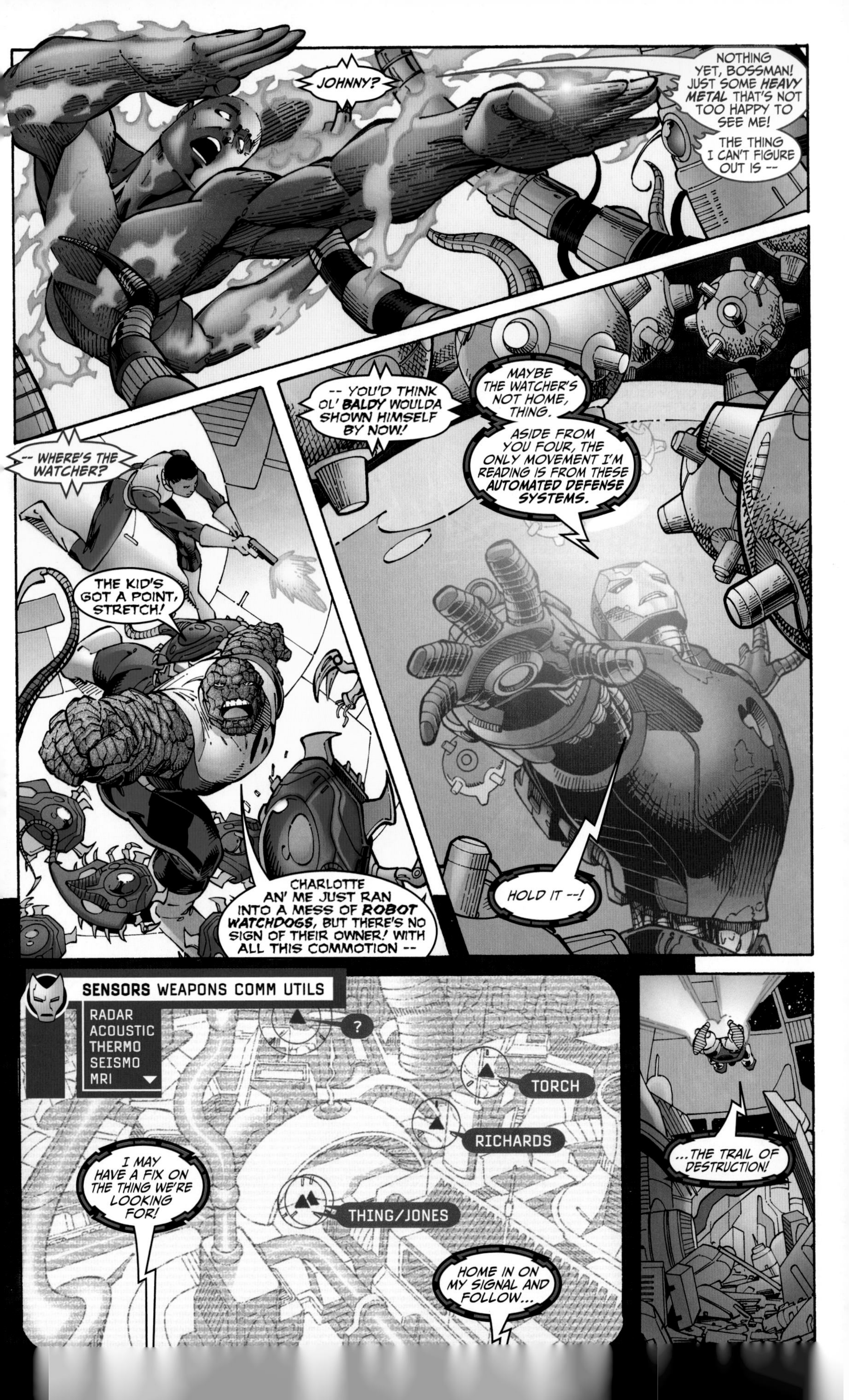
JOHNNY?
NOTHING YET, BOSSMAN! JUST SOME HEAVY METAL THAT'S NOT TOO HAPPY TO SEE ME!
THE THING I CAN'T FIGURE OUT IS --
-- YOU'D THINK OL' BALDY WOULDA SHOWN HIMSELF BY NOW!
-- WHERE'S THE WATCHER?
THE KID'S GOT A POINT, STRETCH!
CHARLOTTE AN' ME JUST RAN INTO A MESS OF ROBOT WATCHDOGS, BUT THERE'S NO SIGN OF THEIR OWNER! WITH ALL THIS COMMOTION --
MAYBE THE WATCHER'S NOT HOME, THING.
ASIDE FROM YOU FOUR, THE ONLY MOVEMENT I'M READING IS FROM THESE AUTOMATED DEFENSE SYSTEMS.
HOLD IT --!
SENSORS WEAPONS COMM UTILS
RADAR
ACOUSTIC
THERMO
SEISMO
MRI
?
TORCH
RICHARDS
THING/JONES
I MAY HAVE A FIX ON THE THING WE'RE LOOKING FOR!
HOME IN ON MY SIGNAL AND FOLLOW...
...THE TRAIL OF DESTRUCTION!

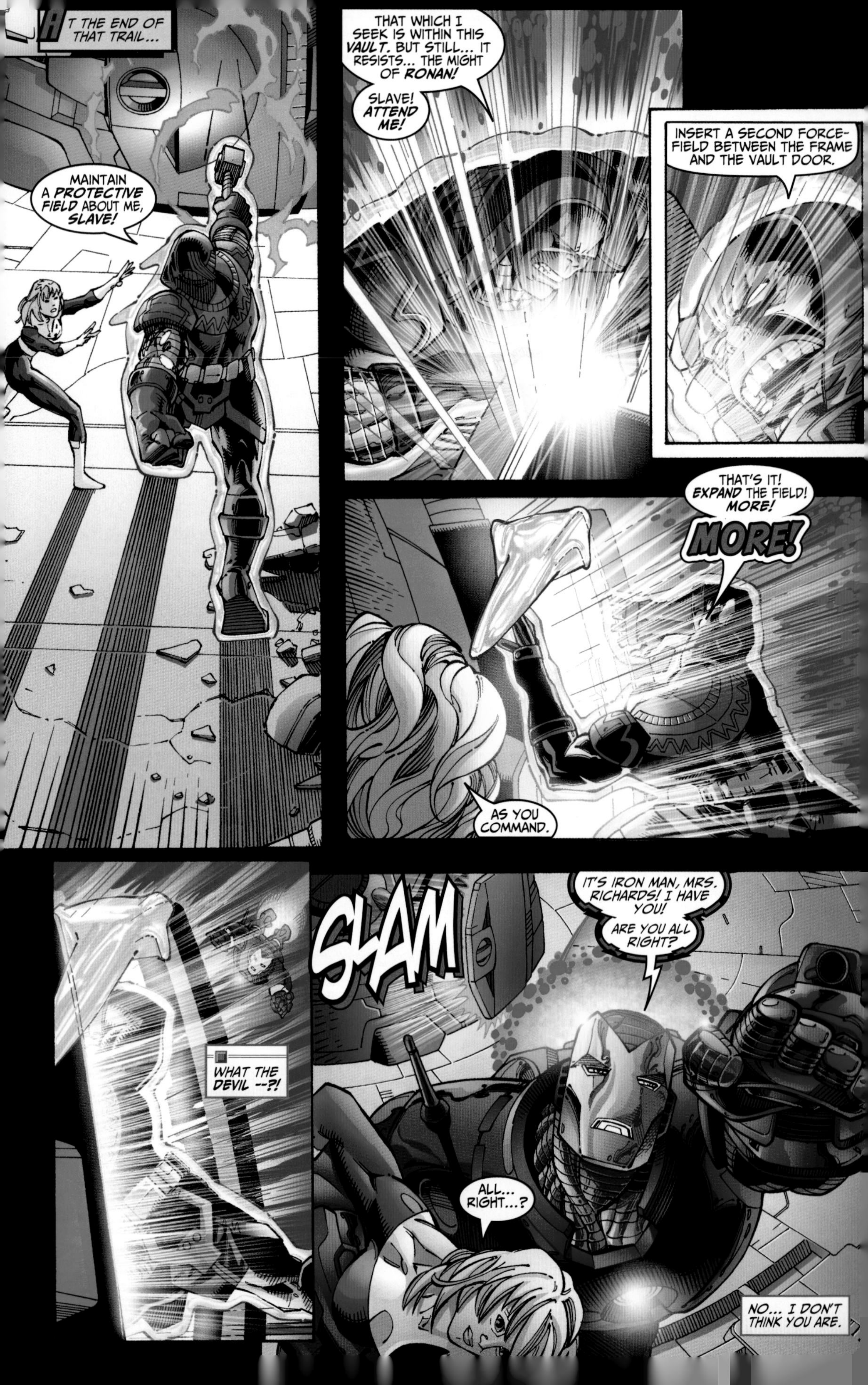
AT THE END OF THAT TRAIL...
MAINTAIN A PROTECTIVE FIELD ABOUT ME, SLAVE!
THAT WHICH I SEEK IS WITHIN THIS VAULT. BUT STILL... IT RESISTS... THE MIGHT OF RONAN!
SLAVE! ATTEND ME!
INSERT A SECOND FORCE-FIELD BETWEEN THE FRAME AND THE VAULT DOOR.
THAT'S IT! EXPAND THE FIELD! MORE!
MORE!
AS YOU COMMAND.
WHAT THE DEVIL --?!
SLAM
IT'S IRON MAN, MRS. RICHARDS! I HAVE YOU!
ARE YOU ALL RIGHT?
ALL... RIGHT...?
NO... I DON'T THINK YOU ARE.

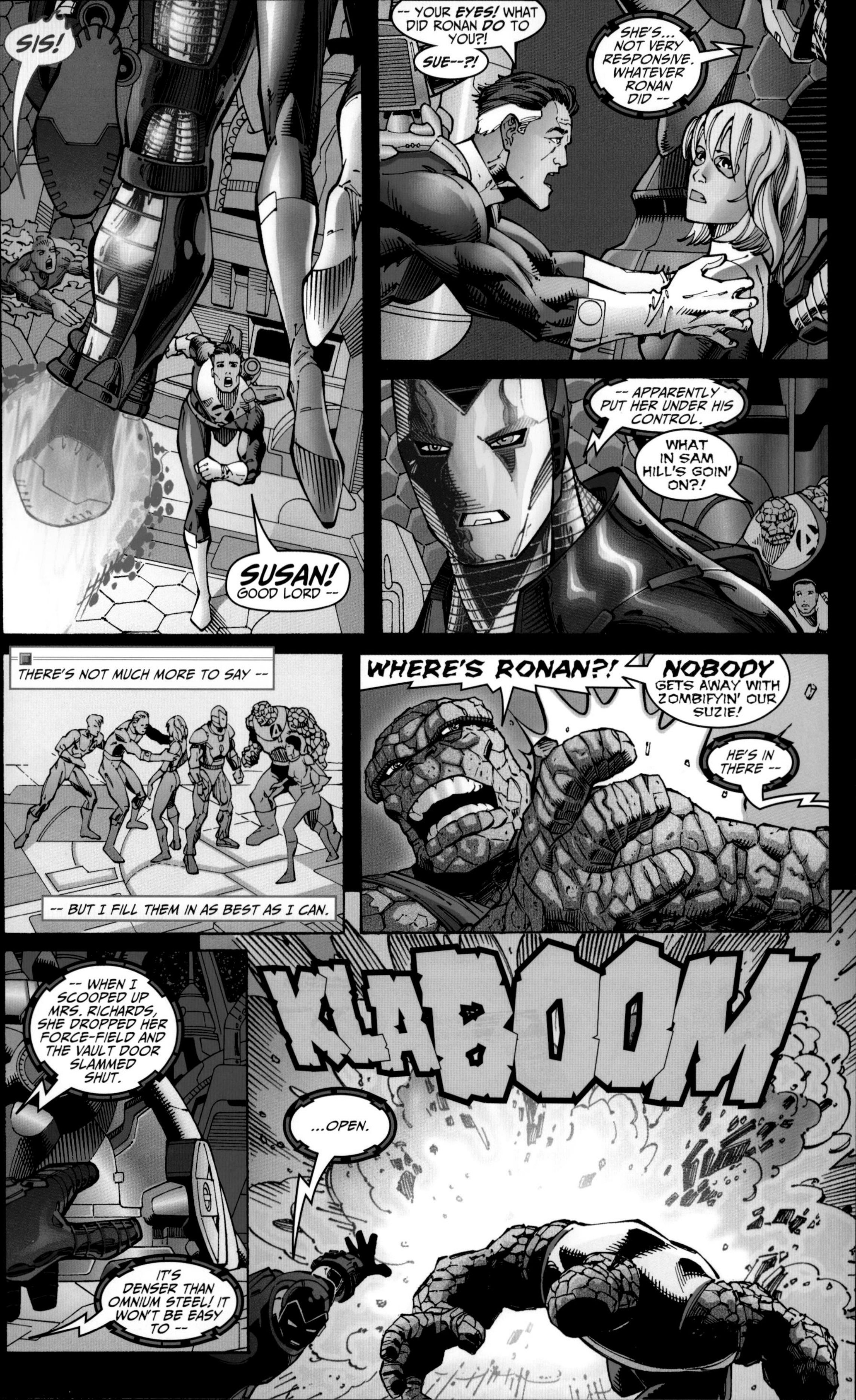
SIS!
SUSAN! GOOD LORD --
-- YOUR EYES! WHAT DID RONAN DO TO YOU?!
SUE--?!
SHE'S... NOT VERY RESPONSIVE. WHATEVER RONAN DID --
-- APPARENTLY PUT HER UNDER HIS CONTROL.
WHAT IN SAM HILL'S GOIN' ON?!
THERE'S NOT MUCH MORE TO SAY --
-- BUT I FILL THEM IN AS BEST AS I CAN.
WHERE'S RONAN?!
NOBODY GETS AWAY WITH ZOMBIFYIN' OUR SUZIE!
HE'S IN THERE --
-- WHEN I SCOOPED UP MRS. RICHARDS, SHE DROPPED HER FORCE-FIELD AND THE VAULT DOOR SLAMMED SHUT.
IT'S DENSER THAN OMNIUM STEEL! IT WON'T BE EASY TO --
KLABOOM
...OPEN.

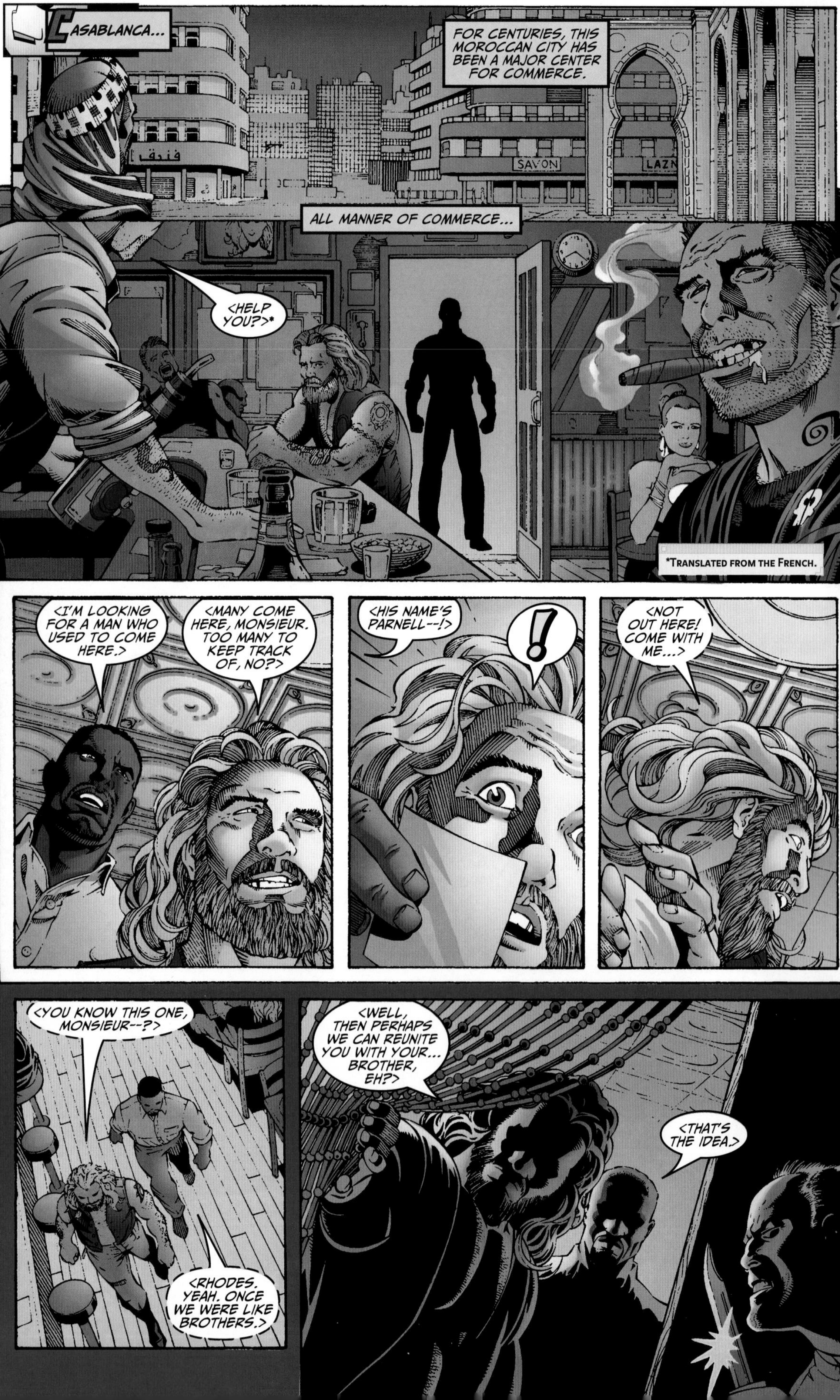
CASABLANCA...
FOR CENTURIES, THIS MOROCCAN CITY HAS BEEN A MAJOR CENTER FOR COMMERCE.
SAVON
ALL MANNER OF COMMERCE...
<HELP YOU?>*
*TRANSLATED FROM THE FRENCH.
<I'M LOOKING FOR A MAN WHO USED TO COME HERE.>
<MANY COME HERE, MONSIEUR. TOO MANY TO KEEP TRACK OF, NO?>
<HIS NAME'S PARNELL--!>
!
<NOT OUT HERE! COME WITH ME...>
<YOU KNOW THIS ONE, MONSIEUR--?>
<RHODES. YEAH. ONCE WE WERE LIKE BROTHERS.>
<WELL, THEN PERHAPS WE CAN REUNITE YOU WITH YOUR... BROTHER, EH?>
<THAT'S THE IDEA.>

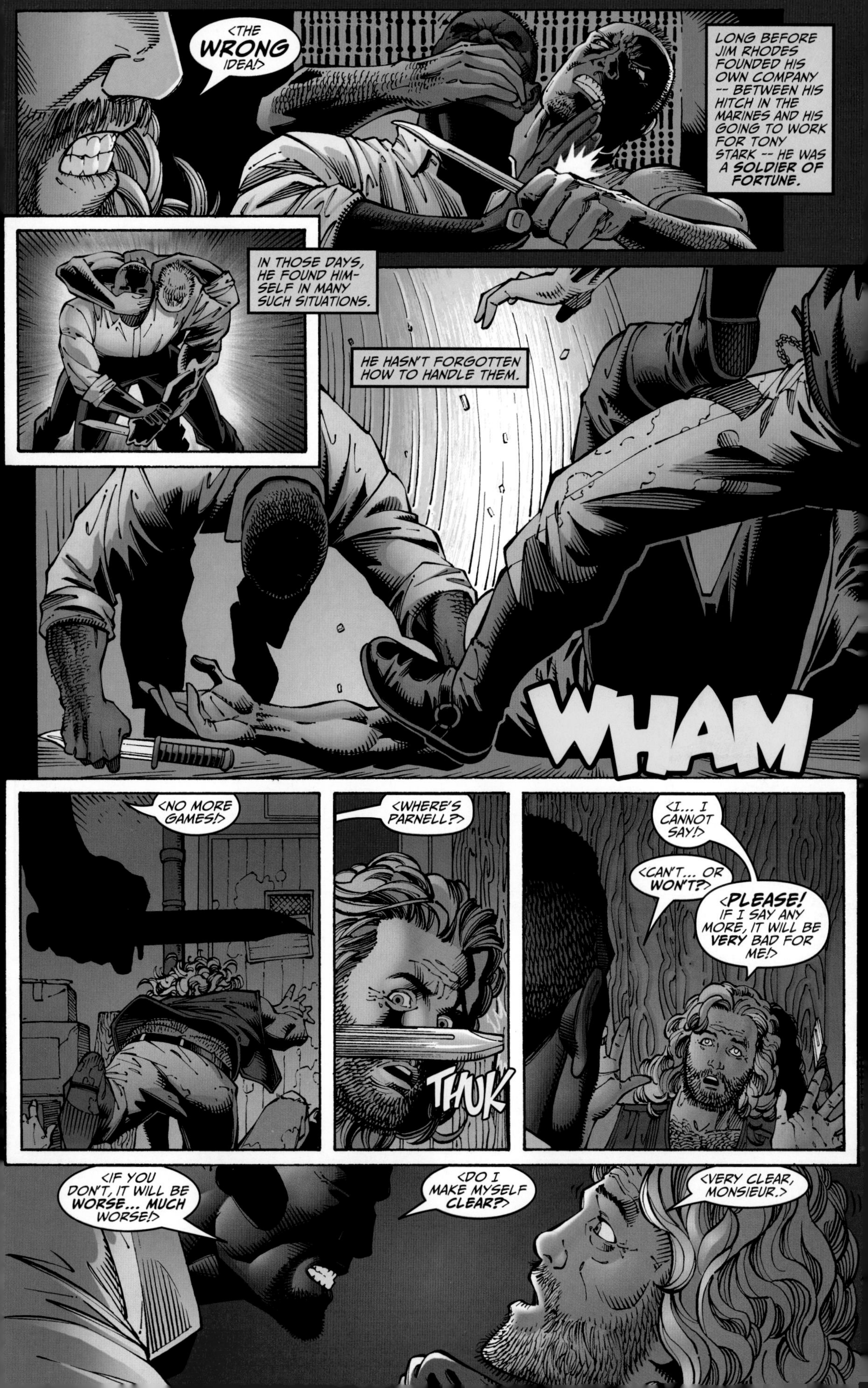

LONG BEFORE JIM RHODES FOUNDED HIS OWN COMPANY -- BETWEEN HIS HITCH IN THE MARINES AND HIS GOING TO WORK FOR TONY STARK -- HE WAS A SOLDIER OF FORTUNE.
<THE WRONG IDEA!>
IN THOSE DAYS, HE FOUND HIM-SELF IN MANY SUCH SITUATIONS.
HE HASN'T FORGOTTEN HOW TO HANDLE THEM.
WHAM
<NO MORE GAMES!>
<WHERE'S PARNELL?>
THUK
<I... I CANNOT SAY!>
<CAN'T... OR WON'T?>
<PLEASE! IF I SAY ANY MORE, IT WILL BE VERY BAD FOR ME!>
<IF YOU DON'T, IT WILL BE WORSE... MUCH WORSE!>
<DO I MAKE MYSELF CLEAR?>
<VERY CLEAR, MONSIEUR.>

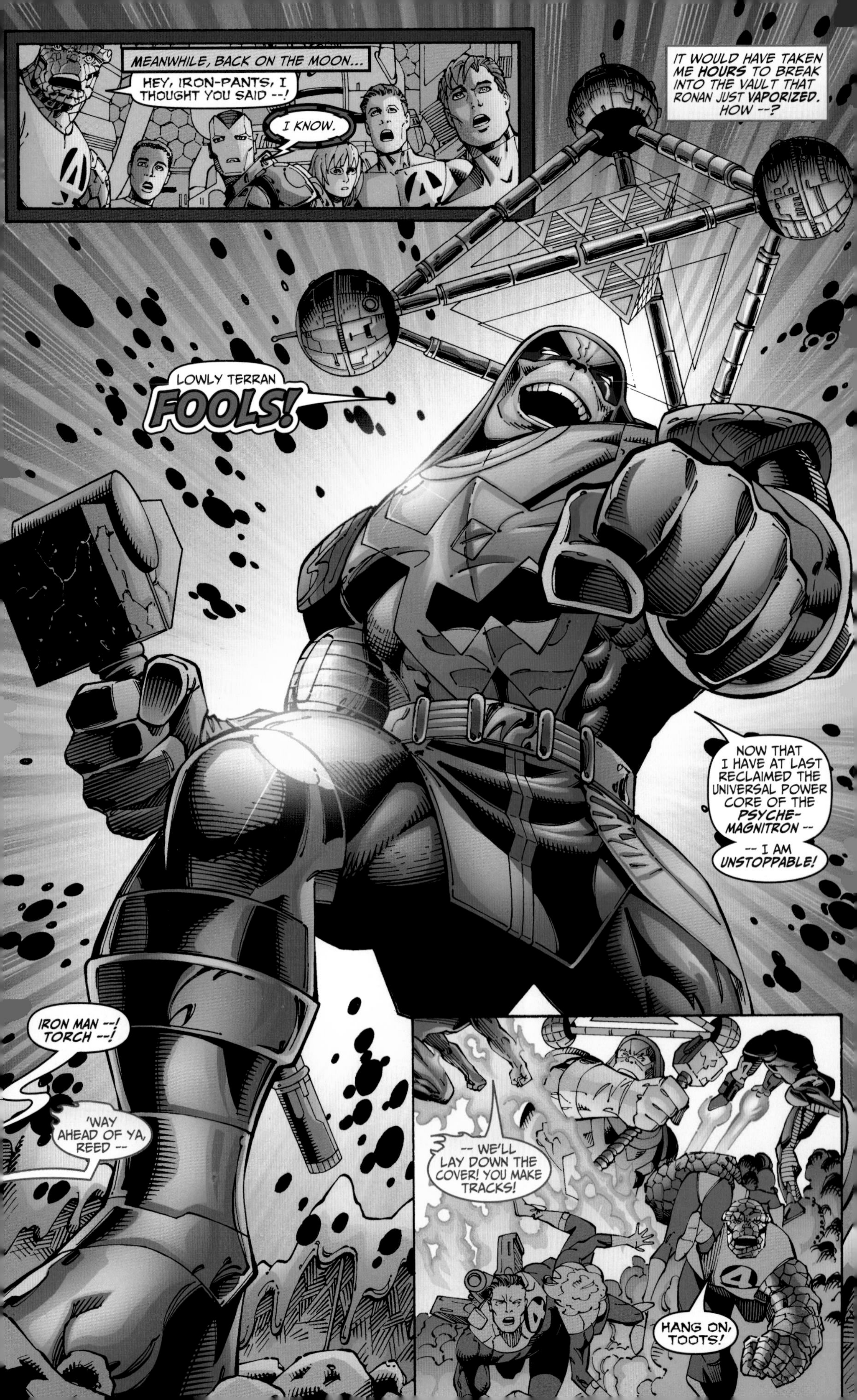
MEANWHILE, BACK ON THE MOON...
HEY, IRON-PANTS, I THOUGHT YOU SAID --!
I KNOW.
IT WOULD HAVE TAKEN ME HOURS TO BREAK INTO THE VAULT THAT RONAN JUST VAPORIZED. HOW --?
LOWLY TERRAN FOOLS!
NOW THAT I HAVE AT LAST RECLAIMED THE UNIVERSAL POWER CORE OF THE PSYCHE-MAGNITRON --
-- I AM UNSTOPPABLE!
IRON MAN --! TORCH --!
'WAY AHEAD OF YA, REED --
-- WE'LL LAY DOWN THE COVER! YOU MAKE TRACKS!
HANG ON, TOOTS!

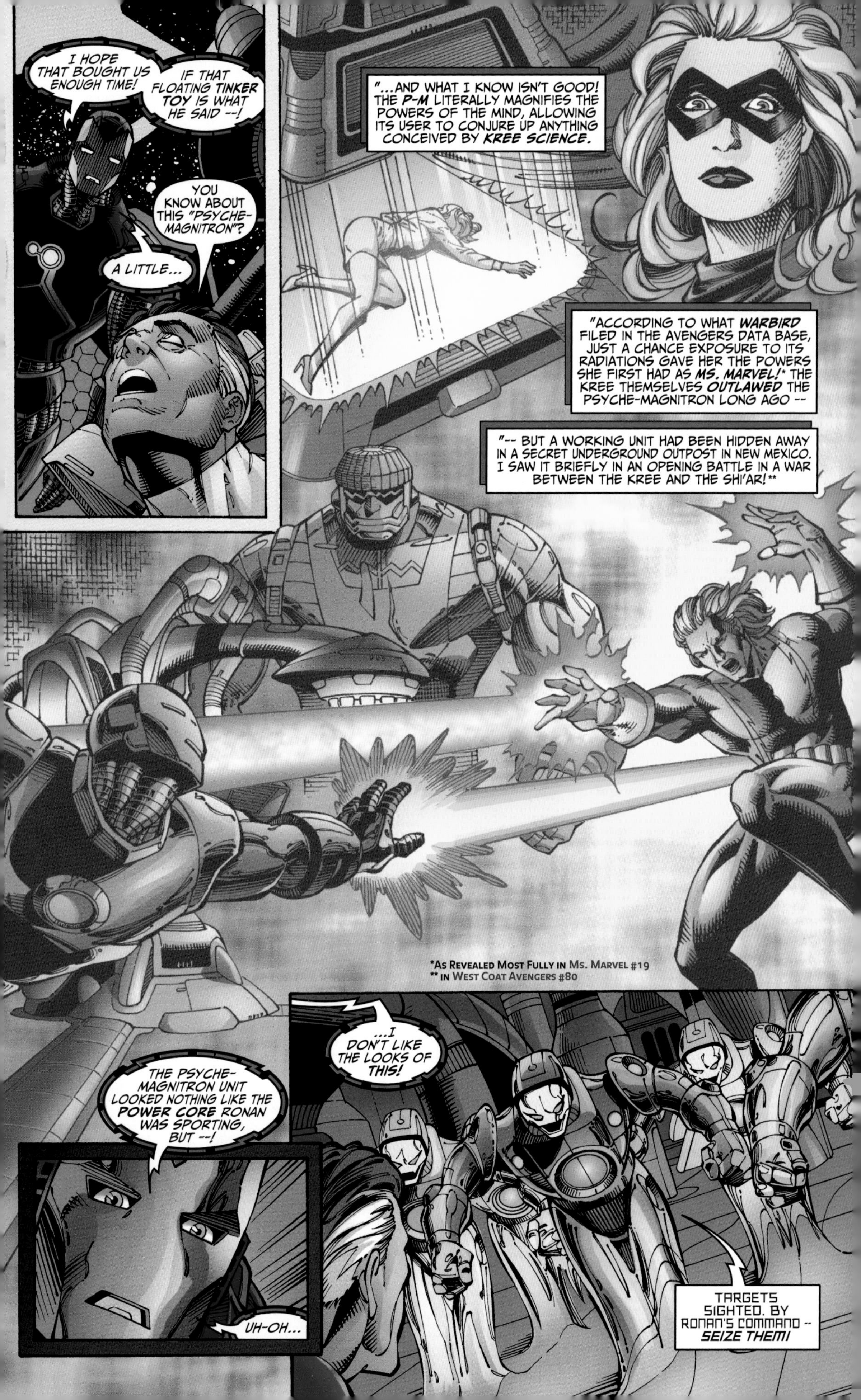
I HOPE THAT BOUGHT US ENOUGH TIME!
IF THAT FLOATING TINKER TOY IS WHAT HE SAID --!
YOU KNOW ABOUT THIS "PSYCHE-MAGNITRON"?
A LITTLE...
"...AND WHAT I KNOW ISN'T GOOD! THE P-M LITERALLY MAGNIFIES THE POWERS OF THE MIND, ALLOWING ITS USER TO CONJURE UP ANYTHING CONCEIVED BY KREE SCIENCE.
"ACCORDING TO WHAT WARBIRD FILED IN THE AVENGERS DATA BASE, JUST A CHANCE EXPOSURE TO ITS RADIATIONS GAVE HER THE POWERS SHE FIRST HAD AS MS. MARVEL!* THE KREE THEMSELVES OUTLAWED THE PSYCHE-MAGNITRON LONG AGO --
"-- BUT A WORKING UNIT HAD BEEN HIDDEN AWAY IN A SECRET UNDERGROUND OUTPOST IN NEW MEXICO. I SAW IT BRIEFLY IN AN OPENING BATTLE IN A WAR BETWEEN THE KREE AND THE SHI'AR!**
*AS REVEALED MOST FULLY IN MS. MARVEL #19
** IN WEST COAT AVENGERS #80
THE PSYCHE-MAGNITRON UNIT LOOKED NOTHING LIKE THE POWER CORE RONAN WAS SPORTING, BUT --!
...I DON'T LIKE THE LOOKS OF THIS!
UH-OH...
TARGETS SIGHTED. BY RONAN'S COMMAND -- SEIZE THEM!

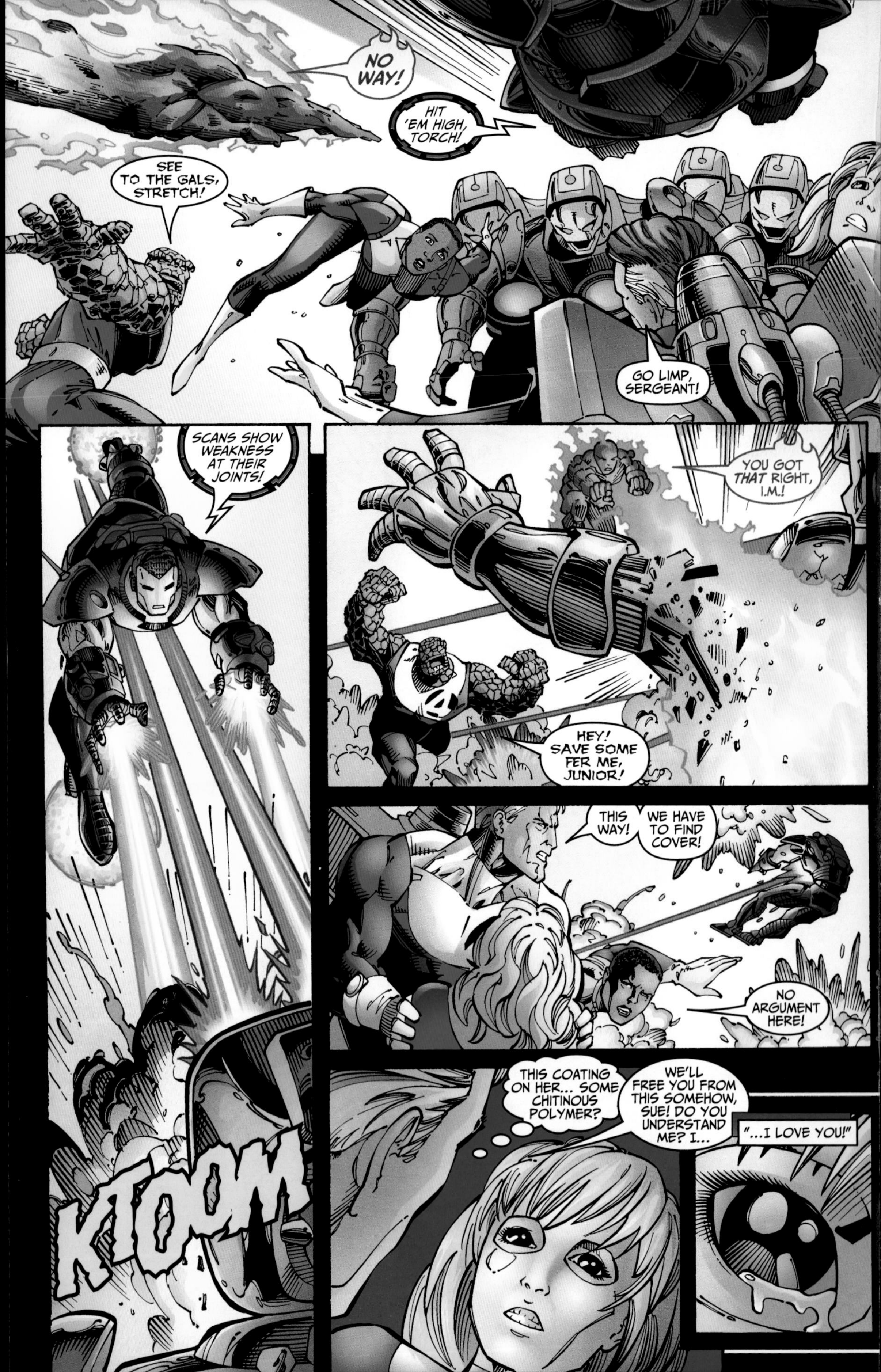
NO WAY!
HIT 'EM HIGH, TORCH!
SEE TO THE GALS, STRETCH!
GO LIMP, SERGEANT!
SCANS SHOW WEAKNESS AT THEIR JOINTS!
YOU GOT THAT RIGHT, I.M.!
HEY! SAVE SOME FER ME, JUNIOR!
KTOOM
THIS WAY!
WE HAVE TO FIND COVER!
NO ARGUMENT HERE!
THIS COATING ON HER... SOME CHITINOUS POLYMER?
WE'LL FREE YOU FROM THIS SOMEHOW, SUE! DO YOU UNDERSTAND ME? I...
"...I LOVE YOU!"

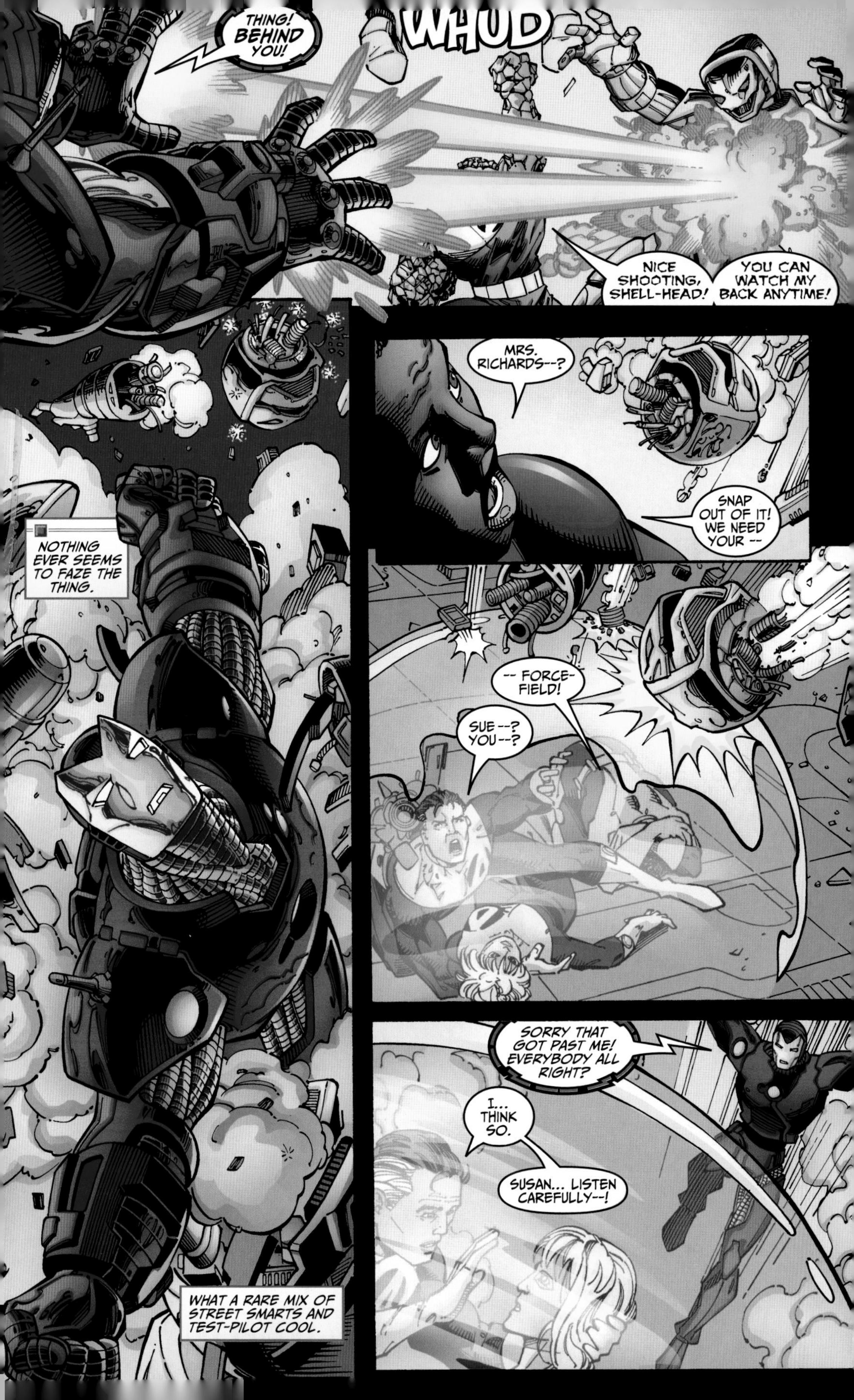
THING! BEHIND YOU!
WHUD
NICE SHOOTING, SHELL-HEAD!
YOU CAN WATCH MY BACK ANYTIME!
NOTHING EVER SEEMS TO FAZE THE THING.
WHAT A RARE MIX OF STREET SMARTS AND TEST-PILOT COOL.
MRS. RICHARDS--?
SNAP OUT OF IT! WE NEED YOUR --
-- FORCE-FIELD!
SUE --? YOU --?
SORRY THAT GOT PAST ME! EVERYBODY ALL RIGHT?
I... THINK SO.
SUSAN... LISTEN CAREFULLY--!

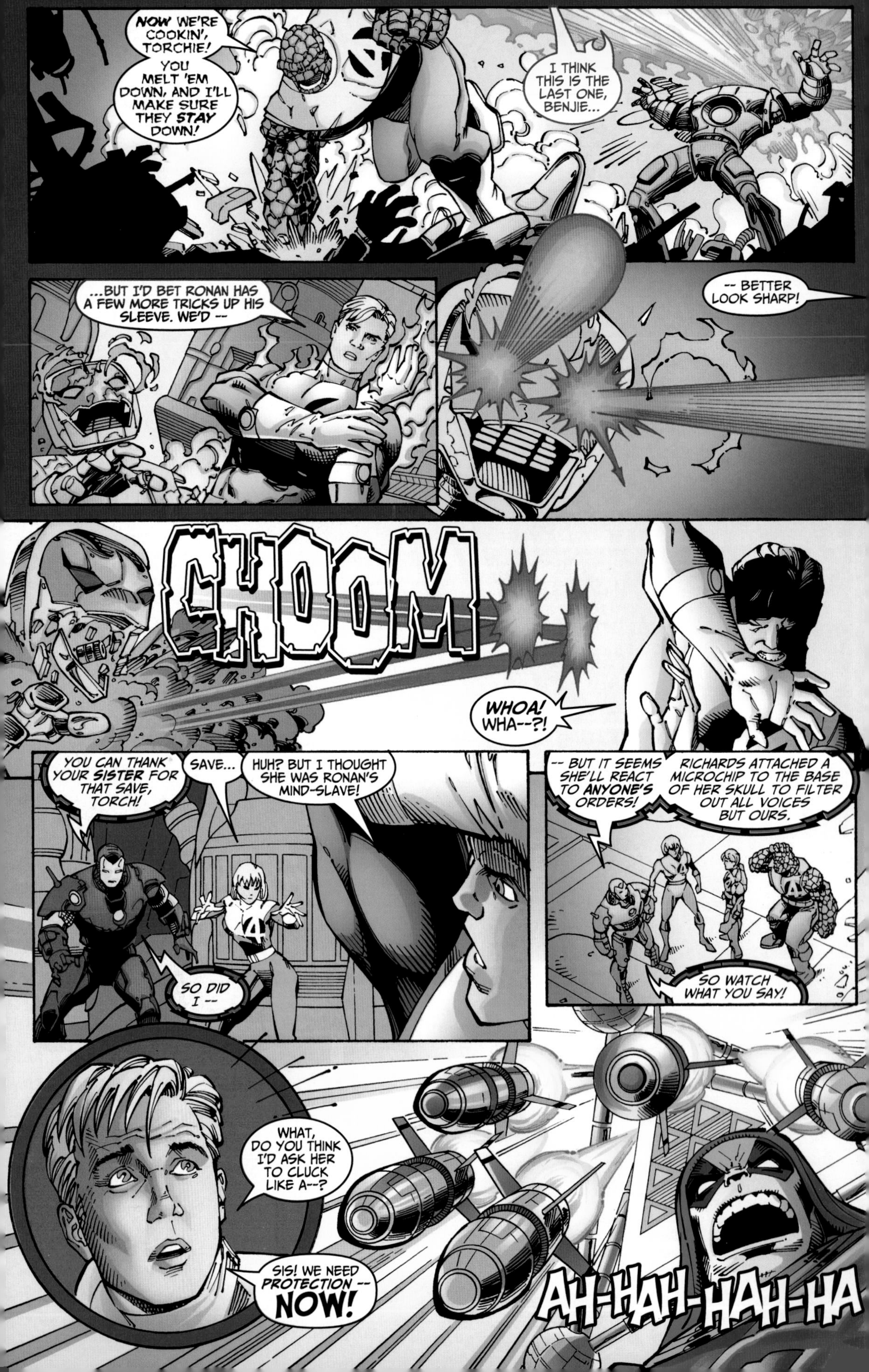
NOW WE'RE COOKIN', TORCHIE!
YOU MELT 'EM DOWN, AND I'LL MAKE SURE THEY STAY DOWN!
I THINK THIS IS THE LAST ONE, BENJIE...
...BUT I'D BET RONAN HAS A FEW MORE TRICKS UP HIS SLEEVE. WE'D --
-- BETTER LOOK SHARP!
CHOOM
WHOA! WHA--?!
YOU CAN THANK YOUR SISTER FOR THAT SAVE, TORCH!
SAVE...
HUH? BUT I THOUGHT SHE WAS RONAN'S MIND-SLAVE!
SO DID I --
-- BUT IT SEEMS SHE'LL REACT TO ANYONE'S ORDERS!
RICHARDS ATTACHED A MICROCHIP TO THE BASE OF HER SKULL TO FILTER OUT ALL VOICES BUT OURS.
SO WATCH WHAT YOU SAY!
WHAT, DO YOU THINK I'D ASK HER TO CLUCK LIKE A--?
SIS! WE NEED PROTECTION -- NOW!
AH-HAH-HAH-HA

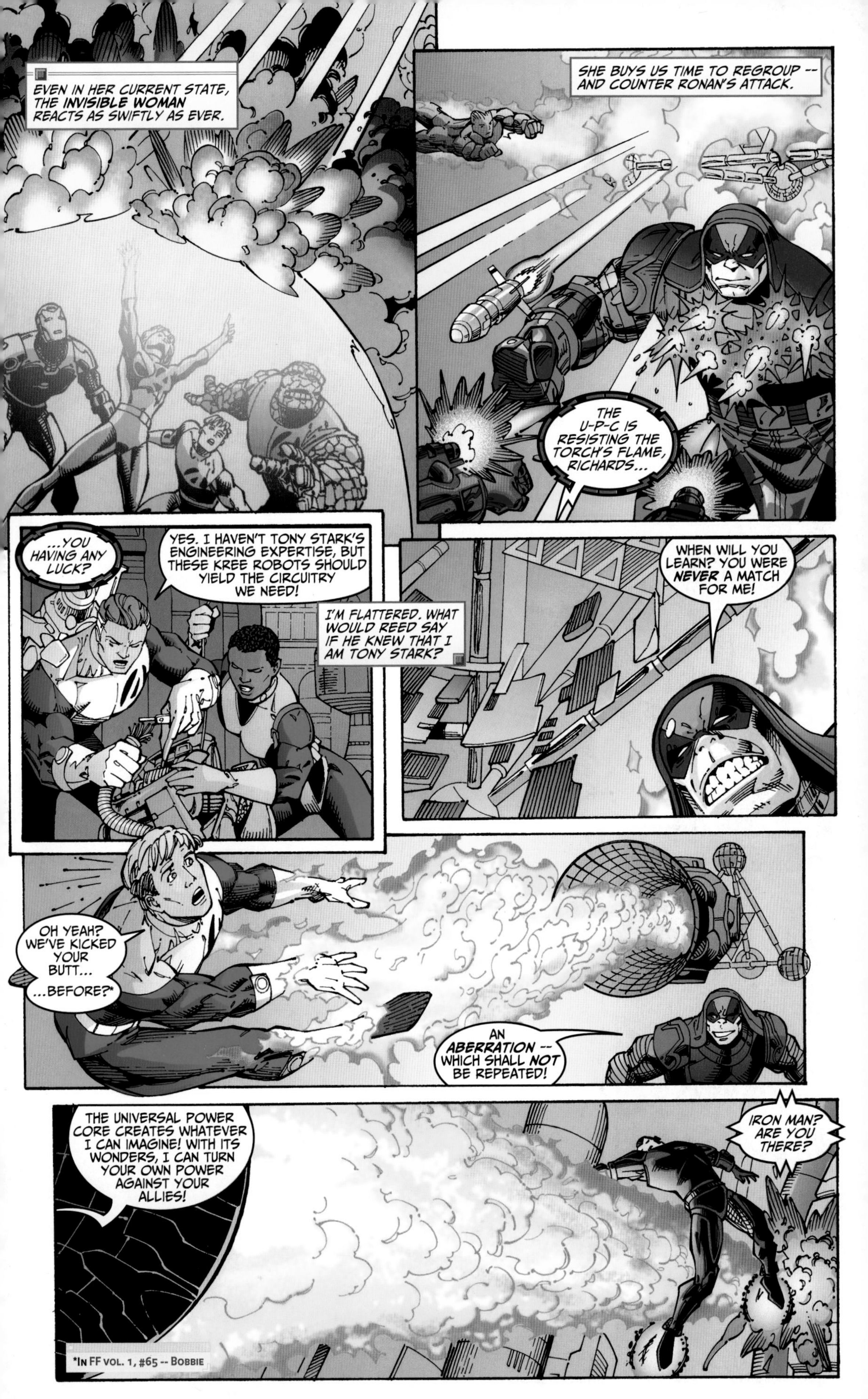
EVEN IN HER CURRENT STATE, THE INVISIBLE WOMAN REACTS AS SWIFTLY AS EVER.
SHE BUYS US TIME TO REGROUP -- AND COUNTER RONAN'S ATTACK.
THE U-P-C IS RESISTING THE TORCH'S FLAME, RICHARDS...
...YOU HAVING ANY LUCK?
YES. I HAVEN'T TONY STARK'S ENGINEERING EXPERTISE, BUT THESE KREE ROBOTS SHOULD YIELD THE CIRCUITRY WE NEED!
I'M FLATTERED. WHAT WOULD REED SAY IF HE KNEW THAT I AM TONY STARK?
WHEN WILL YOU LEARN? YOU WERE NEVER A MATCH FOR ME!
OH YEAH? WE'VE KICKED YOUR BUTT...
...BEFORE?*
AN ABERRATION -- WHICH SHALL NOT BE REPEATED!
THE UNIVERSAL POWER CORE CREATES WHATEVER I CAN IMAGINE! WITH ITS WONDERS, I CAN TURN YOUR OWN POWER AGAINST YOUR ALLIES!
IRON MAN? ARE YOU THERE?
*IN FF VOL. 1, #65 -- BOBBIE

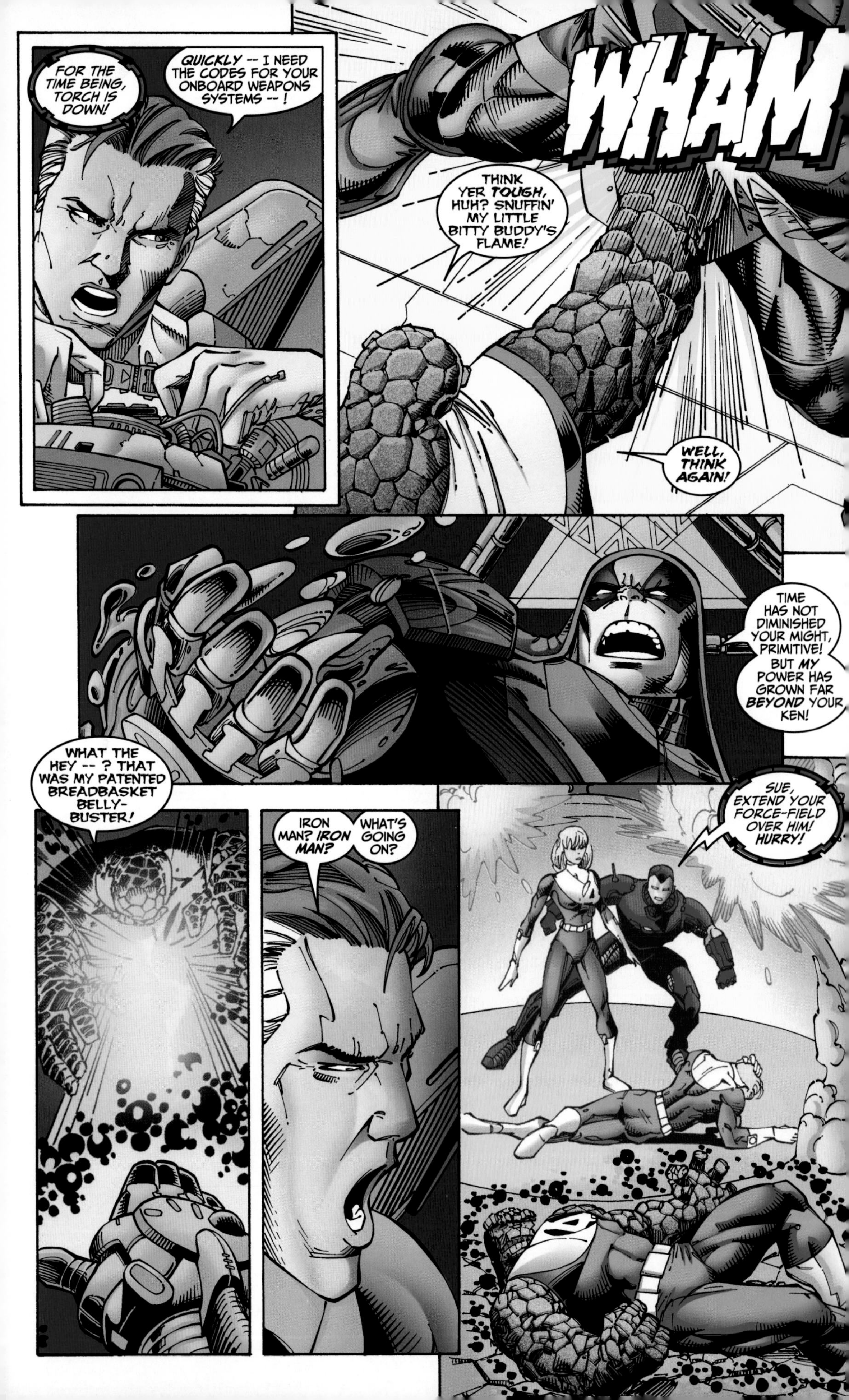
FOR THE TIME BEING, TORCH IS DOWN!
QUICKLY -- I NEED THE CODES FOR YOUR ONBOARD WEAPONS SYSTEMS -- !
WHAM
THINK YER TOUGH, HUH? SNUFFIN' MY LITTLE BITTY BUDDY'S FLAME!
WELL, THINK AGAIN!
TIME HAS NOT DIMINISHED YOUR MIGHT, PRIMITIVE!
BUT MY POWER HAS GROWN FAR BEYOND YOUR KEN!
WHAT THE HEY -- ? THAT WAS MY PATENTED BREADBASKET BELLY-BUSTER!
IRON MAN? IRON MAN?
WHAT'S GOING ON?
SUE, EXTEND YOUR FORCE-FIELD OVER HIM! HURRY!

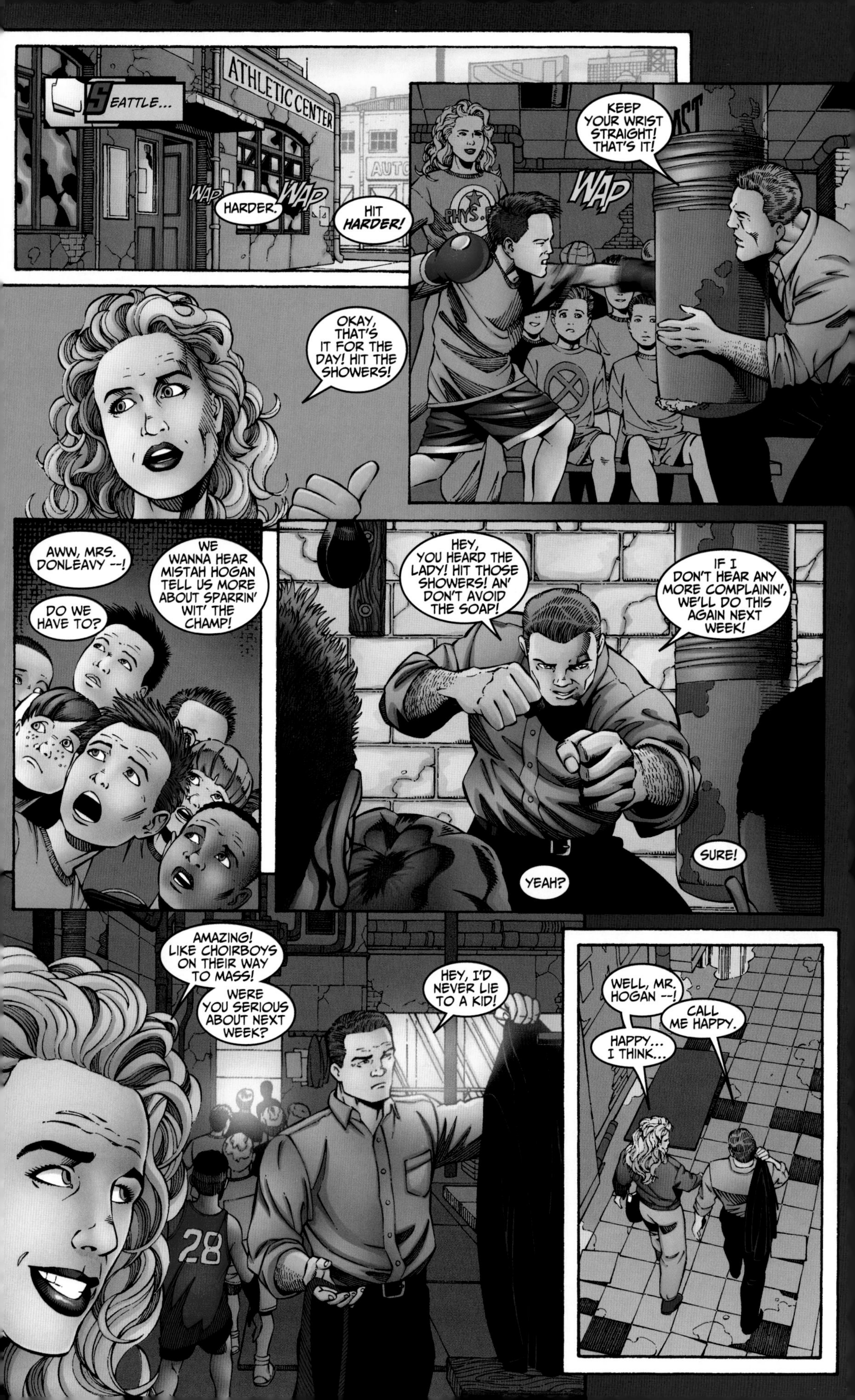
ATHLETIC CENTER
SEATTLE...
AUTO
WAP
HARDER.
WAP
HIT HARDER!
KEEP YOUR WRIST STRAIGHT! THAT'S IT!
WAP
PHYS. E
OKAY, THAT'S IT FOR THE DAY! HIT THE SHOWERS!
AWW, MRS. DONLEAVY --!
WE WANNA HEAR MISTAH HOGAN TELL US MORE ABOUT SPARRIN' WIT' THE CHAMP!
DO WE HAVE TO?
HEY, YOU HEARD THE LADY! HIT THOSE SHOWERS! AN' DON'T AVOID THE SOAP!
IF I DON'T HEAR ANY MORE COMPLAININ', WE'LL DO THIS AGAIN NEXT WEEK!
YEAH?
SURE!
AMAZING! LIKE CHOIRBOYS ON THEIR WAY TO MASS!
WERE YOU SERIOUS ABOUT NEXT WEEK?
HEY, I'D NEVER LIE TO A KID!
28
WELL, MR. HOGAN --!
CALL ME HAPPY.
HAPPY... I THINK...

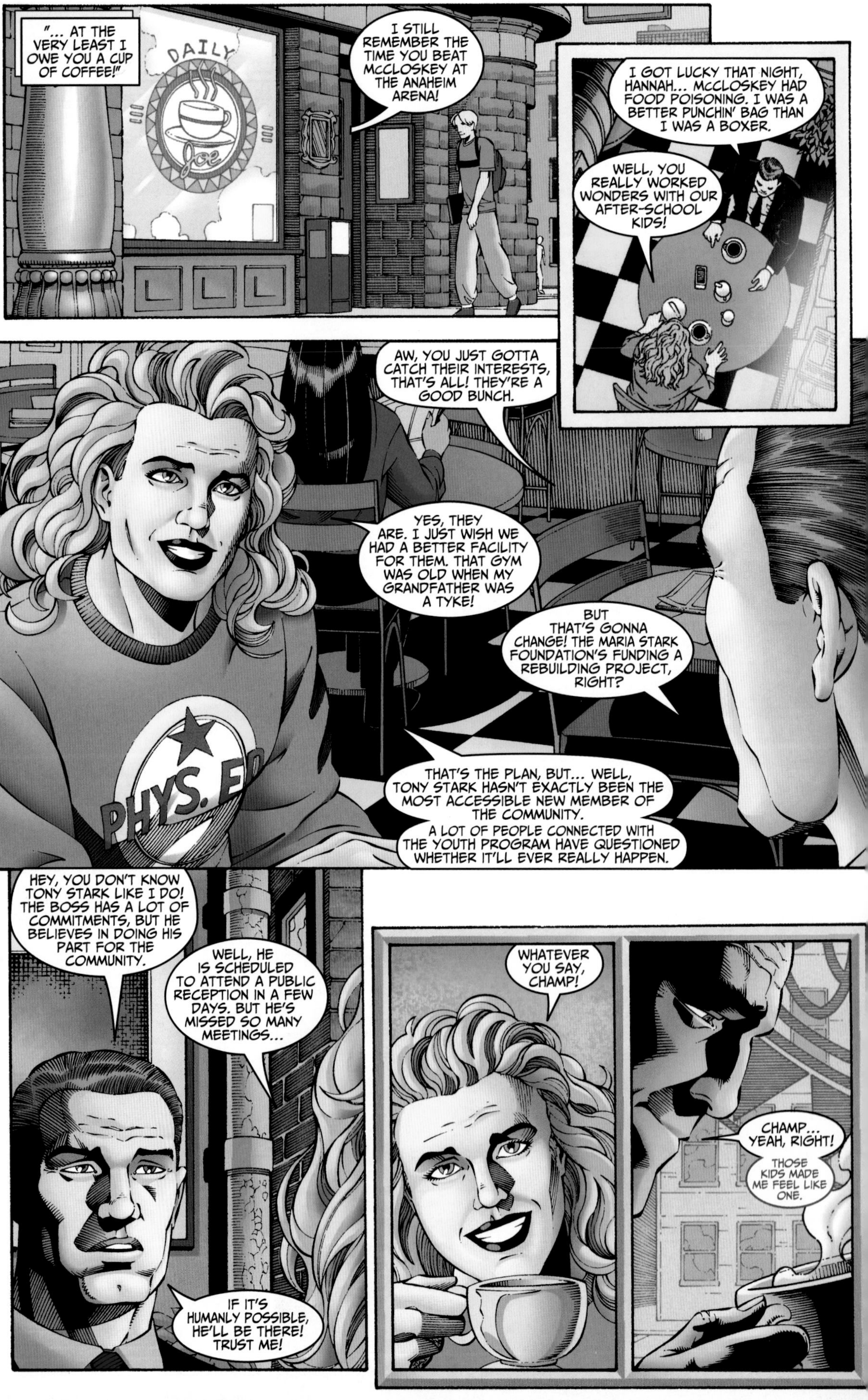
"... AT THE VERY LEAST I OWE YOU A CUP OF COFFEE!"
DAILY Joe
I STILL REMEMBER THE TIME YOU BEAT McCLOSKEY AT THE ANAHEIM ARENA!
I GOT LUCKY THAT NIGHT, HANNAH... McCLOSKEY HAD FOOD POISONING. I WAS A BETTER PUNCHIN' BAG THAN I WAS A BOXER.
WELL, YOU REALLY WORKED WONDERS WITH OUR AFTER-SCHOOL KIDS!
AW, YOU JUST GOTTA CATCH THEIR INTERESTS, THAT'S ALL! THEY'RE A GOOD BUNCH.
YES, THEY ARE. I JUST WISH WE HAD A BETTER FACILITY FOR THEM. THAT GYM WAS OLD WHEN MY GRANDFATHER WAS A TYKE!
BUT THAT'S GONNA CHANGE! THE MARIA STARK FOUNDATION'S FUNDING A REBUILDING PROJECT, RIGHT?
THAT'S THE PLAN, BUT... WELL, TONY STARK HASN'T EXACTLY BEEN THE MOST ACCESSIBLE NEW MEMBER OF THE COMMUNITY.
A LOT OF PEOPLE CONNECTED WITH THE YOUTH PROGRAM HAVE QUESTIONED WHETHER IT'LL EVER REALLY HAPPEN.
PHYS. ED
HEY, YOU DON'T KNOW TONY STARK LIKE I DO! THE BOSS HAS A LOT OF COMMITMENTS, BUT HE BELIEVES IN DOING HIS PART FOR THE COMMUNITY.
WELL, HE IS SCHEDULED TO ATTEND A PUBLIC RECEPTION IN A FEW DAYS. BUT HE'S MISSED SO MANY MEETINGS...
IF IT'S HUMANLY POSSIBLE, HE'LL BE THERE! TRUST ME!
WHATEVER YOU SAY, CHAMP!
CHAMP... YEAH, RIGHT!
THOSE KIDS MADE ME FEEL LIKE ONE.

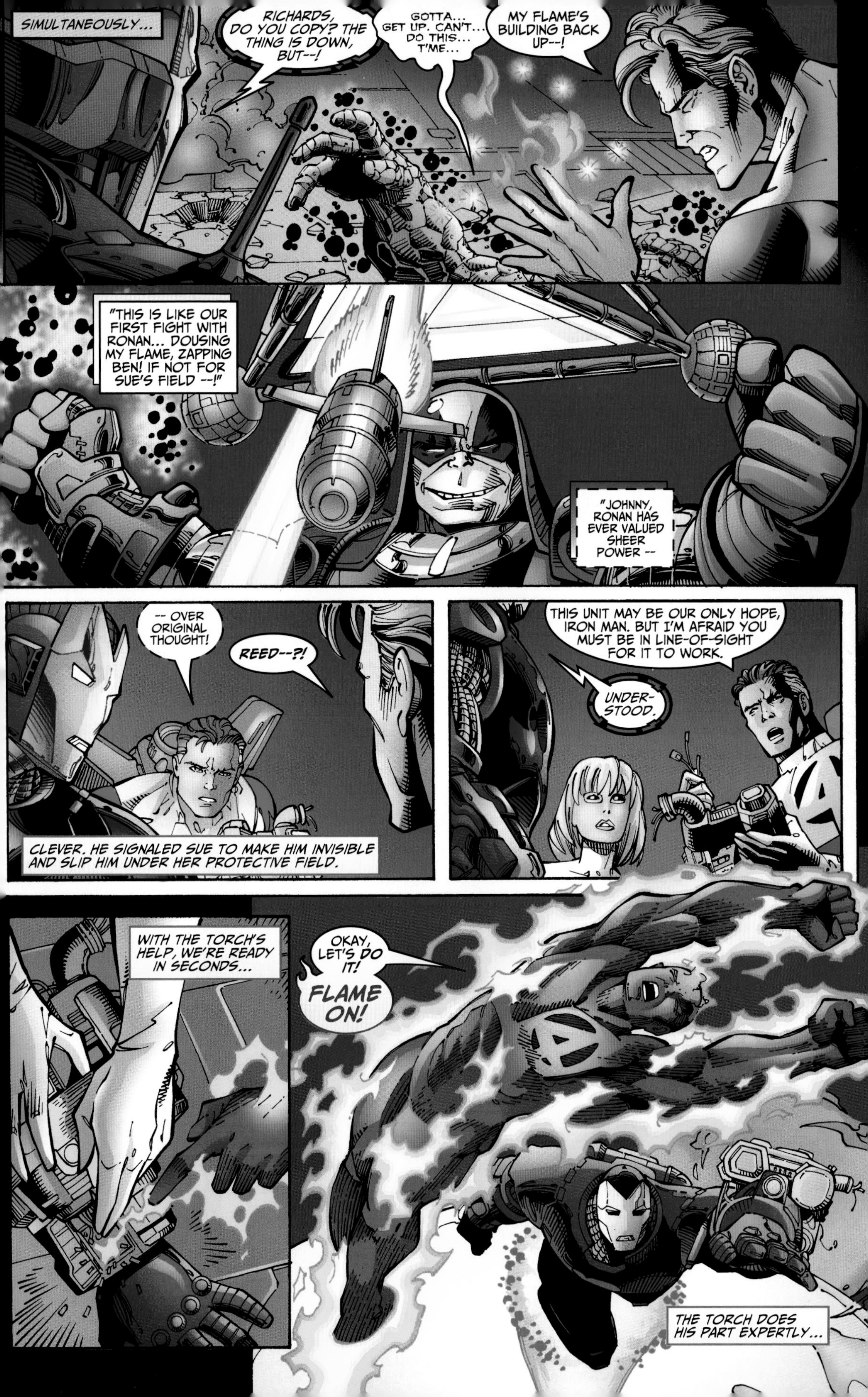
SIMULTANEOUSLY...
RICHARDS, DO YOU COPY? THE THING IS DOWN, BUT--!
GOTTA... GET UP. CAN'T... DO THIS... T'ME...
MY FLAME'S BUILDING BACK UP--!
"THIS IS LIKE OUR FIRST FIGHT WITH RONAN... DOUSING MY FLAME, ZAPPING BEN! IF NOT FOR SUE'S FIELD --!"
"JOHNNY, RONAN HAS EVER VALUED SHEER POWER --
-- OVER ORIGINAL THOUGHT!
REED--?!
CLEVER. HE SIGNALED SUE TO MAKE HIM INVISIBLE AND SLIP HIM UNDER HER PROTECTIVE FIELD.
THIS UNIT MAY BE OUR ONLY HOPE, IRON MAN. BUT I'M AFRAID YOU MUST BE IN LINE-OF-SIGHT FOR IT TO WORK.
UNDER-STOOD.
WITH THE TORCH'S HELP, WE'RE READY IN SECONDS...
OKAY, LET'S DO IT!
FLAME ON!
THE TORCH DOES HIS PART EXPERTLY...

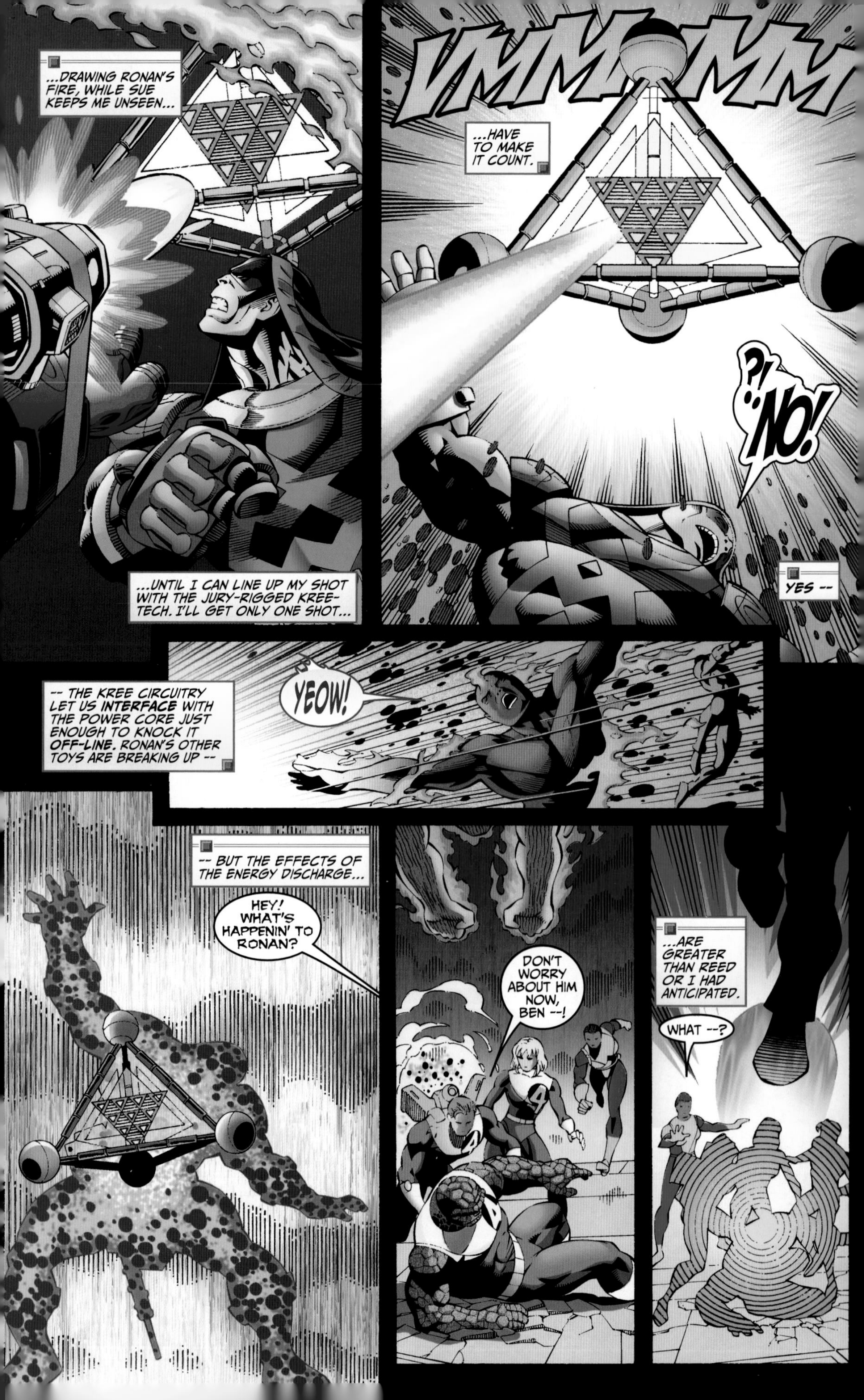
...DRAWING RONAN'S FIRE, WHILE SUE KEEPS ME UNSEEN...
...UNTIL I CAN LINE UP MY SHOT WITH THE JURY-RIGGED KREE-TECH. I'LL GET ONLY ONE SHOT...
VMMMMM
...HAVE TO MAKE IT COUNT.
?! NO!
YES --
-- THE KREE CIRCUITRY LET US INTERFACE WITH THE POWER CORE JUST ENOUGH TO KNOCK IT OFF-LINE. RONAN'S OTHER TOYS ARE BREAKING UP --
YEOW!
-- BUT THE EFFECTS OF THE ENERGY DISCHARGE...
HEY! WHAT'S HAPPENIN' TO RONAN?
DON'T WORRY ABOUT HIM NOW, BEN --!
...ARE GREATER THAN REED OR I HAD ANTICIPATED.
WHAT --?

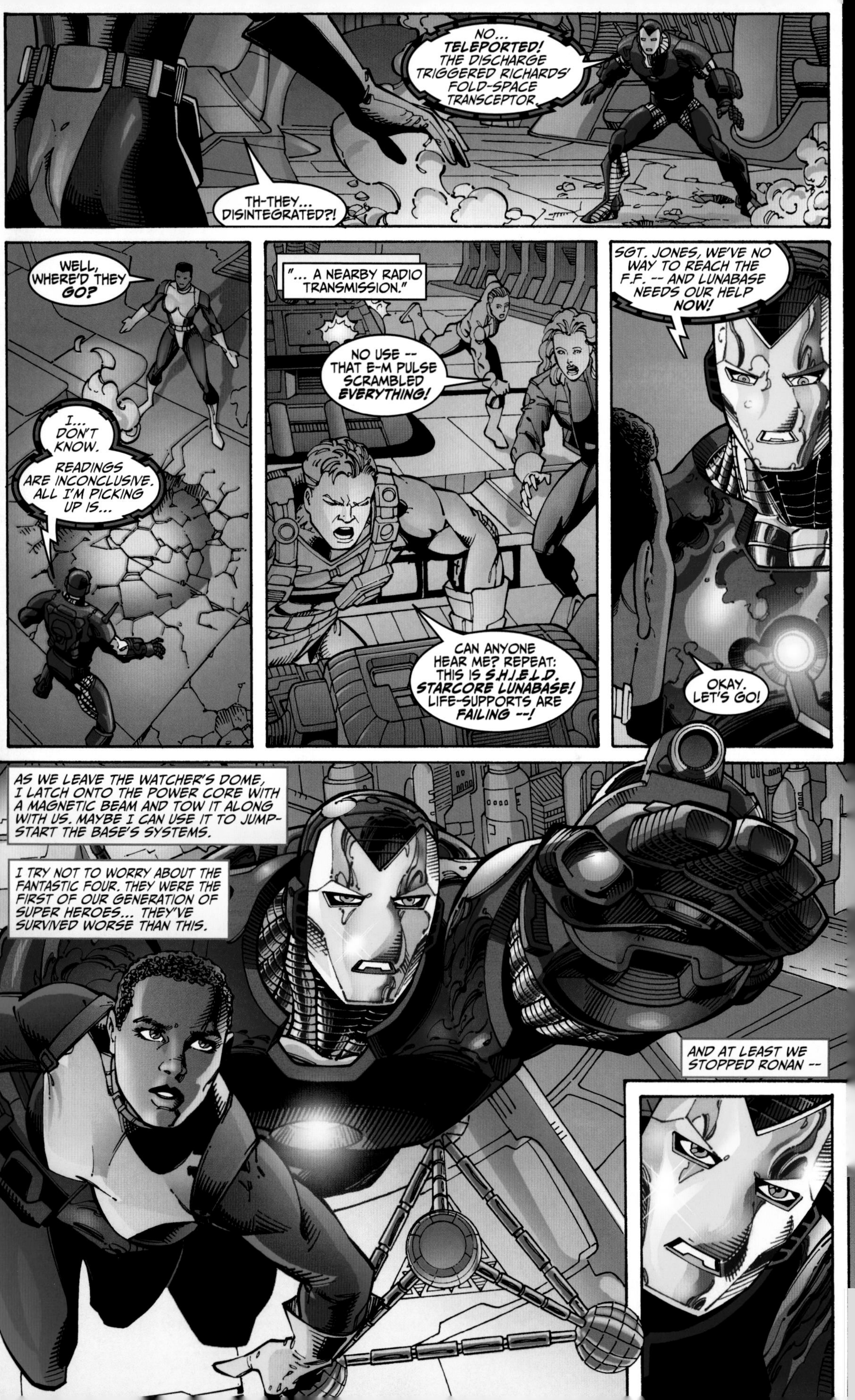
NO... TELEPORTED! THE DISCHARGE TRIGGERED RICHARDS' FOLD-SPACE TRANSCEPTOR.
TH-THEY... DISINTEGRATED?!
WELL, WHERE'D THEY GO?
I... DON'T KNOW.
READINGS ARE INCONCLUSIVE. ALL I'M PICKING UP IS...
"... A NEARBY RADIO TRANSMISSION."
NO USE -- THAT E-M PULSE SCRAMBLED EVERYTHING!
CAN ANYONE HEAR ME? REPEAT: THIS IS S.H.I.E.L.D. STARCORE LUNABASE! LIFE-SUPPORTS ARE FAILING --!
SGT. JONES, WE'VE NO WAY TO REACH THE F.F. -- AND LUNABASE NEEDS OUR HELP NOW!
OKAY. LET'S GO!
AS WE LEAVE THE WATCHER'S DOME, I LATCH ONTO THE POWER CORE WITH A MAGNETIC BEAM AND TOW IT ALONG WITH US. MAYBE I CAN USE IT TO JUMP-START THE BASE'S SYSTEMS.
I TRY NOT TO WORRY ABOUT THE FANTASTIC FOUR. THEY WERE THE FIRST OF OUR GENERATION OF SUPER HEROES... THEY'VE SURVIVED WORSE THAN THIS.
AND AT LEAST WE STOPPED RONAN --

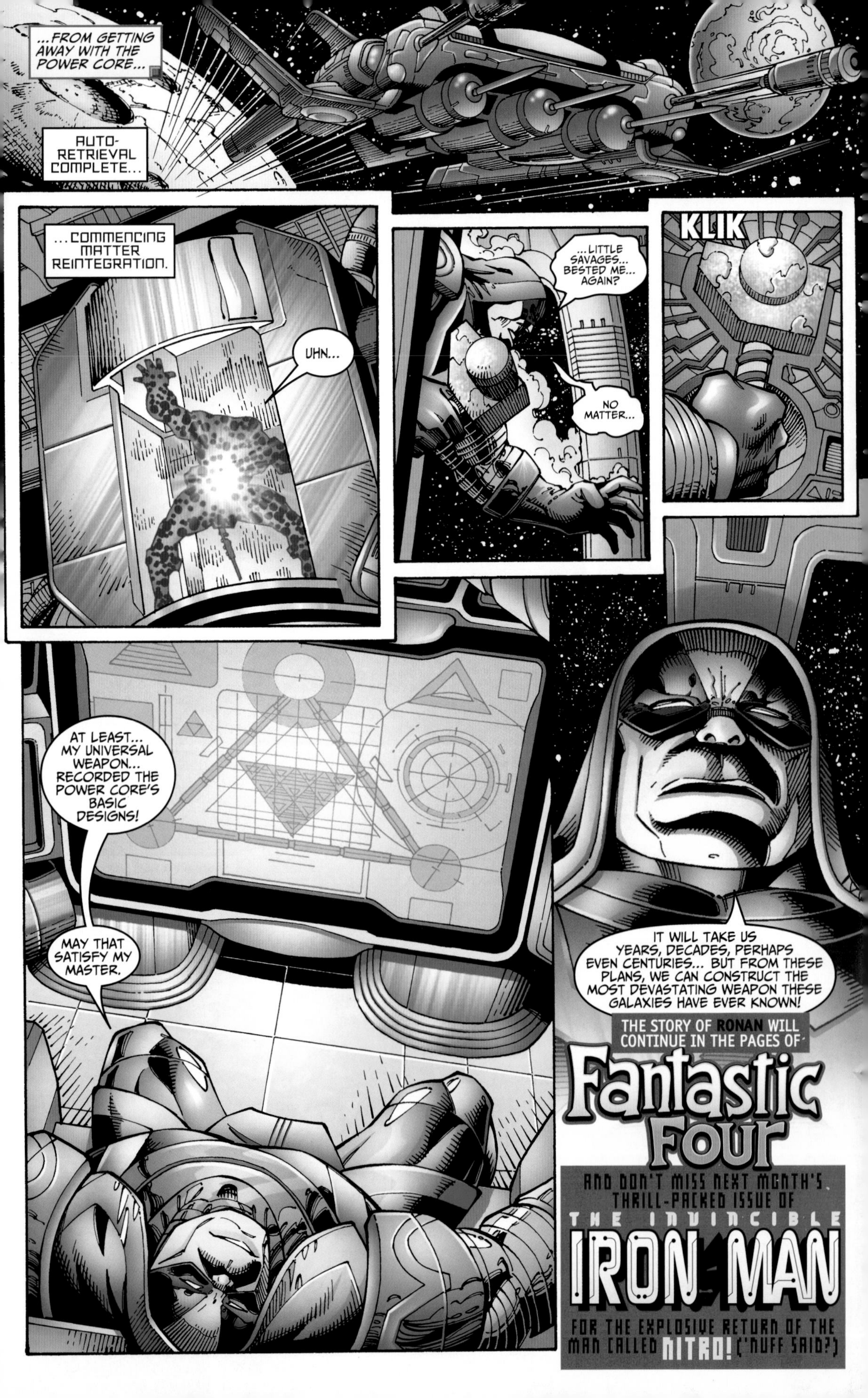
...FROM GETTING AWAY WITH THE POWER CORE...
AUTO-RETRIEVAL COMPLETE...
...COMMENCING MATTER REINTEGRATION.
UHN...
...LITTLE SAVAGES... BESTED ME... AGAIN?
NO MATTER...
KLIK
AT LEAST... MY UNIVERSAL WEAPON... RECORDED THE POWER CORE'S BASIC DESIGNS!
MAY THAT SATISFY MY MASTER.
IT WILL TAKE US YEARS, DECADES, PERHAPS EVEN CENTURIES... BUT FROM THESE PLANS, WE CAN CONSTRUCT THE MOST DEVASTATING WEAPON THESE GALAXIES HAVE EVER KNOWN!
THE STORY OF RONAN WILL CONTINUE IN THE PAGES OF
Fantastic Four
AND DON'T MISS NEXT MONTH'S THRILL-PACKED ISSUE OF
THE INVINCIBLE
IRON MAN
FOR THE EXPLOSIVE RETURN OF THE MAN CALLED NITRO! ('NUFF SAID?)

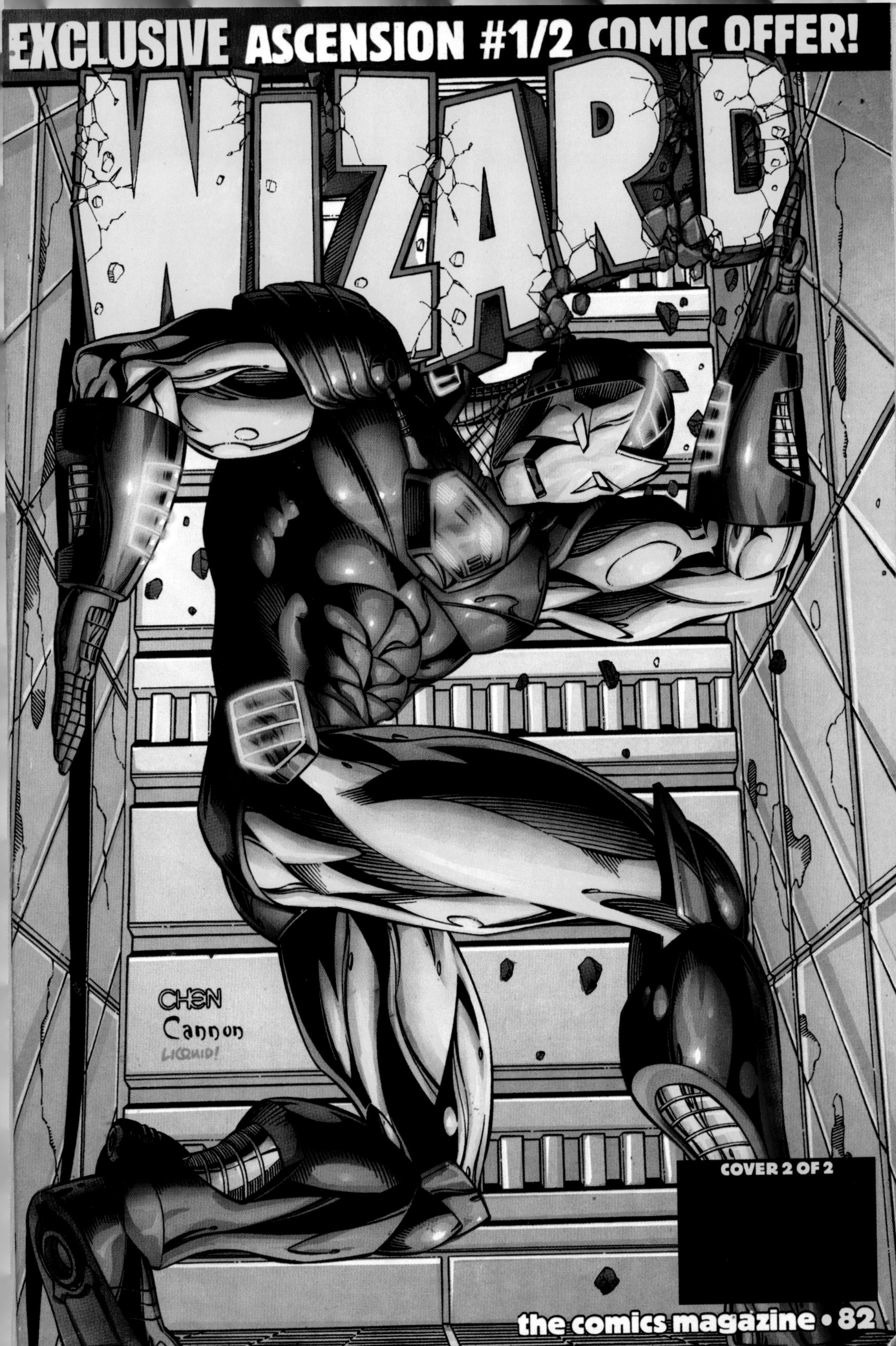
EXCLUSIVE ASCENSION #1/2 COMIC OFFER!
WIZARD
CHEN
Cannon
LIQUID!
COVER 2 OF 2
[redacted]
the comics magazine • 82

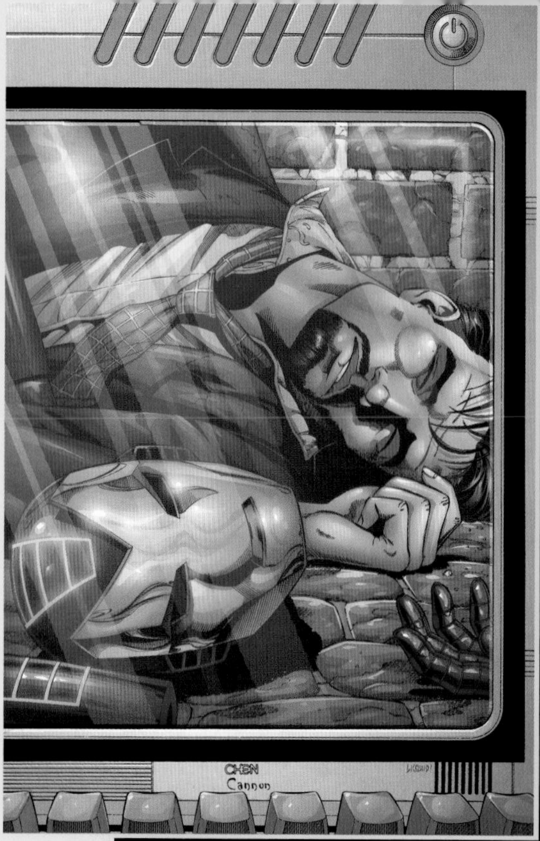
CHEN
Cannon

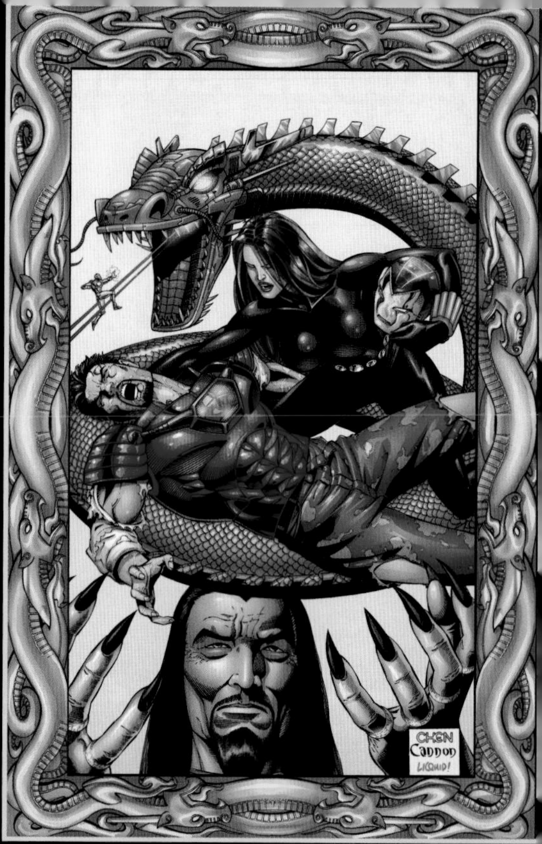
CHEN
Cannon
LIQUID!

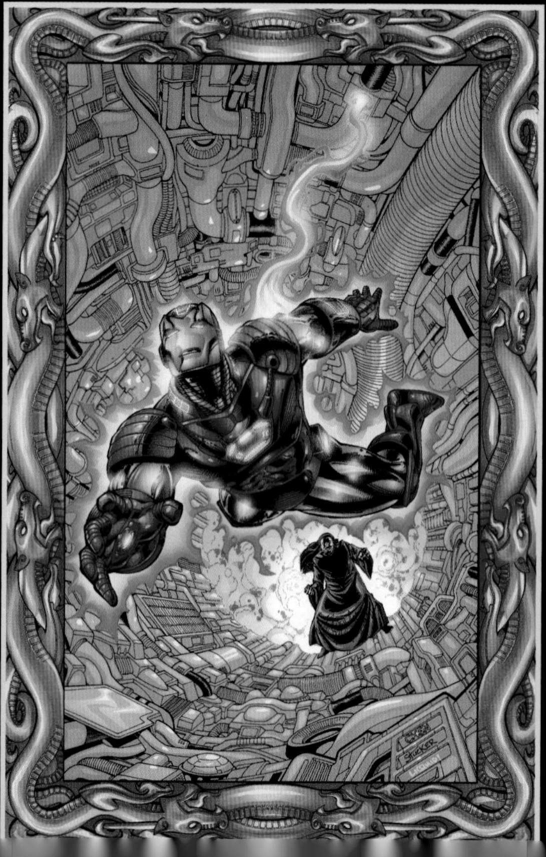

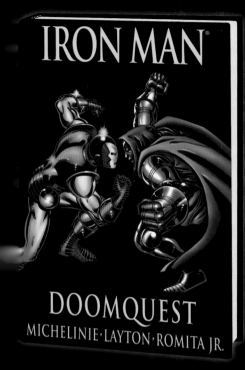

IRON MAN: DOOMQUEST PREMIERE HC
978-0-7851-2834-2

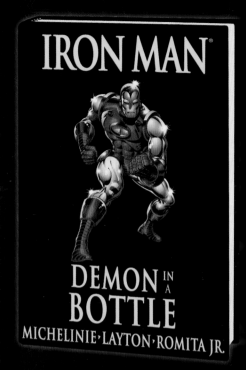

IRON MAN: DEMON IN A BOTTLE PREMIERE HC
978-0-7851-3095-6

IRON MAN: IRON MONGER PREMIERE HC

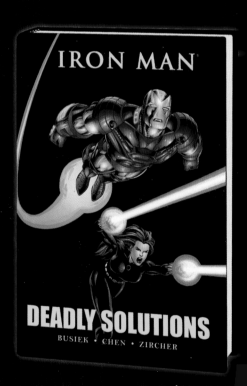

IRON MAN: DEADLY SOLUTIONS PREMIERE HC